CLAIRE NAHMAD is a successful author who has written a number of best-selling books on feminine spirituality, angel communication, meditation, herbalism and folklore. The inner worlds of spiritual percipience have been open to her since early childhood and her intuitive explorations inform her writing. Her books have a strong following world-wide and are frequently utilised in mind-body-spirit courses and workshops. She was born in Yorkshire and lives in a rural area of North Lincolnshire in a tumbledown cottage with her cockerel Coleridge.

MICHAEL REVILL is a gifted medium and visionary who has perfected many hermetic arts. His interests are astronomy, natural history and aviation, in particular the role of the air crews in the Second World War.

The Coming of the Holy Grail

The Exact Location of Heaven's Treasure
and the Promise of its Retrieval

CLAIRE NAHMAD
with MICHAEL REVILL

First published in 2012 by Cygnus Books,
Unit 1, Beechwood, Llandeilo,
Camarthenshire SA19 7HR

Designed and typeset by Bookcraft Ltd, Stroud, UK

Cover image: The Grail Maiden by Dante Gabriel Rossetti, oil on canvas, 1874

Printed and bound by CPI, UK

British Library Cataloguing-in-Publication Data Available

Library of Congress Cataloging-in-Publication Data Available

ISBN: 978-0-95493-268-8

www.cygnus-books.co.uk

This book is dedicated, with all my heart and in loving appreciation of his presence, to Squadron Leader George Carver, who died in combat in July 1944.

Through adversity to the stars

Here lies the hoarded love, the key
To all the treasure that shall be.
Come, fated heart, the gift to take,
And smite the sleeping world awake.

(Text inscribed beneath the painting (one of a series) of Briar Rose
by the Pre-Raphaelite artist Burne-Jones, traditionally believed to
depict Mary Magdalene.)

Contents

CONTENTS

Acknowledgements

We are greatly indebted to Laurence Gardner, who has opened numerous doors for us through his scholarly series on the subject of the Grail. Without the help of his clarification, particularly throughout his book *Genesis of the Grail Kings* (Bantam), we would have struggled in perplexity with much of the material that was given to us.

Special thanks to those who have contributed funds to make this rewrite possible: particularly to May and Ivor Nahmad, and also, with much gratitude, to Olwen and Steve Ballantyne and Daphne Jones.

We will always be thankful to Lewis Carroll for his astounding *Alice* masterpieces, which form a beacon to guide humanity's tentative steps as it enters an entirely new perceptual dimension.

A toast to Johnny Travis, who read the first version of this book with dogged determination, and then re-read it just as thoroughly. Thank you, Johnny, your support meant a lot.

Thank you to Jane Delaford Taylor, who did the same for this rendition whilst I was completing the final stages, and whose encouragement and reassurance were indispensable.

Thanks are due to the writers and researchers Anthony Roberts and Geoff Gilbertson for the illumination their work brought to points in our own.

Thank you to Dianne Pegler for our inspiring discussions regarding the 'crozier of light'.

Thank you to Ann and Geoff Napier, and to Michael Mann, for sorting me out.

Many thanks to Nand de Rijk for kindly allowing us to use her photograph of Lincoln Cathedral at night.

Finally, my heartfelt thanks to our own 'John-man' and to the Grail Circle, without whom this revised version of the story of the Grail would not have been possible.

Preface

This book is about the discovery of the exact location of the Holy Grail, about the mystery of its essence and the wonder of its virtues. It is about the freedom and the unbounded joy we will each individually claim in receiving it, and how we may prepare to receive it. The Grail has not yet been unearthed, but we are certain that it will soon be retrieved from its current resting-place. We are confident that it will be given to the world at the appointed time. The current fortress of official refusal and denial that surrounds the Grail, as far as permission to excavate is concerned, is only in place to protect this most holy mystery until the time is right for humanity to accept it. In a sense, its advent among us has already begun, as we hope our book will show.

Nevertheless, we are entirely convinced that the world will not have to await its retrieval for very long! Every outer indication, every heart-borne message from that deepest source out of which we have sought to draw, confirms and reaffirms this belief. The Grail *will* be given to each and every one of us who is willing to receive it. No barriers of religion or status of any kind can come between those who wish to partake of its blessing, and the inestimable and inconceivable gift of the Grail. It is a free gift from the heart of those who dwell within the mystery of Love. We call this mystery the Christ essence. You may call it by another name or term. It does not matter. The Grail is yours, it is for you if you want to receive it, and it will not be long in coming.

What is the Grail? What were the clues that led us to it? What are its properties, its secrets? What is its great gift to humankind?

How can we prepare for its coming? How will we receive its mystical attributes? What will its effect be on each one of us personally, and upon the world? What is its history? How did it come to be where it now lies, and who placed it there? We trust that this book will provide the answers to these questions.

Although the Grail will always remain an ineffable mystery, it can nonetheless be understood, because its very essence is enlightenment – light itself; light most hallowed, light divine, a light that will chase away the mists and the shadows from our collective consciousness. It is, in truth, a great chalice, a communion cup that will unite the world in brotherhood; but no cup lies buried in the tomb beneath the sacred ground which secretes the Grail. No physical treasure, no gleaming jewel, no fabulously precious chalice, is there. And yet, the most wondrous treasure ever to be given to this planet, and to its human occupants, lies hidden in the vault that contains the Grail.

What rests therein is a great Secret, a Secret that will transform everything, a Secret that will save the world. War-torn and chaotic, seething with grievous suffering as the world is now, indubitably we shall see things begin to change, and change dramatically, once the Grail is given to us. So this is a time for rejoicing, for thanksgiving, and for preparation, in consideration of which, we invite you to join us on our sacred Grail Quest. Put aside all hesitation, all self-limiting thought, because undoubtedly our combined Quest will be crowned with fulfilment!

This is the promise that was borne to us on the breath of the divine, and which we now dare to convey to you. Journey with us, and prepare to receive the Grail.

'Do you know, I've had such a quantity of poetry repeated to me today,' Alice began, a little frightened at finding that, the moment she opened her lips, there was dead silence, and all eyes were fixed upon her; 'and it's a very curious thing, I think – every poem was about fishes in some way. Do you know why they're so fond of fishes, all about here?'

(THROUGH THE LOOKING-GLASS, AND WHAT ALICE FOUND THERE
(CHAP. IX, QUEEN ALICE) LEWIS CARROLL)

Introduction

We would like to make it clear from the outset that we ourselves did not discover the location of the Grail. We were given intimations of its coming, and we have received knowledge of its meaning and its mystery, but we did not pursue or solve the enigma of its whereabouts. The discoverer of the Grail is Callum Jensen, a resident of Lincoln who throughout our acquaintance with him has always remained a shadowy and mysterious figure. He was, almost undoubtedly, aided, directed and inspired in his search by a woman who has a unique aptitude for riddle-solving, cryptology and the esoteric aspect of language, but who shall remain nameless, in deference to her need for protection and privacy.

Unbeknown to us, as I was preparing the forerunner to this book, *The Secret Teachings of Mary Magdalene*, for publication in the latter part of 2005, Callum Jensen had begun to receive tantalising intuitions concerning the site of the buried Grail. The filming of *The Da Vinci Code* at Lincoln Cathedral had encouraged him to look more closely at certain clues he had long contemplated. And, thanks to stroke after stroke of genius on his (and possibly another's) part, gradually all fell into place. Shortly before the publication of the book referred to above, of which Callum had no knowledge, he released his own, short and to the point, revealing the exact resting place of the Holy Grail.

Few people took him seriously. The general consensus was that it was all a bit of a joke, a money-spinner generated by the filming of *The Da Vinci Code* and Lincoln's consequent newly found Hollywood status. We trust that this book will expose just how mistaken that view was.

Our purpose in writing it is to reveal what the Holy Grail is, how it came to be secreted in Lincoln, and how each and every one of us can use it to heal and transfigure ourselves and the world. Our qualifications for writing it, we trust, will be vindicated in the fullness of time. Callum Jensen, always puckish and Merlinesque, has retreated into the enigmatic twilight from which he initially emerged in order to indicate where the Holy Grail lies. We proceed from this point without him, but we salute him for his inestimable contribution to our quest, and we know the world will thank him, and offer him a place in history, for his part in the unfolding of this sacred story.

Nevertheless, Callum has been by no means inactive! A ground-penetrating radar scan was conducted at the site of the buried Grail on 16 April 2011 by a Belgian geologist and archaeologist. The results show something that equates with the dimensions of what Margaret Bailey and I saw when we used our inner percipience to view what was there: a stone chest and a metal box.[1] Of course, the GPR scan can tell us nothing about what might be in the chest and the box; but the chest and the box, shown by the results of the scan, certainly appear to be there.

The Holy Grail contains within its essence four great wonders, called the Four Hallows of the Grail: the miracle of Nourishment, the miracle of Fertility, the miracle of Healing, and the miracle of Immortality. When we truly learn to imbibe these four divine gifts, and that fifth quality, the Grail's quintessence, which is the greatest gift of all and which delivers the other four gifts faithfully to us, we will no longer continue to make a madhouse out of our global civilisation and our tenancy here on earth.

All our problems, even those that currently seem insoluble, will at last begin to loosen their grip and fade into the light which is the dawn of humanity's new day, blossoming in radiance over a new heaven and a new earth.

These stories may be far from history, where one usually reads that such and such a king sent such and such a general to such and such a war, and that on such and such a day they made war or peace, and that this one defeated that one, or that one this one, and then proceeded somewhere.
   But I write what is worthy to be recorded.

(BAYHAQI TARIKH,
6TH CENTURY)

NOTE

1 Our findings, given in the first book about the Grail (of which the present volume is a revision and an extension), describe the stone chest. The metal box was not perceived in similar mundane dimensions, but as a charge of energy that made the soles of the feet tingle. The contents of the box, which comprise earth from the sacred location of the Temple Mount in Jerusalem, were intuited by Michael Revill, and will, we trust, prove to be the source of our percipience concerning the 'uprush' of the Grail forces.

CHAPTER ONE

The Secret of the Ages

*W*hat lies there within, beneath the tomb in the ancient burial ground which houses the Holy Grail?

Imagine, if you will, that the excavation to disinter it has taken place. The vault that secretes the Grail has been opened, and steps lead down to a simple stone chest, waiting in the shadows. A metal object lies close by. The excavators reach the chest, and prize it open with infinite care. What will meet their eyes?

Before we answer this question, I would like to relate a significant dream which came to Margaret Bailey during the time that we were contemplating the mystery of the Holy Grail. The dream offers us a teaching on the purity and power of its essence.

Margaret dreamed that she was leaning over the hole in the ground at the opened site, peering into the gloom of the vault below. A feeling of disappointment washed over her as she thought, 'Oh, after all this build-up and expectation, nothing's there!' Suddenly, from out of the vault there rushed a great plume of brilliant white light like a fire fountain that encircled and glorified all the world.

We must beware, then, of investing the idea of the Grail with physical splendour and riches, with visible spectacularity. The materialist will search in vain for any literal verification of the Grail legend, even though the songs and tales of the troubadours, each and every one, contain some glittering piece of the mirror in which, when once restored to its integrity, we shall behold the truth of the wondrous Grail. Nevertheless, although the dream came as a teaching, it is not quite true to say that there is nothing there. Templar treasure is buried with the Grail. It is traditional treasure, of the kind that worldliness marvels to behold because of its opulence, but it is also beautiful. It consists of 'wonderful things', to quote Howard Carter. It is there, not to be used for selfish purposes, but to help us build a new society and a new economy that is for all rather than the few.

Many, many sites exist across the world where Templar treasure lies. A number of these are steeped in sinister folklore pertaining to the terrifying experiences of those who seek to unearth the rumoured treasure. All such locations are protected by Templar forces, for the Templar brotherhood was familiar with that part of the divine Grail wisdom which it was possible to convey to some members of humanity (particularly the Cathars and the Templars) before it had to be consigned for safety's sake to its sacred resting-place underground. This familiarity enabled the Templars to manipulate psychic forces and to transcend the laws of matter. They used their knowledge to set guards over their treasure, for its proper use lay far ahead in the future, when their garnered wealth would build a new global civilisation that honours and nurtures all people and all life on earth.

The Templars have hidden hoards of treasure that amount to wealth beyond dreaming. When we are ready to use this wealth without greed or self-seeking, when the Grail has driven the shadows and the lowering fog from our collective vision, then the designated sites will give up their treasure. There will be sufficient to create a global People's Bank that will release us from the ferocious power of the current banking system and the stranglehold it has maintained over us for so long.

Within the metal box lying near to the stone chest is a consignment of earth, precious earth from the site of Temple Mount in Jerusalem. This measurelessly sacred site is one of the four great Grail stations upon our earth, currently the most potent of them all, a point where the magical and stupendous Grail power was grounded deep into the planet. The very soil contains and enshrines its sanctified energies.

A portion of this God-touched earth within its metal box was brought in company with the Holy Grail under cover of darkness to the burial place where the Grail would lie as if in enchanted slumber until the moment that humanity was ready to receive the unprecedented awakening it would initiate. A small band of Templars was its escort.

To the first cathedral ever built in Britain, erected upon the site of a church founded in the Magdalene's own lifetime and dedicated to her, it came, in company with, and as servant and protector to, the Holy Grail. The energies within it, corresponding to those of the Holy Grail itself when it was fully alive and active upon the earth, would guard its sacred charge from intrusion, theft and destruction. The metal of which the box is constructed contributes to the protective forces of the soil within it, and activates them whenever necessary. Safe, sealed and sound, the Holy Grail would sleep in the bosom of the earth until its appointed time, secure under the watch of its guardian.

Within the stone chest lies a book inscribed in Latin – the tangible and material Holy Grail itself – which is a copy of an original manuscript; some further documentation; and a little wizened thing, not much bigger than a large nut kernel. As well as the aforementioned Templar treasure, there are also some artefacts which will help us as a planetary civilisation to understand the mystery and wonder of our origins, and which we hope will vindicate the story that unfolds below. Additionally, there are texts relating to the missing 400 years of history which were carefully lopped from the tree of time by the writers – or their copy editors – of the Old Testament. These texts relate to a mighty and glorious civilisation, greater than that of ancient Egypt, which certain factions wanted to airbrush out of history so that important Grail history could be hidden, and so that Moses would not be associated with a certain pharaoh. The timeline these documents reveal is that between circa 1750 BC and circa 1350 BC.

The book is the lost Gospel of John, which was transmitted by Mary Magdalene to John, her brother and amanuensis. It consists of transcriptions from what we shall hereafter refer to as the 'Emerald Tablet'. The book was a combined effort of Mary, Jesus, Tamar and John. Brother and sister in blood as well as in spirit, John transcribed it as Mary spoke it. It is also known as the Book of Love, among other designations. It is the book that the female Pope, depicted in the tarot deck, cradles in her lap, and the book of which a very limited part was known to the Cathars.[1] It comprised the mystery of the Templars, a mystery for which every true Templar was willing to lay down life. It was given to John by Mary and Jesus after Jesus had ascended.

Jesus, through his sacrificial death, had been able to penetrate the hidden and locked dimension wherein the great Secret – the Emerald Tablet – lay concealed by malignant design.

Because of their profound closeness in spirit, Jesus and Mary Magdalene created a polarity between the higher and the earthly planes. They remained in intimate communion despite their apparent separation. Via this beautiful 'satellite link', Jesus was able to read the hidden Emerald Tablet with the help of Mary, who spoke the sacred words it stored within its essence as their conjoined consciousness became consummate with its knowledge. John, faithful servant of the hallowed couple and, as mentioned, brother to Mary, made transcripts as Mary spoke so that a divine book was created.

Jesus, Mary and John's great enterprise could not have been enacted without Tamar, the daughter of Mary and Jesus, with whom Mary was pregnant at the crucifixion. Truly they formed the great cross or tree of the elements with which the Grail is connected (consider the Four Hallows of the Grail), with Jesus (ascended) above in the north, John and Mary standing by on earth as joint receptacle in the east and the west, and Tamar earthing that sacred cross or tree at its foot, in the south, the point that symbolises the sanctified and mysterious underworld wherein dwells the heart of the earth.

Tamar stood surety for the transmission of this sacred book. It travelled to earth on the ray of her light. It was able to come to us because Tamar was able to come to us, via the magnitude, courage and sacrifice of her parents' great mission.

It vouchsafes a secret so precious, so stupendous, so liberating, that, down the centuries, adversarial forces hostile to humanity have done everything in their power (which is the power of the world, the power of materialism) to keep it hidden and prevent us from gaining any knowledge of it. And so it is that we have been denied our divinely granted legacy, that legacy of which the lost gospel tells, and which it, in part, dispenses.

The accompanying documentation in the chest reveals the true status and significance of Mary, the Magdalene, and of Tamar, the daughter and only child of Jesus and Mary. It verifies that Mary was the wife of Jesus, and was the feminine aspect of the Christ as Jesus was the male aspect, and that Tamar was in herself the Holy Grail. (How Tamar is the personification of the Grail, and yet the Grail lies hidden within the vault we describe, will be explained.) Among the documents lies an ancient copy of the entire Gospel of Mary Magdalene, only half of which has ever been recovered. Margaret Bailey brought through the missing half of the Gospel of Mary (with a few minor additions via myself) in our book, *The Secret Teachings of Mary Magdalene*, and it is my firm belief that the manuscript buried at the Grail site will confirm that she faithfully reflected its contents.

The shrivelled nut kernel is in fact a dried human heart, whose identity we can disclose. It belonged to Dagobert, a French king of the seventh century, who was murdered by conspirators in AD 679. We will reveal his intriguing story shortly.

For now, we draw attention to the fact that it is his *heart* which lies buried with the Grail, and that he met his death by being pierced straight through the eye by a lance, which impaled him to a tree. The heart, the pierced eye, and indeed the presence of the lance and the tree, are very important components in our understanding of the Grail.

You might well be inclined to ask: 'Is that all there is to the legendary Holy Grail? Just a mouldy old book, a few documents, and a wizened body part? Is that the sum total of what the world has been waiting, agog, to find down the centuries?'

The answer is, of course, no. Certainly the Grail is inconceivably more stupendous than the contents of the vault, at first sight, suggest; and all of it is not contained therein. The truth is that a part of the Grail already resides *within* each one of us, inside every human heart. Its greater essence is secreted in the higher worlds, in the spiritual spheres, ready to be given to us. The significant point is that within the book lies the vital key to how we shall receive it.

So, the Grail resides within our deeper being, upon the earth, and in the heavens. How can this be?

There is a mystical centre within the heart. Many ages ago, humanity turned away from the guidance given forth from the divine centre of the cosmos, and the entire planet experienced a shift that took it slightly out of alignment with its pole star (referred to today as the 'polar wobble'). Our physical hearts, likewise, began to shift a little off-centre throughout our bodily incarnations, until the physical organ was established where it is today. Nevertheless, the mystical heart centre of humanity has not moved, and is located where our bodily heart used to be. So when we think of this divine heart centre, or chakra, we see it as encompassing our physical heart but yet in the perfect centre of the breast.

The heart chakra is associated with three main symbols: the sign of a cross of light encompassed by a circle of light (the cross is equilateral and touches the perimeter of the circle at its four points); the exquisite form of a rose which dwells fragrantly at its centre – the 'heart of hearts' and the sign of the Holy Spirit which is linked with our breath; and the form of a six-pointed star, called the Star of Bethlehem but, unlike the Star of David, bearing no inner divisions. This star is the light of our spirit, and is our individual connection to, and our individual expression of, divine consciousness.

We can locate our subtle heart centre by gentle, focused breathing, as if we were drawing each breath through the heart; by visualising one of its main symbols; and by allowing the mind to rest easily and softly within the heart, as if tenderly enfolded by it. Contact with this centre is so essential for our reception of the Grail that this little exercise is well worth carrying out for a few moments each day. This is the very best way to begin the Grail quest. Within a short time, it will become undeniably evident that a beautiful consciousness, a distilled perception, does indeed reside within the heart, and it will become easy to understand that it is within this spiritual centre of intelligence that the Grail, our own individual spark or drop of it, is secreted.

That part of the Grail which waits to be given to us from the higher worlds is so mysterious that we will need to accomplish many journeyings, many voyages into the interior of things, before we can bear away the trophy of realisation regarding its secrets. But it is promised to us all that we *will* be enabled to understand, and to make the trophy our own. Of this there can be no doubt. For now, we may conceive of that high essence of the Grail as embodied in and personified by a divine woman, a woman clothed with the sun. She was known on earth as Tamar, the daughter of Jesus and Mary Magdalene.

The third component of the Grail, following on from the mystic centre in the heart and the divine woman or the essence of the Sacred Feminine, is the earth herself.

She is the great Grail Cup, symbolic of our own heart centre, and the power of the Grail inexorably connects above with below, not only in the sense of earth and heaven, but also of the exterior and interior dimensions of the planet itself.

In considering the secrets of the Grail, our attention was persistently and invariably drawn to the sacredness of 'underground' … and we have come to understand that its mysteries and wonders bear some very startling aspects! Be warned that, in spite of scientific calculations regarding the interior mantle and the core of the planet, we will be required to think in terms of a habitable inner earth! And not only are the mysterious inner dimensions of our planet habitable by human beings, but they are so inhabited!

The fourth part of the Grail, that which exists on earth and is hidden in the grounds of Lincoln Cathedral, is in every way as mystical and divine as its other components – the heart, the Sacred Feminine and the Grail Cup of the earth – although it is the only one (so far) that can be located in physical, literal form. Even if in that mundane embodiment it is neither made of emerald nor a table, its true identity is known as the Emerald Table of Destinies, and it is precious indeed. Let our first journey into the interior be in pursuit of this mysterious Table!

NOTE

1   The Cathars were a Christian religious sect who arose in eleventh-century France, espousing ideals of purity and brotherly love. They were the guardians of the *consolamentum* (a limited form of the power of the Holy Grail), which allowed ordinary people to see vividly into, not just the astral spheres (which many individuals are able to perceive), but also the beauty and the magic of the higher spiritual worlds. At the dictate of the Catholic Church, a crusade was mounted against them, and they were brutally slaughtered during the thirteenth century in one of the earliest acts of European genocide. Their final stand was in the citadel at the top of Montségur. It is said that the night before they were forced to leave the citadel to be put to death, four Cathar priests were lowered down the mountain-side on ropes, escaping with the four great Cathar treasures. One of the four secret treasures was a portion of the lost Gospel of John, the gospel which contains the secret of the Holy Grail.

CHAPTER TWO

The Emerald Table

*W*e must penetrate the mists of time, the mists of dimension, to find the mystical Emerald Table. In ancient texts it was loosely described as a uniquely inscribed tablet of ideograms, but it was much more than a stone of carven ciphers. Its spiritual beauty was unsurpassed. It was revered as the ultimate treasure of a lost civilisation. Yet we can trace it back to when it first appeared on earth, which was at the point when the Grail was cut off from the world, cruelly severed by malignant design and by breach of the profoundest divine laws. It was at the time when the human creature sought to kill God, and afterwards, in its ignorance, believed that it had succeeded.

'By this, thou wilt partake of the Honours of the Whole World ... And darkness will fly from Thee ... with this thou wilt be able to overcome all things.' These are among the promises of the Emerald Table, and are direct quotes from transcribed extracts. It is said of the Emerald Tablet that it was testament to all that the earth had ever known and could ever know, indicating that, when humanity had absorbed the full spectrum of its teaching, we would in unison step up a gear and become something more than the sum of our parts. We and our beautiful planet would henceforth surpass our limitations. We would integrate and become truly superhuman, or, as Mary Magdalene expresses it in her exquisite and diminutive gospel, more like a poem than prose, 'fully human'.

It has come down to us from immeasurably long ago, this revealer of the depths of all knowledge; but it was formulated anew by Hermes (the biblical Ham), who translated it from the Book of Thoth, which was in itself a partial rendition of the Emerald Table. In fact, Ham very stringently edited it, for good reason, as we shall see. The idea of Thoth was one which Ham himself imparted as a legacy to the Egyptian civilisation. Nimrod the Mighty, a great king of Mesopotamia, was Ham's grandson, and Nimrod was the father of King Anedjib, the pharaoh of the first Egyptian dynasty, which came into being about 3000 BC. So Ham was the great-grandfather of the king who founded the Egyptian dynasties, and carried the seeds of the monumental Egyptian culture within him.

There is a strange and disturbing story to be told regarding the reason why Ham made transcriptions of the Emerald Table when he did, which was at the time of the terrible destruction of Sumer and the Tower of Babel. Noah, or the king Zi-u-Sudra (the first is the later Hebraic rendition of his identity, the second the earlier Sumerian), had been Ham's firm ally, but turned against him, cursing him and his issue, as the Bible relates. We will reveal in due course why this was so, and why this point in history is so fundamental to the story of the Grail, but for our present purposes we will outline very briefly the turn of events.

Because Noah deserted his former stance and 'changed sides', the real Emerald Table was thrown into jeopardy. A mighty ruler, who despised humanity and wanted to see it fail, stole the Emerald Tablet and, with Noah's help, hid it away, not in a place, but in a locked and concealed dimension that could not be breached by any spiritual or physical technology that the earth could offer. So that no one would suspect his treachery, he created a false Emerald Tablet.

This false Emerald Tablet was so cleverly contrived that it fooled his court, who together with him were its sacred guardians. They failed to recognise it as fake because the king had worked into it many strands of the energy of the real Emerald Tablet, but had secreted a poison and a distortion and a terrifying reversal of energy at its heart.

Realising this, Ham heroically set to work to transcribe only those portions of the false Emerald Tablet that stemmed from the original and which bore within them some necessary illumination for the progress of humanity, discarding the rest. Although he strove with all his heart solely to convey truth from the real Emerald Tablet (those strains of pure vibration from the genuine article which were channelled into the false one in order to deceive its guardians), his success was only partial.

The ruinous energy breathed into it by the king, which was intended to shut down humanity's vision and compress it into a dark and fatal prison of materialism, still pulsated throughout the essence of Ham's transcriptions, albeit much less intensively due to his devoted efforts. Yet humanity needed revelations from what was left of the real Emerald Tablet to survive and make headway.

Therefore, in order to help us discriminate between the true and the false emanations of the king's version of the Emerald Tablet, and also because it was his greater destiny, Ham set up a mystery school and a doctrine based on distinguishing between what he termed 'the Truth and the Lie'. For Ham was Zoroaster, and Thoth was his teacher and guide: Thoth who was known as Ahura Mazda, God of Light, in his Persian guise, and, earlier, in ancient Sumer, Enki the Wise, inspired always by his revered counsellor and wife, Nin-khursag.

It was from Ham's line that Jesus and Mary Magdalene descended (for Jesus and Mary were cousins), who would jointly complete Ham's task by actually rescuing the stolen and secreted Emerald Tablet and handing it back to humanity in an unprecedented gesture of sacrifice and love.

After he had made his transcriptions, Ham still faced the problem of what to do with the actual physical article which was the false Emerald Tablet. Again, he strove with all his might to disconnect its sinister energies from humanity's consciousness. He hid it in Egypt, where it was guarded by a circle of priests and its vibrations were suppressed. Nevertheless, it continued to transmit its muted emanations out into the world, wreaking endless harm.

After the true Emerald Tablet had been recovered many centuries later, unlocked at last from its secret dimension, Tamar took the book of sacred transcriptions with her to Ireland, where she was forced to flee for her own safety. Later we will discuss how the Emerald Tablet was mystically linked with her, for in herself she was and is the Holy Grail. She kept the book safe in a special dûn, a subterranean hall in sanctified ground which was her habitation. Here it was preserved, even after she eventually left her hallowed dûn secreted within the sacred 'inner earth' and travelled to Rome, where she was put to death.

In the seventh century, Dagobert, the French king, transported it from Ireland to Rennes-le-Château, a little French village in the Pyrenees mountain range. It was buried under the church there, which was dedicated to Mary Magdalene, for we must understand that the Grail is a purely feminine energy. Like Jesus, Dagobert died by being impaled upon the sacred tree, lanced to death in a forest. For the sacred book, the Tree of Life, the Tree of the Knowledge of Good and Evil, the male sacrifice to regain what humanity had so sorely lost, and the mysterious Tamar, are all inextricably linked.

Dagobert was the designated guardian of the Grail. Tamar had appeared to him as he slept in her sacred dûn, and had given him his task, entrusting the immeasurably precious Grail to him. Evil forces conspired to have Dagobert put to death in the forest, not only because of his link with the Grail, but also because it was essential for their machinations that Dagobert's bloodline should be destroyed, and another line of descent, much more amenable to the lifeless materialism necessary for humanity's destruction, be set up in its place. To have a Grail-aware monarch upon the throne would eventually spell certain death to their plans. Dagobert's successor was Pepin the Fat, an officious and corrupt burgomaster whose men had assassinated the French king in the forest, and who fitted the bill to perfection.

On his tragic death, Dagobert's heart was enshrined with the Grail by his loved ones, who shared his secret. It contained influences which helped to make the protection around the Grail inviolate.

11

Meanwhile, what of the false Emerald Tablet? It was retrieved from Egypt during the Crusades. The horror of these wars had created a vile wavelength upon which subconscious instructions could be transmitted to certain men, given to black-hearted deeds, comprising a circle of what might be termed anti-Templars. And we see evidence of what always surrounds the false Emerald Tablet – massive human sacrifice similar to the scale upon which it took place during the destruction of ancient Sumer. Always, always, this human sacrifice surrounding the false Grail involves deliberate harm done to children. Devastatingly, we find that the Crusaders killed and ate the children of their 'enemies', roasting them like animals on spits.

The whispered malignant influences from the false Emerald Tablet had put the idea of the Crusades into the minds and machinations of the political and Church leaders who initiated them, because it wanted to be retrieved. It was ready to be removed to a strategic place where it could inflict maximum damage in the future. Of course, through its projected voice spoke the voices of those comprising the circle of darkness whose members hated humanity and wanted to see it perish; a circle whose identity will be revealed.

It was eventually relocated to France, to the very village whose site Dagobert had chosen to protect the true Emerald Tablet. That had been transported to England and the city of Lincoln under the pressure of dire emergency, in haste, in the nick of time, via thundering hooves under the cover of darkness, for its resting-place had been discovered. Sorrowful to relate, it was disclosed by a Cathar priest whom Margaret Bailey saw in a disturbing vision, a member of the *Perfecti*, who had been lured to the dark side. And yet, paradoxically, the Grail was always fated to rest in Lincoln, and a prepared site was ready.

Heading the small band of Templars who rode with all speed, in pacted silence, through the dark of night to rescue the situation (movement by day was too risky) was Robin Hood, among the truest and finest of the Templars. He did indeed exist, and his sacred sign of the arrow protects Lincoln and the Grail to this day, for Robin is still one of the great guardians of the Grail. On the holy road to Lincoln, the road between Scampton, home of the 'Dam Busters', and the cathedral city (whenever travelling this road or any other approach to Lincoln, long before any sort of revelation concerning this story came to me, the thought invariably crossed my mind that I was on 'the holy road to Lincoln', and consequently I am unable to use any other term for it!) there is a recognised bow in the design of the road.

It is sign and symbol of the bow of Robin, true-hearted Templar, guardian of the Holy Grail, whose heart-arrows are still firing to keep it safe, reflected in the beautiful and awe-inspiring flights of the Red Arrows squadron that is based at Scampton and that grace and bless the city.

The false Emerald Tablet was buried at Rennes-le-Château in due course, shortly before the unspeakable Albigensian Crusade began, arranged by the Church. It comprised the first recorded act of European genocide, and it took place between 1209 and 1244 – 35 years of unprecedented atrocity and horror in which the Cathars were virtually wiped out. The whirlwind generated by the same force from the same source hit the Templars in 1307. Both communities were guardians and exponents of the true Grail, and both met their death with unequalled brutality once the ferociously malignant false Grail lay in Rennes-le-Château in place of the true.

What of the transcripts made by Ham, transcripts necessarily of the false Emerald Tablet, yet derived from influences in it that resonated with the true tablet, albeit slightly defiled nonetheless. Scholarly translations of the ciphers of Genesis show that the Emerald Tablet (Ham's edited and very much expurgated version) passed into the keeping of Abraham (formerly Abram) when he went into Canaan, which was why Abram was renamed 'Abra-ham', keeper of the knowledge of Ham.

Beyond Egypt and Mesopotamia, the Table was known to the luminaries of the classical world, especially to Pythagoras and Plato. It was known to the seventeenth-century Stuart Royal Society of Britain (it is worth mentioning that Scotland surfaces again and again in the unfolding of the Grail mystery). The eminent scholars and scientists belonging to the Society introduced fundamental laws of matter to the public domain, such as Isaac Newton's law of gravity, Halley's astronomical revelations and Boyle's law.

All of these illumined discoveries were expressly attributable to secrets deriving from the ancient archive of the Emerald Table.

There is a strange footnote to Boyle's discoveries. Known as 'the father of modern chemistry' who revealed that matter consisted of atoms or 'corpuscles', Boyle had a respected and diligent assistant by the name of Robert Kirk. This laboratory assistant, as well as performing his scientific ministrations with due diligence and excellence, wrote a book called *The Secret Commonwealth*, about a hidden and mysterious race of people, dwelling on and under earth, whom we would recognise as the fairies, the 'shining ones'. It was written not as a book of fantasy, but as a faithful record of attested history as if by an anthropologist. The Grail will reveal more wonders of the inner earth, but the existence of these 'shining ones' is certainly something to be going on with!

It was just prior to this point in history that Sir Francis Bacon stepped forward and dismantled the potent and thriving link between the alchemical mysteries of the Emerald Tablet and the advance of materialist science, which had emerged directly from its source. He did this for a very valid reason. The malignant emanations from the false stone, still present in the transcriptions

13

although very much muted by courtesy of Ham's efforts, would have led to an occult science of such dangerous potency that the nuclear threat pales in comparison.

The Emerald Tablet's essence, the magical 'Chem', also known as the 'Ham' knowledge and, when it was connected with worldly royal succession, the 'Ram' illumination, which is the key to the profoundest alchemical revelations, retreated into the shadows, locked and sealed there by the genius of Sir Francis Bacon. Its off-shoot became the practical positivist science of 'chemistry' with which we are familiar today. It suffers from disconnectedness and blinkered vision, but it is inexpressibly safer than what would have otherwise resulted.

The Emerald Tablet (in the form of Ham's transcriptions) passed into the hands of certain Rosicrucian and post-Templar groups. It came to them and remained with them only in the form of these transcripts, containing, among other esoteric secrets, the most ancient and potent of all alchemical formulae.

At the enigmatic little Pyrenean village of Rennes-le-Château, around which so many mysteries and legends and whispered hints of conspiracy circulate even today, the false Grail lay in waiting. It was in place to reap the harvest of the world wars, knowing that the Third Reich would arise, and that Hitler would send his envoys to Rennes-le-Château to retrieve the false Grail, as indeed history attests. Hitler was directly and consciously connected to the circle of darkness which had originally plotted to deprive humanity of the real Emerald Tablet. The envoys came, but found nothing. We still have our world today to prove it!

Why was Hitler unable to find the prize he so hotly coveted? Just prior to the beginning of the twentieth century, a most intriguing character arrived on the scene at Rennes-le-Château. In a sense he is world-famous now, because Dan Brown provided intimations of him in his famous novel, *The Da Vinci Code*, although, tantalisingly, he gave away very little about the real man in his fictional character of the same name.

François Bérenger Saunière came to the tiny mountain village as a poor parish priest in 1885. When he died, he was a rich man, a multi-millionaire by today's standards, and was influential in the highest social circles. It has been suggested that he amassed his wealth by accepting money for saying masses, which he certainly did.

But the money thus generated by no means accounts for all his riches, and the question arises as to why so many affluent and prominent people of high social distinction wanted to pay so much for this outwardly insignificant priest of an obscure little village in the backwoods to say masses for them.

Saunière was certainly devoted to Mary Magdalene. But he was also paid to create within the little church dedicated to her and its grounds an impressive mirror reflection of Lincoln and the burial site of the Holy Grail. Not only this, but he told the story of the Grail, and even of who threatened it, via his strange and unsettling decoration of the church and the designs he used within its grounds.

On Saunière's instructions, the false Tablet was removed from Rennes-le-Château before, significantly, the commencement of the Great War. Something diabolical was partially dismantled, some growing storm a little appeased. The false Grail passed over the border of southern France into a little Spanish town, where it is guarded today by a secret network of Rosicrucian and Masonic groups. It is known as the Sun Stone.[1] Its storehouse of appalling knowledge associates it with the 'Black Sun' paid homage to by the Nazis, symbolised by their rendition of the swastika, which reverses the spiritual power of the true sun. It is unconscionably dangerous, and may it remain securely hidden until the day comes when it no longer poses any danger to us. We are assured that our prayer will be answered. The unthinkable darkness that it seeks to bring upon the earth and her humanity will never descend. When the real Grail comes to all of us, as it will, the malicious frequencies of the false Grail will disappear like a puff of vapour.

Perhaps Saunière, despite his goodwill and cooperation, permitted something of a self-seeking motive to enter into his mission which allowed the darkness to maintain its strength. Certainly he spent his money on benefiting his parishioners as well as himself, and he fulfilled his designated tasks. Yet something sinister and malicious remained in place at Rennes-le-Château.

Beautiful forces play over it as well as less lovely ones, and it is certainly a special place in a positive sense. After all, it housed the true Grail for five hundred years. Fairy presence and magical happenings are often reported there. But the darkness remains. Echoes from the false Grail still sound their hollow voice with a living and dangerous potency over the landscape.

When Callum Jensen, the discoverer of the Grail, first arrived in Rennes-le-Château more than thirty years ago, he sensed its strange allure. And at the point when he began to piece together Saunière's clues so that Rennes-le-Château finally yielded its secret (and it is by no means certain, in fact circumstances militate against the possibility, that Saunière was ever allowed to know just what and where he was mirroring with his handiwork, although he seems to have known many important and intriguing secrets), Callum and his companions saw an intensely peculiar orange cloud with a menacing aspect drift high in the skies across the valley below the village. Very shortly afterwards, a similar baleful cloud appeared in the vicinity of Chernobyl immediately prior to the nuclear explosion there.

Did something menacing wing across the world, intent on finding a weak spot where it could inflict as much suffering and death on humanity and the earth as possible in a final uprising of retaliation from the false Grail? The lurid, unsettling enigma remains. Yet it seems that it was so. Confirmation from a trusted source has been provided. And, in relation to the Chernobyl disaster, it is disturbing to think that, in the terrible death tally exacted by the Second World War – a war fomented by the forces of the false Grail – the numbers that fell in Russia topped the list by far.

The Bogomils come to mind, those 'lovers of God' (the meaning of 'Bogomils') who gave birth to the gentle Cathars, the People of the Grail, guardians of the true Emerald Tablet who arranged, in company with the Templars, to save it by sending it on to Lincoln when its continued existence was most direly threatened.

The Bogomils originated in the Baltic region and the Russian steppes. They were the descendants of a wandering 'gypsy' ('out of Egypt') tribe who were connected to Miriam, the wife of Moses, when she left her husband behind and took a party of devoted Israelites, the Israelites who came 'out of Egypt', far into the Sinai desert and from there into the Baltic lands, where they eventually spread as a community into Russia and the surrounding countries. The unspoiled boreal forests of Russia and the Balkans were their destination, where they were instructed in the secrets of the Sacred Feminine and Tiâmat (whose infinite wonder and potency will be explained) through a sanctified connection with the Tree of Life, for there were secret brethren in the depths of the forests. Miriam left Moses because he denied her teachings and suppressed them – the teachings of Miriam that bore such similarity to that other, later Miriam that we know today as Mary Magdalene. Both women were mistresses of Grail knowledge.

Whatever the lingering power of the false Emerald Tablet to raise its head and make a final strike at Mary Magdalene and Tamar, perhaps by lashing out at the ancestral grounds of the people who unfailingly loved and supported them, at earth's humanity that they loved so well, and at the boreal forests whose feminine magic its evil essence so utterly deplores, its time is almost over.

It is much more beneficial to concentrate on the beauty, wonder and mystery of the real Emerald Tablet that is coming to us. So, after such a harrowing story, let us continue our quest with some mysterious, beautiful tales of antiquity surrounding the wonder of the true Emerald Tablet. For in examining them, we will move closer to the ultimate secret that it enshrines in its depths.

NOTE

1   The question arises, of course, as to why the human agents of the dark forces were prepared to allow the Sun Stone (the false Emerald Tablet) to lie quiescent in its hiding place at Rennes-le-Château for eight hundred years, until the commencement of the two world wars brought a global opportunity for its hideous power to be wielded. Why not use it at once to bring about their plan of human extinction, especially when so much work had

been done to create global unrest via religious intolerance through the setting up of the Crusades? The answer is that strong and incorruptible agents of the light remained within the esoteric groups associated with the land of Occitania generally (afterwards the south of France) and particularly with Rennes-le-Château whose members had been infiltrated by darkness. They were 'lapwingers' (see Chapter 23) who seemed to embrace the distorted doctrines of the corrupted groups, but who were in fact guardians of the Grail. It was they who secretly tipped off Robin Hood and the circle of true Templars that the contaminated groups had discovered the site of the Grail at Rennes-le-Château and had unearthed the Sun Stone in Egypt, and they who persuaded the other leaders of these groups to secrete the Sun Stone securely in the ground under Dagobert's chuch (later Saunière's) where once the Grail had lain. It was also these reincarnated agents of light who stepped in to ensure that shortly before the outbreak of the First World War, Saunière transported the Sun Stone in secrecy to the Spanish town where it now rests, guarded with great sacrifice by the selfsame brethren of light. They had to use powerful tactics of persuasion to convince the ill-willed group members that what they advocated was in the interests of the dark forces. Although (as we shall see) the great ministers of the dark forces could be fooled, the sinister contingent nevertheless remained active and had to be constantly reined in. During Saunière's lifetime, a fellow priest in the next parish died a horrific, ritualised death, murdered whilst laid out in occult mode, a death which inspired the details of the murder of Dan Brown's fictional Saunière in *The Da Vinci Code*. Many other instances of the descent of the shadow, beginning, as related, with the genocide of the Cathars and the Templars, have been reported in the vicinity of Rennes-le-Château since the Sun Stone was deposited there so many centuries ago: it is a resonance that still lingers today.

CHAPTER THREE

Alice in Wonderland

*I*t is said that initiates of the eternal verities teach that the world's deepest truths are concealed in myth and fairytale. They are given as nourishment to children before their intellect develops to the point where spiritual understanding is rejected, so that throughout their lives they may carry in their psyche some dim gleam, deeply buried, of the soul's mysteries. And it is not only to serve this purpose that fairytale, child's play and story are chosen vessels of the wisdom of the cosmos. A fact that humanity diligently likes to ignore is that the overriding spirit of the universe is one of *playfulness*. The universe responds to us when we are *playful*. It loves to teach us through play. Wonder, like a dreaming child, like Alice, and you will be shown the way forward.

It has been suggested by those who guide us from the spiritual planes that the two *Alice* books by Lewis Carroll: *Alice in Wonderland* and *Alice through the Looking-Glass*,[1] contain the secrets of creation, and focus particularly on the mysteries of the Grail. Those who wish to follow the Grail quest will need to come with us down the rabbit hole deep into the interior of the earth mysteries, and eventually, to pass through the mirror. Like Alice, we have to be prepared to dream, to play, to puzzle and wonder.

Only by such means will we be enabled to step through the mirror and back again, and so attain the Grail; for that is where the Holy Grail lies: beyond the mirror of our perception.

We will come to see, as we progress, just how crucial the interior of the earth is (equating to our own 'interior', the worlds within), and of what great import is the mirror. What a debt we owe to wise Lewis Carroll, the child-hearted Oxford don who was a gifted mathematician and who, through his masterly use of 'nonsense', showed us how to free ourselves from the aggressive, unbending, oppressive dogma of our blinkered perception of logic!

Remembering Alice, then, who fell down a rabbit hole and found herself in a Wonderland which was comically but also mystically structured on playing cards, let us first explore the enigma of the Emerald Table by contemplating the card deck of clubs, spades, hearts and diamonds. Suffice it to say for now that the four symbols depicted in the card deck are the four Grail treasures or Hallows, and indicate the four sacred directions in the manner of the ancient Celtic medicine wheel – akin to the Native American medicine wheel but bearing a slightly different emphasis.

Wonderland, which comprises both subtle and physical creation, incorporating as it does the dimensions of our earth, of the soul worlds and, beyond these, the ineffable essence of the spirit, is structured upon the hallowed and ancient symbol of the cross. Its four arms indicate the four sacred directions, the mystical orientation of our soul.

Wonderland, we see, is the greater reality, the all-encompassing reality, within which, by rights, we should always dwell. It has been stolen from us, purposefully and maliciously, and its polarity has been reversed; but we can regain it. We perceive also that the first thing Alice must do in order to make entry is to go within. We, too, must be prepared to 'go within' if we are to find the Grail.

Alice followed the white rabbit into the rabbit hole which led into the interior of consciousness. He is an emblem of the soul and the white light, the spark of spirit secreted within the soul. Whilst on earth, he is attached to the great wheel of linear time, and he mutters: 'I'm late! I'm late!' as he hurries into the interior. Yes, the soul of humanity *is* late in turning at last to the truth, to the reality of life, which lies within, beyond the boundaries of materialism and materialistic theory. But the good news is that we are not *too* late, and late is certainly better than never! The white rabbit will attain his destination.

This white rabbit, who is a symbol of the soul and who bears the white light, equates with the diamond of the card deck, the 'stone' among its four symbols (remembering our quarry, the Emerald Table). In the mysteries of the hidden people associated with the interior of the earth, the white light of the diamond is the symbol of the sacred north. As our quest proceeds, we will come to understand the deep significance of the North or Pole Star, about its link with Sirius, jewel of the northern constellations, and how its secrets are associated with this pure white light within the heart which we all bear.

We might also mention here that Alice herself is this personified heart centre, following her own white light (the rabbit) within, and that she correlates to the sacred west, where the Grail, or the Chalice, lies hidden; for she is, of course, Alice-Ch-Alice, the chalice which is the sacred vessel, the heart. For now, though, we will return to our task of unlocking the door of wisdom symbolised by the diamond.

If we contemplate the white light that the diamond reflects, and think of the colour spectrum it creates when it divides itself into the seven great rays of creation, depicted by the rainbow (and it will help us in our quest if we bear in mind that the rainbow creates a bridge, a span, or a stairway between heaven and earth),

19

we will see that the green ray is the heart of the spectrum. Three rays occur before it (red, orange and yellow, the fiery colours, often associated with the masculine principle), and three rays come after it (blue, indigo and violet, the cool colours, often associated with the feminine principle).

Uniting these principles is the beautiful green ray, the colour of our earth, for earth is known to esotericists as the green planet (although astronomers call her the 'blue' planet), and of course the basis of life here is our green vegetation. If we connect this heart ray of sparkling green to its source, the white or diamond bright light which gave it birth and which is the ineffable light of the divine that dwells in our hearts and in the heart of all creation, we can see how this green ray is its heart of hearts, its most mysterious essence.

Can we imagine that that green light, most hallowed and secret, is in fact living consciousness? (It would be rather foolish, after all, to think of such a glorious mystery as inert, lifeless and non-intelligent!)

Can we now imagine that that living consciousness could descend into a human vehicle and be born to our earth as a child? The frail and mortal human vessel, drastic as it might be in its limitation and as less than a microbe within the entire scheme of creation itself, might still be able to contain a living drop of that consciousness, of that essence, which could yet connect with its greater source and so manifest through its circumscribed being the glory and the wonder of that source, so that the infinitesimal becomes the infinite.

That mortal vessel, that child, was Tamar, the daughter of Jesus and Mary Magdalene. The white light, the Christ essence embodied in Jesus and Mary, gave birth to its heart of hearts, and brought forth the mystical child Tamar. We will say more about her, but for the present it will advance our quest to bear in mind that Tamar, the Divine Woman, is the green light, the clear and sparkling emerald light that was born from, and is the uttermost heart of, the white light, or the Christ light, which we all bear in equal measure within our mystical heart centre. Now we can understand why this special table, of whose secrets we are in pursuit, is an *emerald* table! The Emerald Table was a representation in language and symbols of Tamar, the Divine Woman, as the Koran is the enlightenment of Muhammad or the Upanishads testify to the light of Krishna.

Another important point to remember about this wondrous Stone is that its earthly expression in the natural world manifests as gold, the precious incorrupt-ible metal that withstands the death forces abroad on earth and gives forth its light undimmed. It is significant to note, in this respect, that, despite its incor-ruptibility, its mundane form does not prevent the lust for gold from overtaking some of those who seek it.

The alchemists' true quest had nothing to do with this gold lust. It was, on the contrary, dedicated to transforming the heavy, poisonous lead of the earthly, corruptible self into the light-bearing, realised Self whose essence was pure gold and whom the death forces could not vanquish. And so the Stone, one of the four qualities of the Grail (Abundance, Immortality, Healing, Nourishment), promises the gift of immortality. It is also known as the Philosopher's Stone, the 'Goldstone'.

However, follow the false path to the Grail, and the quester assuredly will reap death. The false Emerald Tablet is always trying to turn our longing for the spiritual gold of transformation into crude gold lust! This lust takes many subtle forms, and it is wise ever to be on the alert against the iron girder it wraps around the heart. Do not worry, because we are confident that we are approaching the Grail via the true path! But we need to consider the false path, and learn from it.

The story of Midas, whose granted wish arising from gold lust turned his beloved daughter at his touch into lifeless metal best illustrates this cunning plan of what the alchemists called the Stone of Death, manifesting as the False Grail or materialism. The daughter of Midas represents the Sacred Feminine, the presence of Tamar within the heart. King Midas longed for spiritual transformation, but he stumbled against the wiles of the Stone of Death and consequently mistook gold lust for spiritual longing. His heartbreak shattered the hard accumulation of materialism around his heart, he understood at last that his longing was to transform himself into the gold of the spirit, and thereafter his 'Midas touch' became the touch of healing. The Stone of Death had been overcome, and the true Stone, the Holy Grail, shone in his heart.

A beautiful story of the Holy Grail or the Heart of the World bearing the essence of an exquisite crystal comes to us from Fiona Macleod, that purveyor of noble fairy wisdom and the magic of the inner worlds. The story is an ancient one of the people of Iona, the sacred isle. She tells of a noble and lovely fairy people of the north who lived within the dimensions of four mystical cities. Their greatest secret was the treasure that dwelt in a sanctified place in the centre of the earth-mandala which encompassed their region. This was a 'green diamond' that was the heart of a place of wonder known as 'the Glen of Precious Stones'.

The mystery of the green diamond was that it bore at its heart a ruby, of rubescence so pure that no other like it could be found. The green stone is actually a diamond, that pure white diamond of the rays of creation bearing the precious green emerald at its heart. Yet within the heart of the 'green diamond', itself the 'heart of hearts', lies a ruby, or a rose, This is the promise to the material world from the fairy peoples – that matter made perfect (the rose) is the destiny of our planet. A return to Eden, the bringing down of heaven to earth, is what awaits us. And we will find it by embracing the wisdom of the 'Emerald Tablet' and expressing the fragrance of the rose – the depths of knowledge and perception in the heart. For, when it comes to us, we will only understand the wisdom of the Emerald Tablet by the light of our heart consciousness.

A further depiction of the Grail as a stone proceeds from a Teutonic legend which tells how the Grail is an emerald that was the central jewel (note the heart reference) of the mightiest angel in heaven, and how, when the angel fell to earth, this most precious of all jewels in heaven fell with him. This truth-bearing myth is most interesting, because it tells the story of Lucifer ('light'), who became corrupt and fell from heaven.

Could a being, dwelling in light and knowing the mysteries, really enclose his light within the dangerous confines of his ego to the point where his whole perspective darkened, and he lost the route to heaven because he was denied access to the stairway to the higher worlds? And how was it that the precious emerald stone, or table, fell with him?

At the cosmic moment that the godly dream of the highest in heaven descending in perfection to the lowest of the low (for that, we are told, is the true identity of the earth plane and its many astral dimensions) sprang into being, spirit began its long descent into densest matter, and the inconceivable mystery of the story of the falling angel began to be realised upon ever more concrete levels. Eventually, it occurred in a way that our human comprehension might now, in our own time, at last be able to grasp. Let us put this to the test; for there was a fall from grace, and the Emerald Table was lost.

The terrain that now faces us must be crossed, for it is the terrain that requires us to understand this fall from grace and its gravest of grave consequences, in both senses of the word. It is the next stage of our Grail quest.

NOTE

1   These titles actually read as *Alice's Adventures in Wonderland* and *Through the Looking-Glass and What Alice Found There*, but for the sake of familiarity we prefer to use the popular references.

CHAPTER FOUR

The God-Headed People

*E*very civilisation, including and preceding our present era, has had its gods. Those of more recent antiquity (the gods of ancient Greece and Rome, for instance) are imbued with a rich, fantastical history that reflects the foci, and the literary and dramatic cultural influences, of the time. Although there are historical accounts (in contradistinction to the stories of mythology) of direct encounters between mortals and members of the pantheon, these are rare. In general, the gods, although central to the culture of the people, remained at the periphery of the everyday life of human affairs and were perceived imaginally.

The strange thing is that the further back into history we go, the more we find, commensurately, that the reported activities of the gods begin to take on the nature of practical, and sometimes even pragmatic, assistance in human evolution. When we look at the gods of the earliest civilisation known to history, which are those of Sumer in ancient Mesopotamia, we discover that they perform all sorts of quite startling ministrations. These include the precise organisation of advanced human society, the running of municipal affairs, the dispensation of academic, practical and technological education in every field, and, even more astonishing, genetic engineering and the science of embryonic manipulation and refinement.

Can this really be so? Are there really records in existence which verify such things?

Indeed there are, although they were discovered relatively recently – in the first half of the nineteenth century – and there were certain factions at that time (the Church, for one), which ensured that these discoveries were overwhelmingly down-played. The findings threatened the bulwarks of science, religion, history, philosophy, social organisation and the materialistic, patriarchal power of the state.

We have been given a collective name for these Sumerian 'gods', whose histories will perhaps stimulate a worldwide awakening into the reality of our origins.

The reference revealed to us was 'the God-Headed people'. We were taught that they were a human community, albeit with god-like attributes, who had settled on earth prior to the appearance of *Homo sapiens sapiens* humanity, for the distinct purpose of developing, nurturing and monitoring that humanity. We will explain why they were called the God-Headed people, but, for now, it will be as well to bear in mind the huge number of beheadings associated with the Knights Templar and the Grail stories, to say nothing of the French Revolution – and, of course, the monstrous queen in *Alice in Wonderland*, who strides around roaring: 'Off with their heads!'.

To return to the time of the God-Headed people, and to document that crucial fall from grace of which we have spoken in the preceding chapter, we must ask you, as once an elder of the Native American tribes said so beautifully, to walk with us 'back through the dawn-star cycles to a time long distant when the land was not as you see it'. We tell this story in the forthcoming chapters as we have been guided to tell it.

Much of it is verified via inscribed clay tablets from the aforementioned ancient Sumer, a civilisation which arose and flourished with a mysterious brilliancy in southern Mesopotamia from just after 4000 BC until just after 2000 BC.

This corresponds with the Age of Taurus according to astrological cycles, which is interesting, because Taurus is associated with coming into physical being, and the element it celebrates is earth. As we shall see, the Sumerian tablets speak of Adam and Eve, or the *Adâma*, as emerging at the beginning of this time span.

The Sumerian clay tablets and cylinder seals are numerous. Many tens of thousands have been unearthed from beneath the desert sands of ancient Mesopotamia (modern-day Iraq) since they were first were discovered in 1843, although their strange cuneiform language, unlike any other on earth, was not deciphered until the twentieth century. Many still await translation. They can be viewed today in collections at the British and Berlin Museums, the Louvre, and several other locations, and they comprise by far the most extensive record of any ancient civilisation ever discovered.

We do not tell quite the same story as the scholars Zechariah Sitchin and Laurence Gardner, who have examined, and, in the first instance, translated the tablets. Rather, we have discerned a story of many tentacles and astonishing ramifications resting unseen but intact within their revelations. Looking back from the overview of our own time, a sweeping, panoramic pattern emerges. Again, we stress that inner listening, spiritual revelation and visionary intuition (whereby we are actually shown images) have guided us to our conclusions, as well as the more normal forms of deduction. Nevertheless, we ask you to judge our conclusions, not by their roots, but by their fruits!

We have some terrible secrets to reveal from the history of these tablets, as well as many wonderful ones. The discovery of these secrets was so profoundly shocking that it has taken quite some time to summon the stoical wherewithal to write the following account of them.

We regard the disclosure of these devastating secrets as an absolute necessity, however; and as we will show, these deeply disturbing revelations pertain directly to the Grail and our attainment of it. It is imperative that its import is clearly understood before we progress to the final exposure of what has been hidden for so long, with such catastrophic ramifications for humanity.

CHAPTER FIVE

The Dragon Queen and the Anunnaki

*L*et us begin with a much more beautiful emphasis. It is time to introduce the idea of the Dragon Queen. There were several Dragon Queens, all of them vital to history and including among their illustrious company Mary Magdalene herself, but the one with whom we are concerned is Tiâmat, the original and almighty Dragon Queen: 'She who bore them all', according to the Sumerian records. She is not given particularly good press. Her sons are spoken of as 'overcoming' her, splitting her in two and 'slaying' her. In Iraq today (the site of ancient Sumer), she is still remembered in mythology as a composite or even a mistress of the forces of chaos, as a she devil, as a night hag – as Satan veritably personified!

What if we were to say that we have experienced the presence of this Queenly One, the Great Mother Tiâmat, and that she exuded a gentleness, a tenderness, a deep hushed peace and an enveloping and infinite love that was unforgettable and that has stayed with us like a healing benediction? What if we were to say further that we are all dragons, each and every human being born to this earth, and that our dragon essence is our most holy inheritance? For we are indeed light-bearing beings, born of Divine Fire, utterly of the light and in the light, although we have forgotten it.

We were shown that the true meaning of *Adâma* (translated as 'beings of the red earth or clay' and representing both Adam and Eve) is 'fire-beings descending into the clay/earth', 'red' indicating the holy fire whose essence we are, and 'clay' or 'earth' our destination. It is no wonder, then, that according to the ancient clay tablets, the *Adâma* are spoken of as being created at this time, in ancient Mesopotamia in the age of Taurus, the great sign of earth and the labours of earth, signifying the season when all that is 'earthed' from heaven reaches a fullness, a completion, and all earthly labour bears fruit; a time when humanity still possessed knowledge of the heavenly Dragon Queen. We have been given to understand that Adam and Eve, brought forth just after 4000 BC, represented the penultimate stage of a mighty process that began many millions of years ago. The aim of this original and ancient process was to bring humanity (which is divine) right down into the deepest point of earthly matter, where it would be contained entirely in an animal body composed of the physical atoms of earth.

There was a mystical reason why Adam and Eve came into being at this time, over six thousand years ago, and a mystical gift from the Godhead that was enshrined within their creation. We cannot comprehend the supreme significance of Adam and Eve until we understand the nature of this mystical reason and gift. If we try to grasp the great science of human creation in a purely pragmatic and positivist way, we shall surely find only an array of blind alleys leading to ultimate confusion. With the bringing into being of Adam and Eve through genetic engineering at the earthly, physical level of life, and spiritual infusion upon the more subtle planes of being, the omega stage of an alpha process that had begun millions of years previously was almost completed.

We say 'almost', but in fact we can be precise: 75 per cent of the grand architectural design for the creation of humankind was brought to perfection at this time. We became three-quarters finished! In one sense, Adam and Eve did represent a final stage in human evolution, because the pair was given a genetic and soul structure which could successfully contain the precious human essence and allow it to flourish as it should, in full physicality upon the face of the earth. Up to this point, no such genetic and soul structure had been created which would safely allow the human spirit its full expression of divinity whilst entirely contained within a physical body.

However, we have not yet achieved our full potential. The western arm of the cross that is our mystical soul-orientation has still to be won. In Tennyson's poem *The Holy Grail* (for Tennyson was the Grail poet) he describes the great west window of Arthur's Hall at Camelot as composed of clear glass, whilst to the north, south and east the windows were of stained glass, each portraying their own story in exquisite colourful depiction of figures and symbols. The last quarter of our composite human soul, that which is aligned to the west upon the sacred medicine wheel, waits to be completed and woven through mystic design into the substance of the glass. In the coming years, we will become a fully human race; but we need think of no ceiling to our development. When we are fully human, true progress can begin.

To place this story in its proper framework and tell it as the Sumerians told it, we must return to their accounts as they appear in their unique cuneiform inscriptions upon the clay tablets; but first of all we need to establish clearly whose history they detail. The answer is that they speak of a god-people from the stars called the Anunnaki (meaning 'heaven come down to earth') as existing contemporaneously with themselves, although they were aware that these god-people long preceded the Sumerian civilisation.

Although 'Anunnaki' is a generic term for all the god-people, the term is so thoroughly associated nowadays exclusively with the Sumerian reference to the particular god-people who came from a planet called Nibiru that, to avoid confusion, we have kept this reference for the Nibiruans alone among the several groups of star people who settled here. The Sumerians did not mention the other groups. However, we are assured they came, although the Nibiruans (the Anunnaki) were their leaders.

The tablets document the activities of the god beings (our 'God-Headed people') as well as the ordinary people of Sumer, and it is evident from the sober precision and meticulous quality of their reportage concerning the vicissitudes of the god-people that in many instances they are recording history rather than story, albeit a history uncircumscribed by the humdrum parameters of everyday life. The god beings were preceded by a race even higher in evolution than themselves, called the Nephilim, which we shall discuss later. The Nephilim, in common with the God-Headed people, were on earth, but although they could descend temporarily to the physical plane of earth – the outermost reaches of matter where we live today – they conducted their lives in earth's ethereal dimensions.

We might think of the earth as, in fact, many 'earths', all connected, all of the same essence and all the same entity, but spiralling higher and higher into ever more refined dimensions beyond the physical level of life, until the material earth and her lower planes are left behind and the worlds of true spirit begin. Nevertheless, these planes are all connected with, and part of the greater being of, the earth. They comprise her matrix. The home of the star people is not the earth, but a much higher plane hosted by other planets; even so, one day our beloved earth will become a true 'home' planet, when we have done our work and our great task is at last fulfilled – the task of spiritualising the earth until her atoms become spiritual, not physical.

We can indeed confirm that we ourselves, the humanity of today, are the descendants of those star people who entered into material bodies. We *are* the several groups of star people, according to our different races, entirely enclosed in a physical body and living a mortal life on the outermost planes of creation. It is true to say that we have forgotten who we are. One reason for this is the length of time we have been deeply incarcerated in a physical body. As we shall see, we lost the Grail, and in losing it, fell soundly asleep in matter.

Another reason for our amnesia is that our means of remembering (literally, re-membering, or calling together all our scattered members or limbs so that we are fully functioning entities again and can wake up) has been purposely contaminated. Just who this contaminator is will be made known; but we need to understand the length and breadth of the story first, because it is important that we do not miss any of its implications.

Make no mistake, our deep sleep in matter is a dangerous and pathological state for us to be in – the true cause of all our planetary misery and conflagration. It cannot continue indefinitely without the direst consequences, both for ourselves and the earth. This is no prophecy of doom, because, like Alice, we *will* awake. The process has already begun.

What, then, is the connection between the Anunnaki and the Dragon Queen? In fact, the Sumerian tablets begin their accounts of the God-Headed people with Tiâmat, the Dragon Queen, 'She who bore them all' (meaning everyone and everything). The star brethren regarded Tiâmat as their cosmic mother, which indeed she was, but it is clear that she was in existence long, long before they came to this planet, because she is spoken of as their source of origin. Indeed, we can only conceive of her in terms of what we may perceive as the Divine.

In the early days of their adventures on earth, the star brethren embraced their profound, umbilical connection to Tiâmat and lived in peace, beauty and creativity.

Their history as it is given on the tablets implies that there were only one or two generations between Tiâmat and those Anunnaki who brought the new strain of human (Adam and Eve) into being (for the Anunnaki led the mission on earth), but we believe that the period outlined is truly an inconceivable one. This part of the story is symbolic, though not mythical in the ordinary sense of the word.

The story of Tiâmat that the Sumerians tell is a confusing one, because she is cited with reverence as the great cosmic Mother, and then suddenly denigrated and despised as arch-fiend and supreme she-devil. Not only this, but it is clear that although the God-Headed people led the revolt against Tiâmat, and that the earthly Sumerians followed their lead, one or two at least among the highest ranking of the God-Headed people continued secretly to worship and serve her. What was going on? Let us find out!

CHAPTER SIX

The Jewel of the Universe

*W*hen Galileo looked through his telescope and revealed the astronomical truth about our planet, the collective psyche of humanity took a direct hit. There was a feeling, evident in new cultural configurations which gradually pervaded the arts, science and philosophy, that we had been ignominiously demoted from our former privileged position at the centre of the universe.

Yet it seems that we can return to those halcyon days when we believed that we were something special. Although our planet is simply the fourth rock in orbit around an apparently unremarkable star which resides with its solar system in a quiet corner of the universe, it was singled out to fulfil a truly wondrous destiny. Earth occupies a unique and crucial position in relation to the grand central sun of the universe (the great sun that breathes out, which gives us a 'red shift', showing that the universe is expanding and all its stars are rushing away from one another, and that subsequently breathes in, whereby everything returns to the centre).

Earth was chosen as the designated planet upon which a surpassingly beautiful experiment would take place. With dynamic peace, harmony and inspired brotherhood as its all-pervading aim, it was to be colonised by peoples from varying star systems whose humanity represented dramatically different, almost opposing, civilisations and philosophies upon the cosmic scale. Each community from these star systems was aligned to God in its own inimitable and exclusive way, sounding its sole and matchless note in the symphony of creation.

Holistic evolution on these planets comprised such a perfect expression of divine order that all these different planetary peoples lived in harmony with God and with one another. Each had their particular home planet within its individual star system on which to flourish; each had their own 'space'. An advanced system of communication centred in spiritual technology linked them and nurtured an inspired and mutually beneficial intercourse. Each had mastered the dynamics and the rigours of evolution; but what if a sample of the most dramatically differing essences among these civilisations, among these highly individuated notes sounding their vibration throughout the universe, were to be brought together to colonise a certain significantly positioned planet under the most challenging conditions in existence – physical matter? Here, their brief would be to enter into the deepest fastnesses of physical matter – the outermost extremity of creation and thus furthest away from God – and to learn to live together in perfect peace and loving brotherhood as one people, even though the unity they created would consist of very different human races, very different collective windows of perception.

Could it be done? This was the great challenge. Yet the attempt, which was entirely unprecedented, must be made, and the mission must succeed, if universal peace and harmony were to achieve new heights and depths and press on into undiscovered dimensions. For the motive force of creation is ever deeper progress into the limitlessness of love and harmony which is God.

Six peoples came here to establish themselves on earth. These peoples or races differed in colour and were chosen because of their dramatic dissimilarities. Two races came from the same planet in our own solar system; they were the white race and the black, both from Nibiru, or planet X, which we shall discuss presently.

The yellow and the red peoples also shared a single home planet.

We have been given celestial guideposts as to which star systems the races travelled from. The home planet of the red and yellow races was situated in a solar system near the environs of the constellation Hercules. The natural life form into which they entered to express their humanity was that of the ox. The golden race came from a planet near Leo, and expressed themselves through the agency of the lion. The green race (olive-skinned) hailed from a solar system near Perseus. Their designated vehicle was that of the eagle.

As previously mentioned, the black and white races from Nibiru had descended into water-serpent bodies (amphibians) which subsequently developed into beautiful jewel-hued human beings – and, if we can imagine it, there were and are indeed sea dragons upon Nibiru! They comprise an evolved humanity of spiritual might and beauty, expressing grace and poise and mystical soul attributes as well as an exquisite and highly advanced underwater technology. They respire transcendental light. They are not evil or satanic, but are rather amphibious emblems of what humanity is in its essence – the Pendragon, a winged being of divine fire that breathes forth the spiritual light of God. Nibiru itself is said to be winged, surrounded by beautifully shaped systems of cosmic matter that formulate seeming pinions of a fiery dragon, large and sweeping yet angelic in their aspect and expression.

Because of their evolutional progress, and because they were hosts of the solar system to which the other races came as guests, representatives of the black and white races from Nibiru were chosen to lead the great earth mission. Their task was to fulfil the divine plan for members of different star systems to occupy one planet together in brotherhood and harmony. Tiâmat, or Divine Intelligence (Tiâmat may be understood as the great Mother God in whom the Father resides), had decreed that the new humanity – earth's humanity – should now come into being.

At this time, Tiâmat's sacred presence was perceived and worshipped everywhere. She was held in the highest reverence, and no shadow of confused human perception had as yet fallen between her and her children. As the first component of her great plan was put into action, perfect harmony prevailed.

The selected Nibiruans prepared to set forth from their great globe, the twelfth and outermost planet of our solar system, with passion and devotion and high aspiration in their hearts for the mission which was their vocation.

CHAPTER SEVEN

The Coming of
the Nephilim

To return to those early times, when the beginning of life, like a new morning, was stealing as a marvel across the surface of the earth, we see that the first human beings to come here were those known as the Nephilim. They came before the arrival of the chosen peoples from Nibiru, those of the black and white races that dwelt there in harmony. When the divine plan decreed that earth was to receive the grace of selection for Tiâmat's great project, our planet had to be made ready. The Nephilim came to prepare it for its destiny.

We do need to draw a distinction between the God-Headed people and the Nephilim, because they have often been confused and merged. But the Nephilim were not the Anunnaki, were not from Nibiru, and were not from our solar system. Neither were they of the other God-Headed people who came here. They were of a much higher essence.

Reference is made to the Nephilim in Genesis, which states that in the early days of our planet's history, 'they were on the earth', and that they 'found the daughters of men fair', and 'went into them'.[1] This was the root of the confusion, because it was not the Nephilim who took earthly human wives, but the higher Anunnaki and other higher members of the migrant star people, as shall be explained.

The Nephilim (also meaning 'those who came down') were not angels, as has often been assumed. Genesis calls them 'sons of God', but later does refer to them specifically as 'angels'.

We have been shown that this is actually an inaccuracy in interpretation, stemming partially from the fact that 'angel', as well as referring to a divine being, also means 'messenger'. The Nephilim brought the 'message' of God to Mother Earth, which was that she was to give birth to earthly humanity; but they were not angels, although angels accompanied them.

The Nephilim were human beings, but not human beings such as we are today. They were 'fully human', meaning that they were Godlike. They shone with the realisation of all the God qualities that were their birthright, and they were known as the 'shining ones'. Preceding the Anunnaki, they came to our planet in its very beginnings, as life first began to establish itself here. They were its overseers, and they worked with infinite patience and care to nurture and guide its evolution. Eventually they selected a particular strain of that evolving life, to modify and bring to a certain point of development whereby it might receive into itself the precious human seed on its way from Nibiru and other star systems, and so initiate the great cycle of physical human life on earth.

As we know, they chose the simian strain as the most suitable and adaptable animal body according to the needs and demands of the evolutionary patterns of planet earth, and according to the density of the earthly physical matter.

This does not mean that humans descended from apes. No ape ever became a human being via biological evolution, and no human being was ever an ape! (As Laurence Gardner points out, this was never Darwin's contention in any case.)

A certain selected breed of simian was, through the scientific procedures and the spiritual and etheric manipulations of the Nephilim, gradually encouraged to stand upright, becoming *Homo erectus* and, crucially, developing a straight vertical spine and frontal vision.

When this strain was firmly established, a certain number of its members were selected, and work began again, this time with much more emphasis on the finer or psychic vehicles attached to the chakras, which had to be in place before humankind could take up residence within the physical body being so painstakingly prepared for it. (Chakras are energy points or vortices aligned along the spine to the crown of the head, which connect our physical body to the spiritual spheres. Each of our chakras has a subtle body attached to it. Animals have something akin to a chakra system, but it is different from, and simpler than, our own.)

Homo erectus, as a species, was left to gradually die out. The evolutionary dynamic was gently withdrawn from it and it declined over many hundreds of thousands of years. The simian strain from which it was taken, of course, had its own evolutionary path, and continued to develop in line with its true animal nature, as is evident today. When the second creature (the one that, selected from its most advanced members, followed on from *Homo erectus)* had, under the ministrations of the Nephilim, developed its chakra system sufficiently to be able to receive the essence of humanity and house its soul, once again a certain number were selected (those who had achieved the highest standards, as it were), all of them female. Very intensive processes were put in place in order to refine the wombs of these females so that the germ of humanity could be transferred to them, and the life forces necessary to build all the human vehicles, both subtle and physical, could operate unhindered within them.

Throughout this time of selection followed by spiritual and biological procedure, a wonder occurred, to whose particular cosmic synchronicity the Nephilim project was specially attuned.

CHAPTER EIGHT

Planet X

*T*he nature of this wonder was that a complete circle had been turned by earth through the stars, and this event had opened a precisional portal or 'window' between the earth and her twin or mirror-image planet (note again the huge significance of the twinned or mirror image). This twin planet is the strange and secret 'twelfth' planet of our solar system, referred to by Zechariah Sitchin as 'planet X' and called 'Nibiru' by the Sumerians. The work of the Nephilim had from the start been aligned in its chronology to a certain heavenly meeting between planet earth and planet X as they travelled their majestic orbital pathway among the stars.

Although planet X is the twelfth planet of our solar system, it has an important connection with the number ten, as its designation suggests. We would emphasize at this point that although our hands and feet – the extremities of our tactile consciousness – consist of ten digits, in fact they *mirror* one another in twinned sets of five, and that the human body has a pentagrammatical form. Earth has a magical identification with the number five, a number deeply associated with Mary Magdalene.

In its twin relationship with the earth, planet X can be seen as the 'ten' planet, even though its position is the twelfth and outermost planet of the solar system. When the moon is counted as a planet, we find that planet earth, the 'five' planet, is actually the fourth planet of the solar system, as planet X is the twelfth.

Unlike the other members of our solar system, this sibling goes riding off into outer space, pursuing mysterious and heroic paths of its own, before returning for a flying visit and crossing earth's orbital path once every 3,600 years. 360° is, of course, the measurement of a complete circle or circuit, and if we regard each unit of ten years of the twelfth planet's return journey as a single degree, we perceive that the signature of its relationship with its twin, the earth, is that of a circle, and that the circle has a compositional pattern of ten. If, from an imaginal station at the top of the world, we watch this planet hurtle towards us, we might sense that its essence bears a masculine aspect, just as the essence of our own earth is undoubtedly feminine. Planet X is our twin, but it is also our opposite or mirror image.

We might think of it as indeed our twin, yet also our half-brother planet, because it was born of our system but, as it demonstrates by leaving it and returning to some far distant elsewhere, it has two sources of origin. And, wonderfully, it has just been discovered in the field of human biology that twins can have different fathers. Is this the cosmic dynamic that gives to the creative tides of our world its history of prominent mated half-brothers and -sisters? For planet X is the earth's virile, outward-bound, celestial lover from beyond the stars.

We return now to that circuit of the stars which the earth made in the region of her centre, her heart, in her early days, when life had flourished on her surface but she had not yet given birth to her own human children. At this point she was given by divine decree a timely ring of great pulchritude and perfection around her outer body which reflected the magic of the star circuit made by her heart. It was formed from the purest water and consisted of ice crystals exquisite in form. It was put in place for her own protection and the perfect shielding of her prospective children.

On completion of this star circuit she received certain beautiful star emanations into her core which created the necessary conditions for a crystalline beam to pass through her heart, a beam which connected to planet X, homeward bound and due to cross her orbit.

A portal or window was opened by the beam, and as the twelfth planet passed by, it released a fall of life, a miraculous rain of human beings (the Anunnaki) who descended into the finer or etheric spheres of the earth. They did not use space ships, but rather caught the current, as it were, and rode on the serpentine tide of energy that swept and coiled between the two planets.

What we were shown reminded us to some extent of the theory of panspermia, whereby life begins on planets by spore deposits propelled to them on beams of light from established ecosystems on other spheres. Margaret Bailey saw them in a vision as anti-matter spermlike creatures swimming in a line across the skies along the path of the downward-spiralling celestial energy, bound for earth. It is true to say that those human beings who came to earth to aid the Nephilim to initiate our species literally experienced the biblical 'fall'. However, something happened on a profound rather than prosaic level which dramatically characterised the 'fall' in terms of a spiritual darkening, as we shall see.

NOTE

1   See the information under Notes, Chapter 19, The Sumerian King List.

CHAPTER NINE

The Wild Women

*T*his ominous spiritual darkening came much later. In the beginning, the Anunnaki were joyfully welcomed by the Nephilim, their 'elder brethren', who were, though ever young, much older and more evolutionarily advanced than themselves. The Nephilim had 'called' the Anunnaki to planet earth, putting out the divine summons at the right time, when the earth was ready to receive her lover's semen from beyond the stars. Of all the races selected to come to her, they were the first to arrive, because, as mentioned, they were to lead the grand project of establishing earth's humanity.

There were among the Anunnaki mighty kings and queens, great lords of life (the 'higher' Anunnaki), who were given by the Nephilim divine tasks to fulfil on behalf of the earthly communities that would spring up once the female creatures with specially prepared wombs, descendants of the chosen line of *Homo erectus*, had received the Anunnaki essence into themselves and brought forth human children. The Anunnaki who thus entered into physical bodies via the wombs of the designated 'wild women' were the 'ordinary' Anunnaki: younger, less evolved human beings than their kingly and queenly overlords. The higher Anunnaki ruled and held council beside the Nephilim, although the Nephilim continued to direct and monitor the development of earth and her emergent humanity.

Of course, it was not only the ordinary Anunnaki who undertook this strange, beautiful and miraculous journey deep into physical matter. As the other groups arrived from their distant star systems, also comprising ranks of 'higher' and 'ordinary' human souls, the younger or 'ordinary' members of each one embarked on the same unprecedented biological voyage into earthly matter. This consisted of receiving a call, given by divine grace once their decision to take on physical bodies had been made, and following it into a 'Creation Chamber', where they entered a state of perfect peace and transcendent bliss as their consciousness was absorbed into the all-pervading love of the great Mother-Father, that supernal containment in which we are all held during our embryonic stage. The Creation

Chambers were located within the etheric fields of Mother Earth: not within her physicality but within her matrix. They were specially blessed temples, with the Grail force, alight as a flame upon a central altar, powerfully present within. The Grail force was the direct, conscious and pulsating link between God and her-his children, her-his creation.

When the ordinary star people emerged, they were in a body of light, of pure individuated spiritual essence, which could, marvellously, begin to interpenetrate the little physical body being specially built for it within one of the wombs of the 'wild women'. Into the wombs of this second creature, derived from perfected specimens of *Homo erectus*, the 'seed' of humanity (a fertilised egg) was introduced by means of what we can only call 'embryo implantation', although it must be stressed that we do not mean by this the clinical, purely physical procedure that pertains to the concept of artificial insemination today.

The word 'uterus' derives from 'utterer', because it utters the Divine Word from which life springs. By mystical means, harnessing spiritual power, the Nephilim and the higher Anunnaki transferred the human essence of our true ancestors into the wombs of these meek, noble, wild creatures, females of the race that were truly the 'wild men' of history and legend. What eventually came forth from those wombs were simian-related baby bodies containing the human essence of the Anunnaki from Nibiru and of the other four human races from distant star systems chosen to establish themselves on earth, for they are us and we are they. We are star children of the universe, come to earth to learn to live as one and create a harmony as yet unsung in our fantastical history, a harmony that will carry all of creation forward in an unprecedented surge.

Sadly, some of the children born to the wild women despised their sweet-natured, gentle surrogate mothers, although these hairy giantesses harboured a deep, loyal affection and reverence, even awe, for the children they had brought forth so mysteriously. The star children bore some characteristics of their host mothers in that they were strong, tall and generally hominoid. However, the Anunnaki had serpentine features, and the facial characteristics of the other star races also reflected traces of their various origins; neither were their bodies as densely material as ours of today. To enter the furthest reaches of matter, as was our destiny, we had to penetrate its realms deeper and ever deeper. Work continued on this great project over an immense time span. Gradually, these disparate characteristics were refined and absorbed into the new humanity of earth.

The wombs of the 'wild women' were utilised once only, for a single generation, although there were rare cases when they had to be called on again. Generally speaking, however, the single generation plan was adhered to.

Having almost human souls, and souls of great nobility and purity at that, the 'wild women' cleaved to their babies, bonding with them profoundly. They could not be allowed to rear these first human children, because they had no real grasp of their developmental needs. They were allowed to nurse them, however; and they grieved for their offspring when, eventually, they were removed from their care.

The Nephilim remained close to them in spirit, to comfort and sustain them, and to protect them from the varying races of humankind, who would have persecuted them. Under the guidance of their divine protectors, these peaceful creatures became almost supernaturally adept at slipping away into invisibility whenever they were in danger of encountering human beings. They are still in existence today, called, variously, 'Yeti', 'Sasquatch', 'the Abominable Snowmen', 'Bigfoot', 'Wild Men of the Woods', etc. Their numbers were never great, and have never increased. They remain on earth in secret and hidden clans. They have a modicum of language, and a depth of soul that resonates with the human family.

One day soon, when we begin to appreciate the spiritual dimensions of our origins, these clandestine people will emerge from hiding, to allow us to learn how we came into physical being. They are not our ancestors, as their DNA will prove; our furthest ancestors are not of this earth. Yet they will teach us how the evolutionary bridge was crossed. We will find that their DNA corresponds to patterns which are nearly simian and nearly human, yet are neither.

One important fact to grasp concerning the star people, of ranks both higher and ordinary, is that they were androgynes. The Nephilim also expressed this androgynous quality. The male and female essence within each androgyne could separate into individual men and women, but only temporarily, and never completely. There was a certain spiritual plane upon which they always remained connected.

One androgyne in particular was selected to provide blood for the advanced procedures that initially took place involving the 'wild women' and their wombs, and also to provide semen to fertilise the ova that were implanted into them. The feminine aspect of the androgyne provided the former, and of course the masculine aspect supplied the latter. This androgyne was known as Kingu. S/he was of the Nephilim, although s/he had a particular association with the Anunnaki. As we shall see, the Nephilim oversaw the initiation of all human life across the universe. Kingu brought humanity to our own solar system (whose focal point is Venus), and so was an ancestor of the Anunnaki on Nibiru, its outermost planet. With the higher Anunnaki, Kingu led the operation on earth, although many other Nephilim were also involved.

It was, then, semen exclusively from Kingu that was used to fertilise the ova from the star people (the 'ordinary' members among the two races of the Anunnaki from our own star system and the other four races from distant stars). This plan had to be adhered to because ova tended to etherealise the vibrational rate of the particular conception, whereas semen reduced it so that the developing embryo could enter deeper into matter rather than escalating away from it. Therefore, ova from Kingu, rather than semen, would have invested the experimental embryos with the tendency to ascend the vibratory scale rather than to move down it towards the lower vibration of physical matter. The upward tendency of the lower vibrational ova from 'ordinary' ranking mothers and the downward inclination of Kingu's higher vibrational sperm met halfway, harmonising in vibration and permitting a guided and manipulated descent into matter.

This meant that when human ova from the six star races were fertilised with Kingu's semen by means of embryonic engineering, they could, subject to treatments and procedures and spiritually directed mutations, be slowed down in vibration in order eventually to transmute into conjoined physical sperm and physical ova so that the resultant embryos could be implanted into the wombs of the 'wild women'. We stress that it was the etheric expression of the human egg and sperm that the Nephilim and the higher Anunnaki translated into physical biology; without losing a scintilla of its original integrity, it had to be transported down a path of ever-reducing vibrational rate in order to get there. It was an arduous, time-consuming and extremely tricky undertaking.

Some of the mothers' genetic material was mutated throughout this procedure and fused with the star people's ova and Kingu's sperm so that the little embryos could stabilise in their uterine environment, although, as previously noted, in these initial stages of human creation, the resultant physical matter was far less dense than it is nowadays. At a later point in the development of the foetus, the light body that was the essence of one of the star people who had passed through the mysterious processes of the 'Creation Chamber' was introduced into the little foetal body, and anchored into it by means of the available chakra system of the surrogate mother. Angelic presence and intelligence were involved in this great enterprise. Angels of high degree worked alongside the Nephilim and the higher Anunnaki to bring physical human life into creation.

As we have seen, what came forth from those Nephilim-engineered, Anunnaki-assisted, angel-tended wombs were the first of the earthly human strain.

Born to this earth as human babies, they grew, and mated and brought forth babies themselves, who grew in their turn, and became 'the sons and daughters of men' – ourselves. We were still androgynes in those far off days, although, because of the pressure of physical matter, we were a little less closely connected to our counterparts than the star people and the Nephilim. Nevertheless, the connection existed, and it was profound.

So we are all children of Kingu, of her blood and of his semen; and we are all children of mothers who belonged to one of the six races of the star people. All humanity across the cosmos was initially brought forth by the Nephilim; and the Nephilim themselves originated from the blood of God, of Tiâmat, Mother-Father

God who is present and living in each one of us and whose infinite, ineffable and inscrutable spiritual power, the 'holy blood' – not the literal physical expression of it but its ineffable and inscrutable essence – summoned us into being. Indubitably, we are all one.

In telling this story, it tends to sound relatively straightforward, as if the procedures involved were smooth and uninterrupted and took immediate effect. But, of course, many difficulties and obstacles had to be surmounted, and the time span which implemented it was vast, involving numerous civilisations which flourished and passed away.

CHAPTER TEN

The Golden Age

*E*ventually, as the plan progressed, all teething problems were overcome, and the planetary communities flourished in their new physicality. The higher members of the six star groups, led by the exalted Anunnaki from Nibiru, sat in council with the Nephilim. Theirs was a government and a parliament in perfect equilibrium, run on firmly democratic principles, although they were headed by a higher Anunnaki queen-king who was the equivalent of a President. Our present-day democratic model derives not from the ancient Greek ethos but from this vastly more ancient Anunnaki-led Council.

The dimension in which they lived and in which the council convened was an earthly dimension, but was imbued with a higher vibrational rate than earth's physical plane, which is her lowest and slowest. Its name was Edin or Eden. The earthly location to which it corresponded was the region of the North Pole, which in the early days of the world had indeed been as a lush Eden, the high place, sacred and mystical. Within its invisible regions dwelt the Nephilim – the God-realised people – and their lesser brethren the God-Headed people.

The Council of the Star People monitored, oversaw, contributed to and directly intervened in the structures and systems of society evolving among earthly humanity. Led by Enki and Nin-khursag (see page 10), they were earthly human-ity's guides, stewards, benefactors and guardians, and to a certain extent their law makers. They taught them practical knowledge as well as divine principles. Their banner was that of love and service.

They gave every assistance to the developing human communities on earth, but they themselves were bound by their own laws, among which was the strict injunction that Council business must never be discussed with the earthlings. This ruling was in place to ensure that misinterpretation and perceived favour-itism did not arise.

The six races of the visitors to earth now incarnate in physical bodies lived together in harmony, and their axis of life was as a maypole around which they danced and joyfully interwove their own contribution to the human brotherhood of life on earth. There did indeed reign a hallowed and exquisite golden age for a time, extending, we believe, into many thousands of years. During this golden morning of humanity's tenancy of the earth, no form of sentient life was abused or slain. Death did not exist, because when a human being's allotted span of earth time was over, they happily ascended the stairway to heaven once their soul had heard the call. Their physical bodies were modified by the wondrous forces of the Grail until the very body in which they had lived their earth life fused and harmonised with their light body and became one with it. Such was the perfect balance of the five elements within nature (earth, water, air, fire, ether) that corruption and decomposition did not come into play. The physical body raised its vibration and was absorbed into the light. Nothing was left behind.

This comprised the resurrection process that Jesus underwent, not at the time of his death, but within three days after its occurrence, when the impact of his sacrifice partially restored the Grail to earth. Mary Magdalene and their daughter Tamar followed suit, ascending rather than dying when their time came. All three carried the forces of the Grail within them, even prior to Jesus's great sacrifice, which was why they could restore the dead to life. The sublime Grail energies, part of their very consciousness, could undo corruption.

The earth was filled with joy during this rapturous golden age, and her delight knew no bounds or limitation in form. The younger brethren of the six star groups (earthly humanity) walked with angels and spoke with gods, for in those days even the illustrious Nephilim themselves could walk upon the earth in their light bodies, whilst the higher star people of the different races walked among us in manifest forms that we recognised as almost like our own, although their bodies gave off an electric energy which made the physical atoms of earthly humanity tingle and quicken whenever they encountered a member of these God-Headed people, and the finer bodies attached to their chakra systems pulsate, as if stroked with divine fire. The forces that the Nephilim radiated were composed of an entirely spiritual energy and were without this sense of palpable, almost stormy electricity.

At this time, the aforementioned 'secret people', those whom the Celtic seer Fiona Macleod calls 'the clans of the Earth's delight', were abroad among us. Such was the perfection of earthly conditions in those days that they were actually able to manifest as an earthly race. They existed alongside us, not as a human race but as a race living a little removed from human communities, with whom they interacted joyfully. This blissful golden age was a harvest which faithfully brought forth the seeds of its own continuance. What happened to destroy such bliss?

The problem began with the higher star people. It must be understood when considering their dramatic and profoundly shocking fall from grace that the dark adversarial powers were on red alert at this time: powers of the shadow created by God to test our forging of ourselves and ensure that no alloy of impurity is permitted to degrade our soul essence. With the sweeping success of the unprecedented project on planet earth, humanity was bidding fair to make a soaring leap forward in its evolution.

Unless all the forces of darkness were brought to bear on the flourishing progress of the God-forces on earth, they would soon be rendered helpless and completely overcome by an ineluctable inundation of light.

They laid their plans and focused their influences accordingly.

CHAPTER ELEVEN

The Mighty Anu

*W*hen Tiâmat brought forth Divine Father from her ineffable depths, their miracle of conjoinment enabled her to birth her third principle, Divine Child, into being. This third principle that some call the Christ was the first androgyne, the perfect reflection and embodiment of Divine Mother and Divine Father in perpetual union. Having initiated creation with their beloved child, the divine Daughter-Son, Tiâmat (Mother-Father God) sent forth an embodiment of this beautiful androgyne, symbol of perfect harmony and love-birthing creativity, to initiate and bring to fruition the consciousness of all her varied star systems.

Wherever life flourished, particularly in human form, the Christ would nurture its evolution and its return to God; and the Christ, vast, cosmic and ineffable, would express itself through the agency of a Divine Androgyne or, later, a Divine Couple, who would mirror the Christ essence to the required degree upon each plane or planet expressing its own individual microbe of divine creation. A special link of sacred light to the Divine Androgyne or the Divine Couple went through the countless generations of created humanity on every planet where it took root, designating the Divine Androgyne again and again in the rhythm that was needed to feed humanity with the light of the spirit, ultimately linked to Divine Child and God.

The Divine Androgyne designated to initiate, nurture and bless the great earth project was Kingu. However, as we know, Kingu was of the Nephilim.

It was Tiâmat's plan to transfer the sacred role of Divine Androgyne, reflection of the cosmic Daughter-Son, to a member of the higher star people, the Nephilim's lesser brethren. Such a thing had never been attempted before. So far the Nephilim alone had carried and cherished and implemented this most holy trust. Yet the plan for the descent of humanity into the deepest, farthest reaches of matter demanded it. The Nephilim, in their exaltedness, would be a little too distantly removed, too remote, to give the sustenance and teaching that the new humanity would require. It was time to see whether an androgyne among the higher star people was equipped to receive this highest honour.

There is a process by which creation advances that involves a special dispensation. Nature spirals and flowers and dances throughout the universe, expressing her beauty on every level of life, for she is a manifestation of the soul of God, of Tiâmat, as God calls creation into being. The human form has a fundamental geometrical balance and structure that springs into life and refines itself wherever human beings flourish, even the lowliest, because the forcefield of our consciousness and the mystery of our being is a pattern held in the depths of God's heart.

Yet so that we may be one with God's entire creation in the widest, profoundest, and most comprehensive sense, a living form from nature is selected for each new human strain to occupy as it sallies forth on its cosmic adventure. Once this natural form has been chosen as the selected vehicle, it undergoes miraculous processes, as has been explained regarding ourselves and the 'wild women' originally of the simian strain. As the first human babies grow and marry and reproduce with one another, the human essence developing within the body from nature is brought to a certain level of development. And then God vouchsafes a gift of great wonder to her/his evolving children.

S/he directs the Nephilim that brought a particular human strain to life to proceed to impregnate certain selected 'ordinary' females belonging to it with the Nephilim's own seed in order to implant within them, as a direct endowment, the full spectrum of the marvels of their human inheritance. It is as if the Nephilim in an act of love and devotion bend low over the pin-point-sized human flames waiting within the wombs of the mothers selected for this incalculable honour, and, with their holy breath, breathe upon them until each one springs into a uprising column of golden fire.

This process was how the higher star people had come into existence. They were the children of 'ordinary' females from each star system. These 'ordinary' mothers, implanted with ova taken from their own wombs and fertilised with Nephilim sperm, brought them forth as androgynes, sons and daughters of high degree. They comprised the 'higher' group among each people.

The higher group was blessed with a radiance of love and enlightenment and divine power that enabled them faithfully to serve their simpler fellow brethren, helping these brethren to reach the pinnacle of human evolution much more quickly than if they had been left to struggle without such inspiration. The development of the higher and the ordinary human communities was bi-lateral in its progress. The higher group needed the vicarious experience of the journey through life of the ordinary group just as much as the ordinary group needed the example and enlightenment of the higher group, otherwise important evolutionary configurations of spiritual forging and information would have been denied to them.

There was one beautifully radiant androgyne belonging to the higher Anunnaki whom Tiâmat finally selected as the Divine Androgyne destined to bless and teach the prospective humanity of earth: the first ever to be chosen from among the higher star people rather than the Nephilim.

This was the mighty Anu, son-daughter of the male aspect of a Nephilim androgyne named Apsû and an 'ordinary' Nibiruan mother. Apsû was special even amongst the elevated shining ranks of the Nephilim. S/he had not been designated as Divine Androgyne to the Nephilim themselves, for these supreme members of the human race responded directly to the Daughter-Son in the heavens, to Divine Child her-himself with no need for a vessel or intermediary. However, Apsû was Queen-King among the Nephilim, and was deeply revered. Apsû bore a familial relationship to Kingu, who was the designated Divine Androgyne for the higher Anunnaki and indeed all the Anunnaki humanity, both higher and ordinary, on Nibiru. So Anu, through these two specially exalted Nephilim, was son-daughter of a king (the male aspect of Apsû), and the descendant of the Divine Androgyne Kingu.

Kingu stood as guardian and mentor of Anu as s/he prepared for her-his great mission on earth: to descend to the 'five' planet with the ordinary and higher Anunnaki, gather together and unite the other star groups destined to arrive there, oversee, with the Nephilim, the establishment of earthly humanity, and serve the higher Anunnaki and other star people involved in the project on earth, both higher and 'ordinary', as Queen-King and Divine Androgyne.

This was quite a task, but Anu was heralded as the greatest of the God-Headed people in that s/he bore within him-herself the highest essence of the Nephilim, facilitated by the familial link with Apsû and Kingu. S/he reigned in perfect accord and harmony on planet X, and prepared with lofty aspiration to set out on his-her great adventure to planet earth, planet X's cosmic twin, sister, and lover.

S/he came to earth, but never walked the earth, as the other God-Headed people did. From her-his exalted dimension Anu could continue to provide a guiding light for planet X, just as it is perceived by many that Jesus and Mary Magdalene, although long departed from our planet, bathe the earth in their light today.

As chosen light bearer to the new humanity, the Divine Androgyne Anu had been anointed, just as Jesus and Mary Magdalene were anointed as the divine light-bearing couple for earthly humanity during the famous spikenard ceremony at the house in Bethany. Could it be possible, then, that this golden child Anu, selected and nurtured as repository for the descent of the Divine Child, the Christ, could darken and become corrupt? Unfortunately, the answer is in the affirmative, because Anu, or at least the male aspect of Anu, did indeed ultimately reject the baptism of the forces of light that Divine Consciousness or Divine Child had begun to vouchsafe to him and to his feminine counterpart as they began their mission on earth.

CHAPTER TWELVE

Star Fire

S omething happened to Anu, or to the masculine aspect of him, when he came to earth. Although never participating physically in earth life, he nonetheless was affected by, and finally partook of, the imbalance it generated. Yet it was not Anu who fell out of balance, but Annum, the male aspect of the Divine Androgyne. The status of androgyne is indicated by the highly significant feminine 'u' at the end of a name, the import of which is reflected in the *khu,* the ancient term given to menstrual blood, which was revered as the lunar manifestation of the power of Tiâmat: the living waters in which she reflected her glory as manifest Creation.

The trouble began through the new sense of individuation that came to the higher and ordinary star people alike as they entered deeply into their new adventure on earth. Even though the higher star people did not actually incarnate as did their younger brethren (the 'ordinary' ranks), they were the first to feel the stirrings of this trouble. The male aspect of Anu felt it more deeply than his feminine counterpart, and became restless and aggrieved. Likewise, the male aspects of some other members of the higher star people began to feel uneasy, and, for the first time, peculiarly self-conscious.

The problem was that, just as there had been a consequent slackening of the sacred bond between the two aspects of each androgyne who incarnated into physical conditions on earth in order to allow them to benefit from the challenges of individuation that the earth frequencies brought them, so there had been a very slight correlative slackening of that precious bond in the higher dimensions among the star peoples. It was less than that which occurred among the incarnating 'ordinary' ranks of the star people, but, although it was so minor as to be almost negligible, it nevertheless emphasised certain actualities that the male aspect had never really considered before.

The real issue was that surrounding the *khu,* mentioned above, also known as 'Star Fire'. What exactly was Star Fire? The clue lies in the name. Laurence Gardner, in *Genesis of the Grail Kings,* tells us that it was the 'lunar essence' of the 'higher Anunnaki goddesses', which in its material translation was equivalent to high-vibrational menstrual blood. We think this conclusion is correct. Menstrual blood alone carries mitochondrial DNA (a spiritually active substance on the higher spheres), which gives the body cells their fiery 'Pendragon' centre. This DNA is passed on to both males and females alike, of course; but its origin lies only within the female, and it is essential to life, to creation.

The lunar essence of the goddesses (the 'goddesses' being the female members of the higher star people) was akin to physical menstrual blood in a certain sense, and it was received by them within an inner cup which objectified as the womb and which also dwelt in the heart, for the inner substance comprising this sacred cup was multi-dimensional. The Star Fire carried the divine sphere or egg of life itself, the 'heavenly orb'.

The divine spark of life at the egg's centre was engulfed or surrounded, like the white surrounds the yoke, by the individuated life of the dimension upon which that divine life sought to express itself. It enabled the goddesses to conceive and bring forth children in their uterus cups. It was the Star Fire, and it was a direct gift from Tiâmat of her very essence.

It is helpful to remember that humanity, including the higher star people, can only receive Tiâmat's godly essence via the means of water and its principle of reflection, which translates into blood, for blood is essentially water imbued with the essence of spirit. This is why the Star Fire – the fiery dynamic of the imperishable stars[1], which conveys and expresses Tiâmat's divine Dragon essence that is the magic of her sacred creational impetus, her very self translating into creation – has to be given to us through water, or the 'lunar' fluid which is menstrual blood, called the 'living waters' because it is the water that conveys the living God to humanity.

Without the merciful membrane that water creates, without its protective principle of reflection, we would be extinguished in an instant by the almighty coruscating fire of God's essence. This God-imbued water fills the uterus cup, the cup being another rendition of the Grail. The uterus cup, like the cup of Aquarius, is designed so that, at the appointed time, it may release its contents in a miraculous flow or coming forth of individuated life. Although the uterus may be viewed as it functions in the body as an inverted 'u', its true spiritual symbol is in fact the 'u' or cup, because the mirror principle of creation, its water element, causes 'upside-down' imagery to occur on the earthly planes. This principle of mirror reversal is natural and beautiful and God-emanated, and is entirely different in essence from the terrible and deliberate reversals of principle that were later put in action by corrupted members of the higher star people.

The uterus cup was something that the goddesses could actually manifest outside themselves. They did not give birth as we do, through the body. Their sexual experience was one of fusing together with their mate to form an androgyne, whereby they actually entered into one another completely. The sperm and ova would unite through the initiation rod of life, expressed through orgasm. We can equate this rod with the creational pattern of the spine and call it Tiâmat's divine will. It is an extension of her consciousness forming itself into a one-pointed direction or destination, like the spine extending from the brain, but with an added dimension rather like a pointing finger. (This dimension is actually present within the spine itself and is an important component of our spiritual power, but we have forgotten its presence or how to use it.) Divine consciousness is conducted through it and is delivered in the outer spheres as a drop or an orb or a fertilised egg containing the holy flame or the divine potential for perfected creation, as in the embryo. The goddesses would then externalise their uterus cups and take them to the Creation Chamber, over which presided the supreme goddess of the womb (Nin-khursag), mystically linked to Tiâmat.

Within the Creation Chamber was the Holy Breath, the Holy Presence – Tiâmat's presence. Here the babies born to the higher star people would develop, occupying an elevated dimension within Tiâmat's heart until they gave their first cry, thus indicating that they were ready to come forth. Whilst they were developing, the mother felt a strong link with the child through her restored uterus cup, which she carried within her throughout the Creation Chamber pregnancy, even though this precious cup also resided within the Creation Chamber itself as a body of light, expanding with the growing child. It occupied two dimensions simultaneously.

(This beautiful experience of being in two dimensions at the same time is often experienced by pregnant earthly mothers. It echoes the mysteries of the Creation Chamber.)

As well as producing babies, the Star Fire had another sacred purpose. It was actually fed to men of the higher star people so that they could fully enter into the mysteries of God, of Tiâmat, just as the women of the higher star people could by their very nature. It conveyed veritable divine consciousness. When all of Tiâmat's creation was androgynous, this Star Fire was shared in equal measure by each of the two aspects of the individual androgyne, and the male counterpart was not specifically made aware of his dependence on it because the process was so natural and balanced as to take place almost unconsciously. Knowledge of the reality of the situation existed in his consciousness, but he was so perfectly blended with his feminine counterpart that he accepted it as a beautiful truth and manifestation of the Mother's devoted love for the Father that she should so nourish and nurture him. However, after the two aspects had slightly separated from one another, the male aspect was unable to receive it directly, as was previously the case. Therefore, the higher starwomen had to actively feed it to the higher starmen to keep them entirely connected to their source.

It was as full awareness of this reality struck home that there began to be resentful mutterings within the ranks of the higher starmen. That Father God was brought forth from Mother God, and that Mother God was the source of all, began seriously to bug them. Eventually, their ego fell out of balance and its vision darkened. It began to know greed, and to want power and dominion. The roots of this malaise emerged from a misunderstanding of the masculine principle by the starmen. They knew that its origins lay in the feminine expression of life, and because of this they secretly and mistakenly felt that they must somehow be inferior to the female.

Anger, jealousy, and self-justification for these alien emotions started to overtake them. They began to regard the penis as a sure sign that really it was the male who had originated life all along, and not the female. They persuaded themselves that somehow, the female had stolen their true status and instigated a lie about the genesis of creation, putting them deliberately in the shade. They began to associate the penis with reclaiming their power and inaugurating a stance of aggression and dominion over the female. Here was proof in this regal rising of flesh, this lordly dragonhead, they thought, that the masculine principle was king, and lord of all. They looked to their veritable king and lord of all upon the earth planes to implement a new dispensation that would declare this stance in its every rule, regulation and expression. They looked to Anu, not as a complete entity, but the male aspect of him alone, to initiate this (according to them) innovative and glorious revolution.

The name of an androgyne was the defining name, but each aspect always bore its own individual name. The names of the masculine and feminine aspects of the androgyne Anu were Annum and Antu respectively. The male starmen began to press on Annum the idea that his own almighty kingship had been treacherously stolen from him by this false idea that the feminine principle could rule alongside its male counterpart as his equal. The imposter must be ousted! The feminine principle must be shown that she was inferior and dependent on the male principle for her very survival, that this was the true state of things, and not the reverse, as she so outrageously pretended by trying to fool the males that they were reliant on her Star Fire. They had not yet contrived a method whereby they could rid themselves of such shameful dependency, it was true, but that little problem could be dealt with later. Could they count on Annum to lead them and their mission?

Annum, the most severely challenged amongst them because the imbalance which had overwhelmed them fed into his given position of power and tempted him to claim complete dominance for his own gratification and glory, fell from grace at this point. He listened to the tempters. He went under, and his inundation turned history into a channel that continues to torment and degrade us as a planetary community today. Annum was the male aspect of the Divine Androgyne, appointed by Tiâmat to serve her spirit of love and perfection with all its accompanying principles of goodness and righteousness in the most expansive and universal sense, and for him to fail was a dark moment indeed in the history of the cosmos that chilled and saddened its furthest reaches.

By no means did every male aspect among the higher star people androgynes succumb to the new delusion. It was only a small contingent among the Council of the Star People that sought to translate its uneasiness and embarrassment over the Star Fire into a devastating new philosophy. However, it had bagged the king. This minority, led by Annum, now formed itself into a circle of conspirators. Their self-assigned task was to thwart Tiâmat's earthly project and make her appear unworthy. This done, they could then advance their plan for all-male dominion, both upon the surface of the planet itself among the ordinary star people where the new understanding would initiate the required philosophy as a blueprint for all future evolving planetary communities, and among the higher star people themselves. Resistance must be overcome. The universe was to have an exclusively male god, and they would set him upon his rightful throne and eradicate the worship of Tiâmat forever.

The circle of conspirators set to work.

NOTE

1   The dynamic of the 'imperishable' stars is the fiery essence within them that never dies (although it seems to from our limited material perspective), but rather translates itself into higher and higher dimensions, invisible to the eye and to all earthly instruments of registration.

CHAPTER THIRTEEN

The Coming of
the Naphidem

*A*nnum called together his allies in the conspiracy. They consisted of members of all six star races, though their number was small, and they included his son, Enlil. Most of the higher star people comprising the Council (referred to as the 'Grand Assembly' on the clay tablets) remained pure of heart, but they were exposed to the confusion generated by the anger and jealousy of the conspirators. This was given little outward expression, but its prevailing psychic emanations, especially because it originated with the king, created an invisible and bewildering miasma that threw them off course and prepared the ground for their deception.

Annum opened the meeting (as previously mentioned, the two aspects of an androgyne could temporarily separate and spend time apart in bodily form, although they were never sundered in spirit), which was conducted in secret. It was their first formal gathering, and it was the initiation and inaugural meeting of that most sinister of circles whose dark rumour courses throughout history as the Illuminati, the Syndicate and the 'Zionist' plot. The latter title is entirely misleading as the Jewish peoples, coming into being as a nation many thousands of years after the conspiracy had been established, bravely elected to contain its terrible death energies and protect humanity from them until the time when it could rise in unity and throw off its shackles for good. Their original core is of the green race, the olive-skinned peoples who vibrate on the emerald ray and who share a special kinship with the Emerald Tablet itself. Their story is part of the 'high history' of the Grail.

The move carried at this first meeting was to focus on the next stage of the plan for earth's humanity. The conspirators saw that they would gain no ground amongst the rest of the Grand Assembly whilst ever their ordinary ranks, now enjoying life in beautifully evolved physical bodies in a golden age on earth, continued to make such fulsome progress. That must be halted, cast into worse than disorder, and the entire plan appear to fail, before the higher star people outside their circle could ever be persuaded to desert Tiâmat and join forces with them. Once they had everyone on board among the higher star peoples, then they could really get to work to change the order of the cosmos.

Their plot, concocted to bring Tiâmat and her plan for her earth children into disrepute, was cunning and brutal: they would find a way to visit ruination on her strategy involving the impregnation of selected females of the ordinary star people on earth with higher star people sperm.

They had been given a particular leg-up in implementing their plot at this particular point in cosmic history. For the establishment of every other civilisation so far, the Nephilim alone had always supplied the sperm to fertilise the ova of the selected females of ordinary rank. This was provided once the seeded planetary human race had successfully risen from the form in nature chosen for it. That was indeed how they, the higher star people themselves from their planets within various star systems, including of course the present circle of conspirators, had come into being. They had been fathered by the Nephilim but had issued from ordinary ranking human mothers on Nibiru and the other three planets of their origin. Yet the higher star people overseeing the process of seeding the earth with its humanity had been vouchsafed an unprecedented and most sacred trust.

For the first time in cosmic history, they themselves would impregnate the selected females of the race chosen for this new departure – the human race on earth, comprising the six peoples who had travelled here from different planets to populate the earth. It was this sacred trust, invested in them as a gift from Tiâmat and part of her original plan for earth's children, that the conspirators now sought so lamentably to betray.

By brutal technology, by foul ceremony whereby subtle forces are distorted and reversed through diabolical procedure, the corrupted star people, directed by their king, abused the beautiful God-knowledge taught to them by the Nephilim and created horror and monstrosity. They infused the embryos that they engineered with pathological harmonies and discordant, degenerate notes as if with an inflow of weird atonal music. They had not yet learned how to split the embryonic androgyne so that its aspects were born separately as a male and a female baby (in fact the Grail had to be severed before they could do so), but they took the process of slackening the sacred bond between the two principles as far as they could. The angels who attended this work, who should properly have been angels from the highest dimensions of Venus, the creative planet, and other angels bearing godly virtues, were instead angels of darkness summoned by the correlative shadow and evil intent in the hearts of the scientists among the higher star people conspirators.

The abused embryos were returned to their donor mothers on earth, for of course the higher star people were operating from their more refined dimension connected to the planet. Sad to relate, some amongst these impregnated mothers, invested with a greater degree of psychic sensitivity than others, became insane or so distraught during gestation that they committed suicide. Seeing this, the conspirators took steps to ensure that the developing embryos purposely inflicted with such hideous spiritual distortion were carried to full term.

The result was a horrifying race of humanity called the Naphidem (referred to in the books of Enoch and Jubilees). Those of the Naphidem who bravely struggled against their biological and psychic conditioning were brought sharply into line by a series of abuses inflicted on them during childhood, involving sexual and physical cruelty, and also a form of terrifying subliminal maltreatment delivered through unspeakable nightmares. A very small number managed, unbelievably, not to succumb to the great gulf of darkness into which they were continually hurled; but, inevitably, almost all did.

The Naphidem slaughtered numerous communities of earthly humanity, because the twin concepts of superiority and of treating others as worthless had overtaken them, together with a resultant delight in butchery, cruelty, and mayhem for its own sake. Their connection with God was so severely compromised that, for many of the Naphidem, it reached the point of virtual annulment. Once this had occurred, the Naphidem used their mighty powers and titanic stature to indulge in nothing but pure savagery and black magic, or abuse of divine forces. They converted their god powers, inherited from their higher star people fathers, into animalistic and demonic urges. By so doing, they brought destruction on themselves and were 'purged from the earth'. Their angelic and god powers were revoked (for they had also developed qualities akin to dark angelic forces), and they remained (and remain still) in a dimension removed from the earth but not far from it, trying always to regain their status and dominion upon it.

The banishing of the Naphidem into a protected dimension from which they could inflict the least harm on earthly humanity had been ordained directly by Tiâmat.

She had seen the plotters set to work and had known of their intention before they fully delineated it in their own minds, for nothing within creation could be unknown to her. Every opportunity to turn away from their despoilment of her plans had been offered to them. Emissaries of light had been sent forth to call their souls back home to sanity and wholesomeness. Yet, unheeding, the conspirators, by their inviolable free will – the great gift of Tiâmat to her children – turned aside from each heaven-sent chance to make the breakthrough to firmer, higher ground where enlightened vision could once again prevail.

The principle of free-will applied to the Naphidem even though they had been unjustly tampered with. They had been given powers in unlawful measure to carry out with unwavering ferocity and deadly efficiency the will of their masters, the circle of conspirators. Tiâmat, always merciful, has given them grace in that they have been allowed to await the time when an opportunity will arise for their healing and enlightenment. The Naphidem in themselves are powerless, even though they remain highly dangerous. They can only operate through earthly human agents, even though they are always planning to overcome this stumbling block and emerge again in physical bodies adapted to their dimensional needs, for they long with a drastic urgency to be free of the non-physical, dreamlike, vague and misty world to which Tiâmat, for our good and theirs, has confined them. They cannot enjoy their barbarous pleasures and power seeking there, except as if in an indistinct daydream or through floating, nebulous memory, although their memories are never so elusive as to calm their appetite to return to earth. In spite of their extreme savagery, they are highly intelligent and organised, and it is part of the felicity of the Grail forces that the hypnotic sway they hold over us – a feat they have managed even from the depths of their sealed-off world – will at last be rendered impotent.

Even at this early stage, a small number of the conspirators wanted to do away with the experiment of physicality altogether. Annum and Enlil particularly had come to hate the feminine earth and her human children, seeing nothing in the entire project but a degradation of their superior race, the higher star people, as an inevitable expression of the will of the despised Tiâmat. They and a few of their fellow conspirators wanted to prove to the ethereal human races (those existing on a higher plane than that of physical expression) across the cosmos that the God they served was a disgusting one, full of filthy schemes because this God was sourced in the feminine principle, and that only an all-male God that brutally derided and oppressed that feminine principle was acceptable. Their plan to destroy the earth altogether was not shared by every member of the conspiracy, who in some cases did not appreciate the full extent of the schemes they backed.

Nevertheless, as well as putting paid to loathsome earthly humanity, Annum and Enlil were aware that destroying the earth and its human cargo, with its designated destiny to powerfully advance Tiâmat's plan for her creation, would be a hugely desirable feather in their cap. It promised an unimaginable boost of speed and potency to their forward march of domination across the cosmos. As far as they were concerned, the earth and its humanity had to go. Personal gratification and a facilitation of their supreme ambition was the glittering double prize that waited alluringly on the farther shore of such an achievement.

What of Kingu, the Divine Androgyne set over the Anunnaki from Nibiru, in whose footsteps Anu followed when s/he left Nibiru to take her-his place as

Divine Androgyne for earthly humanity? Kingu was the member of the Nephilim appointed by Tiâmat to oversee the project of seeding the earth, and s/he led a group of her-his brethren for the fulfilment of that purpose.

Why did Kingu and the group of Nephilim s/he led not intervene whilst the conspirators were implementing their dark schemes?

Although it was divine law that Kingu should oversee the work they carried out, the conspirators, led by the ingenuity of Annum who was an exceptional scientist and spiritual technician, managed to erect such an impregnable barrier of subtle forces and cast such a deep shadow of obfuscating evil over their proceedings that Kingu her-himself was driven back by its pressure. These means, among other infidelities to her, were also those by which Antu (Annum's female aspect) was kept separated by all but the deepest heart link from Annum as he worked his unholy designs. They wreaked terrible pain and violation on her heart centre, and it was to Kingu she turned for help and guidance at this point.

Together, they saw, although dimly, what Annum was up to, and together, in horror, they went to the Grail temple of Tiâmat and waited therein to hear the voice of God.

CHAPTER FOURTEEN

The Dragon Queen

There, in the temple of the Grail, Tiâmat spoke to them. And what she revealed was more cataclysmic and catastrophic than anything either could have imagined.

Not only were the conspirators attempting to bring down the heart worship of Tiâmat (Mother-Father God bringing forth Divine Child in an act of eternal love, to whom we refer as 'she' for ease of reference) throughout the cosmos, causing confusion and its consequent falling away from wisdom wherever they were able to meet with success, but they were pressing ahead with a plan that was much worse even than this endeavour to draw a veil between her and her children. They intended veritably to split her off from her children – in a sense, to slay her.

Of course, such an act is a complete impossibility. Humanity cannot destroy its source, its containment, and its all. But what it could do was to sever the consciousness of humanity from Tiâmat, so that it would seem to us as if we really had killed God. Earth and heaven were to be split asunder. It was to be done by cutting off their divine connection, the Grail. And this would happen not only on earth, but also on other planets where Annum could gain ascendancy. His mission had already begun, and headway had been made on several planets, where their people were falling under his spell. These peoples, although human, were starting to align themselves with the vibrations of the demonic races, and, if they continued on the same path, would eventually become so negative that there would be little to choose between them and purely demonic beings, the negative polarity of the angels.

Annum wanted to destroy the earth and her humanity because he abhorred the physical expression of life, considering it lowly and obscene. The Naphidem, the human creatures he was seeking to bring forth at the moment by blaspheming Tiâmat's creational laws, would come into being. He would release the Naphidem onto the earth because their behaviour could be relied upon to visit terminal disaster upon the planet. Although he despised the Naphidem, with their squalid desire for physical expression, he would attempt to create a New Man that would rise from their ashes. This New Man would be a kind of Titan as we would understand him today, with all the feminine proclivity for empathy, nurture and moral sensitivity entirely removed from his soul. He would be intended to provide the new mould for developing human communities (non-physical, of course) across the star systems of the universe. He would manifest as a kind of mighty robotic crushing prototypical warrior that would reflect what Annum held in his obsessive and corrupt heart as the true all-male God, a wholly illusory concept reflected to him in ever deepening and strident delineation by the manipulation of the dark forces whose grip had enclosed and so completely mastered him.

Apart from this soul-shattering news, there was personal devastation for both Kingu and Antu on the horizon. Annum, as 'proof 'of his supremacy over Antu, had already taken another wife from among the higher star people. The constant wrenching Antu felt within her heart was the result of Annum's progressive separation from her which eventually allowed this act of infidelity to take place. Without it, Annum would never have been able to separate from her for long enough to perpetrate his dark deeds in tampering with Tiâmat's creation so that he could propagate the Naphidem.

Annum's second wife, Ki, called by the higher star people the Lady of Earth as Antu was Lady of Heaven to distinguish between their differing status, had given birth to Enlil and his androgynous counterpart. Following in Annum's footsteps, Enlil had separated from his feminine aspect as far as was possible and was a devoted member of the conspiracy. Antu already suspected as much. However, worse revelation was to come. She now learned that her beloved son-daughter, the androgyne Enki and Nin-khursag whom she had born to Annum before he took his second wife, was not to be granted the successive king-queenship after Annum's retirement. This inheritance was her child's absolute right, for the royal line of succession was matrilinear.

Worse still, the man elected to deliver the hideous blow which would, to a given extent, disconnect the earth and the consciousness of all humanity belonging to the earth from Tiâmat except for a deep, hidden heart connection which could never be broken, was to be Antu's own grandson. Enki had already donated his sperm so that an ordinary member of the star people on earth could bring forth his child as one of the Naphidem. He did not suspect at this time that the normal, God-ordained procedure of impregnating ordinary star people females with higher vibrational sperm in order to speed up the evolutional process was anything other than just that. An earthly mother was pregnant with his child as they spoke and would soon be delivered of it. And, monstrous as the Naphidem were, this child would be horrific indeed.

At first an androgyne, as normal, the child Mardu would be taken into the care of the court, and would grow up in Annum's palace. Through unspeakable procedure, the male aspect would completely take over his female aspect until it would be as if he were a man with four eyes and four ears – in other words, the components of consciousness of his feminine counterpart would become his.

He would still be an androgyne in a sense, but an androgyne whose male aspect had swallowed or stolen its female aspect for his own use and held it under total subjugation. He would then march on Tiâmat (for there was an actual spiritual and geographical location at the North Pole where the Grail was rooted into the earth, corresponding with the heart centre of the planet and the heart centre of earthly humanity's collective soul) and strike the heinous blow. Afterwards, it would seem as if he were a man and not an androgyne. He would have slain his feminine counterpart in 'slaying' Tiâmat.

His name would thereafter be Marduk, and from his name would issue the title of 'duke', for he would be the leader of the Naphidem, and would insist on being given special honours from Annum and Enlil. Although they would never give him kingship, they would be compelled to make him a sovereign prince in his own realms and on earth according to his demands, for his rabid desire was to rule the earth, and it was this privilege that he would exact in return for striking the blow. He would be the first sovereign prince to rule wholly without a feminine counterpart, for although Antu herself and Enlil's feminine aspect had been forced into a degraded position, they had not been cut off entirely from the consciousness of their masculine counterpart as would transpire in Marduk's case.

Tiâmat comforted Antu and Kingu by assuring them that she would not permit the world to be destroyed, nor allow the Naphidem to take over irrevocably (which was really synonymous with the first situation). However, her children's free will must have its outworking or they would be unable to achieve self-realisation, which was her supreme gift, even if they attained it by having to learn from such dire mistakes.

So Tiâmat instructed Antu not to directly attempt to prevent this grievous history from unfolding, as she would simply be crushed and maltreated all the more without being able to halt it, but instead to hold Annum and all the star people connected with earth, both higher and ordinary, in her heart, which would be the best way to retain for them some half understood connection with God. This was the service Tiâmat asked from her.

If Antu would do this, she would thereby strengthen her beloved child, the androgyne Enki and Nin-khursag. Although they would be sundered at the time of the great disconnection, as would the androgynous human pattern for many ages to come, Enki and Nin-khursag would remain faithful to Tiâmat, and would carry her temple, the true temple of God, forward into the bloody, warring, desperate future of poor humankind, destined to a cycle of endless suffering from now on until the Grail was restored.

Tiâmat also warned Antu that Enki, her adored son, would be called upon to enact a deed which would seem as if it were a monstrous betrayal of her, of his kin, and of Tiâmat. She assured Antu that the deed would be nothing of the kind, but would rescue the dire situation into which her plan for earth had fallen. Tiâmat herself would instruct Enki to carry out this act, and would ensure that it did not break spiritual law. She asked of Antu that she would place her trust in her son and her God unfalteringly, and that she would not be deceived into thinking he had joined the conspiracy and so remove her mother's blessing and spiritual strength from him, because he would sorely need them for the dark days ahead.

Tiâmat encouraged Antu by reminding her that Enki and Nin-khursag had never wavered in their devotion to the true God even throughout all the ructions created by Annum and his conspirators.

They had outfaced Annum's wrath and Enlil's contempt, incurred when the king and his favourite son had not been able to press them into his schemes. Their faith would shine like a beacon forever, and they would steadfastly pave the way for Tiâmat's ultimate solution to the problem to appear.

To Kingu she revealed the secret of the Emerald Tablet. The Emerald Tablet was in Tiâmat's heart, the beautiful ray of love upon which all that was to be fulfilled on earth for her human children was written, cherished and held. She would externalise it as the Emerald Tablet once the conspirators had made the final decision to cut humanity off from her heart by severing the Grail (for an infinitesimal chink of hope remained that they yet might think again and abandon the deed), and give it as her gift beyond price to her beloved children of earth. It was her sure and certain promise to us that our suffering would one day come to an end and that we would receive all the wonders that Tiâmat had in store for us, for they comprised our divine inheritance by her will and intention in creating us. In other words, the Grail would be restored to the earth, for without the Grail, these things could not be fulfilled.

Kingu was to be the guardian of the Emerald Tablet. Tiâmat would birth it into her-his keeping the moment that Marduk marched against her. The deepest sorrow and the deepest wonder would come to Kingu, because, as s/he guarded the Emerald Tablet and, inevitably, sacrificed his-her life in protecting Tiâmat – or human consciousness and its proper recognition of her – Tiâmat would infuse a special dispensation into Kingu's blood. This magical opportunity would arise because of Kingu's willing sacrifice. Without it, the necessary receptacle could not manifest for Tiâmat to fill. It was to be a dispensation of the greatest magnitude, because it would lead ultimately to the rescue of the Emerald Tablet once it had been irrevocably hidden by Enlil, as was its fate.

Of course, Kingu would not 'die', but would re-group in her-his own lofty Nephilim dimension after s/he was 'slain'. Nevertheless, s/he would be ousted with brutal force from the dimension s/he presently occupied in serving earth, and her-his blood would be spilled in a sacrifice s/he was willing to make. Kingu would not die at the time of the delivery of the terrible blow to Tiâmat, but would be overwhelmed by the evil forces present in Marduk, who would seize the Emerald Tablet.

However, he would be required to surrender it to Enlil, and, because Enki and Nin-khursag would still hold some power at court in spite of Annum's unlawful move in making Enlil king, the Emerald Tablet would come under the protection of both Enlil and Enki. They would hold joint guardianship, and the Emerald Tablet would be safe. If Annum and Enlil denied Enki this right, the rest of the Grand Assembly not involved in the conspiracy would be likely to rise against him, and Annum would not risk such danger. The Emerald Tablet, though partially suppressed in its emanations, would at least be secure. But it would not remain so. Enlil would hide it away in an impenetrable dimension, and it would be lost.

This deed lay far in the future. Meanwhile, Kingu, refusing to submit to the new dictate to deny Tiâmat, would be put to death by Annum, charged with 'fomenting rebellion' against him. As Kingu died and her-his blood was spilled, his-her mantle of Divine Androgyne would pass to Enki and Nin-khursag, who would assume it, not as an androgyne but as the Divine Couple for earthly humanity, for all androgynes would now be sundered. The former designation of Divine Androgyne had belonged to Anu, but had fallen from the androgyne once Annum had so dramatically lost his footing.

As the mission of Divine Couple was formally given to Enki and Nin-khursag, Kingu's faithful and loving sacrifice would ensure that the special dispensation Tiâmat had infused into Kingu's blood would pass into theirs, for they were a worthy and devoted receptacle.

This special dispensation was to be a replacement – albeit a very limited and circumscribed substitute, temporary and imperfect, but a replacement nonetheless – for the Holy Grail. The Emerald Tablet was the incomparable treasure that would guarantee the restoration of the Grail, but this dispensation would guarantee that the Emerald Tablet, once it had been stolen and secreted away from the knowledge of the earth and her humanity, would one day be returned safely to them.

And so as the Grail was severed Tiâmat would, by way of Kingu and thence Nin-khursag and Enki, her first Divine Couple, give another, provisional Grail to the earth to act as facilitator until the Emerald Tablet could finally be revealed to the children of earth and the true Grail thereby restored. The provisional Grail was an extension of the holy powers of conveyance of the divine *khu*, and it would manifest as a very special bloodline – the Sangréal.

CHAPTER FIFTEEN

Apsû's Fall

$\mathcal{E}$ verything happened as Tiâmat had revealed to Kingu and Antu. The Naphidem dropped right into the midst of the golden age, overran the earth and slaughtered huge numbers of humanity. The conspirators plotted to sever the Grail, and, as foreseen, chose Marduk (originally named Mardu) as their assassin. Annum, Enlil, and the other conspirators, could not 'kill' Tiâmat themselves because their feminine halves always intervened to prevent this unconscionable outrage. An adult, fully developed androgyne would never be able to achieve such a deed. What was required was a child, of greater evolution than ordinary humanity, who could be instructed and influenced from the first to begin to suppress and oppress his feminine aspect before it could either assert or protect itself. An infant member of the Naphidem would fit the requirement perfectly.

This plan was implemented as soon as Mardu was born. Mardu's male aspect was subjected to an abusive process that mutated his little soul into a potential tyrant. His was a conditioned and manipulated psyche which, through maiming and twisting, began to be purposely trained in the technique of suppressing his feminine aspect. Horrifically, Annum's scheme had its genesis in child abuse, for in order to reject Divine Mother it is also necessary to utterly repudiate the Divine Child within each member of Tiâmat's human creation. This process was all part of the negative-spin magic that Annum used to pursue the new ideal of the penis as supreme originator of all life, and man as lord and master of woman, his sexual plaything.

Air or wind, in esoteric terms, always denotes the mind, and mental images were used to teach males how to pornographise and prostitute females both visually and (as a natural corollary of the process) psychologically. This degradation (which men were taught to assume was their inalienable and 'natural' right) was brought about by powerful black magic, which corrupts images and symbols into oppression and imbalance through bypassing the heart – the chakra that always transforms and releases energy or force into higher consciousness – and proceeding instead via the genitals to the base chakra, the 'foot' of the spine or tree of life. It is another of the beheading processes.

The clay tablets relate that Annum had given the four winds to Marduk as toys for the young 'god' to play with. The 'four winds' with which he toyed represent the Holy Spirit, the Holy Breath, which Jesus and Mary Magdalene shared and which is profoundly feminine in essence. This Holy Spirit breathes through the structure of creation – the Cross – manifesting physically as the four winds, the eight half winds, and the sixteen quarter winds, constituting the organisation of the air element which in particular equates to our mental forces.

Within the spiritual structure of our being, these winds (the Holy Breath) are an expression of the Divine Feminine essence moving through us, as they moved upon the face of the waters at the beginning of time. We see that, through participation in dark ceremony, Marduk reversed the giving-forth nature of the Holy Spirit or Breath. Marduk was taught how to 'toy' with these sacred winds, how to make them his playthings. He did this through abusing the feminine essence within himself by pornographising and dominating her, and feeling the desperate screams of the abused child within himself in a state of dissociation.

This sinister, illusory distance from the spiritual reality of Divine Child and Divine Mother opened his will and his mind to the savage adversarial powers whilst suppressing the ousting of them that would normally have been undertaken by the heart, which as a spiritual centre remained locked, stifled and comatose due to the damage wrought by violation.

Annum chose Marduk, his grandson, to undermine and disempower Enki. Marduk was also chosen as the trained and dedicated assassin of Tiâmat because he carried within him Enki's direct Nephilim blood, inherited from Anu: the Blood Royal which carried within it the rushing and leaping of particular divine possibilities – and the horrendous power of their reversal.

Apsû, king-queen of the illustrious Nephilim whose male aspect had fathered Anu, became aware of what the conspirators were about at the point when Marduk was taken into Annum's court as a new-born baby. The appalling programme of abuse to which the infant was immediately subjected alerted Apsû, for the royal androgyne felt it in his-her blood, in her-his heart. S/he looked with inner eyes at the secret events unfolding on earth, and was filled with horror.

It took some years of earth time for Apsû to fully comprehend what was going on, because Annum so cleverly disguised his tracks. Eventually, Apsû sought consultation with Tiâmat, as had Antu and Kingu. Tiâmat similarly apprised him-her of the situation and sought his-her promise not to intervene by force. The halting of the conspiracy could only be undertaken at this point by higher beings if Tiâmat's earth children were divested of their free will, which would mean annihilation for them as individuated beings centred in their own developing souls. They would not be destroyed, as there is no death. They would return to her heart and re-enter the flame of her light, but they would be lost as individuals.

This, Tiâmat decreed, she would not allow until every avenue had been pursued and every stone turned in an attempt to restore them to sanity and the righteousness inherent in divine love. She herself would ensure that the Naphidem were removed from the earth once all hope was lost for them so that they would be prevented from bringing utter devastation to it. She asked of Apsû what she had asked of Antu and Kingu – that s/he would hold all earthly humanity, its God-Headed people and its ordinary members, even its rampaging Naphidem, in the perfect light of that divine love rather than attempting direct intervention.

Whilst the feminine aspect of Apsû was ready to follow Tiâmat's injunction, the androgyne's male aspect struggled to do so. His protective element came to the fore, and he watched with ever deepening sorrow and disbelief as Marduk underwent his diabolical system of programming and Annum and Enlil came to relish the idea of 'slaying' Tiâmat more with each passing day. Tiâmat's mercy was offered to Marduk, and he was given the opportunity to leave Annum's palace and escape to the mountains, where he would have been cared for by a community of esoteric brethren dedicated to the holy temple of Tiâmat. But so addicted was he to the power and privilege of his position and to the glittering promise of his future that he could not be coaxed away from court. At dead of night, in the silent darkness throughout whose watches he was exposed to his terrible 'conditioning', his soul craved and screamed for such mercy and he would have fled in an instant. Yet by the next morning his tears were dry and he had forgotten, not without manipulative facilitation, the agony and desperation of the lightless hours.

At length, the male aspect of Apsû became so anguished that he decided to exterminate his son and the circle of conspirators he headed. He knew he could not eliminate them without also killing their innocent female aspects, and, furthermore, that via his act, Tiâmat's vital earth project would come to an end and its tragic passing would affect the entire universe. He knew that all these things would directly contravene divine law. Yet still he could not be persuaded to relinquish his intention, so traumatised and outraged was he at the idea of what his son intended to do – his androgyne child, hope and joy of the Nephilim, hope and joy of Nibiru, hope and joy of planet earth, and hope and joy of Tiâmat, fallen, irrevocably, into basest darkness. His heart broke, and he too, like Annum, descended in vibration until his sanity was compromised, although Apsû's male aspect lost his equilibrium through grief and regret rather than selfish pride and jealousy.

Tiâmat, seeing he could not be prevailed upon, instructed Enki to march on him, and, through an exertion of will, 'seize Apsû's crown and cloak of fiery rays' in order to banish him from access to the earth dimension. It was said that Enki killed the male aspect of Apsû, who was known as the First or Primordial Father according to the Sumerians because of his kingship over the Nephilim. In fact Enki did not kill him, but rather assumed his role as representative of the balanced sacred masculine principle after that of Apsû had been banished at the command of Tiâmat. It is true that the etheric bridge which carried him to earth was blocked by Enki so that the male Apsû could no longer find his point of entry, but his blood was not spilled and he was not ousted brutally, as Kingu was.

Apsû's bright crown and cloak of fiery rays were a representation of what Divine Mother had vouchsafed to Divine Father on birthing him into being as an individuated aspect of God. They were the manifestation of his will, his active, creative principle, his kingly insignia just as the divine *khu*, symbolised by the dragon, was her royal signature and vessel of power and authority. The crown and cloak now passed to Enki as the sole bearer of the mark of the true Father God, who neither exulted in war nor sought to dominate Divine Mother, but ruled in equality with her so that they created a perfect ring, without beginning, without end, of divine love, divine joy, and divine harmony.

As bearer of this holy sign of the endless ring of light containing the four-armed cross of creation, which later became the Mark of Cain, Enki should properly have had the backing of the male aspects of Anu, Kingu and Apsû. Yet, after the death of Kingu which was soon approaching, Enki would stand alone. Annum and Apsû had fallen and Kingu could not return. The imperative to restore the correct and balanced understanding of Father God to Enki's own people and to the nations of the earth descended in its entirety on his shoulders. He would have to lead the way.

Antu, horrified at the demise of the male aspect of the great and royal Apsû, took a blow that almost felled her when Annum declared that Enki had killed the First Father. Yet Tiâmat's words sounded in her mind, and the divine *khu* danced through her being. She remained standing. And, because of her strength and devotion, Enki and Nin-khursag were empowered to move forward with their great mission. Had their mother's blessing been withdrawn, they would have foundered.

If the Divine Couple had lost their footing, we would have lost our civilisation, our species, and our world, and the entire plan for creation would have had to be dismantled. Our earth carried within it the potential of the egg of the shining Pendragon, or, conversely, the egg of the poisoning viper. Enki and Nin-khursag now bore forward the torch that would ultimately connect us once again to our highest dragon essence.

CHAPTER SIXTEEN

The Dolorous Blow

*A*fter the removal of Apsû, the conspirators, who thought that they them-selves had brought about his demise and were ignorant of Tiâmat's decree, moved their plot forward. Marduk, honed and prepared, was given the signal to strike the blow that would 'slay' Tiâmat.

We can imagine Marduk advancing on Tiâmat, or on the holy seat where her divine connection to the earth was enshrined, showing her by his flaunting of the usurped kingly insignia (his false authority) that *his* way, his rule, his philosophy (a complete denial of the Sacred Feminine) was to supplant the Great Mother of All. However, Marduk did not act alone. His was the final assault, but before he made it and as it was applied, Annum and his circle were busy configuring unholy ritual: what today would be termed black magic, but black magic taken to its furthermost abysmal degree. They used the power of the masculine principle in reverse-spin mode to implement their will.

Marduk was an embodiment of the male as military aggressor and tyrant, having abandoned all concepts of protector and server. He was the prototype of the new male, the rendition of the masculine principle that Annum and his companions wished to bring into being. Indeed, as Tiâmat foretold, Marduk now demanded of the conspirators that the conditions of his assault on her must be that he was given absolute authority over his fellow gods and granted world dominion on earth.

We will see that Annum, Enlil and the other conspirators sniggered up their sleeve at his stipulations, as they had no intention whatsoever of granting him power over their own clan, the God-Headed people. To them, Marduk was a despised puppet; but a puppet they needed to humour, all the same, and he was indeed granted his 'dukedom' on earth and within his own realm, as shall be explained. Nevertheless, he made clear his insistence on claiming the first kingship of solely masculine rule and advanced on Tiâmat decorated with its insignia, although these would be immediately surrendered to Annum once the blow had been struck.

Marduk, on accomplishing his supreme transgression, stole the Emerald Tablet from the overwhelmed Kingu, to whom Tiâmat had passed it as the Grail was severed, and pinned it in triumph to his own breast (his heart centre). He did this to make the statement that the all-masculine heart had divested the Sacred Feminine, the heart of Tiâmat, of its divine authority and now dominated it entirely. When Annum insisted that this was handed over to him as well, Marduk sulked but obeyed, because he was afraid of Annum and Enlil, the two who had arranged and overseen his dark nights of abuse. Jointly, they held the power of nightmares over him. Marduk would be consoled with his recipience of the rod and the ring, two important spiritual emblems of royal authority; but in his case they would be the false emblems of a false ruler, given as a mere pat on the head for fulfilling his designated task.

The rod, indeed, was the 'Rod of Justice', the lance infused with evil with which Marduk 'killed' Tiâmat and which afterwards became known as the Spear of Destiny that passed from Sumer to Babylon, from Babylon to Rome, and thence to the Jerusalem of two thousand years ago, where it did indeed fulfil a date with a similarly cosmic destiny.

We see in Marduk a Luciferic drive, a being obsessed with his own self-glorification and aggrandisement, a world dominator whose worst example in mundane human terms was Adolf Hitler. Hitler and Marduk were bound by a direct link, as shall be revealed. Although there was a special bond as of slave and master between these two, Marduk's tentacles extended to all tyrannical leaderships throughout history across the globe. As he had insisted, he received his rights of dark dominion.

How did Marduk 'kill' Tiâmat? The clay tablets describe his assault. He advanced, armoured and shielded and wielding a lance or an arrow. His armour and shield were to protect him, not from Tiâmat's wrath as the tablets suggest, but from the hideous and baleful powers he was about to put into play. First, he used the 'four winds' to disorientate and confuse Kingu, who stood by as protector of the Grail and of the holy temple of Tiâmat. Then he reversed the winds, and blew them back through Tiâmat's 'mouth'. The physical aspect of the 'four winds' included not only the winds of the earth's atmosphere, but also the magnetic forces of the planet and the solar winds composed of charged particles that reach the earth. The tablets tell us that it was the action of these winds upon her heart centre which so disturbed Tiâmat that she 'rose up' in remonstrance against Annum. He had been given the gift of the holy light of God, and, through Marduk, had used it against her in an outrageous act of reversal. An unutterably sacred trust had been violated.

Yet it was not Tiâmat who thus rose up against Annum (poor Marduk was always recognised as a manipulated puppet), but the earth herself. For, of course,

Marduk was not raising his desecrating lance against an entity that was embodied as he was embodied, but against the direct, conscious and manifesting connection of the earth and her children to their God.

Nevertheless, because this connection – the Holy Grail – is an entirely feminine energy, the descent of the lance was intended as a purposeful death blow to Mother God. The seat of the connection (Tiâmat's 'mouth') was located at the point on and in the earth of the North Pole, which was lush and temperate in those days and comprised the beautiful continent of Hyperborea. The pristine boreal forests that once graced the serpentine ridges of Hyperborea extended over her borders into what is now Russia and the Balkans. These immaculate forests enshrine many secrets concerning the Sacred Feminine and the Tree of Life.

The entire body of Mother Earth shuddered through and through with the horror of this outrage. The waves of the sea, the powers of the air, the forces of the earth, the living dynamic within sunlight: all rose in an act of cosmic admonishment.

The sea boiled and upsurged in mighty tsunamis. Its surface roiled eerily for a long time afterwards as if something monstrous were about to emerge, for the reversals that Annum had put in place do indeed create unhallowed monsters. The wave form which is inherent in all life, all energy, is the essence of Tiâmat's serpentine emanations. This is the secret of her life and consciousness, of all life and consciousness, and the most obvious and visually evident symbol of her mysteries upon the face of the earth is the sea. The air cracked with strange lightning strikes, as if the sanity of the planet – that which kept all its systems intact and in perfect perpetuation – was itself beginning to hallucinate. The winds howled like a sinister macrocosmic beast in a supernaturally vast and thunderously echoing cavern.

What was meant by Marduk's stated act of 'reversing the four winds' and 'blowing them back through Tiâmat's mouth'? Her 'mouth' was the point where the Grail entered the earth, and the four winds of the Holy Spirit the essence of the arms of the cross of creation in their proper flow within the human heart and consciousness, where we and the earth are linked with God. Marduk had reversed this power and spirit of the heart (for all hearts are one, and connect us to God) by a horrible manipulation of divine forces.

Marduk administered the coup de grâce by shooting his 'red arrow' or lance through Tiâmat's centre or heart: an arrow or lance that had been specially prepared over a great span of time as a mighty symbol of reversal. Tiâmat's heart was located in a mystical sense at the heart of the earth, because although our hearts beat because Tiâmat's heart beats, and all beat in time with hers and rest within hers, there is a special enthroning of her heart at the earth's centre. We will discuss this mysterious red arrow further, for its relation to the Grail, and indeed to our human history, is of vital importance. It bears a positive and a negative aspect, as is clear from its association with both Marduk and Robin Hood. Its red colour indicates that its essence can express the magic of the heart, or conversely be used violently to lacerate and spill blood.

Having applied the profane use of the lance or red arrow, Marduk then tore Tiâmat apart, separating earth from heaven and cutting off humankind from its higher self or heart-centred soul, so that it had to struggle onwards along the path of evolution as one blind, deaf and dumb to spiritual realities. Marduk accomplished this horrendous deed by reversing or rejecting the Holy Spirit, so that it 'inflated' Tiâmat's heart or centre.

This means that he somehow, by reverse-spin magic pertaining to the Holy Spirit, deliberately brought about a highly dangerous situation on earth that could be tipped into catastrophe by precipitation. The resultant situation was not 'natural' in the true sense, but it did arise through the agency of the powers of nature, which in themselves are an expression of the Holy Spirit or Breath. It was at this point that Marduk proceeded to his planned act of precipitation by plunging the 'red arrow' into Tiâmat's centre, or heart. The North Pole became covered in ice, earth's heart and ours shifted slightly off balance (the former is referred to as the 'polar wobble', whilst our hearts relocated a little to the left of centre within us), the Nephilim were forced to detach themselves entirely from the lower dimensions of the planet, and the impact of a body from outer space attracted by Marduk's act of perfidy destroyed huge numbers of humanity. Some 70,000 years ago, his baleful deed descended upon the world.

It is worth contemplating (although perhaps not for too long) this act of ultimate betrayal and unimaginable treachery. We might begin to glimpse thereby how Jesus, on his cross, had to endure the re-enactment of that unspeakable deed, willingly and lovingly accepting its brutal impact into himself, in order to cosmically reverse it. By so doing, Jesus reversed the reversal. And we might also understand why it was unnecessary for Mary Magdalene, in her representation of the feminine half of the Divine Couple whom once Anu had embodied, to undergo the same sacrificial crucifixion. The Sacred Feminine, of course, has undergone continuous sacrifice for millennia, ever since Marduk's blow was struck.

Zechariah Sitchin, in his analysis of the story, considers Tiâmat to be a planet into which the selected aggressor (Marduk, himself also a planet) purposely hurtled, thus splitting her in two. Laurence Gardner, on the other hand, draws on many valid sources to prove that Tiâmat was the original Dragon Queen bearing a serpentine form.

It seems that both these analyses are true, as the human Marduk embodied the forces of Mercury in distorted form. Tiâmat *was* the Dragon Queen, the great originator of life; and the battleground upon which she was rent in two was indeed our own mother earth.

The blow that separated us from Tiâmat is known as the Dolorous Blow. The Dolorous Blow was a beheading,[1] and in consideration of this significant fact it is useful to remember that the name the higher star people used to denote themselves was 'the God-Headed people'. They were not fully God-realised, as the Nephilim were, but they were 'God-Headed' – that is, they could attain a measure of exalted God-consciousness whilst living in an individuated state in a body that could walk the earth, even though its atoms were not physical atoms. In a sense, we can even imagine, just as in *Alice*, that their heads left their earthbound bodies behind, although still firmly attached, of course, and shot off into the heavens! It is a truth literalised for us by courtesy of Lewis Carroll, and it helps us to understand an important inner reality

At this point we would draw attention to the many depictions of Mary Magdalene kneeling by a cross, sometimes in the form of a young tree or sapling, with a human skull at its base; and also to the fact that numerous beheadings were associated with those who upheld her honour and protected her mysteries. These symbols are in place partly to show us, when we are ready to see, that we are descended from and can share the secrets of the God-Headed people, those elevated ones who could attain God-consciousness whilst still on earth.

In those days, the Path of Awe was indeed grandly open to the spiritual stars (meaning the divine mystery emanating from their essence), and we might pause and reflect here that this majestic, star-strewn Open Way *was* and *is* the Holy Grail, for without it we slowly become moribund and fade away into death and darkness. This is the deeper, esoteric meaning behind the biblical quote: 'Without vision, the people perish.' The Holy Grail, the grand open pathway to the stars that links earth with heaven and heaven with earth, *is* vision – vision in all its dimensions and replete with all its aspects of meaning.

We can find the Grail within today by means of individual striving through meditation and inner discipline, but the 'Path of Awe' between heaven and earth is indeed no longer shining and grandly open as it used to be in the early golden days, so that ordinary people could see and sense and taste the radiant essence of the imperishable stars, and walk and talk with angels and receive the palpable blessing of the Holy Spirit. As we know, there can be no Grail without heart-centred consciousness, demonstrated so forcibly for us by the presence of the disembodied heart, King Dagobert's heart, as the Grail custodian.

When the Dolorous Blow 'beheaded' Tiâmat, so severing heaven and earth, or her consciousness (accurately speaking, our access to it) from her body, it put into operation an evil that actually separated consciousness, the inner worlds and the unifying principle itself, splitting asunder what could never be in balance again until healing and re-conjunction took place. From this great act of brutality arose the stories of the Lost Bride, roaming the earth in mourning, awaiting the day when she will be admitted once more into the presence of her 'husband', God, in the heavens.

(As usual, over time the story has fallen into a male bias, with the bride somehow managing to have cut herself off from heaven, being foolish and female, and the male God heroically and 'forgivingly' trying to lift her out of her waywardness!) From this cruel split, too, comes the aforementioned story of the Fisher King, desperately wounded in his genitals where something precious has been torn away from him and which constantly weep blood, so that his whole life is one great supplication for the mercy of healing.

It is this king's agony that Percival witnesses when he goes in search of the Grail. By failing to ask questions of the Grail Maidens (the only two who can usher the Grail back into human consciousness so that a cure can be effected), the king's agony continues, the terrible curse of the wasteland prevails, and Percival, chastened and ashamed, fails to achieve the Grail.

What we need to understand today is that when our forefathers 'beheaded' Tiâmat, she was not decapitated, as of course such a concept applied to God is absurd; but essentially we ourselves were thoroughly decapitated. We lost the link between our true selves and our higher consciousness, between earth and heaven. The energies with which we replenish ourselves in an effort to replace the divine draught that is our birthright are predominantly full of falsity and poison. They shunt humanity from disaster to disaster, and turn the great barbarous wheel of endless suffering with a remorseless hand and a conscious intent.

We are about to learn how to permanently stay that hand and reclaim our magnificent birthright. We ourselves will advance into the status of God-Headed people; and, unlike our foolish forebears, we will surely cherish and protect the Holy Grail once it is restored to us.

NOTE

1 Interestingly, the symbolic Templar story of the Dolorous Blow tells how an unsuspecting knight was hideously tricked into beheading his 'sister', emblematic of his feminine androgynous self.

CHAPTER SEVENTEEN

The Enigma of the Red Arrow

What is the secret of the red arrow that Marduk used to 'kill' Tiâmat? This red arrow can be identified as the lance in the Grail stories that continually drips blood. It is a revered constituent of the Grail mysteries, and it manifests many times throughout our human story. One of its facets is the Rod of Justice, purloined by Marduk and wielded by him as the supreme token of his kingly insignia: a rod which he would convert to the brutal quality of merciless unbending iron in the pursuit of his own self-gratification as would-be ruler of the world.

It is the lance of the Roman centurion Longinus which was thrust through the side of Jesus as he hung on the cross, delivering the death blow and piercing first his spleen (an important chakra, and deeply significant to the nature and meaning of the lance, as the spleen is anciently associated with the forces of wrath which it was his mission to overcome) and then his heart. It is the lance which is Joseph of Arimathea's staff that burst into flower as the venerable sage drove it into the earth on Wearyall Hill at Glastonbury, for when a true son of the true Father uses the lance, it does not cut earth off from heaven but rather unites her with it in bliss. The mysteries of human genitalia, the penis and the vagina, are interwoven into its magic, their culmination, in right mode, its highest power and blessing. In reverse mode, they transmute into a breeding nest of the power of cursing at its rankest and most poisonous.

It is the lance that pierces Dagobert's eye; and, finally (though that is an ill-advised word to use in relation to this mystic lance!), as the Spear of Longinus once again, this time in Hitler's possession and, interestingly, called the Spear of Destiny, so linking it with the hallowed knowledge engraved upon the Emerald Tablet of Destiny or Destinies.[1]

In this context of sacred knowledge, it has another, most interesting aspect in that it relates to what Dr Peter Coveney and Dr Roger Highfield refer to as 'the Arrow of Time' in their scientific best-seller of the same title. Here, they ask the question as to why time points from the past to the future with the precision and focus of an arrow, and compare ideas of linear and circular time. It seems that the unforgiving nature of time, where every nanosecond slips fugitively into the unmanifest as we experience it, is somehow connected with the manipulations of Enlil, the second son of Annum. He was certainly given special status as master and lord of karma and time alongside his father, who gave his name to our calculation of the round of the year.

Our current perception of time is one of Enlil's distortions, in the perpetration of which he was aided by a mind whose scientific vision was cosmic in its proportions (we shall reveal more of this astonishingly gifted scientist in due course). We remain convinced that the nature of this 'arrow of time' (a term originated in 1927 by the astrophysicist Arthur Eddington) has some connection with the misuse of the Red Arrow or sacred lance, especially as two earlier scientists who specifically dedicated their lives to the study of 'the arrow of time' died in sinister circumstances, by their own hand, as a culmination of progressive madness.

Hitler, the very embodiment of the false path to the Grail, was obsessed with discovering the four Grail treasures, certain that when he had attained them, his dream of world domination would be granted realisation.

He managed to obtain a lance which was once the treasured possession of certain ancient kings of Britain and France and which was actually believed to be the Spear of Longinus, the centurion who had killed Jesus by plunging it into his side at the crucifixion.

This spear had, allegedly, assured victory after victory for the great king Charlemagne, but had eventually passed from his ownership into other hands, whereupon his triumphs promptly came to an end. In fact, on the same day that the American 7th Army seized the lance appropriated by Hitler as a trophy from Nuremberg Castle (30 April 1945), Hitler conceded that his mission had failed and, within the confines of his bunker, whose walls were painted with sinister Nazi 'angels' which were actually depictions of the Naphidem, took his own life.

Eerily, Nuremberg was renowned as a centre of toymaking and playthings, echoing associations with Hitler's prototype, Marduk. The lance, rescued from Nuremberg, was eventually entrusted to the Hofburg museum in Austria. On its appearance in Wolfram von Eschenbach's *Parzival*, one of the earliest and most famous of the Grail stories, the lance engenders alarm among the knights of the Grail Castle. They instruct Parzival concerning its malignity, explaining that it is an embodiment of the forces which corrupt and kill that which enables human beings to access their higher spirit – it cuts humankind off from its higher self. In other words, it embodies what reversed the Holy Spirit, 'killing' Tiâmat and eventually banishing the sacred stairway from earth to heaven (one of the Four Hallows or aspects of the Grail – Immortality – and in fact its unified essence).

Although this is indeed so, the spear (or the lance or the arrow) bears within it the magnificent life-giving potential of what it truly is in its positive state. The 'red arrow' which is described in the Sumerian texts has a deep esoteric meaning. It was pure and wondrous in its power before its forces were reversed, and it was given to Marduk by Annum, to whom in comparison he was but a callow youth with no understanding of the potency of that which he wielded, except that it would in some way transfer its unimaginable might to himself.

Robin Hood, a great Templar, certainly knew how to use the power of the lance for the noble purpose of protecting the Grail. The Red Arrows flying team which grace the skies above the ancient city of Lincoln today, creating endlessly significant symbols pertinent to the Grail story among the clouds, unknowingly commemorate this red arrow, this most holy lance, this Spear of Destiny whose forces will one day return to their original pristine state

The carving of the Falling Knight (one of the Grail clues) within the cathedral, who bears it in his back, through his spleen, and points via its agency towards the resting-place of the Holy Grail (from our turbulent past to the glory of our future), tells of the mystery of the Red Arrow, for he awaits the heart-piercing awakening that it will eventually bestow, and that eventually, together with the rest of humanity, he will no longer be able to resist or deny.

NOTE

1   Hitler was determined to find the Holy Grail and the Ark of the Covenant to complete his collection of renowned magical implements. He sensed (or was informed by the hideous 'chiefs' who controlled him from the Naphidem dimension) that each was a repository of unimaginable power. He sent scouts and spies on various missions in an effort to locate these implements. Rennes-le-Château, in the south of France, was specifically targeted. He never managed to procure anything, thank goodness, except for his previous discovery of the Spear of Destiny (which in itself was worrying enough). We have learned from our source that one of the Old Testament Tamars, King David's daughter, oversaw the operation of hiding away the Ark in Jerusalem, in order to further curtail its harmful influence. It is there still. The Ark is almost as dangerous as the false Emerald Tablet, as it grants world dominion. Its history and occult significance will be explained in full.

The equally dangerous Syndicate (see Chapter 66), although it is not able to approach very close, has nevertheless managed to establish subtle contact with its forces (which are vastly diluted, thanks to Bezaleel's art and the efforts of Miriam and the Davidic Princess Tamar), and uses them to stoke unrest in the Middle East.

The Ark represents the seven rays of creation in sinister reverse mode, like a false, back-to-front reflection of the rainbow (the true reflection makes the circle of eternity – of the ring of everlasting life). Its energetic technology is connected in its symbolism to the backwards-dancing swastika of the Nazis, who enshrined the mystic military order (the SS – note the indication of two separated, rather than entwined [Enki and Nin-khursag's seal and sign] rearing snakes) that was the embodiment of the Knights Templars in reverse spin – in other words, their very opposite. The Holy Grail is the divine antidote to the poisonous death-forces of the reversed or false Ark, and will sweepingly overcome their worst menace.

CHAPTER EIGHTEEN

The Kings and Queens of the Grail

*T*he two aspects of Anu, the Divine Androgyne who was Tiâmat's chosen vehicle of light for the earth, were not king and queen as we understand the royal office today, but reigned from above, so to speak. There was no kingly or queenly office, with its direct accessibility to the people, on the actual earth, because until this point it had been deemed unnecessary. There were leaders, of course, but not what might be termed royalty. Whilst all was held in balance, the people of earth could ascend to meet Anu and to worship the light of God, because the Grail was in place to facilitate fully conscious access to the higher planes.

After Annum's treachery, Tiâmat saw that from now on something other than the status quo was desperately required. In the case of earth, the two aspects of the Divine Androgyne could no longer rule only from on high. Their light, circumscribed in its dispersal by the Dolorous Blow dealt to her, was no longer properly reaching those who dwelt on the material plane below. In future, representatives of the sacred Daughter-Son needed to be down on the earth, available to ordinary men and women at the mundane level, dispensing order, justice, protection, and the spirit of the divine, which would shape and inspire communities.

Therefore, although she continued to sanction the appointment of the crucial Divine Androgyne – necessarily transmuted into Divine Couple now that the Grail and with it the human structure of the androgyne had been sundered – she also did something else. As previously mentioned, she gave forth a new dispensation, unprecedented in humanity's earthly tenancy. Starting with Kingu (made possible only by dint of Kingu's supreme sacrifice), passing thereafter to Enki and Nin-khursag and then onwards via a bloodline which would by divine ordinance descend directly to earth, Tiâmat initiated the mystical line of Grail kings and Grail queens.

The titles of 'king' and 'queen' derive directly from the name Kingu. It also exists in the form of 'Quingu'; from this rendition the term 'quayin' or 'queen' emerged, and from quayin came forth 'ayin', the Eye of God or the Divine Focus, for this is what Kingu, the original Divine Androgyne of the Nibiruans who led the earth project, embodied. S/he was the created child of God whose devoted service enabled the Emerald Tablet to manifest into form and to whom the Emerald Tablet was passed. Kingu's sacrifice enabled Tiâmat's specially infused bloodline to come into being so that it could be transported to earth as a temporary but crucial replacement for the severed Grail, passing at last into Cain and his wife, for 'Cain' or 'Q'ain' denotes the sacred 'ayin'.

Such a monarchic bloodline had never come into existence before. The Grail kings and queens were brought into being specifically to nurture the memory and understanding of the Holy Grail, which meant to keep alive human awareness of the all-enfolding love and knowledge of Tiâmat, and of the true Father God contained within her, in humanity's deepest heart. It must not be allowed to forget, Tiâmat decreed, that the root of all is love, our origin and our destiny – even if it were possible for only a small band of the faithful to keep this knowledge alive at any one time.

This sacred and immeasurably precious knowledge, sourced in the Emerald Tablet, must be upheld and secretly passed on from age to age amidst the turmoil and darkness that had descended so barbarously upon humankind.

Tiâmat's true-hearted children would bear forth this knowledge as esoteric teachings, ever striving to reconnect the Grail and restore the Emerald Tablet to its rightful throne in humanity's heart and higher perception. These children – the Grail kings and queens and all who faithfully served them – would be in themselves the very essence of the 'ayin', the Divine Eye which received the light, the sacred truth, the vision and the veritable reality of all things that humanity had lost amidst a sea of confusion and illusion. The Divine Eye is the sanctified inner focus that can receive the light of God flowing from the heart of all things. It is this Divine Eye within us that Enlil has sought to distort and partially blind via the setting up of a device whose secret we shall disclose.

Tiâmat 'lowered the kingship from heaven' so that true-hearted members of the God-Headed people could actually assume kingship and queenship on earth. They would reflect the highest of the high, the sacred Son-Daughter in heaven (Christ-Brigid), for the sake of the reinstatement of the Grail and the Emerald Tablet. Such was the overwhelming obscuration of Annum and Enlil's shadow that these God-Headed kings and queens on earth would not always remember with exactitude the wonder and the blessing of Tiâmat, nor would they entirely realise that they reflected the essence of heaven via Enki and Nin-khursag, whom they would see as lesser rulers than Annum and Enlil. Nevertheless, they would know the truth deep within their soul consciousness and keep its flame alive.

Eventually the sacred kingship and queenship would pass from the God-Headed people to earthly humanity.

It was another phase of Tiâmat's stupendous plan to lower right down to earth, not only a *reflection* of the Divine Couple in the higher realms shining from a mundane king and queen living on earth, but the actual Divine Couple themselves. Many sworn to service in the preparation of this astonishing and unprecedented plan would turn from the path, felled by lies and illusion and the weaknesses within which are always the allies of the shadow, but somehow, through struggle and tribulation, there would remain sufficient of those who remembered and honoured the truth received by the indwelling ayin, where within its heart the human soul touched God, to fulfil Tiâmat's purpose.

Throughout the course of history (and it is worth remembering the impaled Dagobert at this point), adversarial forces would collude and conspire to try to put out that Divine Eye for ever.

CHAPTER NINETEEN

The Sumerian King List

*D*o we have any outer indication of Tiâmat's great rescue mission for earthly humanity, which was the setting up of the royal bloodline? Indeed we have. Tiâmat's instigation of the office of kingship is recorded specifically in the Sumerian King List, a compilation inscribed on fifteen of the Mesopotamian clay tablets at some point after 1960 BC, when the Tower of Babel was razed to the ground, the city of Ur was utterly destroyed along with it, and Sumer simultaneously fell into decline. Its compilation was no doubt inspired as a memorial document of the golden days of the great Sumerian civilisation. The list begins with the declaration, 'When the kingship was lowered from heaven, the kingship was in Eridu'. There follows a complete list of kings from around 29,500 BC until 1800 BC (Laurence Gardner's calculations), together with their seats of dominion.

This enthralling King List marks the interruption of the Flood after recording the reign of eight kings prior to it (at this point stating: 'The Flood swept thereover'). It then resumes with the words, 'After the Flood had swept thereover, when the kingship was lowered from heaven, the kingship was in Kish'. The king who was in power when the great flood came is not named on this ancient list, but other Sumerian texts confirm his identity as King Zi-u-sudra, who equates with the biblical Noah. Therefore, there were nine antediluvian kings of Sumer. Their queens are not mentioned, except when one ruled alone, no doubt because after the Dolorous Blow had been struck, the status of women, among both the higher and the ordinary star people, began to diminish.

One fascinating point concerning the nine antediluvian kings and their queens (all members of the God-Headed people except for one) is that they reigned for a certain specified cycle of time measured in *shas*, meaning a 'passing' and written as a circle (360 degrees).[1] They therefore reflect planet X's 'passing' or crossing of the earth's orbit, which takes place every 3,600 years. However, a *sha* adapted as a calculation of earthly time divides this figure by ten, which gives us the 360 degrees of the circle. A single degree of an Anunnaki *sha* equates to one solar orbit of the earth, making an entire *sha* 360 years in length. In fact, Annum, after splitting off Tiâmat, had to recalculate the calendar, because when the earth began to reverse the direction of her spin from clockwise to anti-clockwise as she registered the sundering of the Grail, there was a period when it seemed as if time stood still. Thereafter, our orbit round the sun was disrupted, a disruption which cooled the globe and caused the Ice Age to begin. The North Pole, which was where the Grail conjoined with the earth and was once a paradise, became a frozen wasteland.

As previously discussed, Anu's masculine name was Annum, and it is from this source that we derive the word *annum* (year), the measure in duration of our solar orbit, recalculated for us by the man who messed it up in the first place. It is also interesting to note that if we divide the original *sha*, a calculation of Nibiruan time which measures 3,600 years, by nine, we arrive at the figure 400, which emphasises earth's sacred connection to the number 4 (the elements) and the Cross of Issue. This figure is also connected with the moon, as the moon is exactly 400 times smaller than the sun, and 400 times closer to the earth. It would seem as if the Anunnaki *sha* is an astronomical calculation relating to both solar and lunar influences as they relate to the earth.

The eight initial God-Headed kings were set in place to rule until the office of kingship could pass safely into the hands of the ordinary star people, the 'normal' human beings of earth, beginning with Noah (Zi-u-sudra). Counting back from the great Ice Age of 70,000 years ago, we can see that it took 35,000 years for human society to re-establish itself under the broken ranks of the higher star people, for of course all fell into disruption after the Dolorous Blow, and reach the point where Tiâmat 'lowered the kingship from heaven'.

After the rule of the eight God-Headed kings, the great experiment began. Tiâmat placed King Zi-u sudra (Noah), the first earthly monarch, on the Sumerian throne. He was not, strictly speaking, entirely of the earthly community, as he and his wife had passed through Tiâmat's Creation Chamber under the care of Enki and Nin-khursag and had been given some God-Headed genes. He had been specially prepared for office, and he was the ninth king to rule on earth.

Nine is an interesting number, as it is the number of the Tower, denoting the Sacred Feminine, the number of the Dragon, and the ultimate expression of 3 ($3 \times 3 = 9$), the trinity of Mother, Father and Divine Child that Tiâmat brought forth from her innermost in order to initiate creation itself. We have just noted how a *sha* (see above), when divided by nine, gives us the sum of 400, a calculation which, in astronomical terms of measurement, links the sun, the moon, and the earth. The Wisdom Keepers of the Australian Aborigines tell of the 'ninth wave', the ultimate expression of spiritual dynamism and creative power, when by divine decree something is accomplished, is brought into being. So it was with Noah, for he and his queen were the foundation stone of Tiâmat's great plan, as we shall see.

After the Flood, therefore, which was the biblical flood instigated by the circle of conspirators, Tiâmat's great project, conceived of her towering love for humanity, continued unabated. Even though Noah's kingship had been purposefully swept aside and destroyed in an effort to prevent her will from being implemented, Tiâmat's resolve – to introduce the first earthly king and queen in the physical dimension of our world who were yet linked through to the higher dimension of the God-Headed people – was again applied. This kingship was a second attempt to establish a 'ninth' king. It was instigated directly after Noah's (Zi-u-sudra's) kingship had failed, when the waters of the great flood had subsided.

Once more it was attacked and overcome, this time not by physical but rather by psychic and etheric inundation, from the same virulent adversarial force that had displaced Noah. The Sumerian tablets relate that it had to be 'destroyed' because of its misdemeanours; however, the flames of the ethical conflagration that consumed it were fanned deliberately, and had nothing whatsoever to do with its king, Ga-nadin-ur, who was a true hero of history, as we shall see.

The resultant onslaught caused the threat of such terrible depredation on both the soul and material levels of earthly existence that Tiâmat, despite the prevailing patriarchal stance among the higher and the ordinary star people, had to install a queen as sole monarch after the second 'ninth' earthly king (the first post-diluvian monarch) fell. There was no other way to remedy the precipitate situation. This queen (referred to on the Sumerian King List as the 'heavenly Nidaba') restored mundane and cosmic balance to the existing civilisation, although she was enthroned only after encountering great difficulties in executing Tiâmat's will, which Nidaba obeyed intuitively, led by an inner guidance of which her conscious self was only semi-aware now that Tiâmat had been 'killed'.

For her grace, her leadership, and her perfectly attuned intuition she was known as the 'heavenly Nidaba', and remembered ever afterwards with reverence and love.

NOTE

1   We have been most intrigued by the authors Christopher Knight and Alan Butler's work on the significance of the existence of the 'megalithic yard', which is a prehistoric unit of linear measurement, extending to precisely 82.966656 centimetres. It was used in the creation of a multiplicity of megalithic structures throughout France and Britain, and was derived from calculating the rate of spin of the earth, based on a geometric system which correlated 366° with the 366 rotations of the earth in a year. In their book, *Civilisation One*, the authors show how this is part of an integrated system which is much more advanced and mathematically precise than any system in use today, and how our imperial and

metric systems of measurement are in fact crude renditions of this original and immeasurably ancient system.

There is therefore a compelling body of evidence which indicates that highly advanced civilisations existed on earth even prior to the Sumerian culture, which of course is what our own source has demonstrated to us. Consequently, we are inclined to believe that, prior to Annum's interference, the measurement of a circle was indeed 366° rather than 360°, and that perhaps the orbit of planet X around the sun is more likely to be 3,660 years rather than 3,600.

What was Annum's objective in thus distorting humanity's cyclical measurement of time? We believe that it partly relates to the home journey of planet X, so that as it passed earth on each of its orbital cycles, some kind of force which this distortion helped to generate would make its successive encounters with the earth progressively more destructive and disruptive to our planet at both the physical and psychical levels of life. Annum took the first steps in reversing the cosmic power of the rainbow (what it is in its true essence rather than its outer physical manifestation), which is Tiâmat's sign and the true 'Arc' of the Covenant. We think that Annum's plan also relates to what is biblically referred to as 'the Beast', which received a severe battering each time planet X passed us by. Annum's plot against the Beast links directly into his objective in distorting humanity's system of cyclical measurement. The number of the Beast is 666 (which we even find in literal existence in the figure of 82.966656 centimetres, the unit of measurement related to the 366° circle or orbit). If we apply numerological reduction (see Chapter 50) to 366, we have a resolution of 6. If we apply numerological reduction to 360, we have a resolution of 9.

The Beast in Revelation in the New Testament is represented as evil, but in fact this is only because its energies have been reversed. There is a wholly good and positive aspect to this Beast when it functions as it should. The good Beast has been referred to as the Rainbow Serpent of the Skies by the Aborigines, and as a great serpent of light by many other ancient cultures, including the Mayans. We think that this Beast of the earth-energies is somehow connected to planetary ley lines (a grid of spiritual and electromagnetic energy that covers the surface of the earth) and to ancient sacred sites, such as stone circles. We know, for instance, that the advanced science of pre-history demonstrated by the megalithic yard understood the complexities of the dimensions, motions, relationships and subtle interrelationships, of the earth, the moon and the sun, that it had measured the solar system and encompassed the knowledge of how the speed of light was integrated into the rotational movements of our planet. This is the key. How the speed of light is integrated into the rotational movements of the earth, and how the great Serpent of Light weaves and coils its way around the planet via the earth's ley lines and sacred sites are one and the same process.

The Mayans (who provided the renowned calendar with its 'end-date' for our present civilisation of 21 December 2012) give us another matrix besides the rainbow and its manifestation of the seven rays of Creation. The rainbow is, of course, the spectrum of the perfect white light from which everything is created. The Mayans saw that brilliant white light as placed above the rainbow, and the sacred blackness as below it. Being, respectively, the total unified radiation of light, and the total absence of light, black and white cannot be considered as 'colours' in the same sense that the rays of the rainbow are colours.

Nevertheless, the Mayan matrix gives us the blue ray as the 'heart' ray, placed at the centre of the nine inclusive gradations between pure light and no light. This is interesting, because, as we shall see as we progress through our story of the Grail, the blue ray is the colour of the priceless 'Stone of Ascension' which resides within our heads (the reason that it is blue is explained fully in Chapter 65). When Margaret Bailey and I see Tamar, her presence is announced by either a beautiful, all-pervading emerald-green light, or by a field of blue and green light (very similar to the swathes of colour, particularly green, which manifest as the northern lights). We think that, although the emerald ray is indeed the true heart-ray, the blue light of the head or mind must be lifted up into that heart-ray, and merge wholly into attunement with it, before the individual can become 'fully human'. The mind keeps its identity as individuated mind, but yet is as one with the green ray. When this happens, the blue ray becomes as beautiful and mystically jewel-like as the green ray. If the mind ray chooses to function on its own, refusing to centre itself in the heart, its colour becomes a deathly, chilling, sinister blue, disturbing to behold. This, we believe, is the esoteric teaching behind the Mayan matrix.

We know that the number 6 represents the 'beheaded' consciousness ('Off with their heads!' screams the false queen in *Alice in Wonderland*), its connection with God (the Grail) lying severed at its feet, whilst the fully human, God-Headed individual who embraces the Grail and whose 'Stone of Ascension' in the head is fully functional, is represented by the number 9. There is also another aspect to 6 in that it is the receptive half of a full circle with its completion in 9; and so we see that 6 in its true aspect has a beautiful and noble function as divine receptacle, and that it is only ignorant human interference which has given it its afflicted and negative connotation. In fact, when we join up the figures six and nine, we can imagine that it is a model of the earth with her two aligned poles in emphasis.

We believe that the Serpent of Light, which is the earth-serpent (the earth's very life-system of energies), is a good and beautiful force in that it is a perfect receptacle for dynamic cosmic energies which it translates into exactly what the earth needs in order to keep her informed and functioning at every level of her cognition as an individuated entity, but that, by dint of the actions of Annum and Enlil, it has been reversed, and, due to the blind and abusive way we use it and attune to it because of our afflicted collective consciousness, it has degenerated into the 'Beast' described in Revelation.

As we shall explain, something tremendous will happen shortly after the time of the 'end-date' to return everything that Annum and his conspirators have put into reverse spin, to positive or forward spin once more. Annum, foreseeing the danger of this (his great hope being that even this tremendous act of the forces of light would ultimately fail because of his ever-increasing hold on human consciousness) wants the great earth-serpent to be impacted in such a way that the baptism of the 'end-date' will be thwarted.

Instead of this mighty baptismal force creating a 9 out of a 6 (a re-heading or resurrection from a be-heading) which is what should happen by divine decree, Anu wants to create a 6 out of a 9. Thus can he be sure that the planet, and humanity with it, will begin to die.

He has, therefore, done something to impose a completely false '9' state upon the earth-serpent, so that, when the great baptism comes, the healing, resurrecting forces that reach it will be thrown into confusion, and it will be unable to revert to its true '9' expression of wholeness, spiritual unity and power. Instead, the poor Beast will be turned on its head to become a '6' creature, an empty vessel incapable of receiving and uniting with its '9' essence because the timing for the descent of this essence, when the Beast should have been in its receptive state, has been thrown awry.

Annum has created this bogus '9' state for the earth-serpent by abusively using the forces of linear time and mathematical manipulation in relation to the process by which the speed of light is integrated into the rotational movement of the earth. By means of such malicious manoeuvring, he thinks he will effectively bag us!

Then is all hope lost? Absolutely not. Although what we ourselves must do as a planetary community cannot be removed from the arena of our responsibility and must be done by a sufficient number of us in order to ensure the earthly survival of humanity and the planet and to secure our freedom, this particular aspect of Annum's cunning plan has already been masterfully dealt with by the ancient Mayans. This beautiful, spiritual and awe-inspiring culture of antiquity perennially fascinates our own, and we continue to pay tribute to its wonders. There is one flaw, however. Why, oh why, people ask, did the Mayans carry out such bloodthirsty and barbarically cruel human sacrifices? We think we can provide an answer to this question.

We believe that it was a particularly severe and painful form of 'lapwinging' (see Chapter 23), undertaken by the noble Mayan culture in order to save the planet in 2012, although we predict that the dramatic 'end-day' event will actually take place in the early months of 2013. Enlil became particularly enmeshed in the plot to wipe earthly humanity out of existence and actually became its ringleader (an apt title, as we shall discover). As he became more terrible and cruel in his wrath and spite and more entirely given over to demonic possession, so did he tighten his control over human society wherever he had managed to gain a foothold, which was virtually everywhere, as he had once been a benefi-cent and reasonably benevolent custodian of the earth and her humanity. As we shall show later on in our story, this usurper king of the God-Headed people was recognised as a deity in Sumerian times, and the same deity is acknowledged by scholarship as equating with the later Mayan god who demanded blood sacrifices of a particularly horrifying nature. Whilst appearing to appease and propitiate this wrathful god, the Mayans were actually keeping him at bay and skilfully dodging the restless gaze of his roving vengeful eye as they dedicated their highest esoteric knowledge and craft to the sole purpose of foiling the evil schemes of Annum, his son, and their followers.

They created by wondrous craftsmanship thirteen crystal skulls, one for each centre of the advanced chakra system which, towards the 'end-date', would begin to become active in humanity (the chakra system relates to the rainbow and the totality of the rays of creation). These crystal skulls will prevent the earth-serpent from suffering the death-strike planned for it via Annum's plan, and will allow it to ascend in glory, becoming the thrice nine (999) creature whose essence accords with its true divine nature. (For an explanation of the hugely significant meaning of this 'thrice' pattern, see Chapter 33). The crystal skulls will also help to break the power and purify the subtle crystals of a vast evil mirror created by Enlil. However, we offer a word of warning – unless humanity responds to the wisdom and love of its own heart centre, which is connected to God, the crystal skulls will not be able to function efficiently at the appointed time.

The beautiful green ray surging from our collective quickened heart centre will activate the blue ray in its fullest and highest measure, and this exalted blue ray (called the 'Stone of Ascension') is the key to activation of the skulls.

CHAPTER TWENTY

Changing the Structure
of the Soul

A fter Queen Nidaba had restored Tiâmat's celestial order on earth and her
reign came to its conclusion, the whole project began again from the beginning, and further God-Headed kingships, with a view to producing a third earthly
'ninth' king, were reinstated on earth as before. Thereafter Tiâmat decided that
new gifts must be given to humanity so that it would not keep missing the mark,
gifts exceeding even those she had bestowed on Noah and the second 'ninth' king,
Ga-nadin-ur; for these two earthly kings had been given distinct powers via her
divine dispensation, even though such powers had ultimately failed to protect the
monarchs from the terrible might of their adversary. Both Noah and the second
'ninth' king (Noah's descendant) had been invested with something very special
indeed. It was their destiny and duty to pass on to others what they themselves
had received; but they must be made strong enough to fulfil their destiny and
duty, and their subjects must also be sufficiently fortified in order that they might
receive it and keep it.

Tiâmat decided that humanity must be provided with an intellectual and soul
capacity that would broaden and stabilise before it ascended into the heights,
in order to establish a sound base that could not, as was presently the case, be
toppled so easily by a too eager vertical ascent into mystical secrets for which
the young souls of humanity were not ready, thereby managing to depose themselves by impure and egotistical design in attaining the treasures of occult
knowledge. Tiâmat would therefore bestow upon us the mundane intellect that
we possess today, in order that we could advance much more safely along the
grand spiritual highway.

From now on, humanity would take three steps forward, and then one step
back, to make sure that it paused, reflected, considered the lessons it had absorbed

and pondered the wider picture before continuing on its way. This method would restore balance and sure-footedness to her poor, ailing human creation. Humankind would thus become as the mountain goat, a nimble, deft and inspired climber, unharried by rocky, steep and arid terrain. Francis Bacon applied the inspired, adroit and neat-handed finishing touches to this epic process.

What this actually meant from an esoteric and creational basis was that, from a certain chosen point onwards, Tiâmat would dispense with the initial structure of the human soul, which in those far-off days was built upon the concept of a tower – tall, slender, and thrusting upwards with great vigour and speed upon a narrow base designed to accommodate this lightning growth upwards – and instigate for it instead the shape of a pyramid. According to this shape the human soul would in future be constructed – its base broad and square, its four pyramidal sides erecting themselves sturdily and steadily upon this safe and sound foundation, and its pinnacle rising only in accordance with the spiritual speed upon which its four strong pyramidal sides progressed.

Our new intellects, although by no means any kind of higher or superior vessel of intelligence than the present humanity already possessed, would provide balance and a steadying hand, even a certain pragmatic blindness concerning spiritual reality. We would no longer be able to snatch the realisation of it out of the air, like a child catching a butterfly in cupped hands. In future, we would have to dig and delve for it.

Nevertheless, although our new kind of intellect would ensure for us a sound, cuboid base upon which to build our awareness, Tiâmat saw that it could and would become a stumbling block.

She therefore, in order to dispense perfect balance, revealed to humanity new secrets, new initiations, new esoteric truth – new yet unaccountably ancient. So far, only the Nephilim and the leaders among the higher star people had been given this revelation of divine truth. However, Tiâmat decreed that humanity should not be deprived of this ultimate blessing. And so it was given forth, perhaps around 3900–3800 BC, and the new humanity emerged once again from the Creation Chamber. For the third time, Tiâmat instigated a bloodline of earthly kingship and queenship from the new humanity which would provide a perfect receptacle on earth for the influences of the overlighting Divine Couple (Enki and Nin-khursag). This time, it worked. And accordingly we may note from the Sumerian King List that there were nine kings prior to the flood, and nine kings after it.

The Capricornian goat, rising up from the sea and climbing the mountain, would be the sign of the new human strain. It would initially have two horns (two aspects of consciousness) as goats have; but, by stages, it would evolve into the one-horned, one-pointed unicorn, receiving emanations from the spiritual stars (the imperishable stars, shining behind the physical stars), its conscious-ness honed into a beautiful unity. The unicorn would be sign and symbol of the Divine Androgyne. Only by such measures would humanity survive, and, with it, the special bloodline that Tiâmat had initiated on earth, the one which would bear such marvellous, hallowed fruit that our eternal survival would be assured thereby, as we shall discuss.

The ninth post-diluvian king (the 'ninth wave', the wave from Tiâmat's heart, her very essence) was Attaba (Adapa, or the *Adâma*) – Adam himself, although we shall see that it would be Eve, his all-important queen, from whom the bloodline actually descended.

Tiâmat decreed that future earthly kings and queens (initially Adam and Eve, who came after the two false starts represented by Zi-u-sudra [Noah] and the second 'ninth' king, who was Ga-nadin-ur, Noah's great grandson), or the sole ruler, if circumstances dictated, would not only reflect the Divine Couple in the heavens, but would be specially linked to them by means of magical ceremony, namely the royal coronation, or sacred anointing ritual. And then what was truly stupendous occurred, by means of the Dragon Queen's further divine decree.

CHAPTER TWENTY-ONE

Tiâmat's Call

*W*hen Enki and Nin-khursag took up the role of Divine Couple after the fall of Annum and the severing of the Grail, they often walked the earth in temporary physical bodies because it was Tiâmat's decree that they should; but as the Grail energies gradually closed down, they were able to do so less and less, until finally it became an impossible feat. It was time for Tiâmat to further implement her unparalleled rescue plan so that it could advance towards its wonderful culmination.

Although Enki and Nin-khursag were faithful to Tiâmat's light to the utmost degree and their contribution to her rescue plan was indispensable, they were yet not mighty enough of soul to pull off the coup against the darkness that humanity, hell-bent on its own destruction, required. The next step, therefore, entailed putting out an SOS call to the highest of the high, to the lordly Nephilim, her pure and incorruptible children who 'stood within the presence of God'. Could there be an exalted androgyne among them, whom she would choose and yet who would freely volunteer to do, not only the utterly unprecedented (for we must remember that we are talking about the Nephilim and not the God-Headed people: the Nephilim whose exalted vibrations prevented them from walking the physical earth except in highly refined ethereal bodies, and even then only when conditions were not nearly so adverse as they had become, and they would become worse), but what seemed the utterly impossible – to descend to earth, *in physical bodies,* and bring the spiritual dimensions in which only the soul could dwell *right down to the mundane level*?

Such a thing had never been conceived of before. The whole point of colonisation of planet earth was, of course, eventually to lift the planet and its dimension of gross matter into the freedom and beauty of the everlasting spiritual worlds. But *this* – this startling plan to put the very opposite into effect first, and bring heaven *right down to earth* whilst human consciousness on earth still languished in the utmost depravity and crudity – could it be done?

It was absolutely vital that it should be done, for only by such means could the Emerald Tablet be rescued and restored to humanity and the Grail re-opened so that the teachings of the Nephilim couple – the teachings of the Christ – might finally be understood. Yet it would entail unique dedication, devotion and self-sacrifice on an undreamt-of scale for the Divine Couple involved, if indeed there existed such a 'couple' (actually an androgyne, who would, in keenest conscious-ness of the continuous agony involved, be required to split apart from one another), even amongst the most illustrious of the Nephilim.

There could be no possible incentive, motivation or reward for the implemen-tation of this Herculean task except that of pure, stupendous, unparalleled love for humanity. This love would have to faithfully reflect Tiâmat's own love for her creation, would have to be commensurate, albeit on a human scale, with the glory of the great Daughter-Son, the Christ (Mummu in Sumerian terms), pure spirit, whom she had birthed out of her own heart as the Divine Fire driving all creation, and of whom all immortals and mortals alike – Nephilim and both higher and ordinary star people (the latter representing people like ourselves today) – possess an infinitely precious spark.

The Nephilim had walked their appointed path. They had evolved over incal-culable aeons on planets other than earth, and had left the travail and brutishness of the lower levels behind for ever – travail and brutishness that had in any case never matched the total degradation of earth. They were immeasurably far above and beyond the earth, and had no reason ever to taste of its sorrow and sordid-ness or to participate in its violence and suffering, let alone turn themselves into personal targets for these degenerate forces

And even if volunteers for this unspeakably daunting, harrowing and thankless mission of torment could be found, how could *Nephilim* ever walk the earth? How could what was made of the highest of the high, of the purest spirit, fire and dew in all its mystical dimensions, be lowered, compacted and compressed into physical, animal bodies? The very experience of that alone would be inappeasable agony. And then to be split apart, to be brutally assaulted by the darkness continually, and continually keep on course until all was finished and perfected although it would cost ocean depths of unending bitterness, ignominy, anguish, sorrow and tears, and might even then be rendered useless at the eleventh hour – how could this be asked of even the highest of the high? Miracles are miracles, but this was something else again.

And yet Tiâmat put out the call. The task of the Divine Couple would be uncon-scionable in its terrifying dimensions. With the special bloodline as their only means, God-graced but still merely a mundane manifestation, they would have to find a way to descend to earth, *without the Grail,* for that would have disappeared by the time of their appointed coming. They would have to find a way to gently lead humankind, who would by now have mired itself in the deepest ignorance, superstition and confusion, back to the path of light.

They would have to singlehandedly break the shackles of the mightiest of the lower forces of earth, forged by the circle of conspirators and their growing band of followers. They would have to find a way to reintroduce the teachings on the divine alchemy detailed on the Emerald Tablet, whereby humankind could perceive that the potential of that divine alchemy existed within each individual soul, independently of any controlling third party, and that the responsibility for igniting and activating it lies with each one of us.

They would have to drive back the worst shadow ever to have fallen on the earth and her peoples, and be ridiculed and despised for doing so. And they would have to bring back the Grail by rescuing the Emerald Tablet, and revealing its final secret, in the most daring bid for freedom ever made on behalf of humanity via an ultimate sacrifice of horrible proportions. Not only all this, but they would have to bring back to earth, *through the agency of themselves*, the infinitely precious drop of Tiâmat's essence, that of Divine Goddess herself, which the earth had lost when the great imbalance was perpetrated and the Grail was severed.

A new heaven and a new earth were needed, and nothing else would do. Tiâmat's essence would have to be brought back to the earth in greater measure than it had ever been given before. A Divine Woman would have to touch down, who, through heavenly cooperation with her sacred parents, would heal the earth and eventually set it spinning the right way again, its negative gyration overcome at last.

How likely was it that an answer would come to Tiâmat's call? Yet come it did. Through unimaginable millennia, the Divine Couple – Jesus and Mary Magdalene – advanced towards the earth, always in training for that most arduous of all missions, the saving of humanity from itself.

Because of circular time, Tiâmat was able to summon them and prepare them in a limitless dimension, in existence before the earth began. They were the two members (androgynous aspects) of the Nephilim, the highest of the high, who answered her call. And when they came to earth, they brought a light whose measure had never been encountered on these planes before, nor ever has since.

Tamar was their daughter – Tamar who was a drop of Tiâmat's essence, of her divine heart. The Dragon Queen would eventually be able to take the earth back into the full embrace of God through the agency of Tamar, the Divine Woman, the Holy Grail, brought to earth via the spiritual majesty of her parents.

The tablets which give us the King List go on to confirm: 'They had not yet set up a king for the beclouded people. No headband and crown had been fastened; no sceptre had been studded with lapis lazuli ... Sceptre, crown, headband and staff were still placed before Anu in heaven ... There was no counselling of its people; then kingship descended from heaven.'

These inscriptions mark the point at which Tiâmat instigated the royal blood-line here on earth, although, as we know, the sceptre had to pass from the higher star people to earthly humanity before it was properly established. Its ultimate design was to provide a biological stairway down to earth, which, at the mystically designated time, the Divine Couple of all Divine Couples, Jesus and Mary Magdalene, would descend in humility and simplicity, touching down in a stable, a cave in Bethlehem, under a star which would gather and merge from all four corners of the heavens until it shone like a full moon and, at the appointed hour, release a serpent tail of light that would point directly over their place of birth – Bethlehem, the 'house' or the 'temple of bread'.

As we shall see, the entire concept of the communion bread is crucial to the story of the Grail.

CHAPTER TWENTY-TWO

Lord and Lady of the Mountain

*I*n the court of Enlil, Annum's wife Antu was not given high status. Her faithless husband, who was once the masculine aspect of the androgynous being that they had expressed together, was seldom at home. He had handed over much of the business of court and council to Enlil, who now entered fully into his usurped kingship. It was virtually a policy of the God-Headed community in this new phase of their history for the males among them to take two wives, just to remind the women that one woman did not equal one man and that they ought to bear in mind their inherent inferiority at all times. It was also a custom insisted on to reinforce to both sexes that the time of the androgyne was well and truly over, and that those dark and squalid days when men had to suffer the outrageous degradation of living and moving and having their being in a state of perfect and consummate equality with women were mercifully behind them.

Antu was a particular target of Annum and Enlil's misogyny because she was intimately linked with Tiâmat, having once been the feminine vehicle of light who dispensed the divine *khu* to Annum when they were an integrated entity. Annum, together with the other God-Headed males, still received the *khu* from his wife, as he would have become seriously disorientated without it. However, there were secret plans afoot to replace it with something else.

Knowing this, Antu in her wisdom gave into the keeping of her daughter, Nin-khursag, the supreme power of the *khu*. This supreme power was a special potency within the *khu* itself which Antu held on behalf of the other God-Headed women, for whilst they all dispensed the *khu*, she was their divine centre and was most intimately linked to Tiâmat.

Although Annum had fallen away from Tiâmat's light, Antu maintained a beautiful and unfaltering devotion to Tiâmat which was crucial to the success of

Nin-khursag and Enki's future exertions, a devotion which now prompted her to pass on the torch of supremacy to her daughter, even though by doing so she would leave herself bereft and even more vulnerable and open to abuse than before. The *khu* is in Nin-khursag's name, which translates in one of its several meanings as 'Lady who is divine keeper of the *khu*' or, put more simply, the Divine Woman, linking her with Mary Magdalene and ultimately with Tamar. Mary Magdalene dispensed the divinely potent *khu* to Jesus, not as a material substance but by subtle infusion through the mouth, when they kissed. (The Gnostic gospels tell of how Jesus used to kiss Mary 'often' on the lips.) Tamar will dispense it to us all by means of a simple initiation ceremony which will be undertaken individually.

Annum had become very dark indeed, and often left earth to retreat to a sinister dimension which may be understood as a location among the physical stars in the constellation of Orion. Many esotericists confirm that there is a cosmic body, a planet or a star, associated with the name of Anu, which is ominously ill-willed towards humanity and continues to plot its destruction. Although Annum's plans for tyrannical control were at first confined to earth, he has since sought to extend his boundaries of dominion beyond earth and her solar system, not without some success.

We need not be in the least concerned, however. We will be shown how to disempower him completely, and his tentacles will one day soon drop away with shrivelling and shrieks. He will be overcome, yet not without our concerted effort.

Antu, valiantly faithful to Tiâmat, held the God-Headed community and earthly humanity in the light of her love. Ki, the God-Headed woman of lower status than Antu whom Enlil had married in flagrant disregard of his wife, loved Antu devotedly and did her utmost to serve her. Together, Ki, Antu, her daughter Nin-khursag and other women among the higher star people worked unremittingly to remedy the prevailing miserable situation of imbalance and oppression that held such sinister and unrelenting sway.

One interesting circumstance should be made clear. Whilst Annum was of the white race from Nibiru, Antu was of the black race. This is difficult to understand from our purely physical perspective here on earth. However, the black and white races on Nibiru symbolised a divine truth conjoining the mystery of the sacred light and the sacred darkness. It was what we might call spiritually natural that the Anunnaki androgyne designated to act as the Christ receptacle for earthly humanity should manifest as a balanced expression of the two races of Nibiru.

Anu, of Nephilim blood, was a child of the meeting and embrace of the spirits of the two races in the higher realms, which on Nibiru translated into something closer to what we would understand as an expression of separate racial identity united in a perfectly balanced androgyne. The two races did flourish separately on Nibiru, but there was also this perfect conjoinment among the higher Anunnaki or higher Nibiruans, just as there was between the higher members of the yellow and the red races who originated on a planet near to the constellation of Hercules.

It shows us how the spirits of the races may be immaculately united as one, and yet retain the perfect expression of their individuality. We might think in this context of Mary Magdalene and Jesus, for Mary, so beloved of Jesus, was of Ethiopian blood, an inheritance from her mother, Mary Jacob[1], whilst Jesus was white.

A gracious friendship between Nin-khursag and Ki was nurtured by Antu from the time of her daughter's birth. It was so close and harmonious that eventually Nin-khursag, newly appointed as Divine Woman as well as just entering into her status as the feminine counterpart of Tiâmat's Divine Couple, also took the title of Lady Earth. This was the rank and appointment that Annum had bestowed on Ki in order to emphasise that his two wives were equal, and that the position occupied by Antu was of no more importance than that held by Ki. It was a swipe at his former androgynous relationship with Antu rather than a grace and favour for his second wife, and was ludicrous, as Antu, Lady of Heaven, was a much more advanced soul than the humble Ki. It was further intended to sow dissension between the two women, as Annum disapproved of powerful friendships between females; they unsettled him and made him paranoid. He would far rather that his women fought over him and were in a constant state of enmity because of him.

Antu, wise and forgiving (though poignantly aware of the brutal humiliations and injustices perpetrated against her) never allowed Annum's psychological blows to fell her. Her strength was in Tiâmat's all-enfolding love. She continued to accept Ki's devotion and allow their solidarity to unfold into an inspired and unusually blessed friendship.

When Nin-khursag took the title of Lady of Earth, it was granted to her by Ki as a token of her honour for Antu and her daughter and a demonstration that Annum's schemes to divide them were impotent.

Nin-khursag was known additionally as Lady of Life and Lady of the Mountain. She had a deep spiritual connection with the earth and was a gifted spiritual scientist who would revolutionise our DNA after the carnage of the Flood had, paradoxically, almost drained the human gene pool dry. She married Enki, Lord of Earth and Waters, her male aspect, after their androgynous bond had been severed. Nin-khursag was the half-sister of Enlil, Lord of Air, and she married him as well as Enki, again in an attempt to establish, through human means, the lost connection between heaven and earth. Her title of Lady of the Mountain referred, we think, to Nin-khursag's association with the high places, the upper dimensions of the spirit. Enlil shared her title, calling himself Lord of the Mountain. To some extent, this was initially his rightful title, because the Grand Assembly of the God-Headed people, under guidance from the Nephilim, had originally appointed Enlil to the role of a lesser lord of karma (the greater lords of karma are beyond what we can conceive of as human beings and encompass both human and angelic consciousness).

In the days before darkness consumed Annum, Enlil was also attuned to the light, and had an important task to fulfil for the peoples of the earth. It was his God-appointed duty to balance the record-book of their karma. Karma might be explained via the old Hebrew dictum, 'An eye for an eye and a tooth for a tooth', or, 'What goes around, comes around'. This is certainly not a cruel or savage law that promotes maiming others in revenge for abuses perpetrated by them, but a simple and fundamental law of balance that ensures the harmonious functioning of creation. It means only that balance must be restored and maintained by equalisation throughout every detail of creation as it manifests and expresses itself.

Thus, if we, symbolically speaking, 'take' an 'eye' or a 'tooth', then we are called to account for what we have done. We must make recompense, and, by an act of healing, restore the balance of wholeness and harmony that we have undermined. This act of healing will require that we give of ourselves, our spirit, our light, in some way that will re-establish the lost equilibrium that we have created. Our act of healing will achieve three objectives: it will return to perfection the disturbed balance of creation; it will make recompense for the suffering, shock and disablement that our deed caused; and it will heal the imbalance or lack of holistic perspective (always generated by a lack of love, whether ignorant or wanton) in ourselves that caused us to commit the harmful deed in the first place.

Afterwards, when Enlil followed in the footsteps of his father Annum and his own soul also darkened, he entirely lost the plot as far as the law of karma was concerned, and began to express this creational energy through a deep imbalance within himself which caused him to interpret it in terms of punishment, blame, retribution and revenge fuelled by anger. Far from setting in motion the spiritual dynamic of balance through equalisation, the expression of anger, retribution, revenge and punishment actually causes the severity of the original imbalance to increase dramatically, creating more and more negative karma which will throw off disruption and chaos until it is resolved. When Enlil began to blank out his apperception of this truth, his title as Lord of the High Places or Lord of the Mountain and his upholding of his status as a Lord of Karma gradually became misappropriated, because his office was removed from him.

Nevertheless, Enlil continued to wield the powers with which he had been entrusted in direct contravention of the spiritual law he had once held in such honour. He became a spiritual outlaw. Eventually, among many other unfortunate consequences of this stance, he began to breathe forth a power throughout the thought spheres of the earth and her peoples which caused human society to become addicted to law making, and to express this addiction in an increasingly unbalanced and obsessional manner. These unnecessary and largely invidious laws enshrined Enlil's warped and virulent perception of the law of karma, a law whose true objective and outworking is the benign restoration of wholeness and peace through a perfect justice which in itself is an expression of Divine Love. He began to use karma as a weapon against us.

At first, all went well, and Enlil was celebrated as a goodly ambassador of Saturn, the dispenser of karma, and a true Lord of the Mountain, pouring influences from on high that were fecund and beneficent. Eulogies were sung, and inscribed in pictorial form and in verse on clay tablets, to the greatness, the magnificence, the goodness of Enlil. Agriculture, civil organisation, and the abundance and fertility of the land and of human communities came under his auspices and received his blessing. One song praises him thus:

You are the lord!
You are a great lord, a lord of the granary!
You are the lord who makes the barley sprout!
You are the lord who causes the vines to sprout!

It is pertinent to say at this juncture that Enlil's half-sister, Nin-khursag, Lady of Life and Lady of the Mountain, was granted just as much power and dominion from Saturn as her brother; but Enlil, from his earliest days as a ruler and leader, developed the habit of denying, ignoring, and upstaging his co-workers, particularly women, and imagining that his alone among the God-Headed people was the starring role. This attitude signalled its extremity by an act of rape which he committed against a female member of the higher star people (Ninlil, Lady of the Wind). Some sources declare him innocent, others denounce him. What remains clear is that prior to his assumption of kingship he was branded a rapist by the fifty great gods and the seven decision makers (leaders in the Grand Assembly) and banished from the city of Nippur, where he was considered, or perhaps considered himself, as chief of the gods. This act of rape, or the accusation of it, marked his spiritual demise.

It is easy to imagine that if Enlil, as Saturn's agent, became unbalanced, the corrupted power of the Saturnine energies would be extremely virulent. They contain the pivotal point of the life and death forces, which, when properly balanced, never culminate in death, but generate the life force in ever greater measure ('I am come that ye may have life, and have it more abundantly', said the Christ, who came into the world through the sacred gates of Capricorn, or the heavenly Goat whose zodiacal tenancy spans the winter solstice, to restore this lost balance). But when the current of the life forces is perverted, through human failings and wanton error of choice, towards death and degeneration, and Saturn's essence is misunderstood, misappropriated and misdirected, Saturn becomes Satan. Saturn's power of gravitation, his power to keep the foetus in the womb, truly becomes an oppressive power of imprisonment. It shackles us in irons.

Whilst Nin-khursag fostered and ushered the forces of Saturn in a mode befitting her beautiful and profound connection to Tiâmat's deepest heart, and was in truth the pure and exalted Lady of the Mountain, Enlil sunk further and further into a morass of his own making, and became a reversed Lord of the Mountain – a marshal of the infernal regions.

NOTE

1 Mary Jacob's mother was Ann, a beautiful Ethiopian woman sometimes depicted as black in ancient images of biblical characters. Ann was in fact the grandmother of Mary Magdalene, not of Jesus. Mary Jacob, Ann's daughter, conceived Mary Magdalene via Matthew Cyrus, a Jewish priest of the sacred Order of Melchisedek, although he was dishonourable in his dealings with her.

CHAPTER TWENTY-THREE

Lapwinging

*E*nki and Nin-khursag had very important work to do together and would bring inestimable gifts to the earthly human race. The problem was that they had to hide their true identity as the new Divine Couple from Annum and the Grand Assembly, because of course both were entirely hostile to Tiâmat's plans and influence. Tiâmat had been banished beyond the veil that separates the higher spiritual consciousness from the earthly dimensions (in this case, even the exalted earthly dimensions where Annum and the God-Headed people dwelt were included in the separation), but of course she continued to exert her godly influence from her straitened position, for all is contained within God. Tiâmat holds the reins of creation in unfaltering hands, and always maintains supreme control; but it was her decision in the beginning to give us free will, and that is a gift she will not countermand or withdraw, because her creation could not achieve its goal without it. Therefore, she permitted her influence over earth to be curtailed by Marduk's act, and allowed herself to be sacrificed rather than her children.

Enki and Nin-khursag had to operate by stealth and cunning. Enki is often seen as a trickster god (although he is referred to as Enki the Wise on many of the clay tablets). We believe that this title gives the key to his 'tricks'. They were part of his wisdom, by which he sought to fulfil his destiny for the sake of the future of the earth without directly antagonising Annum, who was perfectly capable of 'executing' him for rebellion, just as he had executed the unfortunate Kingu.

Enki, in company with Nin-khursag, had to continue to play his hand carefully. This situation was reflected in the life of Jesus and Mary Magdalene, who had to fulfil their mission under the hostile dominion of the Roman Empire and the savage cultural doctrines of the Jewish Sanhedrin court, equating in Enki and Nin-khursag's case to the ever darkening, increasingly threatening conditions of Annum's realm, and to the mounting savagery benighting Enlil's vision and mentality.

Enki had even taken his wise trickery to the point of pretending to make an attempt on Tiâmat's life. We will see how he heard and obeyed her commands after she was ousted, and that all his actions served Tiâmat loyally, with a dedication that risked his status and even his life. We can reasonably deduce from this unswerving devotion that his assassination attempt was indeed one of his tricks. Enki's reign as the balanced masculine principle was always a furtive one.

In the great tradition of the Welsh bards (who are closely associated with Grail wisdom), there are three magical creatures who guard the great truths of the Grail and the higher worlds. One is the dog, who guards the secret; one is the roebuck, who hides the secret; and one is the lapwing, who disguises the secret. The great secret – a vital aspect of which is love and reverence for the sacred feminine – Enki kept concealed and guarded in his heart; but he was most of all the lapwing, bearing within himself its magical essence, disguising the secret as he moved within the courts of his father Annum and within the council of the God-Headed people so that its hidden potency might flourish and be carried into the future.

The first action Annum took after the 'death' of Tiâmat was to declare his intention (subject to democratic approval in the Grand Assembly) that his reign would pass into the hands of Enlil, his second son.

The Grand Assembly raised no objections to his directive, and Enki was powerless to change his decision. From this time on, Enlil, though not yet king in Annum's place, was given greater authority and became one of the leading members of the Grand Assembly. Meanwhile, Tiâmat had begun to instruct Enki and Nin-khursag in the formation of her special bloodline.

Having decided that the higher star people (as represented by himself) were infinitely wiser and better than God, Annum started to conceptualise a God in the image of himself (an arrogant, misogynistic, martially inspired God) that he could deign to worship, and began to influence the other members of the higher star people to join him in his mission. Once he had overseen the operation to have Tiâmat 'destroyed' (for he really believed that that was what he had achieved), we see that the inevitable happened – namely, what was left of the true source of love, wisdom and compassion in his heart began to fail with a frightening rapidity. Within a short time, he was beginning to despise humanity, seeing in them an inferior 'breed' of star people that had been sullied and terminally contaminated by entering into animal bodies. Pure bloods such as the God-Headed people should not have to continue to suffer their brutish existence, thereby continuing the abominable scheme of the degenerate Tiâmat! They were a disgrace to his glorious race! Unless they submitted wholly to every edict of the God-Headed people, they should be eliminated from the earth, the whole project abandoned, and never spoken of again! Such was the sway of Annum's musings and conclusions as he elected his second son as his successor and transferred more and more power to him even before he entered semi-retirement (only as far as the earth was concerned – we have seen that he extended his shenanigans elsewhere, with a view to gaining overlordship of the cosmos).

The God-Headed people, although democratic amongst themselves (except, perhaps, for Enlil, who always found the concept rather difficult to grasp!) were promising fair to become a dictatorship to the people of earth. What a long and sorrowful way they had all come from that point in cosmic history when they had set out from their own planets, balanced by love and a sense of fraternity and equality, higher and ordinary star people alike, at peace with themselves and each other and eager to implement their beloved Tiâmat's edicts! The pull of earth on their innermost souls, of interior conflict and jealousy and the temptation of self-ishness over love, had proven too much for them.

It was at this point, when earthly humanity was becoming subject to the God-Headed people to the point of degradation and slavery, that Tiâmat, from beyond the veil of 'death' that Annum and Enlil, through Marduk, had imposed on her, took a third unprecedented step. She had already given forth the Emerald Tablet. Through her unrecognised influence, she had caused 'the kingship to be lowered from heaven', which had appeared to Annum to be his own decision within the context of the Grand Assembly, but which had actually been secretly motivated, with Enki and Nin-khursag's help, by her silent encouragement. We shall now see how Enki and Nin-khursag were brought to the point, under Tiâmat's direction, where, via the bloodline, they were enabled to bring forth the New Woman and the New Man.

CHAPTER TWENTY-FOUR

Teardrops

*B*efore we begin to describe Enki and Nin-khursag's perplexities and conster-
nations, we must first reveal a deep secret concerning Enki himself. This
is not the 'terrible secret' (which actually relates to Enlil) that gave us so much
heart searching when we first realised its full implications, and which in part our
readers may already have guessed. It is, in contrast, a beautiful secret.

When Tiâmat embraced her need to create, she birthed Father God into being
from her deepest profundity. What came forth from her as the primordial miracle
was her lover and her partner in creation, called into realised being because of her
need for him. Because of this wonder and this conjoinment, she let fall a mystical rain
– we may say almost a shower of teardrops, for this most holy water emerged from
her deepest heart, her most secret centre, the 'holy of holies'. Within this divine water,
among many other potentialities, was the potential to create the physical domain.

Charged with the ineffable fire of God which manifested in the material dimension as radiation, a fire-mist was produced which brought the universe into being
as an ever begetting, ever birthing entity, for, as we know, systems and stars are
forever dying and being born. This stupendous life began in the divine waters,
the 'living waters' that first transformed into suns and planets, and then became
physical life, always accompanied by its ethereal counterpart. Its initial, fundamental expression was that of little, rapidly wriggling fishes, effervescing the
waters so that they bubbled with life.

We might think of Alice in her Pool of Tears (Tiâmat releasing the divine
waters), which soon became filled with a variety of living creatures. Indeed,
Margaret Bailey and I were shown that all life proceeded from a teardrop (the
name 'Tiâmat' means 'saltwater' or 'bitter water' as does the name 'Mary'), and
that the renowned teardrops of Mary Magdalene, far from being expressions of
'remorse' for her 'sins', were rather a symbol of her direct connection to Tiâmat
and to the origins of life itself. She was indeed 'the All', as Jesus reverently and
adoringly named her.

Within 'the All' (Tiâmat the Mother) dwelt the masculine essence of Father God, and when he manifested on earth, in physical life, his primordial expression in matter consisted of these little wriggling sperm or fish, ready to fertilise the fecundity of the Living Waters (Divine Mother) so that they might bring forth all life forms present on earth today. But we must not be one-dimensional in our perception of this great mystery, and think only in terms of biology. When Tiâmat gave forth the divine rain, she released the Father aspect of creation in a great outpouring of her will. This omnipotent movement of divine will was the nature and essence of Father God – will birthed from love and, in its proper balance and expression, ever giving forth and embracing love. This power of will emerged from Tiâmat, and was Tiâmat.

Father God is the principle of the divine will-to-good, part of Tiâmat and utterly faithful to Divine Mother and the creation they have brought forth together. There is no imbalance, no dominance, no wish to undermine, in Father God. He expresses the drive towards organisation, civilisation, the attainment of the heights in human development, achievement and endeavour. In his promptings to scale the heights he manifests as the Goat of Mendes, Tiâmat's chosen symbol (amongst others) for her greatest project – humanity. The Goat of Mendes is the Goat of Capricorn – the Goat Fish or Sea Goat, who emerges from the sea to dwell upon the mountain-tops.

When we think of the essence of Father God entering physical creation in the energy pattern of a fish, should we become literalists and imagine that a fish was ever a God? Surely this would be far too narrow, naive and absurd a concept! It might bear a certain truth in that Father God symbolically clothed himself in fish garb as a devoted acknowledgement, even a proclaimed statement, that he was born of and issued forth from Tiâmat, the Great Mother. It was an affirmation of his love for Tiâmat.

Nevertheless, there did seem to have come into earthly being a divine individual who took the form of a fish man, certainly not the type of fearsome 'creature from the Black Lagoon' that we might first visualise, but a beautiful entity who expressed the godly characteristics of the Son of Light, the Son of the Father. His name was Oannes; but in ancient Mesopotamia, the Sumerians knew him as Uan, or Enki.

This mystery of Enki's two Sumerian names repays deep contemplation, because we see that 'Uan' is almost 'Anu' in reverse. The 'u', representative of the sacred feminine, is placed firmly at the beginning of the name, instead of at the end, where it had been split off by the depredations of the darkening Annum – a declaration within the sacredness of words that the Divine Feminine is the first principle, and not the sub-principle that Annum tried to make it. In other words, we see that Enki (Uan-Oannes) is the positive rendition of his father, that he is indeed the remedy, the antidote to the negative Annum who plotted with Enlil, Enki's brother, to 'kill' Tiâmat and, in so doing, reversed the sunwise spin of the earth as her polar alignment was displaced.

When the shadow of imbalance first fell over Annum, Enki was called upon by Tiâmat to embody the light of the true Father God, because Annum was beginning to reject this sacred task. So it was that Enki, the first true Knight and the original 'Gentle Man', was chosen by Tiâmat to fulfil the Oannes (John) mission. Tiâmat saw that he of all the males of earth, and of those other higher dimensions belonging to it, was the one who possessed the courage, integrity, loyalty, soundness of purpose, and the sufficient depth of unsullied love in his heart, to carry the torch of the true Oannes, the true Father, and never let it go out.

Enki was aided and guided in his great mission by his wife, Nin-khursag, who, it seems, had to argue with him quite a lot to keep him on course! Nin-khursag received within herself the blessing and the grace of God and devoted herself to Tiâmat in the same measure as Enki. In herself she became the first Dragon Queen associated with planet earth, meaning that she carried within her the precious gift of the supreme power of the *khu* and of Tiâmat's Grail lineage – composed of those who remained faithful to Tiâmat's essence, which was Divine Love, and who would, by means of self-sacrifice, step by step, link by link, help to restore the Grail and the true teachings of the Emerald Tablet to planet earth. This lineage was called by the Hebrews the *malkhut* – the 'Kingdom' or 'the place of the Throne'. They recognised it as the ultimate expression of royalty. From another perspective it translates as 'the Blood of the Dragon' – the divine inheritance from Tiâmat delivered via the *khu* and the bloodline. Nin-khursag, supreme mistress of the *khu*, guided and nurtured Enki, and initiated him into the mysteries of Tiâmat and the Father Principle.

And so Enki became the Oannes-man, the Johannes-man, the John-man. In a beautiful ceremony of the deepest magic, Enki was 'swallowed' by the Oannes form, the mighty fish, and became the sacred fish-man. This essence of Father God was indeed, in itself, the Fisher King; and so Enki, the Son of Light, took on his title and became the veritable Fisher King, the Fisher King who showed us, in the dimension in which we could perceive him, that he was wounded, ever bleeding, ever agonised, because his other half (Tiâmat, Goddess, Divine Mother, the sacred feminine) had been brutally torn away from him.

Annum, Enlil and their circle of conspirators, including the Naphidem with whom they were in league, came to pathologically despise the Fisher King and his teachings and would pursue him with malignant intent throughout history.

CHAPTER TWENTY-FIVE

The Angel of the North

*B*oth Annum and Enlil, even at this early stage, continued to feel a certain degree of hostility towards Enki. They did not mistrust him, exactly; but we see that they were made uneasy by him. Enki's very soul emanations, heightened and refined more than ever now that he had dedicated himself to the spirit of Oannes (Father God) and to the service of Tiâmat to a degree never known before on any plane belonging to earth, unnerved them, although they remained unconscious of Enki's true allegiance.

We can see from the preceding woeful history how vital the setting up of Tiâmat's special bloodline was, because it would convey to earth the Divine Couple who would bring a true understanding of Mother God and the Daughter of Light, and Father God and the Son of Light, to our confused, chaotic world, correct its reverse spin, and soothe its desperate suffering into the peace of enlightenment. Many of the lower, and even the higher, star peoples had completely lost touch with any correct perception of Mother-Father God, and pursued instead distorted phantoms of their own making. Father God in particular was almost entirely misunderstood, and Mother God in her highest aspect was almost forgotten. The situation was about to worsen considerably, as we shall see.

'Oannes' reflects the name of Johannes or John; both originate from the same measurelessly ancient source, and it is the Sphere of John, of Father God (sometimes called the Orbit of Sharon, which is its heart) to which the earth was perfectly aligned before the great imbalance asserted itself.

The Sphere of John is associated with the North Star (the Pole Star), and with the mighty star Sirius, which are physical foci for this exalted dimension; in fact one direct link connects them all. It comprises a connection point for the consciousness of Father God to our earthly plane; and in this context it is of note that the diamond in the card pack is associated with the north, as is the 'stone of death' in the Celtic medicine wheel and the stone of the north (the diamond and its heart of hearts, the emerald) which symbolises one of the four Grail Hallows.

The north is associated with the divine masculine, and it is interesting that in Britain, the sacred isle, we have the northernmost symbol of Rosslyn Chapel as a celebration of the masculine principle (reflecting the divine feminine, just as the divine feminine always reflects the divine masculine), and also the sculpture of the Angel of the North, a distinctly masculine figure. In fact, the consciousness of Father God, from the Sphere of John, streams through a mighty angelic medium, and the metallic Angel of the North seems to celebrate this mystery, especially as the mythical tradition of the King (Father God) is always associated with sacred smithship and the Divine Forges; and Enki, Master Craftsman supreme, also bears the same stamp.

We would like to share with you some evocative words concerning the literalness of Enki-Uan-Oannes' existence in our physical world, or at least the human ability to see him and experience his reality from the standpoint of the physical world. We think these words reflect the simple truth of what was perceived in those ancient days. The quotes are drawn from the work of Berossus, a Babylonian priest writing in the third century BC, who compiled a book of ancient lore bearing the evocative title *Babylonica*.

> *The whole body of* [Oannes] *was like that of a fish; and had under a fish's head another head, and also feet below, similar to those of a man, subjoined to the fish's tail.*

It is to be noted that members of the higher star peoples could programme the ethereal atoms of their bodies so that they decreased in rate and produced temporary physical bodies in which they could walk the earth. Here Enki shows us a profound symbol in flesh – that of the human soul swallowed by the Fish, Oannes, Father God. He also shows us his allegiance to Mother God, Tiâmat; for she was of the essence of the salt waters that contained the mystical fish, the living waters of creation which she let fall as a rain of teardrops (water produced from a movement of compassion and love through her heart). Tiâmat was the All; and within the All was contained the Father.

Berossus goes on to tell us:

> *His voice too, was articulate and human; and a representation of him is preserved even to this day ... When the sun set, it was the custom of this Being to plunge again into the sea, and abide all night in the deep; for he was amphibious ... In the daytime he used to converse with men; but took no food at that season; and he gave them an insight into letters and sciences, and every kind of art. He taught them to construct houses, to found temples, to compile laws, and explained to them the principles*

*of geometrical knowledge. He made them distinguish the seeds of the
earth, and showed them how to collect fruits; in short, he instructed
them in every thing which could tend to soften manners and to humanize
mankind. From that time, so universal were his instructions, nothing has
been added materially by way of improvement.*

The 'representation' of Enki does indeed 'survive even unto this day' (with reference in this context to the twenty-first century). Babylonian and Assyrian reliefs
depict the sacred fish-man, and he also occurs in the form of a great statue in
Tiahuanacu in western South America, carrying in his right hand what appears
to be a knife with a sinuous blade and in his left a hinged, casebound book with
what might be some kind of weapon or other contraption protruding from its
top, as though the book were a sheath. We believe that, even though this statue
is in the 'wrong' geographical location, the knife is a representation of Tiâmat's
divine truth and the book is a representation of the Emerald Tablet, with a device
plunged into it like the Arthurian sword in the stone, showing us that, even in
those unaccountably far off days when the statue was first carved, the esoteric
knowledge was in place and recognised which tells us that a male sacrifice would
be necessary to reinstate that divine truth and restore the Emerald Tablet to its
rightful inheritors – the human race.

All of the Sumerian clay tablets affirm that it was indeed Enki who brought
civilisation, education and graciousness of conduct to the Sumerian people, that
strange and magnificent culture which arrived as if from nowhere and rose like
a floodlit tower of progress and learning far above any other contemporary civilisation on earth. Enki was indeed their wise knight, the original 'Gentle Man',
protecting them and bringing them gifts from the deeps of his divine Mother and
Father to help to make them 'fully human', as Mary Magdalene expresses it in her
in stunning, Tiâmat-Oannes-inspired gospel. From the exalted inspiration and
example of this wise knight, the knights of history emerged, especially the knights
of Camelot. They clad themselves in bright silver 'fish-scales' or armour – properly
the reflective armour of the soul mirroring the effulgence of divine spirit – and
strove to uphold the ideals of Enki.

Perhaps we can understand now exactly why the carven figure of the Falling
Knight points towards the site of the Holy Grail (the Emerald Tablet). The Falling
Knight represents the whole of humanity, and men in particular, who fell from
the divine grace expressed, embodied and upheld as a guiding principle by Enki,
the Wise Knight and the Gentle Man. The recovery of the Emerald Table is our
supreme hope and promise.

CHAPTER TWENTY-SIX

City-Under-Wave

*I*t is interesting to note that Enki 'abode all night in the deep'. Nin-khursag often joined him, for they needed the baptismal waters of the ocean depths for their profoundest communion with Tiâmat. As amphibious humans from Nibiru, they were literally within their element in the sighing expanse of the sea. There was also another place that Nin-khursag and Enki would often visit when in fish-garb. To this place they were drawn, as if into a dreamtime of distant memory and tender starlit perception, shadowed yet softly radiant. It was to the sunken Atlantis they travelled, back to the City of Light which was its central jewel.

Hand in hand, they swam in balletic motion around its drowned turrets and obelisks and domes, throughout its mighty halls, its healing chambers and its colleges of instruction, its vast temples and cultural arenas, remembering in both sorrow and delight; for Enki and Nin-khursag had nurtured the civilisation of Atlantis from her beginnings until the coming of the great deluge, when it sank beneath the waves. The civilisation of Sumer was a mirror, though a small and circumscribed one, of Atlantis.

Because of the information on the Sumerian clay tablets, we associate Enki with the Sumerian civilisation of which we have documented evidence from between six and eight thousand years ago. But the darkening of Annum, the fall of Apsû, the 'murder' of Tiâmat and the later appointment of Enki and Nin-khursag as the Divine Couple happened long, long before Sumer came into being.

Apart from its cultural luminosity, its special significance is that it was the civilisation chosen to carry the torch of humanity forward once more after the terrible consequences of the Dolorous Blow (the severing of the Grail).

Enki and Nin-khursag did not visit the drowned Atlantis purely for nostalgic reasons, however. They went to receive a special vibration from a monumental crystal which still survived, buried in the Atlantean mountain range that looked down on the City of Light. Here was a secret dimension wherein dwelt an ancient brotherhood who, with the help of the crystal, fortified them for their special mission. The depths of the ocean held many mysteries for Enki and Nin-khursag. They heard Tiâmat's voice in the surge and fall of the waves, and understood that they, together with all humanity, were the Children of Water, the divine waters of Tiâmat.

We are confident that Nin-khursag manifested, taught and bestowed enlightenment just as Enki did; but, as would befall Mary Magdalene in later days, history ignored her. This was part of the occupational hazard of being a woman after the great imbalance had struck: women were demoted to the invisible content of concepts such as 'man'kind and the universal use of the pronoun 'he' to denote its members, and entirely disappeared into the context of an all-male God. After the depredations of Marduk, the truth of the sacred feminine would become invisible, blacked out as far as men (and very often women) were concerned. The impact of women's visibility would thereafter be channelled in a new way – through the deliberate degradation of the lens of pornographic perception. This little trick could be relied upon to keep the whole system of denial of the sacred feminine in self-perpetuation, and to twist into sinister channels the joy of looking on a symbol of God.

So Enki and Nin-khursag shared this beautiful secret: that they were of Oannes and Tiâmat, they were of the deeps of the Living Waters, they were the golden entwining serpents of the caduceus, and they were the Golden Dragon or Serpent that was later called Poimandres but was first associated with the wisdom of Thoth. The Golden Dragon or Serpent wisdom was later venerated by the Druids, the Knights Templar, the Rosicrucians, the alchemists and the Masons, but initially and particularly, of course, by the Church ('circle') of Jesus and Mary Magdalene. This beautiful, simple, and supremely exalted Church was the very one that was so virulently despised and overthrown by the later Church of Rome, led by Simon Peter's legacy, he who was filled with wrath, who hated women, who wanted (and on one or two occasions actually attempted) to kill Mary Magdalene herself – Mary Magdalene, the feminine Christ. It was this early establishment that harlotised the exquisitely spiritual Mary, airbrushed the toweringly significant Tamar out of historical existence, stamped out the Cathars and the Templars, and condemned as heretical the stories of King Arthur and the Holy Grail.

There was a very clearly defined link and purpose behind all these manoeuvres and abominations – they were not random acts of barbarity committed by an entity that did not understand what it was doing. The unearthly entity that drove them understood the strategic value of perpetrating these obscenities only too well. As we shall see, Peter was its key agent on earth, the 'demon' of whom Jesus spoke when he remarked that one among his disciples was indeed demonic.

Meanwhile, we may reflect on this mysterious and shining truth: that Enki bore the title of Fisher King, the Fisher King who was Oannes or John, first knight and first 'gentle man', the faithful reflection of Father God immersed in the depths of the Mother of All.

CHAPTER TWENTY-SEVEN

Guileful Wisdom

To understand the difficulties of the task that lay before Nin-khursag and Enki, and to appreciate their ingenuity, fidelity, bravery and determination, we need to return to an overview of the nine kingships which were established in Sumer prior to the great flood that was recorded on the Sumerian King List.

First of all, it is important to understand that this particular flood was not the great deluge which sank Atlantis, nor was it the flood that resulted from the rise of the melt-water as the last Ice Age came to an end between ten and thirteen thousand years ago. It was a very dramatic inundation, however, and in fact our source confirms that it was indeed universal. It is also important to understand that this flood of over six thousand years ago was the Flood recorded in the Old Testament.

It is useful to consider here that the Hebrew scribes began to compile their own histories during their captivity in Babylon from 586 to 536 BC under the yoke of the Babylonian king Nebuchadnezzar after he had transported them from Jerusalem, no doubt as an act of empowerment to counter the degradation of slavery. They were potently influenced by the rites and dramas depicting ancient history enacted in the temples and other arenas drawn from the *Enûma elish,* the Babylonian creation story based on earlier Sumerian texts. Thus the Old Testament came into being.

Because the *Enûma elish* was not translated and published until 1876, having been discovered during excavations some years previously, and the earlier Sumerian texts were not deciphered until less than a century ago, this undeniable realisation and the astonishing scope of its implications has only just begun to dawn on Western society. Over the next few chapters, let us look at exactly what happened, according to the story that we perceive as hidden in the Sumerian and later Babylonian texts, and the final Hebraic rendition of both, which includes the story of Genesis and other accounts in the Old Testament.

Concerning the biblical flood of six and a half thousand years ago, recorded in the Old Testament, the Sumerian texts tell us that King Zi-u-sudra reigned in Sumer at that time. He was the ninth Sumerian king, and different from his forbears, as the eight previous monarchs had all been of the higher star people. He was a very special king, as he was the first earthly man to hold kingship. It is not quite true to say, however, that he was of the 'ordinary' star people. He and his queen were the first 'Adam' (a generic term denoting both sexes), the new humanity intended to initiate Tiâmat's bloodline and introduce a new DNA patterning into human genes. Zi-u-sudra and his wife (his half-sister) were both generated by higher star people sperm. Nin-khursag had brought their embryos into being within her 'Creation Chamber', and had transferred them to the wombs of the earthly mothers from whom the necessary ova had been taken.

Within the confines of her Creation Chamber, Nin-khursag, under Tiâmat's instruction and inconceivable mastership, introduced into the new human pair a celestial energy or quickening that gave them, first through their heart awareness and then through their chakra and nervous systems, through their brain and every organ of perception, a new capacity which allowed them to receive one quarter of the supreme consciousness that the ever-loving Dragon Queen had always planned to bestow on her beloved children of earth. Into genetic consciousness itself, Nin-khursag implanted enhanced perceptual receptors, and also shock absorbers and screening processes to block the automatic invasion of the Naphidem at the mental level (although our free will response to them was not blocked).

So it was that, when the time was right for her earth children to begin to receive the new DNA, Zi-u-sudra and his queen were graced from conception with the advanced creational dynamic. They received a perceptual capacity which enabled them to absorb one quarter of the exalted knowledge written in letters of light upon Tiâmat's Emerald Table – that manifested glory which was the heart within the heart of her very essence, and which would enable her created beings to become individually God-realised. This was the promise that Zi-u-sudra took into his soul. From the first, he and his queen dedicated themselves to Nin-khursag and Enki, becoming their staunch supporters and devotees. Zi-u-sudra is better known to us as the biblical Noah.

For many generations prior to this cosmic event, Enlil had been trying to eliminate humanity by means of various plagues and famines, but (as he would also do later on in Egypt) Enki had invariably stepped in, hidden from Enlil's view, and had whispered wisdom, often through dreams, to key community members of the earthlings, so that they found ways to counteract the worst of the evils visited upon them. Enlil did not know that Enki constantly blocked his every destructive move, but his intuition (ever becoming more and more akin to cunning) warned him to beware of the seemingly harmless and generally compliant Enki. Enlil, frankly, wanted to conclude his plan of total extermination of the ordinary star people as quickly as possible, and grew more and more furious as each attempt was thwarted. However, he soon turned the situation to his advantage.

Enlil, Annum and the Naphidem had entered into a pact which involved the two higher Anunnaki leaders surreptitiously enabling the Naphidem to extend their sphere of influence over the peoples of the earth as widely and deeply as possible. (We remember that the Naphidem were prevented from actually incarnating or walking the earth, but were confined in a rather vague, inchoate astral world where they were and are generally unable, thank goodness, to effectively materialise their rabid desires or to experience sensation or fulfilment in anything but a disconnected, dreamlike way. The Naphidem clan can only influence us via their thought-manipulation of willing and susceptible human beings, although it has to be said that they have so far made a good job of doing so within the limitations of their restricted capacity.)

This resulted in warfare, evil-doing and general mayhem on earth, which Enlil capitalised on by declaring to the Grand Assembly that such behaviour must be checked and corrected, and then releasing his plagues and famines upon humanity, as if his true aim were simply to administer enlightenment through karma to errant humankind.

At this point, there was sharp and increasing division among the ranks of the higher star people. Some (a large minority) were entirely repelled by Enlil's style of acting presidency. (Annum always remained in charge, but followed an 'in and out' style of leadership due to his strategy of martial seizure of other planets.) Some feared and resented Enlil, but were unable to assert their authority and effactually defy him. Others were definitely falling under his spell, and openly supported him even though factions were not supposed to arise within the Grand Assembly; they treated those who disapproved of him and his methods with disdain and hostility.

We believe that none of the higher star people, except a few close ministers, had any real idea that Annum and Enlil were in league with the despised Naphidem, or of the hideous nature of their long-term plan. The Grand Assembly still constituted a democracy, and some of the ideals and vision of its members had, to a certain degree, survived the death of Tiâmat; but the seeds of corruption had already sprouted, and were thriving. Nevertheless, everything that Annum and Enlil wished to implement had still to be passed by the Grand Assembly, and in order to win a majority vote, it was necessary for Enlil to deceive, manipulate and mislead.

It was by such means, and by bringing the considerable force of his will to bear, that he managed to persuade the Assembly to agree to a universal flood.

Yet again he had been secretly opening orifices of influence for the Naphidem, through which they eagerly poured their seductive poisons, until certain core groups of the ordinary star people had become so disruptive and chaotic that human society began to disintegrate once more. Triumphantly pointing out that no disaster he had inflicted so far had had the desired effect, Enlil argued eloquently in favour of a mighty inundation.

To the horror of Enki and Nin-khursag, he won the day. Nin-khursag let the Council know how she felt, vociferating her disgust. Enki kept silent, not openly opposing Enlil, but furtively planning his next move. After the meeting had been formally closed, Enki and Nin-khursag repaired to the secret temple where they communed with Tiâmat. Entering into the sacred Silence, they heard her voice. The mighty Dragon Queen instructed Enki, for his own safety and honour, not to directly break the Grand Assembly law, but yet to carry out her will. It was time for Enki to lapwing!

CHAPTER TWENTY-EIGHT

Nine Kings to Rule Them

*W*hat could Enki and Nin-khursag do? The entire human family stood in danger of extinction. Those who managed to survive the flood would have to live post-diluvian lives of savagery and want, reduced to brutishness by scant resources. In the midst of the ensuing social calamity, Enki and Nin-khursag knew that Annum, Enlil and the corrupted higher star people intended to bend the remnant of humanity to their will, and to force its straitened and desperate survivors into slavery. These slaves and their descendants would prepare the earth for the coming of the Naphidem, who, because of Tiâmat's injunction against their inhabitation of the planet, needed certain conditions to prevail, and certain adaptations of human anatomy to be processed, before they could again descend into human bodies and make the world their own.

After they had done so, Annum and Enlil would sit back and watch with approval as the Naphidem, under their king, Marduk, blasted themselves out of existence via the great spiritual law of cause and effect, which the two God-Headed lords had persuaded themselves was in harmony with their atrocious intentions. The fact that they had abused poor Marduk in order to carry out their schemes and had literally promised him the earth as a reward, all the while knowing the cataclysmic outcome of his projected sovereignty, to say nothing of previously deposing Tiâmat (or cutting off our direct route to her) and thereby eventually destroying her earthly human creation, conveniently escaped their attention.

The Sumerian texts, together with many other flood myths from around the world, seem to suggest that the reason for the deluge was not only the misdemeanours of humankind, but an overpopulation problem. The *Enûma elish* tells us that 'In those days the world teemed, the people multiplied, and the great god [Enlil] was aroused by the clamour.' In these stories, Enlil went on to complain that humankind was making such a racket that he could not sleep, and wholesale reduction of numbers was required. We think, however, that this is an incorrect interpretation or, rather, a simplistic spyhole into a deeper truth.

H.P. Lovecraft, the American writer of supernatural fiction, experienced strange encounters with otherworldly beings whom he suspected of attempting to influence him through mind control. His insight into their chilling and unsettling dimension occurred just before and during his frequent subjection to severe migraine attacks. Through the eye of his imagination, he gained deep insight into the Naphidem, who, it seemed, were targeting him in the hope that he would fulfil their objectives on earth. Instead, he resisted them and wrote 'fables' about them which give us a clue as to how they operate, and how, with the help of other undesirables that our informal culture has come to call the 'greys', they link up their own dimension with ours.

They told him that they would teach humanity new ways of maiming, cruelty and slaughter, and that there would be excitement and shouting upon the earth. This idea of the Naphidem causing a huge stir of excitement, of brutal conflict, of shouting, seems to echo uncannily the words of the *Enûma elish*, and of other ancient myths which tell of the time just prior to the great deluge.

We think that the myths reveal how in fact Enlil, having purposely helped to unleash Naphidem influences upon the earth, reported to the Grand Assembly on the objectionable behaviour of humankind, once the mass of it was infected, as the second part of his manipulative strategy. It was not that there were too many people on earth, but rather that far too many people had fallen under the sway of Naphidem domination, which 'teemed' with their followers. Enlil's lack of 'sleep', we believe, should be interpreted as lack of 'rest'; in other words, the great god of corrective karma was kept impossibly busy in his generation of it, and was never able to rest, as there was so much evil-doing on the earth to attend to. The only way he could hope to keep up, and sweep the wicked influences away from the world of men, was to impose a 'last resort' so that humankind, severely reduced and chastened, could be given the opportunity of a 'fresh start' (we are fairly sure that this is how he presented his argument in the Eden parliament!).

It is true that many of the higher star people lost the plot to some degree after Marduk's brutal repulsion of Tiâmat, but it is also true that only Annum, Enlil, and a few others were psychopathic exterminators. The rest, and, at this time, still the great majority, were not. Our belief is supported by the fact that the other gods reacted by 'cowering and trembling' when the floodwaters inundated the world. They were deeply horrified and traumatised, and they clearly had not understood what Enlil planned to unleash on humanity when they voted to assent to his proposal (he had not intended them to understand it, of course).

Although very material in its manifestation, the flood bore supernatural elements, and was accompanied by a burning, poisonous rain. We see that this rain, and the waters which were released, were the very opposite, in fact the illusory death-image (even though it caused real devastation) of Tiâmat's waters of life, her creation of mystical rain falling as 'teardrops' into the abysmal sphere or cup that would hold the universe: the ultimate physical expression of the Grail cup. The flood waters were the waters of death, sent by one who had become, in his own limited sphere of operation, the mirror-opposite of life, of God.

Yet Enlil had invoked the main waters of the flood from a devastating source by a further reversal of divine powers and divine dispensation. Ptolemy, the famous second-century astronomer, geographer and mathematician of Macedonian and Egyptian heritage wrote in his great work, the *Almagest*, of an earth that was the centre of the universe around which fixed spherical transparent bodies moved. Eight of these contained the moon and the stars and two caused the precession of the equinoxes and the alternation of night and day. Whilst Ptolemy made an erroneous scientific calculation in his exposition of the cosmos, he simultaneously tuned into the percipience of what had once been a reality. For there truly had once existed a beautiful, translucent ring around our earth, like a crown or a canopy of ice crystals formed from water of the purest degree in which Tiâmat had infused a blessing of profoundest light – water drawn from her very heart, like the teardrops of creation. This sphere or ring of ice crystals protected us with the absolute strength, surety and devotion of godly motherhood.

Annum had been working for some time on a plan to get rid of earth's perfect crown of protection. Only confusion, fear and degradation rising from the earth in great swathes released by its population, both higher and ordinary, could allow him to achieve his aims, and only then could success be assured by harnessing the sinister technology of the planetary communities he had brought under his sway, honing it into a focal point of pure malice and, finally, being granted a warrant to act. When the Grand Assembly gave Enlil permission to impose his 'cleansing' of humanity, a figurative cheer went up from Annum and his new minions. They could, in cooperation with Enlil, put their plan into action and be confident of its triumphant fulfilment. Lethal contamination and ruin was aimed at the glassy ring.

So came the Flood, and down came the ring of protection, utterly destroyed and displaced. Harmful radiation bombarded us, and hostile encroachers from other planets, other dimensions, were able to reach us. The biblical warning that we do not struggle against earthly foes, but against principals and powers, is a clarion call to rise up against these invaders. They do not only disrupt the lives of many targeted people across the planet, but they infest our minds and our thoughts on a massive scale. They enter into our language and manipulate the power of our words. They have learned how to operate in the subtlest mental dimensions and can transmute themselves into sound waves for the purpose of controlling us mentally, emotionally and perceptually. They have their planets and dimensions in which they live their lives, as we do; but they have a need for a certain energy, upon which they feed and fuel themselves. This energy is that which arises from chaos, horror, extreme suffering and distress, fear, madness, cruelty, and murder, and all that fires up the baser emotions.

As it rises from the earth they are able to ingest it and charge their psychic batteries with its potency. They condition our willpower and make puppets of us, moving us into place like pieces on a chessboard. They call us *goyim* – cattle – and farm us as if we were their property. They are in league with the Naphidem and are of their calibre.

Goyim sounds like 'gollum', the horrible sound that the poor depraved hobbit makes in his throat that gives him his name in J.R.R. Tolkien's famous stories. They are indeed, as we shall see, the great fables of our time, for just as Gollum was once a hobbit but became so degenerate that he was more like a demon, so these 'greys' are human beings, but human beings that are evolving into the profane darkness rather than the sacred light through following the allure of the False Grail (the ring of the story). Gollum indeed in his creator's description of him is portrayed exactly like a 'grey', with his huge lamp-like eyes, his small head and his diminutive, thin, smooth, pale, hairless body. It is not at all reassuring to think of such slimy things slithering all over our thoughts and coming out in our language and intentions, so later we will give some simple exercises to thoroughly oust these unpleasant 'gollums' that make nests of infestation in the ethereal counterparts of our brains! However, for those who would rather not host them, the first step is worth taking immediately, and it is to monitor our thoughts and our language and dispense with negative manifestations, as far as we can, as they arise.

With the translucent crystal firmament gone and the encroachers gaining ground, Nin-khursag and Enki had to act fast to save humankind. Enki had been advised by Tiâmat (who often spoke through Nin-khursag) not to break Edenic law, which prohibited discussion of the higher star people's affairs of council with earthly humanity.

So Enki did not descend to earth and simply tell Zi-u-sudra all about the coming crisis. Instead, he and his consort whispered it to the reeds growing by the river close to the royal residence.

In his dreams, in his meditations (for the king and his queen were deeply spiritual people, and spent much time in contemplation of the inner worlds), Zi-u-sudra heard Enki's words:

Man of Sherpa, son of Ubar-Tutu,
Tear down [thy] house; build a ship.
Abandon [thy] possessions, and seek [thou] life.
Discard [thy] goods, and keep thee alive.
Aboard the ship take the seed of living things.

We see from this quote, derived from the *Epic of Gilgamesh* (Tablet XI), how a spiritual test comes to the king and queen. Will they listen? Will they take heed? Will they be prepared to abandon their great wealth of possessions, to put aside materialism and save themselves, humanity and the human world? The answer is affirmative on all counts, and we may thank this royal pair, a reflection of the Divine Couple Nin-khursag and Enki, and then shining beyond them the heavenly Christ-Brigid, for their keen and true spirituality, for without it, we ourselves would not exist as we do today in our physical world, and would not have been given the inconceivable opportunity of accepting the Grail and becoming one with Tiâmat. Even so, and sad to relate of so noble a soul, Zi-u-sudra did eventually stumble on his path, as we shall see.

We note (as Laurence Gardner points out in *Genesis of the Grail Kings*) that Enki did not advise the king and queen to take pairs of animals on board their ship, but the *seed* of living things.

In other words, the king and queen were being asked to build a great storehouse of clinically preserved material for the sake of future generations – a veritable ship of life to counteract the poisonous death Enlil sought to inflict on earth and her humanity. This was the first covenant with God, and it was commemorated by Zi-u-sudra by the shape of his boat, which was built in the form of an arc, like the arc of the rainbow, Tiâmat's true sign as she shone her glory through the medium of the sacred waters.

This was where Nin-khursag came into her own. It was her great pride and joy that Zi-u-sudra and his queen had followed in her footsteps, and were educated scientists and philosophers like her. (Interestingly, Noah or Zi-u-sudra, a redoubtable scientist, was the first to discover that the earth had actually slipped off her axis, 64,000 years prior to his time, as recorded in the Hebrew Book of Enoch.) This had been her special part in their nurture and culture, and now she rejoiced in helping the royal couple to assemble their submersible boat with its great storehouse of practical and scientific provisions. Enki, of course, played an equal part in this grand procedure. It was indeed Enki and Nin-khursag who together had civilised humanity in its early days, bringing them knowledge of agriculture and the 'distinguishing of seeds, one from another' as part of the full scale of human knowledge. The ark also contained embryonic material which would be implanted in the uteruses of the female animals it carried when Zi-u-sudra and his queen re-established their community.

They were only just in the nick of time. As the last touches were being administered to the ark, the inundation began. Before his crew had laid down their tools, it was under way, and the ship was beginning to float. Whilst the poisonous, acid rain fell, humans and animals (for some domestic beasts were taken on board) had to shelter within the body of the ship, in lamplit darkness. They returned to the womb, as it were, until they could be born again into the sunlight.

It is interesting to pose the question as to why Enlil chose this specific time for his most lethal attempt on humanity's collective life. Did he know about Tiâmat's great plan, already initiated by Enki and Nin-khursag in their bringing forth of Zi-u-sudra and his queen? We believe that he certainly did not know anything about it at this juncture, but that he sensed something major was afoot. All he really knew was that his maddening brother Enki was on the side of this low bred creature, humankind, and whilst he himself sought surreptitiously to destroy it, Enki, he noted, kept succeeding in passing all sorts of ridiculous, unnecessary initiatives through parliament which allowed him to organise the setting up of 'kingships' of God-Headed people on the actual earth to try to help it out, so necessitating his own precious kind to be directly in contact with the vile little things for protracted periods of time. Enlil could not bear that the conjoinment of God-Headed and earthly genes was taking place once more, although he suspected and intuited much more than he actually knew.

He had begun to merge with a virulent demonic entity, perhaps one of the worst, which sprang into being when Tiâmat created humanity in love, and commanded the life forces to flow between them in a supreme act of union which manifests as sexual consummation. This demon was its opposite mirror image, gaining even more power when the androgynes split through the negativity of this impact on human consciousness. Its name is Asmodeus, and we shall discuss it later, although only briefly, as any focus on demons is most unhelpful to the evolutionary impetus within us!

(Demons are merely the 'life' forces of the illusory opposite or mirror image, which had to occur so that creation could come into being. They are waiting to be absorbed into the truth and light of Tiâmat, so that they can become real, not mirror images any more. In the moment that they become real, that Tiâmat's life surrounds and absorbs them, they will be released into their proper angelic form and liberate a new dynamic into the beauty, wisdom and power of creation. Oddly enough, until that time comes, they are actually helping to advance the process of Tiâmat's magical transformation of the mirror image of creation into true reality, but, of course, only if we resist their magnetism, not if we allow it to overmaster us! Naturally, their helpfulness lies in opposition, as they are mirror images.)

So Enlil knew nothing of Tiâmat's mighty scheme, but his demonic impulses, arising from his allegiance with Asmodeus, sharpened his intuitive wits to a murderous degree. It seemed imperative to him to send his lethal flood just at the moment, so to speak, that Tiâmat's plan came into proper operation and her first earthly royal couple, reflecting the Divine Couple at the level of Eden and the Christ force at the profounder level of heaven, was instated.

But, yet again, through her great plan, through Enki and Nin-khursag, through Zi-u-sudra and his queen, Tiâmat snatched her beloved human creation from the jaws of death.

CHAPTER TWENTY-NINE

The Coming of the Grail

*W*e now come to a part of the story that, rather than receiving alteration through distortions and omissions both contrived and ignorant, has been effectively airbrushed out of history. It involves the next king, Zi-u-sudra's descendant: Ga-nadin-ur, and his queen. This king and his consort brought the great city of Ur into being, and the mighty dynasties that later flourished within it were of their seed, although any record of a direct line has been lost because of the cataclysm that overtook them. We need to look into their history, because Ga-nadin-ur is one of the titanic heroes of all time, and Ur, as we shall see, was very important indeed.

When Zi-u-sudra, his queen and his family, together with those colleagues and members of the royal household who had accompanied them, left the ark and set their feet on terra firma once the flood waters had started to recede, Tiâmat sent them the sign of the rainbow. The rainbow, the sign of the heavenly bridge or ladder, is a symbol of the Grail. It reassured the little group of vulnerable human beings that an all-loving, all-powerful God reigned supreme, not the pretender god who had caused so much cruel devastation. Tiâmat promised her children that he would never be able to destroy the world, and that, by following her presence in our hearts through our free-will choice, we would be led out of his dark and terrible incarceration forever.

This was the shining promise, the sure and certain hope, that Tiâmat made to her children on the mountain-top that sublime morning, when the sun shone for the first time after many weeks of gloom in a burst of alchemical gold.

She showed them the rainbow, the Grail, the Resurrection. Afterwards, she told them to go forth and multiply, because it was vital that all the souls who had been driven forth from their bodies by the poisonous deluge should have their path of physical incarnation and reincarnation restored to them. This was the king and the queen's great mission.

A vital part of this mission included the conveyance of their newly activated DNA to all the generations about to proceed from Zi-u-sudra and his queen. This DNA comprised the specially guarded receptacle within us which could safely receive the specified one quarter of the deepest knowledge of all time and all worlds relating to the earth, and which equated to one quarter of the Emerald Tablet. That only they and their children contained it, and their counsellors, servants and colleagues did not, was unimportant, as the children from both strains were bound to intermarry.

Also, a purely physical transference was not necessary. As soon as the new inherent qualities had been 'earthed', so to speak, by implantation within the consciousness and biological systems of heart-attuned individuals such as Zi-u-sudra and his queen, they could be passed on by both psychic and spiritual means to others. (There is scientific evidence for this in that studies have shown that, where one animal in a group is taught a skill which is alien to the usual habits and perceptions of a species, it is transferred 'automatically' to the other animals in the group, so that they all take a step forward in their evolution together. The scientist Rupert Sheldrake's studies with mice confirm this as fact.)

We would like to make clear at this point that those members of humanity who preceded Zi-u-sudra (people from Atlantis, for instance, and those prior to Atlantis) were not in any way 'inferior' to this new strain of humankind. It was simply given greater security, stability and facilitation.

After Zi-u-sudra and his queen had established their new community, many generations passed before Ga-nadin-ur was born. He and his queen were treated and implanted embryos, as were his great-great-grandfather and mother (Noah and his wife). They were the chosen ones, the second stage of Tiâmat's four-part plan. This time, the two specially selected embryos (who would become Ga-nadin-ur and his queen) were given the capacity to receive one half of the divine Emerald Tablet. However, to fully facilitate this process, the Divine Woman, who bore within her some measure of the essence of Tiâmat, must also be given to the earth in addition to the scientific procedures of Nin-khursag; for, as we have learned, no part of the Emerald Tablet can be restored to humanity without her. (Tamar was the final, integral and most perfect incarnation of the Divine Woman; and Nin-khursag, known by her other name of Nin-mah, was the first initiating Divine Woman or Daughter of Tiâmat who began the process with Zi-u-sudra and his queen. The third appears later in our story.) The second Divine Woman would descend to earth through the agency of Ga-nadin-ur and his queen, as their daughter. Nin-khursag took the embryos of Ga-nadin-ur and his queen through the processes of her Creation Chamber, and they were born to different mothers, just as Zi-u-sudra and his queen were before them.

The midway point of Tiâmat's grand plan had been reached. Through Ga-nadin-ur and his queen, humanity now held the potential to realise the consciousness of one half of the mysteries of the Emerald Tablet. However, the work could not be accomplished without the coming of the Divine Woman. The midway point equates to the heart, and it was at this juncture that Tiâmat commanded a woman of purest spiritual potency to descend to earth into a human body, for this Divine Woman contained within herself the Holy Grail, the essence of Tiâmat, the essence of the Dragon.

She would be the mother of the Grail, just as Mary Magdalene was destined to be the mother of Tamar.

The beloved daughter of Ga-nadin-ur was born two hundred years or more after the birth of Zi-u-sudra and his consort. The very early ancient Mesopotamian kings and queens lived an extraordinarily long time, particularly Zi-u-sudra, who was still taking an active part in history several hundred years after his descendant, Ga-nadin-ur, had died. In the beginning, the ordinary star people who were infused with higher star people blood via Nin-khursag's Creation Chamber were given Methuselah-esque life spans. These were withdrawn later, partly because the weight of suffering that humankind brought upon itself, and the consequent need to speed up the frequency of incarnations, conspired to make such an extension of years too weighty a burden.

During his reign, at Tiâmat's injunction, Ga-nadin-ur established the ancient city of Ur and built a magnificent temple ziggurat in its centre. This ziggurat was designed for a special reason. Ur contained the mystery of the Grail, and was a mighty power point of its containment; the ziggurat was built to accommodate its epicentre: a possibility brought about because the heart-point of Tiâmat's rescue plan had been attained and the Divine Woman was drawing close to the earth. The ziggurat of Ur was a symbol of the being and purpose of the Divine Woman who came as a daughter to the king and queen. All this was unknown to Annum and Enlil, who had agreed to Enki's 'idea' that such a structure should be built, and thought that they controlled the residue of the Grail power that it enshrined. Their spies did finally uncover some inkling of Tiâmat's plan, as we shall see.

There were four gargantuan power points belonging to the residual power of the Grail in those days, after the severance of its main spring from the North Pole.

The first, and also its highest and most spiritually potent source, was in Glastonbury, England, its western arm. The second was in Mesopotamian (Sumerian) Ur, its eastern arm, which would later be transferred wholly to Jerusalem and the Temple of Solomon. The third was in France, at the point where Chartres cathedral now stands, its southern arm; and the fourth, today contained within the protection of Rosslyn Chapel, remained located at a spot near the Arctic Circle, its northern arm. The beautiful dancing lights of the Aurora

Borealis, created at the mundane level by the charged particles of the solar winds and the earth's electromagnetic forcefield, show us the remnant of the exquisite Grail presence, rising visibly into the sky like a mystical spirit and regularly manifesting as a robe of hallowed, ethereal emerald green, wonderful to see.

What would eventually become Glastonbury was its purest throne because the land of the Grail (Hyperborea) had actually been brought from an exalted dimension – we would say, from outer space. It was brought here to become part of the land mass of earth expressly to ground the Grail into the planet, as a higher vibration than that of earth was necessary for this to be accomplished. Glastonbury and Rosslyn are a part of what once had been the continent of Hyperborea, and Glastonbury is in itself an energy fountain of unsurpassed purity, as its name, 'the place of the glassy wave', suggests.

Once the ziggurat had been constructed, Ga-nadin-ur and his queen were escorted via its power to the world of the God-Headed people. (Their sovereignty had begun in Kish, but a second palace was built for them in Ur when the city was complete.) Enki and Nin-khursag always accompanied them on these occasions. First, they were taken before Annum (if he was resident), and then to hold court with Enlil. These meetings were merely formalities, in which the two corrupt gods gave the king and the queen somewhat harsh directives concerning their rule and the activity of their subjects – oppressive commandments, the severity of which was intended to maintain strict Grand Assembly control.

The king and the queen would then repair with Enki and Nin-khursag to their secret temple in the woods – the real purpose of their visit to the exalted dimension of Eden. This world was similar to Hyperborea, the once lush and beautiful continent which is now the Arctic, in the time when it was an exquisite paradise of burgeoning loveliness.

Within its supernaturally beautiful expanses there were hills and high peaks, and a strange indigo sea. The presence of the Nephilim and the angels could be felt here, and the handiwork of the nature spirits was wrought in a filigree delicacy of infinite wonder. It was indeed paradise, and it was called Eden, as its reflection on earth had been. The gods had mirrored it on earth once again, after the demise of the North Pole Eden, by nurturing the Fertile Crescent into being (comprising the land of Mesopotamia and the surrounding countries, which once flourished like a garden but nowadays contain huge tracts of arid desert.)

In the secret temple, Enki, Nin-khursag, Ga-nadin-ur and his queen entered the holy silence and communed with Tiâmat, who, on the particular occasion we now home in on, was to give them momentous tidings.

CHAPTER THIRTY

Princess Gra-al

*T*here it was, within the precincts of the secret temple, that Tiâmat told them a most holy gift would be entrusted to them: a daughter of great spiritual power and grace who would conduct one half-measure of the Holy Grail back to the earth, to be kept there in secrecy and protection until its second half could unite with her and return it to humanity in full measure.

In time, the promised daughter was born to the royal couple. She was named Gra-al, which means 'of the essence of the Dragon Queen'. In later times, the Hebraic rendition became *Grael* – the 'essence' or 'blood' of the Shining One (God) or 'the Blood Royal'. 'El' was appropriated by the male gods to denote them-selves, but in fact it originally meant 'shining' or 'fiery one', synonymous with 'dragon' or 'serpent', and the principle it indicated was feminine. The European version of the spelling ('Grail') was, pragmatically speaking, an erroneous and phonetic one, although it bears connotations of a vessel containing nourishment, which is befitting in its symbolism; for nothing accidental can occur in the sacred history of the Grail.

One day the beautiful and exquisitely spiritual Gra-al was summoned to travel up the sacred ziggurat into the presence of Annum, who informed her that he had a suitor for her, and that she was to marry before the end of the year. The suitor was of God-Headed blood, Annum informed the poised and gracious young woman, and it was an honour for her to contract an alliance with him.

Ga-nadin-ur and his queen were initially pleased for their daughter, but their happiness did not last long. When they entered the secret temple in the forest, Tiâmat told them that the suitor whom Annum planned to be Gra-al's husband was of the dreaded Naphidem – Marduk himself! The marriage had three hideous objectives: to eliminate Gra-al's special connection with Tiâmat, to enslave the young princess and her God-granted power, and to bring the swarming Naphidem down the ziggurat of Ur from their own dimension to invade and colonise the earth. Gra-al would be their key.

In ever rising horror, the king and queen listened to Tiâmat's directions. They must send a secret messenger to the country we now know as Britain, to the clandestine brotherhood (of the Sphere of John, directly connected to the later Druids and Essenes) which held power there. Here dwelt a great king, who was the true heart-partner and love of Gra-al. They had met in dreams, and each knew the essence of the other, for they were one, even though they had no conscious knowledge of one another. This great king was the only person on earth who could guard the precious Gra-al. He was her true consort, the one who bore the flame of the Son within himself as she bore the flame of the Daughter.

They must marry, and remain in that far distant, wild, holy and remote island in the west. Gra-al could never come home again, but must remain in deep concealment in what we now call Glastonbury; and all the royal household must be sworn to absolute secrecy as to her whereabouts. The gods *could* be fooled (we know this from many instances in the Sumerian texts), and Tiâmat herself would protect the princess. This plan was urgent, Tiâmat advised them, and must be put into operation immediately. The slightest delay could mean death, not only to their beloved Gra-al, but to the entire human race, to the very earth itself, even to the continuance of all creation.

Tiâmat's instructions were acted upon instantly, and an emissary was dispatched the same day. Gra-al, on the advice of Tiâmat, feigned illness, so that she had an excuse for not ascending the ziggurat into Annum's dimension (where he intended to slowly bind her into the power of the Naphidem), and for staving off her forthcoming marriage for a few extra months. Meanwhile, in secret, the emissary returned with a small party of the 'British' king's men, disguised in Sumerian garb so that they would not arouse suspicion. Amidst terrible but silent grief and lamenting, the beautiful Gra-al bade her final farewells and went out into the night, under cover of the darkness and the soft starlight, and took swift flight, never to be seen again by any of her doting family.

She was borne to present-day England, to the isle of Avalon, where she married her king via deeply sacred rites. A daughter was born to Gra-al, who was named Brigid (*Bri-ghid* – 'Bright One' or 'Shining One'). Brigid was the rose in the heart of the emerald – the sacred issue from Tiâmat's heart of hearts that contained the necessary drop of her essence to transmit half of the Emerald Tablet to humanity.

There was something truly unusual about this child; she was more divine than earthly, more ethereal than she was flesh. Both mother and daughter were so precious to the king that he installed them for protection in his fort, an underground 'castle' consisting of a great cave system which was the interior of the hill that today we call Glastonbury Tor (the Grail Castle). This cave system has now crumbled and the caves have filled up with debris, but it was still partially in existence when Mary Magdalene and her daughter Tamar arrived in Glastonbury with Joseph of Arimathea in AD 36. Like their descendants Mary and Tamar (for we must remember Abraham's distinct connection with the ruling family of Ur, and of course he was of the line that produced the Christ family), Gra-al and Brigid needed underground protection.

The cave system at Glastonbury was used by Mary and Tamar for a few years, but it was steadily deteriorating, and finally the limestone network of caves in the south of France was deemed more suitable to provide shelter and protection. In the end, even these vast caves were not sufficiently safe for the illustrious Tamar, the 'full measure' of the Holy Grail, and she was forced into underground exile in Ireland, the only place where she could be kept safe from those who sought to kill her. The caves in Glastonbury continued to be used as tombs for the noble dead, and no doubt modern excavation methods would unearth some truly astonishing finds.

We also need to remember, as Europeans, our own connection to Ur. As confirmed by historians, the earliest Europeans were known as the *Ur*-people who came from a *Ur*-homeland and spoke a *Ur*-language. The correct pronunciation of Ur is 'yore', not 'er', as most people pronounce it. The pronunciation corresponds exactly with that of 'Eur' in Europe, and indeed the connections between Ur, Sumer and the ancient Celtic world (the Celts were among the first Europeans) are numerous. The Sumerian deities, for instance, find exact echoes in both the Nordic and the Celtic pantheons.

The first Europeans were Indo-Europeans. During the third millennium they expanded eastwards into India. It has lately been proven that old Sanskrit, the early language of India, was actually derived from a source outside the sub-continent, and corresponds to the language spoken and written by a group of Zoroastrians – and, as we shall see, Zoroaster, who is hugely significant to our story, originated from Sumer in southern Mesopotamia, where Ur is located. Similarly, Ur influenced European language and culture. The 'marriage' of Ur and Europe came about through Gra-al and her English king (England did not exist by that name in those times, of course), and it was a cosmic event indeed.

Brigid, the heart of hearts, held the sacred energies of the Grail in safekeeping for the eventual descent of Tamar, the Holy Grail. Both Brigid and her mother possessed supernatural qualities, and were revered as the sacred priestesses of Avalon. Brigid was worshipped as a serpent goddess (meaning she carried the lineage or blood of Tiâmat, the Dragon Queen), and indeed the spiritual presence of the divine Brigid in the heavens (of whom the earthly Brigid was a bright flame or incarnation) was worshipped in these isles for a considerable time before Brigid was born in Avalon. Her name was pronounced 'Bri-ght' or 'bright'. She was the holy Shining One, the woman of the essence of the Dragon or Serpent.

Her mother, Gra-al, was of course also considered deeply sacred and mystical, and we need not explain how her name has gone down in history! She was of the Blood Royal, not only of kingly and queenly lineage from Ur, but the 'heart daughter', the second Divine Woman, of the 'blood' of Tiâmat, of her direct spiritual essence. (It is worth bearing in mind that we are *all* of the Blood Royal, and that the Divine Women both guard and proclaim this most holy heritage for us.) Princess Gra-al was the mid-point, the heart-point, of Tiâmat's great plan to restore the Grail, the Emerald Tablet, to earth.

Nin-khursag and Enki taught Gra-al, and Gra-al taught Brigid, how to enter into the profound and holy dimension of mystical beauty whose doorway was contained in the sacred patterns of water, the creational tool of Tiâmat. Gra-al became the first Lady of the Lake, and her secret world within it carried the energy of the sacred feminine principle, a world of the essence of Tiâmat, and of the daughter of Tiâmat. This was the true Avalon, the otherworldly Avalon shining like a fabulous jewel at the centre of its mundane expression on earth – the true heart of the Mother.

Brigid was an expression of the heart of Gra-al and her king, and was worshipped as the triple goddess. Brigid lived for a considerable time upon the earth, and left a legacy which still endures today in the culture of the Hebrides as the mystic 'Bride', whose name is echoed in the name of these magical western isles. She also gave her name to Britain, and is the essence of the light in its heart.

As Gra-al entered into a blissful union with her king of the wild lands, back home in Ur terrible ructions were about to commence.

CHAPTER THIRTY-ONE

The Forgotten Hero

O f the most mighty and noble Ga-nadin-ur and his equally impressive queen, it is sad to relate that terrible tragedy overcame them. They were inconsolable after the loss of their adored daughter, whom they could never visit in case they were tracked to her far western sanctuary; but worse was yet to come. Gra-al's departure was hidden from Annum for a while, but all hell literally broke loose after her flight was discovered.

Enlil (who always did suffer from paroxysms of rage) and his father Annum were determined to punish the unbelievable presumption of the earthly royal couple who had dared to disobey them. A cataclysmic battle ensued, not a battle such as we know today, where there is physical conflict and carnage, but a battle of mind and will. Truly, it was a battle of black and white magicians, for Ga-nadin-ur and his queen were masters of the mystic arts, as were their predecessors Zi-u-sudra and his consort, although the latter were also practical-minded scientists and natural philosophers.

Annum and Enlil, unbeknown to the rest of both the ordinary and the higher star people, unleashed the Naphidem from captivity in their ravaging, insane hordes, intending that their original plan should not be foiled by the loss of Gra-al and that the Naphidem should fulfil it by travelling down the special ziggurat of Ur (one of the four arms of the cross of the Grail) to completely overwhelm humankind. Ga-nadin-ur, in one of the bravest, most crucial and most selfless feats that history has ever known, stood firm and fast as guardian of the ziggurat, barring and blocking their way, despite the terror and agony they hurtled down upon him.

Terrible eruptions followed in the physical world – traumatised energy expressions such as whirlwinds, the spewing forth of volcanoes, and the rising of waters. This disastrous incident finally killed the lionhearted king and his valiant queen. We have seen him, in full regalia, brandishing a sceptre and dressed in serpent-skin, a noble soul indeed, guarding the entryway of Ur like some Gandalf the White protecting Middle Earth.

He remained in place for long ages after his death, until all danger, even the most remote, was past. If he had not, our world would not have survived; and so we can thank him and honour him at last, from our distant point in history. The memory and inspiration of his beloved daughter strengthened his resolve and put a supernatural steel into his core. His devotion to her taught him how to sacrifice all for the sake of spiritual love. The very title of the city of Ur, which occurred in his own name, was a dedication of himself to Tiâmat, the Divine Feminine, and ultimately to his beloved daughter, even though the city was built before she was born, for he carried intimations of her coming in his heart. The name of Ur was inherited from his forefather Zi-u-sudra whose name enshrined the symbolic 'u' that signified the sacred *khu*.

In the calamity, the ziggurat of Ur was completely destroyed, and the city fell. The Sumerian King List only tells us that this kingship 'failed' (in fact it most certainly did not!), and that the chaos and disruption was so bad that the 'heavenly Nidaba' had to be summoned so that her feminine essence, specially linked to Tiâmat, might set all to rights. The kingship (or queenship, in this case) returned to Kish. Again, all this comprised Tiâmat's directive, acted upon by Enki and Nin-khursag.

Queen Nidaba healed and made pure the poisonous leavings of the Naphidem, who had not been able to break through King Ga-nadin-ur's defences but who had managed to infect humanity to some degree, as usual. Their plan had been to use the Grail ziggurat of Ur as a connecting point with the earth, thereby to enslave humankind by psychic means until such time as the necessary conditions had been prepared for them to occupy physical bodies, and thereafter to take over the world in a final material invasion.

We note that only his queen and Ga-nadin-ur himself had possessed the power – and only then by dint of extreme self-sacrifice and exertion – to drive back the Naphidem foe whom Anu and Enlil had released from their imprisoned dimension so that they could appropriate the Grail entryway to earth.

Thanks to the wonder of Tiâmat's ineffable omniscience and love, we see that a member of the 'ordinary' star people, one of ourselves, had successfully stood firm against the Naphidem in company with his queen, due to the special gifts Tiâmat had unstintingly bestowed on us. Her new pyramidal structure of the soul was working. What incontrovertible proof this is that we are all now safe from them! When the heroic king Ga-nadin-ur finally laid down his great task and service (which was not so very long ago) he gave to us all, by the 'Sheldrake method' (see Chapter 29) an increased strength and insularity against them. They *cannot* encroach upon us – unless we, through our free will, choose to allow them to do so. We have no need to fear them.

The king and queen, bearing the new DNA, had died; but they had managed to convey it by spiritual means to others. This, of course, was also the particular task of Gra-al in Glastonbury. Nevertheless, in order to complete her grand scheme before Annum and Enlil became a huge source of trouble again, Tiâmat released a whirlwind force within the subtle spheres (as though she speeded up time) throughout the eight obligatory sovereignships of the God-Headed people. This enabled her to safely install her final 'ninth', 'ordinary' king and queen on the throne, invested with the DNA which would provide them with three-quarters of the secrets of the Emerald Table, before events became too critical.

She was aided in her response to the new chronological pressure by Enki and Nin-khursag, who, though ousted from their full investiture of power by Enlil, still held great sway in the Grand Assembly.

The necessary eight God-Headed monarchies which occurred after Ga-nadin-ur and his queen fell, passed in the relative blink of an eye, enduring for only ten years each (somewhat different to the eight antediluvian God-Headed kings, who ruled for ten *shas*, a total of 3,600 years, apiece! This enormous difference in time span indicates the measure of Tiâmat's urgency to create the ninth 'wave' so that she might finish her handiwork before Annum, Enlil and Marduk became too obstructive.

And so the time came, in about 3800 BC, when Tiâmat was ready to create Adam and Eve.

CHAPTER THIRTY-TWO

Falsifying the Star Fire

*I*f Enki and Nin-khursag had been forced to 'lapwing' in order to establish and remove from office no fewer than eight God-Headed monarchs in eighty years, their previous efforts were as nothing compared to what was now required of them in bringing forth the third level of the new humanity (the 'thrice greatest') and establishing it according to Tiâmat's directives.

Annum, Enlil and Marduk were still fuming with regard to what they saw as Ga-nadin-ur's terrible crime of disobedience towards them. Never again, they vowed, would they permit higher and ordinary star people genes to be fused, even for the purpose of creating slaves designed to prepare the earth for the coming of the Naphidem. Of course, most of the Grand Assembly still had no idea about their ultimate scheme, and the conspirators were careful to maintain their colleagues' ignorance. They in turn did not realise that Enki and Nin-khursag's aim in creating the new DNA patterning in Zi-u-sudra, Ga-nadin-ur and their queens was actually to bolster and stabilise human beings against both the Naphidem and the depredations of Enlil. They had no idea that any such operation was ongoing.

Enlil himself had brought about Ga-nadin-ur's death, so he had as yet no fears that his own power could be overcome; but he and his conspirators were suspicious, as well as astonished and outraged, to note that Ga-nadin-ur had been able to hold back the Naphidem.

They felt that Tiâmat was somehow involved with this new departure in the endurance and steadfastness of human beings, and they determined that, once and for all, they would disinherit the earth, and themselves, from her power.

This was, naturally, an insane concept. How could God ever be entirely separated from her creation? Even if such a scheme could be realised, the earth and the God-Headed people would cease to exist the moment that the God forces were withdrawn. Yet Annum, Enlil and Marduk, already far down the road of megalomania, believed that they could achieve their objective. By now, God, for them, was a vague deity that they could only understand as equating almost entirely with themselves.

Together, Annum and Enlil had conceived a plan (which did not include Marduk, whom they both despised as inferior, and who as far as they were concerned would in any case eventually go up in smoke with the rest of the Naphidem and be lost). According to this plan, Annum would ascend into the cosmos and extend his area of power over yet more worlds, whilst Enlil remained behind within the earthly spheres to ensure complete domination and an eventual realisation of their plot to seize the earth planet for themselves, in the event that it could be saved from death once it was cleansed of the 'impure' races of earthly humanity and the Naphidem. The problem still remained, however, as to how they would finally organise the invasion of the earth by the Naphidem. Everything had been going so well until the rebel Ga-nadin-ur thwarted them so outrageously! Their rage and resentment continued to rumble and simmer.

Because of their suspicions regarding the continuing influence of Tiâmat, Annum and Enlil had agreed upon an unprecedented strategy: something that Enlil had had in mind for a long time.

They decided to issue a decree making the precious Star Fire, provided for the Edenic community by the goddesses, a banned substance. And yet it was the substance of creation itself, so how could Anu and Enlil effectively ban Star Fire? They could not ban the receipt of the Star Fire by the God-Headed women (the goddesses), of course. What they could do was denigrate it, and refuse to recognise its sanctity and its source, which is certainly what they did.

When the great imbalance struck, the higher starmen began to absorb this precious Star Fire in a different way. Instead of fully accepting it, they admitted into themselves only its power and its potential, rejecting the heart opening it also offered which gave enlightenment into the mysteries of their own feminine or 'Tiâmat' aspect – that aspect which was so deep within them that it could never split off from them because it contained their greater soul, even though, at one level, they had indeed broken away from that same feminine aspect. Nevertheless, a certain measure of this enlightenment still held sway within them at a subconscious level whilst ever they were taking the Star Fire. This 'nectar of supreme excellence' was indeed Tiâmat's very essence, the deepest heart of her mysteries, and it was known as the Gra-al as well as the *khu*.

Some higher starmen, indeed, resisted the great imbalance altogether and consequently did not alter the way they absorbed the Star Fire. These were the Oannes- or John-men, the Wise and Gentle Knights of High Degree. Chief among them, of course, was Enki himself, who was their leader.

What was this Star Fire like? How was it taken? Why was it called a *lunar* essence? The Star Fire was given by a kind of reversed libation. It was poured into the uterus cups of the higher starwomen or goddesses in an act of grace by Tiâmat, the all-loving Dragon Queen.

We can connect this mysterious Star Fire to the source of human consciousness via the teachings of Nin-khursag and Enki, which were espoused with such profundity and inspiration by Ham (Hermes) in Mesopotamia (Ham had a special relationship to the Divine Couple, as we shall see), and by Brigid, the Sacred Priestess of Avalon. They show us that the Capricornian Goat of Mendes, with whom Ham is associated, is symbolised by the sacred pentagram, which relates to Brigid (and, of course, to the earth, to all of humanity, and to Tiâmat herself). This symbol, and the Goat itself, represent Tiâmat's new humanity, being led upwards to its quintessential realisation upon the holy mountain-top by its sacred guides, Hermes and Brigid: Son of Oannes, Daughter of Tiâmat, custodians of, respectively, the divine Mercurial and Saturnine forces destined to lift humankind into exalted consciousness.

When inverted, the pentagram represents the masculine aspect of humanity. It becomes a geometrical drawing of a goat's head, with the two upward-reaching points of the inverted pentagram as its horns, the points at each side sloping downwards as its ears, and the single downward-reaching point as the tip of its beard. According to this ancient esoteric diagram, Tiâmat's Emerald Tablet appears as a precious stone (an emerald) at the top of the goat's head, between its eyes, at the point of the 'unicorn horn' chakra which allows us to receive spiritual emanations from the stars. Although this 'unicorn horn' is one of the two chakras of the double crown chakra, it is closely allied with the pineal gland: the third eye. In other words, the Emerald Tablet shows us in this aspect that it facilitates the reception of the mystical starlight by human consciousness.

When turned the opposite way, the pentagram symbolises the feminine aspect of humanity. The precious emerald occurs in this feminine representation of the pentagram in exactly the same location as before, but now that it is the right way up its two formerly upward reaching points (the horns of the goat) are transformed into 'legs'. So it is between these 'legs' that the Emerald Tablet appears in the pentagram's feminine mode, at the point of the womb and vagina, showing us that the uterus cup is the recipient of the Star Fire, deposited there by the feminine Tiâmat, who contains all principles within Herself. It is the divine function of the female to pass on this Star Fire to the male – literally to feed him with it. When he receives her wisdom, human consciousness throws off its chains, and opens itself to the cosmos, to the divine starlight – to the fire of the stars, or the Star Fire.

The higher starmen men received their gift of Star Fire from the uterus cup of the higher starwomen. It appeared as a substance within the cup, manifesting as the 'living waters' of Tiâmat. It was therefore a lunar substance ('lunar' signifying the principle of reflection), since it was water; but it was red water, because it contained within its mysteries the divine fire of Tiâmat's heart – purest spirit – given to her beloved children by means of reflection, as the moon reflects the sun's light.

Whilst we are in our present state, evolving towards becoming 'fully human' but not yet so, we can receive Tiâmat's divine fire in no other way. If we were given it directly, we would be blinded, burnt up in an instant by its inconceivable radiation and the unconscionable immensity of its power. The moon, the receptive body that contains and reflects the ecstatic sunlight, is the exquisite pearl of the heavens, the pearl of great price, which is the profound symbol of the uterus cup. It is the white-silver chalice or bowl that receives the red fire of the divine – the spirit – and ushers it into mundane human consciousness. It is the Woman reflecting God – reflecting God because it is only the feminine essence that can do so, be it within a man or a woman (it is in both, just as the masculine essence dwells in both). It is the lunar essence, the Star Fire, and it is given by Tiâmat to her feminine children, and by them to her masculine children. It carries within it, in safe measure, the wonder of the sun, the divine Dragon.

To the higher starmen the Star Fire appeared as fluid, but it carried no sense of wetness. It was a spiritual substance, not a physical one; we might say that it was spiritual wine. It had to be given and received in love, or its potency was harmed and diminished. Indeed, in its highest essence, it *was* love. It was taken into the heart by the breath via the mouth. It was this fiery breath that was the kiss of the Dragon Queen. The giving of the Star Fire was a sacred ceremony, and the divine marriage that followed was a marriage of being, a marriage of conscious-ness. It brought about perfect balance, perfect harmony, throughout every aspect of creation.

The ancient Sumerian texts tell of Enki and Nin-khursag drinking a lot of wine and arguing together! This was the half-understood rendition by the scribes of the old tales of the Divine Couple partaking of the Star Fire and discussing the sacred wisdom and enlightenment that they received thereby. Enki was always a little slower to catch on than his conduit and his partner, entailing much animated conversation between the two!

Enlil was having none of all this. He did not want perfect balance, because perfect balance meant that men could not claim to be superior and 'inherit' the cosmos. Symbolically speaking (although there is an occult literalness to its truth) Enlil wanted to cut the moon off from the sun, from Tiâmat.

He had already succeeded in splitting off the earth and the earthly spheres from Tiâmat, so that her creation upon those spheres became less and less aware of the perfect white light that is the spiritual essence of the sun: the Star Fire within its heart, which enables us to attain to our full humanity and which keeps open the 'path of awe' – the Grail. Now it was the moon's turn.

Enlil wanted the mind, the psyche, the intellect, to belong to the masculine principle alone. He wanted to split it off from wisdom, which he saw as the usurping power of Tiâmat, of the feminine principle. He considered wisdom to be stupid and ignorant! He had it in mind that he himself could feed the higher starmen with the white power of the moon, with wisdom, Enlil-style. They needed no more of this contaminating Star Fire filth! Was he not driven by the will of God, whose thoughts, whose desires, were his very own? And so the god of control, oppression and self-glory (what Jesus of Nazareth described as 'the prince of this world') took ultimate root in his heart.

How would he formulate his own version of the white power of the moon, the new woman-denying wisdom? Enlil knew that the Star Fire, in its lowest vibration or most basic form, correlated to gold. This gave him an idea. He hit upon a secret method, which we shall expound later.

CHAPTER THIRTY-THREE

Enlil and Enki

*I*t was in this dire climate that Enki and Nin-khursag had to find a way to persuade Enlil (who, due to Annum's increased periods of absence, had now been granted acting kingship over Eden) to allow their creation plans for humanity to be passed by the Assembly. Tiâmat, in their meditations, in their prayer time within the secret temple dedicated to her, and in those spiritually lucid moments between their sleeping and waking, summoned Nin-khursag and Enki to do her will, as the Sumerian texts relate:

> *O my son, rise from your bed … Work what is wise. Fashion 'servants'* [our quotation marks] *of the gods,* [and] *may they produce their doubles.*

To which Enki replies in due course:

> *O my mother, the creature whose name you uttered, it exists. Bind upon it the image of the gods … Nin-mah* [Nin-khursag] *will work above you … [she] will stand by you at your fashioning. O my mother, decree upon its fate; Nin-mah will bind upon it in the mould of the gods. It is Man.*

Nin-khursag was adored throughout the land. She was called Lady of Life, Mother of All Children, Lady of Form-giving, Lady Fashioner, Lady of the Embryo, Midwife of the Country. Hymns were sung in her honour, such as:

> *Nin-khursag, being uniquely great,*
> *Makes the womb contract.*
> *Nin-khursag, being a great mother,*
> *Sets the birth-giving going.*

Enki, too, was deeply revered, called Image Fashioner, Master of Shaping and Charmer of Making, who delivered his 'repeated incantations' upon the physical substances Nin-khursag used to modify embryos.

It might have seemed to them as if all their skill and craft was at an end, despite Tiâmat's bidding. Enlil and his cronies were adamant that no further indulgence should be shown to the ordinary star people. They were not to benefit any more from God-Headed genetic material. They could not be trusted. Ga-nadin-ur had amply demonstrated that fact, and there was no more to be said on the matter – except that Enlil now, quite suddenly, needed help from the ordinary star people in order to carry out his plan of replacing the Star Fire with another, 'purer' substance that he himself intended to concoct. He needed miners, to mine gold and other precious metals for him, so that this new substance could be manufactured.

After the relatively recent full-scale inundation, the lands comprising the 'fertile crescent' (Egypt, Mesopotamia, and Canaan [Palestine]) were laid to waste. They were still in the process of recovering, and the human population, and subsequently its gene pool, was decimated.

The gods organised the reclamation of the land, but they needed an increased earthly workforce to supply physical labour and to carry out their objectives of reclaiming, rebuilding and restructuring the ordinary star people communities. Most of the Assembly were in favour of allowing the earthlings to rule their own communities through kingship once again. They were still, in the main, basically good-willed towards humanity. They knew little of what had really taken place during the last years of Ga-nadin-ur's reign, when the Naphidem had tried to invade. (Enlil had neatly blamed this on the king's 'subversion'.) All they understood (from their leaders, Enlil and Annum) was that Ga-nadin-ur had been 'rebellious'.

Enki thus saw a wonderful opportunity to lapwing to the best of his ability, and immediately took advantage of it. It was true, he conceded in parliament, that the last two kingships had not been a success. Zi-u-sudra had proved unable to keep control of his people, and Ga-nadin-ur had flouted the will of the Grand Assembly (of course, we are privy to what really happened in each case!). What was required, he argued eloquently, was a modification of the genetic engineering that he and Nin-khursag had initiated with Zi-u-sudra and his queen. They believed they knew where their work required attention, and were ready to bring it to perfection. They would ensure that the problems which arose with Ga-nadin-ur would not arise again.

Enlil was under pressure from Marduk, who also needed more miners so that his own plans of preparing the earth and her gravitational forces for invasion by the Naphidem could be realised. And of course Enlil needed miners himself, for just as dark a purpose. Enki, lapwinging away heartily, 'agreed' with his brother as they sat in council that the new humans should be nothing more than servants, enslaved to the God-Headed community's will and purposes.

He 'seconded' Enlil's view that to allow the earthlings any measure of free will and God-Headed education was asking for trouble. He assured Enlil that the new humanity which he and Nin-khursag planned to engender would be mere workers, bearing the yoke of the God-Headed people. By no means would they be granted liberty. In this way, the Grand Assembly could congratulate itself on their success in achieving their goal of populating the earth, but yet would be free from worry that the new creature would wax strong, aggressive and uncontrollable, vying with the higher starmen and prepared to destroy worlds in order to exercise its selfish and degenerate free will. (It is worth remembering that the behaviour of the manipulated Naphidem had been purposely conditioned in order to deceive the Grand Assembly into thinking that Tiâmat and her plans were invidious.)

Enlil was ready to accede to this plan. As we have noted, he needed workers for his own schemes, Marduk was pressurising him, and he had to appear to those members of the Assembly not under his domination as if he were reasonably good-willed towards the earthlings. Had he come to trust Enki any more than before? Not at all! But Enlil, as we know, had a brand new plan (his own version of the Star Fire) which would neatly nip in the bud any veering towards Tiâmat's influence that Enki might be guilty of. He considered his a wonderful, revolutionary plan. Enlil was really not worried. In fact, at this point, it might be said that he relaxed into a degree of complacency.

Little did he realise that Tiâmat had long foreseen his implementation of his hideous strategy, and had responded by sending Gra-al to earth as a member of the earthly community so that human beings could eventually have the Holy Grail restored to them. Until Tamar (Tiâmat's essence in its completeness) could touch down once again on earth, the earth could not receive the Grail.

But Gra-al, by giving birth to Brigid who contained one available half of its essence, procured its sure and certain promise, and was its heart, although half of her light was shrouded in shadow, and was invisible and inaccessible to us.

And so Enki was formally instructed by the Assembly to approach Nin-khursag, and request that, together, they bring forth the new humanity. Both Nin-khursag and Enki delighted in the performance of this task. It was their third great work in the creation of the new earthlings, and this time, their human creation would secretly be given the noble capacity to receive three-quarters of Tiâmat's Emerald Tablet – to become 'thrice greatest'. Because the halfway stage, the heart point of the potential, had successfully been reached, because the 'ninth wave' had again reached its cusp, the new genetic and soul structure for humanity could be fully realised, and the *Adama* could truly be born. On this third occasion of their endeavours, therefore, it was necessary to do things a little differently.

CHAPTER THIRTY-FOUR

The Birth of Adam and Eve

*I*n this instance of Nin-khursag's and Enki's divinely inspired and divinely guided genetic engineering, Enki's own sperm was used to create both babies (Adam and Eve). Ova were donated by two earthly mothers, as had been the case with the two previous kings and their queens; but this time, when Nin-khursag took her prepared materials into the Creation Chamber, she externalised her own uterus cup and placed the first embryo of the pair within it. Eve was created first, before Adam. When Eve, who was the third Divine Woman, sprang into life within the uterus cup, Nin-khursag took her, by specially protected means, out of the Creation Chamber and down the newly constructed ziggurat of Ur.

Before she did so, she replaced the cup carrying the embryonic Eve into her own high vibrational form. Lowering her vibrations as she descended, she physicalised her body until it consisted of material, fleshly atoms, vibrating on the same wave-length as those of the earthly community. She was received into the Temple of Ur, where six goddesses awaited her coming. There she was tended, and there she gave birth some months later. She was not impressed by the agonies of childbirth!

Nin-khursag had obeyed the directions of the Dragon Queen by following this plan. She imbued the child with her own essence and fed it with her own life force. Through Nin-khursag's ministrations, Tiâmat was able to permeate the foetal Eve with her vital influences and essence to a greater degree than was normally possible, so that Eve carried within her some answering resonance of Gra-al, Brigid and Tamar, and of Nin-khursag, her surrogate mother.

Nin-khursag is deeply associated with Eve in every sense, and in both women, one from the sphere of the God-Headed people and the other from the sphere of the ordinary star people, the presence of the Primordial Mother – Tiâmat, 'She who bore them all' – played and shone throughout them like an eternal flame in a living shrine. Goddesses and angels attended Eve's birth, and the presence of Tiâmat was even more potent than was usual at earthly deliveries. Both children were called the *Adam* or *Adâma,* meaning the divine act of the Star Fire,

Tiâmat's essence or holy blood, descending into the 'clay' or the matter of earth – the animal bodies into which the celestial essence of the ordinary star people had penetrated – by her holy decree. One of the meanings of 'Eve' is 'earth', for Eve did indeed earth the divine force of three-quarters of the Emerald tablet into the body of the planet.

The male child of the pair was called Attaba, and he was brought forth in the same way as Eve. Enki had rebuilt the ziggurat of Ur especially for their coming. The flagging Grail energies were revived to a certain, temporary, degree, and once again the ziggurat was used as Zi-u-sudra, Ga-nadin-ur and their queens had used it in the past: to attain to the elevated dimension of Eden, and to hold counsel, ostensibly with Annum and Enlil, but really, of course, with Nin-khursag, Enki and ultimately with Tiâmat herself in her secret temple in the forest. Attaba became the first priest-king, and held lordly sway over his people. Eve, too, was queenly and regal; but she was in training, and withdrew into the inner life more than Attaba.

Nin-khursag and Enki surreptitiously oversaw their education and instructed them to a high degree, overriding Enlil's dictate and evading their brother's resentful and unquiet eye, full of suspicion again, so that he was ready to erupt at the slightest provocation. Whether they were all on earth or in Eden, Enki and Nin-khursag had to deliver their knowledge to the pair in discreet whispers.

Enki and Nin-khursag often took their sacred serpent form within the Garden of Eden. There was nothing unusual about this. All of the higher star people exhibited their original planetary characteristics from time to time, and, as we know, Enki also used the form of the sacred fish as well as the sea serpent. Throughout all this shape shifting, they retained their inherent, pentagrammatical, human form, as the surviving statues of hominoid figures engulfed in fish-garb attest. Enlil and Annum were also serpentine in essence, but they pretended that its source (Tiâmat) was other than it was.

Eventually, Tiâmat began to instruct Eve in the imbibing of the Star Fire so that, like Nin-khursag, she could receive its supreme power. In one sense, this was a natural, automatic process; in another, the heart centre had to open of its choice entirely to Tiâmat in order to properly receive it. Eve recognised that the Star Fire travelled down two 'trees' to reach her. Both 'trees' were family trees, lineage trees springing forth in joy from, and leading back in mystery to, the heart and the essence of Tiâmat. The beauty and sanctity of earthly trees express this dynamic unfolding of genetic patterns, the stupendous ramification and fruition of the thrust of life itself and its cosmic familial patterns. Trees map our source, and arterially conjoin our origin with our destination. They are manifestations of the Blood Royal (which is the rising sap in all of us) and of spiritual blessing and facilitation – of the wonderful gift of this mighty genetic process.

The Trees that Eve experienced were, of course, the Tree of Life (origin – initiation – life – Tiâmat) and the Tree of the Knowledge of Good and Evil (wisdom – heart – Tiâmat). It was these Trees – and especially the Tree of the Knowledge of Good and Evil, or the Tree of Wisdom, proceeding from the feminine-inspired intuition – that Enlil hated and feared above all else. It whispered to him, and he agonised.

On one or two occasions, his heart was so stricken that he almost gave up his dominion of terror. He resisted it to the point where the merest hint of its intimations drove him into a pathological rage. The Tree was a presence that ate into his heart. His one great aim was to silence its voice for ever – for himself, his followers, and for the despised, doomed earthlings.

He had long since decided that any realisation of, or connection to, this outrageous Tree, and particularly any fostering or nurturing of its rising sap or dedication to the subtle tracery of the foliage of its influences, must be ruthlessly repressed and entirely forbidden. He remained confident that his special white powder would do the trick, as well as the application of new laws and chastisements.

The death of the Tree was Enlil's great strategy.

CHAPTER THIRTY-FIVE

The Tree of Death

*T*he beautiful black and white streams of divine consciousness – positive dark-ness and positive light – that were nurtured and dispensed by the Divine Couple, Enki and Nin-khursag, were related to the Tree of the Knowledge of Good and Evil, and to the Tree of Life. Enki and Nin-khursag contained the teachings relating to these sacred Trees within themselves. The knowledge they imparted expressed the mysteries of the essence of Tiâmat, which was the Tree of Life, and the enlightenment which empowered discernment between the positive and the negative darkness and the positive and the negative light, and all that encompasses wisdom, comprised the Tree of the Knowledge of Good and Evil. The Trees were further connected to, respectively, the Star Fire of the goddesses, and the physical menstrual blood of women.

Annum and Enlil had already begun to denigrate the former and to inculcate associations with it of shame, stupidity and inferiority, and to utterly despise the latter and call it the Tree of Death, because they hated its teachings, and saw the truth it dispensed in exact reverse mode from that which it was. It was at this point that Nin-khursag began to find herself in trouble as she sought to nurture Adam and Eve, and to teach them these truths of the sacred and inviolate Trees in company with Enki, her eternal partner. We must remember that poor Nin-khursag was married to the domineering and wrathful Enlil, as well as to Enki the Wise!

Sad to say, the Tree of Death does indeed exist. Whilst there is an opposite polarity to everything, the Tree of Death should not be what we have made it, but rather a balancing point held firmly within the mastery of the divine light. It should truly be to do with the release of form, of what we no longer want or need and what obstructs us. The Tree of Death as it is expressed today is entirely of our own woeful making. It is a strategic weapon used by Enlil against us, because his agents on earth are careful to perpetuate its – and our – agony.

I learned of the Tree of Death from a friend who is a member of the West African Balanta tribe. Enlil particularly targeted Africa, because it enshrines so much spiritual power and so many mystical secrets. In his indefatigable efforts to gain a foothold there, he initiated a practice which corrupted the sacred power-flow belonging to the Tree of Life and the Tree of Wisdom, combining and reversing both forces. The result was the Tree of Death, created by reverse magic of the deepest and foulest kind.

Tree shrines are to be found in the depths of the sacred forests in Africa, dedicated to the Tree of Death. They are guarded with devotion and the approach of anyone without authority is met with a single warning to retreat and subsequent execution if the warning is not heeded. Under special conditions and circumstances, my friend was allowed to view one of these Tree of Death shrines. The chosen tree is always a denizen of a sacred forest and always an old tree, mighty in girth. A rank smell of death and putrefaction rises from the area of the roots, where the shrine is positioned. Terrible rites of murderous sacrifice are conducted nearby. Because in Africa women are acknowledged as the symbol of life, it is given to an elderly woman to despatch the victim with a knife. Parts of this unfortunate's body, particularly the brain, the liver and the heart, are placed with due ceremony into the shrine. The remainder of the body is cannibalised as a sacred meal.

What is the purpose of these hideous shrines? The answer is simple. They are created to foment and perpetuate wars. Fiendish spirits are invoked to work their terrible arts in stoking the desire for war and bloodlust in those who are targeted. Once initiated, the continuation of the war is fed by further offerings of similar appalling kind to the designated Tree of Death. When my friend was allowed to approach one, the atmosphere and sinister electrical charge around the tree, although metaphysical, made him ill.

The Leaf Master, my friend's guide and tribal 'father', advised him when he first heard of the Tree of Death that even to take a photograph of one of the shrines would be very dangerous. Any kind of effigy associated with it, even a photographic image, would carry and convey something of its monstrous magic. He accordingly did not photograph the tree shine he was allowed to visit, although in fact he would not have been allowed to do so, and might even have been killed had he tried.

From what we understand of an ordinary tree's mighty forces of connectivity, an enshrined tree of ancient and sacred calibre such as are all the Trees of Death would indeed have almost limitless power to foment and perpetuate wars. The day will come when these nefarious shrines are dismantled forever, their unquiet victims healed and released into the exalted worlds of the spirit, and the beautiful souls of the trees set free from the torture and chains of their enforced dark servitude.

Enlil had already started to cast odium on the feeding of the lunar essence of the goddesses (the Star Fire, known as the 'tree' through which Tiâmat manifested: the Tree of Life) to the gods by the time Adam and Eve arrived upon the scene as babies, and eventually banned it entirely. Nin-khursag, although she maintained a certain degree of influence and manipulation over Enlil, began to find it increasingly difficult to bring them up and administer to their care and education as she knew she should. The dispensing of her own Star Fire to Attaba (Eve did not need to ingest it, as she contained it within her own depths, but she was initiated into its mysteries, and its full expression was ritualistically activated within her) became well-nigh impossible under the obsessive watchfulness of Enlil, who knew when she was producing it and began to keep her in confinement, virtually under lock and key, at such times.

Nin-khursag and Enki, in private conference together, decided that the help of another goddess was needed. A very beautiful and powerful higher Anunnaki woman was subsequently approached by them, a goddess of great distinction and a natural high priestess of the feminine mysteries, deeply versed in occult lore of the loftiest order, who had not fallen prey to the confusion Enlil and Annum had spread abroad among most of the other God-Headed people.

Her name was Lilith.

CHAPTER THIRTY-SIX

The Offering of the Apple

*W*hilst Adam and Eve were growing up within the care of Nin-khursag and Enki (from now on we will give 'Adam' his proper name of Attaba), the Divine Couple deemed it necessary, for the reasons described above, to give Attaba into the care of Lilith. She was his nurse, his teacher, his authority and his inspiration, and she fed him tenderly with her own Star Fire. Eve was his half-sister and his beloved companion, and Lilith also instructed her, although Eve was Nin-khursag's special charge. To make the close partnership of the three adults acceptable and less suspicious in the eyes of the other God-Headed people, especially Enlil and Annum, Enki and Lilith married. Lilith was Nin-khursag's twin soul, and there was a deep bond of love and power between the two women.

Lilith was Enlil's granddaughter, and although in a general sense he held females in contempt, he had a soft spot for this exceptional member of the God-Headed community. He was not bothered much by what Nin-khursag seemed to be doing with Eve, as he regarded this sort of feminine bonding to be irrelevant to the affairs of all-important males and thus beneath his notice. He was extremely apprehensive regarding the ministrations of Lilith to Attaba, however. At first, Enlil accepted that she was merely his nurse, and was rearing him to be king of his own kind, according to the overall plan passed by parliament.

Attaba was to be the first priest-king, which, as far as Enlil was concerned, meant that he was to be indoctrinated according to the will and the purposes of the God-Headed community and to have no autonomy whatsoever. He would be the puppet ruler of the earthlings, and the earthlings were to be kept within the bounds of an entrenched slave mentality, by divine decree of the God-Headed people which the priest-king would dispense. This was the designated programme that Enlil believed Lilith was following.

What was really going on, of course, was an entirely different scenario. In private, Enki, Nin-khursag and Lilith were busily educating the royal children to the highest degree and nourishing Attaba with the Star Fire – that spiritual substance which allowed them to fulfil the measure of their true humanity, with all its wondrous legacy gifted by Tiâmat. It was the Dragon Queen's supreme wish and command that the Star Fire fed to Attaba should gradually be replaced with Eve's menstrual blood, imbued with Tiâmat's essence, of which he should regularly partake.

This was because the Dragon Queen foresaw future events, and knew that very soon Enlil would prevent Attaba from continuing to receive the precious Star Fire. Her plan was that the secretions within menstrual blood, which she intended to feed to Attaba and to the future earthly kings of her designated lineage via specially selected priestesses ('Scarlet Women'), would not only esoterically nurture her chosen bloodline, but would introduce into the human gene pool a certain bolstering and fortification of earthly DNA so that the full expression of the sacred feminine principle would always be able to manifest in and through the vehicle of physicality, and the living force of 'wo' or wisdom (conveyed by 'wo-man') would be powerfully protected.

Henceforth, this enriched buttressing, decreed by the Dragon Queen, would ensure that the pure waters of the godly 'wo' quality could no longer be so easily defiled and perverted by the Naphidem. From now on, only if a soul wholly gave itself over by virtue of its own free will to the control of the Naphidem could they fully put to use their wiles and powers of encroachment. Our new pyramidal soul-structure also strengthened and secured our future safety and stability.

Unaware of Tiâmat's insurance scheme, Marduk, Annum and Enlil were indeed at this time involved in appalling experimentation, doing everything within their power to corrupt and pervert the life forces in an attempt to bring about a chemical situation whereby, through interference with the fundamental structure of both ordinary and higher star people DNA, they could create a 'new man'. This plan, they thought, would rid God-Headed blood of Tiâmat's influence for ever. Their monstrous new creature, with its hideous, heretical female counterpart, would initiate a strain in which the wisdom, compassion and heart-enlightenment pouring into the human soul-vessel from Tiâmat could not manifest properly, but was subject to male dominance and distortion via an inherent pattern in the creature's DNA. It would consequently never be overthrown, but would increase generation by generation.

Enlil's investment in the experiments was to make the earthlings into guinea pigs so that, should there be a successful outcome, he might etherealise the process and translate its application to the higher star people. He still fiercely desired the obliteration of the earthlings, who disgusted him because they lived in physical, animal bodies. He saw them as degradations of the God-Headed people, his own noble and superior race, and he would never change his intentions even if the 'new man' experiments succeeded. Annum was of the same mind, although his conquering eye now ranged much further than planet earth.

Marduk pursued the plan with all his might and focus, because on its triumphant culmination depended the future of the ravening Naphidem, who craved release from the misty, dreamlike dimension into which Tiâmat had confined them. If the plan worked, the Naphidem would be able to descend to earth, eventually incarnate into physical bodies again, and enjoy wholesale carnal gratification. Both Annum and Enlil continued to despise Marduk, contaminated as he was in their eyes because of his semi-connection with the earthlings and his lust for material incarnation. Marduk suspected their true attitude (though not their intentions), and loathed them in return; but they served one another's purposes, and so continued to work together in apparently perfect collusion.

In order to block their menaces, Tiâmat dispensed the mercy of the Star Fire to Attaba, provided first by Nin-khursag, and later by Lilith. Eventually, when Eve herself began to menstruate, Tiâmat miraculously captured the full potency of the Star Fire essence in Eve's menstrual blood, translating its physicality into a new alchemy to ensure that she and Attaba could now both begin to benefit from it until the fortification process was complete, and there was no further need for Attaba to ingest it. The menstrual blood had come from Eve's heart which was conjoined with Tiâmat's by means of special attunement, and which beat in unison with that of Attaba, her half-brother and lover.

This heart blood stimulated the heart chakra to release secretions which protected the perfect spiritual attunement of the pituitary, pineal and thymus glands, the head centres which Annum, Enlil and Marduk were specifically targeting. The facilitation of the secretions in the menses enabled a guard to come into being who stood sentinel before these chakras like an angel with a flaming, revolving sword.

Once this had taken place, Enlil lost the power to destroy human beings at will. The conspirators' plan failed. Even though certain overshadowed members of the Edenic community did eventually manage to block the proper expression of the sacred feminine principle, this occurred through distortion, not through the dictates of DNA, and applied only to individuals who wilfully initiated themselves into the service of the forces of the negative darkness.

There came a time, at the point at which Tiâmat, via Lilith, Nin-khursag and Enki, had initiated Eve into the mysteries of the Star Fire, when Enlil was visited by a dream. The dream came to him through the evil auspices of the demon Asmodeus, who was one of the major powers behind Enlil's throne. In Enlil's dream, Asmodeus showed him, through a sequence of symbols, what was happening to Eve, and what was planned for her and Attaba. We understand that Asmodeus, who occupied a very different dimension from that of the God-Headed people, could not speak directly to Enlil, but was able to contact him through dreams and thought-transference. He was, essentially, within Enlil. There is a rendition of Asmodeus in the ancient church at Rennes-le-Château. It has been purposely beheaded because a virulent spirit – a linking thread of Asmodeus's consciousness – actually did take up residence within the statue. As with all other similar demon images in the Templar cathedrals, including the Lincoln Imp (called in the Rennes-le-Château clues 'this demon guardian') Asmodeus is a symbolic representation of the disciple Peter.

Because of his dream, Enlil realised that some 'unlawful' allegiance with Tiâmat was taking place under his very nose. He therefore summoned Attaba (not Eve, as he thought her unimportant, except in so far as she might 'mislead' Attaba), and formally prohibited him from 'eating of the fruit of the Tree of Knowledge of Good and Evil', on pain of death.

Prior to the interview, Enlil ensured that the banned Star Fire would no longer be available for Attaba by placing strict prohibitions on Lilith as well as Nin-khursag.

This 'fruit of the Tree' is symbolised in myth as an apple. In one sense, the apple is the fruit of the rose tree, because both trees belong to the same genus or family. If an apple is sliced in half, a representation of female genitalia can be clearly discerned, and in many types of apple, this depiction also takes the form of a perfect pentagram. The fruit that Enlil banned, therefore, was the fruit of the 'rose tree', or the rosy menstrual blood flowing from the 'tree': the menstruating woman or goddess representing the lineage that reached back to Tiâmat via the family 'tree' which Tiâmat initiated when she brought forth creation.

Poor Attaba left Enlil's mighty presence in fear and trembling. So far, he had not partaken of Eve's menstrual blood, but the ceremony in the temple of Ur in which this act would take place had already been arranged, and was scheduled to take place on the following Friday. (The names of the days were different, of course, but universally the days of the week have always been named after the gods; Friday has always been Goddess day, and has always been associated with fish [Oannes]; so it was the day of the week we would recognise as Friday upon which Attaba would, for the first time, ritually receive Eve's menstrual blood). He returned to the secret temple in the woods, where Enki, Nin-khursag, Lilith and Eve comforted and reassured him. As we know, up until this point, Lilith's (and occasionally Nin-khursag's) Star Fire had been fed to Attaba, but now Eve was about to start her first menstruation, and it was Tiâmat's express wish that Eve's blood, specially infused with the essence of the Dragon Queen, should be given to her half-brother. Eve must give of the fruit to Attaba. Perhaps we may be excused if we repeat the information we have just disclosed.

It was the express wish of God that Eve should give of the fruit of the Tree of Knowledge of Good and Evil to Adam so that he might 'eat thereof'.

Protesting, and still half out of his mind with terror (anyone who encountered Enlil immediately knew that he was not the kind of man to take prisoners!), Attaba told the company assembled in Tiâmat's secret temple that he could not partake of the fruit of the Tree, because if he did, Enlil would kill him.

It was then that Enki escorted Attaba outside for a man to man talk. They entered into the sequestered depths of Eden, where the spirit of nature breathed forth its purest airs and the essence of Goddess surrounded them. There, Attaba found calm, and reconnection to his source; and there, Enki, whispering, because Enlil's spies were everywhere, assured Attaba that, once he had undergone the ceremony in the temple of Ur and had partaken of the 'fruit of the Tree', Enlil would no longer have the power to kill him.

Attaba objected half-heartedly that Enlil had intimated that, although Enlil would certainly kill him for his disobedience if he dared to eat of the fruit, there probably would be no need for him to take the trouble, as the fruit would finish him off anyway. Again, Enki comforted Attaba, and reassured him that the fruit would save him, not kill him. It was not the fruit of death, as Enlil pretended, but the fruit of life. At last Attaba rallied, and his courage returned. Guided further by his beloved Lilith, who escorted him into the Ur temple and presented him for initiation on the designated day, he accepted 'the fruit of the Tree' from Eve, and 'ate of it'.

In that moment, the will of God was fulfilled; and from then on Attaba and Eve carried within themselves the divine mystery of three-quarters of Tiâmat's Emerald Tablet in full measure at the cellular level, and were protected from Enlil's hatred (Brigid, in far-off 'England', was an essential part of this supreme triumph). Enki and Nin-khursag, aided by Lilith, had achieved a glorious victory over the adversarial forces represented by the conspirators. Against monumentally oppressive odds, they, the thrice greatest in the heaven worlds, had infused into Tiâmat's human creation all of the sacred potential that they themselves contained. Now Attaba and Eve were also the 'thrice greatest', and their DNA would eventually bear Tiâmat's immeasurable gift to every human being born to the planet. There still remained the huge issue of human self-will, which humanity itself must conquer, and the towering threat of Marduk and Enlil, who would manipulate it to their advantage. Nevertheless, the gargantuan task depending on the Divine Couple was done, and done admirably. They had acquitted themselves with the highest honour.

CHAPTER THIRTY-SEVEN

The Banishing of Adam and Eve

*T*he important thing now was to keep Enlil in the dark so that Tiâmat's great plan for humanity could continue unhindered. Enki, Nin-khursag and Lilith trained Attaba and Eve in the basics of 'lapwinging', so that the next time they ascended the ziggurat, their state of enlightenment would be hidden from the mighty God-Headed king. Yet although they were made ready with meticulous thoroughness before their next visit to Enlil's court, nothing could have prepared them for the shocking ordeal of what was to come.

Having partaken of the fruit of the rose tree, or the 'apple' of the Tree of the Knowledge of Good and Evil, the next time that Eve and Attaba ascended the ziggurat to enter the Garden of Eden (the environs of Enlil's court), they found that their inner vision was sharpened to the highest resolution of their 'thrice greatest' capacity. Therefore, the enshrouding curtain woven by Annum, Enlil and Marduk's invasive encroachments fell away. Their vision cleared, their understanding was illumined, and they saw in stark relief the unadorned reality that surrounded them.

The Edenic court was still set in a garden of surpassing beauty with a vastness beyond it which, as had always been the case, they were unable to penetrate. Yet, whereas before there was ever a sense of eternal space and freedom, as of a heavenly terrain where the spirit could sail aloft and travel on unhindered wings to a mystical horizon lit with an unfading radiance, the young couple felt that now, looking into it with unclouded eyes, an oppression lurked there.

As if intent on keeping out of sight, a hidden menace slipped invisibly from point to point in a circuitous route to surround them. Their eyes could not see it, but their deeper soul registered its presence and felt its shadow. They had been summoned to appear before Enlil, but their courage entirely deserted them, and they begged Enki and Lilith to hide them from him. Enki, knowing only too well how severe Enlil's wrath would be if he discovered Attaba's disobedience to him, offered to shelter them in Tiâmat's secret temple. It was invisible to Enlil, and Enki and Lilith both hoped that the young couple could regain their strength there until they felt ready to confront Enlil, and perhaps even manage to continue to deceive him. If Enlil was not so deceived, Lilith and Enki knew that indeed the temple would be their only place of safe refuge; and, somehow, both of them sensed a storm brewing.

When Enlil ventured out in the cool of the evening, he came forth alone. He had, in fact, left the Hall of Justice in his palace especially to walk abroad and see where Attaba and Eve were. They had been called into his presence, but had failed to appear. Normally, his servants and ministers, junior members of the God-Headed community, would have sought out the royal earthly couple on his behalf, but on this occasion Enlil dismissed their services. He knew that Attaba and Eve had entered his dimension – his own soul awareness, through its links with his wife Nin-khursag's sensitive apperception, could not help but relay such information to him – so why were they daring to disobey him? Enlil was uneasy. This state of affairs was unprecedented. He needed to discover the reason why, and he needed to do so in secret. Most of his community were still unaware of his ultimate plan, and if it had been foiled in any way, it was better that he should amend the situation surreptitiously, so that they should gather no inkling of his true intentions, nor witness the extremity of the remedies that he would be forced to put in place.

Sensing their nearness, Enlil called out to Attaba and Eve.

Enlil was still some distance from the secret temple in the woods. Lilith and Enki urged Attaba to leave its confines and go to meet the king, so that its existence would remain hidden. It was invisible to Enlil, because it expressed its existence on a higher vibrational wavelength than that upon which, since his coarsening and darkening, he now functioned; but Lilith and Enki preferred not to run any risk of its discovery. They explained to Attaba that they would rather Enlil was diverted away from its precincts than approach any closer.

Whilst Eve was able to stifle her fears, and was ready to appear before Enlil whilst he was still at a safe distance, she could not persuade Attaba to accompany her. Attaba had much more to fear from the irate king than Eve. The prohibition against eating of the fruit of the Tree had been laid upon Attaba, not Eve, who did not need to take it, because she produced it. The 'fruit' was within her, and it came forth from her. It was Attaba, rather than Eve, whom Enlil wished to interview (Eve sometimes attended these interviews with Attaba, unless she was scathingly ordered out of Enlil's presence, which was often the case; otherwise, her attendance was tolerated only if she kept completely silent and stood in the background with her eyes downcast), and therefore Attaba alone who was properly playing truant.

Eve, on the other hand, felt strangely elated. Her heart and crown centres sang. and she was no longer afraid of Enlil. She was coming into her own as a woman, putting on her true womanhood, which meant that her spirit and her deepest soul hit the target of their highest aspiration and connected her consciously with Tiâmat. The Dragon Queen's fire streaked through her, and she became one with her exalted serpent essence. Lilith and Enki, aware of this transformation, instructed her to conceal her spiritual fire and to remain hidden in the temple with them.

Only Attaba must go to meet Enlil.

As the fruit of the Tree of Knowledge of Good and Evil released its full powers of protection within Eve, Attaba was lifted up in vision with her and by her. He saw even more clearly what utter slaves Enlil sought to make of them and all their kind. Now he understood how even he himself, as Enlil's 'priest' king, had been given his priestly role specifically in order to dupe and engulf his people into the debasement of complete bondage and servitude to a cruel and tyrannical ruler, all aspects of their God-given higher nature chained and confined within the dungeon of Enlil's hatred and denial, and mired in his wrath.

Attaba saw that he, himself, had been set on course to initiate a priesthood of damnation and abomination, its purpose to feed demon-like creatures and ultimately to destroy its followers, and would have done so, if Enlil had had his way and Nin-khursag, Enki, Lilith, and, lastly, Eve, had not mercifully intervened. Eve saw with him. They looked through one another's eyes, and their vision was one. They were overwhelmed by Enlil's wickedness, his terrible rejection of God. Indeed, they now had the power of discrimination, the higher knowledge of good and evil, and Enlil, who saw things in exact reverse to them because he could not recognise what was mirrored and what was real, appeared to them at last in his true guise as an ireful monster. And the monster was approaching, closer and closer.

In vain, Enki sought to embolden Attaba to go out and meet Enlil before he advanced any further. Attaba was too desperately afraid to move, even to take his hands away from his face. Enlil, at their very door, stopped in his tracks and thundered his command that Attaba should appear before him. He *knew* Attaba was in the vicinity; he could sense it beyond any doubt. The fact that Enlil could not see where Attaba was infuriated him all the more.

Stumbling to the doorway of the temple, Attaba answered him at last, in timid and tremulous tones.

'Why are you hiding?' was the enraged rejoinder.

'Because I am naked', Attaba responded.

All was lost now. By this statement, Attaba told Enlil that he realised that he was nothing more than a dupe and a slave, and that he knew he had been deceived. All illusions had flown. We think that Attaba was also saying in his fear that he had no defence against Enlil now that the veils had fallen away from his perception, although, of course, because of his decision to partake of the 'fruit of the Tree', he certainly had.

Enlil's straightforward fury now turned ice-cold. The menace in his voice was a blight to Attaba's soul as the great king demanded, 'Who told you that you were naked?'

Something terrible began to happen. As Attaba's fear mounted, his vibrations began to resonate with those of Enlil. The king's tremendous fury and Attaba's tremendous fear entered into an antiphonal relationship and sounded forth the same note. Simultaneously, Attaba cut himself off from Tiâmat's temple, and yet revealed her temple. What Attaba saw and experienced, Enlil now saw and experienced. He saw faintly, as if in shadow form or through a veil of antimatter, Lilith and Enki standing behind Attaba; and he saw Eve standing unashamed at Attaba's side, her eyes unafraid to meet his. From her crown a strange coiling fire scintillated, like a branching tree formed from tongues of brightest flame.

This, more than anything, revealed to Enlil that he was looking into the interior of a secret temple dedicated to Tiâmat. He listened as Attaba verified that indeed he had eaten of the forbidden fruit. His cataclysmic fury knew no bounds.

He tried again and again to kill both Attaba and Eve on the spot by a process of blasting and withering of which he was master, but his psychic blows glanced off them as if he aimed at a mirror image instead of at the very core of their being, which is where he thought he was directing his lethal rays. His wrath made a split in the beautiful etheric matter of Eden, so that it was riven; but Eve and Attaba remained unharmed.

Henceforth, Enlil saw Enki as his sworn enemy (he was not interested in the fact that Enki refused to give any validity to the concept of enmity). Many distorted myths were born in that moment whose conditioning power still holds sway within us today.

CHAPTER THIRTY-EIGHT

Enlil's Wrath

*H*aving always admired and desired Lilith, Enlil now loathed her. Although hatred cannot approach love and could not be further removed from it, there is indeed a thin line between desire and repudiation, or the polar opposites of passion. Enlil now repudiated Lilith, calling her (predictably) a whore, and instigating twisted rumours about her that were intended to arouse disgust and terror amongst the ignorant – namely, that she was a demon who drank blood (because she gave of her own Star Fire to the human Attaba), and that she ate children (because, following Tiâmat's divine decree, she taught Eve to give her menstrual blood to Attaba so that he might imbibe it for his own protection, which of course involved the ingestion of Eve's released but unfertilised ovum).

For Eve, Enlil reserved a similar blasting of the breath of odium. She would become the fallen, evil temptress who led Adam astray and scorned and betrayed the word of 'God' (Enlil!). Following hot on the heels of Ga-nadin-ur's 'betrayal' as it did, Attaba and Eve's disobedience to the higher Anunnaki king seemed a terrible thing to him. He bemoaned and lamented it for century after century; and this was very odd, because there can be no doubt that almost from the start, he never intended anything for us but total and irretrievable annihilation.

This small detail, however, did not stop him from railing against Eve. He cursed her and all womankind, promising her and her descendants distress during menstruation and agonising pain during childbirth. He certainly put abroad the idea, even prior to this event, that menstrual blood was 'filthy' and 'disgusting' (in fact it is absolutely pure, not having gone the rounds of the body and gathered impurities on the way, as ordinary blood has), and he introduced the disempowering idea that menstruation is a 'curse' (in fact it was a curse only to him and his schemes!), although it is a sacred phenomenon, and nothing is more venerable and holy than the 'living waters', as the ancients once knew.

He whispered rumours of virulently evil women, priestesses of a hideous cult, whose consciousness expressed itself in ravening tendrils of the brain that reared

157

and struck like living vipers (his version of the spiritual consciousness of the feminine Tree of Life!), and so the Medusa myth was born, long before the ancient Greeks came into being. As Enlil, through wiles and terrorisation, gained more and more followers on earth, he let it be known that the hair and crown centres of women in particular were offensive to him, reminding him as they did of the moment he beheld Eve in her Tiâmat-centred glory, growing the Tree of Life from her head, as if she were rooted into the highest heavens via that point of her anatomy, which, of course, was true. Enlil also put a dividing sword of horror between woman and her blessed origins (Tiâmat) by seeking to cause her to fear and revile the serpent.

Attaba, of course, was not going to come off lightly either, even though Enlil reserved the worst of his wrath for Eve and womankind in general. Enlil pronounced eternal slavery upon him and his kin (the entire human world) and gave voice to his intention to steal away all the happiness, peace and joy that Tiâmat had planned for her earthly creation.

(All of these things were part of his plan anyway, and measures had been set in place for their fulfilment long before he learnt of the 'treachery' of Attaba and Eve; it was just that, once he had discovered that they were not the pawns he thought they were, he took great pleasure in outlining his true intentions to them – intentions he had taken care to conceal heretofore.)

As for Enki, Enlil simply thought that all these schemes of his younger brother were merely a plot to oust him from authority in the Grand Assembly. He did not forget how outraged Enki had been to discover that their father had given the royal inheritance to himself, Enlil, instead of to him. Enlil set all this down to ego; in other words, he judged Enki according to his own standards. He thought that Enki looked upon Tiâmat as being on his side, as it were, in the matter of Annum's dismissal of his younger brother's claim to the kingly inheritance via the Dragon Queen. He did not realise that self-importance had no hold on Enki's heart, and that all that concerned Enki was centred on his realisation that Annum and Enlil were leading both the God-Headed people, and the earthly humanity which was their precious charge, into the jaws of evil and death. Enlil had no real conception at this point of what Enki really intended, which was to obey Tiâmat's injunction to rescue humanity in its entirety from the doom and destruction planned for it by his elder brother.

Enlil drew the final conclusion that the whole affair amounted to nothing more than a planned political coup. He considered that the empowering of Attaba and Eve according to the old way – Tiâmat's way – was just a ruse of Enki's to gain favouritism, to bring them under his influence and tempt them over to his side.

Nevertheless, Enlil truly feared and despised the Dragon Queen because she reminded him, deny it as he might, that life did not conduct itself according to the principles he sought to force on it, and that the origin of all power, might and omniscience was not masculine, as he purported it to be.

When he discovered the secret temple in the woods which maintained a forbidden link with Tiâmat, he mustered all his forces of destruction and concentrated them on the temple and its mystical connection with his own sphere. We must remember that he was a past master at this art; it was he who gave the red arrow into Marduk's hands to 'destroy' Tiâmat, he who himself in a perverted and deranged act of master craftsmanship forged the beautiful rod of spiritual initiation that the arrow originally was into a reversed weapon of horror, blasphemy and destruction. Yet again, using his 'red arrow', he cut off Tiâmat's link with Eden, now partial and diminished since he had severed the Grail, and laid waste to her temple. From now on, Enki, Nin-khursag, Lilith and Tiâmat's other faithful followers among the God-Headed people would have to find the Dragon Queen in the peace and silence of their own hearts. No dedicated communion point remained in Ur, although, as we shall see, Tiamat rescued its dying embers and moved them to Jerusalem.

After unsuccessfully attempting to kill Attaba and Eve, Enlil banished them from the environs of Eden and closed down the Grail by removing the power of ascension from the ziggurat temple of Ur. This was a natural corollary of destroying Tiâmat's temple, or her conjoining point with the Edenic dimension. Enlil had been of the opinion that the dying power of the Grail (the power of ascension) was now under his and Annum's control, and that this was why it still functioned to some faint degree. He soon found that he was mistaken. Whilst it was true that he 'slayed' Tiâmat by Marduk's hand, and so closed down the Grail energies, Enlil could not re-engage their remnant at will.

The great king Ga-nadin-ur stood guard over the divine pathway between earth and heaven, and, by the grace of his sacrifice, only at Tiâmat's command could the Grail energies flow in either direction. Enlil discovered this fact once Attaba and Eve had been banished, and it was a huge problem for him. How could he now hope to open the floodgates of the Naphidem dimension and allow them down onto the earth, there to wreak their havoc until humanity and the Naphidem themselves were both utterly destroyed, and the earth useless for anything but his own purposes? His great plan seemed foiled again.

Meanwhile, he 'gave coats of skin' to Attaba and Eve. In this regard, it is helpful to remember that, as well as being master of time, Saturn has dominion over crystals, metals, the skeletal structure and the skin. We infer from this that Saturn has rulership over what crystallises and accretes, and over limitations and boundaries. The boundaries of the body are marked out by its skin.

When Enlil gave 'coats of skin' to Attaba and Eve, he bound them fast in their physical bodies, which means that he used his Saturnine powers to prevent them from etherealising their bodies to reach Eden. This power of ascent, once universal, was with difficulty conferred on Attaba and Eve by Enki and Lilith, via the agency of the ever receding Grail. However, it was within Enlil's remit to withdraw it, and consequently Attaba and Eve were circumscribed by their physical bodies and bound into their coats of skin. Except by meditation, no entry to the higher worlds was available to them, just as is the case for present-day humanity.

Eve and Attaba had been humiliated by their experience with Enlil, and felt disgraced by the fact that they now knew they were nothing more than his slaves. Lilith and Enki therefore provided them with royal robes, to remind them always of their true heritage and purpose upon the earth.

These royal robes were similar to the ones that the mighty and noble king, Ga-nadin-ur, had worn when he commanded matters of state, and when he repudiated the Naphidem. They were made up of scales, of intricate and beautiful design, and they were formed from serpent skin.

We would like to make clear that no serpent had suffered death in the obtaining of these skins. They were materialised through the power of magical thought and the manipulation of the etheric forces in matter. Enki and Lilith were eminent shape shifters, and the fashioning and moulding of matter was Enki's special forte. He was the magnificent ancestor of all those who practised smithship in the world, the original grand master craftsman. (Uri Geller is directly of this line and has, for our edification, retained a shred of this mystic power of craftsmanship; he bears the name of one of the ancient Mesopotamian kings.) Thousands of years later, as previously mentioned, the knights who still continued to honour Enki (Oannes) dressed in chain mail or 'shining' armour in reverent memory of these fish or serpent scales.

Enki and Lilith initiated the ancient anointing ritual, beginning with Zi-u-sudra and his queen. They used spikenard, the precious oil which is specifically reserved for rites that balance and conjoin the sacred masculine and feminine principles. It is applied to the head and the feet, signifying the royal and sacred Grail pathway between heaven and earth, and it is associated with ceremonies in which the Grail energies are invoked and spiritual ascension attained. Its creation and application involve no abuse or slaying of animals, and it is indeed this original version of the royal ceremony that Jesus and Mary Magdalene chose, when Mary anointed Jesus, and herself, in her house in Bethany (she rubbed the oil she had applied to his feet onto her own hair).

As we shall discuss, there was also another very important tradition belonging to the kings of the special bloodline that Jesus entirely rejected.

In later times, as the shadow of Enlil fell over the world, the kings of Tiâmat's bloodline, those of her direct dragon inheritance who would ensure the safe arrival of the ultimate king and queen (Jesus and Mary Magdalene), were anointed with the fat of the *Messeh*, the sacred dragon or crocodile. This was an Egyptian ritual of coronation, although the Hebraic word *Messiah*, the anointed one whose coming was awaited, derives directly from it (the Egyptian and Hebraic traditions are conjoined at their roots).

The custom of using animal fat for royal anointing or coronation ceremonies, rather than the original plant oils, which the *Messeh* replaced, was initiated at the express command of Enlil. It is interesting to note that the 'dragon' fat for the anointing ritual was provided by either the crocodile or one of the great monitor lizards, such as the ancestors of the fearsome Komodo dragon, which forms communities today solely on a single Indonesian island and is extinct elsewhere. This highly aggressive animal is reported to have the most malodorous breath in the world, 'death breath', because it often feasts on long-dead carrion. The crocodile, too, is hostile to humanity. That these magnificent creatures should die an ignominious death for the purpose of anointing kings, especially those of the special bloodline, satisfied Enlil. He wanted kingship to express venomous, antagonistic and bloodletting qualities, the 'breath of death', which he admired, rather than the love and unity of Tiâmat's essence, which he despised. Their propensity to rend and to seek nourishment by eating death objectified a reflective truth about his inner nature which craved symbolic expression, and, by the sacred and incontestable law of truth, was bound to be granted such expression.

It was precisely these dangerous qualities of hostility, blood lust and predation that Enlil wished to be psychically transferred to the kings of the special bloodline, not only for the reasons previously outlined, but also for a very specific purpose which shall be revealed. As the Old Testament tells us, he banned the ingestion of blood by his followers. Eve and Attaba's story tells us why he did so; but he was very careful to ensure that his followers should not confuse the killing and eating of animals with taboo activities such as the ingestion of blood. He had a vested interest in the suffering and cruel death of animals, which we shall discuss in a later chapter.

So there were very specific reasons why Enlil chose the fat of the crocodile or the monitor lizard, the *Messeh*, to anoint his kings: he wanted to destroy the power of the sacred spikenard which bolstered and facilitated the divine harmonies between men and women through the rites of the Sacred Marriage, thus activating the presence of the Grail in the heart, and replace it with a substance that did exactly the opposite; he wanted to ensure that his kings were anointed with oil from a slaughtered animal; and he wanted to express his dragon heritage from Nibiru via a highly aggressive, death-dealing saurian, even though, for reasons of expediency, he taught others to revile the serpent.

He also wanted to implant into the coming race with whom he would have special dealings – the Israelites – the conviction that their great prophesied king was of the *Messeh* essence – a *Messiah* manifesting as a fierce warlord who would overthrow the enemies of the Israelites with conquering bloodshed and aggressive dominion. And he wanted to bring all these aspirations about by using the flesh of an animal whose ancestors gave it a direct lineage of predatorial savagery; for the crocodile and the monitor lizard reflect the great saurian creatures popularly known as the dinosaurs, the rampaging lower saurian which is the antithesis of the Pendragon.

Enki and Lilith anointed Attaba and Eve with oil of spikenard in the Ur temple on the designated Friday when Attaba received Eve's purified menstrual blood from her own hands, and thereby 'ate of the fruit' of the 'forbidden' Tree, shortly before they were banished from Eden for ever. When Tiâmat's secret temple was destroyed by Enlil, the Ur temple was destroyed simultaneously. In later years it was rebuilt, and continued as a station of the Grail that contained great holding power, even though the Grail energy was no longer active within it. However, after their banishment from Eden and the destruction of the Ur temple, Enki and Lilith moved the young couple to Eridu, where they remained in kingly and queenly office.

Lilith and Enki dressed their beloved charges in serpent skins, as related, and urged them to enlighten their people to Tiâmat's kindly and beautiful truths, even though they would have to do so indirectly and cautiously in order to avoid the wrath of Enlil. The God-Headed king was indeed still very powerful in his dealings with earth, and was gathering greater strength and momentum with the passing of each day, despite the fact that he could no longer strike Eve and Attaba dead at a whim, which had been well within his capacity prior to the moment when Attaba ate of the 'forbidden' fruit.

Now that the secret temple had been destroyed, Lilith and Enki taught Eve and Attaba how to create a dedicated, sanctified altar to Tiâmat so that they could enter into heart communion with her anywhere, at any time, even though they were no longer able to visit Eden. The altar could be either visible or invisible, but it was always an acknowledgement of, and a withdrawal to, their heart centres. This also provided the means for their future communication with Nin-khursag, Lilith and Enki. Once the Grail had closed down, they, as well as other members of the God-Headed community, could not walk the earth in vibrationally slowed, physicalised bodies any longer. This process was still just possible, but only via great difficulty and highly specialised procedure. It was no longer what we might term automatic, as it had been.

There remained one problem that was particularly difficult to solve. Attaba had fallen desperately in love with Lilith.

CHAPTER THIRTY-NINE

The Master Craftsman

*A*ttaba's problem was that Enki was courting Eve. Enki's 'courtship' of Eve – Eve who was Nin-khursag's spiritual and physical affinity – was part of Tiâmat's plan to strengthen and increase the light of the true Father that Enki bore. Enki's association with her at this time was for the purpose of preparing her for her vital role.

Nevertheless, Attaba felt that, if Eve, his own partner, were to enter into an alliance with Enki for a designated period of time, then Lilith, Enki's wife, should properly become his mate for a while! He had already formed a deep attachment to her, as she had been his nurse and mentor from his earliest days. He admired her beauty and nobility. Lilith revealed to him the necessity of balancing ethereality and physicality by exclusively uniting higher sperm with earthly ova, because, if it were the other way around, the energies of the resulting child would be too etherealised for the purposes of earth, and reminded him that the matrilinear line was the purveyor of the divine *khu*.

Attaba therefore understood that Tiâmat's special bloodline would descend through Eve, not him, and that there could be no union between himself and Lilith. His respect for Lilith's wisdom prevailed, and although he was tested by Eve's liaison with Enki and by Lilith's rejection of him as a lover, he was not found wanting.

His sense of fairness and brotherliness towards Eve never failed, and his upright stance as a true man, an Oannes-man, schooled and enlightened by Enki, helped to rectify to some extent the hold of the great imbalance on earth.

His reign was known and celebrated as a wise era: 'Of the wise one, no one treated his command lightly,' cite the old texts. Enlil took a blow from this noble Oannes- or John-man, and reeled. However, his determination to press ahead with his plan to annihilate humanity did not waver, and he waited in the wings, patient and wily, looking out for his next opportunity.

In time, a son was born to Eve and Enki. He is known in biblical history as Cain, although according to Laurence Gardner's researches, this was a titular name denoting a master craftsman in the sacred, as well as the practical, sense of the word.

We think in fact that it was a royal title, given to him by his father Enki. Enki himself taught smithship to humanity, and was the original craftsman and metallurgist 'par excellence'. This divine inheritance of smithship, of mastery within the Divine Forges, is a sacred state of consciousness, an aspiration of being, that we must particularly address today. Through divining its secret, another will be revealed which has been skilfully and deceptively hidden from us. It also has its practical application in the outer world, of course, and bears both an occult and an extrinsic expression.

Cain derives from *Q'ayin,* which denotes the all-seeing eye (*ayin*), or the consciousness of God in which we all partake, fronted by the Q, which has its root in the planetary symbol for Venus. This symbol represents the sacred feminine, Tiâmat herself. The *ayin* is associated with the lunar essence which flows through exalted females or goddesses: the ineffable Star Fire that translates into higher vision or consciousness. We think *ayin* is also echoed in 'Uan', another name given to Tiâmat's devotedly loyal son Enki who carried the torch of the *khu*. Its earliest linguistic form was Kingu or Quingu, denoting the Divine Androgyne serving the Nibiruans or Anunnaki, from which emerged Quayin or Queen, translating to *Q'ayin, ayin* and eventually Cain.

The name means 'higher consciousness deriving from the Q or *khu'*. The Star Fire, the 'Q', as we know from our study of the pentagram of the Goat of Mendes, is the divine conductor of Tiâmat's consciousness to her creation. It expresses itself in physical matter as menstrual blood, which was often referred to as 'red gold' or 'white (lunar) gold', because it combines and unites the red and the white life forces (as Lewis Carroll shows us via his red and white queens in *Alice Through the Looking Glass*).

Therefore, Cain (*Q'ayin*) does indeed stand revealed as the Grand Master Smith, the supreme goldsmith who works with the sacred Star Fire, having been designated, and entrusted with it, by Tiâmat. It is said that angels attended Eve as she gave birth to Cain, and that these angels were the Virtues, ready to give Cain their inestimable soul gifts. He is the beloved of the Dragon Queen, the true man (John or Oannes) whose spirit rings keen and true as the invincible heavenly sword, (our positive Saturnine lance) and will never betray Tiâmat or his sacred trust. We strenuously make the point at this juncture that the true Cain will only ever use the material of the sacred feminine in plying his divine craftsmanship. No manufactured substitute will ever do! We can deduce clearly now why it is Enki, Oannes's (the Father God in the heavens) true son, who is the original master goldsmith, and not his brother Enlil!

As the receptacle of Tiâmat's consciousness, Eve needed to mate with Enki, the Master Craftsman, to bring forth, as an earthly son, Oannes in the flesh. He would not be in fish or sperm garb, as Enki showed himself sometimes when he walked the earth, but would be an ordinary human man. Cain, and Cain's descendants, especially Tubal-Cain and his son Ham, were vitally important to Tiâmat's special bloodline and to dispensing the light of Oannes to the peoples of earth.

CHAPTER FORTY

Cain and Abel

*A*fter Cain was born, Eve gave birth to two further sons, Hevel (Abel) and Seth. These were Attaba's sons, and difficulties arose between both of them and Enki's son, Cain. The simple fact was that Enlil wanted to destroy Enki's lineage if he could, and, if not, at least denigrate and slander it. He took advantage of Abel and Seth's resentment that Attaba was not their brother's father, and stoked up their uncomfortable feelings about Cain and his entitlement to kingship. The perfect solution, according to Enlil, would be for Abel to kill both Cain and King Attaba, Enki's priests, and then for Abel, his own priest, to seize the throne and the lineage.

Their brother's actual name ('Cain' being a titular designation) was Ar-wi-um, meaning 'place of serpents' or 'throne of serpents'. In other words, Cain was entrusted with the sacred Grail energies, even though, since the Dolorous Blow, the Grail could not manifest in full expression on earth. He married the daughter of Lilith, whose name was Luluwa-Lilith.

Lilith, like her twin soul Nin-khursag, gave physical birth to a daughter who had been generated from an earthly woman's ovum fertilised in the Creation Chamber by Enki's sperm. This daughter (Luluwa-Lilith) was of utmost significance in assisting her husband Cain to ground and stabilise the Grail energies. Without her, the task would have been impossible, because it is the feminine essence alone that can contain the Grail energy; the male reflects rather than contains it.

Because of his connection to the Grail energies, Cain was associated with an area of land upon the earth which provided the sanctified link with God, the ladder between heaven and earth, which the Grail enshrined. Here, the God-given forces he shepherded were grounded deep into the earth, making it a holy place, a mighty power point of the Grail, just as Ur had been before the banishment of Attaba and Eve, and indeed remained so, at an intrinsic rather than an extrinsic level. Via his link with Eve and Enki, his parents, Cain carried forward the power to minister to the grandeur of the Grail energies, and earthed them anew through his wife Luluwa into an expanse of land that stretched between Ur and Egypt – Canaan, originally known as the Land of Cain. The Genesis account calls it the land of Nodh ('land of the Wanderers'), its title prior to Cain's encampment there. The name carried intimations of the solitary mystic wandering in the wilderness to commune with God, from Cain and eventually Abraham and his followers down to John the Baptist.

It was the chroniclers' confusion over Cain's monumental significance and his special connection with the land, as well as some discreet historical rewriting engendered by the influence of Enlil, which led to the misleading account of the story in Genesis. This tells how Abel was 'a keeper of sheep', and Cain a 'tiller of the land'. Both made offerings to God, but, whilst Abel's sacrifices were accepted, Cain's were repudiated. Cain then 'rose up' against his brother, and slew him. Cain was subsequently banished to the wilderness by God, yet to ensure that those who sought to kill him would be warned off, God put a mark on Cain, so protecting him from his would-be assassins. From this story, of course, arises the famous phrase: 'Am I my brother's keeper?'

This is a symbolic, but garbled, account of the story. Let us look at it again, and dig a little deeper.

First of all, it is clear that, as Cain and Abel were both royal princes, they were not, respectively, a shepherd and a ploughman. As a symbolic keeper of 'sheep' (subjects), Abel seems to have held some office of governorship commensurate with his rank (rather as the princes of the British royal family today hold duke-doms). However, his office may have been merely a formality. It appears that Abel, as well as holding a title of privileged rank, was also a High Priest. It is established that the Serpent People (those of the God-Headed people who followed Enki and therefore retained enlightenment) were protected by a legion of warrior priests, who eventually became, thousands of years later, the Children of Solomon, and, eventually, the Knights Templar.

These priests were answerable to Enki, but Enlil also had his own priests and his own temple in opposition to the temple of Enki. Abel was Enlil's priest; Cain, too, had entered into priesthood. Indeed, the post of High Priest awaited Cain, to which he would succeed on his father Attaba's death or retirement. However, Cain, as we would expect from his title, was most certainly a priest who was initiated and instructed by Enki. This is why Abel's sacrifices (which involved the spilling of animal blood) were acceptable to his lord, Enlil, but Cain's were not. The same situation obtained with Abel and Enki. Abel's sacrifices of burnt animals were anathema to Enki, whilst Cain used only honey, corn, herbs and fruits to make heart offerings to Tiâmat via Enki. Of course, Cain did not offer sacrifices to Enlil, and Abel did not offer sacrifices to Enki, so the question of rejection of any offerings never arose. What the scenario in Genesis tells us is that the princes offered sacrifices to two very different lords who had become adversaries, and who were entirely opposed in their stance, their system of values, their philosophy and their objectives.

Having made inroads into the royal family by means of Abel, Enlil encouraged his willing priest to instigate an uprising against his own father, Attaba, and attempt to slay him and his son and heir, Cain. Enlil had never forgiven either Enki or Attaba (to say nothing of Lilith and Eve) for 'plotting' against him, as he saw it, and this coup was his revenge. He wanted to destroy the 'false priest' Attaba (false in his eyes because Attaba had become Enki's priest) and exterminate the bloodline which descended from Enki; first, because the direct blending of higher and ordinary genes which Cain represented affronted him deeply, and second, because he did not trust the plans Enki had for this bloodline. He wanted to see it eliminated, and the bondage and slavery to himself, as practised by the sycophantic Abel (whose historical name, Hevel, means 'puff of vapour') restored. It is worth noting that, at this point, Enlil still remained in ignorance of Tiâmat's great plan for humanity.

Abel obeyed Enlil's command, and led an uprising against Attaba 'in the field', which was literally so, because Abel decided to strike at a time when Attaba was praying in his tent alone and was relatively unprotected. (Tents were a means of erecting a sacred altar to Tiâmat out in the wilds, away from the hustle and bustle of the palace and the 'madding crowds' which milled around public buildings. It was a method of worship which Enki and Nin-khursag had instigated, teaching it to Eve and Attaba after the Grail energies of Ur had been closed down by Enlil.)

The problem for Abel (which, unaware of his own weakness, he actually saw as a splendid opportunity to fulfil his mission in one fell swoop) was that Cain had accompanied Attaba on his out-of-town spiritual excursion, and both men, father and son, were surrounded, as they prayed, by Cain's henchmen.

These henchmen had been instructed by Cain, the master craftsman, in the fashioning of their weapons (only ever to be used in defensive mode). With these superior arms, they easily overcame Abel's rather ineffectual attempt at a coup, and Abel was slain 'in the field'.

We see from this that some of the features of the Genesis account have actually been reversed. Cain certainly did not kill Abel. Rather, Abel tried to slaughter Cain, but was prevented by the royal guard. This was the situation which provoked the angry response 'Am I my brother's keeper?' when Enlil later questioned Cain about Abel's disappearance. (The God-Headed people could not walk the earth in temporary physical bodies any more once the Grail had shut down, but, to high initiates such as Cain, Attaba and Eve, they could appear in ethereal form, such as Enlil now did to Cain). Cain, shocked and aggrieved at the culmination of events, expressed by this retort the scenario whereby Abel had his own keepers (his guards), and Cain in turn had his.

In other words, Enlil, who already knew that Abel had been killed, was accusingly demanding of Cain, 'Where is your brother?' (i.e. 'Why did you not prevent the slaying of your brother?') and Cain replied by pointing out that he, Cain, could hardly have been expected to spring to Abel's defence and become one of Abel's fighting men in order to safeguard Abel's life against the stalwart aggression of Cain's own soldiers, when these soldiers were only attempting to save, not only Cain's life, but also King Attaba's, from the murderous attack on them by Abel himself!

Nevertheless, despite the obvious injustice of the situation, some blame was laid at Cain's door (via the wiles of Enlil) for the death of Abel, even though he had had no personal part in it. Because of the pressure of public opinion, he was banished to the land of Nodh (later called Canaan), which became known as the land of Cain.

CHAPTER FORTY-ONE

The Land of Nodh

*I*ntriguingly, the name 'Nodh' is akin to 'John' in reverse. We will encounter this cosmic playfulness with names and language many times before we reach the end of our quest, just as Alice constantly meets with it in Lewis Carroll's two tales of her adventures. It is a delight to realise how dearly the spirit of the cosmos loves laughter!

Cain's banishment to the land of Nodh, however unfair its cause, was all perfectly in order as far as Tiâmat's greater plan was concerned, because it was here, in the land of Nodh, that Cain, the valiant, lordly and handsome Prince Ar-wi-um, married its queen: the illustrious Luluwa, daughter of Lilith; and it was here, in a very precise spot, that the straitened and reduced Grail energies were earthed anew. The location was what would later become Jerusalem.

Eventually, Cain returned to his homeland to take up the office of kingship on Attaba's retirement. He travelled back, not to Eridu, but to Kish, where his father had repaired in grief after his banishment.

Meanwhile, Enki stood guard over his beloved son (it was he who had alerted Cain to the offensive approach of Abel) as he established himself in the wilderness, and 'put a mark on him' to ward off the incursions of armed assassins, sent by Enlil to slaughter him. This sign was, of course, Tiâmat's sacred sign, the cross of light bound by a circle of light associated with the Ouroboros, which we have previously examined.

Together with the six-pointed star, this cross-within-the-circle is the most potent form of spiritual protection known on earth. It gave Cain 'sevenfold' or complete protection, for the number seven, as the Hebrew chroniclers recognised as well as their Sumerian forebears, was the number which denoted wholeness or completion. Later, we shall learn how to use it for personal protection, for, make no mistake, Enlil is still very much present in the ethereal dimensions of our planet, and still holds the earth under his sway.

The protective circle of the Mark of Cain signifies a serpent-dragon swallowing its own tail – the Ouroboros – a symbol of wholeness, unity, completeness and eternity which portrays the mystical ring. This dragon ring is the way through to higher consciousness. It actually exists, and is not just a concept. The great secret of the master smith in forging higher consciousness (Enki, who passed on his inheritance to Cain and his descendants) is that he stands side by side with the cup bearer, or the bearer of the Grail, the Grail Maiden. She gives him of her sacred essence to drink. The essence is from Tiâmat (formerly manifesting as the Star Fire), and is the consciousness of God. From this essence, the red and the white gold, the master smith crafts his own consciousness. Nothing is wrought that is not wrought of the gold and the precious metals and the magic within them that the sacred blood contains. Any intrusive alloy is rejected outright.

The perfect consciousness of ascension – our own enlightened human consciousness – is to be crafted from this purest gold which streams to us from the God-source. The soul vessel, crafted so purely, from such precious, pristine, noble metals, receives into itself without reservation that spark of divine spirit which dwells in the heart of each one of us and the little spark becomes a star of measureless spiritual light and consciousness which, even so, retains its craft-forged individuality.

The sacred marriage thus takes place, the soul vessel and the spirit become one, and the creature is no longer a creature. It steps through the mirror and finds itself of the veritable essence of the Divine.

CHAPTER FORTY-TWO

The Stone of Death

*I*n his book, *Genesis of the Grail Kings,* Laurence Gardner introduces a most interesting theory. He discusses the lost secrets of the 'highward fire stone', a shining metal or metallic compound which was revered in ancient Sumer. It was known as *shem-an-na,* meaning 'heavenly stone', 'shining stone', or 'stones that rise'. According to his research, it is associated with the tradition of the Master Craftsmen of the God-Headed people, an esoteric consortium with a divine purpose headed by Enki, smith supreme, who passed on his sacred mastership to the earthly kings of his lineage through his son Cain. The tradition passed into the Egyptian line of pharaohs from this source. The pharaohs were fed with a special substance called *Schefa*-food, which was fashioned into conical shaped 'bread' cakes. These cakes were baked from a fine white powder derived directly from gold and other highly prized shining metals, fragrant and sweet to the taste and produced by an alchemical method which was a guarded secret of the Egyptian priests.

As Laurence Gardner points out, the High Priest of Memphis was officially known as 'the Great Artificer', a title suggesting smithship (and, to us, something else; but we will come to that in due course).

The *Schefa*-food of the pharaohs, he explains, was referred to in the Bible under the name of 'shewbread', which echoes the word *shem-an-na* or *she(w)-manna* in that a manifestation of sweet white food 'from heaven', appearing as if by a miracle to the children of Israel in the wilderness, was called by them 'manna' (meaning 'What is it?'), the name 'manna' afterwards denoting 'heavenly bread' or 'bread given by God'.

This manna was probably a product of the tamarisk plant, but it bore a remarkable resemblance to the substance fed to the pharaohs and to the kingly descendants of Cain (for they too received it) in that it was white, sweet, and powdery, and that it seemed to emerge from some magical dimension. The *shem-an-na* or *shew-manna* described in the Bible was not, as was the actual manna that the children of Israel received, a herbal product which was a symbolic reference or comparison to a miraculous, heavenly food, but the shewbread itself, the white powder of gold.

The book of Leviticus in the Old Testament (24:5-7), with reference to the shewbread, says of it, 'Thou shalt take fine flour, and bake twelve cakes thereof'. Laurence Gardner posits that an error in translation substituted the word 'flour' for 'powder', which would have been a more accurate definition of the substance. The shewbread appears within the context of the second Covenant, that which was made by Jehovah or Yahweh with Abraham. The Bible relates that it was present within the Tabernacle, laid out upon a table, next to a candelabra bearing seven candlesticks.[1]

At the time of the third Covenant, made with Moses, wherein the Covenant was codified by the stone tablets which Moses brought down from the mountain, the shewbread appears again.

When the Israelites fashioned their golden calf 'idol' and apparently worshipped the bondage of the body thereby, Moses 'burnt it in the fire, and ground it to a powder, and strawed it upon the water, and made the children of Israel drink of it' (Exodus 32:20). He had, just prior to this belligerent action, pounded down the mountain-side, roaring with rage at the dismayed Israelites, and had even killed some of them, every aspect of which was entirely uncharacteristic of his behaviour. This expression of wrath and killing in conjunction with the white powder is worth bearing in mind.

From the time of Moses, consumption of the shewbread within the Judaic religion became the exclusive right of the priests, although, by their dispensation and according to their discretion, it was still occasionally given to the kings. What had once been reserved for the kings of the special bloodline was later reserved for the priests alone. This is important in considering the shewbread, as is the fact that during the first Covenant, which took place with Noah, or Zi-u-sudra, his queen and their followers, the shewbread did *not* make an appearance. The significant sign in this case was the rainbow, which is linked with the Grail, and with the seven-branched candelabra within the Tabernacle.

One of the reasons that the shewbread or the *shem-an-na* was not present at the time of the first Covenant was because it had not, as yet, come into existence. It seems to have first appeared shortly before the time of Abraham. The renowned priest-king of Salem, Melchizedek, is believed to have given the shewbread to Abraham in an important initiation ceremony (Genesis 14:18) at the time when Abraham, having settled in Canaan, gained victory over invaders. The invasion was led by four kings of the peoples of the surrounding area, who overcame five kings, among them the kings of Sodom and Gomorrah. Lot, Abraham's kinsman, was living in Sodom, which lay towards the plain of Jordan.

Lot was carried off as a prisoner, until Abraham, hearing from an escapee of the warring kings concerning Lot's plight, mobilised an army and came to his rescue.

Because of this military victory, the king of Sodom and others, in particular Melchizedek, honoured Abraham, the kings presenting him with riches, whilst the priest-king Melchizedek, with offerings of 'bread and wine', initiated him as a spiritual leader, blessed by the 'most high God'. Although Abraham's act was undoubtedly both noble and brave, it is worth bearing in mind that it was a military achievement which earned Abraham his honour and standing, and conferred on him an equality of status with the priest-king, so that he himself was equated with this role. This is revealed by the fact that Melchizedek offered him tithes with the sacramental 'bread and wine', a privilege reserved exclusively for the priest-kings descended from Adam.

Intriguingly, the statue of Melchizedek in Chartres Cathedral (France) portrays the royal priest holding a chalice which contains a stone. This is a depiction of the communion or initiatory cup which King Melchizedek offered to Abraham after his victory. Communion is a Christian ceremony, but the offering of the chalice of communion was certainly an established ritual prior to the commencement of Christianity. In the earlier ceremony, communion was with God, the ineffable and supreme, and it was directly associated with the precious Star Fire.

Laurence Gardner suggests that the stone in the cup represents the shewbread, because it was during the lifetime of Abraham and Melchizedek that the Star Fire of the Edenic goddesses was lost to earth, and therefore to the kings of the Grail bloodline, necessitating its substitution with the venerated 'highward fire stone' or shewbread. We have discovered that, in addition to the white shewbread cakes, the Star Fire was symbolised and supplanted afterwards by a mysterious red powder dissolved in wine, as we shall see.

When the Tower of Babel fell and Ur was destroyed, Abraham fled the stricken city with his father and eventually led his followers into Canaan.

It was precisely at this point (the fall of the Tower and the destruction of Ur) that the Sumerian texts report that the God-Headed people left the earth plane for ever, abandoning it 'like migrating birds'. They took with them the facility of dispensing the Star Fire, but, Laurence Gardner states, 'the Master Craftsmen had been well prepared'. Although 'Scarlet Women' – members of the ordinary star people who were special priestesses or adepts of the mystery schools – provided the kings of Tiâmat's chosen lineage with extracts of their menstrual blood for a short time afterwards (which we have seen was associated, as was the original Star Fire, with red and white gold), he explains that this process was soon thrown over in favour of the *shem-an-na*, the 'heavenly stone', which the Master Craftsmen produced by treating gold in such a way that it was transformed into a sweet white powder which could be baked into 'bread' cakes. This white powder of gold contained special properties which, when ingested, stimulated certain centres of consciousness within the recipient.

The statue of Melchizedek in Chartres Cathedral shows the priest-king holding the chalice with its stone or bread just below his heart. His eyes are closed, as if he has risen above the level of everyday consciousness. We might even say that he is in 'the land of Nod'. Considering the link between exalted consciousness and the Star Fire, which was later replaced with the mysterious shewbread or 'highward fire stone', could it be that the substance in Melchizedek's cup (the 'heavenly stone' crafted from the white [and the red] powder of gold) is a representation of the Grail? Is it possible that this miraculous 'highward fire stone' is the Philosopher's Stone spoken of in secret down the centuries, and that the Philosopher's Stone is in truth the Grail itself?

There is little doubt that Laurence Gardner considers this to be so. His research linking the white powder with the Star Fire certainly supports such a conclusion, as we know that the Star Fire provided for humanity a magical link with the consciousness of God. As the link with the heavenly worlds, with God, is the very substance of the Grail, does it not therefore make sense that the white powder of gold, the replacement for the Star Fire which can be made available to us today, must be the Holy Grail?

Laurence Gardner's research and findings are very exciting and compelling. They show us how an ancient temple was discovered at Mount Serabit in the Sinai range by Sir W.M. Flinders Petrie and his archaeological team in 1904. Mount Serabit was formerly known as Mount Horeb, and is the 'Mount Sinai' of the book of Exodus in the Old Testament, the Holy Mountain itself, sometimes referred to as Mount Horeb (Sinai is actually a mountain range within which there are many peaks).

Beneath this Egyptian temple (for the Sinai peninsula was actually an outlying part of Egypt) lay the Cave of Hathor; and it was within the area leading to it that a metallurgist's crucible, together with several tons of a mysterious white powder that the team were unable to satisfactorily identify, was discovered. There can be no doubt, from the considerable evidence presented by Laurence Gardner, who himself is familiar with the process whereby the white powder is created, that W.M. Petrie had stumbled upon an important alchemical temple-laboratory, perhaps belonging to Akhenaten and later to Moses. The temple and the laboratory were sacred to the Egyptian goddess Hathor and appeared to have been used for the express purpose of creating the *shem-an-na* or highward fire stone.

The alchemical procedure which creates the stone is as mysterious as the *shem-an-na* itself.

It is rendered as pure, sweet, fragrant and ingestible – the food of the gods – and, with its remarkable propensities for stimulating our crown-chakras at the point of the pituitary (base of the brain) and pineal (third eye or mid-brow) glands, could it be a food which, in 'feeding our heads', would take us as a planetary society to 'unimaginable' heights of consciousness and evolutional development, as Laurence Gardner posits?

The white powder certainly seems to bear within its essence the Four Hallows of the Grail. It nourishes, because it can be eaten and, as has been shown, it 'feeds our heads'. It secretes properties which are anti-ageing in their application (which *Genesis of the Grail Kings* elucidates), thereby fulfilling the Grail's gift of immortality. It holds great healing potential, because, as Laurence Gardner explains, current research shows that the platinum group metals involved in the process of formulating the *shem-an-na* have qualities which cause them to act as a superconductor, which, when applied to human DNA afflicted with cancer, corrects the deformity of the diseased cells. It gives abundance, because one of the secret uses of the white powder relates directly to a scientific procedure by which base metals can be transmuted into gold. Nourishment, Immortality, Healing and Abundance; all the requisite qualities are present within the stone; and many Grail stories refer straightforwardly to the Holy Grail as 'the Stone', all of them associating the Stone itself with a secret name (*shem-an-na*, shewbread, manna?).

There was every invitation within the impact of all this wonderful discovery for Margaret Bailey and I to feel elated at the revelation concerning the marvellous Stone which would lead to mass enlightenment, for the quintessential quality of the Grail is that it is for everyone who is willing to accept it; and, of course, the white powder could easily be made available en masse. The Stone therefore appeared to fulfil every criterion belonging to the Grail.

Yet we did not feel elated. We felt, on the contrary, very, very uneasy.

Laurence Gardner explains that the sealed burial chambers of the pharaohs were designed as superconductors so that the ancient Egyptian kings would, on death, be enabled effortlessly to enter into a higher dimension, aided by the mystical Stone. (The earliest explorers of the Great Pyramid found only a coffin without a lid in the King's Chamber, empty save for a layer of white powder.) The Stone aids ascension because of its own ascended atoms, which translate into a higher dimension during the repeated heating and cooling sequences of the alchemical procedure.

It was this mysterious quality which the Stone was intended to lend to the burial chamber and to the pharaoh within it, and it was within the confines of the burial chamber that the king's rite of passage to the Otherworld commenced, beginning, in accordance with the Egyptian Book of the Dead, with a question that he must ask. The question was answered, Laurence Gardner tells us, by the only clearly definable hieroglyph on the Giseh plateau, which appears as an inscription near the entrance to the King's Chamber. It depicts the conical loaf symbol for the sacred *Schefa*-food, and reads simply and straightforwardly, 'bread'.

We will recognise the question, because it is the same as that which was asked by the Children of Israel when they were wandering, starving and desolate, in the wilderness, and a mysterious white bread fell from heaven to nourish them: *Manna?* or, 'What is it?'

With regard to the white powder, we ask, *what is it indeed?*

NOTE

1   The chapters in Exodus portraying the Ark of the Covenant describe a candlestick with six branches. In fact, the six branches radiate outwards, three on each side, from the central stem of the candlestick, making seven candle-holders in all. This is borne out by the later instruction that the 'seven lamps' of the Ark should be lit. The *Qabala*, the ancient mystical teaching of Judaism, always portrays the Tree of Life, the focal point of its teachings, as containing the seven-lamped candlestick pertaining to the Covenants of Abraham and Moses.

CHAPTER FORTY-THREE

Rumpelstiltskin

*W*e saw the kings, and not only the pharaohs, being gathered into another dimension, a dimension higher, admittedly, than that of earth, but not nearly so high, nor so pure, as might be hoped.

Who was it who wanted the kings?

As the perpetrator came into inner focus, we saw that he seemed to be a Nero or Herod-like figure, anything but benign, and he wanted – had, indeed, laid careful and highly intelligent, surreptitious plans – to capture them as one would triumphantly gather up kings from the chessboard in game after game of chess, the game of kings. And, curiouser and curiouser, another *Alice* figure came to mind: the Mad Hatter! We shall say more of this tutelary figure later.

For now, I may report that, as we silently contemplated all we knew of the white powder, we saw emerging into view a strange little man, a creature of the depths of the earth, certainly, for he was of gnome or dwarf extraction. He had charge of the material riches of the earth, and he was definitely Saturnine in essence, but of a distorted and unbalanced expression of Saturn's consciousness and energies. He was spinning, spinning, spinning – spinning gold, monatomic gold, or the shewbread. As he spun (and he was helped by shadowy figures, like swastikas, or backwards-shaped spiders – the Negative Spinners) we saw that he spun backwards, so that all the atoms of the gold were put into reverse spin.

With this reverse-spin gold, he was attempting to buy the first-born of the royal household, for he had managed to deceive the queen (the deceived queen equates to wisdom circumscribed and lamed by the arrogant dominion of the intellect) into promising the child to him.

Rumpelstiltskin!

We remembered that the evil little man did not, in the story, manage to attain his goal. According to the tale, he sat in an underground chamber (the Cave of Hathor?), 'brewing and baking' as in an alchemist's laboratory, and as he occultly created the means by which to produce the quantities of reverse-spin gold that would buy him the king, so that the royal child would fall under his influence from the day of his birth, he sang a song, giving a clue to those with ears to hear (for, karmically, he was bound by spiritual law to offer such a clue – the 'clew' that is the silken thread of the sacred spider, the positive spinner which is an aspect of Goddess and the law of Goddess, as in the tale of Ariadne leading Theseus safely out of the maze of the Minotaur):

> *Merrily the bread I'll make,*
> *Today I'll brew, tomorrow, bake;*
> *Merrily I'll dance and sing,*
> *For next day will bring the king!*
> *Little does my lady dream*
> *Rumpel-stilts-ken is my name!*

The gnome's karmically generated promise is that, if the queen can guess his secret name (connected with the name secreted in the Stone, as the Grail legends tell), she may keep the gold, her life, and the child. She may have three guesses, and only three, after which, if she has still not named the gnome, the child will be forfeit to him.

The queen, who was, before her marriage to the king and the birth of their son, a rendition of 'everywoman', or a poor cotter's daughter, had been forced to comply with Rumpel-stilts-ken's terrible demand through force of circumstance. She had been picked up and placed onto the king's steed at her cottage door and borne away with him because he had heard her mother claim that she, her daughter, could spin gold out of common straw (base material). The 'mother' represents the link with the ancestral goddess within every woman, who faithfully bears and guards for her the gift of divine consciousness of the great Dragon Queen or God, and who can indeed give forth the 'red-gold' of the Star Fire, the 'positive-spin gold', if only she could free herself and be lifted into the true dimension of her unfettered soul.

The 'mother' assures her daughter that she can do it, but the daughter has forgotten how. The king promises marriage (the restoration of her rightful heritage as queen and equal ruler) to her, but his stipulation is that she must spin a cellar-full of straw into gold for three successive nights, or she will be beheaded (the power of the Dolorous Blow will again divest her of her rights and her inheritance). So it is that the queen, forgetful of her own rightful royal heritage (the Star Fire), falls into Rumpel-stilts-ken's power, for he comes to her secretly and offers to spin the gold for her (to substitute it), if only she will surrender to him her first-born son.

The queen's loyal handmaiden (the true wisdom or feminine spiritual principle banished into servitude) saves the day. She overhears the little man's boasts, and gives the secret name to the queen, who answers the gnome's question ('gnome' almost equates to 'name' in itself), set to her for the third and final time.

On hearing his name pronounced, the little gnome reveals himself in his true guise, which is as a dangerous and mighty power.

He is bound by spiritual law, however, and cannot hurt the queen or her child. Frothing at the mouth, he releases his wrath and retribution by stamping and 'splitting the earth in two' (he re-enacts the Dolorous Blow), disappearing into the infernal crack he has created, which heals over. The king pays proper court to his queen, the royal child is saved, and the story ends happily. The entire outcome, however, is dependent upon the discovery and uttering of the secret name of the little man.

The 'little man' (actually a considerably mighty man, as the story reveals at its close) was, to our mind, identifiable with none other than Enlil. It is interesting that, in the original Brothers Grimm text, his name is given in three separate syllables, just as the names of the kings often are in ancient Sumer. The story is, we think, clearly a sacred text, as so many folk and fairy tales are. It deals with the matter of Enlil and his plot against Tiâmat's special lineage of kings and queens, which is to steal, via his interference with the consciousness of the kingly line, the inheritance the Dragon Queen has bestowed on every single member of humanity, and then destroy it.

It revealed to us that the white powder, the Stone, was a false stone. It might masquerade as a marvel, carrying within its enticing potentiality divine secrets and gifts that promise to lift us up as a planetary society into heightened consciousness and spur us forward into an unprecedented evolutionary leap, but in reality it is malevolent. Its true purpose was and is to lead us into the jaws of death.

At this point, we may remind ourselves that the hidden people heretofore mentioned, whose wisdom reveals itself in the tarot and the playing-card decks, referred to the Stone as 'the Stone of Death'. There is another Stone, spoken of in the book of Revelation by John the Beloved Disciple in the New Testament:

> *To him that overcometh, I will give to eat of the hidden manna, and will give him a white stone, and in the stone a new name written which no man knoweth saving he that receiveth it.*

> (REVELATION 2:17)

This is properly the Stone of *Daäth,* the divine stone bearing the secrets of ascension and the womb, which is associated with the Emerald Tablet. The other Stone, Enlil's Stone, which is 'taken' in a somewhat similar way to other nefarious white powdery substances, is the actual 'Stone of Death', which attracts with the beckoning of a false glamour. Later, we shall seek out the existence of the true Stone, for although there is a deep connection with the Emerald Tablet (the heart of hearts of the white light), the 'Stone of *Daäth*' is distinct from it, and actually resides within the human head.

To trace the story of the false stone, we need to follow the counsel given in the fairytale of Rumpel-stilts-ken, and find out Enlil's power-name. This enterprise can be fulfilled without difficulty. Laurence Gardner, by means of many scholarly references, has already done the job for us. There can be no doubt whatever with regard to Enlil's later name.

Jehovah.

CHAPTER FORTY-FOUR

The False God

Considering our examination of the accurate Adam and Eve story, it hardly comes as a surprise to learn that Enlil reinvented himself as Jehovah. He is indeed the 'God' of the Old Testament, who cursed the production of menstrual blood and child-bearing through Eve and who banished the couple from entering Eden, pronouncing a sentence of slavery on them both. Of course, this judgment was not quite fulfilled in Attaba and Eve's case, as Enki, Lilith and Nin-khursag protected them and initiated them into the priesthood of the true God. Nevertheless, the wider implications of Jehovah's pronouncement certainly came true, because, since that time, when the Grail finally shut down, humankind has indeed lived in slavery, chained to the illusion of material limitations and ever struggling and toiling to maintain its existence.

Enlil sought complete dominion over the earth and over the Edenic dimension in those times, finally claiming to be the 'most high God' who rules heaven (the higher dimension of Eden) and earth. However, we have to say, with apologies to Monty Python, that he's not God, he's a very naughty boy, and it will be edifying to examine the history of his introduction of the invidious white powder (the False Communion bread, linking us with his consciousness instead of that of God), which has done so much damage over the centuries.

The Nephilim made every attempt to bring Enlil and his conspirators back onto the path of the true light, but they would have none of it. Instead, they forged a link with the dark angels, Brothers of the Shadow, who are highly intelligent and organised, and who have dominion over what we might call the 'Black Lodges', which operate on earth and within many dimensions connected to earth. These dark angels (we might think of them as testing angels), who encouraged and applauded Enlil's darker self from the moment he began to fall, seemed at first, in Enlil's eyes, to comprise God – the all-male, all-commanding, all-conquering warrior God whom he constructed out of his own desires once he (and his associates) had rejected and 'slain' Tiâmat, the true God.

At the point we have reached in our story (the succession of Cain to his 'father' Attaba's kingship after his marriage to Queen Luluwa of Nodh), Enlil was gaining ever greater power and influence, both on earth and in Eden. He was, though, by no means as yet the 'Almighty', as he would eventually 'become' and which would be his favourite title. So things progressed, with Enlil making a certain amount of headway, whilst Enki and his female associates strove to undo Enlil's mischief and to turn both earthly humanity's and the God-Headed people's footsteps on to the path to the true light of God. Unknown to Enlil, he was shortly to receive the biggest boost to his career since the slaying of Tiâmat and the triumph of his near-fatal flood. One of the most significant players in Enki's camp was about to act the turncoat and step over to his side.

It happened in this way. Ham, the son of King Tubal-Cain (descendant of Enki and Cain and famous as 'the Hero of the Good Land') and of Queen Nin-banda (who was in direct descent from Lilith), had been born and had come to manhood when this negatively momentous event occurred.

He was the Archon of the Tenth Age of Capricorn.[1] Capricorn is the tenth house of the zodiac, and its stellar influences are linked with the significance of planet X or the 'ten' planet, the presiding planetary influence on our culture. Ham carried the essence within him of the harmonised, balanced energies and consciousness of Father Saturn, that magnificent and benign centre of stellar intelligence (even though Saturn manifests as a planet in our solar system) who gives to us our base, the fundamental aspects of our physical and soul being.

However, Ham in himself represented the beautiful Mercurial forces. Mercury is 'the messenger of light', the bright little planet which is custodian of the threshold to heavenly consciousness – to the great Sun which is a manifestation of Divine Spirit. The god of Mercury, the spirit that ushers Mercury's forces of consciousness, is known in mythology as Hermes. Ham was the living embodiment on earth of Hermes and was known as such to the ancients, because the name Ham is a rendition of Hermes. He represented the 'divine courier', the part Mercury plays in the Greek and Roman legends. And the idea of the divine courier or messenger, of course, leads us back to the Grail, the magical stairway between earth and heaven.

Ham inherited his great soul-legacy from his mighty forefather, Enki, who also embodied the spiritual consciousness, the spiritual imperative, of the Mercurial forces. For it was the divinely-appointed task of Enlil and Enki to guide God's gift to earthly human beings of the light of heaven, locked for safekeeping in humanity's base, securely and gloriously upwards to its brow centre. This 'third eye' (the ayin) at the point of the brow is the mystical threshold to the exalted, heavenly consciousness bestowed on the unified crown-centre of humankind when it achieves universal enlightenment.

Enlil represented Saturn, whilst Enki embodied Mercury, the golden gateway to the sun. Nin-khursag, beautiful, dynamic and gracious beyond earthly under-standing, was the Divine Woman, the Divine Shepherdess of her brothers' most sacred task. She enshrined both the Saturnine and the Mercurial forces. When Enlil fell into darkness, she stood firm and radiated the exalted Saturnine light with purity and faith so that Enki could continue his mission.

Enlil, leader and conveyor of the deranged Saturnine and Capricornian influ-ences, was Ham's great adversary. Ham is spoken of as Noah's son in the Old Testament, but in fact this information is confused, as is the idea that Noah was born after Adam and Eve. Noah, as we know, came first. He and his queen were the initial pair of Tiâmat's special bloodline, which was designated to produce future kings and queens who would rescue humanity from Enlil and his intention to destroy the human race, and whose destiny it was to carry the evolutionary dynamics of (eventually) three-quarters of the Emerald Tablet to all humankind, via both genetics and the Sheldrake method (see Chapter 29).

When Ham came to manhood, long after the birth of Cain, Zi-u-sudra (Noah) was still alive. Because of their huge contribution to Tiâmat's plan in that they were the founding parents of the Grail bloodline and had ensured humanity's survival via the scientific triumph of the Ark, Noah and his queen were granted an extraordinarily long lifespan (as were Adam and Eve, and all those of the Grail lineage, until Enlil's white powder was introduced). Noah or Zi-u-sudra was a deeply venerated patriarch.

He understood the significance of the Grail (the true Ark of the Covenant, symbolised by the arc of the rainbow), and how its mysteries were connected with the Ark which had saved the day after Enlil's great inundation, when he and Annum melted the protective crystal sphere surrounding the earth and caused the Flood.

It has to be said, however, that his understanding of science veered a little too close to the purely materialistic, simply because this was where his greatest talent lay. Nevertheless, this too narrow and circumscribed focus constituted, in his armour of heightened perception, the tiniest chink. Enlil targeted him, keenly aware that he was on Enki's side and that his nobility of soul and his expertise had richly served Enki and Lilith's endeavours to foil his plans (he remained unaware, at this point, that Nin-khursag, his own wife as well as Enki's, was intricately involved in Enki's enterprises, and indeed often led the way).

At this point, Enlil had no idea of the extent of Tiâmat's involvement in the affairs of planet earth. He did not acknowledge her as God, and therefore failed to see how her hand steered everything, even though he and his cronies constantly worked against her laws. Nevertheless, although they created distress, darkness and confusion, they did not and do not have the power to change Tiâmat's course, or to thwart her ultimate objectives. Ignorant of this, Enlil believed that she only sneaked in her influences occasionally through the back door, so to speak, and that if he held to an unwavering course of ruthless determination, Enki and Tiâmat's other followers would soon lose ground and be overwhelmed entirely.

Enlil's mind, although brilliant, and of course from our standpoint akin to that of a god in a secular sense, functioned almost wholly at a materialistic level.

Because of his lack of both spiritual vision and profundity of perception, he viewed the situation with Tiâmat as almost political. In spite of his insistence to himself that this was so, inevitably his soul depths were touched by his contemplation of her and his awareness of her presence, however much he remained in denial. This secret call to his deepest soul, the entryway where the *nous* resides, was ever answered by him with revulsion, repudiation, wrath and hatred. Nevertheless, the call continued, and does so still, because one day, he will turn and sound the right note in his response.

So entirely is Tiâmat an expression of love that love's will within her cannot be countered. This terrible son, in spite of his grievous crimes, is held within the heart of her omnipotent love and forgiveness, is indeed even blessed by her as one who undertakes a mighty mission, for he represents a polarity we must recognise, and, through free will choice, ultimately reject. Via our choices, we step through the mirror and become real. They are what configure us in the Divine Forges, and with them we forge ourselves into divine womanhood, into divine manhood.

It is not that Tiâmat wants us to suffer, for at any time, at any juncture, the soul can turn from its mistakes to choose afresh, and the spell of the dark forces is thereby broken. But that the opportunity should arise for these dark forces to form themselves into a compelling door and attempt to trick and entice us through it, has to be so, otherwise we could not grasp the opposite or true opportunity to choose real beinghood and boundless and eternal spiritual freedom. Noah had arrived at the threshold of heavenly enlightenment wherein dwells a door straight down to hell, and he was about to throw it wide open.

NOTE

1   Archon, in its oldest sense expressed by the Gnostics, carries within it the idea of divine smithship, and means a king or ruler on earth whose power is second only to God, and whose authority encompasses the actual moulding of the creational forces and the direction of planetary destiny, according to the highest inspiration of the Deity which the Archon receives from the stars as divine directives. Thus the Archonship was the highest state of office on earth.

CHAPTER FORTY-FIVE

The Downfall of Noah

*T*here came a day when Noah (Zi-u-sudra) was meditating alone in his tent. Enki and Lilith had descended to meet him, in their ethereal bodies now that the Grail had shut down and the preservation of its secrets had passed to the land of Nodh, known presently in the time line of our story as the land of Cain. Lilith had offered her Star Fire to him, of which he duly partook. Noah, after offering worship to Tiâmat, put a question to Enki and his two wives, for Nin-khursag was waiting in the background. She was still wary of descending to the lower spheres, because the psychic link between her and her other partner, Enlil, enabled him to some extent to tune into what she was doing. It was imperative to keep him as unsuspicious as possible so that she, Enki and Lilith could continue to function on Tiâmat's behalf.

Noah asked when the three were planning to initiate his own son, Shem, into the kingship of supreme honour within Tiâmat's special bloodline. Shem had been born in Noah's old age, and was now ready to assume the title of Archonship. Ham was currently king of Ur, but since the beginning of his rigorous esoteric and spiritual training for the Archonship, Shem was acting king on his behalf. Neither Noah nor Shem had understood that Shem's appointment would not eventually include the Archonship.

Because of his vast span of years, there had been several other kings of this lineage since Noah had retired from his throne, but, although he had given up his practical office, he was still greatly revered as a kingly patriarch.

Noah was of Enki and Nin-khursag's genealogical creation, born to them (though not of their line) in the House of Shimtî, the Creation Chamber, and he had served Tiâmat, the Mother-Father God, with exceptional merit. He himself had not expected the distinction of becoming Enki's spiritual son and so being granted the status of Archon of Capricorn, but he did expect it for Shem. He was about to receive a terrible shock.

Sad to relate, the old patriarch had another reason for preferring Shem. Shem, the 'shining one', was white, whilst Ham was black. Noah, once he had been thrown off balance by Enlil's gradual encroachment, began to suffer from the blight of racial discrimination. We will see how Enlil manipulated this unfortunate tendency to his own advantage and ruthlessly encouraged aggressive racial patriarchy down the ages.

Gravely, the three God-Headed people looked at one another. They did not relish this moment, although they had known that it was bound to arrive. The time had come to explain to Noah that this special inheritance, the highest honour, was to pass to Ham, not to Shem. The best way to lessen the trauma, the three had decided, was to actually show Noah why Ham had been chosen. He would understand then that the Archon had to proceed from the genetic line concocted by Nin-khursag and Lilith, which was initiated when Nin-khursag brought forth Eve who was delivered of Cain, and Lilith brought forth Luluwa, who married Cain. Luluwa and Cain established the Grail in the land of Nodh, and their line eventually produced Ham. By special arrangement based on a sworn pact, Ham, king of Ur, had relinquished his kingship voluntarily to Shem (known as King Shulgi of Ur) so that he could dedicate himself to the Archonship and its mystical teachings.

Ham would become the first Zarathustra, with his teachings of the true light as espoused by Mazda (Enki), and would kindle the torch to be carried down the centuries which told of the Truth and the Lie. Many others would give their breath to that flame, until, eventually, it passed to its destination: the ultimate lightbearers, Jesus and Mary Magdalene, who would prepare the world for its baptism of divine light and banish the Lie forever.

Therefore, Enki and Lilith escorted Noah, in his light body, back down to the material world, and there, within his tent, they called to Ham to come to them. Ham, who was lodging as a guest in the nearby palace, came at once to their summons. He stood obediently as Enki and Lilith 'stripped him naked', which means, not that they removed his actual garments, but that they showed Noah the image of his soul-force, with its links to Tiâmat and the Grail.

They had not foreseen Noah's response, because Enlil's overtures to Noah had been hidden from them. Enlil had found a foothold in his soul, and had taken pains to carry the ancient king deeper and deeper into a narrowly materialistic view of life. As far as Noah was concerned, *he* (and, he allowed begrudgingly – because male supremacism had already begun to root itself into his heart – to some extent his wife) had saved humanity, had ensured, through his floating laboratory, that the world could be made habitable again.

It was his innovations in genetic engineering and embryonic science which had veritably *permitted* everything and everyone to continue, so that this wretched line from Eve and Lilith, that Tiâmat seemed to be making such an unnecessary fuss about, and which might not be as important as he had first thought, could come into existence in the first place. (Nin-khursag's considerable facilitation of the whole enterprise seemed to fade from his mind and become an erasable detail.)

And now, what were his thanks for saving the world? Total and utter humiliation and dismissal of his own bloodline (from which Attaba [Adam]) had descended) in favour of Cain and Luluwa's lineage!

As Ham's soul qualifications to attain to the Archonship were revealed to him, Noah saw, not the mystery of the Grail contained in Ham's destiny, but only a guarantee that his own son would not inherit, and that the black man would. He gave a great shout of grief and fury, instantly cutting off the presence of his ethereal companions, and calling Shem, who was with Ham's older brother Japhet, urgently to him. They came running, and turned Ham out of Noah's tent, believing that he had somehow dared to injure or insult the revered patriarch.

Later that night, Noah, his son Shem, and Japhet, Ham's brother, sat in conference. Noah explained what had happened, and confessed to them that he was now beginning to think that the visits he had received from Enlil's priest, which he had not welcomed, were at last beginning to make sense. The priest had foretold that his allegiance to Tiâmat and her supporter Enki could only do him harm and lead to disaster for his entire family; and he had been proved right. The priest had gone on to say that, if only Noah would consider paying homage to Enlil, then Enlil would be sure to look after him. Noah, and Shem, who was even angrier about the news concerning Ham than his father, decided to put to the test the priest's alluring words, and see what Enlil could do for them.

Japhet withdrew at this point, and went secretly to warn Ham, because, although he had been shocked by the incident in the tent, he could not countenance taking part in any plot against his brother. Ham, horrified by what he heard, set off immediately to warn his son Canaan of developing events, for he was bound to be adversely affected by them.

Shem (King Shulgi), who a matter of hours previously had been a close friend and staunch ally of himself and Canaan and all those who worshipped Tiâmat, had now turned against them.

Noah and Shem went to visit Enlil's high priest, who at once ushered them into the innermost chamber of Enlil's temple. Here, Enlil appeared, and listened to Noah and Shem's story. They revealed all – Tiâmat's plan, her special bloodline, how it was fed via Lilith's Star Fire, what it was being schooled to achieve. And they also informed him of something else.

Canaan, Ham's son, was called in Mesopotamia King Ur-baba. (We note with interest the Arabic-sounding name; the Arabic peoples as we know them today had yet to appear in the world, but they would proceed from Ishmael, Abraham's son, and the line of Japhet and Canaan.) Due to his father Ham's alliance with Noah and Shem, the kingdom of Ur had been assigned to the latter, whose

Mesopotamian name was Shulgi. This assignment was not necessarily permanent, but had been put in place to honour Noah's life of service to Tiâmat, and, as mentioned, to accommodate Ham's need to retreat into private life in order to prepare himself for his life's mission as the great spiritual teacher and leader known to the ancient Greeks as Zoroaster.

Ham's son Ur-baba (Canaan), who, as his name suggests, should have inherited the kingship of Ur from his father, was instead set up as king of nearby Lagesh (a city state). King Ur-baba, whose forebears had been mighty kings of Ur, shared a familial connection with the acting King Shulgi of Ur. With his kinsman's blessing and royal sanction, Ur-baba founded the city of Babylon just before 2000 BC, building this new site of kingship close to the ancient city of Ur. The project had been instigated by Enki, Nin-khursag and Lilith, who directed Canaan to build a ziggurat temple at its centre, as was the custom in the cities of Sumer.

This temple was to be dedicated to the Father-God, Oannes or John, the gentle and kindly male deity who honoured the Great Mother (as she honoured him). The expression of noble manliness through the principles of the true John-man was a vital and fundamental lesson for men to learn so that the barbarity and conflict engendered by the influence of Enlil and the Naphidem might be countermanded. Tiâmat herself had promised to reawaken the remnant of the sleeping energies of the Grail secreted in Ur and, via King Ur-baba's wife, divert them into the new temple at Babylon as it was being built.

Although it was impossible for Tiâmat to restore the Grail energies to the earth in full measure without overriding her gift of free will to humanity, she would avail herself of every opportunity to give life and hope to her children via the partial restoration of its forces. The construction of Babylon with its central ziggurat constituted such an opportunity. Enlil had blocked and barricaded the flow of the already constrained droplets of the Grail power in Ur; now Tiâmat would relocate this faint emission in Babylon. The name Babylon itself was given, not only as a derivative of King Ur-baba's name, but to honour the founding of this special temple dedicated to the authentic Father ("abba') principle, the John-man whose first duty was always to bend his knee to the wisdom of the heart. It was to instigate the nurturing of an entirely new concept of manhood in the world – a glorious manhood replete with every manly quality, uncorrupted by the wish to slay, denigrate or dominate.

Up to this point, of course, King Shulgi had given every cooperation to King Ur-baba's plan, even helping to fund the enterprise, and lending craftsmen and workers to toil on Ur-baba's behalf.

The city and its temple were by now well under way, and Ur-baba (a natural architect) was present in the metropolis, directing operations. The two kings had planned a gilded period of kindly and equitable rule in the manner of their venerable ancestor Attaba, side by side and, ethically, hand in hand, to set an example to the people of how the John-man should behave. They intended to demonstrate how harmonious and beautiful life would become when men turned for their inspiration on how to conduct themselves to the mighty Oannes, a concept which extended far beyond Enki as an individual, even though he was known by his heavenly father's name Oannes or Dagon (intimating 'dragon'). Their intentions were to be kept secret until they could win a majority of Enlil's supporters over to their side, which promised to be an attainable goal.

The shock that Enlil received from Shem and Noah's information, especially concerning the restoration and diversion of the Grail energies to Canaan's new-fangled Babylon, struck him like a stunning blow. That this could all have been happening under his very nose, for such an appalling span of earthly time, without any proper realisation by him that such an outrageous plot was under way, shook him to his roots. He decided, there and then, that he would destroy Tiâmat's precious plans, and oust Enki, once and for all. He promised Noah, swearing to his word, that Noah's line *would* inherit the ultimate kingship. A kingdom would be built for Shem, a magnificent kingdom which would outshine any that the previous kings of Sumer had ruled. It would extend far and wide – it would encompass the whole world! Enlil would set to work immediately to bring his promise to fruition. All that Noah and Shem had to do was to vow loyalty to him and join his team.

It is sad to relate that the noble old king and his ambitious son were wholly seduced by Enlil's enticements. They agreed to his terms, a ceremony was undertaken, and Noah, with the blessing and facilitation of Enlil, pronounced a curse on Ham's line, embodied in the person of Canaan, Ham's son; Enlil wanted to curse the particular bloodline but found Ham himself, the Archon, too sturdy an opponent to overthrow. At the same time, a promise and a benediction was granted to Shem by Enlil, formally pledging a mighty kingship to him. He wanted to outdo in style Enki and Nin-khursag's trifling gift of an 'acting' kingship. Genesis relates that only Shem was granted the privilege of access to Jehovah, whilst Ham was not, and cites Noah's curse (Genesis 9:25–26):

Cursed be Canaan; a servant of servants shall he be to his brethren ...
Blessed be the Lord God of Shem, and Canaan shall be his servant.

Enlil thus brought down two birds with one stone. When Noah told him that the Grail had been secreted in the land of Cain (formerly the land of Nodh), Enlil immediately decided that that should be his first port of call as far as the gaining of insidious influence was concerned. He had not entertained any idea that the Grail had been concealed anew in the land of Cain, but in the light of the knowledge that Noah had revealed to him, his psychic senses informed him that Canaan, Ham's son, would be intimately involved with the land of Cain, and that it would eventually bear his name. They also sniffed out that the woman he both hated and desired with a ferocious, titanic obsession was involved – that the traitor Lilith was, in fact, a bearer, a holder, of the Grail. It perfectly suited Enlil's purposes, therefore, to have Noah curse the man Canaan, and, through him, curse the land also. We see the baleful effects of his curse today in grief-stricken Palestine.

Curses and blessings (the latter, from Enlil, always given for politically expedient reasons) were bestowed more effectively from Eden if they were given vicariously, through the channel of an earthling. Moreover, as was his wont, he instigated an unpleasant rumour that Ham had committed incest with Noah's wife, his aunt, and that Canaan was the offspring of their incestuous and adulterous union. It was the same old 'mother abomination' story that he loved to spin, and had used in one of its configurations against Tiâmat.

And so Enlil set the scene for today, the point at which he had always planned to ignite the destruction of humanity. He intended to light the touch-paper of its obliteration here, in the land of Canaan, the 'Land of Purple', the land of the royal purple which contained the most holy and royal energies of the Grail – albeit in its reduced, fragmented state – and the royal people of Cain and Luluwa's descent. He hated them in particular because they were the living proof of Tiâmat's plan to oust his own control and save what he found most loathsome – humanity. The day that Noah forsook Enki and Tiâmat, and came over to his side, was a day of both horrific revelation and glorious triumph for the dark-hearted Enlil. A terrible axe fell, its blow delivered by a former hero and champion of the human race.

Enlil lost no time in calling a meeting back home in Eden. In attendance were his most faithful ministers, as well as (unusually) his father Annum, and his nephew Marduk. Enlil revealed all he had learned from Noah, and it was universally agreed that their plan to exterminate humanity, and to render the earth unfit for purpose as far as any chance of re-establishment of humanity's dominion was concerned, must be restructured, made fool-proof and watertight, and put into effect immediately.

CHAPTER FORTY-SIX

The Desecration of the Emerald Table

*E*nlil's first priority was to perfect his own version of the *khu*. It must replace the Star Fire, and be fed to the kings of Tiâmat's bloodline, so that they were thrown off course and confused. It would have to artificially increase their perception and intelligence, of course, or his deception would soon be discovered and overthrown; but it would stimulate the head centres and bypass the heart centre, so that no restraint or overriding commands should issue forth from that absurd feminine obstructer. Having absorbed it for a while, the kings would soon see that patriarchy was the only sane course, and in doing so, they would enter fully into the arena of his influence.

He would make sure that the accursed bloodline, far from producing a king at a certain allotted time who would deliver the nations from the grasp of Enlil's rule (there was even some talk from Noah of an accompanying queen, too, but he discounted such an impotent feminine irrelevance), would instead bring forth a king who, although perfectly equipped for the job he came to do (Enlil could do nothing about that), would be denigrated and spat upon, whose own people would betray him, degrade him and put him to death. Enlil would make an example of him, to show his brother Enki, the whole of humanity, and their filthy female champion, just what happened when anyone dared to challenge the authority of such a great ruler as he.

He mused to himself that he should be able to perfect his technique regarding the white powder fairly soon. He had his own league of master craftsmen that he was training especially for this purpose. He had to supply the finished blueprint, of course, but they would initiate the process on earth, and in doing so, outmatch Enki's irritating smithship guild, which based its technique on all sorts of esoteric lies. Enlil would provide the genuine article.

Had he not come on in leaps and bounds since Noah had encompassed the project with his peerless genius, progressing the Naphidem's experiments with anti-gravity (executed for the sake of creating conditions on planet earth which would comfortably contain and accommodate them once they had taken over) to the furthest point of advanced higher-dimensional technology in his grasp of the principles of production of the white powder? Of course he had! It would be Enlil's glorious, unanswerable, coup d'état! Its subtle contortions of perception would permeate insidiously, invisibly, every belief-system on earth, even the most secret and esoteric, even those which believed they contained the deepest, hidden truths.

Enlil's master plan ran thus: first, he would manufacture his white powder (there was also a red powder involved) and feed it to the kings of Tiâmat's special bloodline so that it could begin to do its work; simultaneously, he would deepen his previously established genial influence in the land of Cain (the future Canaan), so that its people would continue to embrace him as a deity – gaining a firmer foot-hold there was absolutely essential to the successful outworking of his conspiracy, which depended on deracinating the deep-rooted spiritual tradition of Lilith.

Third, he would increase his hold on Ur and its dynasties, because the mystical city of Ur was destined, as he had seen written in his perusal of the Emerald Tablet (which he held [protestingly] in joint guardianship with Enki), to bring forth a great father of nations and of planetary destiny, and this patriarch must be secured as his man.

Fourth (his plan was four-square and four-fold), he would establish and preserve on the face of the physical earth a company of ordinary star people who were susceptible to the worst influences of the Naphidem.

This secret syndicate, relatively small in number but lethally powerful, would clandestinely hold the reins of global political power and worldly wealth through the ages, and would work ineluctably, inexorably – ostensibly under Marduk's direction but really under his – towards the great culmination of his plan, which would extend over the next four thousand years, slowly, steadily, until humanity and the earth were his to destroy (his calculations confirmed that he needed the four-square structure of two thousand years before the coming of Tiâmat's supreme king and queen, and two thousand years after the king's arranged demise, to be sure of his goal). He would integrate all these stages to overshadow every religion, every political system, every social structure on earth; they would look for God, or for some political or humanitarian ideal, or whatever took their collective fancy, and always, always, find him, Enlil, the one true God, the most high, the mightiest of all, dwelling under the surface!

Already, the notion had begun to form in his mind that if he could instigate such a plan of total annihilation and bring it to fruition, then he must indeed be the one true God, for who else could undertake such a mission and be rewarded with success? The crowning glory of this articulated series of strategies concerned the Emerald Tablet itself.

With Noah's wizardry, Enlil planned to cause a rumpus in the Eden parliament between himself and Enki, whereby it would seem as if the Emerald Tablet had been seized by any one of a number of warring factions. In fact, it would not have been stolen at all, but hidden by Enlil in a secret dimension which Noah would open for him alone.

This dimension would be guarded by Enlil's dark angel brethren with a sinister, impassable sword of the death-forces (just as he had sealed off Eden from penetration by the ordinary star people, via an inversion of Tiâmat's own protective measures, after he had banished Attaba and Eve from Eden), only in this instance the protection which secured it as forbidden territory would be invisible and inscrutable. No one, either earthly or God-Headed, would even suspect it existed. And there the true Emerald Tablet would remain, stashed away in complete secrecy, in an impenetrable fortress hidden in the ethers.

No one would know it was lost, no one would ever stumble across it, because no one would be able to breach the fastnesses of the locked sphere in which it was held. It would not be missed or searched for, because no one would guess that it was actually missing. Why? Because, when he triumphantly brought forth what seemed to be the 'stolen' Emerald Tablet, pretending that he had wrested it back from the thief who took it and that it was restored to its rightful guardians (he and Enki) Enlil himself would release a false Emerald Tablet onto the world, an Emerald Tablet or an exalted energy package which would contain only partial truths, flickering with the evocative light of, now the glimmer of truth, now its fugitive, darkly whispering shadow. It would have a hypnotic quality, the power to lull the soul into a sleep or stupor of progressive unrealisation or spiritual unconsciousness.

The false *shem*, the white powder, is how it would be done. The despotism of the white powder would replace Tiâmat's decrees as they were written upon her despicable Emerald Tablet, and Enlil would advance in influence and might and glory, century upon century, step by step. Many people would believe that they could access the Emerald Tablet; the most secret rites would whisper its name.

Those who despised what they saw and knew of Enlil's dominance in the outer world would turn to these rites in the hope that the 'truth' they read in the application of the Stone would at last set themselves and the stricken world free. And no one, no one would know that they did not behold the true Stone, but rather embraced the false one. Even the elect would be deceived. There was no hope of rescue, no hope that the inexorable course of destiny that he had instigated could be altered. The destiny of the despised human race would march to Enlil's tune.

They would pass from the deepest degradation of slavery and suffering into irretrievable destruction!

Nevertheless, all this, however brilliant, constituted plan B. There was another, much quicker and more direct route to his dreams and desires, one that could be implemented without delay. If it failed (which he was confident it would not) the fall-out of its energies could be integrated into the slower but impregnable plan B. This plan, dearest to his heart, involved setting up Shem in the totalitarian kingship he had both envisaged and promised to the ambitious man, and making sure, as he did so, that Shem came under the influence and the tutelage of the Naphidem. Shem would be given Babylon; if possible, he would arrange to have Canaan slaughtered, and Canaan's new kingdom would be given a new name – a name fit for Enlil's plan, and a black joke against Tiâmat's.

Noah, with his wondrous scientific skill, could help Enlil to prepare the earth for the Naphidem invasion (of course, the old king could be fobbed off with some sweetener about Shem, via the Naphidem, holding the entire world in his power, which would certainly seem to be borne out during the early days of the Naphidem take-over). This cherished plan could be implemented throughout the short span of a mere half century, and, considering the secret headway that that treacherous wretch Enki had made, all the while keeping Enlil in ignorance until Noah had mercifully switched sides and come to his rescue, it was the sort of sudden strike that would best comfort Enlil's heart after his trauma of discovery. Certainly, beyond the merest fragment of doubt, Enlil would indeed show Tiâmat just who was Lord of All!

CHAPTER FORTY-SEVEN

The Sham Shem

*A*ction was instigated, and Babylon was handed over to Shem. It ought to be explained that a *shem* (after which Shem had been named by Enlil in preconceived preparation for, not only his royal status, but also his new mystical and spiritual inheritance as the Archon) was indeed, as Laurence Gardner cites, a highward fire stone, revered in ancient Sumer. However, we believe that what this really indicates is not a shining stone *per se*, thus a metal (although it has a definite connection to certain precious metals), but the stone or brick conical towers which preceded the sacred stone ziggurats.

As we have seen, at one time, before Tiâmat's decision to change the structure of our souls because of the ruinous attacks on them by the Naphidem, the human soul was constructed in the form of a tall and slender conical obelisk or tower. These towers were given actual physical shape by the sacred craftsmen (and, at one time, women), the stonemasons and metalworkers (the builders were often in possession of both skills), who constructed them with steep steps progressing from their base to their topmost level. The steps were inside the *shem*, and formed an inner spiral. At the top was a chamber or temple, made of gold, crystal or some metal that shone. It was from this sacred chamber that earthly initiates could ascend into Eden, and members of the God-Headed people could descend into physicality, as previously explained.

When an initiate left the temple to ascend, or a God-Headed person entered it in order to descend, the ethereal energy-release involved would glow throughout the temple, and the top level of the *shem* (the temple) would thus become the 'highward fire stone', or an expression of the Grail. It was this manifestation of the Grail dynamic (the power of the *khu*) that Enlil wished to capture in his own version of the *shem,* which he crafted from gold, or a compound of the noble metals from which the temple was always constructed, to produce the deadly white powder.

We saw him, waiting in his particular dimension (a dimension above that of physical matter, but certainly not of the spirit). As the monatomic (high-spin) gold became weightless, it entered this dimension. We watched Enlil seize it, alter it in some way, adding an ethereal influence which distorts and deranges, and then send it back into the material realm. In the old days, the gold was put into reverse spin by a method, as far as we could see, of transforming all the electrons into positive or forward-spin mode. This, which actually threw the gold into a sinister, negative revolution that created subtle swastika-like patterns, was done at the etheric, not the physical, level. The gold was then returned to the physical dimension as white powder.

The sacred relationship or marriage between the masculine and feminine (positive and negative) sub-atomic particles, giving wholeness and truth of being to the atoms, had been destroyed – but not only destroyed. It was disfigured into a malevolent, mirror-image aspect of its once harmonious holistic self, and it carried the power to conduct its peculiar quality of disruptive malevolence (the masculine and feminine principles in conflict) to the third eye – the organ of perception. Thus wars and hatred, intolerance and abuse, flourished fulsomely, and the ideal of strident patriarchy perpetuated itself.

Even the Grail lineage of kings and queens was unable to prevent or transform this negative situation; when its supreme king and queen eventually did arrive, its king was slain, in line with the perceptual and cultural necessities imposed by Enlil, and its queen was denied and degraded, treated as a whore and an outcast. Their wondrous child, the Holy Grail herself, died of starvation in a Roman prison (the Roman Empire at its most extreme was an objectification in full of Enlil's soul dynamics – his most perfect and illustrious ideal), a symbolism which speaks for itself. Nevertheless, Jesus, John, Mary and Tamar's mission did not by any means fail. It was in fact a majestic triumph – only Enlil has not yet understood this to be so!

Noah's son Shem was the first king to be fed with the white powder. He was its guinea pig (Noah saw this in the light of a royal and religious distinction – his son was the inaugural monarch to be honoured in this way), and its effects were an acclaimed success as far as Enlil and his co-conspirators were concerned. Noah, its main creator, was hailed a hero and warmly congratulated by them. He became the man of the moment, and was initiated into the ranks of the God-Headed people (we remember that his father was a God-Headed sperm donor, and Noah's own brilliance facilitated the rest of the procedure necessary to harmonise his atoms with those of the Eden dimension – notably a skill connected with the Grail, to which interesting fact we shall return).

Shem immediately fell into the power of the Naphidem upon taking Enlil's nefarious substance (the bread of the False Communion). He marks the point where the (sham) fire stone – the white powder – was given to the Grail kings instead of the Star Fire or the menstrual blood. The menstrual blood, in fact, was, according to Tiâmat's purposes, given to the males of the line for an allotted time only. It needed to be administered just until our new pyramidal or zigguratesque soul shape had stabilised and become concrete in form.

Once this had been achieved, Tiâmat ceased to prescribe it. The Star Fire essence from Lilith and Nin-khursag was always on hand, because they did not desert the earth when Sumer fell, as the rest of the God-Headed community did. But in fact Tiâmat was already in the process of refining the Star Fire to the point where both men and women could avail themselves of it in a different way, a process which we can utilise today, and which will be explained in due course.

And so a parting of the ways opened up to humanity: each member could choose freely whether they would partake of the authentic white fire which was the starry essence of the true God, or feed instead upon the white powder, the exclusively intellectual and materialistic forces of consciousness aspiring to a robotic super-intelligence, promoted by the false God and his syndicate.

We must not think that, because the Star Fire essence and, later, the malignant fire stone were given to the monarchs of Tiâmat's lineage, their properties were intended for the rulers alone. Whilst it is true that, as we have explained, a certain DNA patterning had to be preserved because of Enlil's conspiracy to destroy it, and that Mary Magdalene, Jesus, John the Beloved Disciple and Tamar, the Divine Woman who was the embodiment of the Holy Grail, would need to proceed from a specially designated and prepared bloodline, it is also true that the genuine, and eventually the false, fire or light was fed to the kings for another reason entirely.

A king or a queen has a mission of service in that they receive certain spiritual currents, benedictions and endowments from the Divine Source which they then distribute and diffuse at a subtle level among the populace. They are the vessel from which the spiritual wine is dispensed.

We can see this esoteric truth amply demonstrated in the insect kingdom, whereby the queen ant or wasp, bee or termite, will disseminate her organisational commands and energies throughout the swarm by providing her saliva for the workers to ingest (we might call this a form of the Sheldrake method). From this high-powered 'Star Fire' cocktail, the members of the community are instructed how to function. In like manner, from the kings of the Grail bloodline there came forth this stream of consciousness, except that in their case it was a forked river, incorporating the false and the true light. The question remains with us today: which shall we choose?

Shem, thus marking the point where the sham *shem* came into being, conceived a raging disgust for anything to do with the menstrual blood or the Star Fire. Once Enki's man, he was Enlil's priest-king now, and no longer would he have anything to do with Enki, or his wives Nin-khursag and Lilith. From being Ham's respectful deputy as acting King of Ur, and Canaan's good friend and co-devotee of Tiâmat and the Temple of Oannes, he became, because of his original weakness pertaining to self-importance and the later corruption of the white powder, a preening tyrant. A neurosis arose in him, brought to life by the white powder itself, which saw the sham *shem* as an essence born of purity, of wholesomeness, of qualities to aspire to. The *shem* became, as it were, 'sexed-up', the Star Fire anathema.

Many, through Enlil's arranged dissemination, fell under the influence of the white powder of the False Communion, thereby holding up the aggressive, all-conquering warrior in the act of dispensing death (an accurate image of the core of reality within the white powder) as a cherished ideal. The Naphidem breathed their influences through Shem to a greater and greater degree, and day by day he became more entrenched in his slavery to them.

CHAPTER FORTY-EIGHT

The Dark Tower

*M*eanwhile, the extended building programme which had been ordered for Shem's new city of Babylon, a gift from Enlil, came on apace. This half-constructed city was, by rights, the project and the property of Canaan, but he was ousted by Enlil's forces. Later, we shall examine the turbulent, but deeply blessed, history of Canaan.

Everything was done to treat the recently-crowned King Shulgi, now Enlil's high priest, with right royal respect. Shulgi was now no longer only 'acting' king of Ur! Annum, still calling himself 'Anu' as he was convinced he was complete unto himself, came back from his business on another sphere and poured flattering attentions and honours with velvet smoothness upon King Shulgi (Shem's royal name):

> *Let Shulgi, king with a pleasant term of reign, perform correctly for me, Anu, the rites instituted of kingship. Let him direct the schedules of the gods for me.*

The message was clear. Shem (Shulgi) was in favour with the highest of the high. He had arrived.

Noah was filled with happiness, and he was pleased to cooperate with Enlil in every detail whilst such healing balm for his pride flowed forth from the higher Anunnaki king.

What Enlil wanted particularly to do in Babylon (with Noah's help) was to construct, beside the half-finished temple ziggurat designated to dispense the sacred Oannes influences, a *shem* or a 'highward fire stone'. As we have explained, these *shem* structures preceded the ziggurats and the pyramids, and were the first structures to house the Grail energies. They were superseded by the pyramidal structures of later times; however, it was certainly not for the purposes of admitting the ordinary star people into Eden again that Enlil had ordered the Babylonian *shem* to be built.

Enlil's problem was that if he tried to complete and utilise the half-finished temple ziggurat in Shem's new kingdom for his own purposes, Ga-nadin-ur, the great guardian king still present on the inner planes, was standing by on the threshold of the Grail energies with all his increased capacity to protect the earth, not only from the Naphidem, but now from Enlil himself.

The only thing to do, as far as Enlil could see, was to call upon the brilliant scientist Noah to block Ga-nadin-ur's obstruction, to seize the newly awakened Grail forces in Ur which had been prepared by Tiâmat for diversion to the Babylonian ziggurat, and to redirect them to the site of the new *shem* which under Enlil's instructions was being built next to it on revised principles (we might call it a 'one way' *shem*, fit for Enlil's purpose). Enlil could not make use of the ziggurat for his purpose, even with Noah's help, because his use of the physical structure had been banned after his former abuse of it in Ur, and because, out of sheer stubbornness, he could not adapt his soul energies to the new pyramidal design provided by Tiâmat. This custom-built *shem*, his brilliant solution, would receive and activate the redirected Grail forces so that both Enlil and the Naphidem could actually descend to earth and take over.

To this end Enlil had, via his priests now led by Shem, gathered together a great number of his supporters, and commanded them to build the new city with its central *shem* at breakneck speed. (Babylon was within the vicinity of Ur, so that it was virtually contiguous with the old city and on the main artery or ley line sustained by the Grail energies.)

The flourish in the tail to all this strategic brilliance was that Enlil's supporters had been instructed by Enlil himself to take their orders from Marduk for the time being. This terrified them, because Marduk's influence was palpable and very, very sinister, more so than Enlil's, which was like that of a psychopathically authoritarian despot given to fits of rage, and was highly intimidating and unnerving rather than nightmarish. Enlil had by now, however, put into action his plan to cause distracting havoc in the Grand Assembly by secretly plotting that Marduk should appear to 'illicitly' take control of Enlil's own followers whilst an almighty wrangle, specially contrived by Enlil, was going on between Enlil and Enki.

Whilst the Assembly (for the greater part blissfully ignorant of all Enlil's machinations) tried to rectify this situation and reconcile the two brothers, Marduk duly took advantage of the strife (following direct orders from Enlil, whom he always obeyed slavishly, although he also hated him and privately spoke against him) to usurp the official ruling and gain his following among Enlil's supporters, who were themselves under strict orders by Enlil to obey Marduk from now on. Marduk seized the Emerald Tablet, surreptitiously passing it over to Enlil, who, with the help of Noah, hid it in his secret dimension and sealed all entry to its place of concealment.

A little while later, Enlil announced to the Assembly that fortunately he had retrieved the Emerald Tablet, actually bringing forth the false one he and Noah had manufactured between them, which contained some fragmented parts of the living wisdom of Tiâmat, but now had a disguised negative energy current running undetectably in reverse spin throughout its dimensions. This was returned triumphantly to its official place of guardianship – a most holy shrine which constituted a barycentric cup of the divine forces within Eden. Once installed in this centre of gravity (known as the Sacred Chalice), the false Emerald Tablet began to throw out harmful, subversive dynamics which coursed through the etheric structure of Eden, just as Enlil had planned it should.

Meanwhile, Enlil's poor followers on earth, now ruled by Marduk, had begun to extend King Shem's new city (purloined from Canaan) and construct its prominent *shem*. They were all in a state of terror, having been warned by Enlil that invaders were massing on all sides, particularly from the land of Cain, and that if they did not make haste in building the *shem* he had ordered, they would be cast out of Ur and Babylon by the marauders and scattered abroad. Only the *shem* they were building, Enlil's temple, could save them now. Enlil would protect them, but they must work in the sweat of their faces and complete the job swiftly. They were promised that if they succeeded, the temple would enable them to conquer the world; if not, Ur would fall. Enlil needed to get the Naphidem to earth before Ham and Canaan's many supporters in the land of Cain marched against him. They were indeed massing, and mobilising themselves to attack.

CHAPTER FORTY-NINE

Horror in the Heavens

Canaan left his royal palace in Babylon the night that Japhet, crossing the virtually contiguous city boundaries between Ur and the brand new metropolis, alerted him to his dangerous situation. When daylight came, Enlil learned that he had escaped. His shrouded night-time strangler could not be despatched, after all, to solve the problem of King Ur-baba. He could not be followed into the land of Cain, because the influences there were adverse to Enlil. It was true that Enlil had a following in the country; this had arisen long, long ago, before the shadow had so completely fallen over him, when he was paid homage to in the land of Nodh as El Elyon, El Shaddai, with his seat at the head of the great rivers Tigris and Euphrates (actually in Sumerian Mesopotamia, where he was known, of course, as Enlil).

In those days, he was a benign shepherd of the forces of nature, using his status as a Saturnine lord of karma to bless and to encourage the people to attract greater and greater felicity to their lands and their lives. It was this history that Enlil drew on to full advantage to gain a hold in the land of Cain, and indeed he continued to be worshipped there, which seems an enigma, as its people were allies of Enki and Cain, and particularly Lilith and Luluwa. This caused Canaan to be riven, as Eden had been riven by Enlil's depredations. Yet there is the expression of a beautiful truth here.

The mystic land of Cain was destined to hold the memory, the imprint, the buried soul of what Enlil once was, so that the spiritual balance which the two brothers Enki and Enlil represented might be preserved and would not pass away from the earth. This was vital for the future.

However, Enki's followers also amassed there, and they rose up against Shulgi and Ur when Canaan was banished.

The hapless people of Ur and Babylon, with this threat to goad them, were only too eager to take on the yoke of slavery and work to build the required *shem* with its name (the name of the city) before Canaan's supporters struck. They worked at top speed, under the constant whiplash of Marduk, whose petrifying presence was breathed through the priests, especially the high priest, King Shem. The name of the city was to be Shem, in Shem's honour, but to distinguish it from a too literal reference to its central *shem*, the name was translated into a different form. It meant the same, but it had an additional meaning. The truth had to be honoured, and by spiritual law, Enlil could not disguise the meaning and the teaching in the name. The name was in the stone *shem*, it proceeded from it and proclaimed its identity. The name was Babel.

Confusion.

This qualifying name of Enlil's false Emerald Tablet, the dynamic behind the creation of the white powder (for the white powder was created by distorting the truth of the real Emerald Tablet), gives us the defining clue as to its real essence and purpose. It was designed to confuse, to throw off track, to lead to a culmination of full-scale reversal and disintegration. Babel equals Confusion. And within the chosen name for his new city lurked, like a leering grin, Enlil's mockery of Babylon – Babylon that was to have been the home of the great temple to Tiâmat and Oannes – the birthplace of the new John-man.

The unrivalled scientific genius Noah, now fuelled by a demonic inspiration, his nobility of soul completely scrambled and his wisdom in wild reverse spin, was triumphantly successful in attaining all of Enlil's goals.

The reawakened Ur Grail energies were diverted into the new *shem* (the Tower of Babel) and activated anew. The Naphidem gathered, forefronted by Enlil, who was to lead them exultantly down the *shem* to unprecedented victory. Their earthly conduit (just until the earth had been properly prepared for their complete physical manifestation, of course) would be their puppet-king Shem. Noah, ignorant of their long-term intentions, basked gloriously in the moment, his heart swelling with pride in his son.

The first lightning-strike from the Tower of Babel (the *shem*) was a fiery subtle energy that vindicated the new city's name to perfection. Suddenly, the people of Babel, and, progressively, throughout all of Sumer, could no longer understand one another. They were thrown into confusion and panic. Something had happened to their language-centres, located in the right, feminine-orientated brain. What was happening to them? Even their own thoughts were hardly coherent any more!

This, of course, was the first strike of the white powder, which Noah had discovered could be dispensed through concentrating a certain ray upon the atmosphere of Sumer, guided specifically into Babel. It was a necessary preparation to secure the unchallenged victory of the mass invasion of the Naphidem that was to follow. The people scurried hither and thither, in great fear and distress. They put forth a common supplication to the 'most high God'. They thought this deity was Enlil, of course, but Enki, Nin-khursag, Lilith, Ga-nadin-ur and other uncorrupted members of the God-Headed people were standing by. They were horrified by the turn of events, but they held their ground, steady in their spiritual strength. As one, they lifted the people's desperate prayer to God. It broke through the white-powder-induced haze and formed a clear path hewn from their own free will to Tiâmat.

Their pyramidal soul structure stood true and four-square against the power of the Naphidem. Without destroying the point and principle of her creation, Tiâmat could now act.

Enlil descended the *shem* first; but, with the exception of Marduk, who because he was Enki's son, and because of the power bestowed on him by God-Headed reverse-spin rites, had learned how to slip through dimensions, he was not followed by the Naphidem. Tiâmat activated her will, and down came the *shem*, torn from beneath them as they were catapulted back into their own dimension, screaming with pain, disorientation and fury. The etheric doors were closed and sealed. The Naphidem were gone, and so was the *shem*, for it fell promptly into devastation.

Terrible in its clashing might was Enlil's fury as he surveyed the ruins of his plans. Howling with rage, he turned the imploding power of the *shem* on the people. The lethal force of the white powder came into its own as the ray on which it had been disseminated turned it into its most malignant, unexpiated, form. It burst forth as a killer ray, destroying tens of thousands on the spot like a nuclear warhead from some giant celestial god-directed gun. People fell where they stood, their bodies melting like snow in summer. The Sumerian texts vividly recount this desperate time:

> *Ur is destroyed, bitter is its lament.* [Babel was within the environs of Ur, so both cities would have fallen together, and there would have been little distinction between them.] *The country's blood now fills its holes like hot bronze in a mould. Bodies dissolve like fat in the sun. Our temple is destroyed. The gods have abandoned us like migrating birds. Smoke lies on our cities like a shroud.*

and:

> *When they overthrew, when order they destroyed*
> *Then like a deluge all things together consumed.*
> *Whereunto, Oh Sumer! did they change thee?*
> *The sacred dynasty from the temple they exiled.*

It is noteworthy that in both of these texts, reference is made to the destruction of the temple. Because of the link that Noah had created between the *shem* of Babel and the ziggurat of Ur, which had again been rebuilt, both structures collapsed simultaneously. The Ur temple was traditionally the temple of Enki, Nin-khursag and Lilith, serving, in metaphysical disguise, Tiâmat and her bloodline. We think that the specially appointed earthly priests of this temple were those who either were or became kings, some of them ruling contemporaneously in different cities. They comprised the 'sacred dynasty' of the temple, Tiâmat's special royal blood-line, to which the text above makes reference. King Ur-baba, or Canaan, and his father Ham (the Archon), were the most sacred of them all.

Whilst the terrible destruction of Ur and Babel was under way, Tiâmat brought down the 'sword that divides'. This was necessary to prevent Enlil from ascending to Eden again. Had he done so, with his train of God-Headed followers, his power from that celestial height would have been enough at this point to inflict terrible and lasting damage on the earth. The white powder laser had to be disabled and dismantled, a task which Enlil would never have allowed. So Tiâmat barred his way, and effectively trapped him and his supporters upon the earth.

They could still rise to an ethereal dimension above it or within it, because when they descended the *shem* they were not manifesting – and indeed could not manifest, now that the Grail forces had been restricted – in physical bodies. We can confirm that when Enlil and his cronies (not the Naphidem, who were never given the chance to descend) came down the *shem*, they had not been able to physicalise their bodies as they could in the old days of the Grail. They descended in ethereal form. The *shem* that Noah had constructed with the diverted energies from the Ur temple was not able to operate in the miraculous manner of the true Grail ziggurat. His authority could never extend to the actual earthing and reactivation of the true dynamo of the Grail.

So it was that Enlil and his followers became trapped in a dimension which was lower than that of Eden. They could not now leave the earth. Their soul vibrations had become too dense and coarse to allow them to do so. They repaired to a hiding-place, a desolate astral plane possessed of very little beauty, and from there, with occasional expeditions to the physical earth and reconaissances of it, they continued to implement Enlil's plan for the destruction of humankind.

Enlil certainly hadn't finished with Sumer. Wrath and retribution were his main modes of expression, and he now had a field day. For the time being, his new cramped and circumscribed quarters restricted his scale of operations to Sumer alone, but he intended to make the very most of his limited opportunities. He would show the female imposter Tiâmat what he would do to Sumer, her cradle of the new humanity and her central initiating point for all her plans and dreams regarding it!

Meanwhile, Eden itself had to be abandoned. It was not possible for the true-hearted God-Headed people, the ones who had not joined Enlil's corrupt team, to remain there, because it had to be sealed off from the earth.

Spiritual airs could not blow freely throughout its precincts any more. Its energies had to be closed down, and it became a deserted world.

Enlil went on to obliterate Sumer. After the Tower of Babel and the temple ziggurat of Ur fell, and the people cowered in shock, appalled to their roots, Enlil opened the gates of the country on every level, drawing hordes of invaders in as if he sounded a summoning horn. This sudden mass thirst to inflict bloody extinction smacks of Naphidem behaviour, and indeed Marduk acted his part in the doom and downfall of Sumer with relish. He exacerbated, inflamed and incited, until a wind-tunnel opened up within the ethers, and the men of earth were overcome with the Naphidem influences which roared through it into their hearts. Every act of desecration was carried out, and what the white powder left standing, the marauders laid low:

> *The high gates, the roads, were piled high with dead.*
> *In the wide streets, where feasting crowds would gather;*
> *scattered they lay.*
> *In all the streets and roadways bodies lay.*
> *In open fields that used to fill with dancers,*
> *they lay in heaps.*

(SUMERIAN TEXT)

It is very evident from the texts quoted, and from many others, that something of huge and disastrous import happened in Sumer at this time. Afterwards, the land was never as fertile again, and finally the desert claimed much of it. This was no ordinary invasion.

The terrible battle that was fought out at the physical level in Sumer reflected an even more terrifying battle in the higher ethers. This battle was recorded in Revelation, and it shows us that Enki, Lilith, Nin-khursag and others of the true-hearted God-Headed community fought valiantly, with great self-sacrifice, to stay the hand of Enlil, Marduk and the Naphidem, and those members of the God-Headed people who had joined forces with them. This mighty battle was reflected in the First and Second World Wars, where many ordinary, down-to-earth soldiers saw angels fighting alongside them, as if these beings of light fought to drive back some shadowed foe which threatened the human world from beyond the level of mortal combat and the clash of nation against nation. The story of the 'Angel of Mons' is one of the most famous. Many visions of the sword Excalibur were also witnessed at this time. A little word-play gives us 'X-calibre', of which the sword surely was, for X stands for the mysteries of Mary Magdalene and Tamar (thence the Grail), and the mysteries of planet X, our mother earth's lover from beyond the stars.

That this battle should be won was imperative, for on its outcome depended the future of civilisation. Humanity's very existence hung in the balance. All those fighting on the side of the light recognised that if they failed to make that final push to victory, appalling cataclysm would be the result. Would Alice-Chalice, the true authority as the light-bearing influences of the universe, be valiant, or would the false queen, the vengeful maniac who roamed her dominions screaming 'Off with their heads!' win the day?

We stand at such a threshold today.

CHAPTER FIFTY

The Sign of the Beast

*W*hen Tiâmat ordered 'the sword that divides' to split the shadowed and the bright God-Headed people so that the dark-hearted among them were trapped in a lower dimension belonging to earth, and those who were uncorrupted had to leave Eden and the earth for ever, Enki, Lilith and Nin-khursag remained behind with the corrupt members of their community, although, of course, these three enlightened ones dwelt in a different sphere, aligned to the east of the world. They suffered this imprisonment and limitation in order to help their earthly brethren on their upward path to freedom, pledging of their own free will to stay at humanity's side until the terrible yoke of Enlil and Marduk had been thrown off forever. All these incidents comprised a cosmic event, showing us that Noah's *shem* was the means by which the Naphidem most nearly descended to earth since their banishment in the early days. Although the way has been long and hard throughout our history, it is worth considering what strength and resilience, what irresistible spiritual muscular force we are developing in thus struggling against Enlil and the hypnotic power of his false Stone. This is the secret reason why he was allowed to pursue his abominable course, and the reason why, when the Grail is returned to us (which will be very soon) and we throw off his terrible yoke at last, a glory will be released into the heart of the earth and into our earthly lives which will burst forth in unprecedented splendour. No radiance like it will ever have been witnessed before by the earth and her peoples, and all creation will bask in its effulgence.

Our restored connection to the Divine will be deeper and more brilliant than at any time in humanity's entire history. Its keynote will be joy – a joy beyond anything we can presently understand. First of all, however, we must rid ourselves and our blocked perception of this false Stone.

In Revelation, John speaks to us of the sign of the Beast:

*And that no man might buy or sell, save he that had the mark, or the
name of the beast, or the number of his name. Here is wisdom. Let him
that hath understanding count the number of the beast: for it is the
number of a man; and his number is Six hundred threescore and six.*

The number of the beast is the number of the Stone, because the Beast, in this
reversed rendition of its energy, is synonymous with the False Prophet, and the
False Prophet and the Stone are one. It is revealed by the number of a man, which
in numerology is the number 1. The number of the beast is also the number of the
name of a man.

The Gnostic gospels (the bulk of them undiscovered until 1945 at Nag
Hammadi) reveal that the disciple Simon Peter threatened Mary Magdalene's
life on more than one occasion, and tried to rouse the other disciples against her
after the death of Jesus. He spoke of her with contempt, claiming that she and all
women were not fit to be given life (possibly he meant eternal life, but, judging
from Peter's disgraceful attitude to women, and particularly to Mary, it is difficult to be sure!).

Many commentators have believed that Peter was unintelligent, as he is
portrayed as never being able to understand what Jesus was trying to convey. Peter
was indisputably unintelligent, but he was not slow-witted.

He was, in fact, highly intellectual and outwardly very clever, using this stance
as his excuse for despising women and the way they understood the world.

A word of reproach concerning our depiction of Peter came from more than one
critic after our book about Mary Magdalene was released. In fact, the depiction was
not truly ours, but arose from many sources.

When Jacobus de Voraigne, Archbishop of Genoa, set out in search of legend
and tradition regarding the disciples and other prominent saints of the Church, he
visited the places where they were best known in their lifetimes. From such grass-
roots sources, he drew on the most famous and enduring traditions regarding his
quarry. It was from these methods that he compiled a set of names for the disciples
by which they were known according to those most intimate with them or best
acquainted with their personal history – Latin nicknames which had persisted
through the centuries. Peter's was *Exosus*, which translates as 'he who hates'.

We are afraid that things are about to get much worse for Simon Peter than we
ever suggested in our previous book. Jesus had a nickname for him, too. From this
famous nickname, the appellation 'Peter' derives. 'Peter' never was a formalised
Hebrew name. It means 'stone'.

Jesus called Simon Peter 'the Stone'.

This was a man who, as the New Testament and the Gnostic gospels confirm,
was hot-headed and suffered from frequent fits of rage. He was a man of hatred, as

his history attests, and of all things he hated women most. He was often possessed with the desire to kill – especially to kill women. He was generally dictatorial and often assumed unwarranted authority. He hated women's wisdom and he believed exclusively in the supremacy of the intellect, left-brain perception, and all that was masculine.

Is he beginning to sound familiar?

There can be no doubt that Simon Peter was Enlil's agent. 'Upon this rock shall I build my Church', said Jesus in connection with him. But he did not mean quite what the Catholic Church afterwards came to believe he meant. He was declaring, instead, that the Church of Oannes, of the John-man, whom Jesus served, would be raised up upon the false Stone, the hard rock of materialism, and the exalted consciousness of the one would overcome and supplant the death energies of the other. He was announcing the beginning of the end of Enlil's rule. 'Love shall pitch his tent/in the place of excrement', sings the poet Yeats, to apprise us of this situation.

There exists an old system of numerology called the *Ars Memoriae*. It seems likely that John the Beloved, who travelled west and lived in France and Britain for many years (we think he died at the age of 105) would have been familiar with this system. He certainly knew Latin well, because he used it to compile the secret text (under special conditions, as amanuensis to Mary Magdalene) which lies buried in Lincoln, and which is a rendition of Tiâmat's Emerald Tablet – the true Stone. According to this system, the name Simon produces the number 66. Normally, the next step would be to add these figures together, making a total of twelve, and then to add 1 and 2, giving a final total of 3. This is because ancient numerological systems do not exceed the number 9 in their ultimate calculations.

However, the number 9 is a sigil of feminine power. Is it possible that, in the feminine-rejecting Simon Peter's case, the later stages of numerological calculation are not applicable in the evaluation of his name because they come under the dominion of the number 9? This seems a strange and unlikely theory, but if we ride with it we find that the name Peter equals 61. If we push both totals together, (66 and 61), rather than adding them together, we arrive at the number 6661.

If we isolate the odd number, we get 666–1 – i.e. the number of a man (1) whose name is 'Six hundred threescore and six': 666. Furthermore, if we now revert to normal numerological principles and add together the total of numbers representing his name – 6661 – we arrive at 19, which converts to 10 (1+9), which is duly reduced to 1 (1 + 0 = 1) – the number of a man.

Is this too far-fetched? It might be; but the fact remains that Simon Peter hated women and hated the feminine Christ, that he wanted to murder her, that he was Enlil's agent on earth, in place to deflect the inconceivable power of the coming of the Christ (Jesus and Mary Magdalene) away from the immediate rescue of humanity and into Enlil's domain and the pursuit of Enlil's plan of annihilation, that he denied and hated and spoke against Tamar (the Holy Grail), entering into massive rows with Paul when the latter tried to establish her enlightened doctrines into the outlook of the early Church, that he is depicted as 'the beast' (the False Prophet beast rather than the Mardukian beast) in the Grail clues and in Chartres Cathedral, that his name was a byword for hatred and rage, that a 'Simon' (his real name) was mysteriously present in every gospel story which denies and denigrates and harlotises Mary Magdalene and blocks our true perception of her, and that Jesus referred to him as 'the Stone'. The evidence does appear to be mounting, to say the very least!

And yet Peter remains an enigma. We believe that the above accusations against him are true. But he is also cited as a guardian. He stands before the locked gates of heaven, holding the keys. This is indeed the 'key' to understanding Peter. We must overcome his rule, and move beyond him, before we can get into heaven.

Peter has his archetypal part to play in the great cosmic drama in which we all participate in our journey towards ascension.

In our task of delivering what we know of the Grail message to the world, Margaret Bailey and I have both been protected by a 'Peter'. Peter even guards the Holy Grail, because the clue in Lincoln Cathedral that belongs to him is the Lincoln Imp or demon, sitting cross-legged on a spandrel opposite the renowned Angel Choir, and furthermore he is cited in the famous Rennes-le-Château documents as 'this demon guardian'. Why is Peter the guardian?

Could it be that he is telling us that none may approach the Holy Grail, none may enter the gates of heaven, unless they are pure-hearted enough to *recognise* that he is the false Stone, the false Prophet, and thus overcome his illicit dominion, the dominion of materialism, the rock or the stone which he represents? Roll away the Stone, and thereby enter into the true life, he seems to be conveying to us. We will roll away the Stone, in a combined effort of the heart of humanity; and when we do, Peter the Stone will surrender to us the keys of heaven, because the Grail will have returned to earth. The Stone that blocks our path and dims our light shall obstruct no longer.

Peter represents the obscuration that hides and disempowers the precious Stone of Ascension (the true Stone) within our heads when we choose a purely intellectual or brain-centred understanding of and response to life over a heart-centred awareness. More will be revealed of this wondrous Stone of Ascension in the following chapters, but for now we only need to understand the simple truth that the activation of the heart centre is what stimulates the Stone of Ascension within the brain into life.

It is the ego-centred intellect with its death-ray of scathing arrogance which alienates us from our heart centre, and causes us to mistake the Stone of Death

(Peter) for the Stone of Life – the Stone of Ascension in the head which is activated by the heart-wisdom of the wondrous Stone that is the Emerald Tablet.

It was poor Peter's unenviable task to represent this Stone of Death in the universal drama which was the life and the teaching of the Christ, and timelessly to pose to each of us the question: which Stone will you choose? And so we may say a heartfelt thank you to Peter for living out the tragic aspects of his life in order that we might more easily understand the momentous nature of the choice we must make.

Peter's saving grace was that he truly loved Jesus, and longed to serve him, although he saw only half the picture, and was thus led into denying the Christ three times (connected with his denial of Mary and Tamar, and of the three-quarters of Tiâmat's Emerald Tablet, which embodied the wisdom of the Oannes- or John-man that Jesus upheld).

Peter's very real love for what he understood of the Christ, however, assures us that, not only will he be healed and made whole, but Enlil also.

CHAPTER FIFTY-ONE

Abraham

*W*hat happened after the catastrophe and ruination that fell upon Sumer? Despite his murderous rage at the failure of his master plan, Enlil began to implement his fall-back strategy without delay. In fact, to this end, Enlil and Noah carefully preserved the secret of the dispersal of the white powder upon the cataclysmic ray which had destroyed Sumer. Marduk, in consultation with Enlil, moved Babel away from the convulsions taking place in the environs of Ur, and re-established it further west as Babylon. The name 'Babylon' means the 'Temple' or 'Birth-Place of the True Father', for Enki and his wives had founded it as a centre of the Oannes teachings. Now that it had been destroyed and had fallen into Enlil's power, the reinstatement of its name gave it a sinister, menacing twist, whose nightmarish reversal both Marduk and Enlil celebrated.

Enlil, meanwhile, began to pay court to a man from an important dynasty of Ur who happened to be a very good friend of King Shem's – Abraham. Abraham's name at this time was Avram ('he who possesses ram, or high knowledge').[1] King Shem, or Shulgi, we remember, had been devoted to Enki until his father Noah's allegiance had wavered, and finally rejected Enki in favour of Enlil. It was at this point that Avram too changed sides, as King Shulgi was his best friend and mentor.

Avram, a young and idealistic man, passionate yet serene, deeply devout and possessing unusual spiritual understanding, as his name implies, would not easily have been swayed from his former convictions, except for one impacting factor which influenced him deeply. King Shulgi had perished in the terrible ructions that had shaken Babel. Moreover, he had died in Avram's arms.

The king had implored Avram to remember their many cherished conversations by starlight, and to hold dear the ideal which had formulated between them, arising from their lengthy ardent discourses. Both young men were highly intelligent, cultured individuals of advanced education. They practised astronomy and stargazing, and there was nothing these devoted students of the stars loved better than to sit together in the cool of the eastern evenings, poised in the balm and delight of their friendship, stargazing and discussing the meaning of life far into the night.

Shulgi was animated, strident, inspired. Avram was calm and reflective, answering his friend's eloquent arguments with a philosophical gravity and insight which lent an air of spiritual discovery and wonder to their conversations, as though they advanced deep into the marvels of the universe and took radiant flight from the earth. Shulgi's downfall was his mental arrogance, which eventually led him via a disastrous route. Avram's mistake lay in his willingness to capitulate to his friend's ideas of wisdom, which in reality were inferior to his own.

They had conceived the idea of the One God between them. This was in fact Enki's profoundest teaching, which the young men had recently begun to absorb, having now reached the highest degree of learning. Because of the situation pertaining throughout Sumer whereby Enlil was always an ever present threat, the teachings concerning Tiâmat had to be kept concealed as the secret wisdom of a mystery school.

It was these teachings that the young men now embarked upon, drawing their conclusions via the inspiration of the stars, wherewith they experienced intimations of spiritual fusion with the Supreme Being, and the vast cosmic spaces seemed brilliant with intense flashes of communion from centres of exalted intelligence.

When Shulgi fell victim to Enlil's enticements and turned away from Enki and the teachings of his temple, he began to speak to Avram of Enlil as the reflection of the One God, the visible manifestation of the God Most High, whose impalpable presence they had thrilled to in devotion, discovery and spiritual stimulation throughout the peaceful watches of the night, their inner vision nurtured in the inspired bosom of their friendship.

The idea of Enlil as this God Most High troubled Avram, because such an interpretation of spiritual reality was not what he felt he had embraced at the highest point of their exploratory conversations. But it was the reality which Shulgi, the fine, handsome, learned king, his cherished friend, was beginning to espouse; and Avram was moved by the king's new passion. There was in his own family some ancient allegiance to Enlil, stemming from antiquity when several of his ancestors dwelt in the land of Nodh (afterwards called Canaan), and this was another reason why Avram listened sympathetically to the king's ideas.

When Shulgi died in the disaster which overtook Babel, his last words were to Avram. The king begged Avram to continue to honour the One God, Enlil, in memory of their friendship. He perished soon afterwards, in the embrace of Avram, who was profoundly grief-stricken by his loss. Avram left Ur with his father Terah and other members of his family in about 1960 BC, which was when the city, in company with the rest of Sumer, fell to invaders, directly after the Babel holocaust.

For several years he sheltered in the city of Haran, until Enlil was ready to make an onslaught on the land of Cain, now known as Canaan. By this time, Avram had been his loyal subject for some years, and was ready to do his bidding. Enlil called him, and instructed him to go into Canaan with his kinsman Lot. Enlil was very keen to penetrate the fastnesses of Canaan because, with Noah's help, he was able to deduce that after the fall of Ur, Tiâmat had sealed the remaining Grail energies within the special point of Canaan that would later be known as Jerusalem, where a mystical temple dwelt in the ethers. This had always been a holy place, but now that it had replaced Ur as the eastern major arm of the Grail, it was sacrosanct indeed, and consequently very powerful. It was in Canaan that the revered priest-king Melchizedek anointed Avram as a priest-king in his own right after he had driven several enemies from Canaan and achieved a military victory.

Melchizedek was older than Avram, and was a particular friend of Terah, Avram's father. He had familial connections with the great dynasty of Ur from which Terah and Avram had descended. It was this dynasty which Enlil had targeted from the start, although he had made very limited headway. However, through cunning, lies and misrepresentation (mind control was one of his perfected techniques), he managed to squeeze a foot through the door of their acceptance. He had encountered far greater problems with Avram, his main quarry from the beginning; but Shulgi won the day for him at the eleventh hour, and now Avram had been drawn satisfactorily under his influence.

Melchizedek shared Avram's deep spirituality and philosophical insight. A profound and important friendship evolved between them after Shulgi's death, and in many ways the solemn, fatherly Melchizedek, although very different from Shulgi, assumed the late king's place in Avram's affections. To them, Enlil was the Most High God, the supreme deity.

The term 'Most High' is interesting, because it tells us that both Melchizedek and Avram were perfectly aware that there were other gods. If one god is the 'Most High', then there have to be other, lower, gods to whom comparison can be made.

This was a secret trouble in their hearts. Both of them conceived of a Divine Being utterly remote from the political manoeuvrings of the God-Headed people, however godlike they appeared to ordinary mortals.

Both men were of uncommon spiritual bearing. They yearned after the exalted, ineffable nature of the true God, and very often they found her, and directed their actions and values by her moral compass. Moreover, Enki would appear to them in various guises, usually as a simple golden light of purest radiance, and undertake to steer them by the true stars, whose mystical light resonated with the fountain of spiritual brightness springing like a wonder deep in their hearts. This, they knew, was the word of God.

The problem was that Enlil, too clever and guileful to try to overturn all that flowed to them from an incomparably higher source than himself, instead used their confusion to his advantage. He tricked them into thinking that everything they received came to them from him, using many devices to secure his aim. It was very difficult for Avram and Melchizedek to differentiate between the sublime presence of God (what we might understand as the consciousness of Tiâmat-Oannes), and the point where, on their journey from the highest peak of their perception back down to the mundane material plane, they were hijacked by Enlil along the way.

In the end, their ability to discriminate became thoroughly undermined because of the influences of the white and the red powder, and they failed utterly to recognise when they were gazing into the eternal depths of the hallowed eye of God, and when the glaring eyeball of Enlil monopolised their perception!

Likewise, in the Bible, we are given an undifferentiated body of text which one moment flowers exquisitely into the discourse of most holy reverie, and in the next is ranting and stamping with Rumpel-stilts-ken-like rage in an outburst which is unadulterated, unexpurgated Enlil! This shows us that the Bible is indeed a rendition of the false Emerald Tablet – a document coursing with sublime truth often distorted and diverted by Enlil's cunning powers of derangement.

Enlil remained nervous about Melchizedek and Avram's absolute allegiance to him. Their heartfelt response to Enki made him very jumpy, even if he knew how to prevent them from distinguishing his brother's voice from his own. Enlil was careful to nurture that revulsion concerning the ingestion of purified menstrual blood which to some degree he had already established within the two men, and in fact he issued a decree to his followers, headed by Avram, that blood must definitely *not* be ingested from then on, declaring that all blood belonged to him in a blatant move to prevent any further consumption of either the Star Fire or its earthly counterpart.

Enlil was very careful, however, to ensure that his people did not imagine that, just because he was banning the ingestion of blood, he wanted them to become vegetarian. That would not do at all, because the cruelty meted out to animals by their human brethren was one of Enlil's main sources of supply as far as negative karma was concerned. The horror of suffering that arose from it also fed the 'greys', the human extraterrestrials whom Annum controlled and who were working on his behalf to restore the Naphidem. The terrible suffering of animals (which, because of outrageous intensive farming methods, is even worse today) provided him with a rich fund of this lovely negative karma, which he could endlessly utilise to make humanity suffer and to draw the chains engraved with his name which bound them so mercilessly, tighter and ever tighter.

Moreover, the indifference to animal suffering practised by the majority of human beings led directly to an appalling indifference to human suffering, which was even better, because it provided further choice grist to his mill.

Enlil knew well the great spiritual law which decrees that as long as animals are abused and slaughtered wilfully by the hand of humanity, there will be warring and bloodshed between its members upon the earth. Enlil, therefore, breathed forth an influence through the ethers which ensured that vegetarians would be mocked and despised, and even considered perverted and evil (vegetarians became known as those who partook of the 'Devil's banquet', according to the Christian Church), attitudes which in some quarters appear to have remained with our societies to the present era.

Enki's adherents strove to practise harmlessness, which of course included vegetarianism, and so Enlil did all he could to promote the idea that such behaviour was 'unmanly'.

Tutored by Enlil, all things feminine gradually became suspect to Melchizedek and Avram. They seemed sinister, threatening, spooky, and superstitiously horrid. Feminine ritual was associated with ceremonies dedicated to the sun and the moon, which they were taught to consider as anathema. After the initiation rites conducted by Melchizedek, (which involved the ingestion of the red and the white powder), Avram was renamed Abraham ('he' – or 'the Father' or 'Supreme One' – 'who holds the powers of Ham') by Enlil. Abraham was informed that everything that Ham and his son Canaan had 'purloined' from Enlil's followers – the wisdom, the knowledge, the power of the secret Tablet – was now his, by divine right.

Enlil then gave the false Emerald Tablet, or rather Ham's edited version of it, into Abraham's keeping.

NOTE

1 Some traditions tell of the God of Righteousness as bearing the name of 'Brahm' among the Near and Middle Eastern civilisations of Abraham's time. The name is interchangeable with 'ram', as both designations have the same meaning, and relate to the mysteries of the Temple of Enki, or Oannes, as he was also known. Both references are to Masda (Enki), the God of Light, and both passed into the majestic civilisation of the sub-continent of India, where Brahma, Rama and the great fish-man god Vishnu enshrined a mystical understanding of the Divine.

CHAPTER FIFTY-TWO

The False and the True Covenant

The famous Covenant that Jehovah made with Abraham occurred after an earlier Covenant which was made in the land of Canaan (formerly called the Land of Nodh and the Land of Cain) between King Ur-baba (Canaan, Ham's son) and Tiâmat.

The king was deeply troubled concerning the predicament of his beloved friend Avram. Once, King Shulgi, Avram and he had been the best of friends, enjoying a true spiritual intimacy and a vibrant alignment of vision and purpose. When Ur-baba (Canaan) had escaped into the land of Cain, he had hoped that Avram might follow him into exile. Somehow, he had felt certain that Avram would not be seduced by Shulgi's treachery to the temple of Enki, Lilith and Nin-khursag with its teachings on the true God, and to the great ancestors, Cain and Luluwa.

Canaan had been shocked, and, in a sense, heartbroken, when news of Avram's changed loyalties reached him from over the border. Avram and he were cousins as well as close friends, and they had spent many childhood hours together in the court of Ur. Canaan had always believed that there was an unspoken understanding between Avram and himself that Shulgi, although cultivated, eloquent and assured, was the least enlightened of the three friends. When Canaan's supporters in the land of Cain rose up in anger against his banishment (which had been formerly announced by King Shulgi, on Enlil's command), intending to march on Babylon and seize it from the thieving hands of Shulgi (Shem), Canaan's secret hope was that Avram might be rescued from his clutches.

After the fall of Babylon (renamed Babel by Shulgi and Enlil until Marduk moved it westwards and reinstated its former name), Canaan tried on several occasions to make contact with Avram in Haran, where he had escaped with his father. Avram shunned his attempts each time, and when, several years later,

Avram emigrated to the land of Canaan (now named after Babylon's exiled king), Canaan again tried to approach him, with offers of renewed friendship and coop- eration between their respective communities. Canaan's emissary returned with bad news, however. Avram still did not wish to receive him. This was in spite of the fact that Avram had decided to establish himself and his followers in the land of Canaan, not only because of Enlil's promptings, but also because Avram was confident that Canaan would vouch for him and protect him from those in the land who might have defamed him or risen up against him because of his close links with King Shulgi.

Canaan (King Ur-baba), a loyal friend who felt attachments deeply, took his grief to the temple of Enki. He loved Avram as a brother, he lamented to the regal serpent-man and his noble consorts, who appeared consolingly by his side. Now Avram had come into his own land, the land of Canaan, surely the perfect opportunity presented itself for them to come together and oust the curse of Enlil, whose malevolence had left Sumer in smoking ruins, and who would do the same to the entire world, if (perhaps when) he could? Was this not his own mission as a move against Enlil, Canaan asked passionately – to reunite with his dear friend, with whom he had always seen eye to eye and heart to heart, and remove the veils from his eyes? Could not Enki and his consorts do something to bring this about? It was at this point that Enki, Nin-khursag and Lilith gently led Canaan into the holy of holies, the communion chamber where he could hear Tiâmat's voice.

Tiâmat told Canaan that Avram must be allowed to pursue his own path. He had a great work to do for her, she explained, and it was imperative that Canaan should give him every support and blessing, albeit at a distance, even though, in this life, they would never be united in brotherhood again. It was a terrible sacrifice for Canaan's fond heart, but she asked it of him for the sake of the greater good.

She further explained that Avram, now Abraham, would be the father of nations, and that these nations would give rise to three great religions which would shape the world. Canaan was quite right; Enlil had every intention of destroying humanity and the planet, and he had wrested a great secret, a mighty wisdom from Ur and its Grail energies, in pursuit of this goal. In his perversion of this energy, which had already taken place, a weapon had fallen into his hands which would enable him to fulfil his desire. The only way to save the world now was to *contain* his death energies.

Abraham and his wife Sarah, Tiâmat revealed to him, were the designated couple for this gargantuan task. Of the nations which would come forth from Abraham, the Hebrew race would establish itself first, under his aegis (this process had already begun). They were the chosen people, who would bear Enlil forth into the wider world and down the centuries – for he *must* be thus born forth, there was no way to avoid this now that he had become so powerful – and whose inherent national fortitude would prevent him from destroying the world. They would follow him, they would believe in him and, partially, do his will; but they would also throw a powerfully protective forcefield around his most lethal intentions.

Abraham had been deemed fit for this Atlas-like task because of the depth of his spirituality and vision, and because his heart was pierced with strength and verity as if with a keen and true sword.

He and his people would bear this burden to the very end – until all the world was ready to rise up as one and overcome Enlil with the power of the spirit, released and nurtured by the power of the Grail – the only means that would overcome him now that he wielded the power of the reverse-spin Grail: the false Grail.

Yes, Enlil would create a culture and a founding religion that bore his stamp – but the Hebrews would have the strength to contain his hostile energies within a circle of the true God-forces. They would have the potency of spirit to reach up to the spiritual heights beyond Enlil, despite the very worst he could do, and keep his influences and intentions circumscribed within that circle. This great feat of courage required the Jewish people themselves to guard the perimeters of the circle, and dwell in the confusion of darkness and struggling light therein, in order to contain Enlil successfully and absolutely.

A terrible sacrificial price would be exacted in that Enlil's reverse-spin death energies would attract appalling suffering and persecution to the Jewish race, and condemn it to a life of wandering and rejection. The Jewish nation would finally be led back to Canaan, and it would be here, in this very special land containing the Grail mysteries, that a vital choice would be made between the false Grail and the true.

Tiâmat further explained that the land of Canaan would be the birthplace and the homeland of this Hebrew nation, just as it was the birthplace and the homeland of Canaan's followers, originally of the tribe who gathered around and descended from Cain and Luluwa. As Abraham and Canaan themselves were of the same blood and the dearest of friends, except that they had been separated by the stupor and confusion of the senses and perception that Enlil inflicted upon his followers, so would there exist a special brotherhood between the two peoples in Canaan – the Canaanites and the Hebrews.

And just as Abraham and Canaan had been split asunder and falsely cast into the role of mutual enmity by Enlil, so would the Hebrews and the Canaanites eventually be led to despise one another until the day came when Enlil's influences would finally be overthrown. Meanwhile, Tiâmat reiterated her desire that Canaan should bless the endeavours of Abraham as he set out on his difficult and dangerous mission, and keep alive within his own people an awareness of their great destiny.

Canaan, moved in his spirit, accepted all of Tiâmat's decrees; and she made a Covenant with him there on that day, promising the stewardship of the mysteries of the land of Canaan for his people and for Abraham's people and that the rift between them should be healed. She formally conferred on him guardianship of the Grail and sealed her promise once more with the arc of the rainbow.

At the point of the first Covenant with Abraham, however, the concept of the arc was represented simply enough by a six-branched candlestick consisting of seven candleholders. The tabernacle of the first Covenant contained this candlestick, and opposite it, a table displaying the infamous shewbread. The tabernacle was an ideogram of Abraham's deeper soul, of the soul of his future people and the circle of containment in which they would hold the destructive potencies of Enlil. The candlestick equates with the seven rays of the rainbow and the seven chakras of the soul. It is Tiâmat's sign – the arc or Ark. The shewbread, sign of Enlil and the oppositional power of the false Grail, must first be overcome before freedom for Abraham's people could be obtained. The simple tent and imagery were chosen by Abraham, whose soul was deeply aware of spiritual truth, although his intellect and senses hid it from his everyday understanding.

Enlil remained nervous about Melchizedek and Abraham's undivided loyalty to him. For the time being it was not in doubt, but Enlil set about removing every threat to it with a paranoid savagery. He could not forget Attaba and Ga-nadinur's 'disobedience' to him, and he was not going to be caught out again. Enlil, as a final seal of assurance, eventually demanded that Abraham should sacrifice Isaac to him. This was certainly a test of Abraham's allegiance, as the Old Testament records, but in fact Enlil was in deadly earnest concerning the murder of Isaac. (We must make clear that Enlil was indeed a 'god' who demanded human sacrifices, as the terrible propitiatory rites of the Mayans and the Aztecs, and many other tribes around the world whose fearsome godhead equates with Enlil – that dark power of destruction which would not leave them alone until they had mollified his menace with acts of extreme cruelty – confirm. We also ought to clarify that Enlil's presence within these ancient tribes is not merely a matter of recognition through the perpetration of the deeds he inspired, but exists via named entities which scholarship acknowledges are the same 'mythological' being as the Sumerian Enlil.)

Fortunately, before Abraham carried out his intended deed, which would have entrenched him like a helpless puppet under Enlil's dominance, without any further power of containment of his death energies, Enki answered the agony in Abraham's soul and took the form of a ram to stand in Isaac's stead as sacrifice. The sacrifice of this 'ram' to Enlil is hugely significant ('ram' meaning 'one who possesses the highest degree of knowledge'). When Abraham sacrificed the 'ram', he sacrificed himself instead of his son. By this act he pledged deep within his soul that, in order ultimately to save the Emerald Table (in one sense, the 'ram' or 'Ham' – the 'I Am'), and therefore humanity, from Enlil, he would willingly sacrifice his own 'ram' or access to it, and thus be led by a guide and a route that would burden him.

Enki discouraged animal sacrifices as a cruel and degenerate habit, but Enlil absolutely insisted upon them, and thus they could not be avoided by his followers. Enki's act, and Abraham's enlightened response to it, prevented the Hebrews from following a route which would have led quickly to the ripe fruition of Enlil's plans.

From the moment that Abraham happened upon the ram tangled in the bush, he dispensed with the idea of human sacrifice. He thought, of course, that Enki's voice was Enlil's.

Enlil blamed Enki entirely for this intervention. He smouldered, and cursed his brother, but yet was satisfied that Abraham remained faithful to himself, the 'Most High'. Nevertheless, once Abraham had weighed the judgment required of him in the balance of his soul and had given his answer in Enki's favour, Enlil, in this crucial matter at least, was henceforth rendered powerless to force his hand.

CHAPTER FIFTY-THREE

Sodom and Gomorrah

*T*o further secure his man, Enlil needed to do something about the city states of Sodom and Gomorrah. His problem was that these twin cities harboured a culture of enlightenment that was anathema to him and the principles he strove to make fundamental in the lives and psyches of humanity so that his plan of annihilation could move forward unhindered. To make matters worse, both cities now contained many refugees from the remains of Sumer, particularly from the all-important Ur, whose great dynasty had fathered Abraham.

Many mystics and philosophers, many priests of Enki and Nin-khursag, many men and women of science and the arts had congregated within these two city states to form a body of ancient wisdom and progressive knowledge that was quickening with new life and growth. This constituted a real threat to Abraham and Melchizedek's stance as his supporters. Enlil knew all too well that neither of the two men was hostile to these innovative influences, and he remained in terror in case they should be seduced by them. He had already, to undermine the problem cities, inflated the warring situation whereby kings from surrounding states had marched against Sodom and Gomorrah and deposed their kings, which had also presented itself as a convenient opportunity for him to manoeuvre Abraham into winning honour and glory as a chieftain.

Unfortunately for Enlil, the twin cities and the dynamics of their culture had survived these incursions intact. He continued to experience a preponderance of difficulties in effectively stalling the momentum of the intellectual and spiritual movement which was advancing with such brilliance and vigour from within their joint citadels. He saw that decisive action must be taken, and to this end he informed Abraham that he intended to destroy the two cities, as they were both dens of iniquity.

Abraham was deeply shocked, and begged for mercy on their behalf. He implored Enlil to consider the 'good men' within Sodom and Gomorrah (the very group who were rattling Enlil's cage so thoroughly). Enlil's reply to this plea can only be interpreted as a declaration to prove that there were no 'good men' in the city, or at least that there were fewer than five, because the Bible account tells us that he agreed not to destroy the cities if five 'good men' could be found therein. He certainly did go on to destroy both of them, so students of the Bible are left with the impression that Enlil conclusively proved his point that, in actual fact, these 'good men' whom Abraham was so anxious to save were not good at all. How did he do this?

There can be little doubt that Enlil called on Marduk and the Naphidem to do their worst within the two cities. We see the development of a typically Naphidem-inspired situation in a disturbing story concerning Lot and the arrival of two angels in his home. Hearing of the arrival of the strangers, a large group of men of Sodom gathered outside Lot's door and demanded with menaces that the visitors be delivered into their hands for the purpose of homosexual gang rape. The story progresses further into horror to relate that Lot offered up his two daughters in the angels' stead (we think they presented themselves in sacrifice), but the crowd refused this propitiation and Lot himself was set upon and almost dragged into the nightmarish fray before managing to disengage himself and bar the door against the demoniacal mob.

Our source informs us that the two strangers were not angels, but members of the God-Headed people who had used the remnant of the Grail energies in a highly specialised way to materialise their bodies for a short time upon the earth plane (this process was no longer straightforward, as was previously the case). They hailed from the eastern dimension where Enki, Nin-khursag, Lilith and a few other members of the Eden community connected with these Leaders of Light, had retreated after the fall of Sumer. They had come on a special mission: to warn Lot (Abraham's kinsman) and his family that Sodom and Gomorrah were about to be devastated by Enlil via a deadly weapon and that they must flee at the earliest opportunity. They must protect themselves from the fall-out of this blast, which incorporated the need for a shielding of consciousness as well as of the body. They must not look back, even when they were safely removed from the city boundaries, or the destruction of the lethal weapon would fall upon them, for its influences made entry through the eyes.

The two God-Headed men had a particular job to do once the cities had been hit. It was their duty to help Enki and his consorts once more to shut down the ray upon which Noah and Enlil were still able to operate their prized weapon, and to seal and purify the entire area with salt, which is both an earthly and a magical substance with reflecting crystals which countered the energies in the glassy substance that the ray-gun created in the administering of its deadly work. The reason that salt would be necessary as a sealing agent after the destruction of Sodom and Gomorrah, and was unnecessary after the ruination of Sumer (where the crystals in sand sufficed), was because Noah and Enlil had been busy refining the science of their death-ray, and had managed to make it even more deadly. Their express intention was to poison the earth and to permanently destroy a wide area of it, especially incorporating what would come to be known as Jerusalem and Palestine.

The hideous commotion at Lot's door was a Naphidem-influenced group which, although involving a tiny minority, had overrun the two cities and had finally done its designated work by demonstrating to Lot and Abraham (who worked together in their spiritual mission) that the cities 'truly' were infested with a maniacal evil. This group, influenced by Marduk and Enlil, certainly were in pursuit of the two God-Headed 'angels', because they were Enki's envoys. Had they been subjected to battery and sexual assault before they could etherealise their bodies and escape, the resultant trauma and bodily disablement would have prevented them from carrying out their vital task, and the highly toxic and damaging effects of the enweaponed white powder might have caused huge tracts of the planet's surface to be uninhabitable for thousands of years to come.

Due to this terrible experience of the ravening Naphidem-influenced group, Lot and Abraham were convinced that the destruction of the cities was a 'righteous' act, and Enlil saved face and kept his men. Enlil's fate hung in the balance that night in Sodom. Had Lot and Abraham (and, through them, Melchizedek) not been convinced of Enlil's true judgment in devastating the cities, they would have heeded the other warning that came to them with the counsel of the 'angels' that the cities were to be destroyed – that Enlil was dangerous and ill-willed towards the human race. After the visit of the mob, however, Enlil was able to put a very different construction on his decision to use weapons of mass destruction, and Abraham and Lot's understanding of Enki remained obscured and confused. For instance, they assumed that the two members of the former Edenic community who warned them against a Lord of Darkness who 'stood behind' Enlil were referring to a cosmic entity who was actually working against, rather than with, Enlil.

Perhaps it was fortuitous that this was the case, because it was essential that Enlil's insidious influences should remain firmly encircled by the spiritual strength of the Hebrews. Otherwise, our planet may not have survived.

As events transpired, Lot's wife forgot to abide by the angels' advice. She looked back, just once, when she calculated that the little fleeing party had reached a safe distance, and made visual contact with the laser upon which the disseminated white powder was travelling to its target. She was immediately desiccated and crystallised. Enki's envoys encrusted her with salt, fulfilling the same purpose as that for which the devastated cities were packed with salt. Eventually, the Dead Sea claimed them, and the entire area, the lowest point on the earth's surface, became a strange, desolate, haunted place, a 'dead zone', rich only in supplies of pitch, a substance traditionally associated with all things demonic.

Interestingly, this was the location where the Essenes established themselves in later years, although we believe that there was a mystic brotherhood there (of both men and women) even prior to Abraham's time. The lost cities of Sodom and Gomorrah have apparently been discovered on the bed of the Dead Sea. Problems between Jordan and Israel have so far prevented further explorations from proceeding, but if future excavations should take place, it is likely that these two intriguing enigmas would surrender many mysteries. It seems as if there was an alignment with this point on the earth's surface and the place within the earth (which was an ethereal dimension even though it actually existed in the bowels of the planet) where Enlil, his followers, and a number of the Naphidem who at the time of their banishment had managed to escape into the ground, had established themselves when Tiâmat trapped them in the lower earth planes.

There is no doubt that this lowest earthly site was actually a profoundly sacred and powerful interface between above and below, which is why Enlil and the Naphidem settled there. Their presence made it into a wasteland; and the famous esoteric maxim 'As above, so below', applied in weird and unsettling context in this particular application of its meaning.

Enlil and Noah by no means gave up their precious weapon when Enki and his messengers disabled it for the second time. They were determined to develop it to its highest potential, whereby it would (they trusted) one day destroy the world. (Nuclear warheads were created via an escaped strand of this false Grail knowledge, but are not nearly so dangerous as Noah's ray, which has the potential to obliterate all life on earth for ever.) They had already come on apace, as they were piecing together a technique to allow them to make the collective mind of humanity into one great weapon of mass destruction.

Enki had again barred their way, but they would continue with their schemes nonetheless.

CHAPTER FIFTY-FOUR

Enlil's Darkest Secrets

*I*t is time to reveal exactly what Enlil and his associates have done to planet earth. There is no need to worry about the implications of this revelation, because, as we shall disclose, Tiâmat has ensured that everything is in place to counteract and wholly heal the situation, as long as her divine remedy is in accordance with our free-will choice. We are fully confident that there will be sufficient people across the globe who will pledge their allegiance to the forces of the 'one true light' for human free will to properly align itself with this mighty act of divine healing. The ascended master, White Eagle, assures us that 'humanity is coming on in leaps and bounds!'

Our first revelation is that Enlil, with his great accomplice, Zi-u-sudra, has enclosed the earth in a sinister ring of glassy, invisible substance which has been manufactured from his baleful white powder.

It exists in the atmosphere of our planet, and it filters the sunlight, and the spiritual power within the sunlight, so that the *ayin*, the power of God-consciousness residing in our hearts which is our vision of truth, is obstructed. It is not possible to distort this godly power itself, of course, but it is certainly possible to distort and throw off course the awareness within the human soul which accesses it and would normally become consummate with it. This is precisely the function of the false ring (the ring made of the sham *shem*).

The false ring, composed of a refined glass which exists as imperceptible crystals in earth's atmosphere, is actually a mirror. And, looking into the mirror, humanity walking the earth below constantly receives and perceptually ingests the bogus, misleading images that the false mirror throws off, in its power of distortion, confusion and corruption, so that we see things, as it were, the wrong way round. We are plunged within the realm of our perception straight into a topsy-turvy, back-to-front, Alice-in-Wonderland world.

It is possible to rise above this distortion, confusion and corruption, of course, and to see what we should see with our inner vision, our inner *ayin*; the pristine sunlight is eternally pure and undefiled, and can strike our true centre of inner or heart-vision unaffected by Enlil's sinister filter. But it is very difficult and can be psychically exhausting, even traumatic, to maintain steadily and constantly the clear and unsullied truth of the vision of the *ayin* within. The pull of the false reflection hauls us back into its tyranny and we fear to break away entirely.

It was for this purpose – the creation and maintenance of the false ring around the earth, in the upper reaches of its atmosphere – that Enlil commanded his slaves (those on earth who fell completely under his dominion) to manufacture vast quantities of the *shem* or white powder – the false communion bread. It was dispersed into the atmosphere via the malignant ray that Enlil and Noah had used to destroy Sumer, and Sodom and Gomorrah.

Whilst I was visiting an ancient church with Michael Revill, he pointed out the dull, opaque appearance of the stained glass windows from its exterior. We had just been enjoying the mysterious beauty of the glass, with its hallowed lights, like secret treasure or jewelled casements onto the bright dimensions of spiritual worlds, from within the church.

Michael told me that medieval stained glass could be identified by its opaqueness from outside the building in which it was set. This seemed an important point to ponder, and I was struck by the closed and sealed appearance of the windows from outside the church, as if they did indeed express an intention of non-admittance. Shortly afterwards, Margaret Bailey and I learned that this medieval glass was in fact specially conditioned, by alchemical means, to keep out certain sinister elements of the daylight from the sanctuary of the interior of churches and cathedrals, not only to protect the congregation, but also because the locations of such churches were deeply sacred, holy sites far, far older than Christianity, which needed spiritual and physical protection from Enlil's deadly, distorting mirror and its saturated impregnation of malicious intent.

The secret in the glass of the medieval churches and cathedrals which were financed and constructed mainly throughout the twelfth century by the Knights Templar was a pure and beautiful one, mystical and imponderably ancient. Certain branches of alchemical science were used to support and facilitate this divine secret process, but its real application relied on the dispensation of the Holy Breath, the Holy Spirit or Paraclete, which was given in this instance through the art of glass blowing.

The liquid glass was blown into shape by means of tubes. The master craftsmen within the Templar brotherhood used their breath to blow form into the glass, which then crystallised. This puts us in mind of the House of Shimtî, where Nin-khursag, through communion with Tiâmat, provided the Holy Breath to breathe life into human creation, whereupon Enki and she would use their divinely bestowed 'craft' (the craft of crystallisation of form, a Saturnine dispensation) to accommodate, contain and seal the creational essence breathed forth by God.

(Considering Saturn, we might think of the great god Pan, who is a symbol of Father Saturn, blowing with gentle reverence down his magical 'Pan-pipes', and of the crystallisation that occurs throughout the myriad forms of Creation as he does so.)

Through an alchemical method of treating gold and other noble metals, which is akin to creating the negative white powder but produces utterly different results, the liquid metal was transformed into glass. The glass would exhibit a certain hue and quality according to the particular metal used to create it. However, there is a 'missing ingredient' to the process outlined above. We do not pretend to fully understand what it is in all its aspects, but we shall endeavour to share with you what we have been shown in relation to it.

The alchemical procedure via which the glass was made causes 44 per cent of the weight of the metal subject to it, ultimately to disappear and transfigure into vivid white light. It is this light which reappears as the pure and lovely illumination, so mysterious to behold, within medieval coloured glass. When Enlil manufactured the *shem-an-na*, the metals he used were subject to the same ultimate weight loss due to the same dramatic transfiguration into brilliant white light. What, then, was the difference between the two procedures?

The huge differential was the Holy Breath, called *Spiritus Mundi*, 'the breath of the universe', by the Knights Templar. The *Spiritus Mundi* supplied the means of discernment whereby the spiritual student was enabled to distinguish between the true and the false light. The dramatic burst of brilliant white light occurred in both the false, reverse-spin, alchemical method (Enlil's way), and the true alchemical method of pure ascension (Enki's way).

No white or red powder or drug-like substance was created by Enki's way, but the magical, luminous glass, of a depth and beauty of translucency and colour almost synonymous with spiritual vision, most certainly was. Enki's way, significantly, involved breathing in, and thereafter breathing out, the pure white light of the Godhead – the spiritual starlight which makes us Pendragons.

Other wonders were also created by this pure method. Part of the teaching vision given for our interpretation in explanation of Enki's way was a tower of golden coins which were seen as spinning disks, impervious to gravity. From this, we deduce that the anti-gravitational field which produced this effect was created by the godly, forward or clockwise spin of the atoms of gold used by the Master Craftsmen (more properly, Craftspeople, for of course women were also involved) in their Great Work (the esoteric term for the art of alchemy). This positive spin, in overcoming earth's gravity, would reproduce conditions which were attuned to the verity of the true Grail, the path from earth to heaven via spiritual ascension. Enlil's way, whereby the reverse-spin atoms of noble metals are used, created by superimposed and malevolent distortion, draws the unfortunate student onto the path of false ascension – the ascension of the mind, with all its attendant dangers and proclivity for disastrous choices. The anti-gravitational field thus created is dark and sinister – veritably the arena of the horrifying Naphidem.

We reiterate that in these methods of creating the false and the true Grail, the deciding factor between the two was the use of the breath, and of pure spiritual attunement and vision. Breath was used in both procedures. In the first, it was just 'hot air', the inflation of the bellows of the lower self, the self-seeking and self-serving lower dragon, grasping hotly after creational knowledge in order to gain personal power.

This breath was Enlil's, and he used the terrible secret of the reversed Holy Breath, or the power of the 'reversed winds' (we remember that this was exactly how Marduk had 'slain' Tiâmat and destroyed the Holy Grail) to turn the gold into a physical form of diabolical force. In the dimension in which he waited, Enlil breathed this deathly breath into the atoms of the highward-spinning gold as he drew it in. It missed its mark. It seemed to ascend, but only ascended into Enlil's sinister den. It returned to earth as the reverse-spin gold, now permanently transformed into a white powder.

Of course, because its manufacturers are not working specifically for Enlil, today's method of producing the white powder does not give Enlil such direct access to it, and it is transformed into a physical powder whose application conveys several health benefits. It is not the same substance as the false communion bread. Nevertheless, if it is taken as an artificial means of stimulating the head chakras (the 'precious Stone' in the head), severely unhelpful effects are produced which actually work against the process of true ascension. As its discoverer, nicknamed 'Mr Material', proclaims via the ancient system of clue-giving enshrined in nomenclature, let us confine it strictly to the material level of life!

In the second method of alchemical creation, Enki's way, the breath used was the aspiring, Tiâmat-centred, Holy Breath of Divine Love – the breath of the Pendragon. When the white light burst forth, its essence, due to the infusion of the Holy Breath, was of the light of the Godhead; the activated, God-attuned heart of the alchemist used it to set alight the Stone of Ascension in the brain. It seems that music and colour were an integral part of this process.

We have been given to understand that, therefore, human spiritual consciousness directly impacted upon the alchemical procedure and its resultant creations.

They were an example of exalted human consciousness expressing itself, through the giving forth of Divine Love from the heart, in an act of consummation with physical Creation. In other words, they were demonstrations of genuine

Master Craftsmanship. They fulfilled the will of Tiâmat-Oannes in that within them, they expressed the true plan for Creation: that it would realise itself and attain perfection through the direct impact of human, God-attuned, spiritual consciousness. It is as if, in Creation today, God faithfully does Her-His part, but we, in our confused blindness, ignorance and self-will, are stubbornly refusing to do our part. The whole purpose of physical creation seems to be to inspire and empower us to co-create with God in every moment of our lives. When we become properly aware of this, we can begin to learn the true alchemy of life.

Enlil's full repertoire of dark secrets will be revealed in due course, but we would emphasise meanwhile the loveliness and delight of what Tiâmat has in store on earth for all her children, and the wonder of the beautiful secrets which also await revelation. Once we become properly aware of Enlil's shenanigans, we can remove his influences and advance towards our stupendous heritage.

As we know, Ham instigated the ancient Egyptian civilisation. Nimrod the Mighty, Ham's grandson, was the father of King Anedjib, pharaoh of the first Egyptian dynasty, which came into being about 3000 BC. Ham was consequently great-grandfather to the Egyptian nation, but there was another illustrious civilisation, hidden from history, to which both he and Nimrod were founding fathers, that arose in the Land of Cain after 1960 BC. Like twin towers these two glorious cultures rose to their apogee side by side. The Land of Cain was renamed Canaan, after its wise, Tiâmat-centred king, for Canaan (formerly King Ur-baba, son of Ham and deeply influenced by him), true to his forefathers, was a faithful son of Enki's temple.

It was in the advanced and enlightened Canaanite civilisation that Ham made greatest headway with his Zoroastrian teachings. They took root and flourished in Canaan and their purity and motive power was firmly established in this Grail-blessed land whose etheric forces shone invisibly, like a secret beacon, keeping Ham's teachings undefiled and on track long after the nation itself had fallen. Canaan and Egypt could be likened to two brothers, both of extraordinary merit, but Canaan much more spiritually illumined, artistically inspired and morally progressive than Egypt.

It was in Egypt that Ham, who had an extraordinarily extended lifespan, secreted the false Emerald Tablet after the fall of Babel. At this time, access to Eden was blocked to Enlil and his followers, and Eden itself became an inaccessible dimension. Before it was entirely sealed off by a backlash of the natural and spiritual laws that Enlil had broken, Nin-khursag used her *khu* power in extremity, risking considerable personal danger, to seize the malignant Tablet and give it into the safekeeping of Ham. By burying it in Egypt under the protection of a secret order of Enki's priests, Ham was able both to transcribe the genuine parts of it so that humanity could continue to develop and to flourish, and, vitally, to suppress and subdue its death energies, which would have become irreversibly lethal had it been left unattended in Eden.

However, because of its presence, dark powers made headway in Egypt. Over the next four hundred years (from about 1950 BC) Egypt flourished as an enlightened culture, but also as a culture driven by the need to conquer and to acquire material riches. Although Ham directed Egypt's course as well as that of Canaan, Canaan stood strong as the land of the true Grail, becoming the protective, knightly power that prevented Egypt from assuming the global dictatorship that Enlil craved.

For four hundred years the land of Canaan stood firm in its nobility and beauty, exercising the power of restraint over Egypt. Works of art and refined technologies of incomparable pulchritude issued from it to bless and inspire other nations. But Enlil's stirrings in Egypt could not be kept at bay. His own and Marduk's mighty desire to rid themselves of Canaan's thwarting stance reached fever pitch in its surreptitious expression of seditious engineering and manipulation. Eventually, through subversion and other effects of his white powder, a point was reached at which either Canaan or Egypt must fall.

Again, human will chose to preserve worldliness and reject spiritual light, and Egypt devoured Canaan, bringing blight to her own status in so doing, because she herself fell prey to the oppression of invaders from western Asia for almost a century afterwards. Canaan's history has been scrupulously removed from record by virtue of missing texts, purposely deleted from the chronicles of the period. These assiduous deletions pertaining to Canaan's glory and tragic fall were made simultaneously with the mutilations and erasures on artefacts depicting the reign of Akhenaten. They were perpetrated, as we shall see, for the sole purpose of strategically obscuring important Grail history and the huge significance of Canaan as the land of the Grail and guardian of the remnant of its forces.

After the fall of Canaan, Enlil was free to continue with his original plan to bring Egypt to the point where she would be ready to stage a global takeover. (This had been planned for Marduk's reinstated Babylon, but Enki and Nin-khursag prevented the city-state's rule from spreading across the world.)

We shall now advance in time to the coming of the great Akhenaten and his son Moses, the controversial pharaohs who very nearly managed to turn things around and virtually end Enlil's rule so that, when Jesus of Nazareth and Mary Magdalene eventually arrived on earth and brought forth Tamar, the entire planet would have ascended.

CHAPTER FIFTY-FIVE

Moses the John-Man

*T*he story of Moses occurred in a jewelled setting of prime women who power-fully steered his course. This radiant circle of women consisted of Tuya, his great-grandmother; Tiye, his grandmother; Nefertiti, his father's senior wife; Kiya, his mother; Meretaten or Miriam, his wife and half-sister; and Zipporah, his second wife. We will see how they nurtured and taught him, and fought for him valiantly, although the ultimate aim of his mission would fail.

The father of Moses was the son of Amenhotep III. Amenhotep III's ancestor, Ahmose (note *mose*, which has a root-meaning in Egyptian of 'bloodline-offspring-heir') was the king who had freed Egypt in 1550 BC from the degra-dation of a century of oppressive rule by the Asiatic tribe which had invaded after Canaan's defeat. Ahmose had initiated a line of mighty warrior-kings who comprised the famous 18th Dynasty. Amenhotep III's inheritance from his fore-fathers was impressive indeed. They had created an empire of incomparable afflu-ence and power extending deep into Africa and Asia, and although Egypt would rise again in greatness after a period of future decline, the reign of Amenhotep III represented her highest peak of authority.

Enlil had been busily feeding the pharaohs his white powder since Egypt's inception (the refined, technologically unsurpassed substance formulated with the help of Noah had replaced an earlier, cruder, experimental and less effective version), and he had great plans for Amenhotep III's inheritance of the cusp of Egypt's wave of supremacy.

He happily anticipated that this would be the point where a global takeover would gradually be secured, and the release of the Naphidem was set to follow. But, as usual, Enlil had reckoned without Enki and Nin-khursag.

Almost four hundred years before Amenhotep III's time (his regnal years were circa 1420–1355 BC), when the land of Canaan had risen to glory under the auspices of King Ur-baba (otherwise known as King Canaan), Joseph, he of the coat of many colours and son of Jacob who was also given the name Israel, entered the court of the pharaoh of Egypt after being sold into slavery by his brothers. Enki and Nin-khursag had come whispering to Jacob-Israel after his encounter with the angel-adorned ladder on the mountain, which was of course a vision of the Grail. Enki had struggled at Jacob's side all night as Jacob contested with Enlil, for the 'angel' to commence the famous struggle was indeed Enki's dark-hearted brother, who desperately wanted Jacob as his man. However, with Enki's help, Jacob had won the day and turned resolutely to the Temple of Tiâmat and Oannes. Guided by Enki, Jacob left Canaan with his extended family to settle in Egyptian Goshen in the Nile delta, for he needed to be in place to fulfil Enki's plan.

His son Joseph, also guided by Enki, interpreted the pharaoh's dreams and imparted much wisdom to him, proving himself a Merlinesque figure of knowledge, vision and prophecy. (We find invariably that an expression of Merlin precedes a manifestation of the Grail.) The pharaoh responded by heaping honours on him and protecting his father's people, the children of Israel (Jacob). Joseph was held in such awe and reverence that he actually founded his own dynasty within the court of Egypt, so that after him his descendants consecutively became the designated 'wise man' connected to each succeeding king, counselling him and his court.

The first-born son of the preceding Joseph bore his father's name, either in actuality or as a titular designation, and grew up to bear his status. This situation persisted for four hundred years, until the time of Amenhotep III.

During the reign of Amenhotep III's father, Tuthmosis IV, the great 'Joseph' of the court was Yusuf-Yuya (the hereditary Joseph's Egyptian name). He was born almost four hundred years after his legendary ancestor of the coat of many colours. Tuthmosis IV made Joseph or Yusuf-Yuya Grand Vizier or Governor of Egypt. Joseph or Yuya married Tuya (great-grandmother to Moses – again, note the hereditary name embedded in that of Tuthmosis), and they ruled Egypt together under the aegis of the pharaoh. Tuthmosis IV was withdrawing into spiritual contemplation and quietude and needed a wise and trustworthy deputy to deal with his worldly affairs. Yuya and his wife were obvious candidates; and indeed it was this inspired couple who guided and informed his inner contemplations, which comprised the teachings of Enki. His son, grandson and great-grandson would follow suit with incremental emphasis and intensity.

Tuya was the daughter of an important Egyptian priest. Although she was Egyptian and had a royal inheritance, she had an ancestor in Esau, Jacob's brother, and was of a line of women designated as 'the King's Ornament'. This enhancing quality referred to her status as a 'wise woman', because within the Egyptian court there was a tradition of 'wise women' as well as 'wise men', particularly throughout the course of the hidden four hundred years. Both Yuya and his wife were devout members of Enki's temple, and Tuya carried a Dragon Queen inheritance from

Nin-khursag who was associated with the Egyptian goddess Neith. Throughout the time of their governance, Egypt was ruled, and Yuya and Tuya's children were brought up, within the light of Tiâmat's wisdom.

We are, in fact, observing the emergence of a secret sisterhood here, with Tuya as its very significant successor, for it had always existed. However, with the arrival of Tuya it properly came into its own.

Tuthmosis IV's son, Amenhotep III, was, like his father, moved in his heart by the enlightenment and teachings of the Grand Vizier and his wife, and when he became pharaoh he married Tiye, Yuya and Tuya's daughter. Thus the Temple of Oannes became firmly established within the precincts of the royal court of Egypt; and it was headed by women of high spiritual degree. These noble queens moved into place on Enki and Enlil's chessboard to prevent Enlil's forward march towards world domination and to bring to fruition the carefully laid plans of Enki and Nin-khursag. When Callum Jensen, the discoverer of the location of the Grail, releases his book, *Synchronicity and the Scarlet Saint,* it will be seen how the queen of the chessboard of the Grail clues led him unfailingly to its resting-place.

Bitter must have been Enlil's lament as he viewed what was happening! Just as he had brought Egypt nicely to the brink of her potential for world dominion, the grand arm of Canaan reached right into the royal household and deposited Yuya and Tuya as joint controllers of Egypt's deepest dynamics! Tiye, their daughter, married the pharaoh and took charge of Nefertiti, the daughter of Amenhotep III by another of his wives, and brought her up under the banner of Tiâmat. She would later marry Amenhotep's son by Tiye, the succeeding pharaoh, who would be drawn deeply into the light of her influence. Together they would have a daughter, Meretaten, blessed especially by Tiâmat and granddaughter of the great matriarch Tuya, who would marry Moses himself and steer both him and Egypt entirely away from the course that Enlil had so assiduously, with such bright glaring hopes, created for them both.

Moses would be given the chance to rule the world, as was his inevitable birth-right; but he would choose to fulfil it in a very different manner from that which would have realised Enlil's aspirations and dreams.

There must indeed have been gnashing of teeth and rending of garments as Enlil watched the dramatic events of the closing 18th Dynasty unfold! For him, the whole scenario promised to be a disaster from start to finish. And yet there was a shadow of a chance of redemption for his schemes – no more than a flimsy cloud drift, but there nevertheless. Enlil, in the wings, awaited his chance.

Amenhotep III adored his wife Tiye and revered her counsel and vision. As far as the pressures of the culture of the day allowed, he upheld women's rights. 'From of old, a daughter of the king of Egypt has not been given to anyone', he replied brusquely to a letter of request from the king of Babylon, thus quashing his hopes that his own favour of sending a royal Babylonian bride to Egypt would be returned. Tiye had told her husband all about Babylon!

Tiye oversaw every one of her husband's diplomatic marriages, and, from their obvious focus on their Egyptian wives, it seems that both Amenhotep III, and his son Amenhotep IV, paid only cursory attention to their respective harems. Both pharaohs scrupulously avoided war, although Egypt's position at the pinnacle of might and wealth smoothed their path concerning this aspiration. Amenhotep III was rather regarded as a mighty upholder of lawfulness.

Amenhotep III and his son, Amenhotep IV, ruled jointly for a few years. This co-regency was undertaken so that the father could initiate his son gradually and surely into the mysteries of Enki's temple, where the relationship between the true Father God and his enlightened Son was of vital importance.

Amenhotep IV was taught that the Father and the Son were sourced in the great Mother. He had seen his father undertake the Christing ceremony, where he was ritually born as the Son of Light, the living embodiment on earth of the sun in the heavens.

This Christing ceremony, fundamental to the Temple of Oannes, was reinstated by Amenhotep III. He resurrected it from earliest Egyptian history, where it had flourished before it was supplanted by other ceremonies more in keeping with the influences of Noah's new and improved version of the white powder and the emanations of the false Emerald Tablet, buried in Egypt shortly after 1960 BC. Amenhotep IV would take this original sun ceremony further into the resonances of its true meaning, as we shall see.

When his father died and Amenhotep IV succeeded him, he ascended to the throne with Nefertiti as his queen. Nefertiti was the daughter of Sitamun, Amenhotep III's sister, whom he had married at an early age in order to assume the rightful title of pharaoh. Sitamun had given birth to Nefertiti, but had died shortly afterwards. It was after this event that Amenhotep III married Tiye, who became his chief consort, the 'Great Royal Wife' of the pharaoh, and who took little Nefertiti so warmly and influentially under her wing.

If Amenhotep III had doted on Tiye, Amenhotep IV's devotion to his wife was unprecedented in its intensity. He lavished love and praise on her, calling her Great of Favour, Mistress of Sweetness, Beloved One, Mistress of Upper and Lower Egypt, Great King's Wife Whom He Loves. Images of the royal family show them enjoying intimate scenes of domestic bliss. At least three important artworks depict, respectively, Nefertiti bestowing the power of the *khu* on her first daughter Meretaten, and Meretaten twice giving the *khu* to her father the pharaoh.

It was conferred via the breath by a kiss on the lips, as Mary Magdalene would transfer it some seven hundred years later to Jesus, for through the grace of

Tiâmat's ministrations the Star Fire could now be given by subtle means via a loving kiss.

Indeed Meretaten was the chosen vehicle of light, destined to be mistress of the spiritual forces of the *khu*. She was the Divine Daughter designated by Tiâmat to bring forth the wonder of what was known as the Sapphire Tablet, and as such she continued the line from Nin-khursag to Gra-al, to Brigid, to Eve, to Luluwa (Cain's wife), down to herself, a line which would eventually consummate its descent in the blaze of glory that was Mary Magdalene and her daughter Tamar, the Drop of God-essence that enabled the Emerald Tablet to return to earth. Of course, within the special line of descent down the ages were many other women, lesser but still vitally important beacons, such as those who surrounded Moses.

The famous Sapphire Tablet, called the *Schethiyd* by the Quabalistic masters, was next in status to the Emerald Tablet (to think of the order of the rays of the rainbow is to understand why). Meretaten was appointed to dispense its teachings to humanity with her consort Moses, until Jesus and Mary's appointed time came to descend to earth by means of the special bloodline and restore the Grail to humanity. If Meretaten and Moses had succeeded, the entire planet would have ascended two thousand years ago.

In the fifth year of his reign, Amenhotep IV took a dramatic and unprecedented step. He publicly proclaimed the truth of the Temple of Oannes and asserted his vision of one ineffable God above and beyond the teeming Egyptian deities. He named himself after this inscrutable deity and became Akhenaten, 'Knowledge of the Aten'.

He strove to introduce the philosophical concept of a unifying principle in which everything that could be conceived of was contained, but, distinctly anticipating Buddha, he posited that this omniscient, omnipotent principle could not be found with the physical senses, but could be discovered only through the mystical wisdom of inner percipience. He used the symbol of the Aten, the sun disc sometimes depicted as eight-rayed which is an esoteric representation of the inner unifying eye (the *ayin*), to illustrate the new philosophy to his people. Within the Aten shines the mystical star which exists as a potent reality within the human heart, the Grail within us that connects us unassailably to God.

The number 8 is deeply associated with feminine divinity, and is a symbol of the continuous flow of divine life and consciousness. Ultimately it is the Caduceus, the 'kissing serpents' conjoined at the point of the mouth, the heart and the genitalia, circulating the *khu* between them and creating the Staff of Life or the Sacred Tree. This idea of the eight-rayed Being (as in the seven tones of music being completed in the octave, or eighth note) permeates the entire Gospel of Mary, which is in perfect harmony with Buddhist philosophy in its deeper aspects. The gospel is an exquisite expression of the realisation of the 'Aten', of its gentleness and its all-permeating quality of absolute goodness and love as the soul purifies itself throughout its seven circuits, and takes flight into the spiritual starlight at the eighth level, becoming itself a being of Star Fire, the Pendragon. Osiris himself (connected with Oannes) was the heavenly shepherd of these pure stars of brilliant light, ushering them back into the heart of the One, the Aten (Tiâmat).

Unfortunately, because of the emanations of the false Emerald Tablet in their midst and the insidious workings of Enlil's white powder, the vision of Tiâmat was blocked to the majority of the Egyptians.

They conceived of her especially through Isis and Hathor, and worshipped the 'rising power' (ascension) these goddesses represented. Their religion and culture incorporated a multiplicity of magnificent, stupendous and beautiful aspects, and was in some respects much more advanced and admirable than our own, but inevitably it had its blind spots and its dark side. The problems which had dogged all civilisations since the advent of the great imbalance shadowed its progress, and a certain succession of priests had been careful up to the point of Amenhotep III's reign, upon which Tiye and Tuya prevented it, to continue to feed its rulers with the conical bread cakes (the false *shem*) so that particular influences were disseminated and broadcast to the people by the pharaohs.

Akhenaten not only promoted the idea of monotheism via the Aten, he banned the worship of Egypt's numerous gods, although he allowed the honouring of the 'God-touched ones' such as Hathor, Isis, and of course Thoth, whose teachings he espoused. He was simply insistent that they were not God, which of course was entirely consistent with Enki's teachings.

However, Akhenaten banned entirely even the mere honouring of particular 'gods'. He had lists inscribed of their faults and drawbacks as compared to the perfect Aten and the spiritual enlightenment that flowed from this prime source. These denigrated 'gods' were those that tended towards materialism and the encouragement of self-seeking. In particular, Akhenaten condemned the worship of Amen, and we may guess just whose rites and influences the concept of this deity had fallen under. Akhenaten was at particular pains to point out to the Egyptian people that this supreme deity was not God at all and, in fact, was not even God-touched!

To counteract the unbalanced masculinity from which the Egyptian culture suffered and its consequent rigidity, Akhenaten encouraged the artists, sculptors, scribes and artisans of his reign to create flowing, dancing, intimate and naturalistic images which celebrated the spirit of the Sacred Feminine. He had depictions of himself purposely feminised to express the divine androgynous nature of his union with Nefertiti.

Nefertiti played a prominent role in the introduction and perpetuation of the new religion, actively becoming its high priestess under the tuition of Tuya and

Tiye. As Antu had done so long ago, Nefertiti sacrificed her special presidency over the *khu* in order to pass it on to her daughter, little Meretaten, inspired and star-bright even in her earliest youth, for this child was the chosen one, the supreme daughter whose prominence would only be succeeded by the ultimately illustrious Mary Magdalene, destined to bring forth Tamar – known in her deific mode as Derdekea, the Drop. Nefertiti knew that a son of Akhenaten, a son she would not bear and to whom Meretaten would be half-sister, would be her daughter's spouse, and that they had a great work to do together for the world. Nefertiti looked to the future with both joy and tears, for Meretaten's triumph would bear her loved ones away from her, not least her adored husband.

Enlil's cage was thoroughly rattled by all this, and he was in an agony of resolve to rectify matters, especially as his psychic vision revealed to him that Moses was ineluctably coming down the line. Throughout Akhenaten's years of rule, his enemies massed and mobilised themselves. Enlil hurled every disaster upon Egypt that he could muster.

Each succeeding problem that thenceforth menaced the lives of the people was blamed on the sweeping ordinances of the pharaoh to desert the old gods and the old ways; and his adversaries, already numerous, multiplied and closed ranks.

His antagonists eventually forced him to abdicate in favour of Smenkhkare, his cousin. However, this cousin was found to be in partnership with Akhenaten in all things philosophical and religious, and he too was ousted after holding office as pharaoh for only a matter of weeks. The beautiful city of Akhetaten, translating as 'horizon of the Aten', which Akhenaten was building as an act of devotion to God, saw both monarchs literally driven out of town one after the other. It was to have been an early 'new Jerusalem', a forerunner of the Holy City. Almost 2,000 years later, Camelot would be built upon the same principles of joyful celebration, abundance, social cohesion, and religious and philosophical enlightenment.

The two ousted pharaohs, 'feeding-brothers' because they had shared the same wet nurse, were literally driven deep into the wilderness. The Midianites, whose land stretched east beyond the Sinai wilderness, came to their aid and gave them shelter and succour. They were descendants of Esau, Jacob's brother, and shared a familial and religious affinity with the Israelites in Egypt.

The Israelites – the children of Israel or Jacob from whom the dynasty of 'Josephs' originated – were very influential during the reign of Akhenaten and Nefertiti and enjoyed high royal favour. This had generally been the case for four hundred years, since the time of the first Joseph of the coat of many colours, but they were elevated to highest distinction during Akhenaten's regnal years. Akhenaten, under the tute-lage of his wife Nefertiti, his mother Tiye and his grandmother Tuya, championed their homage to the Temple of Oannes that taught its devotees to honour and love the one true God, the Mother-Father of purest light and ineffable divinity.

The High Priest of the Israelites sat often at Akhenaten's table and was given favoured distinction at court. Akhenaten referred to him as 'brother', both as a term of endearment for a treasured friend and because of the blood-tie that connected him to the children of Israel through Yuya. This situation, inflamed by Enlil's influences, who wanted the Egyptians back on side as soon as possible, caused the Egyptian court officials and eventually the Egyptian people to feel that their own state religion had been ousted in favour of a usurping foreign influence. In reality, it had returned to its roots; but Enlil was on hand to dispense amnesia and xenophobia and so conveniently obscure the fact.

The Midianites, descendants of Esau, were not so firmly centred in Enki and Nin-khursag's enlightenment as the Israelites. Enlil had managed to make some headway among them, and his plan was to throw Akhenaten on their mercy and into the heart of their influence, as had indeed occurred. The John-man who was coming – the feared and despised one according to Enlil – could be reared amongst the Midianites and the danger he posed safely absorbed by them. That was his contingency plan if his current plan A failed to work. However, his preferred scheme was a good one and he fully expected to pull it off. As usual, he hid it in his heart and waited.

CHAPTER FIFTY-SIX

The Basket of Rushes

Nefertiti did not leave the royal court when Akhenaten and Smenkhkare were driven out of Egypt. She remained behind to care for her six daughters and to continue to exert her influence over the state. Another important role she played at this time was that of covert observer, listening in clandestinely to the new domineering Egyptian authorities who threw their weight about objectionably at court and within the Halls of Counsel and who tried, but never quite managed, to treat her with scorn. She would then report back via secret messenger to Akhenaten and Smenkhkare, who were hiding out with the Midianites. Many loving messages passed between Akhenaten and Nefertiti as well as official business. They felt their separation keenly.

Tiye, who had outlived Amenhotep III, took over as unelected but accepted regent for the time being, but her edicts were constantly overridden by these same Egyptian authorities: a group of generals, Enlil-led, who had plotted against the king for years and had exerted dominance during the last twelve months of Akhenaten's reign and the three or four months that Smenkhkare had held power. They had been responsible for rallying the army and the people against the pharaohs and finally ousting them. Once the monarchic line of the 18th Dynasty had ended with the death of Tutankhamen, the royal bloodline would be abandoned in favour of a dynastic rule of such generals, which was exactly the way Enlil wanted it. Among their company was a young and ruthlessly ambitious military official, afterwards named Horemheb, who was destined to sever the throne of Egypt from the royal bloodline.

Intuiting that the time was drawing near when the young John-man would be born, Enlil activated his plan. As mentioned, Akhenaten had been a devoted friend of the High Priest of the Israelites, who had held sway at court. It was his power and influence that the generals had been obliged to overcome before their schemes for ousting the pharaoh could be brought to fruition. They put it about that the Israelites were planning a coup to take over the land and make the High

Priest king of Upper and Lower Egypt once Akhenaten had fled, and that it was the High Priest all along who had drawn Akhenaten so dramatically off course. Their allegations were afterwards disproven, but the propaganda had done its work. From that point on, the Israelites were treated badly by a suspicious populace, and racism reared its head.

Having prepared the ground, at the time when he knew that the birth of Moses was imminent Enlil influenced the generals to issue a proclamation that the Israelites must, as an act of contrition for their treasonable plots, cast all their new-born sons into the river as a sure and certain guarantee that they did not intend any member of the next generation to accede to kingship. The Israelites, denigrated and abused and in a very vulnerable position in Egyptian society, had no choice but to obey.

However, Enlil had made a very grave error. Because of Noah's revelations to him when the old patriarch deserted Enki's cause, Enlil had considered that this coming prophet of the Temple of Oannes who would be declared king and lead his people – and eventually the world – to freedom, would be born of the Israelite bloodline which had descended from Cain into the Canaanite people; and of course the children of Israel were Canaanites.

Akhenaten himself was indeed of this line, inheriting it from his mother Tiye, the daughter of Yuya and Tuya, who both had Canaanite ancestry.

But somehow Enlil never suspected that the prophesied Canaanite child, whom he knew in the depths of himself was soon to be delivered because he could feel it like a danger signal running through his every nerve and sinew, would be the first-born son of a pharaoh. All he knew was that this coming child was of the Canaanite strain and was likely to be the king that would turn all his plans to dust. The revelation of the Palestinian birth some 650 years later was yet to be dealt with by him, when again he would instigate a similar edict via Herod. Meanwhile, this child of the present time promised fair to be the great foretold menace and must be eliminated without fail.

In the land of Midian, Kiya was preparing to give birth. Akhenaten had married Kiya, Nefertiti's half-sister and therefore his own, with his senior queen's blessing. Nefertiti, strong, resolute, proud and courageous, beautiful and magnanimous and of an exquisite clarity of wisdom and intellect, passed on her role to this young woman who was destined to play the next part in the great chain of events that would culminate in Bethlehem. Nefertiti knew that she would be separated from Akhenaten, and that Kiya would bear Moses to him. Kiya had already given birth to Akhenaten's first son, Tutankhaten (afterwards known as Tutankhamen). Nefertiti stood firm, although her destiny cost her sorrow, loss and bitter tears.

Queen Kiya had an interesting heritage. Her father was the pharaoh Amenhotep lll and her mother was a Mesopotamian princess, very much connected to the lore and traditions of the God-Headed people. The dynasty to which her mother (Gilukhipa) belonged originated from Cain and Luluwa and their famous descendant, the spiritual luminary Ham. The family had strong connections to King Canaan and the land of Canaan (now called Palestine), and had been of the wandering people who followed, first Cain and Luluwa, and then their descendant Canaan.

They had instigated the fabulous civilisation that arose there and burned incandescently for five hundred years.

Queen Kiya's ancestors could therefore be traced back directly to Enki, Nin-khursag and Lilith (through Eve, the daughter of Nin-khursag and Enki who bore Cain; and through Lilith, who bore Luluwa to Enki). She was thus graced with a Dragon Queen heritage from both Nin-khursag and Lilith, and echoed the name of Queen Ki, Lady Earth, second wife of the (once) great Annum, and Lilith's mother's name, the enigmatic queen of the netherworld – that unendingly mysterious world beneath our feet in all its unfolding dimensions – who was called Eresh-Kigal.

The sacredness of the earth and its most mystical point – the Grail – is emphasised in Queen Kiya's name. She was known at the Egyptian court as 'the Royal Favourite; the Child of the Living Aten'; and these titles were bestowed upon her because of her very unique and exceptional connection to the Dragon Queen, who is referenced in each case. Nevertheless, she truly was a favourite of Nefertiti, who relinquished Akhenaten to her as a sacred trust, for she knew that her time with her beloved husband was fast drawing to a close, and that Kiya's was just beginning. Both women were conjoined in sisterhood both earthly and spiritual in its essence.

There is in Queen Kiya's name the suggestion of a 'key', and in all its senses this designation may be applied to her. She was the 'greatly beloved' of her parents as well as of Nefertiti, who nurtured, protected and tutored her. Later, she would become the 'beloved of Amon', the beloved of Akhenaten. She carried the heritage of the royal houses of Egypt, Canaan and Mesopotamia, all contiguous countries, and all bearing the secrets of the Grail, for it was from Egypt, with its older Mesopotamian and land of Nodh connections, that Jesus and Mary Magdalene drew succour for their mission.

(The Lord's Prayer is a rendition, almost word for word, of a much earlier hymn to Osiris. Jesus and Mary were brought up together in their early years in Egypt, Mary Magdalene prepared for her spiritual assignment in a temple in Alexandria, Tamar herself was born in this Alexandrian temple, and both Jesus and Mary often quoted texts from the sacred teachings of Isis during their three-year undertaking. Both baptism and communion were associated with the rites of Isis, as was the couple's sacred marriage in Bethany. When we learn that Tamar, the Divine

Woman and the Holy Grail, is linked intimately with the identity of Isis, this comes as no surprise.)

Kiya, through her daughter, the sister of her son Tutankhamen, who married one another, consolidated the succession which would ultimately descend to the Royal House of Judah, to King David and eventually to Mary Magdalene, Jesus, Tamar and John, the Four Sacred Persons of the mystical cross represented on earth, each of them of this bloodline. However, as she gave birth to Moses, her second-born son, the great mission of her own lifetime came to fruition.

Enki and Nin-khursag came to Akhenaten and Kiya some weeks later, and instructed them as to what they must do. They must place their tiny newborn in a basket of rushes sealed with pitch, and place him in the reeds near to Queen Tiye's bathing place along the river. She had been alerted, and was eagerly awaiting the arrival of her grandson. She would retrieve him as soon as he had been hidden, and tell her story to the court.

The king and queen, apprised of Enlil's intentions, cried out against this. It was a crazy plan! Enlil wanted every newborn son of the Israelites dead, and it would seem to everyone, especially the ruffianly Egyptian authorities, as if Moses were an Israelite baby. How could Enki and Nin-khursag ask them to sacrifice their little son so carelessly and cruelly?

Nin-khursag explained that there was an Akkadian influence, headed by a noblewoman who was a member of the secret sisterhood, within the Egyptian court that would associate the discovery of Moses with the discovery of Sargon the Great of Akkad. This woman would remind the court of the ancient mystery associated with a child thus drawn out of the water, and the sacred teaching that identified such a child with a deity. The court would then become afraid of enraging the deity should they murder the child, and the baby would be adopted by Queen Tiye, who would bring him up in the royal household as if he were preparing to ascend to the throne as pharaoh. There would be an edict against his assuming the throne, of course, because he would be considered an Israelite, but this difficulty might eventually be overcome.

Because he had been found in the water, as if cast adrift by an Israelite mother who could not bring herself to actually commit the act of drowning her son herself, his true identity would never be suspected. Throughout his childhood, the Israelite High Priest would act as his father, tutoring and initiating him into the Temple of Oannes. In this way, their son would return to the royal household and be brought up in honour and distinction as a royal son at court under the supervision of Enki-attuned Tiye, Nefertiti and the High Priest. There was no other way available to secure such an outcome. And one day he would return to them.

Akhenaten and Kiya agreed at last. Their little son was placed in a basket of rushes sealed with pitch, carried back to Egypt secretly by night and placed among the reeds along the river. The secret sisterhood undertook a lengthy vigil so that Enlil would not be able to view what was about to happen. It was too dangerous to despatch a messenger, for the messenger might be captured and the truth forced out of him, resulting in certain death for the child.

The Israelite High Priest himself escorted the baby in the basket to Egypt under the cover of darkness, and then melted away into the shadows, for it would imperil the mission if he was spotted at the riverbank and the baby was afterwards discovered there. It was little Meretaten, Moses's sister, who watched and waited until dawn, armed with a stick to drive off any rodent or predatory animal that might come too close.

There Tiye came, secretly summoned, at break of day. She 'found' him, and drew him out of the water, whereupon his remarkable history began.

CHAPTER FIFTY-SEVEN

Fleeing Egypt

*I*n the royal court, controlled mainly by the generals and the priests but still supervised and influenced by Queen Tiye and Queen Nefertiti, the child was accepted as the adopted son of Queen Tiye, for the reasons that Nin-khursag and Enki had predicted. The generals were simply too cowed by fear of the supernatural to intervene. All the symbols surrounding this child were of Tiâmat, but she had been so long forgotten that the generals never recognised them. They were there, nonetheless, comprising the ark: the great symbol of Tiâmat in the act of creation; and the reeds from which the basket was woven, for the reed is a feminine emblem. It was the voice of the reeds – the voice of the winds – that Nin-khursag and Enki employed to speak to many of their followers on earth. And of course water is the supreme symbol of Tiâmat as she reflects her glory to her children, using its soft mysterious membrane to protect them from the inconceivable might of her divinity.

The child was given the name 'Moses' – 'drawn from the water' in the language of the Israelites but also sharing an Egyptian etymology. In fact, the root of the name Moses is interesting, as it derives from more than one source. It is an ancient form of the name Osiris, which is connected with Oannes. As well as its 'drawn from the water' derivation, it also indicates a son or an heir.

In total we have the implication of a son or descendant of Oannes, the fish-man who emerged, or was drawn from, the water. In other words, we have a John-man, a Son of Light. We think that the biological process called osmosis is linked with the names Osiris, Oannes and Moses. Tiâmat's blueprint for the creation of humanity, and of biological life itself, as her magically impregnated water became blood which carries the mystery of the *khu* and of metals and other substances within it, relied on the procedures of osmosis. We are all 'drawn from the water' and crafted from the elements of life.

Moses was watched suspiciously by the court officials as he grew to manhood. Eventually Queen Tiye died, and some years later, receiving news of Akhenaten's death in Midian, Queen Nefertiti, grief-stricken, also died. She arranged for Akhenaten's body to be returned to Egypt and properly buried before her demise. Moses was shaken by her death and mourned it. Although there were rumours that he had entered into a liaison with her, their closeness was a purely spiritual affair.

Prior to the death of the great queens, the generals and the priests had consulted with one another and decided begrudgingly to allow Tutankhaten accession to the throne, as long as he changed his name in honour of the former supreme deity in Egypt (Amen, who was a conduit for Enlil), denounced his father and the Aten, and turned his back on the holy city of Akhetaten. Nefertiti took these decisions for him, as he was only nine years old, barely two years older than Moses. She knew that if Kiya's son had refused the conditions exacted, his death would have been quietly arranged.

So Tutankhaten became Tutankhamen, and took office as pharaoh. He died ten years later, and his death did after all occur under suspicious circumstances, as the idea that he had been murdered by a blow to the head has been discounted. (What appeared in an x-ray photograph to be trauma to the skull revealed itself, on closer inspection of his mummified body, to be a ball of resin.) His enemy in the royal household appears to have been Ay, who held high office at court during Akhenaten's reign. Ay was the youngest son of Yuya and Tuya. Their eldest son Anen, who would normally have assumed the position of the titular 'Joseph', was in this case passed over in favour of Ay, although under Amenhotep III, Akhenaten's father, Anen was made High Chancellor of Lower Egypt, High Priest of Heliopolis and Divine Father of the nation.

However, Ay was, so to speak, set aside for Akhenaten. He was paid the supreme honour of the designation 'Father of the God', meaning that he was chosen as Akhenaten's first priest. He became the next 'Joseph', although his name, a loose form of Yuya or Yusuf, was given to him to denote the sacred *ayin* or 'God-consciousness', the new yet ancient consciousness Akhenaten sought to promote.

For many years Ay was indeed a passionate devotee of Akhenaten, the Temple of Oannes and its understanding of Tiâmat as the Aten, but, relentlessly targeted by Enlil, after Akhenaten's banishment he lost his footing. Holding court with the generals and priests of the realm who were champions of Enlil, he was persuaded to accept the white powder according to his 'divine right' as chief priest. Once he had done so, he was fatally tempted by the worldly possibility, inflamed within him by the manipulative promise of the generals and priests, that he himself would become pharaoh after Tutankhamen's demise. At the time of the offering of this promise, Ay was already elderly, whilst Tutankhamen was still a teenager. And as soon as Tutankhamen fathered a son, Ay knew his opportunity would be lost.

True to his new allegiance with worldliness and self-seeking, Ay arranged the death of the young king and married Tutankhamen's youthful widow, Ankhesenamen, to secure his accession, although from the tone of her letters, sent out to various kingdoms immediately after Tutankhamen's death in a frantic attempt to secure a husband who was not of the Egyptian administration and who in particular was not Ay, this was a terrible fate for her. She suffered deeply, for she and Tutankhamen had been a devoted couple who secretly upheld the vision of the Aten, although they had been forced to publicly denounce it. They placed their reliance on Moses to rescue the nation from the future rule of the generals and the death of Tiâmat's special bloodline in Egypt. Ankhesenamen's babies to Tutankhamen, miscarried or stillborn, were not delivered lifeless without the intervention of Enlil. All was orchestrated by the Anunnaki king, who was desperate to end the royal succession and secure the throne of Egypt under the rule of his man.

'How the mighty are fallen' applied to Ay as to so many others in the epic history of the Grail. A four-hundred-year-old tradition faltered and collapsed under his watch. 'I was one favoured by his lord every day. My name has penetrated into the palace, because of my usefulness to the king, because of my hearing his teaching.' Such was Ay's boast, inscribed within his tomb whilst he was still serving Akhenaten, for the construction of the tombs of the Egyptian great were begun long before their actual demise. Ay resumed important building projects originally begun by Akhenaten as soon as he became pharaoh, dedicating them wholly to his own glorification by having Akhenaten's and even Tutankhamen's names erased and his own name inscribed over theirs. Thus we see how utterly he afterwards forgot the king's 'teaching' (the teachings of Enki).

Akhenaten and anyone to do with him, even his son, was now anathema, by explicit degree of Enlil via his mouthpiece, Amen, who existed in the etheric dimensions of earth and was one of his followers. Despite his harrowing of Ankhesenamen, Ay died without issue. He was the last of the line of the great Josephian statesmen, a family tree he felled with his own blows, for although his elder brother could have supplied the next 'Joseph', the pharaoh generals who followed Ay and who were not of the royal bloodline had no interest whatsoever in allowing the continuance of the Josephian dynasty. The removal of such a huge hindrance to his plans – for all the 'Josephs', even Ay in his earlier years, had been priests of the Temple of Enki, priesthood and statesmanship not being mutually exclusive – was one of Enlil's main objectives from the start of his Egyptian enterprise.

During the years of, first Ay's brief four-year kingship, and then of the next pharaoh, General Horemheb, Moses was left without a protector in the royal court. The High Priest of the Israelites, who had been a father to him in Akhenaten's absence, still stood by his side; but by now the Israelites were shunned and abused in Egypt, and had fallen into bondage. Due to Nefertiti's influence, and allowed by Ay before his complete descent into treachery, Moses had become a military commander. One day, whilst overseeing troops, Moses witnessed one of his men begin savagely to beat an Israelite on some trivial pretext. The situation in Egypt had deteriorated into one of the first pogroms against his grandmother Tiye's bloodline, afterwards known as the Jews, which history had witnessed.

Moses, in his anger, set himself bodily against the Egyptian, which inadvertently resulted in the abuser's death. When an account was made of the incident to Pharaoh Horemheb, he turned on Moses.

Although ordinarily such an event would have been considered merely unfortunate but well within the remit of a commander, Horemheb demanded that Moses pay for the life of the Egyptian with his own. Horemheb had been tipped off by Ay that there was something mysterious and undisclosed about Moses. Ay had not been told of Moses's true parentage as Tiye and Nefertiti sensed that the statesman was no longer a sound vessel for their confidences, but Ay had nevertheless picked up a distinct aura of threat to his own position embodied in Moses. He had conveyed this to Horemheb, who did not forget it. Besides, as Moses appeared to be an Israelite and was obviously prepared to defend the lives of his own people before those of Egyptians, it was decided that his influence at court must be immediately curtailed. The queens had gone, followed by Ay, who had cherished a passing and somewhat furtive respect for Moses. There was nothing to protect him now, and the people had long been muttering about their fears of some kind of armed uprising of the Israelites, who might perhaps align themselves with a smaller kingdom on Egypt's borders populated by her enemies. Moses's act of inadvertent homicide gave Horemheb just the excuse he needed.

Moses fled into the wilderness and travelled to the land of Midian, east of the Sinai mountains. However, he did not leave alone. Before making his escape he married Meretaten, his half-sister and Nefertiti's eldest daughter. The couple were welcomed by Lord Jethro, the Midianite leader; Kiya, Moses's mother; and Aaron, his uncle. Meretaten was formally honoured as Moses's royal wife, and given a Hebrew name in addition to her own – Miriam.

Lord Jethro had a daughter, Zipporah, one of seven sisters. Meretaten (Miriam) and Zipporah shared a soul kinship, and it was not until Moses had also married Zipporah, and the two women were united as 'sisters', that his true mission could begin. This extended beyond the introduction of the teachings of Aten (the concept of the mystery of the one God) to the exalted rites of receiving enlightenment from what could be given, via Miriam, Kiya and Zipporah, of the Sapphire Tablet from Tiâmat herself. Tiâmat would give this gift so that humankind could move steadily forwards on the road to ascension until Jesus and Mary met them at a certain point along the way and delivered the integrated whole of the Emerald Tablet and the Divine Woman, Tamar, to earth. Thus, with the death forces already partially overcome before their arrival, there would be no need for the horror of the crucifixion, or for the catastrophic wave of human, animal and planet suffering which would culminate in the two world wars, and would not abate even after these twin peaks of suffering had ravaged human civilisation.

And yet Moses's marriage to Zipporah came at a price. From Lord Jethro's perspective, the alliance was crucial because it cemented Moses into the Midianite tribe and gave Jethro the twin influences over Moses of father-in-law and of beholdenness because he had given his daughter in marriage. Moses fell deeply in love with Zipporah, and felt within himself the spiritual righteousness of their impending union. Miriam, too, rejoiced in the idea of their marriage. This was a happy time for Moses, a sweet interlude of rest and renewal before his great labours began. He spent many hours in the company of Miriam and Zipporah, and absorbed much wisdom from them in preparation for his formidable task.

All the time, without their knowledge, except for the intuition of the two young women and Kiya, Jethro watched them, studied them, and heard the voice of Enlil speak in his heart.

CHAPTER FIFTY-EIGHT

The Smoking Mountain

*J*ethro was a descendant of Esau, twin brother to Jacob. They were sons of Isaac, who was the son of Abraham. Esau sold Jacob his birthright for 'a mess of pottage', and whilst on the run from Esau, who felt as if he had lost his birthright through trickery, Jacob witnessed as in a dream a great ladder between heaven and earth. All night he had watched angels come and go upon it, whilst a mighty 'angel' wrestled with him until morning, seeking to consume all his strength. As dawn broke, Jacob was at last victorious in his struggle with the 'angel' (actually Enlil), proving that he had the power, the will, and the devotion to bear the secret of the Grail, and to continue to contain and thus minimise Enlil's death forces whilst the vital bloodline progressed through the kings of the Davidic lineage to its glorious destination in Bethlehem. For, of course, Jacob's vision of the ladder connecting heaven and earth was a vision of the Holy Grail.

'This is a terrible place, for it is the House of God', Jacob pronounced upon returning to normal consciousness. We may remember these evocative words as we ponder the Grail clues, for their quotation in the Mary Magdalene church at Rennes-le-Château certainly plays a part in pointing out to us where the Emerald Tablet lies today. Jacob meant that the site of his experience was the inconceivably holy connecting point between the planet and God, between humanity and God, which does not have an absolute geographical location, but is established by the presence of the divine forces of the Grail creating an arc, or a bridge, or a ladder between heaven and earth as an outpouring of ineffable love which enables us to ascend.

It was the willing awareness, acknowledgement and reception of this divine love that the death forces blocked and 'slew' so many thousands of years ago.

As we know, Jacob's brief from Tiâmat, amongst many other imperatives, was to lead the Children of Israel (Jacob's family) from Canaan into Egypt, to the root of their spiritual conjoinment. Here was the seat of many esoteric traditions which had been passed down from Enki (the Egyptians called him Thoth) and which belonged to the mystical rites of Isis and Hathor, both Dragon Queens in Egyptian guise. The role of the twin brothers Jacob and Esau was to unite the two great civilisations of Canaan and Egypt, into whose royal bloodline the descendants of Esau would pass, eventually producing the Amarna kings Akhenaten, Smenkhkare, Moses (unacknowledged), Tutankhamen and Ay, the first three of which were so vital to the eventual manifestation of the Sapphire Tablet.

The plan was that, though Canaan would fall, Moses and Miriam would arise to lead the children of Israel (Jacob), protected and preserved in Egypt, back into Canaan, where they would reestablish the progressive and enlightened civilisation in the land that Tiâmat had dedicated to the preservation of the Grail. Miriam and Moses would rule both Egypt and Canaan after receiving the Sapphire Tablet on Mount Horeb. The light of the two combined nations would spread across the globe. Through Egypt, Africa would come into her own and the Tree of Death would be healed and released into the light of the spirit. The hidden light in Britain with its point of release in Glastonbury, accompanied by the light at Chartres and Rosslyn and all resonating with the light in Jerusalem, would arise and take fire until the entire world was bathed in the radiance of Tiâmat, the Mother-Father. Thereafter, Jesus and Mary would descend to bring forth the Emerald Tablet and restore the Holy Grail.

Mount Horeb, upon whose utmost peak the Sapphire Tablet would descend into the keeping of Miriam and Moses, was famous for its turquoise mines, the blue-green stone being an exquisite symbol of the Sapphire Tablet gradually melding into the purity and pulchritude of the Emerald Tablet.

When Tiâmat, from the burning bush, described Canaan as 'the land overflowing with milk and honey', she described the land where the Sacred Feminine would once more come into its own through the proper dispensation of the *khu*. The Star Fire or the *khu* was a manifestation of spiritual gold, and it was sweet and fragrant to the taste, as was Enlil's false rendition of it. Moreover, the goddesses of the higher star people, before the rejection of Tiâmat, fed their lovers not only on the Star Fire flowing from their sacral centre, but with a special secretion of milk which flowed from their heart centre. This was the deeper meaning of the mellifluous and abundant flow of 'milk and honey' to which Tiâmat alluded. In other words, Canaan was to be restored to its hallowed status as the seat of Tiâmat from which the nourishment of the 'milk and honey' flowed, and this time Egypt would stand strong and sheltering at her side, their twin flames conjoining to become one rather than the latter seeking to destroy the former. And so the symbolism of the twins Esau and Jacob is revealed in its esoteric sense: an ultimate upholding of one another rather than quarrels and threats and stealing of birthrights. However, although Tiâmat shone upon the descendants of Esau as she shone upon those of Jacob, there was at least one among the former who succumbed to the machinations of Enlil: Jethro, Lord of Midian. Enlil particularly focused his attentions upon the Midianites, sensing intuitively that they would have the power to influence the dreaded John-man who was coming.

Jethro, most definitely Enlil's man, began immediately to inculcate a notion of indebtedness in Moses. In doing so, he followed Enlil's orders. We make a mistake if we think too narrowly in terms of good and evil, however, for Jethro was certainly not evil, but duped and unenlightened. Although there were many admirable traits in his character, equilibrium between the male and female principles was glaringly conspicuous by its absence in his philosophy. Jethro hinted that Moses could repay the Lord of Midian's hospitality to him, Miriam, Aaron, Kiya and his late father, as well as Jethro's 'gift' of Zipporah as his bride, by allowing him access to the Mount Horeb temple which enshrined the sacred Cave of Hathor.

This temple, vast and complex, had long served Egypt's pharaohs and queens, and Moses, due to the number of his father's supporters who had continued to press for his reinstatement in Egypt and who guarded it, inherited charge over it. Miriam and Zipporah were to journey there shortly, Jethro pointed out, and he would be grateful to Moses if he could make use of the temple himself, as he had some plans for alchemical work which he was anxious to carry out for reasons of a religious nature. Jethro explained that he had a certain amount of gold which he would need for his devotional work, but he would require assistance in his procedures from the servants of Moses attached to the temple. Moses was glad to agree, and despatched one of his retinue to instruct the temple guards to grant access to Jethro. (Because Miriam was a priestess of Hathor, her right of entry together with a female companion would not have been questioned.)

Both Miriam and Zipporah (who knew her father only too well) were greatly concerned about Moses's decision, and sought with all their energy and skill to overturn it.

The temple of Hathor in the holy mountain (for the whole of Mount Horeb was sacred to the great goddess Hathor) was a place which enshrined mystical energies rising from the earth and spiralling out into the stars and beyond to the highest dimensions. Ceremonies had been enacted upon the mountain in loving worship of the Great Mother since humanity had first been born to the planet. The great peak itself was an entirely feminine energy, and it was with the warp and weft of such divine forces that Nin-khursag had woven into human creation the pulsing signals from the spiritual starlight which were Tiâmat's blueprint for her earthly children, who would reside in bodies made from the earth so that they could love the earth, and, through loving it, find her, the great Dragon Queen, at the centre of all – in the molten heart of the earth, in the auriferous sun, in the ancient and ever-new starlight, and in the mystical light within their hearts.

These were the very energies which Enlil sought to reverse, and his wholesale infiltration of the temple of Hathor was a major triumph for his schemes. He, Annum and Marduk had already ensured that the mighty connection with God, visible to all and freely available to all, had been severed from human awareness by the Dolorous Blow. However, Enlil knew that to increase his reverse-spin power, he had to seek out those places upon the earth where the Grail energies – the connection energies – still existed, though in a muted form, hidden, secret and veiled since Marduk's action. They were still all-powerful, still ultra-potent fountains of beauty and truth, still expressions of the unfettered eternal feminine, and Enlil loathed them and desired to reverse them with all the corruption in his heart. He had already instigated the production of the white powder in the temple of Hathor, but only intermittently, surreptitiously, and in small measure, by back-door means. Now his expectations were much more ambitious.

Unfortunately, Moses was deaf to the remonstrations of his wives. He did indeed feel indebted to Jethro, and was acutely aware that he might well need to call on Jethro's goodwill and generosity yet again in the uncertain times to come. Zipporah was a bond between the two men, Lord and Pharaoh, and in some respects a tug of war. Jethro used her to bend Moses to his will, whilst she herself made strenuous efforts to awaken her husband to the full implications of his divine vocation and to steer him away from the hooks with which Jethro sought to barb him.

Moses had been protected from the nefarious red and white powders so far by the powerful ministrations of Nefertiti, whose authority had prevented the priests from dispensing it to him. Her contention had been that as Moses had been sent by the gods, and was not a member of the Royal Household by blood (she knew the truth, of course), it would therefore offend the gods if he was to receive ritual food not intended for him. The priests would have argued against her, but she was too powerful. Nefertiti's popularity, her royal status (which seemed unusually potent), and her mighty soul forces all conspired to silence them and stop them in their tracks. She commanded them by various means of reiteration not to mess with either Moses or herself. They obeyed.

Jethro, despite the indefatigable efforts of Miriam and Zipporah to prevent it, was given gracious permission to use the Temple of Hathor as he would, and Moses bound a workforce to his service. Jethro also employed many of his own priests and craftsmen, for he had been given a tremendous task to fulfil. Enlil had ordered him to create vast quantities of the white powder. Jethro must oversee its production, and arrange for it to be stored in readiness in chambers within the temple.

Enlil explained to Jethro that Moses was to be sent out by 'God's will' (he meant himself, of course) to rule the world, and he, Jethro, would be his first minister.

The white powder was a 'holy' weapon which would guarantee military victory after military victory.

The Lord of Midian was further told that Moses did not know that he would rule the world as yet, or even that he wanted to, but it was Jethro's God-given task to slowly enlighten him to his true mission. A gradual, insidious conquest was what was required, Enlil advised him. He knew Jethro could do it, but Enlil issued a solemn warning. Jethro would have to be on his guard against the women! Meanwhile, he was to commence the manufacture of the white powder without delay.

We would ask our readers, in consideration of what we have revealed concerning Enlil's distorting mirror, to take special note of the fact that huge stockpiles of the sinister white powder were produced and stored in this temple-laboratory, to be discovered many centuries later by the (very much puzzled thereby) archaeologist W.M. Petrie and his team. Shortly after Moses had ascended the holy mountain, the royal temple that Petrie discovered had been made inaccessible by a mighty weight of rubble and had lain hidden for over 3,000 years.

Enlil and Noah together devised an unprecedented plan and used vast quantities of the white powder to create an astonishing weapon (a vast mirror made from refined, reverse-spin crystals which surrounded the earth, and is still in place and active today). For this they needed enslaved miners, which were procured for them by Jethro, just as they had been by earlier agents in ancient Sumer, when the white powder first came into production.

The manufacture of the white powder was also in progress to create other kinds of weapons of mass destruction, which as children of the nuclear age we can all better understand, even though they far exceeded nuclear power. Nevertheless, the particular weapon to which we make reference and which was the result of such unsurpassed wizardry is so subtle and so all-pervading that we could never have guessed, without direct guidance, that such a phenomenon ever existed, let alone that it is still present amongst us in our own time.

Once this great work to produce the white powder commenced, Mount Horeb sometimes glowed with the inner furnaces lit at Jethro's command, and roiling smoke often hung over the mountain, giving it a strange and sinister grandeur, as Genesis relates.

CHAPTER FIFTY-NINE

Dark Egypt

*A*fter his marriage to Zipporah, Moses encountered the 'burning bush' upon the sacred mountain of Horeb. Enki and Nin-khursag appeared as a golden fire which gave forth a preternatural burst of light but did not consume or injure. Tiâmat spoke through them, communing with Moses's heart and inner vision, telling him that she was 'I Am That I Am', the 'I Am' within him that was his link to Mother-Father God and that was all-powerful and incorruptible – the true Grail in his heart which Enlil could never obscure unless he was given permission to do so via the free will of the soul. He must now enter into his 'I Am' with all the strength of his spirit, Tiâmat told him, for his great work for humankind had begun.

Tiâmat's communion with Moses tells us that she was truly 'Jehovah', or 'I Am That I Am', the literal translation of the name. Moses was instructed to remove his shoes and stand barefoot upon the mountain, for it was sacred ground. Marvellously, the mystical charge of the Emerald Tablet which contains the secret of the forces of the Grail can be sensed by the soles of the feet at the Grail site in Lincoln. And at Glastonbury Tor there existed anciently at its foot the beautiful little 'slipper chapel', where pilgrims climbing the Tor would leave their footwear so that they could climb and descend the sacred mount barefoot, retrieving their discarded shoes on their return journey. (The Tor was considered sacred by pilgrims because of its association with Joseph of Arimathea, the disciples and the two Marys, Mary the mother of Jesus and Mary Magdalene, whom old texts confirm as coming to Glastonbury shortly after the Crucifixion and establishing the very first church or kirk (circle) of Christ, made of wattle and daub, at Glastonbury.) Tales of antiquity relate how a divine energy could be felt through the soles of the feet, like a zinging uprush, and of how it was considered disrespectful to God to block its course through the body and the soul with shoes. This uprush of force was, of course, the remnant of the severed Grail, for Glastonbury was its purest station on earth.

The true Jehovah appears from time to time in the Bible, but, sadly, the imposter Enlil, who encouraged men and women of religious faith to think of him as Jehovah or Yahweh, manifests much more often. He is marked by the unmistakable stamp of rage, aggression, retribution, hatred, prejudice, judgementalism, spite and arrogance, by his threatening, domineering and dictatorial stance and his sinister demands for sacrifice. He delivers death and suffering in a mood of self-congratulation. He is the epitome of heartlessness (of course), and he is an excellent example of what God is not, for we are certain that the true God manifests the very opposite of the qualities cited above in Her-His immeasurable goodness and mercy.

Tiâmat instructed Moses to return to Egypt and rescue the Israelites, whom the new pharaoh had cast deep into bondage, for he would need this faithful congregation to work with him in order to perform his great and God-given task. He would prove that he was Egypt's lost – and genuine – pharaoh by performing certain pharaonic rites which, via Tiâmat's blessing, would assume the distinction of miraculous feats.

These pharaonic ceremonies were rituals which descended from the tradition of Enki and the Serpent People (the higher star people who followed Enki and Nin-khursag). They associated the snake (the serpent, the dragon) with the magical Grail qualities of transformation, healing and creation.

Therefore, the three miracles consisted of transforming a rod (the sacred lance in its true, positive mode) into a serpent; manifesting a dread disease (leprosy) and then showing how the heart made all things whole and perfect (the hand was put forth as leprous, was taken to the heart centre, and came forth again whole); and turning water into blood, the very creational dynamic Tiâmat used to bring earthly humanity into being, especially, as mentioned, by a form of osmosis (Osiris-Moses).

Although Moses was given the instruction to appear before the current pharaoh in office (rightfully, of course, it should have been he himself who reigned over Egypt), he actually passed the job on to Aaron, who travelled back with him to the Egyptian court. This was because Moses, after receiving appropriate training from his wives, was the conductor of the God-force which gave rise to the miracles, and preferred to remain undisturbed, in a meditative state, whilst they were performed; and so Aaron became his spokesman.

We think that the reason the pharaoh consented to Moses's request that he should lead the Israelites out of Egypt was that he felt threatened by the return of the rightful pharaoh, around whom many stories of wonder circulated, particularly concerning his birth as one of the gods come to earth. The plagues that blighted the land when Moses was denied his request served to reinforce the pharaoh's sense of this extraordinary man's supernatural grandeur.

Akhenaten was the first of the kings known as the Armana dynasty. This dynasty ended with General Horemheb, who banned the concept of the Aten (note the Anunnaki 'ten' reference within the word), prohibited any reference, even verbal, to Akhenaten, and removed the Amarna kings (the dynasty originated by Akhenaten) from the formal King List. Wishing to stamp out the culture, the influence and the historical memory of the Armana era and its Tiâmat-centred religion (the devil, for him, was in the blood as well as in the man Akhenaten), he destroyed and dismantled all of its monuments and other records. These fragments had to be skilfully pieced together before the existence of Akhenaten was discovered as a figure of Egypt's past in 1926.

The real bugbear was Moses, and it was his history and influence in particular that the pharaoh was instructed to entirely obscure and figuratively spit upon. Even Nefertiti's portraits were collected, mutilated, hidden and arranged so that her image hung upside down, the ultimate insult to royalty in ancient Egypt which carried a penalty for treason. Viewed today, the defacing and obliterations are so disturbing that they seem to reflect a psychopathic mentality rather than mere vandalisations. However, the Enlil-influenced Horemheb actually reigned and died in Moses's lifetime, during the years that he was in exile. Therefore, it was not only the past that Horemheb and his puppet-master Enlil were so desperate to wipe out, but any possible future for Moses and the Aten.

When Moses returned to Egypt with Aaron, a new dynasty, the 19th, had succeeded the 18th Dynasty rulers, of which General Horemheb, dying without an heir, was the last. Its founding pharaoh was Ramesses I, the pharaoh who received Moses and Aaron and observed their three miraculous rites.

He was so unnerved by these that he afterwards had a stela placed within the Cave of Hathor, where he knew that Jethro was working under the sanction of Moses. (Since Horemheb's time, Moses's temple guards had relinquished their defence of it on his behalf, as they had been required to admit Horemheb's agents, to which, because of Jethro's wishes, Moses had consented. Horemheb had, indeed, changed his name to equate with the name of the holy mountain as a dominant gesture to the escaped Moses, on whom Horemheb had decreed death, that he was the rightful overseer [Hor-*emh*-eb, meaning keeper or warden] of the mountain and its powerful temple.) This stela described the new pharaoh, Ramesses I, as 'The ruler of all that Aten embraces', just to let Moses know that, first, because of the three pharaonic rituals he was thoroughly impressed by Aten, Akhenaten's 'god', and second, that Moses ought to be aware that, despite his status as proper heir to Egypt's throne, Ramesses was pharaoh nowadays and intended to remain so, even if it meant an obligatory tipping of his cap to 'Aten'. The fact that he refers to the Aten as simply the name of a god, however, suggests that he had no real grasp of Akhenaten's and Moses's philosophy and spiritual percipience.

The spiritual meaning behind the return of Moses to rescue the Israelites reflects a constant truth. First, Moses (the higher soul) is rejected and cast from power (his flight from Egypt) by the claims of the lower soul, the little earthly self that is not the 'I Am', and that responds to the claims of the world and its self-seeking values. The lower soul seeks to eliminate all references within its greater consciousness to the lost higher soul (Horemheb's eradications), but fails to obliterate its poignant memory. The higher soul then returns to lead its confused lower self out of 'dark Egypt' (the body and its materialistic claims) to the 'promised land' – exalted consciousness and the pure realms of the spirit, attained through the act of ascension whilst still living in a physical body.

Apart from an expression of the smiting anger and psychopathic disgust of Enlil, and Horemheb's own anxiety that he might be ousted by Moses's growing number of supporters, there was another reason why Horemheb was so meticulous in his eradication of the Amarna dynasty from all official records. Miriam, as we shall see, gave birth to a daughter in her mature years. This daughter did not appear until after Horemheb's death, but nevertheless, General Horemheb was Enlil's dedicated soldier and followed his orders unquestioningly, supplying Jethro with most of the gold he needed to create the great stockpiles of white powder.

Enlil saw that the daughter of Moses and Miriam might give birth to rightful heirs to the throne of Egypt. He saw that these heirs could well give rise to a new religion in Egypt which would merge with Christianity at its inception, and keep it pure and resonant with the children of Tiâmat who founded it. The double strength of this undefiled religion would of a certainty bring down his best-laid plans. Therefore, Enlil was painstaking in his measures against such an outcome. And he wanted to be sure that future generations, particularly our own, when he hoped his most lethal plans would be realised, would never understand the connection between Miriam and Moses, the Sapphire Tablet, Mary Magdalene and Jesus, and the Emerald Tablet that awaits our retrieval in the burial ground of St Margaret's at Lincoln Cathedral.

As it transpired, these heirs of Moses and Miriam never did return to Egypt. They travelled to the Baltic regions, and the secrets of the Grail were entrusted to the descendants of their followers, many of whom derived from the tribes of Canaan, whose ancestors were Cain and Luluwa. In the far distant future, Tamar, the blessed one, the Divine Woman who was the Holy Grail, embraced these God-touched, wandering people as their queen and goddess, becoming known to history as the Queen of the Gypsies.

Her people, due to the forces he mustered against them, were as relentlessly hounded, persecuted, despised and slandered as Enlil could have wished.

CHAPTER SIXTY

Moses and the Dragon Queen

*A*nd so Moses and Aaron, having duly impressed the current pharaoh, led the children of Israel out of Egypt into the Sinai wilderness. Lilith materialised like a beautiful benediction before Miriam and led them all safely via a secret route through the Red or Reed Sea, bestowing the blessing of this mystical place upon each one through the agency of Miriam. She caused illusion to fall upon the pursuing pharaoh, Ramesses I, who had accepted Moses and Aaron at first, after conceding that the Aten was a source of true godly power and authority (as the stela he ordered to be erected in the Cave of Hathor at this time bears witness; interestingly, Ramesses I is recorded as an enemy of the Aten, and so he was, until the last year or two of his life).

Seeing this heart-opening towards the Aten in Ramesses I, Enlil, alarmed, had arranged that the pharaoh should be bombarded with *Schefa*-food so that he would turn against Moses. (There are several instances in the biblical story relating to Moses of 'God' deciding to 'harden the heart' of the pharaoh; when we realise just who was masquerading as 'God', and the precise means he used to thus harden hearts, everything becomes clear.)

Enlil had every intention of also bending Moses to his will, but he had not succeeded as yet in spite of all his efforts, and he was thoroughly disgusted with the pact Moses had made with Tiâmat through Enki and Nin-khursag via the ridiculous burning bush incident, although he had only been able to view it from a distance.

He thought he would quite like to have Moses slaughtered as he was so unfit for purpose (Enlil's purpose), and so rid himself of the threat he represented once and for all. After Moses and the Israelites had been rescued by Lilith, however, he reverted to plan B (he would much have preferred Jethro to take over from a deceased Moses, but he just did not seem able to procure this desirable outcome). Ramesses lost his way and perished in the Reed Sea, but Egyptian anger was not quelled, and his successors continued to wage war against the hapless Israelites.

The Reed Sea was a place of beautiful spiritual poignancy to which the Isle of Avalon and the river Tamar in Devon, England (originally a river of reeds) were mystically connected. The reed is associated with the Divine Feminine, with the Voice of God, which whispers in the ear in a hushed, small voice like the wind in the reeds, and with the Holy Breath or Spirit. The Druids revered it to the extent that they regarded it as one of their sacred trees. Lilith had retired to the ethereal dimensions of the Reed Sea after encountering much trouble and tyrannical behaviour from Enlil. She had eventually married him, for the express purpose of protecting Enki and his work for humanity from the havoc that Enlil sought to wreak upon it (her presence was a distraction to him). Her refuge was this lonely, wild, lovely place of reeds.

The designated time for Moses and Miriam's ascent of the holy mountain arrived, and they set off alone, after undergoing certain ceremonies sacred to Hathor, and anointing one another with spikenard, the precious oil for the head and the feet that was the ritual perfume of the Sacred Marriage and whose fragrance whispered of the secrets of the Grail. Although Akhenaten banned the worship of a multitude of gods in Egypt, there were certain deities whom he had viewed, not as gods, but as sacred routes to the Aten.

Hathor was deeply revered as such a supreme and shining one, and it was in her honour that the Israelites, led by Miriam and sanctioned by Moses, fashioned a golden calf as an altar. Hathor was represented in the Egyptian pantheon as a divine cow who gave her cosmic milk to succour the universe. (Our source tells us that Mary Magdalene bears a close association with Hathor, whilst Isis is an expression of Tamar.)

This golden calf was never intended as an image to idolatrise, but as an important symbol and a mental focus. Miriam and Zipporah were greatly relieved that a quantity of the gold in the temple of Hathor, waiting to be transformed into white powder, could actually be used for other, much more salubrious, purposes! The idea of building a calf rather than a cow was, amongst other symbolism, to remind the children of Israel that Hathor was a blessed and beloved daughter of the Great One – the Aten – not the overarching Deity herself. It also related to the fact that Miriam actually took on the identity of Hathor, so that Hathor shone through her, and spoke through her; and that Miriam was pregnant at this time as if with the calf of Hathor.

One of the most significant reasons for the golden calf, however, was that it was also a symbol of Rebecca the great matriarch's link with the divine Hathor. Rebecca was the mother of Jacob, who became Israel when he slept upon the mountain-top and was given the vision of the Holy Grail. This moment, which it was hoped would eventually result in Moses's true ascension with and via Miriam, and their triumphant return with that part of Tiâmat's knowledge or spiritual infusion, the Sapphire Tablet (her consciousness made manifest) which could be restored and vouchsafed to the world until Jesus and Mary Magdalene came to rescue the stolen Emerald Tablet, was a very special one for the children of Israel.

Their glorious matriarchal inheritance (we remember that this was always the significant line of descent, whose true status was overthrown by Annum and Enlil in favour of the male line) was about to come into its own. From this day forth, they were to be known, not only as the children of Israel, but as the children of Hathor (Rebecca). The literal translation of 'Rebecca' is heifer or cow – not the humble bovine but the sacred Hathor herself.

Rebecca's name was about to be transposed, as Jacob's was, from its mundane to its sublime resonance, and her children were about to receive the divine blessing whose potential she had always borne for them. From Rebecca's lineage, as well as her illustrious sons, came Miriam and, eventually, Mary Magdalene and Tamar – the Holy Grail – herself. This was Rebecca's promise, and her gift, which was about to be bestowed upon the Israelites. In the event, it would remain with them in an openly declared sense for only a few days.

There was a further reason why the symbol of a golden calf was used as a focal point for the ceremony that the Israelites would undertake whilst Miriam and Moses ascended the holy mountain to receive the Sapphire Tablet. The golden calf, like the golden lion of Judah and the lion that was the Egyptian Sphinx, was one of the four figureheads of this special nation that was destined to rise from Moses and Miriam to unite, not only the four corners of the globe, but the four natural creatures whom the six human races from the stars had entered into to forge and progress their humanity: the noble steadfast ox; the royal and magnificent lion; the powerful, lordly, clear-visioned creature of flight, the eagle; and the wave-esque serpent of higher consciousness whose form can be seen in the waves of the sea but whose ultimate expression is in divine fire – the dragon.

We are each specially attuned to one of the four, but it is our destiny to express them all in their higher spiritual mode through our adaptable simian heritage. Then we truly become the Adama, and the Adama becomes the Pendragon. At this point, we can say that we are fully human.

It was ultimately very fortunate that a calf was indeed the requisite symbol for the portent of the moment, because in fact Jethro would not permit the Israelites to have any more gold than was sufficient to make a small calf! He was entirely disapproving of these ceremonies to Hathor, and, stamping around with a dark face, tried strenuously to dissuade Moses from permitting them or ascending the mountain under their protection and inspiration.

The orgies that the Israelites were said to have indulged in never took place. Instead, a great prayer went up from the people, calling on the Great God, the beloved Aten, the ever-loving Mother-Father, to deliver the world from confusion, and to accept the spiritual essence from their hearts and head centres so that the designated portion of the Tablet of Light might be received and understood by Miriam and Moses, no matter how many blocks, scramblings, etherical techno-viruses and general interferences Enlil had imposed. (Most of them knew nothing of Enlil as an entity, because he masqueraded as God, so of course they did not identify him by name; but they were aware that some sort of shadow, conscious and intelligent, had fallen over humanity since its earliest days.)

We might say that these rites of Hathor, conducted in such devotion by the Israelites, caused the spirit of the Grail to descend and created the conditions by means of which the sanctified Grail forces could be maintained until Miriam and Moses had fulfilled their commission upon the mountain-top.

These ceremonies were indeed the pure rites of Hathor essayed by Miriam, created as a superconductor for the prayer and spiritual aspiration of the people, so that Tiâmat could reach them in the fullness of her presence and they could embrace her essence in full consciousness in order to receive the Sapphire Tablet. As we have said, these rites, led by Kiya and Zipporah below and designed to aid and uplift the royal couple, were to be maintained until they descended with Tiâmat's consecrated Sapphire Tablet ... but the rites were obstructed and inter-rupted as they made their descent.

Miriam and Moses, leaving their companions behind, reached the sanctified mountain-top. There, they were blessed with a beautiful realisation of Tiâmat.

Well might Moses have been portrayed with the horns of exalted perception by Michelangelo! These horns depicted, not only his own attuned crown chakra, but the inspired consciousness of the goddess Hathor, whose beautifully curved bovine horns were in themselves symbols of her perfected lunar consciousness (the Star Fire). This outflow of supreme consciousness, Hathor, through Miriam, directed to Moses, as though she gave him the true Star Fire essence, as in the old days of Sumer.

Kiya and Zipporah were Hathor's conduit in the valley below. The power of the rites they conducted ascended like incense to carry the couple into heaven. Thus uplifted, Moses and Miriam, through their unicorn's horn chakra, received Tiâmat's living spirit – her star-emanations, which are received in the *ayin* and the heart but which, just as at Stonehenge, are best recorded for the sake of posterity in the stuff of stone – the body of the earth herself, which creates an earthly eter-nalisation of them.

In their heightened state, Moses and Miriam were able to 'read' this wondrous stone, vouchsafed to them by Tiâmat, because the light of their consciousness resonated with the light secreted in its miraculous heart.

Upon this tablet of stone, of purest sapphire which reflected a light of scintillating diamond brilliance, appeared miraculous letters of light – the revelations of the spirit written in matter, sometimes effulgently golden, sometimes of the bright whiteness of angels. Yet the description is symbolic only, because the *ayin* and the heart in their connection with the stone understood in deep still wells and unscaleable bright heights beyond the world of form and intellect.

The stone tablet was sapphire because it revealed, in part, the mystery of the Emerald Tablet. The latter was of a higher spiritual frequency than the former, being the heart of hearts of the ray of white light which streams from Tiâmat's consciousness and is an emanation of it. We note that the blue ray's position in the seven rays of the rainbow – the seven rays of creation – is one degree nearer to the earth, one step down, from the green ray. This was the knowledge that Moses and Miriam received. Its essence married with the green ray and faithfully carried its vibration.

We might say that it was a further revelation of the Emerald Tablet, but not the Emerald Tablet in its entirety. The attainment of that wonder must wait for the descent of the Divine Couple; but, nevertheless, Moses and Miriam were certainly a receptacle for knowledge so beautiful that, had they been able to retain it, the entire planet would have been ready for ascension at the time of their coming. It is worth thinking again of the holy mountain and its abundance of turquoise, the mystical blue-green stone that was sacred to Hathor and which the Egyptians used for many of their magical ceremonies. The blue ray correlates to the mind, and the green to the heart. When the mind bends its knee to the heart, the blue ray is in perfect harmony with the green, and the mind thus reflects heart-consciousness. This heart-consciousness is the very essence of the Holy Grail.

Moses and Miriam began their long descent.

Until Moses was about half way down the mountain, his feet sprang upon the ground as if they danced and sang. He rejoiced in an atmosphere of complete equilibrium and loving devotion with Miriam. Then he entered a clouded level of the mountain path, where the smoke from the furnaces of the temple of Hathor (so sadly profaned) billowed and created a hanging garden of mists. He lost sight of Miriam and could not perceive her at all.

There stood Jethro, Lord of Midian. He had first done his utmost to disrupt the rites which were being essayed below, and had then hurried up the mountain at Enlil's command. (It seems that even the name of his place of origin indicates that he was a man who stood at the mid-point of the life forces, and, according to the dictates of his soul, would either ascend or descend. Unfortunately, he chose to descend into the shadow. The name is also reminiscent of midden, which of course is bovine excreta, as though this is what he had reduced the potencies of the temple of Hathor, and his own spiritual perception, to.)

Jethro came forward, as if to assist Moses, who suddenly felt unaccountably weary. The stone tablet he clasped to his heart (neither large nor heavy) dragged at his arms. He saw that Jethro offered him bread and wine, which he wished to accept because hunger and thirst had swiftly come upon him; but he felt that he should not relinquish the stone tablet, which was dancing with light as if he cradled an angel. Jethro agreed to place the bread and pour the wine into his mouth, so that there was no need for him to let go of his precious burden.

As if she appeared in a dream, Miriam stepped out of the swirling mists. She begged Moses not to touch the bread and wine, because they were derived from evil substances. There was terrible danger within them. She implored him to trust her.

Jethro then spoke up. What Miriam meant by this assertion, he explained, was that there was an exclusively masculine energy in the bread and wine, which had served men well for many ages. It was about time that Moses availed himself of it. He had a mighty mission to fulfil for God, and here he was, being ordered about by his wife, a mere woman!

Jethro begged Moses to consider just how the children of Israel had fallen away from his command. They listened to no one but Miriam nowadays. It was a disgrace, the way they hung upon her every word. Even Zipporah, his own daughter, who had been reared to know better, would obey Miriam before she obeyed Moses. Was he really going to allow this sorry state of affairs to continue? The children of Israel had been entrusted to him by God, and he was permitting them to slip away from him. Would he not partake of God's ritual of the bread and wine, as in the old days, and reclaim his dignity? It was high time he took the Israelites in hand. There they were, down below, led by the women and involved in shocking orgies that revolved around pagan worship of idols. Was Moses not going to reassert his manhood, with the help of the bread and wine, and put a stop to it?

Uncertainly, for he still hesitated, Moses allowed Jethro to give him the reverse-spin bread and wine, so that he received the reverse-spin communion. Miriam cried out against it, but Jethro's words had hit home. Moses *was* jealous of Miriam, and wished to dominate her.

He swallowed.

CHAPTER SIXTY-ONE

The Angry Eye

I mmediately, the stone tablet Moses held seemed to jump of its own volition out of his grasp (without his knowledge, his own nerves and reflexes had rejected it). It smashed into many pieces upon the mountain-side. To Miriam, it was as if the Sapphire Tablet was their child, for the rites of the Sacred Marriage had taken place upon the mountain-top, and God had given the precious Tablet into their keeping through the power of their attuned ecstasy. She ran away weeping down the winding path.

Enlil then made his presence known to Jethro and Moses, and in a blaze of strange and lurid light, his ethereal form appeared among the rocks. Moses was confused. Was this the great presence whose embrace he had felt upon the mountain-top, come again to help him renew the tablet he had broken? Perhaps it was.

He listened impotently whilst Enlil ordered Jethro to wait for his son-in-law at the foot of the mountain. Enlil and Moses had business to conduct.

Enlil instructed Moses to hew a second stone. This stone was another block of sapphire, a black sapphire with a strange, sinister red light in it, like an angry eye (true black sapphire actually reflects pure light). Enlil subsequently did something to the stone (he 'wrote' something in it). After Enlil had finished directing a certain cosmically powerful force into it, all the flesh of Moses which was unprotected by his clothing glowed with a potent radiation. This noticeable glow did not abate for some days, and in fact killed him a year or two afterwards.

As Laurence Gardener points out, there exists incontrovertible evidence which confirms that the Israelites must have moved into Canaan or Palestine ('the Promised Land') very soon after Moses had received the Table of Testimony upon the holy mountain. As we know, Moses did not live to see the children of Israel cross into it. He died of radiation sickness, from which he would have been protected (through the resonance of his own bodily atoms with the reverse-spin forces) had he at any time accepted Enlil's plans to make him ruler of the world. As he did not accept them, Enlil, with characteristic callousness, left him to die slowly, a process which commenced from the moment of his encounter with Enlil on the lower half of the mountain.

Enlil then instructed Moses to inscribe the 'laws of God' upon the stone, which Moses did. These were just the laws of the Negative Confession, and they were nothing remotely remarkable because they were already in existence in Egypt, and had been for some considerable time. They were sensible, pragmatic laws, put in place to govern society. Although they followed the ordinances of God, they were not quite the inspired revelations of God, because they did not lift their students into the consciousness of God, whereupon everything would have become clear. (The Christ Consciousness speaking through Jesus and Mary repeats these laws in the Gospel of Mary, in their true form, where they are perceived as emanating from the heart of Divine Love.)

In fact, Enlil was not in the least interested in these commandments. He actually issued over forty of them, rather than ten. They were *commandments*, and they were almost all set out in negative mode ('Thou shalt *not*'), which would have made him proud at one time, but he had more important things on his mind just at the moment.

He had been careful to impregnate the glassy stone with something very deadly, something unimaginably powerful, which, once activated, would lead the Israelites to world domination in no time (relatively speaking). It made the Sapphire Tablet (Enlil's replacement) into an immeasurably destructive weapon of war, and its emanations could not only be physically harnessed, they could be psychically harnessed as well. In addition to its unspeakable material attributes, its terrible power was pregnant with the ability to turn the entire, collective mind of humanity into one giant weapon of mass destruction.

This terrible, lethal stone, Moses bore down the mountain. And as he descended, he grew more and more outraged, with a horrible, self-perpetuating wrath which seemed to enter him as a possessing spirit, at what Jethro had told him about the behaviour of the Israelites (which was actually complete fabrication, designed to tempt him to recoil from the sacred feminine forces and see them as unclean and unholy, as well as to cast a slur on his experience of the Sacred Marriage with Miriam on the mountain-top). When he reached the foot of the mountain, Lord Jethro and Miriam were waiting for him. There ensued a blazing row, in which Miriam stoutly defended the rights of her people, which Jethro wanted to erode by imposing upon them all sorts of laws and constraints which belonged to his own community, and which had been inspired and powerfully moulded and influenced by Enlil. In other words, the laws were repressive, constricting and burdensome, designed to lead to the creation of an inharmonious, cruel and oppressive society.

Jethro persisted. These were the *laws* of God, he bellowed in staccato tones – the *laws*, the *laws* of God, the *laws*! Moses *would* honour them! And, cowed and weary and unaccountably sad, Moses accepted these endless, tedious laws.

They were not exactly bad laws for the most part, but they were angled and designed to be applied in such a way as to maintain the materialistic, uninspired, status quo. There would be no change for the better.

Miriam was heartbroken and horrified. She had to make a stand. She caused an uprising, and, on Jethro's recommendation (the man had virtually taken over) Moses had her imprisoned. The only secure place (Miriam was a very determined woman, and there were many prepared to rescue her) was inside the mountain, within the temple of Hathor. Here she was confined for seven days, and thank goodness she was, because what transpired by her hand within that fateful week managed to save the world. It was not saved in the way that Tiâmat and her exalted company had laboured to make possible through the advent of Moses and Miriam, had Moses only listened to his intuition, but it was saved nonetheless.

Once Miriam had been marched off, Moses set to work on the Israelites. He was filled with an inextinguishable rage, an unreasoning fury, especially considering his former stance (Margaret Bailey and I have witnessed just such a huge surge of irrational rage towards a woman from a devoted male friend after he had taken the white powder – and we must remember that today's version of the white powder is not nearly so disruptive and deadly as Enlil's original recipe.) This rage was the only thing that seemed to give him new life and energy, for immediately prior to it he had felt distressingly drained. He roared around the camp, decrying Hathor and threatening everybody. (The Bible says that he even maimed and killed some of the Israelites.)

Moses denounced the very idea of the children of Israel also becoming the children of Hathor. And then he dragged the sanctified golden calf onto the fire, built up the flames, and proceeded, following Jethro's instructions, to melt the symbolic object down and create the white powder from it.

He forced the children of Israel to drink it in water (there was no time to bake the conical bread cakes, because his aim was to turn the people against Miriam and bring them swiftly under Enlil's control). Enlil must have hugged himself in high glee as he watched this procedure. He had bagged the children of Israel! Through his influence on Abraham, he had thought they could never be won over to Tiâmat, but after Jacob's almighty struggle on Mount Bethel all the generations of his issue had turned resolutely to her. And now, what had helped to inspire the minds and lift the hearts of the Israelites towards Tiâmat via the art of symbolism would deftly serve to place them utterly in his power!

Henceforth, the Israelites' beautiful worship of the Aten – the Aten which contained All, the Aten which was Tiâmat bearing Oannes within her – would be brutally diverted to worship of 'Adon'. Adon means 'lord', and in this new context it meant, very specifically, Enlil!

Deep within the confines of the abused temple of Hathor, Miriam wept. But her weeping and her sorrow were not passive. She had work to do, and she must work fast.

Summoning the power of the 'I Am' within her, the will-to-good of which she had a thorough command and understanding via her spiritual sisterhood with Hathor, Miriam sent forth a focused force which shattered the glassy 'sapphire' stone that Moses had brought down from the lower part of the mountain. Afterwards, she entered into the deep fastness of the Cave of Hathor, and, kneeling there, sensed the potency welling up from the centre of the earth, the power beneath. This was the force which Enlil sought to bend to his will and purposes in his production of the white powder. Alone in this sacred place, Miriam called on Tiâmat; and she called upon the Holy Grail.

Miriam was of the line descended from Queen Gra-al, as was Moses, Aaron, Kiya, Nefertiti and Zipporah; and yet it was she, Miriam, the chosen one, who held the power secreted in a profound place within her – the power of the Grail.

Miriam called, and her prayer was answered. A gleam of spiritual light brought a beautiful illumination, a flame of brilliant, liquid clarity, to the utter darkness of the sacred cave. Tears of relief and thankfulness fell from Miriam's eyes like crystal rain, glancing through the light and the darkness of her environment. She knew now that all would be well; not perfect, not as it could have been – but all would be well, all would be restored to its rightful course. Miriam entered the unfathomable silence, and dwelt in peace with Tiâmat.

CHAPTER SIXTY-TWO

The Ark of the Covenant

*B*efore Miriam was released from imprisonment, a divine message had been clearly received by Moses. He must give instructions for an ark to be built in which the shattered stone should be placed. (Moses brought only one stone down from the mountain. Tiâmat's stone was lost. The idea of two stone tablets relates to the confusion over the whole incident upon the mountain.) It was to be called thereafter the Ark of the Covenant. This message seemed to come from Enlil, and in some respects he did have a share in it. Enlil wanted the Covenant to be placed in an ark, and he also thought he influenced the design in that a *shem* – a tall conical tower, like a church steeple – was included in the finished vessel. These were to honour Noah and Shem respectively. But Enlil had been fooled.

It was time for the Ark to save the world again, just as it had done in Noah's early days. In this instance, however, it would not be a floating vessel, but it would be, as formerly, a vessel of containment. It was Enki and Nin-khursag who placed the idea of the Ark, ostensibly as homage to Noah, in Enlil's mind (he overlooked the significance of the fact that the seven rays of creation expressed in the rainbow arc was Tiâmat's sign), and Enki who whispered to Moses in his dreamless sleep that he should employ a certain craftsman to carry out the work who had been marked with distinction by God. This man duly offered himself for service, a young man hailing from Egypt, with relatives in Canaan.

He was the son of Uri, one of Moses's most important ministers. He believed there was a special service for him to perform in relation to his craft, for he had been shown in a dream that he must build a precious vessel to help Moses in his great work.

The young man's name was Bezaleel, a master craftsman and goldsmith. It was said of him that he had been filled with the spirit of the Elohim (the highest angels) in wisdom, understanding, knowledge and mystical craftsmanship. He was put in charge of the construction of the Tabernacle and the Ark, in which, as well as the crumbled Table of Testimony (which still contained its 'angry eye' intact – the epitome of the reverse-spin *ayin*), the 'hidden manna' and the 'shewbread' were to be housed. A distinction is drawn between these two, as well there might be. One was the bread of heaven, the other the bread of hell.

What was the 'hidden manna' that was placed *opposite* the shewbread (a most important, mirror-image point)? We think the clue is in the tamarisk plant which deposited the manna in the wilderness for the children of Israel to eat. It is simply, so simply, just that – an extract of a plant or herb equating to a wholly *natural* food. The Bible tells us that the manna was placed in a pot of gold, equating to the pot of gold at the end of the rainbow or Ark. The idea of the pot of gold at the end of the rainbow is an ancient Celtic theme, and, as we shall see, the Celts or Gaels descended directly from Aaron, pharaoh and cousin of Moses, and devotee of Miriam. This evocative image was part of Enki and Nin-khursag's teachings, which enshrined many mystical lessons within the symbol of the rainbow, and it is from Aaron and his esoteric knowledge that the story of the pot of gold at the end of the rainbow travelled down the Celtic line of inheritance.

This pot of gold was, literally, at the end of the Ark. What was within it? Did it contain some miraculous, heavenly food, worthy to be called the 'hidden manna'? Yes, it did. What was in the pot of gold was another golden substance, a properly ingestible one – honey!

The point of the honey (which is a complete food, and has many astonishing properties) is that it is of the yield of the good earth, and is a product of that most magical creature of such high significance to the alchemist – the bee. The bee, of course, belongs to a community which is presided over by a queen, and its harvest is one of pure gold: honey. The bee is striped with bands of darkness and light in perfect harmony and accord, creating an immaculate balance. The bee vibrates with the sacred 'Aum'. It is miraculous, because, according to scientists, its body weight and structure should make it unable to fly. And yet it flies, because it has overcome the restrictions and limitations of materialism, of matter.

There is a further secret concerning the bee. Esotericists say that it is not of earth, but that it has its origin on Venus, the only planet in the solar system to spin clockwise, and from where all humanity in our system was generated. The bee gathers pollen from flowers (flow-ers) to serve the queen and create the hive's yield of honey; and the white substance from the tamarisk plant which the Israelites found in the wilderness and called *manna*, meaning 'what is it?', was, of course, akin to pollen. The Israelites' question was provided with the answer, 'It is bread from heaven'. The crucial point is that they asked the question; and their soul (represented by Moses and Miriam) answered them in good faith. The lesson to be derived from this incident is that before we feed our bodies and our souls, we should question the authenticity and nature of the food of which we are about to partake. Then, if it is sham food or shewbread, it will be revealed to us as such by our soul.

It is interesting that the old form of the English word 'show', a form actually used in the early English translations of the Bible, is 'shew'. And so we see that the shewbread is showbread, sham bread. It is the sham *shem*. Its promise of heavenly, miraculous nutrition is all a show. It is hellish bread, not heavenly bread.

The difference between the shewbread and the hidden manna is so simple – a lesson for an innocent child. The good earth herself will feed us; she contains the 'hidden manna'. If only we will eat pure, nourishing wholefoods, foods which require no killing and bloodshed, foods which contain and promise no false 'mystery' (such as is the enticement of the false Divine Woman, the Whore of Babylon, who would feed us with substances that drug us), foods which contain instead the goodness of the earth, then we will absorb and imbibe the true alchemy, the hidden manna. This lesson resonates with every level of our being. The earth herself contains the 'hidden manna', the food of ascension; it is natural, pure and good. We must learn to eat such food if we are to ascend. All the processed foods, especially from the slaughterhouse and from factory farms, must go. We need to ask, 'What is it?'

We must learn the true danger lurking in unwholesome food. The fact that our supermarket shelves are groaning with such produce is a grand master-stroke of Enlil's reverse-spin genius. These foods spell decay and degeneration, of the soul as well as the body, and whilst ever we slay animals, there will also be human bloodshed upon the earth. We are asked to turn down all food that drugs us and chains us in manacles of materialism.

In the Ark, opposite the hidden manna or the pot of gold at the end of the rainbow, sits the ominous shewbread upon its table (the table which is a rendition of both the false Sapphire and Emerald Tables). Enlil has learned how to feed that shewbread, like a needle in the vein, into every system that supports our human communities. Let us no longer keep such a table!

We must remember that the choice is ours: the hidden manna – or the shewbread.

It is our belief that humanity is now ready to choose the hidden manna, the alchemical manna – the pot of gold at the end of the rainbow. As soon as we truly realise just what sort of a table we are presently gathered around and eating from, we will be ready to overturn it – just as Jesus overturned the shewbread or materialistic tables contaminating the sacred entrance into the temple. And, of course, this materialistic table that Jesus taught us to overturn without the least hesitation or compunction is the very opposite of the Emerald Table – the real altar of truth within our hearts. Meanwhile, we may ponder upon the bee, the pot of gold or honey, and the hidden manna: the bread of heaven. Such wonderful truths will arise from the potency of these symbols when our understanding fully embraces them!

Over the Tablet of Testimony, the stone table which Enlil had given to Moses and which Miriam had shattered, Bezaleel, who had been tutored in the mystical arts relating to craftsmanship by Enki, built the beautiful 'mercy seat' (an apt name indeed). This 'mercy seat' was guarded by two great images of angels, members of the Cherubim. They were traditionally placed at entrances to consecrated places as spiritual protectors. Tiâmat decreed that her faithful servant Bezaleel should put them in place above the fragments of the false Table of Testimony, that tablet of stone which had been infused with such guileful and sinister intention by Enlil, and given to Moses as if it constituted the Emerald Tablet itself. The Cherubim are in possession of many eyes, which enable them to stand guard comprehensively, protecting from above, below, and all around, and are of the *ayin*, the sacred consciousness of God.

So mystically skilled, so potent in his soul was Bezaleel that he was able to fashion images into which the spirit of the Cherubim actually entered.

The angels needed some kind of form with which to withstand the terrible frequencies emanating from the shattered table, which, according to the composition of the statues and the artistry with which they were made, helped them to throw a protective forcefield around the hideous energies of the stone fragments, so that they were contained within a ring of light. The entire Ark of the Covenant was forged from metals which, after being alchemically treated by Bezaleel and his servants, fulfilled a similar function. Much lavish finery was demanded by Enlil for 'his' Ark; but even its *shem* was designed around Aaron's 'budding rod', the magical serpent rod or lance which Tiâmat had blessed. And so Bezaleel appeared to obey Enlil's directives, but was secretly faithful to the wisdom of Miriam and the true God.

Enlil, thank goodness, was fooled throughout, and although in Exodus he is seen to encourage Moses in aggressive acts of warfare:

> *behold, I drive out before thee the Amorite, and the Canaanite, and the*
> *Hittite, and the Perizzite, and the Hivite, and the Jebusite. Take heed*
> *to thyself, lest thou make a covenant with the inhabitants of the land*
> *whither thou goest, lest it be for a snare in the midst of thee: But ye shall*
> *destroy their altars, break their images, and cut down their groves ... For*
> *thou shalt worship no other God: For the LORD, whose name is Jealous,*
> *is a jealous God: For I will cast out the nations before thee, and enlarge*
> *thy borders.*

(EXODUS, 34:11–14 & 24)

the divinely inspired skill of the alchemist Bezaleel ensured that the Israelites were protected from the savagery of the stone.

By Tiâmat's mercy, through Bezaleel's magical sealing and containing skill, via Moses's last determined stand, they never understood the cosmic power for ill they wielded, nor did they ever call upon its lethal potency.

The sort of ranting demonstrated above is typical of Enlil, and one can imagine him fairly frothing at the mouth as he revels in the prospect of ethnic cleansing, counsels poor Moses and the Israelites strictly against peace negotiations or judicious, peaceable conduct, and incites 'his' people to religious hatred and violence, topping all with a maniacally egotistical chest-beating concerning his right to total allegiance, and a big bribe, designed to appeal to the worst in human nature, to encourage the Israelites to express it. And he gives his name at last – not Jehovah or Yahweh, 'I Am That I Am', but a name that means 'Jealous'!

All of the passage quoted above relates in reality to Enlil's desperate lust to win the Grail-favoured land of Canaan for himself, and his fevered attempts to ensure that the Israelites did not worship at the altars of Enki, Nin-khursag and Lilith and were not swayed by their teachings, for theirs were indeed the true altars in place in Canaan, although others existed which belonged to immigrant communities that enjoyed a measure of the religious tolerance that the teachings of Enki sought to promote. Peace, tolerance, progressive cooperation, devoted service to the best and the highest within that was God in their hearts – these principles held the field in Canaan. No wonder Enlil carefully groomed the Israelites against responding positively to such a happy and harmonious scenario! The altars raised to Enki, Nin-khursag and Lilith were not dedicated to them as Gods, but as inner teachers of their temple who provided a conduit to the vision of the one true God.

It is true that these dreadful outbursts endorsing savagery and warfare are hidden within the endless listing of Jethro's Midianite laws, which are of course Enlil's laws (he obsessed about law-making, and nothing delighted him more than to craft them for every conceivable human activity, so that the miasma of his oppression might linger everywhere, over everything). Nevertheless, it might make us pause and wonder how we could ever have been deceived into thinking that these irate explosions of venom were the word of God. Enlil, wanting to impress the Israelites with his own grandeur as their god, made sure that the Ark of the Covenant seemed very beautiful and impressive in all its rich array and magnificent apparel. In truth, only the mercy seat was beautiful in every aspect, although Bezaleel's art was unsurpassed. What was within the Ark of the Covenant was a terrible travesty, the darkest talisman of the ravening death forces.

Enlil, of course, did his very best to groom Moses for world domination.

He wanted Canaan, and within it Jerusalem where the powers of the Grail were secreted, to be the centre of a global autocracy run by him via the Israelites – for the same old reason, of course, which was to eventually release the Naphidem onto the planet. Whenever the Israelites gathered for battle, when they marched into their promised homeland to claim it, the Ark of the Covenant was unfailingly borne before the troops on a litter (there were two rings on either side of it for staves, so that it could thus be carried). Despite his very best efforts, Enlil could never turn the heart of Moses towards a lust for global power, nor could he ever properly communicate to the Israelites through Moses just how cosmically potent the Ark of the Covenant was, or how they should use it.

The spiritual power of Bezaleel's art, which contained the highest angelic potencies as well as those of Enki and his consorts, soared above all, and the exquisite mercy seat, the seat of divine power over which the beautiful presence of Tiâmat brooded, poured forth the mercy of celestial protection, and kept the Israelites, and the world, safe from its hideous potential.

CHAPTER SIXTY-THREE

Miriam

*A*s Miriam was at last escorted out of her prison, she caused a vibration to sound deep in the bowels of the earth. It brought a fall and a crumbling of stone which effectively buried the temple of Hathor and sealed off all access to it. She had warned everyone present in the temple to flee it beforehand. They heeded her warning, because Miriam was an adored figure among the Israelites, and even among the Egyptian servants of the temple, to whom she was still their rightful queen.

Miriam's huge relevance to Moses's mission has been overlooked to the point of absurdity in the Old Testament. The children of Israel esteemed her and followed her guidance more than they valued and listened to Moses, and it was this uncomfortable truth which prompted Moses to swallow the red and the white powder when it was offered to him by Jethro, and, ultimately, rush down the mountain, engage in a furious row with Miriam, order her incarceration, and then, after venting his ungovernable rage further on the innocent Israelites, force-feed them the white powder himself.

Miriam was the chosen earthly daughter of Tiâmat, and from the first, even before she was born, she was deeply identified with Hathor, and received this deity's blessing in her secret cave.

Intriguingly, there is a direct line of association extending from Tiâmat, to Hathor and the star goddesses, to Rebecca, Jacob's mother, to Meretaten or Miriam, to the Queen of Sheba, to Mary Jacob, and at last to Mary Magdalene. Mary Magdalene was the ultimate and supreme 'daughter' of this line, the Christ daughter who, in a mystical sense, gave birth to her 'mother', Tiâmat or Tamar, thereby returning the most Holy Grail to earth, just as Jesus, the divine son, handed the priceless Emerald Tablet back down to John on earth, John who represented Oannes, the Supreme Father. And so the ineffable Daughter and Son handed back the divine authority to the Mother and the Father, whose foolish children of earth had managed to disconnect themselves from it.

It is important to understand that the bloodline itself is not sacred, and it is special only in that it facilitates the descent of highly evolved souls, reaching up as a heavenly staircase even to the most exalted among the Nephilim. It is a sort of halfway-house rendition of the Grail. We stress this because we believe it is essential to avoid harbouring superstitious beliefs concerning the bloodline, which would smack of racism and materialism. It progressed through many souls with feet of clay, as well as many whose divinity had spread its wings, before it reached its ultimate goal.

A text of great antiquity called the Book of Jasher records the historical details relating to Miriam. Although the Old Testament scribes wrote their version of the story centuries after it had occurred, Jasher himself had the advantage of being present as a witness to what he wrote. He was with the Israelites before they left Egypt, his birthplace, and was royal staff bearer to Moses. He seems to have been a trusted and punctilious servant, and his book was highly respected by the ancients.

Allusions to it in Joshua and Samuel cite it as an invaluable reference book concerning the grass-roots history of Moses, but because of its controversial aspects it was strategically ignored when the compilers of the Old Testament made their decisions regarding inclusion and exclusion of available texts.

The Book of Jasher makes it incontrovertibly clear that it was actually Jethro, not Moses, who became the mouthpiece of 'Jehovah', and that Jethro's strident will effectively sidelined Moses's authority. Jethro began to detail his own traditional Midianite laws to the Israelites, including the Commandments, as soon as Moses reached the foot of the mountain, as though all power of command belonged to him.

There has been some controversy regarding the Ten Commandments since the Egyptian Negative Confession was discovered. It suddenly became uncomfortably obvious that these laws which Moses had received on the holy mountain were neither original nor particularly inspired. It is somewhat tempting to imagine that the muttered comments from some of the less devout Israelites in the crowd around Moses once he had descended the mountain might have included 'Tell us something we don't know!', 'Is that what we've traipsed all this way to hear?' and 'We could have told you all that before you set off and saved you the trouble of the climb!'. These people had been educated and cultured in magnificent and esoterically-adept Egypt, and, quite frankly, they would have heard it all before.

Of course, now we know that Enlil could hardly be bothered with what went on the stone tablet, and that he just gave Moses something to write to keep him occupied whilst he was busy infusing a commodity of an unimaginably different nature into the stone, everything becomes clear.

In full realisation of this, Miriam asserted her will against Jethro's encroachment when Moses could not.

The Book of Jasher clarifies that as her husband stood helplessly before them at the foot of the mountain whilst Jethro took over and began to pontificate, the Dragon Queen in Miriam stepped forward in a blaze of conviction, demanding to know why the ancient traditions (the rites which had their genesis in Enki and Nin-khursag's temple in ancient Sumer) were to be supplanted by those of another, younger nation, one considerably less established in the sacred wisdom of the mystery schools. 'Shall Jethro instruct the Hebrews?' she vociferated. 'Are the children of Jacob without understanding?'

Jasher states specifically that 'the voice of the tribes of the congregation was on the side of Miriam'. It was at this point that Moses, feeling more and more out of control of the situation, particularly relating to the dimensions of his rising anger which was swiftly taking on the proportions of a fit of madness, ordered that Miriam should be imprisoned. The Israelites lamented his decision, and would not leave him alone concerning it. Jasher further reports that: ' the people of Israel gathered themselves together unto Moses and said, Bring forth unto us Miriam our counsellor.' Even the terrible incident of being force-fed with the white powder did not break their allegiance to this woman, whom they considered their leader.

Aaron, in particular, valued Miriam highly, and set her authority above that of Moses. It was Aaron who gave his sacred rod to Bezaleel to provide the model for the *shem* included in the Ark of the Covenant – and he gave it at Miriam's behest. Aaron consulted and conferred with Miriam constantly, and we see that Moses had struggled with his ego regarding Miriam from the beginning of their relationship, alternately adoring and resenting her. Aaron was the founding father of the Scottish and Irish Gaels (a title very similar to 'Gra-el', the Hebrew rendition of Princess Gra-al's name), via his daughter, Princess Scota, who generated the race.

The Gaels commemorate Miriam and her supremely royal Dragon Queen heritage in their own inheritance of her flame-red hair, for she, Aaron and Moses all belonged to the Egyptian royal family in descent from Ham, which, of course, had its origins in Mesopotamian antiquity. Esau, their nearer ancestor, is reported as also inheriting this fiery red hair.

The Book of Aaron, whose author was Hur, grandfather of the illustrious Bezaleel, tells us:

> Miriam from hence became the admired of the Hebrews; every tongue sang of her praise. She taught Israel; she tutored the children of Jacob – and the people called her, by way of eminence, the Teacher. She studied the good of the nation, and Aaron and the people hearkened to her. To her the people bowed; to her the afflicted came.

It is worth noting that, although Enlil constantly hijacked the Israelites' perception of the Aten and strove his utmost to translate it into his own currency, it was indeed the Aten (Tiâmat – in whom Moses perceived and worshipped the Eternal Father as well as the encircling, mysterious Feminine: the void, the unutterable mystery, which Akhenaten called 'the Aten'), that the children of Israel worshipped and set at the centre of their lives. Even though they were forbidden to speak the word 'Aten' in favour of a direct reference to himself – 'Adon', or 'Lord', Enlil was finding this 'one God' business a double-edged sword. At first he had encouraged it, because one of his favourite imperatives was that *he* should be set above all and adored as the 'most high God'.

Now it seemed as though the whole concept was highly dangerous, and kept opening up the consciousness of the people to the despised Tiâmat!

Enlil, in the end, had been terrified of Abraham's conception of the One God (derived from Enki's original teachings), because it kept slipping beyond his command, reaching to Tiâmat and almost restoring the earth's connection to her. He had managed to deal with that emergency successfully, and, after applying himself with the full force of his power and cunning to the problem of Moses, he had also latterly managed to bring Moses's perception under his dominion, even calling himself by Tiâmat's name ('I Am That I Am', or Jehovah, and YHWH, the Tetrad, the Four Sacred Persons), and was acknowledged by Moses when he did so. As far as Enlil was concerned, he seemed to have brought the situation under control, and had accomplished his mission.

He afterwards pirated Enki's idea, espoused and proclaimed by Akhenaten and his family, of the One God, and had people worship him as such, because he preferred it despite its dangers and drawbacks relating to Tiâmat. He had, in fact, been attempting to get his followers to think of him as the One God for centuries, and had imposed all sorts of injunctions and threats to try to persuade them to do it. Although they accepted the concept, in practice they stuck steadfastly to the idea of the divine Tetrad, because the symbol of the Four Divine Persons – Mother-Father-Daughter-Son – was an ancient understanding of Tiâmat, whose memory their souls unconsciously craved. It was not until after the time of Moses, when Enlil had finally hijacked Akhenaten's spiritual teachings, that he began to be worshipped by his devotees as the One God.

Because of the heartbreaking state of affairs, Miriam parted from Moses when she was eventually released from prison (poignantly enough, on the eighth day, associated with Ascension).

She conferred with Aaron, and he, as a royal priest, agreed in his lifetime to block the custom of feeding shewbread to the kings who would arise from the established nation of Israelites in Canaan, so that they might be delivered of its curse.

(He also did his best to prevent the priesthood from ingesting the shewbread, but because of the strong contingent initially headed by Jethro, his valiant attempt was unsuccessful.)

Despite Jethro, the original vision of Moses continued to inspire his people, and some aspects of his mission were partially triumphant. Ultimately, he listened to Aaron, and grieved for his beloved lost wife. He eventually gave his support to Aaron's condemnation of the shewbread, especially as he intuitively knew that the substance which had harmed him and caused his painful, lingering death was connected to the white powder. Through his sacrifice and his aspiration, the Israelites maintained the spiritual strength to hold Enlil in containment, and to prevent his destruction of the world.

Miriam, with many devout followers, wandered in the Sinai wilderness, and in Canaan, for many years. She gave birth to her daughter, the 'calf of Hathor', who further secured the renewed grounding of the Grail energies in that country. Often, on her travels, Miriam would order a circle of small stones to be laid out on the ground in a specific location. A triangular shape built of similar stones would be placed inside the circle, and in these rings of stone Miriam taught her people regarding the secrets of ascension (in later years this knowledge travelled with her followers to the gypsies of the Baltic regions). We believe that such triangles exist invisibly in many of the stone circles of Britain and elsewhere.

When Miriam died, the Israelites were distraught – not only her own personal followers, but her wider supporters. The Book of Jasher relates that she died in Kadesh:

> *The children of Israel mourned for Miriam forty days; neither did any man go forth of his dwelling. And the lamentation was great, for after Miriam arose up no one like unto her; … and the flame thereof went out into all the lands … yea, throughout all Canaan; and the nations feared greatly.*

High up on the east corner of Lincoln Cathedral – the eastern side of the building which enshrines many Grail clues within its rising sun symbolism of promise and hope and new beginnings – a strange stone head looks out towards the Grail site.

It is another of the intrepid Mr Jensen's discoveries, and at first it seems a disconcerting spectacle. Certainly, and understandably, he designated it as a 'she-devil'. Clearly feminine, covered in thick, black, snaking hair and sporting a pair of horns, it is faceless, for its face has been torn off. Literally defaced, it looks down in its gouged state, a blank enigma reminiscent of the defaced statues of Nefertiti, the queen whose portraits were hidden away and hung upside down as an ultimate statement of dishonour.

Her husband, Akhenaten, was similarly disfigured, and referred to, when he was mentioned at all, as 'that damned one' and 'the rebel'.

This portraiture in stone that hangs so high on the cathedral's east corner is a depiction of Meretaten, daughter of Nefertiti and Akhenaten, who with her Egyptian hair and the horns of Hathor, the goddess whom she represented on earth, looks down protectively upon the Grail site, for she is truly one of its most illustrious guardians; Meretaten who was Miriam, who drew the Sapphire Tablet from the heart of Tiâmat, and who whispered intimations of that coming one that was her namesake – 'Miriam' or 'Mary' Magdalene.

CHAPTER SIXTY-FOUR

Down with Enlil!

*A*s Alice and the March Hare argued between them at the Mad Hatter's tea-party, it is important to say what you mean, and to mean what you say. We hope you will join with us when, in honouring their advice, we chorus 'Down with Enlil!' We might well add, 'and about time, too!', for this historical point we have reached where we can entirely oust him has been a long time in coming.

Of course, ridding ourselves of Enlil does not mean deposing anyone, or marching against a foe in an act of war. The glorification of war in all its many differing aspects is exactly what Enlil has promoted down the centuries. The war that we are required to fight is of the subtlest kind, because it necessitates mastery of our lower self. That is the level of life under Enlil's control. It is where his tenta-cles are wrapped around us in unrelenting malice.

When Miriam closed off access to the temple of Hathor, the production of the white powder became a problem. It could still be manufactured, of course, but not in the quantities that the refined energies of the Cave of Hathor made possible. After Moses and Aaron banned the ritual ingestion of the white and the red powder by the kings and did their utmost to block its dispensation to the priests, the preparation and administering of the powders became subject to severe restriction. Canny as ever, and still with Noah very much on board, Enlil and his followers found a way to feed its substitute to those people on earth who came under his sway.

The beautiful *khu* could be given etherically, through loving mouth-to-mouth contact, as indeed it was given to Jesus by Mary Magdalene, who 'kissed her often on the mouth', according to the Gospel of Philip. It was this sacred act that Enlil and Noah artificially replicated in horrible mimicry. They used subtle, astral means, so that those who were willing could receive the false communion via a kind of etheric feeding tube, directly into the chakra-system. Here it takes on the colour of a violently bright, eerily beautiful gold, being the ethereal part of reverse-spin gold. Its effect is not quite as spectacular as the physical powder, but it performs its function efficiently enough.

Miriam's dramatic effect on world history in one of its aspects was that, once she had acted against the distribution of the white powder, it was no longer given as a birthright to the kings (even occasionally including queens and princesses) and therefore broadcast automatically to their respective nations. Although, via Enlil's machinations, the kings continued sometimes to receive it, especially if they expressed pronounced spiritual greatness (such as King David), the procedure was by no means wholesale, as it had been before.

The huge significance of this is that, once the white powder could no longer generally be fed to the kings as a physical substance, it could forthwith no longer be imposed on anyone without their consent. The subtle white powder, fed into the consciousness via the etheric body in concentrated degree by Enlil's revised method, could now be wholly rejected by the recipient. The priests, of course, continued to broadcast it etherically on Enlil's behalf, and many of the populace who thus received it did not reject it outright. Even those who refused to receive it were afflicted and handicapped by it – a situation which very much persists today. Nevertheless, the threat of overwhelming obstruction to human free will was removed, and the global prospect brightened. Enlil was frustrated in his attempts to lure us into a helter-skelter descent of his perpendicular path of doom.

We have within our heads a magical stone, like the toad stone of legend which folktale relates is played over by many mottled hues of gold. It is indeed, although the colour of the stone, as we shall see, is actually a heavenly, bright sapphire blue, as was the *Schethiyd* that Moses carried down from the mountain. The *Schethiyd's* resonance with and partial activation of the stone in the head is what would have brought enlightenment to the peoples of the world, had Enlil not interposed his will.

This stone in the head, at the physical level of life, comprises the slightly more than 5 per cent dry weight of noble metals (members of the platinum group) which exist naturally within the human brain. These metals are iridium and rhodium in what Laurence Gardner calls the 'high-spin state', which is not the negative spin that Enlil imposed on his powder, but what can and should be the high-spin state of true ascension, as long as we are careful not to get waylaid and tempted off-course into Enlil's waiting dimension! It is this stone which will be fully activated by the Holy Grail, when we receive the blessing and the teachings of the Grail (the teachings of the Emerald Tablet).

It is this stone, too, which Enlil wants to make dysfunctional. To this end, he dispenses the white powder (seemingly more dangerous than the red, although the red certainly plays its part in focusing the death forces) via subtle means to the susceptible people of earth (a considerable number of us). Not understanding how to conclusively refuse it, we take the false bread, the false wine, to a greater or lesser degree, and receive communion with the false god, the god of retribution, violence and wrath, of both unconscious and wanton cruelty, of materialism, intolerance, self-seeking values and the self-perpetuation of misery – the god who makes the darkness glitter as if with the promise of good things. The ethereal substance of the white powder, with ruinous precision, perpetuates the denial and repudiation of the Sacred Feminine within men, and the obscuration of its beauty and potency in women. That was the imperative motive that fuelled its design. This false communion creates the 'mad hat' of Enlil, a dark enclosed tomb which sits as an ethereal shadow over the Stone of Ascension within our consciousness and within our actual heads, sending it into a death-like sleep so that we build our world as if in a confused dream.

In *Alice in Wonderland,* the Mad Hatter admits to Alice that he has damaged his relationship with Time (Father Saturn, whose positive forces Enlil chokes, distorts and reverses), and so the backwards-rotating, nonsensical world Alice finds herself in is frozen in time, unable to progress.

The point at which time froze was six o'clock, which is of interest, not only because six o' clock is definitely *not* the usual Victorian tea-time hour (Lewis Carroll wrote during the Victorian era, during which 'tea' – a pot of tea with sundry sweet and savoury snacks – was served between 3 and 5 pm), but particularly because the figure 6 is the reverse of 9, the number of the soul and of the Divine Feminine. Somehow this divine number has been turned on its head and petrified in a death-like trance. It seems that the Mad Hatter, presiding over the tea-party (human society), is an expression of the spell under which Enlil holds humanity. He teaches us that whilst ever we wear the 'mad hat' of Enlil, the cycles of human development will really take us nowhere, because, despite the appearance of progress, we will just endlessly repeat the same old mistakes until we eventually destroy our civilisation.

In his book, *Fingerprints of the Gods*, Graham Hancock draws on convincing evidence to show that advanced human culture is much older than we imagine, and that we have visited catastrophe on ourselves over and over again.

In the varying traditions of many contemporary tribal peoples across the globe, such a worldwide catastrophe is forecast for the very near future.

We say that humanity can and will transform what is so direly predicted, because, thanks to the Grail, we are about to dispossess ourselves en masse of our 'mad hats'.

It is worth noting that the atmosphere around the earth, which gives us our beautiful blue skies, represents just over 5 per cent of the weight of the earth, the same ratio as the iridium and rhodium content within our brains. These exalted metals in their high-spin state, which constitute the Stone of Ascension within us, create the ethereal atmosphere in the brain which, when activated correctly, will integrate our earthly brain with the ascension of our individual conscious-ness. It can easily be seen why this is the meaning of the sapphire blue ray which Miriam and Moses received from Tiâmat at the summit of the holy mountain. The ethereal part of our brain, correlative to the atmosphere of the planet, is what will carry us upwards, once it is activated by the knowledge of the Emerald Tablet.

This knowledge can only be received, understood and sparked into operational life by the heart, our own Emerald Tablet or Grail residing within us; but it is the mind, the sapphire, which must prepare and attune itself and kneel in service to the heart, before the heart can come fully into its own and give forth its spiritual life-forces. Therefore, our mind needs to receive the Emerald Tablet as teachings or in book form, so that we may stimulate its essence within us, and translate its spiritual knowledge into a form which we can faithfully apply to our earthly lives. The profounder essence of the Emerald Tablet cannot be received or understood in the earthly mind, but only by the God-attuned intelligence which dwells as a spiritual flame, deep in the secret recesses of the heart. When both forms of intel-ligence, the earthly and the divine, begin to work together within us, the power of the heart is no longer obstructed.

In preparing ourselves for the Grail, then, we need to overturn Enlil's rule. How do we get rid of Enlil? We stop feeding him and his power-source! We do this by awakening from our heavy sleep in materialism (imposed by his design) and opening our consciousness to the spiritual reality of life. We do it by ridding our lives of cruelty in all its aspects – our own, perhaps unconscious, cruelty to others – our cruelty and violence of language, our cruelty and violence of thought; our cruelty to ourselves in imposing alienating value-systems on our lives which we flog ourselves mercilessly to maintain; and the cruelty inherent in our everyday lives through the exploitation of abused workers, of animals (whose terrible collective suffering, which we ourselves thoughtlessly inflict, is even greater than that of human beings) and of the planet.

We do it by properly honouring and obeying the sacred feminine principle, which encourages us to be wise, to be nurturing and merciful, to see things by the light of the intuition and to be unafraid of the astonishing realities this light will reveal, and which will entail a final laying-down of the male supremacism that still exists and is still part of the societal framework and mores of our countries, in the West as much as in the East. Then the sacred masculine principle will arise in its true guise and glory, and men will come to see in wonderment who and what they truly are.

We do it by sacrificing our need to be angry and resentful, contemptuous and demeaning, towards others, by recognising that we are children of the same all-embracing God and that this Divine Spirit loves each one of us equally, whatever and whoever we are. We do it by halting the urge within us to dominate or dictate, and by allowing an unshakeable respect for others, an empowered harmlessness, an inspired and loving tolerance, to flower within our attitudes to life.

We do it by calling on and trusting our inner strength to resist the temptation to bow helplessly and succumb before those principles or those persons who would dominate or dictate to us. And we do it especially by refusing to bow to the tyrants of fear, shame, self-doubt, and the tyranny of the will of the little self – the self of earth which is not the 'I Am', called the self-will or the lower will – which always wants to dominate and dictate to us.

Yet, most of all, we do it by reclaiming our most holy dragon heritage, granted to us from our very beginning in an ineffable act of love by Tiâmat, which we have allowed Enlil to take from us.

In this mighty and sanctified undertaking, we reconnect with the God-sourced magic in our hearts which will guide us with perfect, unfaltering steps through all of the above-mentioned accomplishments, so that we achieve an ideal balance between the boiling chasms on either side of every principle we seek to embrace and express. And we do it by cheerfully forgiving ourselves on the occasions when we 'fail' to live up to all these high expectations! Failure is not failure; it is delayed success, a further stepping-stone to success. Forgiveness is magical. When we forgive ourselves, we take away the burden that would otherwise turn us away from our path of attainment.

It is time to learn how we can each become a dragon again – an exalted creature of spiritual light, breathing divine fire, expressing its right royal inheritance.

Let us transfigure ourselves into dragons!

CHAPTER SIXTY-FIVE

Transforming Ourselves into Dragons

*T*he first thing we must remember as we set out on the mission of restoring our own Dragonhood is that Enlil has no power over us. This may seem a strange assertion when we look out on the world and see him riding so high on the cusp of the waves of power. Everywhere, it seems, Enlil has made his mark and claimed his dominion. Yet it is true to say that he may wield over us only that measure of power which we, consciously or unconsciously, are willing to give into his hands.

Enlil has created a terrible smoke-demon of fear which oppresses and demoralises us. As the spearhead of all the confusion, anxiety and darkness of the material world, he can only too easily seem all-powerful. It is what he strives to make us think. But in actual fact, he is impotent. The death-forces he embraces are, to state a truism, without life. They have no impetus of creativity. Of course, this does not mean to say that if we make a gift to him of *our* life and creativity, he cannot capitalise on them to the highest degree. He still has some control over our karma, although the judgment aspect of a lord of karma has been removed from him entirely. What he can do, and revels in so doing, is to hurl at us devastating thunderbolts of the negative karma we ourselves create. He cannot operate outside cosmic law, but he can apply it in such a way as to make life much darker and more distressing and difficult for us here on earth than it was ever intended to be.

The initial step on our journey, therefore, is to cut Enlil down to size and to reclaim the 'I Am' that exists within us. We do this very simply, through the breath. We may think of the House of Shimtî, meaning 'breath-wind-life', Nin-khursag and Enki's miraculous 'Creation Chamber', designated as such because it contained the essence of, and linked them to, God. We might bear in mind that the translation of Lilith is 'wind spirit', and that, as the Divine Couple progressed their crucial mission, the Gnostic gospels tell us that Mary Magdalene and Jesus kissed often on the mouth, sharing the Holy Breath.

The breath is deeply magical, and, if we would become dragons, we need to know how to use it. We need to breathe fire – the right sort of fire, which is light. As dragons, we breathe easily and without effort from the centre of our bodies, yet ensuring that we gently fill our lungs to their capacity, and peacefully empty them (we cannot entirely empty them, because a small residue of air must always remain within the lungs). In doing this, people sometimes find it easier to visualise their lungs filling with air and expanding to the sides, rather than thrusting out at the front of the body. We focus on our breath to calm and steady the mind.

We now attune to the 'I Am', the great 'Aum' of Buddhism. When we assert our 'I Am' selves, we begin to stimulate the divine inner fires which allow us to assume our true Dragonhood. Enlil, we must remember, wants to force us into our lower saurian-hood, whereby we become the tortured dragon of wrath bound on the wheel of its own self-destruction, the opposite of the divine Ouroboros. This wrath-dragon of the lower self is an entirely earthbound creature, sub-human and divested of all the magnificence of its spiritual heritage.

We tame it with the breath and the reclaiming of the 'I Am', which allows the royal dragon, the Pendragon ('head dragon' – in more than one sense, when we consider the Stone of Ascension), to come into its own.

We now choose any quality of the higher self of which we stand in particular need. It might be courage or strength, peace or harmony, love or kindness, patience or endurance, clarity or joy – any one of a vast number of exalted spiritual states which we are finding difficult to achieve or maintain. We then intone the simple mantra:

I AM Divine Peace

or:

I AM Divine Love

or:

I AM Divine Wisdom

etcetera, etcetera; whatever it is that you feel you need in order to banish the shadows from your life. The mantra is said whilst focusing on your breathing and on your words. Say it peacefully, slowly, powerfully. Say it many times, until it becomes a rhythm pulsing through your mind, effortless, resonant, musical.

There is a special form of the 'I Am' which is particularly potent. It is the mantra of the Holy Grail, because, of course, the Grail is the Resurrection, our own personal resurrection from the tomb in which Enlil has sought to constrict us for so long: the rolling away of the Stone of Death from the door of our prison:

I AM the Resurrection and the Life.

Of course, the 'I AM' is not a reference to the little self of earth, to which feelings of grandiose self-importance might attach themselves. The 'I AM' is our God-self, our Pendragon self, which cannot be swayed by petty egotism, but remains always noble, always humble; because it is centred in humility, humiliation cannot wound it. Select a mantra and repeat it for a few minutes each day, or whenever you have need of it. Thus will you begin to re-establish the power of the dragon that Enlil has sought to leach away from you.

To become dragons, we also need to reclaim the unwavering gaze of the dragon: the Ayin, by means of which it can control its own inner cosmos and work spiritual miracles within its own environment. This unwavering gaze is the focus of the mind; and it is the mind we must learn to still and strengthen, so that it may begin to reflect the many hues of the Ineffable One, the heavenly Dragon Queen.

To clarify the mind so that we may reflect the eternal flame of the Divine, we need to meditate regularly. Five minutes each day makes a good beginning, although, as you come to enjoy meditation more and more, you will probably wish to extend this period to twenty minutes. If five minutes a day is too much for you at first, simply start with two. The important thing is that it is done.

> *We take for our first meditation symbol the beautiful form of a rose. It is our Dragon Chalice, from whose depths we absorb our sacred and divine Dragon heritage. The rose is pink, because it harmonises the red and the white life forces, and we see it blooming in the heart centre. Gently stabilise your inner focus upon the rose in the heart, and inhale its pure fragrance. Assume a rhythm whereby you breathe in the perfume of the rose, all the while keeping your inner gaze upon it, and absorb the entirety of its healing, calming, inspiring essence. Then breathe it out to the world. Just spend five minutes doing this peaceful exercise, or longer if you wish to.*
>
> *Our next symbol is the eternal flame. It is the power of our Dragon form. (It is only necessary to work with one image each day, changing it as you prefer.) See a flame of liquid light curling into the heavens. This mirror-bright flame might be a candle-flame, the shape of two hands joined in prayer; or it might rise from some mystical source in the interior of the earth, ascending like an angel of purest light. It might be a flame like the northern lights, dancing its spirit dance in a swirl of mystical colours. This flame, too, is in your heart; breathe in its light, flood your entire being with its brilliance, and then breathe it out to the earthly world, for its blessing and healing.*

Our third image is a sword of hallowed light. It is our Dragon keenness of spirit. Its blade of glory points upwards. We feel it in our spine and wield it in our hearts, and we can reach into the heart centre and take it, still pointing upwards, in our hand. We dispel the shadows that press in upon us with this sword. It tames the dragon of the lower self. It fills us with courage. Fear in all its manifold forms is driven away. See its light shooting upwards in a streak of spiritual purity and beauty. If we ever seek to use it selfishly or violently, we shatter the sword. We can still use the breath in conjunction with the sword, for we breathe in its holiness, its surety, its protection, and then breathe out these peace-yielding gifts to the world.

Our final symbol is that of Silence. This is the Dragon-stone, the Stone of Ascension. We might find this concept too obscure to be able to cope with it in meditation purely as a state of being. If so, we can imagine it as a ring of immaculate light, as of the vestal light in the brilliant flash of diamonds.

Go through that ring of light as if you crossed the threshold into a gem of unimaginable radiance, as if you stepped into the heart of a boundless star. Dwell in the light, and be aware of your breath and the pulse of your heart. This is the rhythm of Silence, this is the pulse of Silence. Dwell in the hallows of the Silence, and send forth its pulsation of creative love into the human world that struggles below the heavens.

We will note that four symbols are given. They are the four symbols of the Grail, our Dragon heritage. They will help us in our bid to reclaim it. If difficulty is experienced with the idea that the symbols exist in the heart, just see the image as if face to face with it, with an inner knowing that its dwelling-place is the beautiful shrine in the heart centre.

When we sit for meditation, we ensure that we are comfortable and relaxed, and that our spine is as straight as possible (support it if this gives greater ease). When we emerge from meditation, we have to be careful to seal our higher centres, for our own protection. This just takes a few seconds. In imagination, hold the symbol of a bright silver cross of light enclosed within a circle of light over the two crown centres, the brow centre, the throat centre, the heart centre, and over the solar plexus.

The symbol of the cross of light within the circle of light is the great Sign of Tiâmat. It is the Mark of Cain, or kingship ('Cain' or *Qayin* translates as 'king' or 'queen'). It is the symbol of the royal or exalted Dragon, the symbol of our highest humanity. We can use this great and glorious symbol as a mighty form of protection. Practise creating it in an instantaneous sweep of the imagination. Stand within the intersection of the cross, at its heart, where a star of the fire of God burns with a measureless light. No darkness, no evil, can withstand this light. It must halt, turn back, hide its face. Assume your Dragon heritage, merge with the light of the star, and know that nothing can touch you. You are a child of God. You cannot be harmed or overcome. Nothing evil can come near you. All is well.

We also need to use the magic of the true Ark of the Covenant in overcoming Enlil and his army of dark-orientated entities and human beings who seek to usurp our rightful inheritance of the earth. They enslave us by filling our minds – our thoughts, emotions, percipience and attitudes – with fear, intolerance, distaste, harshness, dread, unhappiness, criticism and negativity, from which anger and even violence and desecration arise.

To counteract the unpleasant activities of Enlil's invading army, we nourish ourselves with the food of the gods. This 'nectar of supreme excellence' is, in earthly terms, simply honey, for honey has an unsurpassed ethereal counterpart that nourishes the soul. The magic of the Sacred Feminine and the *khu* is within it. Its essence is gathered from flowers, just as the Scarlet Priestesses were the flowers who fed the *khu* to the earliest kings when the human pattern of the androgyne was split. It is indeed a form of natural gold.

However, although it is very good to take physical honey in balanced quantities, we can use its ethereal qualities with great effect to thwart the intentions of the interlopers. We do this by first softening, making gentle, the negative thoughts or feelings that come swirling into our soul-space – our mentality and emotional self. Soften and make gentle the way the inrush of negativity has made you feel. Now turn the focus of the *ayin* – the inner eye – to the thought of honey. It is utterly sweet, like the balm of a new day or evening birdsong. It is not cloying or saccharine-sweet, for its sweetness turns the soul to God. Its sweetness is the divine antidote to the burden of degradation and disgust, or the burning sting of distress, that the negative inundation has created within you. Take the ethereal essence of honey, like an angelic thought, deep inside your mind and soul, into your emotional self, into your suffering nervous self. It will actually soothe away an acid stomach or a sense of bitterness in the mouth and throat. It gets rid of the deposits of misery and sullenness and general negativity that envelop us from within. It gets rid of the gloop and mire of mind-controlling influences. Take in ethereal honey, take in sweetness, and feed it to your heart and mind. Feed it to the *ayin*, and look out at the world through softened, gentled eyes, through sweetened vision.

Now let the honey flow from your heart and mind into your language. Dare to use this new language! It takes away the tongue's need to lash and flail. It transforms the wormwood in our everyday linguistic constructs. It cleanses and purifies. It is the secret of the true Ark of the Covenant.

You can do the same with pain, sickness and irritation. Pour honey into the site of distress, ethereal honey from the gardens of paradise. It is the kiss of God, the touch of the angels. It will help you. Think of an inundation of honey, mellifluent, cradling you in gentle sweetness. Your very bones will respond.

The beautiful six-pointed star, described in the first chapter of this book, is the supreme key to the reclamation of our Dragonhood. It is the 'Aten', the perfect star that shines from the mystical heart of the sun. Its light is the issue of God. It is formed from two equilateral triangles, one with its pinnacle pointing upwards, and the other with its pinnacle pointing downwards. The merging of these two triangles creates the six-pointed star, but, unlike the Star of David, it bears no inner divisions. The fusion of the two triangles creates a flawless unity. It is expressed in a great blaze of supernal light.

The star is within our hearts. We find it by focusing gently on the breath, and letting its light shine forth. The star in our hearts connects with the great, blazing star in the heavens, the six-pointed star of the spiritual dimensions, for truly they are one. Having created the star, having summoned it into being, we know that the star is in our hearts, that we stand within the heart of the star, and that it also shines above us in the overarching skies of the spirit. These realities exist simultaneously.

Now we can project the light of the star. We do it with the out-breath, with the gentle, steady focus of the mind, with a blaze of love from the heart centre. If we find it difficult to feel love on command, then the trick is to *act* as if we are feeling that current of love. When we act with true intent rather than in order to deceive, the act itself forms a channel through which higher beings can nourish us with the genuine essence of what we are expressing. This is the crucial difference between dramatic art and sham, and the secret as to why great actors can move us so deeply. We act within ourselves, within our hearts, as if we conjured the outflow of love with a magical command. We know that it is there, we have faith that it goes forth from us – and it does.

There are special hours at which we can make a supreme connection with the star. They occur at the points of 3, 6, 9 and 12 o'clock throughout the 24-hour cycle. Twelve noon, the meridian, is the most powerful of all, being the heart centre of the day. If, whenever we can, we take a two-minute or even a one-minute break from whatever we are doing, and send forth this light with a spoken blessing on humanity and the world so that it encircles the planet, we will prepare ourselves and the earth for the coming of the Grail.

We can project this light into our homes, our places of work, to local and international trouble spots, to people who are in need of help. The light may be radiated to animals, to places in nature, to gardens, even to individual trees and plants. It is never forced on anyone, nor is it projected to bring into being any personal preference concerning another person's behaviour or decision. It is simply a free gift from the heart, for the recipient to accept or refuse as they will.

Our dragon nature, our higher self, scintillates far above the pushiness and desire for control which belong to the ego, and brings that ego, the little earthly self, into the heart of the greater self, so that its humanity and its connectedness with earth remain, but its inharmonious aspects do not. They are caught up, transformed into a perfect energy, pulsating in rhythm with the divine light of the star – the light of God.

As we use the star, we will receive absolute confirmation of its truth and reality, and of the actuality of the spirit and the higher worlds from which it shines.

We will no longer be tempted to think that the dull veil of the earth dimension is all that exists, or that we are helpless, impotent creatures living finite lives on an insentient ball of rock. We are dragons, and the worlds which are our birthright are glorious and infinite.

A number of people have been working with the star for several decades now (and some long before that, because the star is an ancient and eternal symbol). Not all such people may think of themselves as dragons – but in ethereal vision their astral forms are revealed as replete with many-coloured flourishing dragon crests and streaming manes of unfathomable light, with swirling tails or wings like outspread tongues of flame dancing through their auras. Truly we are dragons, and our Dragonhood is waiting for us to consciously assume it once again.

It will benefit us hugely if we carry out a simple exercise, designed to do a great work.

We have forgotten the divine crozier within us, which is part of our supreme legacy from Tiâmat and which connects us to the beautiful Tree of Wisdom (called in the Bible the 'tree of the knowledge of good and evil') in her heart. So that we might be led back into the pure sheep-fold of that ineffable heart, we need to properly reconnect our awareness, our consciousness, according to the shape and conductive power of our crozier. Only by so doing will we re-charge our unicorn's horn chakra, located at the top of the forehead at its mid-point, so that we might once again take our part in the grand symphony of the stars, and receive the grace of exalted, starlit consciousness, our link restored at last to the roots, the foliage and the fruits of the Tree of Divine Intelligence, the Tree of Wisdom.

We can do this work, either standing or sitting with the spine straight and relaxed, with a clear quartz crystal (a tumbled stone or a point), or by a simple act of visualisation:

Reconnecting to the Sacred Tree

Just see the brilliant white light of the spirit running up the spine to the base of the brain, progressing over the head to the first crown chakra (actually located at the point of the crown), to the second crown chakra, the unicorn's horn at the top of the forehead at its mid-point, and then dipping to the third eye chakra, which is situated in-between, and a little above, the eyebrows. The light comes up the spine, curves over the head, and dips to the brow, forming the shape of the divine crozier, or shepherd's crook. Hold this radiant form gently and firmly in your inner vision for a moment. That is all there is to it. If you wish to use the clear quartz crystal, simply cleanse it by washing it swiftly under the cold tap each time you use it, and place it on the point of each chakra as you do the visualisation exercise. Let the exercise flow, and your will and intention will do the work for you.

Practising this exercise once or twice a day will prepare us to receive the Grail and facilitate our enlightenment.

Alice Through the Looking-Glass ends with a question, a kind of manna ('What is it?'). Alice-Chalice wonders whether her dream of passing through the glass and back again was her own dream, or that of the Red King (the red, Saturnine king being a symbol of Enlil). 'Which do you think it was?' asks Lewis Carroll astutely. To answer his question, we must awaken to the truth.

Then it will be Alice's dream we live and move in – the dream of the triumphant soul – and no longer that of the Red King and his topsy-turvy, false mirror-image, reverse-spin, completely nonsensical world.

CHAPTER SIXTY-SIX

The Syndicate

*A*s we look towards the discovery of the Holy Grail, there is one difficult and unpleasant subject we must broach. It concerns what is known as 'the Syndicate'.

This deeply sinister group has been given many titles in the past. Hitler called it in general terms 'the Zionist plot', which is darkly amusing, as he was completely under the dominance of its highest levels of authority.[1] He did not give it its title, however. It was in existence long before he rose to power (on its hidden wings), and its first priority was to eliminate the Jewish people – Hitler's 'Final Solution'. The reason for this was that, at some point in the last few hundred years, Enlil discovered the truth about the ancient and kingly Jewish race.

He had always believed that they *promoted* him and his cause, and that the Jews would lead him to world dominion down a straight and rapid track. Imagine his horror, therefore, when he discovered that, far from promoting him, they were actually *containing* his terrible death energies, and actively *preventing* him from attaining his cherished goal! By now, we can imagine the howls of wrath that must have ensued!

As far as Enlil was concerned, he had put paid to the great threat to his plan which Tiâmat had instigated with her bloodline. The exalted king it was intended to accommodate (he ignored the queen) had been and gone, slain by his own people, as Enlil had carefully arranged. He thought, being so far out of touch with the eternal verities, that the Christ mission had been a total failure. He had thought that he was merrily on his way to the end of the road. And now he was beginning to discover that those whom he had always considered as his obedient agents of destruction were actually the *protectors* of humanity. We believe that the story of David, the protective shepherd-boy who slew the giant Goliath with a 'stone' and thus entered into his kinghood, is a symbol of the Jewish people's secret mission. It depicts the Jews keeping Enlil and the Naphidem at bay from humankind by the use of a special stone (in the sense that they contained the white powder via Bezaleel's art within the Ark of the Covenant, and so used the giant's own 'stone' against him). Enlil was outraged!

The so-called 'Zionist plot', in one sense, was nothing more than the hot and murderously hostile pursuit of all those who strove to follow Enki and Nin-khursag's teachings (the teachings of Tiâmat-Oannes, the teachings proceeding from the Divine Light) and those who were of Tiâmat's special bloodline down the ages, because, although the branch from Mary Magdalene and Jesus ended with Tamar, the greater family line, known today as Rex Deus, of course continued. The huge aim and objective of the bloodline was to deliver to earth this Divine Couple of Divine Couples, but even after it had achieved its goal, it still produced incarnating souls who had a service to perform for humanity. Enlil was determined to exterminate these people and stamp out the bloodline forever.

Once he had learned that the Jewish race was blocking him rather than furthering his cause, his main priority was to get rid of it entirely.

Until it was gone, he had no hope of succeeding in his dark enterprise. With great cunning, therefore, he and his cronies arranged the release of a reverse-spin piece of intelligence – that there was a dread organisation, headed and financed by racist and radical Jews, to crush all other races beneath their feet and take over the world. In other words, what Enlil had formerly believed was secretly really happening via his own devices but was in fact a nonsense (i.e. that he himself was riding on the backs of the Jews towards a triumphant global takeover) was now spread abroad as a terrifying rumour, designed to inflame the lower minds of those who could be thus manipulated, and prompt them to wipe out the Jewish people forever. (The actual fundamentalist Zionists are nothing but a smokescreen to give weight to this rumour, being in themselves a small number of Jews, not quite as strong in spirit as their more muscular kin, who had fallen prey to Enlil's hypnotic hold).

Enlil did not leave things to chance, although he bore in mind that there was more than one way to skin a cat and consequently always had several cunning plans up his sleeve. Throughout many centuries he plotted the exact course that history would take (providing, of course, that humanity would fall into line according to his allurements and manipulations – but he was very confident it would – after all, it always had done so in the past ... Enlil was sanguine on this point). However, if we look into the machinations and manoeuvres of the Syndicate, we must not expect to find a simple array of darkness versus light, of black versus white.

Enlil is nothing if not subtle; but even so, even though he plotted barbarity after barbarity, confident that he could drive us like cattle (the Syndicate's scornful name for us is 'Goyim' – cattle) into whatever sinister enclosures he chose to prepare for us, Tiâmat's hand, unseen and unsuspected, was always on the steering wheel.

The destiny of the earth did not slip out of her hands, as perhaps it seemed to do, and as Enlil was convinced it had. Although our own free will would make us become as Enlil's foolish cattle, although he did his very worst and surpassed himself at every turn, yet Tiâmat would lead us to a place in history that we would recognise as a turning-point – a wondrous, miraculous turning-point – where all the ill and evil that Enlil had inflicted on the world could be overturned as in a moment, and humanity could march in triumph towards the glorious destiny she had planned for us before time began, when she held us within her heart as a golden principle, a divine and cherished idea.

There is a single quote which might help us to better understand the twisted confusion that is the Syndicate:

> *For our contention is not with the blood and the flesh, but with dominion, with authority, with the blind world-rulers of this life, with the Spirit of Evil in things heavenly.*

> (EPHESIANS 6:12)

Certainly, many good people and many genuine idealists have been involved, in one way or another, with this Syndicate. It seems just as certain that they had no idea of the real nature of its power or its ultimate objectives. One feels the touch of the true light forces, of Tiâmat-Oannes, in such infiltration of the Syndicate! The light and the dark forces work together for long-range good; the highest initiates of the dark forces, the angels and overlords of their structure, know this, and are only disguised as creatures of the darkness. Their lesser minions do not know, and must eventually be redeemed from their ignorance. The humans among them (which of course include Enlil and Marduk) are also entirely hostile and given over to the destructive forces – except for that tiny, tiny glimmer at their heart centre, impossible to extinguish despite all their efforts – the little flame of their humanity, the tiny dragon flame which proclaims them as beings of light, however far they may have sunk into wickedness.

No human being can actually be *of* the evil forces, counted among them as truly one of their legion, even though it is only too clear that certain members of humanity can be completely taken over by them and work with all diligence for them. Evil, however, is only a temporary measure. We are under its heavy-duty tutelage only until we finally decide, on a collective basis, that we really don't want a reverse-spin world and a reverse-spin consciousness any more!

It seems questionable as to why Enlil accepted an influx of light into his dark Syndicate. One reason seems to be that he welcomed such an ingredient because it then became much easier to fool even the most exacting and discerning among us into thinking that his designs really were schemes of light. (We might consider, for instance, just how invigorating and recuperative it must have been for the

German people to be led forward by Hitler, with his visions of a new Germany, in his early days of leadership.) We have to learn how to test the waters and differentiate between the False and the True Grail. We look for lies, for unacceptable actions and philosophies, and most of all, we look and hearken to our souls – which if we take them regularly into the mystic Silence will calmly and reverently enshrine the light of the spirit – to give us the unfailing signal as to whether or not we are in safe hands. This is how we sniff out the lurking presence of Enlil.

A second reason was that there was still a dim flicker of light within Enlil himself. Sometimes, he seemed to express this to a limited extent. Yet, sadly, it was always overcome by the false light to which his soul was lashed (by bonds he himself created) as if to a monstrous navigator. We do not wish to give a misleading impression here, because Enlil is by no means in two minds about what he wishes our destiny to be. He intends to exterminate us. Similarly, the intention behind the Syndicate is entirely malevolent and corrupt, even though good-hearted, enlightened people and groups have become enmeshed in its terrible purposes. The false bread and the false wine were fed to these bearers of enlightenment to disconnect them from their inner compass, their intuitive wisdom. This has always been the source of its hideous strength. From the first, the Syndicate learned the art of a diabolically ingenious puppetry, and knew how to make even the spiritually elect dance to its appalling tune.

This is why our contention truly is 'with the Spirit of Evil in things heavenly'. It is this Spirit of Evil which prevents heaven from descending to earth, which prevents us from ascending into our heavenly spiritual heritage, and which therefore prevents the coming of the Grail. But we are about to rid ourselves of the ignorance which allows it to prevail, and thus will we see its miasma lift and disperse and become as nothing.

All that this 'evil' comprises, in the simplest terms, is the downward pull of matter itself against the natural spiritual tendency towards ascension and the return to God. H.P. Lovecraft has described it as being 'coterminous with all space and coexistent with all time'. In other words, it is utterly of the material plane and is an influence within matter itself. ('Matter is a force to be reckoned with!' Jesus declares in the Gospel of Mary.) It moves in the opposite direction to the affinities of the spirit. Therefore, what is most pure can become loathsome and corrupt, what flames forth from the heart of highest ecstasy can become virulent pain and suffering. We must conquer the reversals of matter before we can step through the mirror and become real. Until then, illusion persists, making us its collective dominion, and our 'White Knight' (the will, movement and direction of the soul when it obeys the ordinances of the spirit) will blunder, will keep being unseated, will concentrate on irrelevances, will carry all its confusions forward as burdens which hinder its progress, and will use its vision and powers of creativity in entirely pointless enterprises, just like the White Knight in *Alice Through the Looking-Glass*.

NOTE

1   It is interesting to note that the Nazis, and in particular their inner brotherhood of the SS (symbolising the unentwined or separated serpents, in contradistinction to Enki and Nin-khursag's symbol, which is the caduceus), were the reverse-spin opposite of the Knights Templar. The Nazis also modified their symbol of the Eagle so that it represented the reverse of the Eagle of St John. Although some confusion did latterly enter the ranks of the Templars, and although members of its outermost circle did not properly understand the Order's true aims and objectives, our source assures us that the inner circle of the Knights Templar was indeed pure and noble, entirely dedicated to fulfilling the ideals of Oannes and accepting Tiâmat-Oannes as God.

Himmler selected a site in a remote mountainous location and built a castle in a strange triangular design, intended to facilitate the inundation and destruction, Tower-of-Babel-style, of the new pyramidal soul-structure that Tiâmat had provided for humanity in order to protect them from the invasion of the Naphidem. (The Naphidem, of course, were the driving force behind Hitler and the Nazis.) An inner temple was created in the triangular castle where, on a central altar, an 'eternal flame' burned. This flame was actually a gas flame, and the acoustics of the temple were designed so that the hiss of the gas flame was aggressively amplified.

Within the temple the twelve highest-ranking SS Nazi officers would sit in meditation on twelve thrones surrounding the hissing flame. Black arts were set in motion to try to seize psychic control of the human chakra system, which, since Tiâmat's gift to us of our pyramidal soul or chakra system, has been preparing itself for the activation of thirteen main chakras rather than its former use of seven. The twelve SS officers represented twelve of the chakras, whilst the hissing flame represented the central heart chakra. It hissed with the fury and thunder of Enlil, the lower dragon or dinosaurian principle, which wishes to overpower via its own might and hostility. (We remember that Enlil began his black magic practices long ago in pre-history by distorting humanity's awareness, understanding and reverence for the heart centre.) Himmler himself was called 'the Crystal Knight' and kept a crystal in a secret place in the triangular castle. Knowing, as we do, Enlil's manipulation of crystals and mirrors in his plot to destroy humankind, we can imagine to what dark purposes this crystal was dedicated.

Hitler was in conversation one day with Rauschning, the Governor of Danzig, on the topic of mutating the human race (it was Hitler's aim to reintroduce the Naphidem to earth via genetically mutated human vehicles, in a horrible perversion of Enki and Nin-khursag's God-sanctioned work in the House of Shimtî). The Governor, not being privy to Hitler's sinister esoteric knowledge, pointed out to him that all he could hope to do was to assist Nature via genetics and trust that she herself would create a new human species for him.

'The new man is living amongst us now! He is here!' Hitler declared triumphantly. 'Isn't that enough for you? I will tell you a secret. I have seen the new man. He was intrepid and cruel. I was afraid of him.' Rauschning described Hitler as 'trembling in a kind of ecstasy' as he uttered these words.

Rauschning also recorded a further disturbing account: 'A person close to Hitler told me that he wakes up in the night screaming and in convulsions. He calls for help, and appears to be half paralysed. He is seized with a panic that makes him tremble until the bed shakes. He utters confused and unintelligible sounds, gasping, as if on the point of suffocation. The same person described to me one of these fits, with details that I would refuse to believe had I not complete confidence in my informant.

'Hitler was standing up in his room, swaying and looking all round him as if he were lost. "It's he, it's he," he groaned; "he's coming for me!" His lips were white; he was sweating profusely. Suddenly he uttered a string of meaningless figures, then words and scraps of sentences. It was terrifying. He used strange expressions strung together in bizarre disorder. Then he relapsed again into silence, but his lips still continued to move. He was then given a friction and something to drink. Then suddenly he screamed: "There! There! Over in the corner! He is there!" – all the time stamping with his feet and shouting.' (*Hitler m'a dit,* Hermann Rauschning, 1939.) After these horrifying episodes, Hitler would fall into a deep sleep and, on waking, would be normal again.

All of the details above are attested history, with the exception of the reason we have given for the twelve SS officers seated in thrones around an amplified hissing gas flame supposed to represent the flame of eternity (that they actually did so is well documented). Such is the result of human and Naphidem association. In case anyone should begin to suspect that Marduk was not so bad as Enlil after all, as it was not the Naphidem chief's intention to exterminate us, it is as well to bear in mind that the difference in intent between the two men is simply that of an eliminator and a sadist, one of whom wishes to kill his victims outright, the other of whom wishes to keep them alive to satisfy his appetite for corruption, degradation, and torture.

CHAPTER SIXTY-SEVEN

The History of
the Syndicate

We will take up the history of the Syndicate in 1776, when on 1 May Professor Adam Weishaupt of Bavaria founded the Bavarian Illuminati (the 'illumined' or 'shining ones'). Its great aim was to establish a world government which would fall under the influence of Marduk (whose puppet-master, pulling Marduk's strings, was Enlil). Marduk would then manipulate humanity into admitting the Naphidem back into their favourite dimension – that of the physical earth. (We must remember that, as there are light and dark dragons, so there are positive and negative 'shining ones'. The positive shining ones are true, beautiful, just and pure, and work for the good of humanity. The false Illuminati weave tissues of lies, are hideously contorted in their philosophies and aims, perpetrate terrible injustice, and work towards the destruction of humanity. We might think of them respectively as denizens of the True and the False Grail.)

Funded by the recently established House of Rothschild ('Wrath's child', and, even more interestingly, 'Red Shield', the literal translation of the name), Weishaupt was ordered by a certain group of enormously wealthy and influential financiers, industrialists, military commanders, politicians, scientists and churchmen (as well as representatives of other religions) who had entirely come under Enlil's tutelage and control, to reconstruct their inherited Luciferic doctrine into a new long-term plan for world domination. The plan would incorporate the measured but sure destruction of all religions, governments, philosophies and value-systems of every society on earth, to be fomented by a polarising of the world population into fanatically opposing factions.

Wars, insurrections and revolutions were planned to bring this situation into being. It represented Enlil's long-term plan B, steady but sure, the one upon which he would rely should his and Marduk's more dramatic and ambitious attempts (such as the Nazi takeover) be met with failure.

The Bavarian Illuminati began to plot the course of human history across the globe. The hidden Syndicate (Enlil, Marduk, their God-Headed and Naphidem supporters, and their human puppets on earth) had done its utmost to direct human affairs for thousands of years, and Enki, Nin-khursag and Lilith had in turn done their very best to stymie their shenanigans, as we know from examining the ancient history of Zi-u-sudra (once such an ardent follower of Tiâmat), Ga-nadin-ur, Attaba and Eve and their descendants. However, the founding of the Bavarian Illuminati seemed to mark a shift. Enlil's control and power-bases on earth became suddenly much more overt, and his tentacles tightened around many of the European secret societies of alchemists, Freemasons, Rosicrucians, Jewish cabbalists and others who were the bearers of genuine hidden knowledge, but who now stumbled in some respects and began to fall into confusion, so that a dark aspect fell over them. The false communion of negative-spin bread and wine did its work, and the Freemasons particularly were thrown into disarray.

Masonic precepts of universal brotherhood and equity, their knowledge of the true craft of life and its divine origin, began to be overlaid by élitism, political squabbling, and a narrow, materialistic, self-seeking philosophy. Their potent mysticism and magical rites slipped away into the obscuring mists of forgetfulness and non-comprehension, and here and there, in some of the groups mentioned, the shadow of unwise and even black magic separated them from the inner sun that had blazed with divine truth since their inception.

These groups were, in the main, the remnants of the Templar brotherhood, the order of knights savagely annihilated by the Church and the king of France early in the fourteenth century. On learning that the Templars were planning to re-introduce the true Church of Christ, which had been lost to the world two hundred years after the Crucifixion and which was, strictly speaking, the Church of Tiâmat-Oannes, the Roman Church, behind the façade of Philip the Fair, denounced them as heretical and exterminated them. These impulses within the French court and the Roman Church were, of course, fed and manipulated by Enlil.

Whilst the Church of Peter, like Peter himself, did at least strive partially to fulfil the teachings of the Christ (Jesus and Mary Magdalene represented this ineffable Christ Being on earth), the Illuminati were wholly evil in their intentions. Everyone in the inner circle of the Order knew exactly to whom they paid allegiance. In effect, Enlil was playing one group off against another (always a favourite trick of his), because an 'earlier' Illuminati had formed itself as an antidote to the aggressive superstition of the Church, which, for instance, almost had Galileo burnt at the stake because he reported what he saw through his telescope.

The Church was so hostile to the progress of science that certain key thinkers and scientists organised themselves into an underground group with the aim of securing the advance of knowledge and reason.

This was, of course, a good and progressive development. The only problem was, that, abandoning the very science and reason they sought to uphold, some group members decided that they ought to set themselves in diametrical opposition to the doctrines and creed of the Church itself, just to prove how much they held it in disdain – and became Satanists! Whether or not this was originally just an act of black humour is difficult to determine.

Unfortunately, certain rites were essayed, and Enlil and Marduk were only too happy to be invited to take over the control of this early Illuminati (the true Syndicate, or false Illuminati, was of course instigated many centuries before the Illuminati of scientists and thinkers formed themselves during the Renaissance). The element of magic or spiritual illumination in science thus had to be disconnected from it with all speed, or there would have been a planetary catastrophe from which the earth could not have recovered. The great master Francis Bacon (who worked with Shakespeare and indeed with a secret brotherhood to release certain wisdoms and esoteric knowledge to the world via his plays) undertook this mighty task. The current materialistic, positivist sciences are the result of his work. Whilst this prevailing philosophy is in itself a great stumbling block to our collective enlightenment, it was a very necessary act of damage-limitation.

To return to Professor Weishaupt and the Bavarian Illuminati: a perusal of their recorded chronology tells us that they had scheduled the French Revolution to commence in the year 1789. We have solid evidence for this because Weishaupt's re-organisation and updating of the Syndicate's ancient plot was transcribed and put into book format by Hans Zwack, a German Illuminatus, who entitled the work *Einige Original-Schriften*. In 1785 a copy of the book was despatched by courier to a group of French Masons who were involved with the Illuminati, and who were occupied with fuelling and inciting the movement towards a decisive and very bloody revolution. The courier (Lanze) was struck by lightning as he rode through Ratisbon, on his way from Frankfurt to Paris.

He and his steed were incinerated, but the book with which he had been entrusted was unscathed. It was passed to the Bavarian government, who searched the homes of all the members of the Illuminati.

The organisation was declared illegal, and its Masonic branches were disbanded.

The following year (1786) a book was published exposing the conspiracy (*The Original Writings of the Order and Sect of the Illuminati*). Even so, nothing could stop the forward motion of the stampeding dynamics the group had initiated. The Revolution *did* take place in 1789, and it was just as gruesome and bloodthirsty as both Enlil and Marduk could have wished, although it also, to a certain extent, destroyed the false ideals of rank and privilege, which stem from materialism and were never intended to attach themselves to the service and self-sacrifice of royalty. It effectively closed the door upon any king or queen of Tiâmat's special bloodline ascending to the French throne, because, of course, the throne itself was permanently unseated. Over a thousand years previously, the French king Dagobert had been assassinated, and a man without proper legal claim had been elevated to kingship. Dagobert had a son, and it was the fear of his descendants that led Enlil to instigate a revolution in France, for Dagobert carried the secret of the Grail.

Another reason for the Revolution, as far as Enlil was concerned, was to detach the French from a spiritual realisation that was their natural inheritance, and to set them at odds with England via Napoleon. As England and France were the two most powerful countries in the world at the time of the founding of the Bavarian Illuminati, Enlil was afraid that the progressive impetus in both countries might lead them to rediscover their own spiritual brotherhood, and with it the deeply buried esoteric tradition of the true Church of universal brotherhood.

This trepidation was the motivating factor behind the instigation of the Crusades, of the destruction of the Cathars, and of the annihilation of the Knights Templar; and, as we can read in the extant documents of the Illuminati, it was also the motivating force directing the two world wars, the establishment of communism and fascism and the appalling devastation of the atomic bombs. When Enlil brought in his own world government, he wanted to ensure that there was no faction anywhere that he had left untouched and impervious to his influence, ready to rise up against him at the last moment. Thankfully for us, there always was a sanctuary whose doors Enlil could never force – the sanctuary of the human heart, where the holy of holies resides. Enlil thought he could draw a veil over humanity's realisation of its heart and the God-force within it. All over the world, humanity will show Enlil at last that he has made a big mistake in his assumptions.

Because Enlil wants a world government, some people (who of course know nothing about Enlil, but are aware of the calibre of the Syndicate and its ultimate intentions) have assumed that the establishment of such an authority would be an evil. It may be unwise to think in these terms. It would seem that a world government, with each nation enjoying its own identity and culture and partaking in a unified governance of international affairs, is probably the only way to secure justice and liberty for all. It is not structures in themselves which constitute the huge threat to human freedom and happiness, but what lies within them, what lies at their heart.

Any world government with Enlil at its helm could only ever wear the sham appearance of a democracy, because it would be run, first by the Syndicate, and eventually, quite blatantly, by Marduk.

In 1840, the notorious General Albert Pike, an American Freemason, came into office within the hierarchy of the Syndicate, and was eventually promoted to leadership. In 1859 he began to draw up a new military plan which would improve on Weishaupt's original. It was Pike who delineated the vision of three world wars, all of them to be implemented by the end of the twentieth century[1]. Global history has followed Pike's plan to the letter – except for the third world war. This was to be fought over religious extremism, and although those involved in the Syndicate have done their utmost to inflame this war (which they dutifully began on schedule) into a worldwide conflict, they have not succeeded.

This is the great signal which confirms that humanity is at last beginning to turn away from the mesmerising, hallucinatory dispensation which Enlil sends to us through the ethers, so that we fall into stupor and discord, and act according to our lower nature. This is the great signal that we are making ourselves ready to receive the Grail, and that its time draws closer. 'Those with ears to hear, let them hear', is a refrain sounded by Jesus throughout the Gospel of Mary. 'Hear' and 'ear' are within the word 'heart', and in one sense the heart is indeed a listening organ. There is no doubt about it; humanity is beginning to hear, and to pay heed.

Pike's ultimate plan was that, after strengthening the forces of communism across the world, it would then be held in check, to be unleashed in the final holocaust. Pike particularly laid emphasis on its nihilistic, materialistic, and totalitarianistic traits rather than its positive qualities, which he wanted to ensure held only false promises of justice and equality.

His new draft of Weishaupt's plan included the founding of the state of Israel to inflame racial and religious hatred in the Middle East, so that the opposing factions would annihilate one another in a nuclear war (the secrets of the atom bomb were to be disclosed to the scientific world by Enlil's supernatural agents during the course of the two world wars). Judaism and Islam would thereby be thrown into total confusion and meltdown.

The Syndicate would then unleash the most unsavoury aspects of communism upon the world, and a new war would begin between communists and Christians. The Christians would be allowed to win this war, but it would effect the complete collapse of society everywhere, and create a wholesale lapse into brutishness and degradation. Into this shattered, fragmented, desperate planetary society, unable any more to believe in any of the gods it once upheld, Marduk would triumphantly descend.

General Pike (whose name identifies the pike, the mass exterminator among freshwater fish and their most dangerous predator – a fit symbol for the would-be destroyer of Enki, and his link with Oannes the Fish-Man and the Apse, the magical source of earth's freshwater) wrote a letter to the leader of the Syndicate who preceded him and who acted as his mentor, the Italian Freemason Giuseppi

Mazzini. The letter is held today in the archives of the British Museum. It is dated 15 August 1871, and a quote from it reads:

We shall unleash the Nihilists and Atheists, and we shall provoke a formidable social cataclysm which in all its horror will show clearly to the nations the effect of absolute atheism, origin of savagery and of the most bloody turmoil. Then everywhere, the citizens, obliged to defend themselves against the world minority of revolutionaries, will exterminate those destroyers of civilisation, and the multitude, disillusioned with Christianity, whose deistic spirits will be from that moment without compass, anxious for an ideal, but without knowing where to render its adoration, will receive the pure doctrine of Lucifer, brought finally out in the public view, a manifestation which will result from the general reactionary movement which will follow the destruction of Christianity and atheism, both conquered and exterminated at the same time.

NOTE

1   It is interesting to note the continuous progression and interplay of Enlil's plan A and plan B in his operations (see Chapter 46). Plan A was the quick route to success, plan B the much longer, quieter, insidious route, drip by drip, step by slow, measured step, to which he unfailingly returned whenever his numerous attempts at plan A failed. The instigation of the First World War belonged to plan B, the second to plan A, which would, Enlil hoped, result in a world coup by the Nazis and deliver plan A by speedily returning the Naphidem to earth en masse. Yet, if by some unlikely chance (he surmised) this particular and most ingenious rendition to date of plan A failed to come off, then both plan A and plan B would meet in glorious triumphant union in his manipulated third World War and at last facilitate his 'final solution' for earth and her humanity. This planned third World War, of course, will never happen. Although there is more work for us all to do, the earth's vibrations have already been raised, and therefore Nibiru's return is set to completely destroy Enlil's magic mirror and imposed reverse spin. However, although the ring will be destroyed immediately, the changeover from reverse spin to positive spin will take a considerably long time to come into effect. Nevertheless, the passing of Nibiru or Planet X through earth's orbit in 2013 will initiate the process. Each time he passes is a time of special spiritual opportunity for the earth and humanity. If we count back 3,600 (or 3,666) years to his last passing, for instance, we arrive at the time of the rise of Canaan, the glorious land of the Grail, which, had it not been brought down by its 'brother' Egypt, would have lit the Grail flame in its other three major stations (Rosslyn, Glastonbury, Chartres) in preparation for its complete re-establishment in AD 33.

CHAPTER SIXTY-EIGHT

Bilderberg

*T*he Bilderberg Group is the best known branch of the Syndicate today. It was formed in 1954 at a hotel in Holland of the same name. The Bilderberg Conference (which nowadays takes place at various locations) is an annual event attended by leading financiers, industrialists, media tycoons, business moguls, members of the nobility and of European royal families, high-ranking soldiers and scientists and leaders of secret (and sometimes even fundamentalist and overt) religious orders, who all come together to decide how the world (particularly the Occident, although its tentacles are by no means restricted to the West) should be run, and in what direction it should be manipulated. It is an entirely private affair, and is always protected by armed guards.

The Bilderberg Group is famous for the invitations it issues to join its fraternity and attend its conferences to small-time politicians and others who then go on to become world leaders, or major players on the world stage. There exists film footage of very contemporary prime movers in global affairs aboard a coach heading for a Bilderberg Conference prior to their election. Even more worrying is the fact that, once in power, these men have been careful to instigate policies and make decisions which are perfectly in tune with Adam Weishaupt and General Pike's master plan.

It is very likely that many of the individuals thus elevated to power have no real idea of the terrible evil behind the Syndicate. They know enough to understand that the organisation can propel them to power, and they are content not to question quite how such a feat is managed.

They think, no doubt, that once they have power, they will be their own man or their own woman, and do a lot of good in the world. Not so! They will find themselves forced to obey the directives of the higher authority within the organisation. If they should fail or refuse, events and situations will rapidly militate against them and threaten to strangle them in an invisible noose until they turn in the specified direction. The white powder is dispensed to them in ethereal form at the Bilderberg meetings. First their minds and souls are primed to receive it, and then it is given in material form, often literally in wine and bread. The subtle systems within the chakras perform the required reverse alchemy, and the false *khu* actually comes into being within the physical body. Once its recipients have accepted it (for it can be refused and rejected), they are henceforth no more than dogs in training on a choke-chain. Any power for good that they may implement will bring more chaos and reversals than benefit to the given situation. Their autonomy of soul and impetus of vision is lost to them.

There is no doubt that the overt evils and distresses of the world – Mafia activity, drug-peddling, illegal arms dealing, prostitution and paedophile rings, corporate greed, wholesale murder, assault and rape, assassinations, genocide, the brutal regimes of certain governments, etcetera, etcetera, and especially the hidden malevolence of the world which controls all the misery and oppression in its establishments and organisations – are linked to the tentacles of the Syndicate, and are fed and organised by them. When we finally see the picture for what it truly is, humanity will be astonished by the sheer scale and the horrible perfection of these vast administrations of the dark powers. Nothing is arbitrary. Nothing is random.

Evil is a complex system, a gargantuan organism functioning on many different levels, with many spheres of bio-diversity co-existing in mutual dependency upon its bi-lateral source, which combines a reverse-spin energy emanating from an ethereal dark realm perpetuated and fed on earth by consenting humanity. Its life support system is circular and cyclical.

Certain ceremonies are performed that feed these tentacles of evil. They generally circulate around sadism and sexual abuse perpetrated against children, women and animals, although the rape and degradation of men are also involved. Elaborate rituals involving child abuse have been implemented for thousands of years. Such ancient ceremonies are unconscionably powerful, but because their adherents are written off as deluded 'Satanists', their activities are not taken seriously. And yet the members of such groups stretch back over countless generations, long before 'Satan' was conceptualised. Children are born into the cult, which is worldwide but has ancestral branches, and designated either as sexual fodder or 'breeders'. These latter children, constantly impregnated and subjected to ritual abortions from the age of twelve or thirteen, provide subjects for sacrifice and cannibalism.

Sometimes, the 'fodder' children are also sacrificed as well as the foetuses. Children disappear. Excuses are made. Local authorities either overlook the missing children or forget them. Both 'fodder' children and 'breeders' as well as their parents, who are always willing participants, are taught how to cope emotionally and psychologically with their unspeakable nocturnal activities whilst running outwardly normal and successful lives. Occasionally, something goes wrong with this occult conditioning, and there are involuntary escapees, such as Rosemary and Fred West and the 'Moors Murderers'. Pornography, even the so-called 'soft' variety, directly feeds into this black vein. No one has understood this terrible cycle for what it truly is. Rather it is tolerated happily, as if it is innocuous.

One thing is certain – we will never, no matter how hard we may try, bring down this almighty structure by force of arms or law, or by any attempt to outwit it.

It sometimes seems as if our universal fixation on crime fiction, be it cinematic, televisual or literary, stems from an anxious need to believe that to do so is really possible. Sadly, it is not. Although law enforcement helps to keep society functioning, it cannot disable this great unquiet beast. The same is true, even more so, of the Syndicate itself. It cannot be brought down by worldly means. Evidence melts away, strategies backfire, focus disappears, trusted agents become confused, corrupted, or simply refuse to continue. All attempts to fight back are disabled and disempowered.

One day it *willl* be dismantled, but we cannot attack it via conventional means. In fact, we must learn not to attack it at all. Commensurate in popularity with crime fiction is our hero fiction, the good comic-book champion who is ready to be our saviour and rescue the world. Again, this approach of passive reliance on an aggressive force which is on our side will not work. There is only one way to overpower Enlil, and that is by personally refusing his methods of retribution and retaliation and living by the light of the star, the source of divine fire within us which transforms us into our higher dragon or Pendragon selves. It is the force of love. Each individual effort is needed to foster, to faithfully honour, and to unstintingly give forth this divine force of love.

When we do this, when we reclaim our Pendragon status, it will be Enlil's turn to suffer disablement and to become disempowered, confused and confounded. The wisdom of the heart is what will free us from him and the inestimable psychic structures of darkness that he maintains.

If we try to use our mind, our intellectual reasoning, to overcome him, we will be drawn into the darkness, bound and manacled as quickly as a spider trusses up its prey. Our vision will shut down, our inner compass will spin madly out of control, and the jaws of his trap will close with a triumphant snap. Only when the power of the mind is absolutely allied with the heart, and is in devoted service to it, may it be used against the tyranny of Enlil. (The procedures outlined in Chapter 67 will help in this respect.)

Furthermore, we strongly and earnestly advise our readers not to focus on the Syndicate or to make it a project of study. It is very tempting to do so, because in one sense it is a gripping story – the conspiracy of all time, the conspiracy of conspiracies. Yet we ourselves, possessing a degree of forewarning and having summoned all the forces of light for protection in setting out to research it in good faith, have soon become disconnected from our source and cast up on the shores of confusion, cold and shivering with a toxic soul-fear. To banish such fear we have to keep our *ayin*, our soul focus, on the absolute power of the light.

The Syndicate, or at least its dark overlords, have honed the art of *mind control* to a fine art. This is why the mind leads us – anyone and everyone – into such peril when we approach the problem of the Syndicate with a mental or an intellectual probe. All the unfortunate ailments of the mind come to the fore when we allow our mentality to explore the Syndicate too deeply; obsession, anxiety, paranoia, confusion, fixation – all come crowding into our field of vision.

As the true Grail gives to humanity four wondrous gifts (Abundance, Healing, Immortality and Nourishment) so this organisation belonging to the false Grail steals from us in four ways, causing an acute energy-loss to the point where the soul becomes distressed.

These four thefts committed by the false Grail are perpetrated by the spectres of Fear, Self-Doubt, Self-Will and Shame. They are the four veils which must be removed before we can receive the Grail, and they correlate to the Four Horsemen of Doom who inflict on us the gifts or the Four Hallows of the Grail in reverse spin – Famine, Pestilence, War and Death.

Every writer who has produced a book on the subject of the Great Conspiracy seems to have fallen into a trap of some sort. A tendency to right-wing extremism asserts itself, or else everyone connected with esotericism is tarred with the same brush of condemnation as the Syndicate, as though any group who declares itself less openly than the Women's Institute must surely be evil! Sometimes, a book will begin in a state of commendable equilibrium and end with a right-wing rant, as though its author's judgment had become unbalanced whilst actually writing it (which we consider to be highly likely). At the very least, there is a jarring misinterpretation of symbolism, and a sinister cloud of suspicion seems to descend through the writer's mind on the true as well as the false light, casting everything awry. (Perhaps it would be wise not to make this chapter too long! …)

The Syndicate represents the great separating force, that which separates us from God. It has been assembled for that very purpose, and is supernaturally expert in its field. It makes wisdom appear as a terrible stupidity; higher vision takes on the guise of naive gullibility, and what we should trust most, we suddenly doubt with a lurch of horror. The path of fear, paranoia, and fragmentation of the soul suddenly seems the only sensible route to pursue. The voice of panic masquerades as the voice of prudence.

Let us beware the arrogance and the misplaced curiosity which might tempt us to think that we are strong enough to handle the challenge the Syndicate represents! If we are in any sense below the level of a deity, we assuredly cannot. Focusing on it through curiosity is the way of destruction of strength and centredness. We can only defeat it by protecting the mind from its own tendency towards self-will, and thereby overcoming its refusal to aspire to the 'I Am' power of the higher will, the God-force within the heart. Let the mind be gently absorbed into the heart, and the tentacles of the Syndicate will no longer be able to reach you.

There is a safe method of studying the calibre and the secrets of the False Grail, which will reveal all that the Syndicate seeks to hide and obfuscate without leading the mind into danger and treachery. This secure exposure of the False Grail will be revealed in the next chapter. We will end this chapter with a quote from Alice, who gives short shrift to the mind-befuddling techniques of the Syndicate:

> Alice sighed wearily. 'I think you might do something better with the time,' she said, 'than wasting it in asking riddles that have no answers.'

CHAPTER SIXTY-NINE

The End of Days

*A*t this point, it would probably be worthwhile to sing along with the White Rabbit in the film of *Alice in Wonderland,* just to help ourselves wake up to a crucial fact:

> *We're late, we're late*
> *For a very important date!*

We are certainly late in organising ourselves for a very important date, but, as has been stated before, we are not too late to rectify the situation.

The date is early 2013, and the event is the return of planet X, which will cut through earth's orbit as it travels around the sun and sets off into outer space again, not to be seen for another 3,600 years. Mercury will also feel its impact, but then we must understand that the Luciferic influences stem from the unharmonised emanations of the planet Mercury, just as Enlil represents the unharmonised forces of the planet Saturn. The transformer, as always, is human consciousness.

The true plan of God was for Enlil to conduct the divine light buried in the earth and in the human base chakra upwards into the keeping of Enki, who would then glorify human consciousness with its transformational essence, for Enki and Enlil represent the forces of Mercury and Saturn. Due to Enlil's terrible failure and humanity's foolishness in following his dictates, we got a 'Satan' (Enlil) and a 'Lucifer' (Marduk, who, being Enki's son, enshrined the forces of Mercury, albeit in highly negative mode) instead! Marduk had been selected from earliest infancy to 'slay' Tiamat and join forces with Enlil precisely because Enki carried within him the Mercurial forces destined to bring the light of higher consciousness to humanity. These Mercurial forces were inherited by his son, who was duly taught to throw his inheritance into dissonant, distorted mode so that humanity was largely blocked from receiving the gift of enlightenment dispensed by Mercury.

This appalling situation, of course, was ameliorated by Enki's rescue plan activated through his spiritual son, Ham or Hermes. Thankfully, the impact on Mercury will bring it into an alignment with earth which will help us to overcome our dissonance with Mercury, expressed in our unfortunate attraction to Marduk, which runs so rife in our world. Outer, bodily reality is an objectification of inner reality, the true reality, and what happens in outer space is a reflection of the dynamics occurring in inner space.

As planet X slices through our orbit, it will have a profound effect on our own planet. First and foremost, it will completely shatter Enlil's sinister ring, and will eventually set the earth spinning clockwise again, as she did many thousands of years ago. Planet X's cosmic kiss will be felt by us all; we will have to hold on to our hats, but we are assured that there will be minimal disruption on earth. At some point towards the end of the year 2012 the returning planet and its course for earth's orbit will be visible and calculable by even amateur astronomical observers.

We should not fear or dread planet X's return. He comes as our White Knight, to rescue us from the terrible malice of Enlil and his kiss of death. If our planet was left to spin anti-clockwise without eventual change of course, if the terrible reverse-spin gold ring was not shattered, Enlil – who, as we know from his physical and ethereal production of certain nefarious powders or negative-spin gold, has learnt to harness the power of the planet's negative spin in his own special way and was the agent of its changeover from positive to negative spin in the first place – would claim total victory.

We ought at this point to say a few words concerning the End-Dayists, who have been made aware of planet X's return by the scientific predictions of the astronomer Dr James McCanney, who, as far as we understand, is not an End-Dayist himself, but was prepared for altruistic reasons to leak information, against the American Government's specific instructions, about the approach of planet X. The End-Dayists are a Christian cult who believe that planet X will destroy the earth, but that they, being good, will be saved at the eleventh hour by 'Yahweh' (Enlil), who will sweep them off the earth into heaven, whereas the rest of us, being bad, will have to perish in the flames and carnage of planet X's fatal impact. If only they could see into the heart of what they call their 'God'! It is as fearful as Mordor.

If, as appears to be the case, the End-Dayists are incarnate on earth in physical bodies, if they were born of woman, then they must forget the idea that any mercy or 'saving' will be available from Enlil (whom they call YAHUVEH). Enlil loathes the human race, and his aim is simply this – to exterminate it and to exterminate the planet that supports it. He laughs us all to scorn, his dupes as well as those who are awake to his sinister reality. He has deranged ideas that he is God, and can control the universe. Believe us when we say that this is not a well man we are dealing with.

Enlil is not God, and he cannot control the universe. He can only control *us* if we allow him to do so! His control must be brought to an end, not through outer belief that he is an impostor (which will look after itself), but through our triumphant reclamation of the spiritual light, the true God-force, within our hearts, the awareness of which he has darkened and confused and set into reverse spin.

Enlil is already panicking, because his master plan is off course. No third world war over religious intolerance has begun, despite his best efforts, even though he encourages our leaders to make repetitive statements about 'the war on terrorism'. There is a dark occult power in the bandying of these words alone. Additionally, it is an attested fact that certain right-wing 'Christian' religious extremists from the West have in disguise infiltrated many fundamentalist Muslim cells, stoking up fear and hatred of Christianity and Western countries, and inciting them by all kinds of means to commit horrors and depredations they would otherwise never have conceived of. There is, therefore, a secret bi-lateralism in this 'war', and the fundamentalist aggressors are certainly dupes of the hidden power of the Syndicate, even though they think they struggle against the worldly power of Western civilisation. They are actually pawns in Enlil's game.

Meanwhile, the End-Dayists, of whom there are more than 63 million if sales of their literature are a true guide, play their part. One of their number, a Texan billionaire, is busy furnishing plans to multiply nuclear warheads within Israel, spurred on by the fact that his cult want to bring about the end of the world as soon as possible, imagining that thereby they are helping to fulfil the Scriptures!

This third world war 'should' have started at the beginning of the new millennium. '9/11' was specifically devised to bring it about. According to the strategies and calculations of Enlil and Marduk, by the year 2013, the destruction of society, accompanied by horrible planetary emanations from our own earth that we ourselves would have created, ought to have been well under way. If this had happened, planet X would not have been able to ride through the skies to save us. Instead, because of these noxious planetary emanations and the electromagnetic jarring caused by them, his impact would have caused terrible devastation and wholesale loss of life and he would not have succeeded in destroying Enlil's reverse-spin gold ring. His failure would have been due to the fact that, in order to shatter the ring, a certain spiritual vibration as well as a physical one needs to be conveyed by him to the earth which, because of humanity's afflicted state, she would have been unable to receive. All this would have brought about the magnetic point of human woe and despair Enlil and Marduk are relying upon.

General Pike (see the preceding chapter) was informed that this global catastrophe would be the prime cause of humanity's turning away from any genuine idea of God. He hid it from all but his closest allies because as little warning as possible of planet X's impact could only boost Enlil's plan. According to this plan, humanity would not know what had hit it. Civilisation would have begun to descend into chaos in the early years of the new millennium prior to the hit, and therefore nobody would have been watching the skies, and nobody would have seen planet X coming.

Enlil would thereby be in a position to reap the full benefit for his plan of what would amount to wholesale shock tactics of a kind never before encountered by the peoples of earth. We have reason indeed to salute Dr McCanney for depriving Enlil of this strategy. Thanks to his courage, we now seem to have it on scientific authority that planet X is indeed heading towards us.

Although, because Enlil could not risk moles or leaks concerning such intelligence, the Syndicate themselves knew nothing of the planet's return except for those of its members who held the highest office, he was confident that the very small number of people who would inevitably be made aware of it some years before its strike would be in his pocket, and could be influenced to keep quiet (he obviously reckoned without the good doctor!).

However, the point at which humanity would be brought to its knees and would cry aloud to a seemingly unresponsive God (see Pike's letter above) was indeed planned to be that at which planet X would strike, thereafter causing conditions on earth to seem like doomsday. Only by means of such planetary anguish could Marduk (Lucifer incarnate) persuade humanity to create the psychic opening through which the Naphidem could descend to earth. (We must understand, however, that Marduk, godlike as he is, is a human being, as is Enlil. The forces that drive them can be understood as two mighty angels of darkness, one of whom is Lucifer, who possesses Marduk, and the other we might call Ahriman, who possesses Enlil.)

Even bearing in mind the horror of all this, it is quite amusing, in a dreary sense, to see how Marduk and Enlil are forever contending against one another. We remember that they hated one another, although they worked together in perfect collusion, with Enlil remaining very much the dominant one of the pair.

Marduk had to dance to Enlil's tune, but secretly thought he could rise to a position of equality with Enlil, and, moreover, persuade humanity to despise him, once Marduk and the Naphidem were safely back on earth. Marduk (erroneously) did not associate humanity with the Naphidem, and yet he vaguely sensed approaching danger.

Marduk was afraid of Enlil's power, and was, to some extent, aware that Enlil sought the annihilation of humanity. Marduk thought this was a bad idea. Why destroy humanity, when it could be kept alive for fun, and taught new ways of torturing, violating, degrading, oppressing and murdering one another, and, even more importantly, heaping up what it would etherically create thereby on altars dedicated to the Naphidem, whom humanity would feed with its anguish and worship and adoration? As far as Marduk was concerned, Enlil was just being a spoilsport. There was no need to kill humanity, when it would make such entertaining Goyim (cattle).

With these thoughts in mind, Marduk decided that he was the good 'god', and Enlil the bad 'god'! He was allowed his own headway with the Syndicate, because Enlil's plan from the first was to eliminate humanity by permitting the Naphidem to descend in triumph, and thereafter to corrupt it to the point where it brought self-destruction upon its own head. This self-destruction was intended to include the Naphidem in its grand sweep, because Enlil hated the Naphidem just as much, if not more, than ordinary humanity itself. Marduk, of course, knew absolutely nothing about Enlil's drastic and sweeping 'Final Solution' for the Naphidem as well as for earthly humanity, but he suspected his austere, lordly colleague of some kind of undisclosed plot.

In another letter written by General Pike, dated 14 July 1889, he explains to the Grand Masters of his Palladian Councils (groups practising rites of revised Masonry that he himself founded):

> That which we say to the crowd is 'we worship God'. But it is the God that one worships without superstition. The religion should be, by all us initiates of the high degrees, maintained in the purity of the Luciferian doctrine ... Yes! Lucifer is God. And unfortunately Adonay is God also ... for the absolute can only exist as two gods. Thus, the doctrine of Satanism is a heresy: and the true, and pure philosophical religion is the belief in Lucifer, the equal of Adonay: but Lucifer, God of Light, and God of Good, is struggling for humanity against Adonay the God of Darkness and Evil.[1]

It is plain from this excerpt, which plays the two 'gods' off against one another, that General Pike knows who 'Adonay' (from Adon, Enlil's preferred name, meaning 'Lord') is. He is the god who proclaims himself the One God ('Jehovah'-Enlil), and he is the god of Satanism, who, according to Pike's letter, makes the same claim; in other words, these two entities are one, who is Enlil.

Reading between the lines, we can see that Marduk (equated with Lucifer), is already selling the idea to his beloved Syndicate that he himself is God. He could not summon the nerve to deny Enlil as co-ruler (we are fairly certain that Marduk would never have dared to make even these co-ruler claims face to face with Enlil!), which seems to be why General Pike understands the Absolute as 'manifesting as two gods'.

Marduk, who calls himself 'Lucifer' ('the Supreme Light') when he communicates with the inner circle of the Syndicate, has portrayed this 'other god', Adonay (Enlil), as dangerous and ill-willed towards humanity, which of course is correct.

However, Marduk is obviously putting himself forward as a 'good' god, struggling to overcome Enlil's power, with humanity's interests at heart!

Marduk liked to comfort himself with this kind of name-calling and diatribe against Enlil, believing himself (again, erroneously) to be secure and insulated from Enlil's angry eye within the protective confines of the Syndicate. Even so, Syndicate members themselves were uncomfortably aware that Marduk alone did not direct the group. Mazzini, Pike's mentor and predecessor, wrote to a friend:

> We form an association of brothers in all points of the globe. We wish to break every yoke. Yet there is one unseen that can hardly be felt, yet it weighs on us. Whence comes it? Where is it? No one knows ... or at least no one tells. This association is secret even to us the veterans of secret societies.

This, of course, was the impalpable influence of Enlil, the merest hint of a whisper of his ice-cold breath, the quivering of the veil of his invisible domain, darker than the deepest night. Marduk organised the Syndicate, but he took his orders from Enlil.

When we consider the machinations of Enlil and Marduk, and ponder on the Syndicate, we are in danger of being dragged down by the oppressive, strangling, anti-creative death forces that they represent, as mentioned in the previous chapter.

We need a safer course of study, one that will enlighten us rather than lure us with barbed hooks disguised as morsels of nutrition into the darkness.

CHAPTER SEVENTY

One Ring to Rule Them All and in the Darkness Bind Them

*I*t is now time to drink a toast to Tolkien! This masterful John-man wrote his epic, *The Lord of the Rings*, to throw a profound illumination upon the nature, principles, dangers and powers of the False Grail. He was an orthodox Catholic, and had no overt knowledge of the history of events as we are disclosing them … and yet he knew everything, as his great work of imagination silently proclaims. We can study his literary marathon in as much depth as we like without falling into the least danger. We will be given a panoramic view of all we need to know concerning the False Grail, including a guided tour of its mysteries, and we will be magnificently protected throughout.

It is most telling to relate that, when asked to what historical era the environment of his tale might belong, Tolkien replied that he would place it somewhere around 4000 BC. This, as we know, is precisely when Anu and Enlil's dark plot against humanity began to cast its deepest shadow in the form of the creation of the reverse-spin gold, after Enlil had discovered that the 'new humanity' (Adam and Eve) had not been brought forth by Enki and Nin-khursag as mindless slaves for the use of the corrupt contingent of the God-Headed people, but as initiated, Tiâmat-consecrated beings with the full range of potential necessary to attain supreme beinghood. ('It is the time of Man!' proclaim the kingly characters in the book.)

Enlil went on to create his malevolent ring from the reverse-spin gold, which he placed around our planet in the form of subtle, undetectable crystals in the higher atmosphere, where it still exists today.

It is at this point that we might play a simple word game and pause to ponder on Tolkien's name. If we read the last two letters and conjoin them with the fourth and fifth in reverse or mirror order (en-ki), the result is interesting, to say the least! The other 'name within a name' in mirror reversal is Lot, the learned man from Ur who held high status in Gomorrah, and who was visited by two angels, come to inform him that the 'citadel of ancient knowledge' in which he lived was about to be horrifically destroyed by the Dark Lord via fiendish and magical weaponry.

It is as well to become accustomed to this capering and cavorting of language known as the 'rabbit language' or the 'mother tongue', because it is an ancient art pertaining to names in particular, which are charged with their own life. For instance, 'Adam Weishaupt', the first overt leader of the amalgamated Illuminati (even though it was known as the 'Bavarian' Illuminati) means: Adam (the first man), *Weis* (to know), *Haupt* (leader), and seems to read as: 'the first man to be known as leader', indicating that the Syndicate, after thousands of years of secrecy, became a fully manifesting earthly organisation at that time. (This cipher within Weishaupt's name was discovered by the authors Anthony Roberts and Geoff Gilbertson.)

As Quayin or Cain represented the true eye or the *ayin*, the Eye of Horus of whom humanity is the 'pupil', associated with the Star Fire (whose symbol was the eye) and a sigil of the Grail, so this symbol of God-consciousness became distorted by the negative-spin agencies into the false eye, the false Grail. This eye is more commonly depicted as an eye within a triangle.[1]

By no means is it necessarily a negative symbol, as its esoteric meaning is 'Doorway to the Light'. The great question is: which light? It can indicate the doorway to the spiritual light, the ineffable light of God, or it can refer to the false light, the light of Lucifer and the Luciferic Illuminati. In other words, the doorway specified can open onto the serpent-ladder of light stretching upwards into the heavens, or it can creak slowly ajar onto the head of a great negative snake and take the duped spiritual seeker on a slithery ride down to degenerate depths. Which way will the eye in the pyramid go? Which direction will it choose? The false eye relates to the imbalance of materialism (the downward pull of matter), and within its glittering gleam can always be found the desire for authoritarian power and control. The symbol of the eye in the pyramid appears as the *reverse* of the United States Great Seal, and in 1933 (we note the 33 degrees of Masonic symbolism) President Roosevelt introduced it as the *reverse* sigil for the one-dollar bill.

There is a rather spooky story attached to the adoption of this symbol.

It seems that while Franklin, Adams and Jefferson were collaborating on the design of the Great Seal, there was some disagreement, and Jefferson took a turn around the garden to imbibe some fresh air and clear his head. Suddenly, a tall man dressed entirely in black, arrayed in a sweeping black cloak which hid his face (virtually a Black Rider!), appeared before Jefferson and gave him a piece of paper, advising him that he would find it meaningful and appropriate. The stranger then disappeared into a thicket, whilst Jefferson was left staring down at the piece of paper, which depicted the emblem of the eye in the triangle. Jefferson rushed back indoors and presented the sigil to his colleagues, who immediately agreed to adopt it.

This story demonstrates the need for cosmic balance between darkness and light, which must be harmonised in the heart.

The United States has a great choice to make between the doorway to the Grail (the 'good dragon') and the doorway to the snakehead (the 'negative dragon'). The prophecy of this choice was integral to the very founding of America. Currently, the eye in the triangle sigil seems to incline more to the dark side. Anthony Roberts and Geoff Gilbertson call it the 'all-seeing burning eye of power and control that would one day dominate the world'. This appears to hold sway at present. What Enlil has severely underestimated is the huge reservoir of goodness, of simple love and purity, within the collective human heart (after all, we are Tiâmat's children, not his!). It is true that it is heavily obscured at the moment; but we are assured that it is there, and that humanity is already turning towards the light, towards the heart. Remember how awry Enlil's plans have turned! There is no doubt that we are on track and heading steadfastly towards the return of the Grail.

We can return to Tolkien's epic tale and think of that great eye within a tower (in this case, within what preceded the pyramid – the tall, straight tower known as the *shem*) which constitutes the Dark Lord of Mordor. This is the evil eye – the Luciferic eye which is also the eye of Enlil – the besieged and manacled *ayin*, prevented from becoming the prepared organ for higher consciousness or the Stone of Ascension in the head. The whole of the Dark Lord's terrain is a vast evil forge. Just as Cain is the good, true and just craftsman, building the pure and light-filled human soul, the individual human consciousness connected to the Star Fire, so the Lord of Mordor, Sauron (*saur* – the lower self or dragon, the rampaging dino*saur* of earth), is the evil craftsman, constantly battling against the creative forces and seeking to undo and undermine their progress.

Not only is Mordor an evil forge, it is a hideous *forgery*. It is the constructor of the Untrue and the epicentre of Lies. We think that the very name *Mordor* whispers an echo of the actual name of that dark and ireful dimension in which Enlil and his followers dwell, described so aptly by Tolkien as a place where loathsome worms (manifestations of the lower dragon) slither beneath the surface and undermine the integrity of the very ground beneath one's feet. It is a name linguistically very similar to the words 'murder', and 'mort' or death. Mordor and its lord forged the ring. This ring, which must be cast into the Cracks of Doom, is the False Grail and all its power. It was found by an innocent swimming in the water (originally an Oannes man, until he became the Falling Knight and plunged from grace), and it overwhelmed him and turned him into a subhuman creature whose only source of intelligence was his own evil – the anti-Oannes man – Gollum (linguistically close to *Goyim* – cattle or driven creatures, just as poor Gollum was desperately driven by his rabid, all-consuming desire for the ring).[2] It can only be overcome by being returned to its source. Then it shall no more have dominion.

What does this mean – returning it to its source? It means that we give back the Luciferic and Ahrimanic gifts which have been given to us. Everything in our nature which acts against the heart comprises these gifts. We give them back to Enlil and Marduk[3], and we become free. False pride, selfishness, condemnation, anger, hatred, authoritarian power and domination, etcetera, etcetera, we return to its source. This can be done in simple, everyday ways, but its impact will be monumental. We do it by refusing to accept the 'gift' (really the takeover, because the dark forces steal rather than give, although they are very good at disguising this fact) in the first place.

We decline to take on board the dark energy, the dark expressions, the dark thoughts and acts of the lower dragon – our lower 'Sauron' selves. When we do this, we return it to its source.

The surefire method of succeeding in this task is to nurture our higher Pendragon selves in the way we have previously described – to turn to the light, to exercise that moment of choice when we can most powerfully choose to repudiate the darkness, to use the star constantly in our everyday lives, and to have absolute faith that there are shining beings of the one true light stretching their hands towards us to help us onward and upward in every conceivable situation we may encounter.

NOTES

1   The eye in the triangle is a depiction of human consciousness within its chakra system (the *ayin* in the pyramid). It is the sigil of the new soul-structure with which Tiâmat provided us when the depredations of Enlil and Marduk overcame the earth-vulnerable *shem*, the tall, thin, conical tower shape upon which human souls were previously structured. The priceless jewel, or Stone of Ascension within the head, is the sign of exalted human consciousness rising above and beyond the triangle of the chakras, until it is free to walk among the stars. The eye above the apex of the triangle is therefore Enki's sign, whilst the eye enclosed in the triangle is Enlil's sign. As has been discussed, the latter sign is only evil when the eye is actually imprisoned within the triangle, unable to rise because it has fallen into the trap of the reverse-spin powers. When this occurs, the precious Stone of Ascension in the head eventually becomes subject to a full reversal and descends

in degradation to the feet – Enlil's final victory, because if this happens he has success-fully beheaded those who aspire to be God-Headed people (ourselves), and he can laugh in triumph as he beholds our God-given Stone of Ascension – our very God-head itself – lying worthless, atrophied and disconnected at our uncomprehending feet. Enlil may be prone to victorious belly-laughs at our plight (and he has given forth many of them), but only because he does not understand what will happen on a worldwide scale when humanity begins at last to realise its mistake and moves to embrace the Grail.

2   Gollum calls the ring his 'precious' and is utterly besotted with it. It is a symbol of his lower self, the little 'I' of earth, which the forces of materialism tempt us to adore and indulge to the extent where we become selfish, self-seeking and narrow-minded, utterly bound to the earth and incapable of rising into the reality of the spiritual worlds, from where we draw our life, vision and ultimate redemption. From this point on, the soul becomes corroded and corrupted, and can only embrace death.

3   Sad to relate, a small number of the *Perfecti* (the Cathar priesthood) fell into Marduk's power. He appeared to them as a God of Light, and unfortunately they were unable to differentiate between the true light of the spirit, and the false light of illusion. Marduk had a plan of his own. As we know, he had always hated and resented Enlil, and suspected that Enlil wanted to kill humankind (whilst remaining oblivious that Enlil also intended to eliminate the Naphidem, of whom Marduk was chief). Marduk concocted a plot within a plot. He would win the Goyim (cattle, or humanity) over to his side by persuading those members of earthly humanity over whom he won influence that he was the 'good god' and Enlil was the 'bad god'. Masquerading as a god of 'pure' light, he wormed his way into the Cathars, the Templars, the Rosicrucians, the Masons, the alchemists, and other esoteric groups who existed to preserve Enki and Nin-khursag's truth: the truth of Tiâmat the Mother and Oannes the Father, and of the Daughter-Son of Light, their divine child. He made small or great headway according to the strengths and weaknesses of the groups he encountered. This led to a rift between these esoteric groups. Some stood their ground, others became contaminated. Where even a chink appeared in their armour, some organi-sations fell, horribly butchered, as in the case of the Cathars, Templars and 'witches' (femi-nine wise ones or mystics). Enlil smiled approvingly whilst Marduk schemed. Marduk's plot was taking the Naphidem chief exactly where Enlil wished his footsteps to fall, although, of course, Marduk believed Enlil was ignorant of his intentions. Instead, Enlil did exactly what he wanted with the strength and influence of the defiled esoteric socie-ties, particularly with the global banks, which were a direct legacy of the Templars (there were no banks until, originally for altruistic reasons rather than for profit, the Templars founded the principle which led to their establishment in the seventeenth century).

We note with interest that, of the two men who set up the Bilderberg movement in 1954, one was George Ball, a businessman who later became the managing director of Lehman Brothers Incorporated. This establishment was the first US bank to collapse in 2008, so setting up the domino effect for the others. The idea behind the calamity was to fan the flames of global chaos by instituting financial mayhem.

CHAPTER SEVENTY-ONE

A Ring of Pure and Endless Light

*W*hat of planet X's return? Will it cause mayhem on earth, even if we reclaim our Pendragon status?

It will cause some practical problems and strange weather manifestations, but there will be no devastation or disaster. Its effects will be apparent but minimal. Its impact, however, will be cleansing and therapeutic, and many imbalances on earth will be healed. The terrible ring will shatter forever. The sure and certain promise of positive planetary spin will come into being.

Although we should do all we can to keep our planet and its atmosphere pure and unpolluted, we are advised that it is not carbon emissions that are mainly responsible for current meteorological disturbances and peculiarities, but the electromagnetic effect on the sun of planet X's return, which is then translated to earth as a consequence. Our weather patterns will return to normal a few years after it has passed us by on its return journey to outer space. Although we certainly must bring to an end our destructive, polluting behaviour towards our beautiful earth (especially with regard to the destruction of the rainforests), the future of the planet is assured. In the future there will be some inundation and loss of land, but our compensation will be that new lands will arise from the sea, which will actually regulate and stabilise rising sea levels. Some parts of Atlantis will emerge permanently from their watery grave (although not necessarily at the time of planet X's return) which will put paid to a lot of tiresome argument!

In the Gospel of Mary, there is a wonderful teaching about ascension and the seven circuits of the soul, which of course refers to the chakras. We have to cleanse and energise our chakras with the inspiration of divine love, with the influx of Pendragon consciousness. What planet X will leave behind him when he cuts through our orbit is a great streamer of cosmic matter (we are not going to say debris). This cosmic matter will surround our planet, and we will experience some (bearable) turbulence for seven years as we pass through it. Seven years – seven circuits of the soul. This is our great mission – to cleanse our own chakras, and those of our beloved planet, as we make each of the seven circuits through planet X's streamer of cosmic matter. During these years, the Grail, by public demand, will be retrieved and, we hope and trust, the divine secrets of the Emerald Tablet revealed and absorbed.

We will have many chances to express brotherhood and helpfulness, disinterest and generosity, during these seven years – both to our neighbours and within a global context. All humanity will come together to pull one another through these years of trials and testing. But it will not be soul-destroying and terrible, as Enlil would wish it to be. It will be challenging, but by no means will civilisation break down. We will be able to do the normal things of everyday life. We will sail through the experience if we concentrate on meeting one another's needs rather than our own. In fact, it could all be quite good fun; and we will find ourselves insisting more and more, as the years go by, that life on planet earth *is* fun; not commercialised, substance-fed fun hooked up to all sorts of strange manipulations and control, as it is at the moment, but real fun for everyone, which is quite different in essence, and much, much, more potent.

Yes, we will succeed in our mission of universal chakra healing and cleansing, even rather magnificently. And when the seven years are done, and the potential of the Grail has been recognised (as indeed it will be), something truly wondrous will happen. The streamer of cosmic matter will grow brighter during each of the seven years, reflecting more and more light, crystalline and dancing, like the clearest starlight. And then, finally, the wonder will come into being.

A ring of pure and endless light will form in perfection around our planet, breathtaking, beautiful. It will be the most exquisite of all the cosmic phenomena the world has ever seen. And it will be permanent; a ring of celestial love, delicately pearlescent, a band set with pearls of wisdom and reflective Star Fire, given by planet X to honour his lover, the earth. It will look rather like Saturn's ring, but it will wear an aspect of even greater heavenly grandeur and cosmic beauty.

Within this exquisite ring, which will give our nights a soft and magical glow that blesses the darkness, we will be perfectly safe, immaculately protected, from the incursions of Enlil or any other hostile influence …

… At one, at peace, all danger assuaged at last, and the Grail lifting us ever closer to heaven and its boundless stars.

> *For I dipped into the future,*
> *Far as the eye could see;*
> *Saw the vision of the world, and*
> *All the wonder that would be.*

(ALFRED, LORD TENNYSON)

The Whore of Babylon

he Whore of Babylon is the fourth profane person of which Revelation speaks. These four, the Dragon of Wrath, the Beast, the False Prophet and the Whore, mirror in reverse shadow-image the Four Sacred Persons who are realised to their fullest potential in Mary Magdalene, Jesus of Nazareth, John the Beloved Disciple, and Tamar the Holy Grail, and who announce, and are associated with, the Four Hallows of the Holy Grail.

The Whore of Babylon is the false, distorted and reversed expression of Tamar, who is the Divine Woman and the personification of the holy *khu*. The Dragon of Wrath is the reversed Pendragon, and the Beast is the state of humanity deprived of the *khu*. The False Prophet or Stone deceptively mirrors the true Stone – the Emerald Tablet with all its gifts and revelations and divine infusions of enlightenment wrought from the pure and living light of Tiâmat. The Whore of Babylon deceptively mirrors the Divine Woman:

> So he carried me away in the spirit to the wilderness: and I saw a woman sit upon a scarlet-coloured beast, full of names of blasphemy, having seven heads and ten horns. And the woman was arrayed in purple and scarlet colour, and decked with gold and precious stones and pearls, having a golden cup in her hand full of abominations and filthiness of her fornication: And, upon her forehead was a name written, MYSTERY, BABYLON THE GREAT, THE MOTHER OF HARLOTS AND ABOMINATIONS OF THE EARTH.

> (JOHN: THE REVELATION, 17)

This prophecy shows us how the civilisation rises that Enlil controls, and will (so he plans) ultimately control so that he can lead it to utter destruction. The civilisation is led and inspired by the *false* Grail, who is a harlot. She gives and receives the life-forces without love, in return for money (materialism). She symbolises the closed-down heart centre, the very reverse of Tamar the Divine Woman, she of the emerald-green radiance who represents the mystical heart in full expression of its God-centred forces. (We might think of the divine Tree of Life and its twin-companion, the Tree of the Knowledge of Good and Evil [Wisdom] in full leaf, the cusp of their utmost expression.) The false Grail, the harlot, is the opposite shadow-image of love, and she shows us how the sacred feminine principle has been denigrated and perverted, transmogrified into a carnal lackey, when her true standing is that of highest queen. The harlot colludes with Enlil and rides him, demonstrating that the power of the false Grail, the spiritually deranged consciousness arising from the powers of reversal contained in the white powder, and the soul's refusal of the light, actually control Enlil, although this mighty red dragon, full of conceit, thinks in opposite terms – that he is in control.

Together they create a formidable malevolence, because in her hands the Whore of Babylon wields the false Grail cup, the ultimate blasphemy of the true Grail. It mocks the Star Fire, and the giving of the Star Fire, in a unified symbol.

It shows us the gold, the symbol of exalted consciousness which is used to make the white powder; the precious stones which represent the high regard and desirability with which the white powder is esteemed; and the pearls, the lunar jewels which are both an emblem and a confirmation that the white powder is indeed a mockery of the Star Fire, for it is masquerading as the essence of wisdom from the source of God.

Yet look who the Whore that puts the substance in the false Grail cup really is – 'the mother of harlots and abominations of the earth'.

The Whore is the ultimate degradation of the sacred feminine, from whom all misconceptions regarding the feminine arise, because she is a degradation of God, of Tiâmat herself. She holds forth the false Grail, the deadly potentiality of all loveless actions, policies, responses and behaviours, the four gifts of the Grail in reverse spin, forced into this mode at the point when Tiâmat was 'slain' and the Earth herself began to spin anti-clockwise: death, disease, famine and the wasteland. These shadow gifts of the false Grail operate on every level, so that the high tides of despair, uneasiness, hopelessness, and savage emotional and psychological want with their devastating social expression which course throughout our world are constantly sustained and never truly appeased.

Why is the Whore associated with Babylon? The answer to this question seems to be that it was Enlil and Marduk's special aim to pervert the course of the hated, Tiâmat-dedicated, Oannes-aspiring Babylon, and that Enlil's false Emerald Tablet (the very essence of the Whore, as the true Emerald Tablet is the very essence of Tamar) had been conjured into being synonymously with the purloined and hijacked Babylon itself.

Babylon had been built to house the temple to the true Father, expressed in the Oannes-John man, as part of Tiâmat's great plan to deliver humanity from Annum and Enlil's tyranny. Enlil and Marduk renamed it Babel ('confusion') in mockery of its original name, to show that it would henceforth be a centre dedicated to the forces of the white powder, or the new consciousness for humanity that they were determined should gain ascendancy. They were at this time working on a 'new man', a creature which they had designed to arise from the basic human vessel walking the earth (the ordinary star people). This new man would, according to their plans, one day house the Naphidem, so that they could walk in flesh again, as in the good old days.

Thankfully, their plan did not succeed and attempts to create the mutated new man were abandoned (until the Nazis resumed the procedure towards the middle of the last century).

However, the idea of a new Babylon as a temple of Marduk and a seat of his power was not one that the Naphidem king was prepared to relinquish once Babel with its terrible objectives had fallen. The energies of the false Emerald Tablet were now abroad, and they needed a focal point so that they might more efficiently be broadcast to the world and to future generations and civilisations. Babylon, Marduk decided, was obviously destined to be their cradle. With Enlil's blessing, he moved the entire project into the west, and, once the mayhem of dying Sumer had diminished, he began building again until Babylon was re-established under his power. It flourished and became a great city state, as we know.

There were many admirable aspects of Babylon (the Naphidem, after all, are human, and there are always gifts of greatness to be found in the human soul, even if these gifts are ultimately corrupted), but it secreted within its belly a certain influence, like the power granted to King Midas, to turn everything into gold – the reverse-spin gold. Babylon was the embodiment of Marduk's secret dream to build a capital from which the entire world would one day be ruled, initially in a metaphysical rather than an actual sense, and then, once the Naphidem were back on earth, directly.

We know that this was exactly and literally what had been planned for Babel before Tiâmat brought down its infamous Tower and scuppered such plans. Marduk, child-like, found it hard to give up his dream; and so Babylon (impudently given its former, Enki-inspired name as a resonating war-cry of Marduk's and Enlil's triumph, because it had been successfully seized from the enemy and rededicated to the false Grail and the establishment of a very different kind of 'Father') carried a certain breath, a certain air, of the fragments of that dream. Good things arose from Babylon, but a shadow ever lurked and beckoned at the heart of every one of these jewels of human endeavour. The Whore of Babylon, the first kingdom dedicated to the white powder, was born to this city precisely because it was so dedicated.

When the three Wise Men attended the birth of Jesus, the one born in Babylon brought gold. It was intended, in one sense, as a gift of the white powder, offered to Jesus so that the Divine Couple might transform it. Jesus entirely rejected it, and instead attuned his whole being, of whom Mary Magdalene comprised half, to the true symbolism of gold. The fourth Wise Man bore pearls, emeralds and sapphires, but he died of natural causes on the journey to Bethlehem. We can deduce from the clue of the jewels he carried that he was coming to honour the first Christ-child, Mary Magdalene (Jesus followed twelve days later), but so virulent were the forces ranged against her from the beginning that this fourth Wise Man was not allowed to complete his journey.

There is further confirmation in the passage quoted that the Whore is the false Grail, holding up the mockery of the Star Fire, for of course she is in herself the false *khu*. The colours purple and scarlet, associated with royalty and the Star Fire, are also connected with alchemy and the Philosopher's Stone, sometimes called 'projection powder'. (We would like to make clear at this juncture that we are certainly not condemning alchemy as a dubious practice, but rather suggesting that Enlil has introduced some kind of scrambling influence, which can project adherents of the art, and of other esoteric arts, down an opposite path from the one they originally sought, leading them into complications, dangers, and often simply a dead-end, not always recognised as such; this power of perversion arises from Enlil's false Emerald Tablet, the one he released into the world at the time of Marduk's take-over, when Babylon was born.)

Certain metals which have been altered in their elemental structure by the alchemist's art of heating and cooling, or refining, form a substance which, it is said, is soluble in glass before the glass reaches melting point. The substance, on contact with the softening glass, washes throughout it and transforms its transparency to a rich, translucent ruby red, which gives off a vivid purple fluorescence in the dark. When this jewel-red glass is ground to powder in a mortar of agate, it translates into a form of the famous Philosopher's Stone or 'projection powder'.

Thus we have the white and the red powder, both of which are used in the tradition of alchemy to facilitate ascension, or to provide a form of the Holy Grail.

What we would say at this point is that there is indeed a great mystery involved in what actually happens to matter itself when human consciousness, grounded in a physical body, takes flight in an act of ascension. By some means most deeply mystical, we can co-create with God at this point via the sacred stone, the Philosopher's Stone, which resides within our heads, within our brains. In the future as we begin to receive the Grail, so that many of us undertake ascension, inevitable changes in the structure of matter will occur which will advantageously affect our civilisations and the nature and philosophy of our currently positivist, materialistic sciences. However, we would stress that, before we can reach this level of existence, we have to be very clear, as a planetary society, that some kind of quick-fix via the application of certain powders, either white or red or both, is not an option!

The alchemists who ascended in consciousness after preparing and finally transmuting their various metals in the crucibles within their laboratories did so because, after many, many years of patience and inquiry sourced in an appropriate spirit of reverence in which they consciously strove to reach towards God, they experienced a transmutation of consciousness itself. This came about because, through their long years of experimentation, they finally demonstrated to themselves certain sacred cosmic truths, which they were thus able to comprehend and recognise through their own facilitation. This protracted realisation is, indeed, a beautiful way to receive such truths, because their nature, although wondrous, is also devastating, and the unprepared mind might succumb to disintegration or displacement under the pressure of such divine revelation.

Alchemy, therefore, is a method of achieving transmutation of consciousness by means of preparing and subduing the mind to receive the gold of the spirit, and as such it is akin to Buddhism.

Can we imagine the joy and the wonder of the alchemist coming to him like a sunburst as he sees, enacted before his very eyes, the perfect validation of those principles which prove that the mystery of God lives within matter itself, and that his own being is veritably of God rather than matter, and thus has the power to transmute matter? In the ecstasy proceeding from the marvel of that moment, enlightenment or transmutation comes to the true alchemist; but it is a heart-piercing, or a realisation within the heart, which stimulates ascension, not the ingestion of or radiation from a red or a white powder.

It is at this point that the true, God-given *shem* in our heads becomes active, and allows us to directly impact and configure matter with our thoughts.

It is a relic of this inherent power that Uri Geller (whom we believe belongs to the bloodline of the ancient Mesopotamian kings descending from Enki and Lilith) wields in bending metals and bringing forth the sprouting life from seeds: a power we are certain that Noah and his queen possessed in all its comprehensive dimensions, as well as all those of Tiâmat's special bloodline who were known as the Master Craftsmen. Enki, Nin-khursag and Lilith used this power to directly manipulate and mould matter (we remember that Nin-khursag was called 'the Lady of Form-Giving', and that Enki was known as Image Fashioner, the Master of Shaping and the Charmer of Making). It seems that Uri Geller, if he recognises such a destiny, may have much to teach us about our divine inheritance.

If we try to employ material means to ascend, as is the case when drugs are used, we most probably will ascend, but it will not be an act of flight, whereby we use our own wings and follow the light in the heart to our destination. There are many, many astral dimensions, some of them very sinister indeed, into any one of which we may be propelled if we use drugs, or if we use the white and the red life-forces contained in the two powders as drugs (i.e. material means used to lift the unprepared mind and soul away from the carnal dimension).

We may at first tend to visit the more (superficially) attractive astral planes, but inevitably there will come a point where we begin to struggle in the nastier spheres, and it is all downhill from there. The problem is that Enlil and Marduk, with the help of Noah, have prepared an intensely ominous and baleful dimension for those of us who might be tempted to think that ascension is all about the use of the red and the white powder (and of course the meaning of this statement is not limited to literal reality, but translates into all kinds of applications).

If we use a material substance inappropriately, or indeed a materialist mentality, we will find that we enter dimensions very much inhabited by shadow-beings such as the Dragon of Wrath, the Beast, the False Prophet and the Whore of Babylon. Some people, seduced by the glamorous otherworldliness of these beings, might feel they would benefit from encountering them. But how much fun is it likely to be, to undergo famine, pestilence, the wasteland, and death? Think of how we experience these things on earth. That is the fundamental reality of how we will experience them on the deceptively glittering astral planes, only with more terrifying intensity!

One reason why the Whore of Babylon is called Mystery is because she attracts people in just this way. She calls them into her essence (she seduces them) because they are attracted by the lure and glamour of occult and esoteric 'mystery'.

It is good to wish to be consummate with mystery, but we must first take care to leave behind the false values arising from egotism – an urge to grasp something desirable for our own self-gratification – or we will come away with a bad case of metaphysical pox rather than enlightenment, which will show us just how definitively we failed to leave the earth behind after all! As the Gospel of Mary shows, when we truly ascend, we ascend on wings of the spirit, and we bypass all the greedy hands reaching out to us from these astral spheres, waiting to grasp us and draw us in. When we can safely pass them by, which the Grail will teach us to do, we will be free of the threat engendered by Enlil and Marduk forever.

There may be another reason why the Whore of Babylon is called Mystery. Perhaps it is because, when we contemplate her, we might receive the intimation that we should be seeing something else, that her wretched and ravening identity is hiding a deep and beautiful truth.

331

And so, surely, it is; because when the Whore image is fully understood, its reverse spin can be dispensed with. The unscathed spirit of the eternal feminine then takes form in the mirror of our perception, and Tiâmat shines forth in the glass. What we understand of her steals on the soul as a benediction and a profound peace as her encompassing love assures us that all will be well, for even the strongest of the dark forces must halt, fall back, and ultimately surrender their authority to the ineffable light of the Dragon Queen.

Alice, The Dragon Queen, and the Tree of Life

*W*e will let Lewis Carroll speak for himself, after pointing out that the pigeon is of the dove family – the dove of the Holy Spirit which descends on the waiting soul as that quality of 'peace that passeth all understanding' – the peace of the Paraclete. The pigeon is the only bird to secrete 'milk' to feed its young. The esoteric rather than the literal argument here is that the Pigeon is unaware that the treasure it brings forth from its depths is for the nourishment of its Pendragon self in its aspiration towards ascension, and is not brought forth simply so that it may keep on reproducing its little earthly lower dragon self over and over again in a repetitive and unprogressive cycle (the latter being the state of soul and consciousness that Enlil tries to inculcate in us). The Wonderland Pigeon is, of course, the dove in its mundane, uninspired manifestation (with all due respect to pigs, we might say that there is a pig-headed element to it!); however, although its attitudes leave a lot to be desired, it still seems to know a thing or two, as we shall see:

> *'Come, my head's free at last!' said Alice in a tone of delight, which changed into alarm in another moment, when she discovered that her shoulders were nowhere to be found: all she could see, when she looked down, was an immense length of neck, which seemed to rise like a stalk out of a sea of green leaves that lay far below her. 'What can all that green stuff be?' said Alice.*
> *'And where have my shoulders got to? And oh, my poor hands, how is it I can't see you?' She was moving them about as she spoke, but no result seemed to follow, except a little shaking among the distant green leaves. As there seemed to be no chance of getting her hands up to her head, she*

tried to get her head down to them, and was delighted to find that her neck would bend about easily in any direction, like a serpent. She had just succeeded in curving it down into a graceful zigzag, and was going to dive in among the leaves, which she found to be nothing but the tops of the trees under which she had been wandering, when a sharp hiss made her draw back in a hurry: a large pigeon had flown into her face, and was beating her violently with its wings.

'Serpent!' screamed the Pigeon.

'I'm not a serpent!' said Alice indignantly. 'Let me alone!'

'Serpent, I say again!' repeated the Pigeon, but in a more subdued tone, and added, with a kind of sob, 'I've tried every way, but nothing seems to suit them!'

'I haven't the least idea what you're talking about,' said Alice.

'I've tried the roots of trees, and I've tried banks, and I've tried hedges,' the Pigeon went on, without attending to her; 'but those serpents! There's no pleasing them!'

Alice was more and more puzzled, but she thought there was no use in saying anything more till the Pigeon had finished.

'As if it wasn't trouble enough hatching the eggs,' said the Pigeon; 'but I must be on the look-out for serpents, night and day! Why, I haven't had a wink of sleep these three weeks!'

'I'm very sorry you've been annoyed,' said Alice, who was beginning to see its meaning.

'And just as I'd taken the highest tree in the wood,' continued the Pigeon, raising its voice to a shriek, 'and just as I was thinking I'd be free of them at last, they must needs come wriggling down from the sky! Ugh, Serpent!'

'But I'm not a serpent, I tell you!' said Alice. I'm a – I'm a –'

'Well! What are you?' said the Pigeon. 'I can see you're trying to invent something!'

'I – I'm a little girl,' said Alice, rather doubtfully, as she remembered the number of changes she had gone through that day.

'A likely story, indeed!' said the Pigeon, in a tone of the deepest contempt. 'I've seen a good many little girls in my time, but never one with such a neck as that! No, no! You're a serpent, and there's no use denying it. I suppose you'll be telling me next that you never tasted an egg!'

'I have tasted eggs, certainly,' said Alice, who was a very truthful child;
'but little girls eat eggs quite as much as serpents do, you know.'
'I don't believe it,' said the Pigeon; 'but if they do, why, then they're a
kind of serpent: that's all I can say.'

(CHAPTER V, *ALICE'S ADVENTURES IN WONDERLAND,*
LEWIS CARROLL)

Exactly!

The Cheshire Cat
A Dissertation Written
in Wonderland

*W*e would like to offer here, for those to whom it might appeal, a little dissertation written in Wonderland. Some of these ideas are not new, and it will be abrasively clear to our readers by now that we are neither mathematicians nor scientists. However, for the fun of it, here goes:

We will start with the black dot, which seems to be massively important (only what sort of mass?). We think, a very strange sort of mass; however, we will not allow ourselves to be deflected from the point …

We posit that

- the pupil of the eye, or the *ayin*
- the nucleus of the atom
- the decimal point
- the contracted universe

are all the same thing!

This tiny point contains all dimensions, even the concept of dimension. For instance, if a single atom were as big as a giant planet, its nucleus would still be an infinitesimal point. Therefore, perhaps size and dimension are all illusory.

This might be the reason why, traditionally, fairies delight in appearing to human beings as terrifyingly huge or very small, and then suddenly changing their size dramatically. They are teaching us that size in itself is an illusion.

- The pupil of the eye expands and contracts.
- The decimal point expands things if it moves in one direction, and contracts things if it moves in the opposite direction.
- The universe expands into everything, and contracts into the black dot or let us say, the decimal point.

The decimal point not only contains all size and dimension, it *controls* them. (Moving forward, it expands; moving backwards, it contracts.)

We think that Enlil has somehow contrived, via this secret of the *ayin,* and of the nucleus of the atom, and of the decimal point, which is enshrined in his reverse-spin mirror, to make small things look big and big things look small. Trying to respond appropriately, we move in a direction to *minimise,* but we *maximise* instead – and vice versa. We think that Enlil has hidden his mirror from our cognition by moving the decimal point to a position that we would never suspect within the confines of our normal rationality. We need to ask Alice's advice on this!

One character from Wonderland has come forward to show us the way; namely, the Cheshire Cat. Our lesson seems to be about dimension and size, and the wrong, misleading or opposite reflection of dimension and size.

Just like the initials of the Cheshire Cat – the CC – the two halves of a circle (the circle whose centrepoint is the dot) show that the ring or the circle has been cut in half instead of maintaining its God-given form and thereby sustaining the creation of the continuous energy flow within the integrity of a circuit or a circle. (We actually see the circles coming forth from the dot, as if it were emitting them. We think that what we see is the Ouroboros, the essence of the power of the sacred ring which Enlil seeks to pervert or reverse.) This cleaving in half is the Enlil principle – the same principle he used in order to change all the positive and negative pairs of electrons (male and female) in his high-spin gold to exclusively positive (male) electrons at the ethereal level.

Enlil's aim was to create an exclusively masculine scenario or dimension, or at the very least, a masculine-dominant one which obscured and denied the feminine principle. To do this, he ensured that instead of creating the sacred marriage of the circle or circuit with the components of the circle, the circuit would be cut so that its halves lined up like this – CC. Although their equality cannot actually be impaired or removed, one half nevertheless *stands behind* the other half and is obscured and overshadowed by it. If this situation persists for long enough, degeneration, death and destruction is the result.

We see that in the case of the Cheshire Cat – the CC – his *body* disappears, but his *smile* remains in the physical, visible dimension. This is the wrong way round – his *body* should remain in the physical dimension – the special dimension prepared for it by Tiâmat – but his *smile*, the impression of his spirit, should easily disappear from it without encountering any difficulty or delay in slipping between dimensions.

In other words, the Cheshire Cat fits into earthly reality the wrong way round, because his body vanishes and his smile remains!

This teaches us that Enlil has learnt how to reverse the qualities of dimensions or, rather, how to hide what should be visible within a dimension, and show what should not be there, or should not be there in a certain expression or context. He has hidden half the decimal point behind the other half – CC – so we can't see the real world! We can't see the emanation of Tiâmat's consciousness in its true expression.

The brain can be fooled by Enlil's reverse-spin, or fool's, gold, but the *eye* or *ayin* cannot – hence the huge significance of Dagobert's eye. However, we know that Dagobert's eye was put out, or run through by a lance. This does not matter, because there is an ethereal eye of the spirit in the brain – the Stone of Ascension – whose point of consciousness is the chakral 'third eye' (to show our 'thrice greatest' status). This eye cannot be fooled and cannot be put out, simply because it *is* the decimal point in all its purity, indivisible and incorruptible and unbeguilable by Enlil. It is the pupil, the nucleus, the contracted universe, the decimal point, Tiâmat's consciousness itself – the sacred *ayin*.

We have found the Cheshire Cat to be a most helpful and instructive beast. He seems not to mind in the least that we may have cracked the enigma behind his smile! However, it is not in the nature of Wonderland to run out of possibilities. His disembodied smile still seems to be a knowing one ...

An Appeal

If you have been inspired by the information in this book, you can choose to join us on the Grail quest by writing to HRH the Prince of Wales at Highgrove and requesting that, as patron of Lincoln Cathedral's Fabric Fund (a position he will hold until 2016), he expresses support for the project of excavation at the Grail site.

Please also write to the Dean of Lincoln Cathedral at the address below:

The Very Reverend Philip Buckler, Dean of Lincoln
c/o Ms Angela Chappell
Fund Development
Lincoln Cathedral
4, Priory Gate
Lincoln
LN2 1PL

A courteous, brief letter, keeping to the crucial point, is best. It seems that only public demand will retrieve the Grail, so adding your voice to this call will be of real service.

> ... *slowly he lifted his arms and opened them wide.*
> *'It's a gift!' he said.*

(J.R.R. TOLKIEN, *TREE AND LEAF*)

Further Reading

Gardner, Laurence, *Genesis of the Grail Kings*, Bantam Press, 1999

Jensen, Callum, *Synchronicity and the Scarlet Saint*: soon to be released

(Callum Jensen has also made a movie-documentary about the clues that led him to the site at Lincoln cathedral: *The Murder of Mary Magdalene*, 2010, available from Amazon)

Nahmad, Claire and Bailey, Margaret, *The Secret Teachings of Mary Magdalene*, Watkins, 2006

Sierra, Javier, *The Secret Supper*, Simon & Schuster, 2006

In Memoriam

We would like to honour the memory of Margaret Bailey, who died in June 2011 and express our warm appreciation for the contribution she made to the book *The Secret of the Ages*, upon which this book is based, and for the inspiration she was to all who knew her.

Male
Sexual
Abuse

Male

Sexual

Abuse

A Trilogy of Intervention Strategies

John C. GONSIOREK

Walter H. BERA   Donald LeTOURNEAU

SAGE Publications

International Educational and Professional Publisher

Thousand Oaks   London   New Delhi

For information address:

SAGE Publications, Inc.
2455 Teller Road
Thousand Oaks, California 91320

SAGE Publications Ltd.
6 Bonhill Street
London EC2A 4PU
United Kingdom

SAGE Publications India Pvt. Ltd.
M-32 Market
Greater Kailash I
New Delhi 110 048 India

Printed in the United States of America

Library of Congress Cataloging-in-Publication Data

Gonsiorek, John C.
    Male sexual abuse : a trilogy of intervention starategies / John C. Gonsiorek, Walter H. Bera, Donald LeTourneau.
        p. cm.
    Includes bibliographical references and index.
    ISBN 0-8039-3716-4. — ISBN 0-8039-3717-2 (pb)
    1. Male sexual abuse victims—Rehabilitation. 2. Teenage sex offenders—Rehabilitation. 3. Male prostitutes—Rehabilitation.
I. Bera, Walter H. II. LeTourneau, Donald. III. Title.
RC560.S44G66   1994
616.85'83—dc20   94-11731
                                                            CIP

94 95 96 97 98 10 9 8 7 6 5 4 3 2 1

Sage Production Editor: Yvonne Könneker

Contents

Acknowledgments

Special thanks goes to William J. Doherty and Mac A. Baird for permission to adapt their model of levels of family involvement in family-centered health care to adolescent sex offender families. Their article, "Developmental Levels in Family-Centered Medical Care," appears in *Family Medicine, 18*(3), pp. 153-156, 1986, and is used with the permission of the Society of Teachers of Family Medicine.

The Victim-Sensitive Offender Therapy Model was originally presented as a chapter by Walter H. Bera, titled "The Systemic/Attributional Model: Victim-Sensitive Offender Therapy" in J. M. Yokley (Ed.), *The Use of Victim-Offender Communication in the Treatment of Sexual Abuse: Three Intervention Models,* Orwell, VT: Safer Society Press, 1990, and is used with the permission of the publisher.

The opening extract of the epilogue is from *A First Zen Reader* by Trevor Leggett. Copyright © 1960 by Charles E. Tuttle Co., Inc. Used by permission of Charles E. Tuttle Co., Inc. All rights reserved.

Valuable comments on previous drafts of this manuscript were made by Craig Allen, Debra Boyer, Bill Friedrich, Stephen Grubman-Black, Mary Koss, Brenda Vander May, Larry Morris, and Stephen Mussack.

*　　*　　*

I wish to thank my life partner, Jim, for his patience, love, understanding, and support; Nicholas Kozel, for typing, editing, and computer assistance; Brenda Vander Mey for encouragement and wise counsel during a difficult period; Charles Silverstein, for his example of courage and tenacity; Walter Bera and Don LeTourneau, for their friendship, collegiality, and patience; and M., for teaching me more about the effects of abuse and recovery than any book or expert could.

−J. C. G.

                    *   *   *

I wish to thank my family, Jane and Sophia, for their deep love, patience, and support in the creation of this book. Thanks to those who read early drafts and provided valuable comments and support: mentor and friend William Doherty and Gail Ryan and William Friedrich, whose clear feedback came at a critical time. Thanks to Fay Honey Knopp, who provided critical early support in the development of the victim-sensitive offender therapy model. Special thanks goes to old colleagues and friends Mike O'Brien and Ruth Matthews, who read the early drafts and, as part of PHASE, stimulated and supported the development of many of the concepts presented. Finally, thanks to John Gonsiorek and Don LeTourneau for their friendship and intellectual honesty; and to the many victims, offenders, and their families who taught me what is needed in healing.

−W. H. B.

                    *   *   *

I wish to thank Mike, without whose badgering and support I never would have found my way in the world of hustlers; Michael (Seattle) and Gabe (Los Angeles), for acting as insightful sounding boards over the years as I have thought out boy prostitution; Debra Boyer, for reviewing an early draft and offering support and insight; the staff of the Center for Youth Development and Research, for helping to teach me the praxis of youth work; Michael Baizerman, for being a mentor, friend, and colleague who would not let me get away with intellectual laziness; Jackie Thompson, with whom I have shared much and whose work and research have informed and shaped much of what I have written; Walter Bera and John Gonsiorck for believing in me and teaching me much of what it means to be male in this culture; and to all the young people I have worked with on the streets who taught me so much, thanks for sharing your stories with me—to those who did not make it, your stories are not forgotten.

—D. L.

Introduction

This book describes three clinical intervention approaches to working with adolescent and young adult males who are victims or perpetrators of sexual abuse. These perspectives differ both in the populations for whom the applications are intended and in the style and theoretical orientation of the intervention techniques.

Part I: Assessment of and Treatment Planning and Individual Psychotherapy for Sexually Abused Adolescent Males describes assessment, treatment planning, and individual psychotherapy with primarily young adult or later adolescent males who have been sexually abused. The theoretical perspective draws upon adaptations of Heinz Kohut's self-psychology. In terms of technique, this perspective often employs interventions from a cognitive-behavioral perspective.

Part II: Family Systems Therapy for Adolescent Male Sex Offenders proposes a model of family systems therapy for working with adolescent males who are perpetrators of sexual abuse. A variety of family systems perspectives and techniques are synthesized into a victim-sensitive therapy for offenders.

Part III: A Model for Working With Adolescent Male Prostitutes relates a model of working with male street youth who are engaged in prostitution. The detached youth work perspective is derived from an older social work tradition best articulated by Gisela Konopka, and recently adapted by Jackie Thompson. The intervention described falls more under the rubric of youth work, not therapy. Indeed, the population described is generally viewed as untreatable in therapy.

Male Sexual Abuse is not a primer on sexual abuse of children. Finkelhor's *Sourcebook on Child Sexual Abuse* (1986) attempts to do that. The two-volume series by O'Donohue and Geer, *The Sexual Abuse of Children: Theory and Research* (1992a) and *The Sexual Abuse of Children: Clinical Issues* (1992b), offers a thorough and well-documented grounding in the complexities of this field.

Nor is *Male Sexual Abuse* a comprehensive view of males as victims of sexual abuse. *Males at Risk* by Bolton, Morris, and MacEachron (1989) fits best in that category. *Male Sexual Abuse* is not written for a lay audience, as is Lew's *Victims No Longer: Men Recovering From Incest and Other Childhood Sexual Abuse* (1988); nor it is a self-help book for sexual abuse victims such as Nestingen and Lewis's *Growing Beyond Abuse: A Workbook for Survivors of Sexual Exploitation or Childhood Sexual Abuse* (1990). These and similar volumes published in recent years effectively address such topics.

Our intent is to provide a diversity of clinically sophisticated points of view in working with adolescent and young adult males involved as victims or perpetrators of sexual abuse. The intended audience is mental health and human service professionals. The sexual abuse field needs greater sophistication in clinical approaches than the first wave of writings produced. We also believe a greater emphasis and respect for diversity of ideas is needed; the field has moved prematurely and somewhat dogmatically to a level of purported consensus about childhood sexual abuse, unwarranted by the nascent databases and clinical explication currently available.

We do not attempt, except in the most rudimentary manner in the Epilogue, to coalesce our three different perspectives. Indeed, they have been developed in a divergent, not convergent, fashion. Some readers may find this unsatisfying. The intent of this book is more to raise questions than to give answers, and to stimulate, not to conclude, discussion.

We come from a variety of backgrounds. John C. Gonsiorek is a traditionally trained clinical psychologist who works primarily in the areas of sexual orientation and sexual identity, and sexual exploitation by health-care professionals and clergy. In the area of sexual abuse, his primary focus has been on young adult and late adolescent males

1

Historical and Background Perspectives on Adolescent and Male Sexual Abuse

THIS CHAPTER ADDRESSES issues that are typically neglected, avoided, or misunderstood. For a comprehensive historical perspective, readers are referred to the work of Vander Mey (1988, 1992a, 1992b) and the references cited in this chapter. This chapter critiques some internal contradictions in the sexual abuse field; places the concept of adolescence in a historical context; raises the often neglected issues of diversity, erotophobia, and homophobia; and introduces recent understandings about sexual orientation.

The study of sexual abuse is a relatively new field, at least in its current incarnation. Masson (1984) describes an effort to explore this area almost 100 years ago, as well as its eventual suppression. Yet, much writing on sexual abuse lacks historical perspective. It appears that this area emerged suddenly as victims came forward in the 1970s. Writers with more historical grounding point to Freud's "discovery" of sexual abuse in his early work and his later refutation of it. This is important not only for its historical significance, but for its theoretical import. The refutation of the reality of client reports of sexual abuse is a central component in Freud's theory of the unconscious. Arguably the most powerful theoretical structure in mental health, the psychoanalytic perspective is predicated on the belief that reports of childhood sexual abuse generally are not real. Psychological

3

perspectives appear to have a history of extremism in the ways they view sexual abuse.

Methodologically sound research on sexual abuse is expensive and more challenging to undertake than most endeavors in the behavioral sciences. An adequate empirical base is only beginning to emerge in a few areas. One might anticipate that, under these circumstances, theoretical and clinical perspectives would be cautious and tentative. Instead, they display a distinct tendency to be overreaching, conclusive, and dogmatic. This is a common failing in the behavioral and social sciences; however, the study of sexual abuse displays it to an unusual degree.

For example, there is no parallel in the behavioral sciences to the assertion made in some quarters early during sexual abuse theory development that "victims never lie." The assertion itself is not surprising; one might expect this from the popular press. What is surprising is its pronouncement by some mental health professionals and behavioral science researchers as a rationale for incomplete assessment or sweeping conclusions when the available database was insufficient. Even after malpractice actions against mental health professionals have skyrocketed in the area of sexual abuse/child custody situations, some mental health professionals continue to assert that they "can tell" who is telling the truth even in the most adversarial and contentious sexual abuse/child custody situations. Whether victims do or do not lie (or, more correctly, which victims respond with what degree of veracity under which circumstances) is an empirical question not conclusively answered and inadequately researched (see chapter 3 for further discussion of this subject).

Theory and treatment in the area of sexual abuse tend to stand apart, unintegrated with the main body of theory and clinical practice in the behavioral sciences. For a problem perceived to be so damaging, its conceptualization and remediation have often been asserted in minimalist and simplistic terms. If the initial observations and findings about sexual abuse are accurate (and we believe they generally are), how abuse experiences affect victims, what paths result in certain individuals perpetrating, and how all involved can experience meaningful remediation of their problems and pain are as complex as anything in the behavioral sciences or clinical practice.

We do not purport to offer a sophisticated historical analysis of how this pandemic of simplistic thinking came to be. Part of the problem may be that the forces that are most effective at bringing attention to a neglected issue are often not the most effective at explicating and integrating it. While the field of sexual abuse would not exist without feminism, as chapter 2 argues, feminist perspectives alone seem unable to conceptualize the diversity inherent in sexual abuse, and to create clinical models that can respond to that diversity.

Initially, it is important to take a broad perspective of sexual abuse. A number of historical and theoretical concepts important for understanding adolescent males as victims and perpetrators of sexual abuse are discussed below.

Males as victims and perpetrators of sexual abuse cannot be understood without a grounding in the pervasive erotophobia, denial of diversity, and homophobia of our culture, and in the development of sexual identity. Most sexual victimization of males is very likely done by males. While this creates no simple prediction about the sexual orientation or sexual identity of either victim or perpetrator, American culture's homophobia and stereotyping become mobilized by these situations. Understanding this homophobia is an important component to understanding the causes of adolescent male sexual abuse.

THE HISTORY OF ADOLESCENCE AS A CONCEPT

In late-20th-century North America, most individuals, including most mental health professionals, are likely to view the life phase known as "adolescence" as self-evident and, without question, "real." Adolescents are seen as a class of humans, as distinctive as infants, children, and adults, that faces unique developmental challenges and shares common psychological processes. Training programs in the health and behavioral sciences increasingly treat adolescence as a distinct area of specialization. Indeed, much current knowledge about adolescence has developed because areas such as developmental psychology and adolescent medicine made the assumption that adolescence is a distinct entity worthy of study.

It is important to realize, however, that this was not always so. Some historians argue that the concepts of adolescence and even childhood are relatively new: "It seems more probable that there was no place for childhood in the medieval world" (Aries, 1962, p. 33).

Aries (1962) suggests that the concept of childhood as a distinct phase of human development emerged in the Middle Ages as a complex distillation of social, religious, economic, and political forces. In particular, the development of the concept of childhood was linked with "the growing influence of Christianity on life and manners" (p. 43). As time passed, the importance of a nuclear family to the social order (as opposed to the more amorphous extended families of earlier times), coupled with the use of the concept of childhood to further religious ideas, crystallized into a concept of childhood as a fragile stage in human existence. In the 18th and 19th centuries, these two trends merged with others (such as concerns about cleanliness, hygiene, and physical health and the need for predictable training and education of the workforce) to strengthen the concept of childhood.

As the 19th century progressed, the nuclear family as the central social unit began to have increasing political, social, and economic importance. A rationale for the nuclear family was to provide protection and development for children. With the emergence of organized medicine and the increasing medicalization of social issues in the late 19th century, the concept of childhood as a distinct real entity became more urgent, warranting not only the attention of the family but also the attention of the helping professions to ease and monitor children through the transitions, conceptualized as increasingly difficult and fragile, to adulthood. In this process, adolescence as a distinct period of life and development began to emerge.

This particular structuring of both the family and childhood as distinct entities is neither universal nor inevitable. As some historians (Veyne, 1987) note, during other historical epochs, such as the Roman period, the basic role and structure of the family as well as the existence and conceptualization of a childhood period, while accepted, were construed so differently as to be qualitatively distinct. A historical perspective suggests that not only the family but the conceptualization of developmental stages is rooted in a social, political, economic, and religious context inextricably bound to time and place. (See Calvert, 1991, for a history of childhood in the United States;

deMause, 1982, especially chapter 1, for a general history of child-hood; Hart, 1991, for a history of children's rights; and Radbill, 1974, for a history of child abuse.)

This is not to suggest that conceptualization of childhood as a distinct entity is a mere cultural figment of the imagination. Indeed, some argue that conceptualization of childhood as a distinct period is a hallmark of civilized societies. Rather, the strength of the conceptualization of childhood, and even more so its particulars and structure, varies across time and cultures. This is even more true for adolescence, a relative newcomer as a distinct entity and less stable as a fixed concept.

Throughout the majority of history, persons were considered fully adult at a time in life that is now labeled adolescence. Even in cultures and historical periods that have a transitional phase between childhood and adulthood, this phase appears to be briefer than our own conceptualization and the transition to adulthood was made at an age younger than ours. This was true in our own society until the industrial revolution and remains true in many third-world countries today. As Veyne (1987) describes, the Romans (who had a conceptualization of childhood, although not like our own) rapidly transited children into full adulthood during a period that we consider mid-adolescence, ages 14 through 16. Today's research on differences in family structures across ethnic, class, and racial groups begins to capture some of this idea of variance, but often does not recognize the magnitude of possible variability once cultural and historical variation are added. In other words, current concepts of diversity are blind to the effects of time and historical development.

Moreover, in the 20th century there appears to be a trend to prolong the duration of adolescence, particularly among upper-socioeconomic strata. Adolescence no longer ends at age 18, the traditional legal beginning of adulthood, but increasingly extends through the college years. Our society is not only ambivalent about when an individual is accorded the rank of adult, but also capricious, as shifts in the legal age for the consumption in alcohol over recent decades suggest. (Ironically, one of the few relatively stable hallmarks of adulthood has been the age at which one can join the military.) The development and expansion of adolescence runs contrary to a trend toward earlier physical sexual maturation that began in the late 19th century in industrialized societies. Consequently, the biological hallmarks of adulthood have steadily diverged from the cultural concept of adulthood.

Adolescence Today

In its current North American conceptualization, adolescence is generally viewed as an intermediate period between childhood and adulthood that is catalytic, in that both psychological and biological development reach a kind of crescendo, more or less setting into place the physical and emotional framework of the human being who will now be deemed adult. Most developmental psychological theories posit explicitly or implicitly that adolescence is the last great burst of development, after which the variations of adult development are relatively minor. Despite recent increasing interest in the complexity and strength of postadolescent adult development, there is little evidence that these adult development theories alter the primacy afforded childhood and adolescence in theory.

It would be simplistic to conclude that because there are historical, political, economic, and social bases of the current conceptualization of adolescence, and because adolescence as we understand it in late-20th-century North America may not be universal, adolescence is therefore less "real." Most viewpoints that adopt this perspective, often known as social constructionist or deconstructionist, at times imply that dissecting such influences somehow renders a concept transparent, null, or less real.

Not only are adolescents depicted as immature and incapable of adult decision making, adolescents themselves generally accept this view. Current cultural institutions expect and tolerate immature behavior from adolescents. Large social structures such as educational institutions, the legal system, health care, and the family accept and promulgate this reality, as do adolescents. The fact that adolescence may be culturally constructed as a psychosocial reality does not mean that it is easily discarded, that it can or should be discarded, or that, for individuals operating within this cultural context, its reality and power are diminished.

Sexual Expression

There is probably no area conceptualized more distinctly as a purely adult prerogative than sexual expression. In our culture, sexual expression is reserved for adults, specifically heterosexual, married adults. Sexual expression is not seen as a proper adolescent prerogative; rather adolescent sexual expression is construed as an institutional and psychopathological problem requiring a response from parents, schools, clergy, physicians, mental health professionals, and the court system. The intent of this concern is to understand, categorize, legislate, pathologize, cure, and ultimately suppress adolescent sexuality.

This view is widely held, despite the fact that throughout human history individuals were fully sexual, reproducing at ages that are now viewed as too immature to permit sexual expression. One does not have to look far to see the tensions and incongruities of this view. Skyrocketing rates of adolescent pregnancy and sexually transmitted diseases suggest that whatever position one takes on adolescent sexuality, the effectiveness of its repression is without doubt a failure.

The Social Constructionist View

The current view of adolescence is relatively new. For example, a comparison of age-of-consent laws in the United States in the last 100 years suggests that not too long ago in a more agrarian, less industrialized, society, sexual expression and marriage were deemed appropriate activities at an age at which individuals today are deemed incapable of such activities on the basis of their "psychological immaturity."

While some more politicized commentators have referred to this incongruous state of affairs as a "colonization" of childhood (Mendel, 1971), such radical deconstructionist or social constructionist perspectives miss the point. All cultures have powerful internal rationales for what they do that are pervasively encoded into the social structures and individual psyches of members in that culture. One is hard-pressed to find cultures that do not utilize such ultimately arbitrary structures. As Berman (1982) notes, such radical social constructionist perspectives offer only "a world historical alibi for the sentence of passivity and helplessness" (p. 35).

However, there is an appropriate use for social constructionist perspectives. At a point of rapid social, cultural, and political change (which is a fair description of our time), the most basic assumptions not only can shift but probably are shifting; in Berman's (1982) phrase, "all that is solid melts into air." The mental health disciplines have been especially myopic in this regard, glibly describing observations that may be astute about white, North American, English-speaking, middle-class, mid- to late-20th-century culture as universal truths about human nature. While ambivalently and incompletely embracing the "minor" variations of ethnic, race, and (to a lesser extent) class diversity within one culture at one point in time, mental health perspectives quickly dismiss as ridiculous the possibility that "major" variations of change over time and cultures unlike Western ones might be so extensive as to demand a revision of basic conceptual categories.

THE PRESENT SOCIAL CONTEXT

The discussion so far has focused on historical challenges to current conceptualizations about adolescence. One could argue that current realities about the lives of some adolescents are alone sufficiently incongruous to challenge our notions of adolescence. Current realities regarding adolescence are considerably more grim than musings on the historical context:

- Every 8 seconds an adolescent drops out of school (552,000 in the 1987-1988 school year)
- Every 14 seconds a child/adolescent reports being abused or neglected (2.2 million in 1986, up 66% since 1979)
- Every 26 seconds an adolescent runs away from home (1.2 million per year)
- Every 7 minutes a youth is arrested for a drug offense (79,986 per year)
- Every 2 hours a young man between 15 and 25 is murdered (4,233 in 1987)
- Youth of color and/or poor youth represent a disproportionate number of these youth

The catalog of similarly somber statistics is extensive (Children's Defense Fund, 1990).

Because of demographic changes, the United States faces a future in which children and youth will be a shrinking share of the population. There will be 14% fewer young people in the 18-24 range in the year 2000. Nearly one third of the nation's 18- to 24-year-olds will be from minority groups, compared to less than one quarter in 1985. Today, more than 12 million children and youth have no health insurance. The earning power of young males has dropped sharply since 1973. Foundations, business, education, health, and welfare groups have issued reports that warn of the impending problems from society's inability to create environments for young people that foster growth and development.

Kurth-Schai (1988) presents a conceptual continuum to describe contemporary paradigms of children in society. On one end of the continuum is the image of children as victims of adult society. The assumption in this image is that children are vulnerable and in need of adult protection. The most obvious examples include the numbers of children who are physically, sexually, or emotionally abused and, more recently, who have joined the ranks of persons with AIDS. In this image of children, those who are not overtly victimized may be sentimentalized as "economically/socially worthless but emotionally priceless."

At the other end of the continuum is the image of children as threats to adult society. The assumption in this image is that youth are dangerous and in need of adult control. Images of youth as threats to established political, educational, and moral conventions have been perpetrated by youth participation in civil rights and antiwar protests during the 1960s, classroom violence during the 1970s, and gang warfare during the 1980s and 1990s.

In an intermediary position on the continuum is the image of children as learners of adult society. The assumption in this image is that children are incomplete, incompetent, and in need of adult guidance. Because guidance can include elements of both control and protection, this paradigm can be used to support philosophical/political positions associated with either of the other two positions. This image has gained academic endorsement in modern child development theories: for sociologists, through theories of socialization; for anthropologists, through theories of enculturation; and for psychologists, through universal stage theories. All assume that human development is orderly, predictable, and universal. All are blind and/or antagonistic to the historical perspectives and assume the "reality" of the categories they utilize.

Kurth-Schai (1988) points out:

> By conceptualizing children as objects of sentimentalization we trivialize their thoughts and actions. By seeing children as objects of socialization we obscure their social insight and environmental-shaping competence. By regarding children as victims we obscure their potential for adaptations and survival. By perceiving children as threats to society we ignore their potential as catalysts for positive social change. (p. 117)

Toffler (1974) notes:

> The secret message communicated to most young people today by the society around them is that they are not needed, that the society will run itself quite nicely until they—at some distant point in the future—will take over the reins. Yet the fact is that the society is not running itself nicely . . . because the rest of us need all the energy, brains, imagination, and talent that young people can bring to bear on our difficulties. For a society to attempt to solve its desperate problems without the full participation of even very young people is imbecile. (p. 15)

Adolescent Sexual Abuse

Given current conceptualizations of young people and gender stereotyping, young males are more likely to be considered threats to society and young females are more likely to be considered victims of society. Sexual abuse of males complicates and muddles these stereotypes (i.e., Are they victims or offenders? Are most offenders victims? Are they potential offenders?). As a result, sexual abuse of males elicits much resistance; it is more threatening to current conceptualizations of adolescence, gender, and social structure than most people can easily articulate.

Many theories of sexual abuse treatment for children and youth (both males and females) fail in three key aspects:

1. By viewing youth as victims, threats, or incompetents, these theories fail to be client driven, not allowing the client to create meaning or to have a proactive role in treatment.
2. By failing to recognize the economic, social, and developmental realities of young peoples' lives, these theories ignore environmental factors that mitigate or counteract many treatment strategies; these environmental factors may be a cause of presenting problems, instead of, or in addition to, intrapsychic issues.
3. By focusing on the dysfunctional, these theories often overlook creative adaptation and factors that foster resilience.

The reason why many survivors of abuse do not begin to heal until adulthood may be more related to our culture's incapacity or unwillingness to empower, listen to, and respond to young people than it is to the inability of these survivors to address those issues until adulthood.

DIVERSITY, EROTOPHOBIA, AND HOMOPHOBIA

Even as a relatively accurate description of the conjunction of a particular culture and time, current perspectives on sexual abuse still have problems. North American society, the context in which current knowledge of sexual abuse has developed, is not only pluralistic but becoming more so. Most information about mental health practice in the behavioral sciences, including sexual abuse, describes a subset that is primarily white, English speaking, and middle class or above.

There is not only political injustice in this state of affairs, there is also scientific inaccuracy. It is simply poor science to develop theory and practice on samples wherein certain classes of individuals are overrepresented more than their numbers warrant. In particular, it is in the areas of class, cultural, ethnic, and racial diversity that concepts relating to the nature of adolescence, the role of the family, and the nature of childhood reflect greater diversity than current scientific knowledge encompasses (see Homma-True, Greene, Lopez, & Trimble, 1993, for elaboration).

Another factor that complicates any discussion of adolescent sexual abuse is our culture's pronounced erotophobia. Our culture is obsessed with sex, yet phobic and deeply distrustful of sexuality. Considerable attention is focused on sexual behavior rather than on the integration of intimacy and sexuality. North American, particularly U.S., society is deeply ambivalent about sexuality, so much so, that the United States lacks the basic sex education school curricula considered minimal in most Western industrialized societies.

Sexual faults deserve a penalty in the public eye far greater than the most egregious financial or political corruption. Concern about the influence of the media on children and adolescents focuses on sexual material, although most empirical studies suggest that such material is most problematic in the area of interpersonal violence. The deeply embedded erotophobia in our culture makes discussions of sexuality, particularly adolescent sexuality and even more particularly adolescent sexual abuse, problematic and complicated.

Homosexuality in American Culture

Most men who are sexually victimized as children or adolescents are so abused by males (see chapter 3). This belief mobilizes our culture's extensive hostility to homosexuality even though this situation is no more representative of homosexuality than situations of sexual abuse by adult males of female children are representative of heterosexuality. Yet the cultural myths persist to such an extent that they must be factored into any understanding of adolescent male sexual abuse.

In our culture, most individuals are socialized, to varying degrees, to be negatively predisposed toward homosexuality. The range of these negative biases extends from denial that homosexual individuals exist to indictments of homosexuals as diseased, sinful, or criminal. Allport (1954) discusses the general nature of prejudice and its effects, while Herek (1991) addresses the complex social psychological processes that perpetrate such stereotyped perceptions. As Herek notes, an extraordinary amount of organized bigotry, random violence, and discrimination is directed against individuals who are homosexual or perceived to be homosexual.

"Homophobia" refers to an irrational and distorted view of homosexuality or homosexual persons. Among heterosexual individuals, homophobia is commonly manifest as a prejudice or general discomfort with homosexuality, developed and maintained through the psychological processes described by Herek. The intensity of these feelings is modulated by a number of factors, including personal history, contact with homosexual individuals, and individual psychological makeup. For example, there appears to be an inverse relationship between levels of homophobia and interaction with gay and lesbian individuals (Staats, 1978; see Herek, 1991, for discussion of the complexities of this finding); that is, certain kinds of contact with homosexual individuals reduces homophobic bias. As a result of the pervasive homophobia, in situations of sexual abuse where both the victim and the perpetrator are male, there is a distinct tendency for the same-sex aspect of the interaction rather than the exploitative aspect to predominate in the minds of most observers.

SEXUAL IDENTITY DEVELOPMENT

Another area that warrants explication in understanding the male adolescent experience in sexual abuse is the development of sexual identity in males. This area is generally one of considerable confusion for both lay people and professionals. The field is itself in a somewhat disorganized state. (For a comprehensive look at sexual identities across the life span, D'Augelli & Patterson, 1994, is recommended.) The first problem in understanding male adolescent sexual abuse is the general confusion that exists about sexual identity.

Shively and DeCecco (1977) divide sexual identity into four components: biological sex—the genetic material encoded in chromosomes; gender identity—the psychological sense of being male or female; social sex role—adherence to culturally created behaviors and attitudes that are deemed appropriate for males or females; and sexual orientation—the erotic and/or affectional disposition to the same and/or opposite sex. It is important to note that the first three components bear no necessary relationship to sexual orientation in any given individual; however, each has been confused with sexual orientation.

Confusion frequently arises between sexual orientation and sexual behavior. Engaging in either same- or opposite-sex behavior is not always a good predictor of ongoing disposition to same- or opposite-sex behavior; nor is it a good predictor of a psychological sense of identity as bisexual, homosexual, or heterosexual.

A number of different psychological processes impinge on this. Many individuals who have significant same-sex interests deny these on account of societal or intrapsychic pressures. There is therefore a class of individuals who engage in same-sex behavior but deny or distort to themselves recognition that this indicates an ongoing same-sex desire. A different situation occurs in individuals who are oriented toward the same sex, but who deny this to themselves and become heterosexually involved as a part of this denial. In this situation, sexual behavior may be directed toward the opposite sex while fantasy life and affectional disposition may be directed toward the same sex. Finally, there is a class of individuals who may engage regularly in same-sex behavior for reasons other than erotic attraction to the same sex, who retain full awareness of this, and who assume incorrectly that this represents a same-sex erotic preference. It should be noted that the division of sexual orientation into categories such as homosexuality, heterosexuality, and bisexuality is currently viewed in some quarters as inaccurate and in need of revision. (Gonsiorek & Weinrich, 1991, provide discussion on the definition and scope of sexual orientation.)

For the purposes of this discussion, the original research on males by Kinsey and his associates (Kinsey, Pomeroy, & Martin, 1948) makes the relevant points. They found the following:

- 50% of the population is exclusively heterosexual in both activity and fantasy.
- 37% of the population has had at least one overt homosexual experience between adolescence and old age and an additional 13% have had at least incidental homosexual fantasy without behavior.
- For at least a 3-year period between the ages of 16 and 55, 10% of the male population has been predominantly homosexual.
- About 4% of the male population is solely homosexual beginning with adolescence and continuing through adulthood.

The Kinsey data clearly indicate a discordance between homosexual behavior and a stable ongoing pattern of homosexual practice. Taken at their most extreme, these data could suggest that of all males who have had at least one homosexual sexual experience, only one in nine will be exclusively homosexual throughout their adult lives (the 37% figure versus the 4% figure). Similarly, the number of individuals who are predominantly homosexual for at least a 3-year period is 2½ times the number of individuals who are exclusively homosexual throughout their adult lives (the 10% figure versus the 4% figure).

Descriptions of homosexuality in prison note individuals who engage in homosexual behavior for prolonged periods of time, but, when given a choice of sexual opportunities outside prison, engage only in heterosexual behavior. The point is clear: Sexual behavior at any one point in time, or even for an extended period of time, is a weak predictor of ongoing sexual interest and behavior throughout the life span, and bears no necessary relationship to self-identification as homosexual, heterosexual, or bisexual.

Coming Out

A related issue is the coming-out process, or the development of an identity as gay. This area is important both to recognize those individuals who are undergoing such a process and to recognize those who are not, as the predominant same-sex nature of much sexual abuse of male adolescents can often obscure this difference. Following is a cursory introduction to this area. (Readers are referred to Gonsiorek, 1988; Gonsiorek & Rudolph, 1991; Malyon, 1981; and Martin, 1982, for further information.)

Boys who eventually have predominant same-sex orientation are raised in the homophobic culture described above. In individuals who eventually become gay, these antihomosexual prejudices mobilize a series of psychological processes that occur in addition to the other developmental events of childhood and adolescence. Boys who will eventually become bisexual or homosexual often develop an awareness of being different at an early point in their lives, often in childhood. They may not understand the nature or precise meaning of this difference, but they quickly learn that it is negatively regarded. As these boys mature, they reach a fuller understanding of the nature of this difference and also of the negative societal reaction to it. These negative feelings are often incorporated into self-image, resulting in varying degrees of internalized homophobia. These negative feelings about a part of one's self—that is, sexual orientation—are often overgeneralized to encompass the entire self. Later effects may range from a tendency toward self-doubt in the face of prejudice to unmistakable overt self-hatred. This process occurs later and in addition to earlier developmental processes; that is, it is overlaid on a full range of preexisting personality development.

This internalized homophobia can have various expressions. Some individuals can overtly experience it and may consciously view themselves as evil, second class, or inferior on account of their homosexuality. They may abuse substances or engage in other self-destructive or abusive behaviors. Because overt internalized homophobia is so psychologically painful and destabilizing, it is probably less prevalent than covert forms. Few persons easily tolerate conscious self-deprecation. The covert forms of internalized homophobia therefore are likely to be the most common. Such individuals appear to accept themselves, yet sabotage their own efforts in a variety of subtle ways.

In adolescence, however, these psychological processes are likely to be underground. Denial of same-sex interests often predominates and has a number of effects. Teenagers who eventually become gay or bisexual often withdraw from typical adolescent social experiences. Socializing with either gender can be emotionally difficult: Interaction with persons of the same gender may arouse strong sexual or emotional feelings, while interaction with the opposite gender may be a painful reminder of the absence of heterosexual interest. As a result, teenagers who eventually become gay or bisexual may avoid the interpersonal experimentation that is an important developmental task of adolescence. This suppression and repression of same-sex desires and interests is often accomplished at the expense of normal adolescent interpersonal skill development.

Denial tends to be problematic, as adolescent sexuality is somewhat diffuse. That which is being denied is a moving target. As a result, denial often is generalized beyond sexual areas. As sexual drive increases during adolescence, greater intrapsychic energy is required to maintain denial. The effect of this escalating emotional blockade is that some adolescents who eventually become gay or bisexual reach adulthood as strangers to their own inner emotional life and have developed habits of constricting any strong feelings. So, while homosexuality per se is clearly understood as a nonpathological variation in human sexuality (see Gonsiorek, 1991, for a review of this literature), some adaptations to it are psychologically constricting and in that sense pathological. The same can be said for heterosexual and bisexual variations.

When emergence of same-sex interest does occur, it is almost never as a result of a conscious decision. Typically, a strong emotional or sexual interest toward someone of the same sex emerges in a way that breaks through the denial. For teenagers who eventually become gay or bisexual, the coming-out process is initiated by a defensive collapse that often represents the beginning of a shift in that individual's core sexual identity. As a result there are likely to be dramatic levels of emotional distress. There appear to be gender differences (Gonsiorek, 1988; Gonsiorek & Rudolph, 1991) in the direction of males being more dramatically and floridly symptomatic due to differences in sex-role socialization. Males also tend to sexualize these conflicts to a greater extent than females.

The coming-out process as an overt event is triggered by defensive collapse in an individual who, in order to maintain repression of same-sex interests, has been avoiding interpersonal skill development typical in adolescence and has become increasingly alienated from his or her own emotions. Not surprisingly, individuals in the coming-out process, particularly men, often go through a period of considerable emotional turmoil. It is important to note, however, that homosexuality and psychopathology are not intrinsically related (Gonsiorek, 1991), and that most individuals after a period of temporary distress appear to weather this crisis and proceed with their lives.

Sex-Role Stereotyping

Sex-role stereotyping is also an important consideration in understanding adolescent male sexuality. Most studies on social sex roles suggest that these roles are most rigidly defined and behaviorally prescriptive during adolescence. While social sex roles are complex in their effects and individuals vary in the degree to which social sex roles are adhered, there is a general tendency for males in this culture and adolescent males in particular to view sexual expression apart from intimacy and, perhaps more importantly, to view sexual expression as a male prerogative. Put another way, most male adolescents view sexual contact as something that they have willed or chosen except in situations of obvious force. This creates a situation where adolescent males are often unaware of the interplay between sexual and other emotional needs and of the subtleties with which sexuality can be manipulated. This represents a particular way in which adolescent males can be vulnerable to sexual abuse.

SUMMARY

Sexual abuse of males presents a significant challenge to our perception of adolescence, gender, and social structure. Understanding how other times and places view human development, the role of diversity, how homophobia functions, and the development of sexual identity can facilitate more open, inclusive, and useful perspectives in this area.

2

A Critique of Current
Models in Sexual Abuse

THIS CHAPTER BRIEFLY OUTLINES and critiques some current models for understanding sexual abuse. The term *model* is used loosely not to refer to a distinct school of thought but to ideas that appear to be consistent with and represent a relatively cohesive view of sexual abuse or certain aspects of sexual abuse. These models are presented with broad strokes, to outline core beliefs that impinge on the area of male abuse. Some, especially feminist and psychoanalytic perspectives, contain variations and elaborations far from the ideas described here. Our interest is in describing the assumptions, limitations, and points of tension and paradox of current models.

Most of the discussion focuses on feminist models, the dominant perspective today. Psychoanalytic models, which generally preceded feminist perspectives, are discussed briefly as a point of comparison. Profamily models usually represent a lay perspective, although they may be more present in clinical practice than their scarce representation in professional literature suggests. Propedophile models are discussed at some length, partially because their explication can help disentangle sources of some of the homophobic bias described in chapter 1, and partially because they are usually ignored in the professional literature, and so operate as underground models.

FEMINIST MODELS

The field of sexual abuse would not exist if it were not for feminism. At a time when North American culture viewed sexual abuse as a rare and arcane phenomenon not worthy of serious discussion, feminist advocates, theoreticians, and researchers courageously and tenaciously insisted on the reality, relatively high frequency, and deleterious effects of sexual abuse. Developing from the late 1960s to the present, feminist models, through increasingly diverging perspectives, represent the current dominant models in the area of sexual abuse.

In feminist perspectives, sexual abuse is usually seen as a variant of the ways in which men control and oppress women. Feminist perspectives, then, view sexual abuse as overwhelmingly perpetrated by males upon females. These models implicitly or explicitly minimize male victims and female perpetrators or recast them as mirrors of the male perpetrator/female victim model without recognizing that they may have unique characteristics. Although some feminist models can accommodate a differential understanding of types of sexual abusers, these are generally posited within a sociopolitical context of sexual abuse as an example of the oppression of men upon women. Vander Mey (1988, 1992a, 1992b) offers comprehensive analyses of feminist perspectives on rape, incest, and sexual abuse.

Feminist models usually have as their ultimate goal the righting of sociopolitical wrongs, of which sexual abuse is merely an example. As this is essentially a political and moral perspective, those who disagree with aspects of feminist perspectives tend to become suspected of sociopolitical corruption. Feminist perspectives implicitly or explicitly carry with them a "siege mentality" in which individuals are either for or against the "right" cause. If an individual is deemed against the right cause, then, feminists believe, his or her opinions are lacking in credibility because they are suspect. Feminist perspectives have a difficult time accommodating divergence of opinion or empirical information that do not fit their framework.

Feminist perspectives are, at their core, a political and social change paradigm. Indeed, that is one of their strengths. At a time when sexual abuse had no scientific data or theoretical respectability to support it, only sheer political will could have been effective against the intransigence of the professional communities surrounding this issue.

Once feminist models forcibly opened the issue of sexual abuse to scientific inquiry and the development of clinical practice models, the preeminence of the political rights of women increasingly developed into a hindrance. Restricting scientific discourse to theory, research, and practice that is congruent with a limited sociopolitical perspective is poor science.

Clinical practice, in particular, has at its core the ethical requirement and legal structure for practitioners to operate in the best interests of the individual patient, in a specific sense. The tendency to view the realities and rights of some patients as more legitimate than those of others due to their disenfranchisement, and to construe the best interests of the patient in an overarching manner focused on general political goals for certain classes of clients, leads to an ethically compromised and legally vulnerable clinical practice.

The paradox is that science and clinical practice do not seem to be (or at least have not been) able to work themselves out of the ruts they periodically create without a nonscientific, nonpractice driven challenge—that is, political will. The beneficial effect of the challenge by political will leads to the establishment of a more holistic and less biased science and clinical practice; which, paradoxically, ultimately rejects the excessively narrow claims of the political will that corrected it. The field of sexual abuse is at such a juncture as more paradoxes and contradictions emerge within feminist perspectives on sexual abuse.

A central tenet of feminist perspectives is that women are not seen as flawed, deficient versions of men but as whole, complete, and different entities in their own right. Yet, feminist perspectives often resist viewing the perceptions of male victims of sexual abuse as the touchstone to understanding male experiences. Instead, models of sexual abuse are derived from the experiences of female victims and are often held dogmatically.

Similarly, research suggests that those individuals who are victimized are not entirely random but include a disproportionate number of individuals noteworthy for their vulnerability prior to the actual sexual abuse. In keeping with their broad sociopolitical perspective, feminist models view the effects of abuse on victims as relatively monolithic, because the meaning of abuse is ultimately monolithic in this sociopolitical sense. The possibilities that some individuals may suffer minimally from abuse, that the effects of abuse may be diverse, and, especially, that abuse may intermingle with preabuse life experiences and problem areas are difficult for many feminist perspectives to accommodate.

The myth that male victims usually become perpetrators is a misconception not applied to female victims. Simple political slogans that sexual abuse is something men do to women become complicated by a full array of psychosocial problems, issues of equity and justice, and other concerns of which the rights of women are only one part.

An irony of some radical feminist perspectives is their insistence that victims of sexual abuse are purely and entirely victims. This seriously underestimates the real damage that childhood sexual abuse can cause. The propensity of some individuals to develop chronically self-destructive patterns as a result of their victimization is perhaps one of the most horrifying effects of victimization, as it increases the likelihood that victimization will continue in the future. Once such patterns are established, individuals with such patterns are ill-served by focusing solely on the wrongs done to them, rather than on how the wrongs done to them have led to self-destructive patterns that they now continue and bear personal responsibility to alter.

The role of the therapist within feminist perspectives is often to assist the client in undoing the specific damages caused by the abuse and to educate the client about broader sociopolitical issues and empower the client to act on those. Clients who may disagree with or have mixed feelings about the larger sociopolitical feminist viewpoint can sometimes be perceived as holding their opinions as a result of abuse or larger political oppression. In other words, differences of opinion are prone to be pathologized.

Feminist perspectives on therapy with abused clients are paradoxical in this regard. Although these perspectives endorse advocacy for the rights of clients, clients can be infantilized and treated as diseased or incompetent if they have substantially different viewpoints on larger sociopolitical issues. Similarly, although treatment is empowering for the specific effects of abuse, it can become intrusive and infantilizing if it assumes the therapist knows best what the sociopolitical larger picture is, and if a goal of therapy is to persuade the client of this. Feminist therapies run the risk of becoming what they aspire to remedy, that is, oppressive and controlling therapy.

Feminist therapies often implicitly assume that the rights of some people, such as women or victims, are more important than the rights of others, such as men or perpetrators. This creates another paradox in which the sexism and male privilege of "traditional" male therapists can be replaced by reverse sexism and moral privilege of radical feminist therapists. As a result, a range of actions from legislative remedies to suggestions made in therapy are undertaken in which the possible harm to others is considered as significantly less important than the potential benefit to women. In so doing, feminist perspectives erode their own moral basis. By substituting moral righteousness for raw power as the basis for privilege, they open the possibility that others with different value systems can assert higher moral privilege and thereby also decide, as some feminists do, that some human beings are more important than others.

These criticisms are primarily directed at the more radical feminist theorists in this area (Dominelli, 1986; Mackinnon, 1987; Rush, 1974). However, to the extent that moderate feminist theorists are silent on these problems, it is fair to characterize the problems outlined here as generally true of feminism.

We do not perceive these problems as failings of feminism; rather, as successes, albeit ironic ones. This development of a need for more heterodox and integrated theory and clinical practice and less politically restricted discourse on sexual abuse could never have come about without the single-minded insistence on the reality and seriousness of sexual abuse provided by feminism. Feminism is now challenged to take its rightful place as a necessary, but by itself insufficient, building block of a more eclectic, diverse, clinically sophisticated, and theoretically complex field of sexual abuse and to relinquish its role as the arbiter of the field.

Challenges to feminist perspectives have been most acute in the field of male sexual abuse. Victims who are not female and who do not necessarily respond as female victims do, and perpetrators who are not always male and not always powerful adults and whose motivations can include ignorance, stupidity, misinformation, and confusion as well as malice, arrogance, and insensitivity require even-handed explication. We have little doubt that sexual abuse is done by men to women more often than any other dyad. But other dyads exist, are not rare, are of equal human worth and scientific interest, and should be understood on their own terms and in a multiplicity of ways, not merely from feminist perspectives. If the field of sexual abuse is to obtain scientific respectability and its practice models are to obtain clinical integrity, sexual abuse in all its diversity must be understood and integrated.

Feminist views are not only articulated by women. Some recent writings on male victims (Hunter, 1990; Lew, 1988) are within a feminist framework in that they assume global, pervasive, and monolithic effects of sexual abuse; have a high advocacy component; treat therapy as a generally extensive process with elements of "therapist knows best" about phenomena outside therapy; and have a difficult time accommodating interactions with pre-sexual abuse damaging experiences. Such writers have adapted the core of feminist perspectives while changing aspects of the context. Not surprisingly, this male-feminist perspective is relatively inarticulate about a broader sociopolitical agenda, as the internal contradictions of adopting some but not all of the feminist perspective leave it without a clear sense of direction.

PSYCHOANALYTIC MODELS

Psychoanalytic models include a variety of perspectives that in some ways provide a mirror image of feminist perspectives. These models tend to minimize the specific effects of abuse experiences and maximize, in line with standard psychoanalytic thinking, the earliest developmental events as central. For example, a sexual abuse situation that began in the latency period (the modal time for abuse experiences to start) or later would a priori be deemed less important than earlier history because most of the individual's psychological structure had been laid down prior to the abuse. When effects of abuse are discussed, they tend to be subsumed as examples of other, more historically based, issues.

Analytic perspectives are hostile to political or client advocacy and generally view such perspectives as countertherapeutic. Analytic therapy is nonintrusive and nondirective, with little explicit attempt to shape or guide the therapy experience, although such passivity may mold in its own ways. Analytic perspectives often assume a point of cure, a feature they share with feminist perspectives. These two perspectives differ, however, in that analytic perspectives explicitly view the point of cure as a resolution of the broader intrapsychic issues of which the abuse may be merely an example, whereas feminist notions of cure involve, usually implicitly, not only a resolution of the specific abuse but also far-reaching changes in consciousness in which a broader feminist sociopolitical perspective is adopted.

The rejection of the reality of sexual abuse by Freud in his development of the theory of the unconscious, although unevenly accepted by modern proponents, gives psychoanalytic perspectives a tendency to minimize or ignore the reality of child abuse. Analytic perspectives are capable of handling issues prior to the abuse in a sophisticated and complex manner, but they tend to so minimize the abuse that they often waste this advantage.

Proponents of psychoanalytic models view intrapsychic change as the only truly profound change. For victims or perpetrators of sexual abuse with significant behavior problems, as many males present, this perspective offers little to ameliorate symptoms until a client is "ready" for intrapsychic change. Psychoanalytic perspectives often translate their failure with such situations into pessimism about the treatability of individuals who do not respond well to its techniques.

Analytic perspectives tend to be limited by perspectives of culture, social class, and worldview; all the more so for their tendency to assert their universality and dismiss such concerns. The applicability of these perspectives beyond the Eurocentric upper-middle-class confines on which they were developed has long been suspect.

PROFAMILY MODELS

Profamily perspectives are often, but not always, associated with right-wing political movements. A core feature of these perspectives is the assumption that the family and larger social structures are primary and the individual is subordinate. To disagree with this view is to invite social chaos and societal collapse. Therefore, sexual abuse situations that are congruent with this political perspective are not only emphasized but demonologized; sexual abuse situations that run contrary to this political perspective are minimized or denied. Specifically, intrafamilial sexual abuse is minimized. When admitted at all, the welfare of the family as a unit, not the individual who has been abused, is asserted as paramount.

At the same time, nonfamilial sexual abuse, particularly sexual abuse perpetrated by males perceived to be homosexual, is considered a threat of the first order and its destructiveness is maximally emphasized. Because sexual abuse of males, more often than that of females, occurs in a nonintrafamilial context, profamily models are paradoxically sensitive to sexual abuse of males. The one paradigm these perspectives can easily admit, that of a nonfamily member male abusing a male victim, appears to be more represented in male abuse situations. The relative lack of concern for female victims is consistent with these perspectives' pervasive sexism.

Profamily perspectives are riddled with contradictions. Advocacy in the intrafamilial context is considered an intrusion of the state on the most sacred institution—the family—whereas no degree of advocacy is unwarranted in responding to sexual abuse outside family confines. This is not as contradictory as it appears, however, because the guiding principle is that the rights of the family and social institutions are paramount. This guiding principle unites these perspectives.

Therapy within profamily frameworks often runs a significant risk of unethical practice. The ethics codes of all major mental health professions share a requirement that the services rendered be in the best interests of the client. This is the basis for the entire ethical and practice structure of the mental health professions. Profamily models implicitly, and at times explicitly, deny this basic assumption, stating that the welfare of the family and of traditional social institutions are paramount and the individual's welfare must be subsumed to these institutions. Children and adolescents are ultimately viewed as property, to be handled in a way best suited to the family and other social structures. Legally, this perspective often runs into conflict with child protection statutes, which generally mandate reporting of child abuse and neglect regardless of circumstances or effects on families or other institutions.

PROPEDOPHILE MODELS

Propedophile models assert that the repression of childhood and adolescent sexuality is damaging to minors and therefore to society. As part of the broader liberation of children and adolescents, free sexual expression is encouraged. This sexual expression includes the "right" of children and adolescents to be sexual with adults.

These models suggest that treating minors as incapable of consent in relationships with adults is another aspect of disempowering minors and depriving them of their rights. Within these models, the negative effects of child abuse are viewed as illusory or fabricated, either to discredit pedophiles or to squelch childhood sexuality; or as a misunderstanding, in that society's negative reactions to childhood sexuality, not sexual contact between adults and children, cause negative effects.

Propedophile models claim to be uniquely sensitive to the needs and rights of minors, and at times claim to provide the emotional support and nurturing denied children and adolescents by a heartless society (O'Carroll, 1982). Minors are conceptualized within these models as primarily sexual in their needs. The possibility that minors may have areas of vulnerability and fragility, may be vulnerable to manipulation, and may confuse sexual and nonsexual needs are viewed as distortions. Paradoxically, then, propedophile models, which begin their arguments based on a wish to support childhood sexuality, end up supporting sexual access of pedophiles to children.

The propedophile movement devotes little energy to encouraging the right of children and adolescents to be sexual with each other or to be seen as individuals motivated by needs other than sexual. Ironically, propedophile models share with profamily models a view of children as property; however, profamily models view the appropriate use of children/property as in the best interests of the family and the state; whereas propedophile models view the best use of children/ property as in the sexual interests of pedophiles.

COMPARISON OF THE MODELS

The different models operate in different contexts and with different profiles. Prior to feminist models, child abuse models did not exist; there was primarily denial about child sexual abuse. (Although some researchers tried to direct attention to incest in the 1940s and 1950s; see Vander Mey's 1992b discussion of the work of Riemer and Weinberg.) Isolated pockets remain where service delivery systems deny the existence and seriousness of child abuse, sometimes but not necessarily out of any organized perspective such as the profamily or propedophile models; more often, simply from denial. These are fading rapidly, at least in professional circles. By and large, feminist models predominate.

Analytic models tend to keep a low profile, except in areas where analytic perspectives predominate, in which case anything other than analytic perspectives are viewed as simplistic, second-rate, and "not really therapy." When confronted with strong opposition, however, analytic perspectives tend to avoid conflict with feminist perspectives. Rather, they withdraw into the background, generally acting acquiescent or passively scornful toward feminist perspectives. Through their passivity, assiduous avoidance of advocacy, focus on the importance of factors prior to the abuse, and lack of directiveness with clients, analytic models tend to undermine feminist perspectives.

Profamily perspectives are generally the province of so-called Christian psychotherapists and other religiously oriented providers. Profamily perspectives are weakly represented in the mental health professions but assert occasional power in the legislative arena and in the courts. They can marshall their few professional experts and mobilize them effectively to serve as experts in key cases. Profamily perspectives can operate as a powerful lobby and directly challenge feminist perspectives in lobbying for legislation and social change. Although they are underrepresented in mental health, profamily perspectives can, through court cases and legislation, affect mental health services. The ability of right-wing profamily lobbyists to control the political agenda regarding adolescent pregnancy, birth control, and health care throughout the 1980s and early 1990s, despite opposition from health-care providers, is a good example. The role of these perspectives in the mental health professions is more as a devil's advocate; these models were the first to challenge the assumption that victims never lie. Although scholars of intelligence and integrity exist on both sides of the repressed memories versus false memory controversy, much of the subtext and public discourse on this debate is increasingly assuming a feminist versus profamily cast.

The propedophile movement is the most curious one in terms of its position and profile. Although it claims to have a database (Sandfort, 1982, 1983, 1984; Sandfort, Brongersma, & van Naerssen, 1990), the movement is generally regarded as fringe and without empirical foundation (Finkelhor, 1990a). The propedophile movement has virtually no clout politically, and is not well represented among mental health professionals or among feminists. It derives its weak power base from its peculiar relationship to some segments of gay male communities and by occasionally playing on the sympathies and support of "liberal" academics. It suggests few therapeutic strategies; its focus is on sociopolitical change for the benefit of pedophiles, although ostensibly for the rights of children.

The propedophile movement claims that the repression of pedophilia is similar to the repression of gay men and lesbians, women, and racial and ethnic minorities; if one repression is allowed, all will follow. This movement argues that, by analogy, the empirical foundations for overthrowing the illness model of homosexuality and racial and sexist stereotypes apply also to pedophilia, although besides analogic reasoning no data are behind this, as there are for the obsolescence of these other stereotypes. Under the guise of academic inquiry and criticism, this perspective is portrayed as having scientific credibility (see Sandfort et al., 1990; and Tsang, 1981).

Segments of gay male communities have frequently served as the launching pad of the propedophile movement. In a sense, the propedophile movement can exist only because of homophobia and the repression of homosexuality. The analogy that if pedophilia is repressed then homosexuality will also be strikes a chord in some gay males who are aware that homosexuals are the only remaining minority group where bigotry remains acceptable and officially sanctioned.

The propedophile movement may also capitalize on the existential experiences of some gay males. Many gay men can clearly recall a period in their own adolescence in which they were isolated, cut off from any support, their sexuality vilified and repressed, and their level of psychological functioning impaired. Peer support for emerging same-sex feelings was simply not available for most gay adolescents. Some gay adolescents resolve this dilemma by seeking out the adult gay community, some of whom provide support and a remedy to external oppression, and others of whom merely provide sexual contact or, at times, frank sexual exploitation.

Even in these latter situations, for the gay male adolescent who has experienced disparagement as a result of his sexuality, this valuing of sexuality alone may be powerful and positive enough to override, at least temporarily, exploitative aspects of the interaction between the adult and the adolescent. Whether or not a particular gay male has directly experienced this, he often knows this to be real from vicariously understanding the experience of his peers. Many gay male adolescents are keenly aware of their isolation and wish for contact, sexual and otherwise, with other gay males.

The propedophile movement exploits the oppression of homosexuality by playing up the fear that lack of acceptance of pedophilia foreshadows increasing intolerance toward homosexuality. On a deeper level, the propedophile movement resonates in the life experience of some gay men, who recall a time of intense isolation and longing for contact, sexual and otherwise, with other men. In this sense, there is a grain of truth, albeit distorted, in that the repression of adolescent sexuality can be damaging and its expression can be healing. The solution the propedophile model offers, however, is an exploitative one. But compared to the further repression of homosexuality, it may seem like the lesser of two evils for some gay males.

A genuine solution to the repression of adolescent sexuality involves full civil rights for homosexuals and the creation of support services for gay and lesbian youth in which they are afforded the same interpersonal opportunities and exploration that heterosexual youth are. The propedophile movement, however, deflects gay male communities from these goals by its focus on the sexual access of pedo- philes to youth.

The relationship between the propedophile community and the gay male community is paradoxical and complex. Some gay men find it virtually impossible to reject the propedophile movement until there is greater support for homosexuality; yet, in not rejecting the propedophile community, the gay male community elicits political rejection because of its perceived support for child abuse. The gay male community rarely conceptualizes these issues clearly. The propedophile community, whether consciously or not, exploits this dilemma artfully. In this way, the relationship of the propedophile movement to gay male communities is parasitic, not symbiotic.

Strengths and Weaknesses of the Models

The strength and value of feminist models are their unyielding insistence on the reality of sexual abuse and its damaging impact. The weaknesses of feminist models are their tendencies to bring sociopolitical concerns not necessarily directly related to a particular client into the therapy of that client and to be insufficiently sensitive to the history and personality factors of the individual prior to the abuse experience; and to restrict scientific discourse to that which is politically correct and congruent with feminist perspectives. This insistence on the reality of abuse is not obsolete; as discussed in chapter 3, greater questioning of this basic reality appears to be in the offing, as the false memory syndrome advocates sort out whether they will offer a scientific corrective to politically correct ideology and assumption, or right-wing "disinformation."

The main strength of psychoanalytic models is their ability to conceptualize the individual in a rich psychological context where a variety of historical and personal factors can be used to understand and treat the individual. The primary vulnerability of psychoanalytic models is their suspicion or outright rejection of the reality of sexual abuse effects or, in some more modern formulations, minimization of the trauma of the abuse while earlier historical factors are maximized. In addition, dynamic perspectives can run the risk of financial exploitation of clients as the nondirective, leisurely therapy style is inefficient. These models can be a disservice to individuals, many of whom are men, whose sequelae of sexual abuse include disinhibition and acting out problems because of the models' inability to provide sufficient structure and direction for such clients.

The profamily and propedophile perspectives do not have a great deal to offer in a direct sense, although both offer a nugget of truth amid their self-serving rhetoric. Profamily perspectives are exquisitely sensitive to understanding that sexual abuse occurs in a series of contexts—family, community, and societal—all of which have a stake in sexual abuse. Profamily perspectives react instinctively to the tendency of some mental health professionals to be unnecessarily overbearing and discounting of the importance of such contexts.

Propedophile perspectives are the most clear in espousing the rights of minors, including the rights of minors to be sexual, and are perhaps the clearest voice for the reality of adolescent sexuality. However, propedophile perspectives use this as a rhetorical device, a distraction from their systematic misconstruction of the rights of children, by equating the rights of children with the alleged right of pedophiles to have sexual access to children.

Neither the profamily nor the propedophile perspectives offer much of substance to mental health practice. Each does, however, remind mental health practitioners in a convoluted way of some blind spots and limitations in their assumptions.

THEORY-DRIVEN VERSUS
CLIENT-DRIVEN MODELS OF TREATMENT

The economics of services for abuse victims and their political implications are also worthy of consideration. The analytic model offers individuals who have been sexually abused the same slow-moving, expensive, inefficient therapy of unknown but generally long duration that it offers everyone. The economics of analytic therapy has been one of the strongest reasons for its distrust by policy makers and its perennial attraction to entrepreneurial mental health providers.

However, feminist therapies increasingly run the same risk. When broad-ranging change in consciousness is a therapeutic goal and other therapeutic goals range far from the client's presenting problems, the client who came because of victimization may end up paying the therapist to inculcate him or her into the therapist's political agenda. We suggest that therapy that is unnecessarily prolonged, particularly for reasons external to the immediate needs of the client, is itself exploitation, a form of economic oppression, regardless of the sophistication, alleged righteousness, or urgency of its theoretical rationale.

The three clinical intervention models discussed in this volume differ in this regard. The goal-oriented, focused quality of these models tends to make the interventions briefer and more focused on therapeutic goals. These approaches are difficult where intervention goals are expansive, either in an intrapsychic or sociopolitical sense.

The models critiqued in this chapter are theory driven. As a result, goals extraneous or tangential to the individual have an increased probability of being included in interventions derived from them. The likelihood of unnecessary economic burden to the client increases as a function of the degree to which a model is theory driven.

The three models described later are client driven. The role of theory is subsumed to a source of suggestions; heuristic devices to inform, but not dominate, an intervention plan that is individually tailored. This factor plus the willingness to recombine therapy models into hybrids to maximize change decrease the likelihood of unnecessary economic burden for clients. Attentiveness to the economic implications of interventions is an important concern for all clients, particularly for individuals who have been victimized.

It is our observation that many therapists are relatively insensitive or inattentive to this concern. We reject arguments that therapists as a group are naive about economics. Rather, it is our observation that entrepreneurially driven therapists attempt to act generally in the best interests of their clients except when their economic self-interest is involved, in which case they generally act in their economic self-interest. This is a weakness of the mental health and human services industries that is merely exaggerated and more sharply drawn in clinical work with sexual abuse victims. It is unlikely these concerns will be resolved soon or easily as the number of therapists increases and competition increases for the already besieged health-care dollar.

One of the effects of therapists who operate primarily in their economic self-interest with sexually abused clients is a tendency to overdiagnose in order to obtain authorization of continued treatment. To the problems and stresses already experienced by the abused individual can sometimes be added unnecessary or overpathologizing diagnoses that have a significant impact on the individual's future insurability in health, life, and other insurance situations.

Managed health care, with its very different but still very entrepreneurially based system, can impose a different kind of dilemma for victims seeking treatment. Entrepreneurially based therapists in the private sector receive maximum economic rewards by prolonging treatment as long as possible. Entrepreneurially based managed health-care systems derive profit from keeping treatment as short as possible. Managed health-care systems that are not quality conscious can provide inadequate levels of service for sexual abuse victims. Ironically, even though private health-care providers and managed health-care systems often see themselves as opposite, if they are insufficiently attentive to clients' needs and quality of care, both share a tendency to short-change the client, albeit in different ways, due to their particular economic motivations.

SUMMARY

This chapter critiques ideas and models, both manifest and latent, in the sexual abuse field. If we have added complexity and ambiguity to readers' understanding of this area, then this critique has been effective.

3

Male Victims of Sexual Abuse

THIS CHAPTER REVIEWS some of the basic theoretical and empirical understandings of male victims, and will serve as a database for further discussions. This review is not comprehensive, but focused to be most useful for ideas developed later. Readers seeking comprehensive reviews should consult Bolton, Morris, and MacEachron (1989), Finkelhor (1986), and the two-volume series by O'Donohue and Geer (1992a, 1992b). Konker (1992) summarizes the lack of theoretical consensus in the field of child abuse and offers an anthropological perspective.

DEFINITIONS OF ABUSE

As Finkelhor (1986) notes, definitions of abuse vary widely in the research literature. Compared to the definitions used in clinical practice, however, they are relatively consistent. There is almost no standardization of definition in clinical practice.

Particularly with adolescent sex offenders, it is important to factor in the overlap between true situations of sexually abusive adolescents versus childhood and adolescent sexual exploration when defining sexual abuse. The typology of male adolescent sex offenders discussed in chapter 5 suggests a continuum starting from a gray area to clear situations of sexual abuse. It is important to note that on the other side of the gray area is normative nonpathological sexual exploration between adolescent peers that is often accompanied by considerable confusion, much clumsiness, a full range of both positive and negative affects, and a full range of sequelae.

As noted in chapter 1, ours is a deeply erotophobic culture. One effect of this is an increase in the likelihood that adolescents, during normative sexual exploration, will not be able to handle their sexuality well. As a result of cultural erotophobia, adolescent sexual expression is often labeled as psychopathological, especially if it is same sex.

The field of childhood sexual abuse must struggle with the important distinction between normative sexual exploration in adolescence and childhood and abuse. This distinction is not easy, but it is imperative. If this challenge is not met, the field of child sexual abuse runs the risk of becoming an "enforcer" of cultural erotophobia. Overly broad definitions can label all adolescent sexuality as abuse or abusive, or recapitulate cultural bigotry, as in homophobia or stereotyping adolescents of color as hypersexual.

A disturbing trend we have noted is the tendency of some therapists to use purely subjective definitions of sexual abuse. Although there is no consensus on an absolute definition of sexual abuse for research purposes, the various research definitions that exist are relatively objective (see Finkelhor, 1986, pp. 22-27 for definitions). Theoretical positions that label a situation as abusive if others react badly to it, if it creates any negative affect, or if it does not fit how "normal" sexual or interpersonal relationships are theorized can be dangerous. Such therapists place themselves in the role of enforcing cultural erotophobia. In an erotophobic culture, most sexual exploration by adolescents receives negative reactions from someone and has some accompanying negative affect and sequelae, and the form and nature of the interactions are displeasing to some people. Comparable to the risks of some feminist therapists seeing as therapeutic the inculcation of clients into a particular construction of reality, therapists working with adolescents are challenged to make certain they operate in the best interests of the specific adolescent client, and not in the service of any particular worldview.

We believe the tensions over adolescent sexuality are primarily a cultural problem. To label them as problems of individual psychopathology is a political act, and a deeply regressive one. After a period of sexual excess in the 1960s and 1970s, the 1980s ushered in a period of sexual repression. Both stances are extreme. Practice styles and theoretical models that are overly aligned with either extremity are flawed. Competent theory and practice in the area of sexual abuse are vigilant of the potential for therapists to become agents of social control and cultural fads, rather than agents of scientific inquiry and therapeutic healing.

PREVALENCE

Although research on male victims of sexual abuse has not been as extensive as research on female victims, its amount is respectable and dates back to some of the earliest studies. As discussed by Peters, Wyatt, and Finkelhor (1986), studies of prevalence are problematic due to varying definitions of sexual abuse, different modes of questioning, differing sample characteristics, and varying response rates.

The prevalence rates of sexual abuse, based on studies from the United States and Canada, vary between 3% and 31% of males and between 6% and 62% of females (Peters et al., 1986). In most broad community studies, female victims are from 2½ to 4 times more likely to have been sexually abused than males; however, in studies of college populations, females are about 1½ times more likely to have been abused than males.

The studies that show the highest percentages of males as victims of sexual abuse are four of the earliest reports. Freud (1896), in the period when he believed client reports of sexual abuse, describes one third of sexual abuse victims as males. Hamilton (1929) found prevalence rates of 20% for females and 22% for males, whereas Landis (1956) found prevalence rates of 35% for females and 30% for males. A study by Bender and Blau (1937) also suggests an equal male/female risk. The predominance of female victims is concentrated in the more recent studies, with the exception of the Tobias and Gordon study (1977), which suggests equal risk. Some (Kempe & Kempe, 1984; Plummer, 1981) have theorized that boys are more likely to underreport sexual abuse, and therefore the "real" prevalence is roughly equivalent.

A number of studies suggest increased reporting of male sexual abuse. The American Humane Association (1981) found that sexual abuse reports have risen over the years and that the proportion of male victims reported has increased. Finkelhor (1979) surveyed 796 college students and obtained a sexual abuse victimization rate of 9% for males and 19% for females. In 1980, 15.7% of sexual abuse reports were from males; in 1984 that number increased to 21.7%. Of 2,627 people contacted in a *Los Angeles Times* random phone survey (Timnick, 1985), 16% of the men reported being molested as children. In a large (N = 2,019) British sample, Baker and Duncan (1985) report that 12% of females and 8% of males recount sexual abuse before the age of 16.

Self-report studies from perpetrators suggest a higher rate of male victimization than studies based on victim reports. Freeman-Longo (1986) reports a prevalence rate for female abuse of male children of 40%, and Petrovich and Templer (1984) a rate of 59%, based on retrospective reports in a sample of male rapists.

The current literature suggests that in most populations studied, female victims outnumber male victims, but the specific ratio is not easy to determine, and may vary significantly between different samples. Some have argued that the admission of victimization is at odds with sex-role stereotyped masculinity so powerful in adolescence. Because most sexual abuse of male adolescents is likely perpetrated by males, avoiding the appearance of homosexuality imposes a significant constraint on boys reporting their abuse (Freeman-Longo, 1986). Others have commented that society is more sensitized to girls being victims because of the perception of boys as strong and girls as weak and that victim status and role are "reserved" for females (Vander Mey, 1992a), whereas males are not permitted to express vulnerability and helplessness (Nasjleti, 1980). Clearly, there are many unanswered questions in the empirical literature. Although there are insufficient data to determine if the arguments for severe underestimation in males are true, the arguments are consistent with other known features of male adolescent behavior, and so warrant serious consideration.

Setting aside the issue of male/female differences in prevalence, the range of sexual abuse cited in the studies is roughly of a factor of 10, that is, a range of variation that is unacceptable for informed decision making. The public policy implications of knowing whether the prevalence of sexual abuse for women is 6% or 62% are enormous.

The reaction of some researchers to methodological problems in prevalence studies is peculiar. In the volume by Finkelhor (1986), otherwise characterized by a cool objective tone, personal attacks on particular researchers appear to be limited to researchers who advocate equal prevalence for boys and girls (see pp. 61-64). Finkelhor and Russell (1984) appear intent on making certain there is little deviation from childhood sexual abuse being predominantly conceptualized as something that males do to females. Although Finkelhor and his associates seem sympathetic to the notion that rates of sexual abuse may be underestimated across the board, they seem overly protective of the idea that many more girls than boys are sexually abused. In a field where much research is weak, studies that conflict with the prevailing notion of female predominance in victimization are singled out for weaknesses that many studies share.

Allen (1990) comments on the increasing recognition of female perpetrators of sexual abuse. His discussion raises an interesting possibility. If one assumes that sexual abuse perpetrators of either sex act consistent with sex role stereotypes (this is a reasonable assumption, as research suggests many sexual abuse perpetrators are quite conventional in their sex role stereotypes), it may be the case that female perpetrators perform sexual abuse in a more "female" manner, that is, in a less goal-directed, violent, or overtly genital manner. Examples of this might include exhibitionism, both overt and subtle; seductiveness; caressing; and fondling, as opposed to acts of penetration and violence and clearly orgasmic activities.

If female sexual perpetration is underestimated because definitions of sexual perpetration are geared toward describing male perpetrators, the data on prevalence of male and female child victims might be skewed. For example, if female perpetrators consistently select more male victims and the observation that males underreport as compared to females is empirically validated, then prevalence estimates may require substantial revision.

It is our belief that male victimization and female perpetration are likely to be a minority of the sexual abuse situations, although not a small minority. What this means, as Allen (1990) points out, is that there are millions of cases of this "minority" situation. Clearly, any viable conceptual framework of sexual abuse must be able to accommodate the full range of sexual abuse experiences, both the majority and the minority. It is for this reason that we believe that feminist perspectives, which were crucial in the early development of this field, are insufficient in the current phase of theoretical development.

The Truthfulness of Child Abuse Reports

In the early years of current interest in childhood sexual abuse, it rapidly became an article of faith that the truthfulness of self-reported victims could not be questioned. To do so often elicited pejorative labeling, such as "minimization theorists," from child abuse advocates. Such advocates imply that raising questions about the truthfulness of abuse reports is tantamount to saying that abuse does not exist. We believe this is an extremist position.

Historically, questions about the truthfulness of child abuse reports have occupied a central role. The "discovery" by Freud, and earlier by French mental health practitioners (Masson, 1984), were revolutionary. Equally revolutionary was Freud's complete repudiation of his previous theory. This repudiation occupies a central place in psychoanalytic theory, as it is a core feature in Freud's theories of the unconscious and the Oedipal struggle. It is unwise to take a position that all reports of sexual abuse are true. Historically, extremist positions about such matters seem to fall in and out of fashion.

The late 1980s and early 1990s have seen the latest twist in changing fashions, with the emergence of "false memory syndrome" (False Memory Syndrome Foundation, undated; Freyd, 1992; Wakefield & Underwager, undated), which allege that many cases of childhood sexual abuse are lies or distortions, often created by overzealous therapists. This perspective legitimately points to the error of assuming that sexual abuse must have occurred when there is no memory of it because of the existence of certain symptoms common in sexual abuse victims. However, it appears to go beyond this in its suggestion that remembered or even clearly substantiated cases are generally suspect.

In fact, there are sound methodological and empirical reasons to believe that the recollection of repressed memories of sexual abuse is considerably more complex than a simple slogan of "victims never lie" (Briere, 1990, 1992; Doris, 1991; Faller, 1990, especially chapters 5 and 9; Goodman & Bottoms, 1993; Jones & McGraw, 1987; Loftus,

1993; Loftus & Foley, 1984; Meyers et al., 1989, especially pp. 32-127; Perry & Wrightsman, 1991; van der Kolk & Kadish, 1987). The field of sexual abuse may be reaching a stage comparable to Freud's doubts before he "recanted" and denied the reality of abuse memories. Our view is that both extremist positions are unworthy of scientists and health-care professionals.

There is a middle position that can be exemplified by a classic film, *Rashomon.* In this film, based on a medieval Japanese tale, two individuals come upon the scene of a rape-murder. The crime is reported to the authorities, who interview the two witnesses, the alleged murderer, and the murder victim, who is represented through a medium. Each individual tells an internally consistent and entirely believable story. Each individual's story differs in significant details. The movie ends with the narrator bemoaning the human condition, complaining that truth and reality are impossible to ascertain and that all is chaos. Although we do not share this last conclusion, the movie makes an important point.

The truthfulness of a report of sexual abuse is very difficult to ascertain in a number of situations. In most situations of sexual abuse reporting, this is not the case; rather, the truth is relatively easy to come by because of multiple victim reports, incriminating circumstances, material evidence, and the like. It is important, however, to admit that gray areas exist for a balanced understanding of sexual abuse phenomena. Examples of these gray areas include situations between early and older adolescents or between late adolescents and young adults where the older party is developmentally immature. In these, immaturity, clumsiness, and insensitivity can be recast as coercion and abuse.

Many areas may appear gray, but on careful examination are not. Chapter 7 presents a methodology with a purpose of uncovering the truthfulness of what occurred in a sexual abuse situation. Similarly, Schoener and Milgrom (1989) describe a technique in situations of client-therapist exploitation that can sometimes uncover greater degrees of accuracy in situations that appear gray. Neither of these methodologies is foolproof, and cases remain where it is impossible to ascertain what occurred. These situations occur predominantly where there is a single alleged victim or when victim reports become contaminated. A noteworthy example is the famous Jordan,

Minnesota cases (see Hechler, 1988), in which contamination by prosecuting attorneys and therapists working for the prosecution rendered much of the evidence from alleged multiple victims unusable.

Similarly, in situations of client-therapist exploitation, we have seen situations where alleged victims of the same perpetrator are placed in the same support group. In the process of obtaining support and advocacy, stories that were initially dissimilar become strikingly similar, making truthfulness harder to ascertain. Given the preponderance of simplistic theory in the area of sexual abuse (i.e., the belief that victim effects are monolithic and that if a person does not show a predictable pattern of effects then he or she is "in denial"), there is a danger that attempts to provide support and clarification for victims can instead provide a kind of secondary victimization in which alleged victims are told what to believe, think, and feel, or are labeled as psychopathological.

It is our observation that truthfulness cannot be separated from a sociopolitical context. In a period when victim reports, whether of childhood sexual abuse or client-therapist exploitation, are not believed but rather discredited, individuals who make reports have a very high probability of being truthful. This is a context in which there is no benefit from making a report of abuse, truthful or not, and making the report is an uphill struggle. Not surprisingly, the few instances of false reporting in this context are likely to be situations in which the false reporters have significant problems with reality. This is an environment in which any reporting, true or false, is likely to bring neither justice nor benefit to the reporter.

It is important for child abuse and client advocates to realize that when their advocacy efforts are successful, as they generally have been, the sociopolitical context changes. When justice and accountability for victims become possible or even standard, when criminal sanctions are strengthened and civil statutes are amended to allow for easier recovery of damages, the context changes.

In the past, the context was one in which it was more or less true (with the exception of those people with poor reality testing) that victims almost never lied. When there is greater justice and accountability in the system, at least two possible effects occur. There are greater sanctions against perpetrators and it is possible (although it is certainly not clear empirically) that some potential perpetrators might be constrained from perpetrating. More importantly, some individuals might have greater motivation to claim victimization when it did not occur or to exaggerate victimization, as there is the possibility of obtaining significant damages monetarily and of harming alleged perpetrators in other ways, such as via licensing board complaints.

To put it another way, in an environment where victim reports are not believed and there is little justice for victims, only a crazy person would make a false report, and there is little constraint on potential perpetrators. In a situation that approaches justice and equitability, constraints on potential perpetrators might be effective in some cases; more importantly, there are sound reality-based reasons for some people to file false or exaggerated victim complaints.

Therapists who treat victims of abuse in a simplistic monolithic manner contribute to this situation. Sloganeering, such as anyone who engages in inappropriate behavior has a progressive out-of-control illness and will necessarily reoffend, any vaguely remembered emotional discomfort in early childhood is indicative of sexual abuse, particularly if it is not well remembered, and the like tend to create distortion, especially when popularized as "scientific." These belief systems, particularly when reinforced in a support group, can shape and even manipulate a client's beliefs and create retrospective falsification of vaguely remembered events.

We continue to believe that most victim reports are true; that a class of perpetrators exists who reoffends until forcibly prevented from doing so; and that there is some truth to simplistic myths about child abuse. These viewpoints describe a subset of abuse situations, not the entirety of them. A pressing need in the area of child sexual abuse is to develop the conceptual and theoretical capacity to deal with gray area cases without resorting to extremist positions of denying the possibility of abuse or embracing it when there is insufficient clarity to make such determinations.

BARRIERS TO IDENTIFICATION OF MALE VICTIMS

Once boys realize that something sexual has happened to them that was confusing or inappropriate, there are no clear avenues for clarifying their confusion. Rape crisis centers and other victim services are generally staffed and identified as resources for women. The advertisements, literature, and atmosphere of an organization can prevent male victims from coming forward.

Some organizations have significant cultural barriers to recognizing male victims. Organizations identifying themselves as feminist or as having a feminist ideology are readily able to identify and support females oppressed in a world controlled by males but may have difficulty recognizing the adolescent or young adult male victim of sexual abuse—especially if that abuse is perpetrated by a female, or if the male victim is sex role stereotyped and not "feminist." Male victims of sexual abuse can be silenced by the gender stereotyping of both patriarchy and feminism.

When the need for services for male victims of sexual abuse is acknowledged, a fear of competition can develop. Providers who serve predominantly female clientele are at times resistant to address the issues of male victims because their services are already overburdened with female victims. This competition for funding has been recognized as between those who serve people identified as "offenders" and those identified as "victims."

Mental health services providers suffer from a lack of awareness of the extent and nature of male victimization. As a result, they fail to ask questions in a way that is sensitive to male experiences and perceptions. (See the section in this chapter, The Effects of Sexual Abuse on Males, which suggests that interview formats, as opposed to checklist formats, may be more sensitive to male experience, as men have greater resistance to describing abuse effects.)

The media and arts in general fail to identify male victimization. This lack of realistic images in the media prevents males from having models with which they can identify, and thereby feel less alone. *Deliverance* and *Ode to Billy Joe* exemplify this insensitivity to male victims; in *Prince of Tides,* sexual involvement of an adult male with his female psychotherapist is depicted as beneficial. A significant lack of research and theory addresses the issues of male victims.

Primarily as a result of cultural gender stereotyping and homophobia, a number of myths concerning sexual abuse have led to its lack of recognition and therefore underreporting by both victims and health professionals (Dimmock, 1990).

Myths About Male Sexual Abuse Victims

You Cannot Make Males Have Sex Against Their Will. For children and adolescent males, as with young females, the majority of sexual abuse is perpetrated by family members, known persons in authority, relatives, or friends. The victim is tricked or manipulated by someone whom they trusted. The experience most often results in a feeling of confusion. With older teens and young adults, sexual abuse often occurs with force. This is especially true when the victim is in a residential, correctional, or armed services setting and is threatened by someone who has power and authority in that context.

If a Male Has an Erection and Ejaculates, He Consented. Male children and adolescents can experience erections in a variety of situations. In cases of abuse, the male adolescent may ejaculate; this is confusing for the victim. It may also be difficult for others to believe his report about this experience. Manipulation or trickery, whereby the victim "goes along" with a situation, in no way implies consent. Rapid ejaculation is often described by victims as the way to get through the abuse quickly.

All Males Who Sexually Abuse Boys Are Homosexuals. A number of research studies show that the vast majority of sexual abuse against boys is perpetrated by heterosexual identified males or females (Groth & Birnbaum, 1978). This myth equates sexual abuse with sexual orientation, and sexual abuse with sexuality; such myths are no longer tolerated in regard to female sexual abuse victims but continue regarding males.

If Abused by a Male, the Abuse Occurred Because the Boy Is Gay or Acted Gay. This particular myth causes considerable anguish and confusion for boys. The victim sometimes ascertains the pedophile's focus on the typically androgynous qualities of young adolescents. The offender may say "how smooth your skin is" or "how pretty you look," leading to misattribution of blame and responsibility onto the victim. For adolescents who are experiencing some sexual identity conflict or are at the beginning of a coming-out process, this myth adds a considerable burden.

If Abused by a Male, the Male Victim Will Become Gay. Some correlational research suggests that male victims of sexual abuse are twice as likely to engage in same-sex behavior (Finkelhor, 1984; Johnson & Shrier, 1985). It must be emphasized that this research is "correlational," and no direct causal factor has been determined at this time. One rationale may be that a young male who is in a coming-out process may have been read as such by a pedophile, who takes advantage of this special vulnerability of a child or adolescent in a homophobic society (see chapter 4).

If Forced or Tricked by a Female Into Being Sexual, the Boy Should Consider Himself Lucky. This myth is perpetuated by a number of teen "sexploitation" films that depict older or adult females as sexual with adolescent boys. Although many adolescents (and society in general) initially have a difficult time perceiving this situation as abusive, there is no evidence that the gender of the perpetrator eliminates or diminishes effects of the abuse.

If a Boy Is Sexually Abused, He Will Become an Offender. This is sometimes called the "vampire syndrome," which holds that once abused, a boy will become an abuser. This myth is often offered as an explanation of how men become sex offenders. As suggested by the PHASE research (O'Brien, 1989) and other studies (Becker et al., 1986; Fehrenbach et al., 1986), only a minority of adolescent sex offenders in outpatient treatment programs report being victims of sexual abuse. (Chapter 5 provides a typology of adolescent offenders that demonstrates differential motives and behaviors.) This myth is readily applied to male but never to female victims, who are viewed in a comparatively benign manner. Neither clinicians nor the general public assume that female victims have an enhanced probability of becoming a perpetrator. This myth reflects gender stereotyping that males play aggressor and offender roles, and females play passive or victim roles.

Boys Are Less Hurt by Sexual Abuse Than Girls. This myth reflects gender stereotyping that boys are stronger, tougher, and not as emotionally vulnerable as girls. Ironically, this sexist stereotyping has been promulgated by some feminists (Rush, 1980). It implies that if boys are abused, the abuse will not affect them as much. In fact, both boys and girls display symptoms that reflect psychological and physical trauma when they experience sexual abuse (Friedrich, Beilke, & Urquiza, 1988; Woods & Dean, 1984). Although some research suggests the nature of effects may be different, it does not suggest the severity is less. For boys, such sexist stereotyping often encourages repression and denial.

Boys Can Protect Themselves From Sexual Abuse. This myth seems to view sexual abuse as a correlate to physical assault, whereby "tough boys" should be able to defend themselves physically. This reflects the stereotyping that if a boy is threatened, he is expected to defend himself and his manhood (Block, 1983).

Males Are Initiators of Sex; if Abused, They Got What They Were Looking For. Gender stereotyping implies that males are initiators or aggressors of sexual encounters. In reality, males are as vulnerable as females to seduction by manipulation or force.

FEMALE PERPETRATORS OF SEXUAL ABUSE

Virtually all the literature on sex offenders describes male offenders, and there is little doubt that males are the majority of sexual perpetrators. The prevailing view has been that female perpetration is rare; Finkelhor and Russell (1984) conclude that females account for about 20% of perpetration on males. However, there are good reasons to consider that females may not be such a small minority of perpetrators.

A number of researchers have raised the possibility of greater amounts of female perpetration on males. Justice and Justice (1979) suggest that the appearance of lower rates of female perpetration is due to female perpetration assuming a different form and mimicking child care through activities such as exposure, fondling, and sexualized physical interactions. Groth (1979) expresses a similar view and suggests that bathing and dressing children can mask more varieties of female perpetration than can typical goal-oriented male orgasmic behavior. Children are reluctant to report, especially if the perpetrator is a parent, and males may be even more reluctant to report as a group.

Knopp and Lackey (1987) found that female perpetrators account for 51% of male victims in their research. Johnson and Shrier found that 60% of their adolescent male victims were sexually abused by females. Allen (1991), comparing female and male perpetrators, found the women to be less aggressive, had more troubled histories, more often selected male victims, and were less willing to admit sexual abuse perpetration.

Finkelhor and Russell (1984) reviewed the clinical literature and report that approximately 24% of all male victims and 13% of all female victims are sexually abused by females acting alone or with a male partner. Clinicians have reported that female sex offenders are usually nonviolent, the abuse is not explained in terms of power and authority, and no psychosis is found in mother-child incest cases (Marvasti, 1986; McCarty, 1986).

Fehrenbach and Monastersky (1988) summarize findings on 28 female adolescents referred to an outpatient juvenile sexual offender treatment program over a 7-year period. None of the subjects were self-referred. Less than one half (39.3%) had been adjudicated for the referral offense or another sexual offense. Referral offenses were either rape (53.6%) or indecent liberties (46.4%). Rape involved oral, anal, or vaginal intercourse, or penetration of the victim with an object or finger. Indecent liberties involved sexual touching between offender and victim, short of penetration. Modal age of the victims, with the exception of one adult victim, was age 5. The victims were all known to the offender, with the majority occurring while the subject was baby-sitting. Ten of the offenders assaulted males, sixteen assaulted females, and two assaulted both sexes. About one half of the female offenders had reported histories of being sexually abused themselves. The authors report that, unlike female sexual offenders of previous studies (McCarty, 1986; Wolfe, 1985), these adolescents committed offenses without coercion from male co-offenders and starting at an early age.

Typology of Female Offenders

Mathews and her colleagues developed a preliminary typology of female sex offenders based on a study of 14 adolescent and 16 adult female offenders (Mathews, 1987; Mathews, Matthews, & Speltz, 1989). This typology is presented in abbreviated form below. The first three types are termed "self-initiated" by the female offender, and the last two are termed "male-involved," and include a male in the commission of the offense.

The Exploration/Molestation Type

The exploration/molestation type is usually a younger adolescent with a young male child (6 years or younger) in a baby-sitting situation. Abuse occurs one or a few times and involves fondling the victim.

The Predisposed/Severe Abuse History Type

The predisposed/severe abuse history type can be an adolescent or adult female with a severe sexual and physical abuse history, who commonly has substance abuse, depression, and personality disorder diagnoses. She is apt to have clear deviant sexual fantasies, minimizes and rationalizes the sexual perpetration, and commits abuse in a forceful, repetitive, and ritualized manner. Fondling, exposure, finger penetration, and oral sex are common abuse behaviors.

The Teacher/Lover Type

The teacher/lover type is an adult female, and victims are usually teenaged males (age 11-16), who may be the perpetrator's own child, stepson, child's friend, neighbor, student, or "friend." Deviant fantasies and projection of blame are apparent, with the abuse described as a "love affair." This type appears most similar to Groth's fixated or regressed pedophile type.

The Psychologically Disturbed Type

The psychologically disturbed type is usually an adult female who may abuse a peer-age adult or child of either sex, with participation

but no coercion by a male cohort. This type tends to have a significant history of psychological problems, conduct disorder, or antisocial personality that is a contributory factor to the sexual abuse.
The abuse may be initiated by either the male or the female, occurs
alone or with the partner, and tends to be more violent than the above
types.

The Male Coerced Type

The male coerced type is usually an adolescent or adult female
intimidated or threatened into the abuse behavior by a boyfriend or
husband, who generally initiates the abuse prior to the female's involvement. The victims are familiar children, adolescents, or adults chosen
by the male initiator.

We focus on female perpetrators in this discussion because their
existence is minimized or denied in most discussions. Sexual abuse by
females is as complex as abuse by males, and may well approach it
in frequency.

THE EFFECTS OF SEXUAL ABUSE ON MALES

There appear to be striking gender differences in phenomenology
and effects of sexual abuse. Considerably more males than females
are sexually abused outside the home; female sexual abuse is more
characterized by intrafamilial incest situations, which is less characteristic of male victims (Finkelhor, 1986). There are other suggestions
that force plays a greater role in the sexual abuse of males (Pierce &
Pierce, 1985, p. 195).

There also appear to be gender differences in the effects of sexual
abuse. Although some studies suggest that males are less adversely
affected (Fritz, Stoll, & Wagner, 1981), this does not appear to be
entirely accurate. Johnson and Shrier (1985) describe approximately
two thirds of the males in their sample as reporting that sexual abuse
was adverse in its impact. Finkelhor (1984) reports that, although two
thirds of girls rate the effects of sexual abuse as adverse, only one
third of the boys do. Even in the Finkelhor study, however, male victims
scored lower on a sexual self-esteem inventory than female vic-

tims. Woods and Dean (1985) suggest a more complex pattern; male victims in their research report fewer adverse initial effects but, on greater scrutiny using a more intensive interview procedure, a greater percentage report negative effects. Friedrich ct al. (1988) found that of those boys who viewed their abusers positively, this effect was reduced significantly over time. From a radical feminist perspective, Rush (1980) asserts, based on feminist theory and not data, that boys are less affected by abuse than girls.

There are some suggestions that the particular effects reported differ between boys and girls. Boys appear to respond more often with acts of aggression (Gomes-Schwartz, Horowitz, & Carderelli, 1990; Tufts New England Medical Center, 1984), whereas girls tend to respond more with depression (Conte, Berliner, & Schuerman, 1986). Urquiza and Crowley (1986) report few differences between men and women, with some exceptions. Women are more often depressed, whereas men more often have aggressive fantasies toward others and report a greater sexual interest in children. Because there are suggestions that the frequency of behavior problems secondary to sexual abuse increases with time (Friedrich et al., 1986), and males display more behavioral problems, male effects may again be masked. Rogers and Terry (1984) note sexual identity confusion, insecurity about masculinity, and recapitulation of victimization as unique effects on male victims.

Citing studies by Conte, Berliner, and Schuerman (1986), Tufts New England Medical Center (1984), and Kelley (1988), Finkelhor (1990b) emphasizes that most studies show little differences between males and females; however, most of these studies utilized a symptom checklist format that does not appear to be especially sensitive to revealing sex differences. It is noteworthy that most of the studies that show specific male effects tend to use interview rather than symptom checklist formats (e.g., Woods & Dean, 1984). If it is true that males have a more difficult time admitting to sexual abuse or perceiving the effects of sexual abuse, then greater effort is required to elicit histories and effects of sexual abuse from them. Part of the difficulty in obtaining clear sex differences may be due to a presumption in the research that victims speak directly and freely about their sexual abuse experiences and effects, an assumption that may be more true for females than males.

In studies on client-therapist sexual abuse, there are suggestions of similar patterns. Gonsiorek (1989) comments on the extreme reluctance of male victims, particularly adolescent male victims, to perceive sexual interaction with a therapist as abusive, especially when the therapist is female. He describes situations where male victims of female therapists maintain denial that the interaction was exploitative even when presented with information that they were one of multiple victims. This information is often effective at breaking down the denial about victimization of female victims, but less so with male victims.

O'Brien (1989) found that 37% of 170 juvenile sex offenders surveyed were victims of sexual abuse. This figure is comparable to other surveys of outpatient adolescent sex offender treatment programs (Fehrenbach et al., 1986). In O'Brien's study, nearly one third of the respondents reported that the sexual abuse was perpetrated by a female. In order of frequency, the perpetrator was a baby-sitter, a relative (such as an aunt), a sister, and the mother.

In a study by O'Brien (1989) examining the sexual abuse victimization rate of adolescent sex offenders, the results are as follows: 42% of incest offenders, 40% of child molesters, and 29% of non-child molesters (e.g., exposure offenders, obscene phone callers, or acquaintance rapists) were themselves victimized. These outpatient figures reveal only a minority of adolescent offenders as victims. They are different from residential or prison population statistics (Groth & Burgess, 1979), which report significantly higher rates of victimization (see Bolton, Morris, & MacEachron, 1989, pp. 81-85 for a review of this area).

As with the truthfulness of sexual abuse, it is important that a gray area be developed in understanding the effects of sexual abuse victimization. In the area of male victims, volumes such as the ones by Lew (1988) and Hunter (1990) have played an important role in opening the field and providing the crucial step of giving permission for male victims to speak about the reality of their abuse. However, these volumes, like similar ones on sexual abuse of women, are simplistic because they suggest a relatively monolithic, invariably severe, and global characterization of victim effects.

A good theory about the effects of sexual abuse victimization must be able to take into account a full range of effects, a continuum from virtually no adverse effects to psychologically devastating ones. Such a theory is presented in chapter 4. Preliminary findings in the empirical literature indicate that the longer the abuse, the greater the trust violation; the more sadistic or brutal the abuse, the worse the effects. Finkelhor (1990b) notes that one quarter to one third of child victims report no adverse effects.

SUMMARY

When viewed through the lens of sexual abuse of female children, sexual abuse of males is seen as a rare phenomenon, similar to the abuse of females but less frequent. As sensitivity to the particular characteristics of male victims and female perpetrators increases, such sexist assumptions are likely to change. It would be surprising if males were a large majority of child sexual abuse victims and females a majority of perpetrators. However, greater recognition of female perpetration, near gender parity of victim prevalence, and greater appreciation for unique male victimization effects and clinical needs are likely.

4

Diagnosis and Treatment of Young Adult and Adolescent Male Victims: An Individual Psychotherapy Model

THIS CHAPTER DESCRIBES a method of assessment, treatment planning, and treatment for male victims of sexual abuse in an individual psychotherapy model, using techniques derived from cognitive-behavioral perspectives and theory derived from the self-psychology perspective of Heinz Kohut. The target populations are late-adolescent or young adult males who are independent of their families or whose families are not accessible or amenable to treatment. Typically, the sexual abuse experiences are not current but removed in time, and the client presents with symptoms related to his sexual abuse. Clients vary in the degree to which they attribute their current symptomatology to the aftermath of sexual abuse.

Most sexual abuse of males occurs in latency or adolescent years; however, most victims do not then seek services. Rather, the typical course is that most boys and young men bury the abuse experience, and attempt to avoid its aftermath. They often seek assistance some years later, often in young adulthood, when they encounter problems, usually relational or interpersonal in nature, and/or perceive adverse effects of the abuse. This population is the focus of the therapeutic strategies described here. For those boys and early adolescents who receive therapeutic services shortly after the abuse, the material here is less applicable, as it is meant for an older population and family and systemic intervention strategies are generally preferable with younger populations.

The material presented here is not the "correct" way to assess and plan treatment, nor is it the correct way to undertake psychotherapy with young adult male victims. Rather, it is an example of how to apply assessment, treatment planning, and psychotherapeutic techniques, extant and established, thoughtfully and in an effective manner to the particular challenges presented by male victims of sexual abuse.

The chapter concludes with an attempt to understand the experience of male victims of sexual abuse through a self-psychology framework. Again, this is not offered as the correct perspective on male victims of sexual abuse but as an example of understanding sexual abuse in a more theoretically rich manner and integrating it with a "depth" theory in psychology.

A word about terminology is in order. "Psychotherapy" is used throughout this chapter to designate the intervention strategies described. That word is chosen to reflect the emphasis in the model described here on linking current problems with past history. It is not intended "territorially," that is, to imply that only persons with particular degrees, training experiences, or the like can make use of these ideas. The focus is on the behavior and conceptualizations of the therapist. Although this does assume a theory base and skill level in the therapist, it is not specific or exclusionary in this regard. In fact, the model presented is itself a hybrid of different theoretical and technical styles.

ASSESSMENT

As Bolton, Morris, and MacEachron (1989) note, careful assessment is the prerequisite for appropriate treatment planning in the area of sexual abuse. They argue that assessment should be multidimensional and yield direct implications for treatment. Further, they suggest a number of areas that should be assessed, including the nature of the abuse, the type and severity of problems that ensue from the abuse, and the strengths and skills of the person being assessed. We recommend their approach as a sound introduction to assessment of male victims, but with some modifications.

Psychological Testing

Psychological testing is not always necessary or desirable; but when it is done, it should be done cautiously and well. Psychological testing is a complex skill, rendered more commonly than well, with as much potential to hurt as to help. For those adept at this skill, this discussion can raise and clarify some difficult issues; for those who do not provide psychological testing services themselves, it can assist them in making more informed and discriminating choices about the best uses and limitations of such services for their clients. Matarazzo (1986) points out that testing alone is inadequate; psychological testing is useful only to the extent that it is integrated with other sources of information, and its implications filtered through clinical judgment.

Generally, psychological testing can be useful early in treatment when the presenting problems are complex and/or confusing, when the client's ability to describe his history and/or psychological state is poor, or when there is a known history of clinical risk or volatility, such as suicide attempts or decompensation, such that a quick and thorough database is desired. Later in treatment, psychological testing may be useful if the therapy becomes inexplicably "stuck," if unexpected new information arises that confounds an earlier treatment plan, or if unexpected symptoms or behaviors occur in therapy.

Psychological testing is probably not worth the expense when clients present with a relatively full information base, either from their self-report or from other sources; or when the symptom picture is relatively uncomplicated and congruent with known history. Routine testing in all cases may pose an unnecessary financial burden on some clients, and will often be redundant with what is already known.

Because the field of sexual abuse treatment is so young, it is important for a therapist to use the best validated and most established psychological measures, on the principle that when a field is new and quasi-experimental, this should be counteracted whenever possible by utilizing established techniques. Novel and specific psychological measures are often recommended or utilized with sexual abuse victims; problems with this approach are twofold.

First, they are too specific. The treatment of sexual abuse victims and theories about the effects of such abuse are at an early stage of development. Assessment should therefore cast as broad a net as possible. Specific tests implicitly focus the assessment process on the relatively narrow range of measures that such tests are capable of detecting. The assessment process then becomes prematurely narrowed toward the assessment of a relatively small number of variables. The tests that capture the broadest possible range of information are the most desirable.

Second, the tests used should be among the most highly validated and well understood. Specific tests tend to be marginally validated or narrowly validated on limited samples. This tends to be true of specific and limited psychological tests, as they tend to attract less research interest precisely because of their specificity.

There is a noteworthy psychometric dilemma in such decisions about testing. In general, the more narrow a construct that a test measures, the more likely the instrument will capitalize on particular features of the population on which the test is standardized. What such a narrow instrument measures, then, becomes contaminated by error variance particular to the population on which validation occurred. This is a problem with all psychological testing and measurement. More broad-ranging instruments however, because of the multiple variables they measure, tend to be standardized on multiple populations. Initial results on target populations often appear promising with single variable measures, and the measure is then often utilized before adequate cross-validation occurs. If and when the necessary cross-validation does occur, validity often shrinks to a level where enthusiasm for the instrument is considerably diminished (see Greene, 1981, for a good introduction to these concepts).

An example can illustrate this point. Suppose one has a theory that male victims are unusually prone to sexual inhibitions and one develops a 20-item test of sexual inhibitions secondary to male sexual victimization. Suppose that this test is initially standardized on a number of samples of male sexual abuse victims in therapy, and the results appear promising; that is, male sexual abuse victims score higher than a sample of nonvictim males.

It would be too early to conclude that the test has any necessary validity. For example, loss of libido is a common sign of depression, and the instrument may really be measuring the higher degree of depression, including loss of libido, that is common in psychotherapy samples. If the sexual inhibition measure were part of a larger battery of established tests, correlations with measures of depression and other variables could document this possible area of contamination. With single measure instruments, it is too tempting to conclude erroneously that one has effectively measured a variable.

The ideal assessment battery consists primarily of broad-ranging, well-validated standard psychological test instruments. These can be supplemented by more specific single variable measures if these are of interest to the assessor. Our recommendation, however, is that specific measures never be utilized alone, as they are often not adequately validated for diverse samples. Further, there is no way to place these narrow measures in a fuller psychological context without a broad-ranging psychological assessment.

The battery we recommend includes a Minnesota Multiphasic Personality Inventory (MMPI) variant: the MMPI-II (Butcher, Dahlstrom, Graham, Tellegen, & Kaemmer, 1989) for adults and the MMPI-A (Butcher, Williams, Graham, Archer, Tellegen, Ben-Porath, & Kaemmer, 1992) for adolescents, and a well-validated projective instrument such as the Exner System Rorschach (Exner, 1986). The MMPI is recommended because of its unparalleled ability to screen quickly for major elements of psychopathology. It is our view that there is still no instrument that can screen as effectively with such little time required of the assessor. The Rorschach provides the most in-depth psychological description of the defensive style, functioning level, and conflicts of an individual, provided the administration and interpretation are competently rendered. This means that the assessor must utilize correctly the Exner scoring system and interpret the Rorschach within the confines of that system.

In some cases, this battery will be incomplete. The MMPI, although unparalleled at describing psychopathology, tends to provide minimal, flat descriptions of individuals who have little overt symptomatology; the MMPI is not intended to measure different kinds of normal personality variables. The Rorschach, although adept at describing areas of psychological conflict and defensive styles, gives less, but still some, information about normalcy. Therefore, in many situations, another test is in order specifically to measure more normal personality variables.

It is our view that the California Personality Inventory (CPI) (Gough, 1987) is unparalleled in this regard. It is well validated and adequately standardized, and provides a broad-ranging description of normal personality variables.

In some situations, other measures may be in order. For example, with certain populations, rapid and detailed assessment of Axis II problems, that is, character disorder pathologies, is desirable. This is a weakness of the MMPI variants, which do not differentiate among character disorders well; similarly, the Rorschach, although it addresses the kind of problems inherent in Axis II diagnoses, rarely yields a clear diagnostic formulation of characterological problems. For the purpose of differentiating among kinds of Axis II problems, the Millon Clinical Multi-Axial Inventory (MCMI-II) (Millon, 1987) is probably the most effective choice.

It should be noted that the MCMI-II, however, is not an appropriate instrument to assess broadly the presence or absence of psychopathology. The intent of the MCMI-II is to differentiate varieties of personality disorders. The MCMI-II generally assumes an Axis II disorder exists and proceeds to describe it. It is limited in describing mental health problems apart from character disorders and where no psychopathology is present. The MCMI-II can serve as a useful adjunct to the MMPI when working with populations with a high rate of Axis II disorders, such as those in court or corrections systems.

All of these tests are extensively validated on a diversity of populations and provide very broad descriptions of personality functioning, and their strengths and limitations are relatively well understood. More specific limited measures may be appropriate, depending on interview and testing findings. When single variable measures are used embedded within a comprehensive battery as described above, the established measures can anchor the less validated ones.

These recommendations may come as a surprise to individuals who work in the area of sexual abuse. Most of the instruments recommended here are considered "old-fashioned" and are somewhat suspect as a result. We feel this is not a relevant objection. The assessment of sexual abuse victimization presents difficult clinical and ethical challenges. These more established old-fashioned assessment instruments do present a problem of relevancy in the area of sexual abuse, in that few variables they measure directly address sexual abuse concerns. The instruments that do appear to address such concerns more directly, however (i.e., meet the criteria of relevancy), tend to be more specific and less validated.

We believe the best response to this dilemma is to use the strongest available instruments and supplement their weaknesses regarding relevancy by careful interviewing. Relying solely on assessment instruments of questionable validity does not truly address the question of relevancy; it merely obfuscates it by giving a false sense of security that something has been adequately measured, when in fact it is usually unclear what has been measured and how it fits with other attributes of the individual.

Specific instruments in isolation are likely to confirm only what the clinician already believes he or she knows, which violates the most commonsense principle of psychological assessment: that it should suggest things one does not already know. Otherwise, the considerable expense and bother are not worthwhile. In addition, theoretical development is inhibited by narrow instruments; broad-ranging instruments can suggest relationships one would have never expected. We feel this quality is especially desirable in a fledgling area of practice.

No assessment should be attempted without a careful articulation of the central question in every assessment situation: What is one trying to assess? We suggest two central assessment concerns. The first is an assessment of serious psychopathology. Current theories about sexual abuse effects posit the possibility of relatively severe mental health sequelae. An assessment can rapidly ascertain if these are present to optimize treatment planning and manage risk to the client.

The second assessment concern is to describe generally the personality style, defensive patterns, assets, and liabilities of the individual. Individuals who have been sexually abused have a psychological history prior to the abuse, and this history interacts in often unpredictable ways with the abuse experience. A general description of personality functioning can begin the process of mapping this basic information.

The first concern can most efficiently be assessed by an MMPI variant, supplemented in some populations by the MCMI-II. The second concern can be addressed over a complete range of strong-to-poor psychological functioning by a combination of the CPI and the Exner-scored Rorschach. Those who enjoy the challenges and risks posed by single variable measures may want to experiment with ones that seem relevant to the experience of male victims, provided they are embedded in a battery of standardized instruments like the ones described above. Alternatively, one can obtain such information from interviews.

A word of caution. The American Psychological Association's *Ethical Principles of Psychologists and Code of Conduct* (1992), *Standards for Educational and Psychological Testing* (1985), and *Guidelines for Computer-Based Tests and Interpretations* (1986) make a number of related points (see also Pope, Butcher, & Seelen, 1993, for details on these and related issues for the MMPI variants). Appropriately trained psychologists must always be in charge of psychological testing. Even when psychologists delegate such activities to others, psychologists retain responsibility—this responsibility cannot be delegated. Psychologists are also entirely responsible for the decisions made about the appropriateness of instruments used. Not only are clients poorly served by poorly chosen and rendered psychological testing, but the professionals involved can make considerable trouble for themselves.

An important and informative tension exists about the use of psychological testing. Standard psychological practice and assessment were, for many years, insensitive to the area of sexual abuse. Many individuals working in the area of sexual abuse are suspicious of traditional practice, and appropriately so; indeed, the area demands all the skepticism and creativity its practitioners can muster. However, if psychological assessment is performed at all, it ought to be performed well. Careful psychological assessment is typically a tedious and rather stodgy process that often does not attract the interest of many practitioners. Yet practitioners who work with sexual abuse victims often need to know the kinds of information that cannot be easily or quickly ascertained in interviews alone; hence the need for psychological testing.

Those skilled in psychological testing are challenged to utilize these measures in the most effective way, and to do so in a manner that corrects for the insensitivities of the measures toward sexual abuse victims. Those not skilled in psychological testing are challenged to find those who have such skills and who can use them in ways that benefit their clients.

Interviews

Psychological Testing and Interviews: Relative Merits

Psychological testing and interviewing both work best in relation to the other. Psychological testing is a rapid way of learning things from initial interviews that one does not already know or one cannot easily or quickly assess because it is not entirely in the awareness of the individual. Interviews are best at obtaining individual details of history that do not easily collapse into the discreet variables measured by sound psychological testing instruments and obtaining information on how the measured general tendencies of an individual are uniquely manifest.

Two examples illustrate these points. Psychological testing, although it can comment on ongoing propensities of individuals, usually functions best as a description of the individual at one point in time. Certain clinical problems that are by their nature variable over time are therefore difficult for psychological testing to measure. Bipolar affective illness, manic-depressive disorder, is a good example. Most psychological tests more or less accurately describe the current mood state but almost never capture the range of affective swing that is central to this disorder. Similarly, psychological testing can describe some of the propensities for certain kinds of interpersonal disturbances commonly found in Axis II character disorders but rarely gives the level of detail required to make an accurate and specific Axis II diagnosis. In both cases, interviews, careful history taking, and perhaps corroborative interviews are needed to develop an accurate understanding of the person's functioning over time. Some diagnoses rely heavily on history, others rely more on the symptom picture at one point in time. Most psychological testing, especially paper-and-pencil, objective instruments, work better with the latter.

Another area where psychological testing has difficulty is in circumscribed disorders, such as the paraphilias or sexual perversions. Generally, the more circumscribed and specific a problem area, the harder it is to measure without considerable cross-validation research on different populations to eliminate the population-specific error variance that often contaminates promising measures. Many of these diagnoses are best determined by careful interviewing, clear understanding of symptoms, and verification from external sources of corroborative information, such as police reports and victim accounts.

Well-interpreted psychological testing, on the other hand, can have an objectivity that is less easily swayed by the reactions one may have to a client in a prolonged series of interviews. A valuable feature of psychological testing is its ability to suggest what clients are unable to describe because they are not aware of it. Both psychological testing and interviews have strengths and weaknesses and are best used in conjunction with each other, with a clear understanding of the powers and limitations of each. As Matarazzo (1986) notes, an assessment process is considerably more complex than mere test interpretation, involving skilled integration of multiple sources of information by an accountable assessor. Dahlstrom (1993) offers a concise overview on the proper uses of testing.

An Approach to Interviewing

Later in this chapter, a theory about sexual abuse effects is presented. To preview one part of that theory, we hypothesize that a class of individuals (not all sexual abuse victims) exists whose history of emotional deprivation and psychological injury prior to their sexual abuse make it more likely that they will be sexually victimized, due to their enhanced vulnerability combined with the ability of some abuse perpetrators to "read" such vulnerability. In line with this theory, we recommend extensive interviewing to differentiate levels of problems that may have arisen from different kinds of abuse, deprivation, or psychological trauma. This includes a detailed history from childhood, focusing on patterns of emotional support or deprivation in the family of origin, and a detailed history of all significant interpersonal relationships.

Detailed questions about what occurred during the abuse, what it was like for the victim, and effects the victim has noted are important. It is our observation that many individuals who have been victimized are not fully aware of its impact on them; however, we also suggest it is inappropriate for therapists to fill in these gaps with hypotheses derived from the relatively young theories in this area.

Rather, the incompleteness is valuable in its own right. It serves as a clue to understanding what may be submerged and the varieties of distortions and defensive operations the client uses. It can suggest what might be significant about what is verbalized versus what is unspoken, and what these mean. The client's description of the abuse, with its bumps and warts, is not flawed. It is the distillation at one point in time of how the client understands what happened to him and the coping resources he brings to bear on those experiences. The difficulty and therefore the challenge for the interviewer is that this distillation cannot always be easily teased apart from actual and complete "truth." The task is easier if the therapist keeps in mind that the goal is to understand the client, not to verify a favorite theory, and that truth may be as elusive clinically as in *Rashomon,* but consistency is often a realistic goal.

Corroborative Interviews

A partial solution is corroborative interviews. Interviewing the spouse of the victim, other family members, close friends and associates, romantic partners, and others who have a detailed observational base of the client can provide useful information about effects about which the victim may not be aware. Again, the outcome is a more consistent hypothesis, not necessarily the truth.

Case Example

    Greg, 22, requested psychotherapy to help sort through the effects of being sexually abused by his mother's father. He had had a dim recollection of the events for some years. What precipitated his coming into therapy at this point was his attendance at his younger sister's substance abuse program's family week, where she told him that she had also been abused by the same grandfather. Initial interviews gave the impression that Greg had a fairly detailed and accurate knowledge of the abuse, much of which was admittedly spurred by discussions with his sister and her memories, but a good deal of which Greg appeared to recall on his own. However, he also reported episodic deep depressions that came and went for no apparent reason. He talked about these only with reluctance, which was unlike him, as he was generally non-defensive in therapy.

After the third abrupt unexplained depression, the therapist suggested a joint interview with Greg's wife as a way to understand these episodes further. At one point in this interview, the wife stated as if it were obvious and self-evident, "You know you always get these after you have any interaction with your mother. It has something to do with her." This was new information for Greg, although he agreed that the pattern his wife observed was true. He became increasingly depressed talking about it in the joint session. Psychological testing was sought at this point; it suggested long-standing depression, with likely linkages to early emotional deprivation.

The next few individual sessions produced new material that proved to be the key to understanding these mysterious depressions. Greg began to recall that his mother, on at least two occasions, walked in on the sexual abuse by her father of Greg; not only did his mother not interfere with her father's abuse of her son, but she subtly accommodated her father in this abuse. Greg also began to verbalize very early memories of being ignored for long periods in his crib while his mother sat immobile nearby, perhaps seriously depressed herself. For Greg, the impact of these memories rivalled the impact of the abuse per se.

Interviews can obtain a detailed understanding of the coping strategies employed by the victim. This is an area where both strengths and deficits are explored. A typical pattern is that victims utilize coping strategies that are suited to the victimizing environment but are often not adaptive outside that environment. Some victimized individuals develop areas of real strength and high functioning in areas of life that have been untouched by the victimization, sometimes as a compensatory device.

A careful history of relationships, with corroborative interviews if possible, can be very useful. Many clinicians working with victims of sexual abuse report that intimate relationships can be the most sensitive in mirroring the effects of sexual abuse. Whom one chooses, whether there are elements of exploitation versus mutuality, how and whether conflicts are resolved and the nature of conflicts, the longevity of relationships, how relationships begin and end, repetitive areas of stress within relationships, the subjective experience of connectedness, the parts of relationships wherein the client holds back, and sexual functioning within relationships are all rich avenues for exploring the impact of sexual abuse. Particularly with males, who often do not perceive effects as clearly as women, a detailed relationship history can set the stage for understanding effects of which they have not been aware.

Diagnostic Formulations

Case Example

Paul, 21, was a gay male who had a pattern of choosing unavailable men. In adolescence, he almost exclusively fell in love with heterosexual men; however, as he developed a gay support system, he received feedback that this was self-destructive. Paul partially incorporated this feedback but began to choose as the objects of his interest gay men who were in relationships or not interested in relationships. The only relationship in which he had not been abandoned was one in which a man he was dating left a relationship he was already in for Paul, at which point Paul terminated the relationship.

Paul could articulate his depression, anger at his family, and sexual dysfunction (he could not tolerate being touched while asleep or even sleepy and he connected this to the fact that the stepfather who had sexually abused him usually initiated the abuse when Paul was asleep). Paul had no recognition, however, of his active avoidance of intimacy, focusing on his perceived inadequacies and the "impossibility" of finding someone in the gay world as explanations for his relationships.

Although Paul's relationship history had been obtained in bits and pieces over the course of six sessions, the therapist suggested at the end of the sixth session that he would like to spend the next session getting more detail about Paul's relationship history. In this interview, the therapist focused Paul's discussion on the unavailability of his choices and how hard Paul worked to pursue such impossible situations. Paul was able, for the first time, to conclude, "Sometimes I think I just pick men who just can't give me what I want."

Mental status exams can be helpful in determining significant current symptomatology. Ideally, assessment should be sufficiently thorough not only to map out the particular effects of sexual abuse and current functioning but also to diagnose accurately on both Axis I and Axis II, should these exist (American Psychiatric Association, 1994).

Many clinicians who work in the area of sexual abuse often display a distinct dislike for making diagnostic formulations, particularly on Axis II. The reason often articulated is that such labels tend to blame the individual for the effects of the abuse, and the Axis II labels in particular tend to shift the blame to the victim. Although we endorse such vigilance in making certain the victim is not blamed for his own abuse, we believe that, in this situation, reluctance to make diagnostic formulations is misplaced.

An unwillingness to diagnose problems for which there is clear evidence tends to underestimate the effects of sexual abuse. Sexual abuse is so damaging because it can elicit or create diagnosable mental illness, among its other possible effects such as constriction of educational and vocational opportunity. The appropriate response to the unique complexities of diagnosis in victims of sexual abuse is not to resent the diagnostic process and render it poorly but rather to render it with skill and sensitivity to the particular issues of the victims.

In addition, some perpetrators do not randomly select those whom they victimize but rather choose individuals who are vulnerable. In other words, mental health problems existing prior to the abuse are likely to be overrepresented in individuals who later become sexually abused. At least some of the perpetrators select victims for vulnerability. It is precisely this vulnerability that will eventuate in later diagnosable disorders and/or interact with the abuse history to create certain diagnostic disorders.

Thorough Assessment

Sexual identity and sexual orientation can best be assessed in terms of perception of identity and in terms of behavioral and emotional experiences with the same and opposite sex. Male victims are apt to differ from female victims in that their victimization is more likely expressed through male socialization. Males in our culture are socialized to respond in ways that include more acting out, problems with behavior control, and sexualization of problem areas. Because male sexual abuse victims often express sequelae in ways consonant with male sex role socialization, areas of acting out, impulsiveness, and self-destructiveness within sexual expression and across different areas of life functioning should also be assessed.

Case Example

Bob, 23, came from a chaotic family where he was sexually victimized as a child by a young aunt, an older male neighbor, and two male cousins. Bob had chronic difficulties with properly asserting himself, particularly on the job. He was meticulous and a perfectionist, who would be assigned more than his share of work. He did not protest this but instead became increasingly angry and resentful, which he directed toward his wife. Bob was particularly ashamed about his temper outbursts and alluded vaguely to "flying off the handle," but gave the impression that this consisted solely of episodic verbal abuse.

About 3 months into therapy, Bob came to a session despondent, and announced that his wife had left to stay with her sister and was discussing separation. After obtaining permission from Bob, the therapist conducted a phone interview with the wife, in which the therapist learned that Bob's abusiveness was not merely verbal; when he became enraged, he destroyed property in the house on a regular basis. The incident that led to the wife's moving out was an evening when Bob came home from work especially frustrated, picked an argument with his wife, and then systematically destroyed a collection of orchids she carefully tended. Bob was deeply ashamed of his inappropriate outbursts, because he associated them with the behavior of one of his abusive cousins. At the same time, however, he minimized the impact these had on his wife. The therapist had neglected to do a careful assessment of acting-out problems and corroborative interviews in the beginning of the treatment, and so was surprised by these events.

Thorough assessment interviews can be therapeutic in that the client tells his story in detail for the first time and frequently has a variety of reactions to it. The simple act of the therapist taking a profound and detailed interest in the client's life and obtaining information without prejudgment can elicit a variety of complex emotional reactions from the client. It is usually wise, however, for the therapist to refrain from active intervention at this point except in a broadly supportive way that facilitates the assessment process or to intervene in crisis or near-crisis situations that require immediate attention. It is preferable to wait until the assessment process is complete and the therapist can offer a formal treatment plan before embarking on active intervention strategies.

It is important to conceptualize assessment as not merely data gathering but as a vehicle for conveying to the client the first impressions of what the interactions with the therapist will be like. The optimal stance for the therapist during this process is to be direct, thorough, and interested in all aspects of the client's life. The therapist may ask challenging questions and at times be pointed in his or her probing but should not jump to quick conclusions and should elicit and value the client's understanding and explanation of what his life means to him. This is the first set of experiences in which the client can see that the therapist is genuinely interested and proceeds with caution and respect. The effects of sexual abuse can be conceptualized as an injury to the sense of self. Many individuals who have been sexually abused had previous injuries caused by emotional deprivation and other situations.

The importance of conveying to the client early on that he is of great interest to the therapist and will be treated with care and respect cannot be underestimated. It not only provides a framework for later interaction, it serves as an anchoring point against which the internal negativity and hostility toward the sense of self, which is present in many sexual abuse victims, can begin to be focused and directed. Paradoxically, the interest and respect shown by the therapist both makes it safe for the client by creating a healing environment and begins to mobilize the negativity within the client to undermine this environment in which the self, which is partially unacceptable, is treated consistently well.

FORMULATION OF A TREATMENT PLAN

Once a treatment plan is formulated, it is important that the client fully comprehend and agree to it. Although this is a truism in practice with all clients, it is especially pertinent in working with victims. An individual whose trust has been violated is often especially sensitive to coercion.

It is not uncommon for a therapist to have a more comprehensive view of the areas needing treatment than does the client. In particular, therapists are often more persuaded of subtle effects of sexual abuse and expect multiple effects in the victim's life. Therapists are often distrustful of the client's description of low levels of sequelae. However, a recent review of research suggests that approximately one third of victims of childhood sexual abuse are nonsymptomatic, even at follow-up (Finkelhor, 1990b).

This is partially due to the tendency of clients who have been victimized to be unaware of some of the effects of victimization. However, there are situations when these are distortions on the therapist's part, as theory and practice in this area are overinclusive and tend to "see too much." It should not be assumed that any discrepancy is merely the client's denial, although it may be. We have observed an unfortunate tendency in many therapists to believe it is their prerogative and even obligation to press clients who have been victimized into accepting the therapist's view of how the abuse has affected the client and what should occur in treatment. We disagree with this strategy.

In situations where the client and the therapist disagree about goals and treatment plan, we recommend that the therapist, in a straightforward fashion, explain the rationale for his or her recommendations and discuss differences with the client; if differences remain, then the therapist should defer to the client's perspective whenever possible.

This does not mean that the therapist should agree with the client's perspective if that is not what the therapist truly believes. Rather, the two agree to disagree but formulate a plan in which goals that are mutually agreed on can be addressed. The therapist can take the position that if the client is correct, then, on completion of this limited treatment plan, the therapy is done. If the therapist is correct and the client ends therapy too early, goes out into the world, encounters problems stemming from unresolved abuse sequelae, and realizes that more work lies ahead, the client is welcome to return. The client and therapist can then recontract and formulate a new treatment plan.

Case Example

Aaron, 17, sought therapy at the suggestion of his brother. Both had been abused as children for a period of months by an adolescent female baby-sitter. The brother was in therapy and persuaded Aaron to come for an assessment. A careful evaluation, including corroborative interviews with Aaron's mother and current girlfriend, found few or no symptoms suggestive of sequelae of sexual abuse, although all parties seemed to assume that hidden effects must be present, primarily because the brother had significant effects.

Aaron's agenda appeared to be a simple one, namely to tell his story, to obtain some educational information about sexual abuse, but not to continue in therapy. The therapist appropriately outlined the possibility that more subtle effects might be present but also acknowledged that a significant minority of individuals appear to experience no sequelae; and invited Aaron to return should there be problems at a later date.

Approximately 4 years later, Aaron again sought services from the same therapist when he was making a difficult vocational decision that involved relocation and a complicated career shift. The therapist had an opportunity to follow up on the possibility of sexual abuse sequelae and again determined that there was no evidence of any sequelae. The therapist also learned that Aaron's brother discovered later in therapy that he had been sexually abused previous to the baby-sitter by an older male neighbor, whereas this had not been the case with Aaron. The diversity of sexual abuse effects between the two brothers began to make sense.

Case Example

Carlos, 23, appeared for an evaluation at the suggestion of a cousin when a priest who served the parish in which Carlos grew up was prosecuted for a long history of sexual abuse of altar boys. This cousin had been abused for a prolonged period by this priest, and made a formal complaint. Carlos told his cousin that he too had been abused. Although Carlos was cautious about coming in for an assessment, he agreed to do so.

The assessment suggested that Carlos had some significant areas of possible sequelae. In particular, he had a history of going to sexually oriented bookstores and public cruising places, where he allowed men to perform fellatio on him, even though he identified himself as heterosexual. These behaviors seemed related to periods of stress and conflict in his marriage. Carlos refused the therapist's recommendation for therapy, stating he understood after talking with his cousin about their mutual abuse why he did such behaviors and he was confident he would no longer do them. Furthermore, Carlos did not want his wife to become aware of these behaviors. The therapist reiterated his perception this might be a significant problem warranting treatment, suggested what Carlos might look for if the problem worsened, and left open the possibility for Carlos to return.

Eighteen months later, Carlos returned, stating he had been arrested in a sexually oriented bookstore by an undercover police agent. Although his attorney quietly settled the charge, Carlos was deeply shaken by this close call with public exposure, and detailed to the therapist an even more extensive history of anonymous sexual behavior with males, which was incongruent with Carlos' perception of his sexual identity as heterosexual. Carlos requested the therapist do "some sort of behavior modification to cure this homosexual thing" and resisted examining the issue in any depth. The therapist declined to offer Carlos the treatment he sought, stating it was inappropriate for his problems.

Carlos returned 2 years later, stating he had sought services from a Christian psychotherapist who did aversion therapy to "cure homosexuality." Although Carlos initially experienced some reduction of same-sex behavior from this treatment, his sense of shame and self-esteem problems worsened and his cycles of sexual acting out deepened. This time when he appeared for services, Carlos was willing to look at the full range of ways in which the sexual abuse may have affected him, including his sexual orientation confusion. The therapist believed that his gentle and respectful handling of the disagreements about the treatment plan with Carlos made it possible for Carlos eventually to return for substantive therapy.

We refer to this approach as a "dental model" of mental health practice: One year a person may need a cleaning, another year a filling, the next year a root canal. The fact that different goals are the focus of the treatment at different points in time does not decrease the legitimacy of any of those goals or place either party in the position of having to be right or wrong. We believe it is imperative that, if therapy with victimized individuals does nothing else, it should model a relationship of trust and respect. The exceptions to these recommendations are situations where the client's plan for treatment is contraindicated or objectively harmful. Disagreement with the therapist's favorite theory does not in and of itself constitute objective harmfulness.

Further, it is our view that the belief of some therapists that they know more than the client does about his sexual abuse is arrogant. Clearly the therapist is—or ought to be—expert; but in the area of sexual abuse the knowledge base is thin and highly impressionistic. One therapist's expertise may be another's incompetence, narrowness, or countertransference. The problem is that the field in which the therapist is expert is murky. We recommend therapists be non-defensive about this, as it is no one's fault—it reflects the development of knowledge in this area and the field's immaturity.

At the end of the assessment process, the client and the therapist agree on particular therapeutic goals. Complete agreement on all goals the therapist views as important is not necessary, but the therapist must believe that those goals that are agreed on are clinically sound and relevant. At times there may be insufficient agreement between the client and the therapist to proceed. In such cases, it is recommended that the therapist lay out his or her perceptions and recommended treatment strategies and rationales, listen to the different points of view from the client, seriously consider those, and discuss them with the client; but if no common ground is reached, then the therapist should decline to treat the client.

This happens most typically with clients who have unrealistic expectations about a rapid cure in therapy, who conceptualize their role in therapy as a passive one, or who have become philosophically aligned with certain theoretical perspectives or self-help movements. They might insist, for example, that the therapy focus solely and exclusively on issues such as "healing the child within" or "helping recover from codependency." The idea of mutually agreed-on therapeutic goals does not mean that the therapist surrenders his or her judgment but rather that the two parties find areas of genuine agreement. If these cannot be found, therapy cannot proceed.

Case Example

Ralph, 24, presented for therapy with the request that he be given "heavy-duty psychological techniques" to help contain his sexual acting out. Ralph had been sexually abused by his stepfather and had a history of sexual interaction with female prostitutes once or twice a year on business trips, which he felt was out of character for him and about which he felt considerable guilt. For the past year, he had attended a sexual addicts' group facilitated by a charismatic leader whom the therapist regarded as an ill-trained cult figure. This leader believed that any sexual expression other than monogamous heterosexual sex was "addictive" and would "eventually destroy you." Included in the prohibited activities were any masturbation and all sexual fantasies if they were not of one's monogamous spouse.

It was the therapist's assessment that this extremist and shaming perspective further eroded Ralph's behavioral controls, increased his difficulties maintaining adequate self-esteem, and exacerbated his problems. The therapist outlined to Ralph the reasons for his concerns and disagreements, made a number of alternative suggestions, and informed Ralph that what the therapist had to offer and what the group had to offer were different in philosophy and style and that Ralph would have to make a choice because the two treatments would likely clash. Ralph opted to obtain individual psychotherapy from a therapist recommended by the group leader.

It is important, both from an informed consent perspective and as an aspect of respect shown the client, that the therapist be explicit. There will be times when the therapy causes more upset and disruption than relief of symptoms and times when the therapist will ask the client to do difficult things. It is also wise to clarify that therapy will be an active process and that no change will occur unless the client actively participates.

An Individual Therapy Model

This individual therapy model is a hybrid, in that the conceptualization of client problems is in line with the self-psychology theory; however, the therapist's behavior and interaction with the client are more akin to a cognitive behavioral style. In other words, the therapist thinks dynamically but acts pragmatically, in a goal-oriented fashion. This model is meant for late adolescents, young adults, and older men who are functioning more or less independently of their families of origin.

The intent of this therapy is to reduce symptoms that the client presents within a framework of producing dynamic change in the sense of self. These two features taken separately are considered necessary but not sufficient conditions in working with sexual abuse victims. Symptom reduction alone does not address the unique characteristics of sexual abuse victims, such as their propensity for repetitive interpersonal difficulties. Given the possible depth and pervasiveness of the effects of sexual abuse, it is reasonable to assume that symptom reduction runs the risk of problems reemerging at a later date. Similarly, dynamic change alone provides no way to ascertain if the client's change process is merely intellectualized or emotionally integrated. The ability of the client to reduce symptoms and apply coping strategies learned in therapy to a variety of new life challenges is considered in this model to be the best test of whether dynamic changes are truly integrated.

Individual therapy is central in this model; although group, couples, and family therapy modalities may be used to amplify individual therapy, they are auxiliary. The use of these other modalities is briefly discussed later. This is not to suggest that individual therapy is necessarily the optimal choice for a given client, but that if multiple modalities are used, they be coordinated and consistent.

Early Stages

The initial stages of interaction involve taking a thorough history of the client and in particular, reflecting on how the past history of sexual and other abuse currently affects the client's life. A picture of current symptomatology should be mapped out and the reasons why the client presents for therapy now should be discussed.

Typically, individuals who have been sexually abused have been living with this history within some sort of equilibrium. When they seek individual therapy, often something has occurred to disrupt that equilibrium and increase symptoms. A thorough understanding of these reasons and events can clarify a number of important points. The coping strategies and vulnerabilities of the client can be illustrated, and initial ideas of the most efficient points of entry into the client's experience of having been sexually abused can be suggested.

Most individuals with a history of sexual abuse who have managed to lead their lives with reduced or no symptoms in at least some areas have struck some balance between their history and coping strategies. The immediate situation that has increased symptomatology provides an important opportunity for the therapist. It allows the therapist to get underneath those coping strategies in a way that is acceptable to the client, as opposed to battering down the client's defenses in areas where these defenses have been effective. In other words, the circumstances of the immediate situation can reduce the sense of violation during the therapy process. They also signal to the therapist possible related areas that are ripe for the next interventions, presuming the client continues in therapy.

Equally important is understanding what has worked well in the client's life. Areas of high functioning and good coping strategies can provide a context for understanding the overall fragility or strength of the client, as well as a context for mapping out the areas of defensive adaptation that may not be amenable, at least not quickly, to therapeutic intervention.

Implicit in this discussion is the assumption that the therapist should not dismantle the client's defenses. What is suggested here is that the therapist approach only those defenses that have already failed and respect those that are working well. The rationale for this approach is twofold: it conveys to the client a sense that he will be respected and not violated, and it reflects a therapeutic stance in which the client is seen as an individual who has been besieged by certain events and who has evolved a pattern, however flawed, of coping with those events, that warrants respect.

The therapy process, whenever possible, should improve functioning level, not erode it. The client's sense of himself in day-to-day functioning is crucial. If there are areas in his life where he feels competent and proud of his functioning, these are areas to be encouraged, not undermined, even if the functioning strategies are problematic. In this model, therapists who believe that breaking through the client's defenses for the "therapeutic good" of the client are not seen as acting with more thoroughness but with disrespect, poor planning, and lack of imagination and understanding. Such therapists are seen as not adequately strategizing how they can most effectively work with the areas of vulnerability the client presents while respecting the areas of strength the client has carved out. If the client does not perceive maladaptive aspects of what he considers a strength, the therapist might use examples from the client's experience to suggest these aspects. The therapist's "hunches," "experience," or "theory" alone are insufficient. The client's experience weighs the most.

Case Example

Fred, 26, came from a family in which there was extensive physical and sexual abuse and alcoholism. Despite the emotional and economic poverty of his background, he was very proud that he completed college and achieved a middle-level management technical position at a large corporation. He was particularly proud of what he perceived to be his "strength." As the therapist began working with him, Fred began to form the perception that a good deal of his "strength" really consisted of a variety of intellectualized defenses against a profound underlying depression. These defenses caused considerable emotional constriction, which apparently led to chronic dissatisfaction from his male spouse about Fred's aloofness and coldness.

Auxiliary couples treatment was not effective in altering this pattern. Fred perceived that the couples therapist and his male partner wanted him to be "weak." The individual therapist determined it was unwise to push Fred at this time on this issue. Some weeks later in a one-to-one session, Fred began to explore tentatively his sadness and disappointment in himself regarding an incident with his 4-year-old son from an earlier heterosexual marriage. His son came to him for support and comfort following an altercation with a peer. Fred saw that his aloofness clearly wounded his son, who then sought support from Fred's partner. For the first time in a therapy session, Fred teared up, but he rapidly began to compose himself. The therapist decided to take a risk with this opportunity and asked Fred if he really wanted to do to his son what was done to him.

Fred began crying profusely but then became panicked at his "weakness and loss of control." The therapist redefined this "loss of control" as progress and reassured Fred that his well-established patterns of reinstating control would not likely desert him; he might learn a more sophisticated and flexible way of maintaining control if he could stay with these feelings for a while. In the following sessions, Fred discussed physical abuse and emotional coldness from his biological father, whereas before Fred's emphasis had been on the physical and sexual abuse he received from a stepfather. Fred spontaneously noted he could see the legitimacy of his partner's complaints.

Behavioral Assignments

The initial assessment, because of its thoroughness, often elicits considerable historical material. In this model, it is recommended such material be pursued if it seems relevant to current life problems, but that it not become the sole or even primary focus of therapy. Rather, we recommend that early in therapy, the therapist strategize behavioral tasks for the client to do as homework assignments. The selection of these initial assignments is important. The ideal assignments are ones that involve a current problem area in the client's life which is a clear example of a long-standing dysfunctional trend and is theorized to be related to the aftereffects of sexual abuse, other damage to the sense of self, or deprivation. The ideal assignment targets initial behavior change in a pattern that represents how the client currently functions out of a historically damaged sense of self.

Equally important, these initial assignments should be chosen for a high likelihood of success. Part of the intent of this assignment is to give the client an initially successful experience with behavioral change. This is why a thorough understanding of the client's functioning level during the initial phases is so important. Without this information, it may be difficult to predict the likelihood of success in these assignments. Considerable care and planning are crucial to this therapy model. Spontaneity may have a role in the therapist's style but not much of a role in the therapist's strategies.

Case Example

Kent, 24, was repeatedly passed over for raises and promotions on his current job and treated with considerable verbal sarcasm by a male supervisor. Nevertheless, the supervisor and others in the office understood that when a difficult job needed to get done, Kent was the person to do it. This had been an ongoing pattern with Kent, and indeed had been the reason he resigned a number of jobs in frustration and anger. He had never been able to discuss his dissatisfaction with supervisors. The first behavioral assignment started by helping him clarify in therapy his dissatisfactions with the current job and how his passivity may have played a role in this dissatisfaction.

Kent eventually understood this was not simply a situation of unpleasant coworkers and supervisor but rather an interaction between their behavior and his own. The therapist assisted Kent in targeting reasonable appropriate assertive requests of the supervisor and then role playing them in therapy. After these were refined, Kent carried out the assignment. Results were mixed: Kent performed well, albeit with some passive-aggressive aspects that were not effective; the supervisor was responsive to some but not all of Kent's requests and reduced but did not eliminate sarcastic remarks.

As important as planning the assignment was its recapitulation. Over the next few sessions, time was spent reviewing Kent's performance, examining his expectations about what changes were reasonable, and targeting the next behavioral assignments. The initial tasks provided an opportunity to discuss the maladaptive aspects of Kent's passivity, withdrawal, and passive-aggressive style; challenged his idealized and grandiose expectations of his ability to change the world; and connected these themes to how his sexual abuse as an early adolescent by a minister affected him and resulted in poor coping strategies.

Ideal assignments exemplify chronic situations in which the client acts in a self-defeating way that seems linked to his history of abuse and any earlier damage to his sense of self. The specific examples initially chosen, however, should be relatively uncomplicated and "safe bets" for successful experiences. Even though the assignment is relatively simple, it should be treated cautiously. The situation is reviewed in therapy, the client develops some understanding of his and the other person's role in the problem, and the situation is role played. This increases the likelihood of the experience being successful and ensures that the client's perceptions of the events are reasonably accurate. Treating a client concern, even a minor one, as worthy of careful planning is an important message.

These "simple" initial assignments are not simple in their meaning for the client; there is often a surprising amount of resistance. The reasons for the resistance are processed and the client is reminded that little can occur in this therapy without his active participation. Once the client begins following through on assignments, gradually more complicated and challenging assignments are given until the client experiences significant affective responses. This sometimes occurs early, although a few assignments may be needed. Examples of these responses include a recognition of anger at other events in the client's life, feelings of sadness at having been cheated and deprived, or a sense of insight or connection to earlier events.

If this process continues with the affective responses processed and the client gradually being given more assignments, a point will usually come at which the client begins to experience directly his negative sense of self. This can take the form of a lack of confidence in relatively simple assignments, feelings of not being worth the positive outcomes of the assignments, feelings that progress in therapy is not "good enough," or similar distortions. What is happening dynamically is that the areas of life in which the client is functioning with a low sense of self are being slowly remedied and replaced with the client acting as if he has a positive sense of self.

Although the client may initially be elated and have a sense of empowerment, this is often followed by the negative sense of self emerging as strong resistance. In other words, a parallel history begins to develop that is based on a positive evaluation of the self. This eventually creates conflict with the prevailing negative sense of self.

Middle Phase

Simultaneous with behavioral assignments, the historical issues that emerged in the initial phases are pursued in the middle phase of therapy. Part of the therapy sessions is spent planning for and processing the assignments, and part is spent discussing longer-term issues. By the time significant negativity emerges from the behavioral assignments, the client has begun to process historical issues that can be brought to bear on understanding the negativity.

In this model, the behavioral assignments serve a number of functions. They begin to create a parallel history in the client's life in which he secs in his own experience that he is capable of mastering tasks he thought were not possible earlier; the behavioral assignments serve as an engine that drives a more dynamic integration. When chosen carefully, the behavioral assignments will not only address real problems in the client's life but will produce a variety of meaningful emotional responses, the integration of which begins to make the client more whole.

Resolution of the negative sense of self involves letting the client experience it directly. Typically, this negativity has been defended against and the client backs away from it when it emerges. The client is encouraged to "let it have its say," to experience and integrate the accompanying affect, and to analyze them in a cognitive-behavioral fashion (cognitive restructuring, see Beck, 1976, and Young & Beck, 1982; rational-emotive approaches, see Ellis, 1962, and Ellis & Greiger, 1977; structured behavior changc, see Phillips & Weiner, 1966), whether this negativity is what the client wishes to support or to counteract.

Throughout this process, two events require careful management. First, although it may temporarily slow down to give more time to process and resolve affective responses, the process of changing behavior in the present does not stop. In other words, forward momentum is maintained in the behavioral change, despite the affective responses. The negative self is not allowed to stop the behavioral development of a positive self.

Second, it is important to make certain that the anxiety elicited during these processes is not discharged by acting out. The earlier careful assessment of acting-out potential becomes crucial. Often, when these affective responses do not occur, the client has been discharging the accompanying anxiety in some other way. If acting-out anxiety is occurring, it is important that this be blocked.

Case Example

Mark, 19, came from a family background of sexual and physical abuse and significant alcoholism. Therapy seemed to be progressing surprisingly well given his history; he appeared to handle initial behavioral assignments well and historical issues were being explored. Mark seemed to be handling these seemingly meaningful changes and discussions in stride, with little distress and no emergence of negativity toward himself. The therapist inquired generally about acting-out behaviors; Mark reported none.

A few sessions later, the therapist received an emergency phone call from Mark; this had not occurred previously. Mark was mysterious on the phone about what had transpired but was clearly upset. The therapist saw him later that day on an emergency basis. With considerable embarrassment, Mark revealed he had begun a sexual affair with a female coworker about a month into therapy. Her boyfriend had discovered it, followed Mark after work, ran him into a ditch, and showed him his shotgun, which he promised to use on Mark if he had further contact with his girlfriend. Mark returned home, had a series of panic attacks, and called the therapist.

In the next session, processing focused on Mark's distrust and fear of rejection by the therapist in not discussing this earlier. Information also emerged that self-destructive affairs to avoid affect were a pattern for Mark. Mark and the therapist agreed to a contract in which Mark would tell his best friend and the therapist when he began to plan an affair.

Mark canceled the next session at the last minute; this was unlike him. The therapist called Mark; after initial defensiveness, Mark began crying, stating he had "fucked up his therapy like he fucked up everything in his life." With much difficulty, the therapist persuaded Mark to return. Over the next sessions, Mark expressed considerable self-hatred. Eventually, his long-standing pattern of placating male authority figures by being "perfect," followed by sexual acting out, followed by his withdrawal from the male figures because he believed they would reject him if they knew, was explicated and processed in light of other aspects of his family background.

In Mark, the lack of the expected emergence of negativity against the self raised the possibility that this negativity was being discharged instead of being experienced. Although attempts to evaluate this

produced no information, when it did emerge, Mark used his deception with the therapist as a vehicle for self-attack. Making a contract to
contain his acting out produced anxiety and more deception and pre-
cipitated a crisis. The crisis was eventually put to therapeutic effect,
but it was a risky point in the therapy. If the therapist had been rejecting or critical of Mark for his deceptions, or had been too lax in limiting the acting out, the therapy might have ended poorly.

It is important that the therapist be forgiving of errors the client
makes both during the behavioral assignments and in the processing
of the affective responses. The therapist's typical response to errors
should be one of acceptance coupled with an expectation that, despite
these errors, the client will maintain forward momentum. If levels
of depression or anxiety reach the point where the client begins to
experience functional impairment, breaks can be taken and a more
supportive therapy temporarily put in place; but when the client is
able, the forward progress is again resumed. The therapist communicates to the client that the client will be able to cope with the
situation. The negative self can be experienced but not allowed to
interfere substantially with development of a positive self.

Case Example

Bill, 21, had been sexually abused during childhood and adolescence by his pediatrician, who was also a neighbor and family friend.
He did not want to file a complaint or reveal the name of the pediatrician in therapy. Bill's goals were to improve his relationship functioning and eventually to confront the physician. The therapist cautioned
Bill early in therapy that his plan of a one-to-one confrontation without support or knowledge of friends, family, or authorities placed an
undue burden on Bill, and agreed to proceed only if Bill was open to
considering other options if his original plan proved ineffective.

After making some significant improvements in his relationship
with his girlfriend, Bill began discussing confronting his abuser. After two sessions discussing his ambivalence about this, he came to the
next session distraught. He had become angry at the pediatrician after the last session, had seven beers, went to the physician's home,
and demanded $5,000 to help defray the cost of therapy. The physi-
cian calmed Bill down, offered to send him instead to a colleague

who would treat him free, offered Bill more beer, and then seduced him. This was the first time Bill had had sexual contact with the physician in 5 years.

In the session, Bill was confused, harshly self-critical, and deeply ashamed, stating he should have listened to the therapist all along and filed a complaint with Child Protection and the Medical Board, and suggested they do so immediately during that session. The therapist responded by cautioning against impulsive decisions, and recommended that a few sessions be spent discussing complaint routes and what they meant to Bill before taking any action. The therapist also rejected Bill's harsh assessment of his failure, and commented that although his particular plan of handling the situation had not proven effective, Bill's general tendency to take charge of his life and decisions had been a hard-won fight for him given his history, and was a valuable trait, even if his rendering of it was too inflexible. Bill had gotten in over his head in this situation, and the most positive response would be to learn from his errors, not to attack himself, act impulsively, or surrender his judgement to the therapist's.

In the next 2 months, a number of issues were processed. The pros and cons of various complaint routes were explored, the need to temper but not eliminate Bill's stubbornness and rigidity were discussed, and his episodic impulsiveness, particularly in the face of anxiety and perceived failure, were explicated. Although Bill eventually decided to pursue formal complaint routes against the pediatrician, the process afforded the opportunity to demonstrate to Bill that he was acceptable even when he erred, and to challenge his rigidity productively. Bill later commented that he appreciated the therapist not taking advantage of him when he was down by immediately contacting the authorities, and that this incident was pivotal in his being able to trust the therapist, because his initial motivation in complaining was to please the therapist, whom he feared might reject him because of his errors.

Selection of the assignments and a sense of what might be coming during the affective responses are crucial to the success of this process. A clear sense of timing about when to "let up" is also important. A therapist who is dogmatic, unforgiving, or insensitive will fare poorly. This process, when done well, accomplishes a number of things. The client can see from his own experience that he can make significant behavioral changes; that he can make errors and recover from them; and that he can experience strong affective responses and weather them without disruption of his behavioral progress.

The therapist derives from this process a clearer understanding of the client's coping patterns, strengths and weaknesses, areas of resistance, and typical ways of defending against change. Behavioral assignments are goal oriented, even though the emotional impact on the client is pervasive and sometimes profound. Not uncommonly, as this process requires numerous judgement calls, the therapist may miscalculate by not pushing the client enough, pushing the client too hard, being judgmental about mistakes, not being sufficiently challenging, or being too challenging about possible distortions in the client's understanding. This process works best when the therapist is relatively transparent about what occurs in therapy and why. Similarly, the therapist is straightforward about errors, admits them, and reformulates accordingly.

Case Example

Tom, 25, was sexually abused by a priest in his pre-adolescent years, by an older male sibling in early adolescence, and by a female high school teacher in mid-adolescence. In addition to sexual abuse, there was a history of emotional deprivation. Both parents were highly career oriented, and Tom spent much of his childhood growing up in different cities where his parents were assigned for employment. Most of his care was provided by his older male sibling, and Tom himself provided a great deal of care for younger siblings. Not surprisingly, he presented with considerable pseudo-maturity and had little recognition of the degree to which his own emotional needs were not met.

Therapy initially progressed very well. Tom effectively addressed a long-standing, self-defeating pattern of not finishing school work and was quite elated when he received a B.A. after finishing up a large number of incompletes. Next, he made an effective and articulate complaint to the diocese that employed the priest. Even though the minister was deceased, Tom found considerable resolution in having his complaint heard and acknowledged by church authorities. Tom attempted to track down the high school teacher, who had in the meantime changed school districts. He contacted Child Protective Services in the teacher's new county, who told him that the case was too old to prosecute but assured him that they would open a file on her and monitor her closely.

Tom's next goal was to confront his brother, but he became somewhat hesitant and self-doubting, which had been uncharacteristic of him in the therapy. The therapist encouraged Tom to press on and did not attend to Tom's hesitations. Tom made a reasonable plan to confront his brother and rendered it well. However, the brother's response was demeaning. Tom became extremely depressed, hopeless, and had serious feelings of worthlessness. He believed that he was a failure. He was sophisticated enough to appreciate that his brother was very difficult, and did not blame himself for the brother's poor response, but instead felt worthless because of his severe, and to him inexplicable, depression. At that point, Tom's therapist decided to obtain a consultation.

The consultant suggested to Tom's therapist that he had been inattentive to Tom's suggestions of wanting to slow down before tackling his brother. Tom had had the role of a parentified child in raising his younger siblings, and the consultant suggested that Tom had slipped into the role of being a "super client" and the therapist had unwittingly encouraged this and had been insufficiently attentive to the striking lack of distress and difficulty Tom experienced as he progressed through one therapeutic success after another. The consultant suggested further that Tom's depression might be related to a feeling that his therapist, like his parents and brother, was inattentive to his emotional needs; this depression was partly historically related and partly related to an error on the therapist's part.

The therapist, in exploring this further, also recognized a countertransference issue. The therapist himself had been sexually abused by an older cousin. Part of the therapist's inattentiveness to Tom's suggestions of slowing down before tackling his brother was perhaps related to the therapist's eagerness to have Tom confront his older brother, something the therapist had never done with his older cousin.

As suggested by the consultant, the therapist in the next session discussed the idea that he had been insufficiently attentive to Tom's hints of wanting to slow down before tackling his brother, and this might be related to his depression in that it was another neglect of Tom's emotional needs as he tried to please an authority figure. The therapist also let Tom know that this blind spot was due to the therapist's own countertransference, which he planned to pursue and resolve in his own supervision. As suggested by the consultant, the therapist did not disclose the nature of the countertransference.

Tom's depression significantly resolved over the next two sessions and he described that for the first time, he felt that he could "be a mess" and be acceptable and that someone else could take care of him. It appeared that the consultant's view of the dynamics of the situation was reasonably accurate.

In this manner, not only does the client see he can manage a trial-and-error process, but he observes the therapist doing so. The point is not to create errors on the part of the therapist but to recognize that in this active, directive strategy there is some likelihood that errors will occur, and the therapist should respond to them in a way congruent with the way the therapy is conducted.

It is important to note that transparency about the therapy does not mean transparency about the therapist. In the example above, detailing the nature of the therapist's countertransference would have been a strain on the therapeutic boundary. Rather, the client is kept informed about what is going on and why but not about the therapist's personal issues. Hence the client was informed that the therapist made an error because of his own background and that the problem was being addressed in supervision, but not what these issues were. This way of doing therapy shares a cognitive-behavioral bias that the most effective treatment is nonmysterious: The client understands what transpires and why. Therapeutic progress and the means by which it is achieved are the client's to keep while boundaries are maintained and modeled.

Later Stages

After the client has accumulated some experience in making positive behavioral changes in the present and emotionally integrating them, this model is applied in situations that have more historical import. Specifically, the therapist and the client begin to plan how to address parts of the abuse history directly using these strategies.

An effective tool is the use of letters directed toward the perpetrating individuals or others who enabled the perpetration. These letters are not vehicles of communication to those individuals but rather a journal process in which the client can record various feelings he experiences in imagining communication with these individuals. The intent of this exercise is to give the client a more full and complete understanding of his affective response to the individuals in question and also to clarify what he wishes to say to them.

With these issues clarified, the therapist and the client can begin to explore a variety of options to obtain some resolution of the historical abuse situation. The therapist does not a priori assume that any one solution is better than others. Solutions range along a continuum from directly interacting with the perpetrator, with or without the therapist present, or with other family members or support people, to interacting with other individuals in the system in which the perpetration occurred, to having the story be heard and acknowledged by significant others, to writing a final unsent letter in which the reaction of the client to the abusive behavior is described. In other words, the options range from the most direct to the purely symbolic. The goal of this procedure is to assist the client in having emotional resolution in a context in which his experience is acknowledged, where he receives support and validation, and where emotional integration can occur.

This part of therapy can be particularly tricky. The intent is to help the client have the optimal experience for resolving the abuse. As this is an adult client who is removed in time from the abusive situation, and the abusive individuals or enablers are not part of the therapy process, it can be difficult to judge the most efficacious options. Corroborative interviews with spouses, significant others, friends, siblings, or other family members can assist in planning this and should be utilized when appropriate. At this point in the therapy, many clients are sophisticated enough to do their own corroborative interviews and data gathering about the options. Whenever this more empowering option is available, it is generally preferred. It is important to make certain that the client does not make an impulsive decision but an informed one about which option is the best.

In situations of doubt, the recommended strategy is to choose the option with the highest likelihood of success, carry it through to its resolution, and process it in therapy; if this has not been sufficient, then move to more risky options. Options that seem high risk and prone to failure are generally not encouraged in this model; although if the client is intent on pursuing them, the therapist might outline the pros and cons and help the client process this. In other words, the client might choose to pursue an option with which the therapist disagrees. In keeping with the stance of empowering the client, the therapist should not interfere with this, although the therapist can insist it be discussed before and after action and can offer his or her opinions and cautions prior to the choice.

Case Example

Ted, 25, had been sexually abused by a stepfather. He found the initial behavioral assignments difficult and was resistant but followed through and made a degree of progress in his primary relationship and his work situation that exceeded his expectations. Ted became hopeful for the first time that he could manage himself.

Ted outlined to his therapist a plan to confront his stepfather. The therapist was cautious and not encouraging of this plan because of Ted's three siblings; his younger brother refused to discuss the sexual abuse (and Ted strongly suspected that he too had been abused by the stepfather), his older sister was openly supportive of the stepfather and hostile toward Ted, and his younger sister, with whom Ted had the closest relationship, appeared to very passive and dependent and vacillated between supporting Ted and supporting the older sister, depending on who talked to her the most at any point in time. The therapist commented that Ted's plan warranted caution because Ted had little clear indication of support within the family, and the family history suggested that both the stepfather and the older sister could be explosive in their behavior and affect. Ted's mother, with whom he had had a strong relationship, was deceased.

Ted's only support in the family was an aunt in whom Ted had confided about the abuse as an adolescent and who contacted Child Protection. This aunt then took Ted in. Child Protection did not intervene because Ted "was too old and a male anyway." As the therapist and Ted discussed the pros and cons of the situation, they continued to disagree. The therapist told Ted that although she remained uncomfortable with the plan, it was Ted's prerogative to pursue it and she would be there to support Ted and process the situation should Ted decide to implement it.

On the surface, the meeting between Ted and the stepfather was disastrous. Ted, who was gay, was vilified by his stepfather, who told him that the sexual abuse was another example of his "sick faggot imagination" and refused to discuss it further unless Ted agreed to undergo counseling at an organization affiliated with the fundamentalist church where the stepfather was a deacon. His older sister sided with their stepfather, verbally abused Ted, and pressured the younger sister to side with the stepfather and shun Ted. A tense situation persisted for a few weeks until the younger brother, who had been brought into the family dispute by the older sister, announced to everyone that he too had been sexually abused by the stepfather, at which point, the younger sister clearly threw her support behind Ted and his younger brother. The stepfather and older sister announced that they would disown all three of them for being "perverts and liars."

These events required a few months in therapy for processing and integrating. However, at the end, the therapist came to the conclusion that Ted's course of action was reasonable and told Ted that. Ted had correctly assessed that his older sister was intractable, his younger sister unpredictable, and his younger brother inscrutable; and that his strategy, although high risk, was the only one available if he wished to deal directly with the abuse history, which he did. Later, Ted told the therapist that the therapist's acknowledgement of the reasonableness of Ted's judgement had been a major boost to his self-confidence.

Throughout this process the client has the option of disregarding or delaying certain options. It can sometimes be useful to take a break from therapy before pursuing certain options. Sometimes, as clients feel more effective and powerful and have a growing sense of themselves as competent and worthwhile, they begin to tackle behavioral changes in their lives during their therapy but without input from the therapist.

Case Example

Matthew, 18, had considerable confusion about his sexual orientation, and discussed early in therapy the pros and cons of exploring same-sex relationships, which he had never before had. He opted to delay this exploration. After a series of successes in handling school-related challenges, assertive situations with friends and family members, and a confrontation with his abuser, his previous therapist, Matthew announced that one night he had gone to a gay bar and had his first sexual experience with a man, none of which had been discussed in therapy.

This situation presented an important therapeutic decision point. The style of the therapy had been one of mutuality and enhancement of Matthew's personal choices and power. Spontaneously applying concepts learned in therapy was consistent with the therapeutic style, and welcome. The therapist's challenge was to strike a balance between affirming and encouraging Matthew's self-directed choices, yet raising appropriate questions. These included whether Matthew's choices were well planned or impulsive, whether Matthew emotionally integrated the experience, whether these experiences were self-defeating, or whether Matthew used them to deflect anxiety or create a crisis that distracted from other, more pressing situations.

The therapist's response to Matthew was to inquire about his planning process and why he had not discussed it in therapy. The therapist learned Matthew had planned this situation well, including obtaining information on and implementing safe-sex procedures, but did not mention it in therapy beforehand because of his shame regarding same-sex desires. With this clarified, the therapist commended Matthew for his sound planning, particularly about safe sex, and suggested that Matthew's shame about same-sex feelings interfered with emotionally integrating them, which then became a therapeutic focus.

One of the long-term goals of therapy is to assist the client in making the bridge between skills learned in therapy and their application in the outside world. At times, when the behavioral change process starts "cascading," the therapist's role is to help the client become better at mastering his own change process by helping him attend to issues of pacing, emotional integration, sound decision making, and the like.

Matthew had done well in most of these areas, requiring only a nudge to begin to integrate emotionally his same-sex experience and desires. His way of offering a *fait accompli* in therapy, but nondefensively, suggests a level of initiative, autonomy, and trust that signalled he was nearing termination. (There also may have also been age-typical issues of establishing autonomy with an authority figure.)

Throughout these processes, the therapist must tend to the symptomatology, affective state, and trust level of the client. The goal is to push the client to make significant behavioral changes and to integrate emotionally—but not too hard. Mild distress or slight increases of symptomatology are acceptable in this model, but when there is any significant drop in the client's functioning level, the therapist should pull back from more difficult material and move into a supportive role. The therapist can be relatively transparent about this process, working cooperatively with the client to ascertain when the stress has become too much and making joint decisions about this. For many sexual abuse victims, the levels of coping they have achieved, however flawed or incomplete, are an important accomplishment. Therapy should not undermine them. The intent of this model of therapy is to build on what the client has already achieved, not eradicate and replace it. Whenever possible, some forward momentum on behavioral change is maintained, even if only symbolic.

Case Example

Steve, 23, had been abused by an uncle and aunt who raised him; the uncle physically and sexually, the aunt physically. Both had been alcoholic most of their adult lives and were deceased. Prior to living with the aunt and uncle, Steve had experienced considerable emotional deprivation; his biological father had abandoned the family and his mother had died when Steve was 3.

Steve made reasonable progress in therapy, reducing a persistent sexual dysfunction, retarded ejaculation, which troubled his current same-sex relationship. His next goal in therapy was to speak with a number of his relatives about the abuse. Steve was particularly ashamed about the sexual abuse because it occurred from ages 11 through 17. He spent time processing that the sexual abuse was not his fault and addressing his concerns that his poorly educated relatives might blame him, as the uncle was viewed within the family as being a saint for putting up with his abusive wife. Steve was planning a rare visit to his home state in the coming month to talk to his family.

Suddenly, Steve's company was acquired by another and he was laid off without warning a month before he had been promised a

highly desired promotion. Steve was devastated, because he had
worked hard and had no warning.

Steve and the therapist discussed the pros and cons of delaying his
talk with his family. The therapist was particularly concerned because
Steve tended to be overresponsible and unaware of the emotional impact of stress on him. Steve agreed that the sudden changes in employment were very stressful, but felt he had worked hard in therapy
to prepare for this visit and he needed to "do something" to address
the history of the abuse directly.

The therapist hit on a compromise solution. A long-time dream of
Steve's was to learn to play the flute. His aunt and uncle had forbid
him to learn music because they viewed it as "unmanly." Learning the
flute had, for a long time, been a symbol for Steve of something he
might do when he was free from the constricting influence of his
family. Steve and the therapist discussed this as a symbolic but nevertheless powerful action that might satisfy Steve's need to "do something" while he delayed interacting with his family to a less stressful
time in his life. Steve took flute lessons. These served as a useful
bridge until his employment situation improved and became a symbol for Steve that he was autonomous and independent of his family.

Termination and Continuation

Therapy can end at varying points in this model. The change
process for clients is conceptualized as one in which they simultaneously come to greater understanding of the effects of the abuse in
their lives, learn behavioral change strategies to alter these effects,
take appropriate steps to address directly historical material as it
becomes manifest in their lives, and continue this process in an
ongoing fashion. The point of ending is not a point of cure nor a
remaking of the client but a process of setting in motion a more or
less stable parallel track of functioning in which the self is enhanced
and affirmed. As a result, there can be different points of ending. In
the words of Arendt (1955), "We can no more master the past than
we can undo it. But we can reconcile ourselves to it" (p. 21).

Some clients end therapy when they have made simple behavioral
changes in their lives. They may be feeling better than before and do
not want to "risk it" by pursuing more volatile material directly

related to the abuse. If the therapist has an opinion about the advisability of pursuing or not pursuing this material, he or she is free to offer it. In any case, the recommended therapeutic stance is to congratulate the client on the progress made and to welcome him to return later if needed. This is true whether or not the therapist and the client disagree about the advisability of pursuing historical material.

Other clients continue therapy through behavioral changes, and continuing through emotional integration of certain aspects of the abuse. It is important for such clients to understand that even though they have done impressive work, they are not "cured," but have addressed the known issues at hand. It is important for such clients to realize that ramifications of the abuse undetected by both the client and the therapist may emerge at a later date. The client is free to return without any implication that therapy failed. Rather, the new material is understood as exemplifying the complex nature of abuse effects. The past therapy would be conceptualized as having been successful given what was known by the client and therapist at that time. New issues can be addressed building on the success of the earlier therapy.

Case Example

Ed, 22, had been in 10 months of therapy 2 years previously addressing chronic unassertiveness, sexual acting out, episodic alcohol abuse, a history of sexual abuse by his biological father, and considerable emotional deprivation. It was not easy for him, as he was prone to panic attacks, but he made reasonable progress and felt confident and competent in ending therapy.

Ed returned when he developed his first long-term relationship with a man. He had done a good job asserting his needs early in the relationship, but as intimacy increased he became fearful of abandonment and worried that if he asserted himself, his partner might abandon him. He became increasingly unassertive and resentful, which peaked when he and his partner began discussing living together and could not agree on a neighborhood, type of apartment, and the like. Ed also felt dejected, believing that he had undone his earlier therapeutic progress.

The therapist disagreed, reminding Ed that his progress had been real. The therapist explained that it was unlikely that Ed's fears of abandonment and difficulties managing intimacy and autonomy could have occurred earlier because he had never had an ongoing relationship before. The recent problems were consistent and understandable from Ed's history. The therapist suggested to Ed that the earlier progress was his to keep, as he had maintained his other improvements; the new situation reflected problems that were earlier unknown. The therapist suggested Ed continue in therapy to address these, which he did.

The client may wish to return to therapy at a later date to address issues truly or seemingly unrelated to the abuse; returning to the original therapist is safe and relatively efficient, as there was a positive relationship and is a shared understanding about the client's history. These are examples of the dental model of therapy described above.

This is not to suggest that all points of ending are necessarily sound. Situations in which the client is avoiding important material in either the behavior change process or the exploratory part of the therapy, situations where the client appears to be acting out or experiencing poor behavioral controls, or situations where the client abruptly stops for no apparent reason are undesirable. The recommended therapeutic style remains respectful, transparent, mutual, and flexible.

The therapist can describe his or her observations and understanding of the current situation, and suggest to the client what he or she considers the best course of action. The client's input is solicited and discussed. If the situation is resolved to agreement, then the termination proceeds or the therapy continues. If the client and the therapist remain in disagreement and the therapist has attempted to understand the client's view but the client continues to want to terminate, then the therapist can state that even though he or she believes it inadvisable to terminate, the client is welcome to come back at a later date for any number of reasons, including to process this disagreement further, to address new areas that have arisen, or to continue the treatment plan as recommended by the therapist.

This therapy model is not one in which the client primarily identifies, expresses, and catharts affect related to the abuse experience. Simply emotionally reliving the abuse experience is viewed as an irresponsible therapeutic goal. There is significant danger of regression; such catharsis does not necessarily lead to improvement in functioning level or increased behavioral skills; and there is no guarantee that catharsis will result in integration. Therapeutic approaches that posit affective experience as primary, we believe, run the risk of not only causing regression in the client and eroding functioning level but inculcating in the client a counterproductive sense of being a helpless victim—a rationalized version of the negative sense of self that is a core problem of the client.

The effects of the abuse and deprivation on the sense of self are considered primary and central as the focus of therapeutic efforts. The underlying affect is not considered central but more as a series of cues. An assumption is made in this model that affect is useful only to the extent that it is informative, integrated, and utilized effectively for behavioral change. Affective expression in and of itself is neither therapeutic nor untherapeutic. It can be either depending on the context and circumstances; however, it can be volatile, and requires careful management because of its "regressive pull."

THE ROLE OF OTHER THERAPY MODALITIES

Many clinicians who treat male victims of sexual abuse primarily utilize group therapy. The individual therapy model described here does not typically make use of group therapy, although it could in some circumstances. These include when the group is run by a professional leader; when the goals of the group and individual therapy are congruent; and when the client is in need of what group therapy can offer.

It is our view that group therapy is most effective as a way to educate clients about sexual abuse, to provide support, and, to a limited extent, to function as a "social laboratory" to address interpersonal deficits. Other than for these goals, we are not enthusiastic about group therapy as the primary treatment for a number of reasons.

The individual therapy relationship described earlier, although goal oriented and directed, is nevertheless a deeply intimate one. Both the therapist and the client, especially the client, are vulnerable, and the trustworthiness of the therapist in periods of success and failure is a central therapeutic tool. For clients who have experienced the violation of trust that is central to sexual abuse, this interaction is uniquely powerful, cannot be duplicated in a group process, and is more akin to the kinds of intimate relationships the client will face in the real world. Group therapy diffuses the intensity of the interaction; on the other hand, a highly distrustful client too fragile for individual therapy might find a group with a strong leader and a focus on education about sexual abuse a more tolerable first step.

It is our observation that much group therapy tends to be more dogmatic than our model, in that particular goals and ways of achieving the goals are assumed best for those who have been sexually abused. The model presented here is more individually tailored and nondogmatic.

Although the intensity of support and group structure can be powerful in making certain kinds of therapeutic gains, they can also freeze the client into a relatively low level of functioning in which the role of victim is perpetuated. Clients may not learn to become independent centers of initiative but may remain on some levels passive and dependent on group approval. It is also our observation that only the most skilled group leaders are unable to prevent a group, particularly a long-term group, from functioning at the least common denominator of group members' functioning and affective levels. In other words, those clients who are most damaged and un-able to get beyond chronic feelings of anger, self-attack, disappointment, and rage are often unwilling to let others move on to other levels.

Given the historical self-help emphasis of many sexual abuse treatment programs, this may not be a popular perspective. We believe, nevertheless, it is a sound one. We view it as unwise for professionally trained therapists to abdicate their responsibility to assess accurately and thoroughly and to develop individualized treatment plans for their clients because of the pressures of self-help movements. If a therapist has nothing more to offer a client than a duplicate of what a self-help movement can offer, such a therapist should direct their clients to self-help groups, where they can get comparable services for free.

Some high-functioning individuals can partake of self-help approaches; obtain the support, education, and feedback that such approaches are best at offering; and proceed, without therapy or continued dependence on the self-help organization, to make effective changes. We are objecting, rather, to "therapy" that gives little more than the offerings of self-help movements or that suggests that clients who have been sexually abused are intrinsically unable to lead their lives without therapy or self-help movements. The model proposed here can accommodate the limited and purposeful use of self-help groups, although not in a random or primary fashion. It can also accommodate individuals who need little more than what self-help groups offer and individuals who need no therapy.

Couples and family therapy can occur congruently with the individual therapy model described here, although clearly in an auxiliary manner in serving to corroborate information or focus on limited goals of change within the system. These types of therapy tend to diffuse the intensity of the therapeutic style described here.

We suggest that therapists be deliberate and judicious and plan well in utilizing therapeutic modalities. This model assumes that individual therapy is central, with group, couples, or family components as auxiliary and selected for congruence with the individual therapy goals and style. Other models suggest different choices. If treatment plans are carefully and individually rendered and congruent, then a variety of viable and helpful approaches can be used to treat male sexual abuse victims and, sometimes, even the same client.

THEORETICAL IMPLICATIONS OF THIS MODEL

Having outlined a clinical model that draws on self-psychology, we now suggest some areas of theoretical synthesis between certain aspects of self-psychology and current understandings of sexual abuse, especially the effects of sexual abuse. We think this is important for a number of reasons. The field of childhood sexual abuse risks becoming a clinical backwater by its lack of integration with more general theoretical structures available in mental health. An example illustrates this point.

There have been some attempts to create a specific sexual abuse trauma syndrome. These efforts have generally not been successful nor accepted broadly, partly due to their lack of specificity. Most of these attempts utilize overinclusive symptom lists with an additional requirement of a historical factor of sexual abuse; this, however, does not change the lack of specificity in the symptoms.

Other attempts have involved the application of posttraumatic stress disorder (PTSD) to childhood sexual abuse. The concept of PTSD may have some merit, as it could bring conceptualization about the effects of childhood sexual abuse closer to mainstream conceptualizations; however, it appears this particular syndrome may be a poor candidate in relation to sexual abuse.

Although PTSD has been applied to a number of situations such as spouse battering (Walker, 1989), it is a concept developed on Vietnam-era veterans; to a certain extent, it still bears the marks of its relationship to that specific group. If the conceptualization of PTSD is generalized to capture more fully the experience of other groups, it may be useful. At the current time, it seems somewhat off-track with the experience of sexual abuse victims.

Finkelhor (1990b) criticizes the use of the PTSD diagnosis on a number of counts: It does not fully capture the experience of sexual abuse victims, it has a misplaced emphasis on the affective realm, and it ignores cognitive effects. A PTSD diagnosis incorrectly suggests that sexual abuse victims who do not have PTSD are somehow less traumatized. There have been some attempts (Conte & Schuerman, 1988) to structure symptoms presented by victims using symptom check lists. Although these approaches can be helpful in summarizing what is known, they are essentially atheoretical and simply rearrange or cluster the data.

A core problem in these conceptualizations is that they are not sufficiently psychological in their approach. The sexual abuse experience is not only central to these concepts, it predominates. Sexual abuse happens to individuals who have histories of other experiences, personality characteristics, cognitive styles, and important historical events that may or may not resonate with the sexual abuse experience. Put another way, most conceptualizations pay insufficient attention to the fact that the experience of sexual abuse is filtered through individuals who have other characteristics unrelated to the abuse.

Finkelhor and Browne (1986) suggest a conceptual model for under-standing abuse effects that effectively describes social environmental factors in abuse. Their model could be enriched by intrapsychic understandings of the abuse experience for victims, as much as the more intrapsychic ideas outlined here require understanding of social environmental factors to place the individual in context.

Wedding these two perspectives can provide a framework for understanding some anomalies in research on sexual abuse. For example, Finkelhor (1990b) discusses the fact that most studies on the impact of sexual abuse have found that varying percentages of victims are symptom free. These percentages generally run from 20% to 30% of abused children. Although some researchers have theorized that effects are delayed, there is no empirical support for this idea. Finkelhor concludes, "a final conjecture, and the one that seems the most plausible, is that the asymptomatic children are the ones who have suffered less serious abuse and have adequate psychological and social resources to cope with the stress of abuse" (p. 328).

Browne and Finkelhor (1986) note that asymptomatic children are abused for a shorter period of time, receive support from adults, come from well-functioning families, do not experience violence, and are not abused by a father figure. Such findings can serve as a bridge to developing theoretical explication and clinical integration of their meaning. We suggest that a developmental psychological perspective is necessary to round out a social environmental, abuse-centric perspective.

Theoreticians have not fully addressed the specific effects of sexual abuse. Sexually abused children have characteristics prior to the abuse, some of which may be conducive to symptomatology or psychological distress, and some of which may immunize against distress. A good theory about the effects of sexual abuse must differentiate specific effects of sexual abuse from factors prior to the abuse.

In addition to the theoretical need for such theory, there are pragmatic needs. In civil law, in which sexual abuse victims attempt to obtain financial compensation for damages received from the abuse situation, a crucial legal concept is that of proximate cause. Legal counsel for the victim must show to a reasonable degree of scientific certainty that not only do symptoms and areas of distress exist in the abused individual, but they were likely caused specifically by the abuse and not by other factors before, during, or after the abuse experience. A good theory, then, must be able to take into account preabuse historical factors, the specific nature of the abuse experience, and experiences after the abuse to create a model that can predict a range of different outcomes.

We offer in the remainder of this chapter some theoretical suggestions to that end, using the self-psychology perspective of Kohut. We outline relevant features of Kohut's theory, apply them to sexual abuse experiences, and test the theory on some current conundrums in the research on effects of sexual abuse. We offer this particular theory as an example of the more broad-ranging theoretical integration we believe needs to occur. Abuse-centric/sociological and intrapsychically oriented/psychological perspectives are both needed.

A Self-Psychology Perspective

Simply put, a narcissistic injury is a profound blow to one's self-esteem. For the majority of sexually abused children, sexual abuse is an experience in narcissistic injury. Sexual abuse is a wounding both by commission and omission. The abusive acts are damaging in a variety of ways (Finkelhor, 1990b; Tharinger, 1990); the failure of a perpetrating adult figure to respond in the best interests of the child and the typically confused or inadequate response from other adults to the abuse are damaging by what does not occur. The result of this neglect and devaluation is a loss, in many cases drastic, of self-esteem, initiative, and legitimate entitlement. The self is prone to fragmentation, enfeeblement, and disharmony.

Provided the child arrives at the point of sexual abuse not otherwise psychologically crippled or severely traumatized (e.g., from prolonged involvement with pathological parents or other toxic childhood experiences), the narcissistic injury (if it is brief) can be a temporary, albeit nontrivial, wound—a developmental challenge to be mastered. Because this wounding occurs relatively late in childhood compared to other critical developmental events, its effects are likely to be less damaging. As sexual abuse continues over time, has violent or other damaging features, or is associated with other varieties of abuse or neglect, its ability to damage increases.

The child who has been chronically narcissistically injured through-out childhood by events prior to and separate from those described here, however, reaches the abuse experience in a different and highly vulnerable state. To these victims, the narcissistic injuries of sexual abuse are met not as a developmental challenge to be surmounted but rather as another danger that threatens to shatter an already tenuous psychological constitution. These fragile children and youth make up a majority of the most severely disturbed casualties of sexual abuse, those for whom a resilient response is beyond their personal resources, and for whom the narcissistic injury of sexual abuse is a *coup de grace* leaving them emotionally debilitated. We theorize that these individuals make up most of those whose postabuse histories are characterized by the worst symptomatology.

Kohut (1971, 1977, 1984) writes extensively on narcissistic injury and develops an analytical psychotherapy for the healing of narcissistic injuries, or self-deficits. Although he writes generically of the narcissistic injuries in children as a function of unresponsive, unempathetic, and unavailable parents, his theoretical model can be applied, if not exactly then heuristically, to the narcissistic injuries of sexually abused children and youth.

This discussion simplifies Kohut's theory of self-psychology, and the theory's application to the narcissistic injuries of sexual abuse is inexact. We apply Kohut's concepts to a later developmental period than that on which he developed his theory. Nonetheless, we believe these ideas can help create a better understanding of the complex effects of sexual abuse on a full range of children and youth.

Self-Psychology Applied to Sexual Abuse

From a self-psychology perspective, sexual abuse is seen as a narcissistic injury that can create distortions ranging from mild to severe in the sense of self. The degree of narcissistic injury is likely to be a function of both characteristics of the abuse and characteristics of the abused child. The length of time the abuse took place, the degree of violence, the sadism of the abuse, and the amount of violation of trust and personal boundaries are all likely to be important factors that will predict a range of severity, from mild to devastating, of the specific effects of the abuse experience.

There is also a range of postabuse effects. These are related to the response of family and other adults to the abuse experience, psychotherapy to remediate the abuse experience, and positive or adverse experiences with the child welfare system and the courts. These also range over a broad continuum. The cumulative effect of the postabuse experiences may eventually be sufficient to reverse the negative effects of the abuse, if the abuse is mild enough and the postabuse experience is positive enough. Whether or not this desirable state of affairs is common, it is possible.

Our model can take into account a third factor, the preabuse history. As a number of research studies have shown, children who are abused are not a random group. Rather, children who come from dysfunctional families and who have experienced other and earlier narcissistic injuries are overrepresented in the group of children who become sexually abused. We are not suggesting that all sexually abused children have had previously narcissistic injury. We are suggesting some sexual abuse perpetrators, usually the more planning, chronic and cunning ones, ascertain the vulnerability of their intended victims and choose accordingly.

Such individuals have relatively well-developed abilities to determine which children are likely to be vulnerable based on the degree to which they have been narcissistically injured. Other groups of offenders who may be more situational, less planful, and more clumsy may select previously narcissistically injured children less effectively or may select intended victims in a random manner with no attempt to pick the more vulnerable victims.

Therefore, depending on perpetrator characteristics, a range of intended victims is chosen, from most damaged to nondamaged. The net effect of the choices of the different perpetrator types, however, is that children who are narcissistically injured are overrepresented among children who are sexually abused.

Further, this theory predicts that preabuse history is an important, but not sole, predictor of the effects of the abuse. In other words, given a predictable level of abuse, preabuse history produces a range of effects from mild to severe. This can occasionally be seen in situations of a repetitive, fixated sexual perpetrator with multiple victims in which the perpetrator performs essentially the same acts in the same manner with a variety of victims. Because the specifics of the abuse in this situation are more or less constant, preabuse history is the most precise predictor of the ultimate outcome and gives the widest range of outcome predictions.

When sexual abuse cases are summed together, however, it is difficult to pick out the preabuse, postabuse, or abuse factors as a group because of their high variability within each category. It is for this reason that much of the research literature is so hard to interpret. Other than situations of repetitive, fixated offenders with multiple victims (providing consistency in the abuse effects) or a sexual abuse advocacy system in a particular locale that provides a comprehensive set of services in a predictable fashion to abuse victims (providing consistency in the postabuse effects), preabuse, postabuse, and abuse history vary widely in most situations. This results in masking differential effects.

Application of This Perspective to Some Conundrums

This theory can also be helpful in explaining certain anomalies in the literature. For example, Finkelhor (1984) and Johnson and Shrier (1985) found that sexually abused males engage in more homosexual behavior than nonsexually abused males. This effect is considerable. In the Finkelhor study, there is a four times greater likelihood of homosexual activity; in the Johnson and Shrier study, males who were sexually abused identified themselves as homosexual seven times more often and bisexual six times more often than the non–sexually abused control group. This has led some researchers to speculate about the validity of the stereotype that sexual abuse causes homosexuality.

However, an understanding of the literature on homosexuality contradicts this. Although the causes of different sexual orientations remain unclear, it is clear that whatever its causes, sexual orientation appears to be set in place by early childhood, definitely before latency. Most sexual abuse occurs in latency or after. This suggests that sexual abuse is not causative of homosexuality; rather, that sexual orientation is likely to have been in place prior to most instances of abuse.

But a conundrum remains. What then can explain these findings? This conceptualization of narcissistic injury has been applied to the coming-out and identity development experiences of gay men and lesbians (Gonsiorek & Rudolph, 1991). Using a similar framework to the one presented here, Gonsiorek and Rudolph suggest that the disparagement of homosexuality extant in the culture and its internalization in children who eventually become gay, bisexual, or lesbian produces a kind of narcissistic injury, occurring later than most and therefore generally less severe, but that poses certain developmental challenges that are played out during the coming-out process of gay men and lesbians.

Returning to the data of Finkelhor (1984) and Johnson and Shrier (1985), the following explanatory mechanism can be derived. A class of sexual abuse perpetrators more or less carefully selects children who are most vulnerable. In the rubric described here, that is likely to mean children with the greatest degree of narcissistic injury. It is already clear from the literature that children from dysfunctional families, with alcoholic parents, and the like are overrepresented among children who become sexually abused; that is, they are selected by certain sexual abuse perpetrators. We suggest that if the disparagement of same-sex feelings in the culture produces a kind of narcissistic injury for youth who become gay, lesbian, or bisexual, then certain sexual abuse perpetrators can read this as a vulnerability and select pregay youth as victims. In other words, perpetrators who operate in this manner consistently select for vulnerability no matter what its cause, whether toxic families or the damaging effects of societal bigotry.

Earlier chapters of this book speak of the need for information on child sexual abuse to work effectively across the ranges of diversity. As Wyatt (1990) notes, "Although initial reactions to sexual abuse may not reveal ethnic differences especially when black-white comparisons are made, there may be some aspects of ethnic minority children's lives that affect long term adjustment to these traumatic experiences and prevalence rates as well" (p. 338).

Wyatt (1990) describes how racism has particular effects on black children. She recounts the stereotypes of many researchers that black children are more sexual, and notes that black children experience the effects of racial discrimination as much as their parents in their social environments and schools. Furthermore, racial and ethnic minority children observe the disempowerment of their parents and as a result have the normative idealization of parents disappointed. Although Wyatt does not conceptualize her descriptions in a self-psychology framework, much of her discussion can be reconceptualized in this manner. Namely, racial and ethnic minority children endure narcissistic injuries in childhood and later as they begin to perceive and experience the effects of racism and ensuing economic oppression.

This conceptualization is akin to the one by Gonsiorek and Rudolph (1991) on gay and lesbian youth as it posits narcissistic injuries that occur later in the developmental sequence. The effect may be to increase the vulnerability of those racial and ethnic minority children to those sexual perpetrators who seek signs of such vulnerability in their victims. More importantly, this conceptualization can serve as a vehicle to understand interactions between the effects of external societal bigotry, preexisting personality variables, and sexual abuse.

This model can also serve as a guide to treatment. Once a careful assessment is made of the injuries endured at the three levels (preabuse, postabuse, and during abuse), then a treatment plan can be made accordingly. For example, treatment of an adolescent sexual abuse victim who has suffered significant narcissistic damage prior to the sexual abuse is likely to be more long term than an adolescent victim whose preabuse experiences were benign.

The effects of these three levels of narcissistic injury are not simply additive. For example, one would theoretically expect that the experience of narcissistic injury and toxic parenting prior to sexual abuse experiences might produce a general deficit in coping skills and sense of self. An adolescent with such a history would have not only quantitatively more damage but also an impairment of coping abilities that makes specific effects of sexual abuse more overwhelming than they might otherwise be. Further, a damaging family might be more likely to respond poorly in the postabuse period and be less able and thoughtful about mobilizing appropriate resources for the victim. In reality, the effects are more complex than an additive model can accommodate.

Similarly, an adolescent coming from a high functioning family who experiences abuse from a randomly selecting impulsive perpetrator might have a positive outcome, particularly if this high functioning family is adept at mobilizing quality resources in the post-abuse period.

To return to the legal considerations noted earlier, although the legal system would like to make relatively simple distinctions between the damage caused before and during the abuse, these effects are not so simple. However, the model based on self-psychology outlined here does allow a framework for beginning to differentiate damages from causes. It might also serve as a vehicle to educate the courts that simple either/or determination of percentages of damages is not always psychologically meaningful or sensible.

SUMMARY

The model presented in this chapter is client driven, not theory or politically driven. The model is informed by theory specific to sexual abuse but is not driven by it. This model can accommodate variation along gender, racial, ethnic, sexual orientation, class and other lines. To utilize this model effectively, careful assessment and history taking are crucial. The treatment recommendations that derive from this model have a high probability of being individually tailored. This model taps into a in-more depth psychological approach that can function as a complement to more abuse-centric, sociological perspectives.

We appreciate that our suggestion of preabuse history as an equal partner in understanding abuse effects runs counter to current theory and practice in the field. We anticipate that this perspective will be misconstrued by some as "blaming the victim." We reject this criticism.

Our view is that abuse-centric perspectives that posit that sexual abuse is reliably a more powerful event in the lives of victims than any, or even all, other events in the individual's life are thoroughly implausible. There is no evidence to warrant subsuming all other events in an individual's developmental history to these relatively late-occurring events. In fact, there is no known developmental, psychological, or behavioral event as powerfully predictive of later functioning and psychological structure as sexual abuse is alleged to be by some abuse-centric theoreticians and practitioners. Further, such an atomized, fragmented view of sexual abuse victims is not conducive to a therapeutic process of rendering the person whole again.

Such abuse-centric perspectives, because of their psychological barrenness, produce little direction for clinical treatment.

The horror of sexual abuse is precisely that it "gets under the skin" psychologically and can elicit powerful interactions with preexisting issues in the victim. Clinical theory and practice have the obligation to grapple with these complex issues.

PART II

Family Systems Therapy for Adolescent Male Sex Offenders

WALTER H. BERA

5

Clinical Review of
Adolescent Male Sex Offenders

THIS CHAPTER BRIEFLY REVIEWS the common clinical issues observed in adolescent sex offenders, focusing on the prevalence of family issues reported in the literature. Adolescent sex offenders are defined and demonstrated to account for a significant percentage of sex crimes. Family issues are theorized by many clinicians as a major factor in adolescent sex offender development. A general model of the adolescent sex offender etiology is presented in an attempt to organize the clinical literature in a logical manner. The chapter ends with the explication of a descriptive adolescent offender typology that connects the individual, victim, and family factors reviewed.

This chapter should be read in the context of the historical and background information on sexual abuse and critique of certain models provided in chapter 2. Chapter 3, on adolescent sexual abuse victims, is also useful with regard to a number of clinical issues shared by both populations.

Definitions of Juvenile Sex Offenders

Sexual abuse can include all forms of forced, tricked, or manipulated sexual contact. Such behaviors include sexual intercourse, cunnilingus, fellatio, anal intercourse, and digital or other intrusions into the victim's orifices. They can also include the intentional touching of

113

a victim's private parts by the offender. There are also "nontouch" forms of sexual abuse such as obscene phone calls, messages or drawings, sexual exposure, voyeurism, and fetish-associated burglary, such as stealing female underwear.

A juvenile sex offender can be defined as a youth from puberty to the age of majority who has committed one or more of the above-mentioned acts (Ryan, 1986). The clinical literature on this population uses the terms *juvenile, teenage,* and *adolescent* interchangeably. Recently, preteen sexual perpetrators have been identified and are sometimes included in references to "juvenile sex offenders." These younger offenders are not, however, the focus of this chapter or book.

Groth and Loredo (1981) suggest criteria for defining the juvenile sex offender. They include the age relationship and social relationship between the persons involved, the type of sexual activity, and the types of coercion used in the offense.

Case Example

Larry is a 13-year-old who had been reported for "playing doctor" with a 5-year-old neighbor girl he had been baby-sitting. On investigation, it was discovered that the doctor game involved fondling and oral sex. It was ascertained from interviews with the girl that the events had begun 5 months previously, when Larry began baby-sitting. She reported that the abuse occurred on almost every one of Larry's bi-weekly baby-sitting visits. Larry told the girl not to tell anyone, because these were "secret examinations" and they would both get in trouble. He always rewarded her for being a good "patient" by playing whatever other games she wanted and giving her a lollipop—just like the real doctor.

Juvenile sexual abuse is legally defined by the statutes of the state in which the abuse occurs. These codes typically define a juvenile offender as someone who is below the age of majority, usually age 18, who has committed a sexual offense. The sexual offense statutes are variously titled: criminal sexual conduct (e.g., rape, child molestation), intrafamilial sexual abuse (e.g., incest), lewd and lascivious communication (e.g., obscene phone calls).

A contact-type sexual offense is often defined by criteria such as a power differential between offender and victim (e.g., age difference, greater physical size or mental capacity, position of authority), sexual contact between family members, or use of force, intimidation, or trickery to manipulate a victim to perform a sexual act to which he or she would not otherwise consent. Noncontact sex crimes are legally defined under a variety of statutes, some of which may not be "sex" related (e.g., fetish burglary may be tried as a burglary charge, or window peeping as a trespassing charge).

Increased Awareness of Adolescent Sex Offenders

Increased reporting of sexual abuse has led to a significant increase in the number of sex offenders arrested and adjudicated. The U.S. Department of Justice (1993) reports a number of important statistics. In 1992, 97,761 rapes were reported in the United States, with 51.5% cleared by arrests. There were 83,997 other sex crimes, such as child molestation, reported. From 1988 to 1992, the number of rape arrests increased 4.9%, and arrests for other sex crimes increased 9.5%. Of the 1991 U.S. prison population, 3.5% were incarcerated for rape and 5.9% were incarcerated for other sex crimes.

The percentage of people imprisoned for sex crimes is high in certain states. For example, the Minnesota Department of Corrections (1993) shows that sex offenses make up the leading index crime, accounting for 21% of the prison population. The U.S. Department of Justice (1993) shows that sex offenders are among the highest recidivists of all criminal types.

Simple imprisonment has not been an effective deterrent, with recidivism rates for sexual offenders averaging 19.5% and ranging from 6% to 35% in one survey of 11 studies (Finkelhor, 1986). As a result, prison-based programs have been developed across the country to treat sex offenders and are showing some success (Knopp, 1984). Prentky (1989) makes a case for treatment as an ultimate cost reduction by estimating the expense of investigating one offense and treating one victim at about $80,000. Nevertheless, the cost of incarceration and treatment for such a large population of inmates is substantial, and new approaches for early intervention are clearly indicated.

This awareness of the need for early intervention has led concerned clinicians and researchers to focus attention on the juvenile sex offender. Previously, juvenile sexual misconduct was minimized or ignored by supervising adults as naive experimentation or clumsy exploration. As a result, sexual offenses committed by juveniles were severely underreported (Knopp, 1985).

That has been changing. U.S. Department of Justice (1993) juvenile arrest statistics show a 17% increase in U.S. forcible rape arrests and a 28% increase in other sex offense arrests (e.g., child molestation) from 1988 to 1992. In 1992, 5,369 forcible rape arrests and 16,632 other sex arrests were reported for juveniles. Juveniles make up 16% of all arrested rapists and 19% of those arrested for other sex crimes.

Child sexual abuse reports demonstrate that more than 50% of the molestation of boys and 15% to 20% or more of the sexual abuse of girls is perpetrated by adolescents (Rogers & Terry, 1984; Showers, Farber, Joseph, Oshins, & Johnson, 1983). Based on surveys of victims, 20% to 30% of all rapes and 30% to 56% of all cases of child molestation can be attributed to adolescent sex offenders (Brown, Hill, & Panesis, 1984; Deisher et al., 1982; Fehrenbach et al., 1986).

The importance of intervening with the juvenile sex offender is demonstrated in a study by Abel, Rouleau, and Cunningham-Rathner (1986) in which adult sex offenders reported an average of 380 sexual crimes. On average, adolescents currently being evaluated report substantially fewer victims. Several studies (Abel et al., 1986; Gebhard, Gagnon, Pomeroy, & Christenson, 1965; Smith, 1984) report that approximately 50% of all adult sex offenders admit that their first sexual offense occurred during adolescence.

Knopp (1985) suggests the following advantages of early interventions with juveniles:

1. Deviant patterns are less deeply ingrained and are therefore easier to disrupt.
2. Youth are still experimenting with a variety of patterns of sexual satisfaction that offer alternatives to consistent deviant patterns.
3. Distorted thinking patterns are less deeply entrenched and can be redirected.
4. Youth are good candidates for learning new and acceptable social skills.

5. Public safety is improved by preventing further victimization.
6. Fiscal economy is enhanced.

As a result of the increased awareness of adolescent sexual offenses, there are now more than 700 specialized juvenile sex offender treatment programs in the U.S.; approximately 20 were identified in 1982 (Knopp, 1985; Knopp, Freeman-Longo, & Stevenson, 1992).

Adolescent Developmental Issues

The clinical understanding of juvenile offenders can be complicated by the fact that normal adolescence is often a stressful time in the development of sexuality (Leaman, 1980). Puberty usually begins around age 11 in boys and girls, and major physiological changes are usually completed by the late teens. Production of sperm begins. Boys often experience "wet dreams," which may be psychologically disturbing. During these years, body configuration changes and an increase in hormone production arouses strong sexual feelings in adolescents. Sexually oriented dreams and fantasies may be frequent and intrusive. Masturbation may be an activity that the adolescent views as shameful.

Adolescents often begin to assume rigid gender roles—roles that are strongly influenced by their peers and society (Berger, 1974). Opposite-sex friendships, dating, romantic attachments, and sexual experimentation become increasingly important. Normal adolescent conflicts over independence and separation from the family may also be expressed in a sexual mode. Teenagers may use sexual relationships to put distance between themselves and their families.

There is evidence with regard to sexual abuse, adolescent pregnancy, abortion, and sexually transmitted diseases to indicate that teenagers frequently become involved in sexual activity without adequate information about birth control, sexual relations, and other sex-related concerns. Parents report that they provide little or no information on sexuality and sexual abuse—often because they did not receive such information themselves as adolescents. This reflects society's general erotophobia or discomfort with sexual issues, especially regarding teenagers. When teenagers are successful in achieving developmental milestones, they are able to enter young adulthood with a secure self-image and feelings of self-worth. A failure of healthy adolescent maturation is the development of sexually victimizing behavior (Strong & DeVault, 1992).

HISTORICAL OVERVIEW OF THE ADOLESCENT SEX OFFENDER

The majority of studies and publications concerning sex offenders pertain to adults. Adolescent sex offenders have received less empirical study; however, a growing body of literature does exist and is worthy of review for the practitioner or researcher who is serious about becoming acquainted with this arena of sexual deviancy. Due to limitations of space, a lengthy review is not attempted here. Instead, a brief historical review is designed as an introduction to this literature base. The reader is encouraged to pursue further exploration using the sources cited here as well as the bibliographies of these sources.

In the earliest references to adolescent sexual deviance, criminally victimizing behaviors are not distinguished from "sexual misbehavior," which includes status offenses or socially unacceptable behavior. These early studies reflect the cultural erotophobia and homophobia discussed in chapter 2. For example, in 1943, Doshay studied 256 juvenile sex offenders treated in New York Court Clinic and found little recidivism as adults. However, many of the referral problems of his sample were behaviors that adults at that time believed were problematic for youth (such as a peer-age consenting sexual contact) but would not be termed *offenses* or *abusive* today. Markey (1950) examined 25 boys and 25 girls referred to a juvenile court for "immorality." The age range was 13 to 17, with an average age of 15.2. From extensive testing and interviews, he concludes that sexual symptoms are not in themselves evidence of morbid sexual development but represent poor personality integration. He describes family trauma as the primary source of sexual maladjustment. Maclay (1960) describes 29 boys who committed sexual misdemeanors. He concludes that boys who indulge in sexual delinquencies come from homes that fail to give them adequate emotional support.

Research began to gain greater specificity in the late 1960s and 1970s. Shoor, Speed, and Bartelt (1966) describe 80 adolescent child molesters. They conclude that such offenders are loners, have minimal social peer group activities with boys or girls, and prefer playing with younger children; their main work experience is baby-sitting younger children. They typically have little sex education, are socially and sexually immature, and have distorted family relations and personality patterns.

In one of the first studies to report on behavior clearly defined as illegal and abusive, Groth and Loredo (1981) studied 26 male offenders between the ages of 15 and 17. Fourteen of these boys were convicted of rape and 12 of child assault. A modal description of the convicted adolescent offenders in this study is a 16-year-old boy of average intelligence. He usually carried out his assault alone, and the victim was usually a female a year younger than he. Weapons were used in about one third of the offenses. Drugs and alcohol played a minor role. About three fourths of the offenders had committed a previous offense. The average educational level was 8th to 9th grade.

The 1980s saw a huge increase in the number of programs for adolescent sex offenders. The decade began with a handful of known adolescent sex offender treatment programs, a number that grew to more than 700 in 1992 (Knopp et al., 1992). The quantity and quality of the clinical literature increased as well. Davis and Leitenberg's (1987) review of this literature highlights some consistent findings:

1. Adolescents account for a large share of the sex offenses committed in the United States, with the most conservative estimates being about 20% of all cases.
2. Nearly two thirds of victims are younger children, with the vast majority being acquaintances or relatives of the offender.
3. In general, victims are more frequently female than male, with the proportion of female victims lower in cases of child sexual abuse and greater in cases of noncontact offenses such as exhibitionism.
4. More than 95% of reported adolescent offenders are male. (Note that the in-depth study of female sex offenders only began at the end of the 1980s—Mathews et al., 1989.)
5. Adolescent sex offenders more frequently present a history of being physically abused and probably sexually abused when compared with other groups of adolescents,.
6. Adolescent sex offenders, compared to other delinquent youth, have similar current and past signs of behavioral and school disturbances.

7. Adolescent sex offenders claim to have had more sexual experiences, including consenting ones, than comparison groups of adolescents.

8. Preliminary relapse statistics and uncontrolled treatment outcome statistics are encouraging, with typical rates of less than 10%.

9. The research on adolescent sex offenders, behavior, and victims is still in an early stage. Studies involving matched comparison groups are lacking.

The Adolescent Victim/Offender

For some time, the "sex abuse victim turned sex offender" theory of sex offender etiology enjoyed widespread popularity, perhaps because of its simplistic, intuitive appeal. However, the rates of offenders with sexual victimization backgrounds are not high enough to justify this as the only etiology, and in cases when the offender is a former victim, it is probably not a complete explanation (Becker & Kaplan, 1988; O'Brien, 1989). Physical and emotional abuse are also common in the lives of young sexual perpetrators but have not been adequately reported. Such abuse may be a significant contributor to sexual abuse. Furthermore, there are no good studies on the percentage of victims who become offenders, though it is clear that most do not. Nevertheless, the study of the victim/offender adolescent is important for both its treatment and its prevention implications.

Reported rates of sexual victimization among adolescent sex offenders vary greatly. Brannon, Larson, and Doggett (1989) reviewed the incidence of sexual abuse among 63 incarcerated male juvenile offenders. The average age was 16.1 and only 11 were officially charged with a sexually related offense. Seventy percent reported sexual abuse; females accounted for 58% of the perpetrators and males for 42%. The reported abuse included fondling, intercourse, fellatio, and sodomy, with some of the abuse being brutal. Petrovich and Templer (1984) found that of 83 adult rapists studied, 59% were abused by a female prior to age 16.

Fehrenbach et al. (1986) found a 19% prior sexual victimization rate among the sex offenders they studied. The authors suggest this is an underestimate because it is the result of the intake interview, and admission of abuse increases as trust grows in therapy. Gomes-Schwartz, Horowitz, and Carderelli (1990) found a 38% victimization rate among sexual offenders, whereas Becker et al. (1986) found a 23% victimization rate. O'Brien (1989), in a study of 170 adolescent offenders, found a 37% rate, with approximately one third reporting victimization by a female.

Allen (1991) suggests that barriers to recognizing child sexual abuse by women are the result of the cultural norms and deep-seated beliefs held by professionals and society in general. These barriers include overestimating the strength of the incest taboo in women, overextending feminist explanations of child sexual abuse, and over-generalizing the lack of reports of child sexual abuse by women.

Gilbert (1989) reviewed the limited clinical literature on sexual abuse among siblings. Sister-brother incest is the most reported form of sibling sexual abuse and typically occurs in dysfunctional families in which parents are physically or emotionally unavailable. Many of these homes are highly sexualized (e.g., children witness adults engaging in sexual intercourse).

These statistics indicate that a significant percentage, and even the majority, of perpetrators were female, but only recently have researchers begun to study female perpetrator populations (Mathews, 1987; Mathews et al., 1989; McCarty, 1986).

In O'Brien's 1989 study, although 37% of adolescent offenders reported direct sexual victimization, the highest rates are among incest offenders (42%). Extrafamilial child molesters or those who molest children who are not in the family, as in a baby-sitting or playground situation (40%), report victimization as a child, as do non-child molesters, such as the acquaintance rapist, exposer, and window peepers (29%). O'Brien also found that adolescent incest offenders tend to come from families judged much more severely disturbed than other offender types as determined by a clinician's rating.

Significant Family Systems Issues

Many clinicians and researchers working with juvenile sexual offenders see dysfunctional family systems as significant in the etiology or maintenance of sexual misconduct. Chaotic family systems with role confusion are common. Father-son relationships in particular are strained or nonexistent.

When reviewing the literature on dysfunctional family dynamics associated with many juvenile perpetrators, the danger of backward causality and inappropriate overgeneralization from captive clinical, residential, or prison populations must be kept in mind—there is a need for research from general population samples and nondysfunctional family samples or controls. The following overview is presented as an aid for clinical mapping of juvenile offenders and their families.

Knopp (1982) surveyed nine model treatment programs for adolescent sex offenders. Based on therapist observations, dysfunctional or chaotic family systems often played a significant role in contributing to the offender's pathology, fathers were emotionally and physically distant, and father/son relationships were inadequate. Family resistance to acknowledging sexual victimization and exploitation, minimization of the significance of the child's offenses, and blaming the victim were common.

Awad, Saunders, and Lavene (1979) discovered significant family issues in the 24 male juvenile sexual offenders compared to 24 other delinquents matched for age and social class. Family instability, psychiatric disturbances, and unsatisfactory parent-child relationships were common characteristics in the sex offenders. Seventy-nine percent of the sexual offenders experienced long-term separations from at least one parent. Clinical ratings of the juveniles' relationships with their families reported that 36% of the mothers and 63% of the fathers were seen as rejecting, and 26% of the mothers and 50% of the fathers were seen as emotionally detached.

Burgess and Holmstrom (1975) and DeFrances (1969) report that at least 50% and possibly as many as 80% of all child victims are sexually abused by people known to them. Parents, stepparents, brothers, sisters, or other relatives are responsible for 30% to 50% of all sexual abuse cases reported. These researchers conclude that, because of a child's trusting relationship with the offender, the use of physical force is rarely necessary to engage a child in sexual activity. Such cooperation can be obtained through the offender's position of dominance, a bribe or reward, a threat of physical violence, or other pressure or persuasion.

DeFrances (1969) estimates that poor supervision by parents and failure to set proper controls for a child or adolescent's behavior is a contributing factor in over 70% of all cases of sexual abuse, whether perpetrated by adolescents or adults. One third of these families have a history of a prior sexual offense involving a family member. Eleven percent of the mothers stated they had been child victims themselves. DeFrances concludes that for an adolescent growing up in such families, the sexual abuse behavior in which he or she engages may be an attempt to fulfill needs that are normally met in other ways; for example, the abuse may be motivated by a need for love, affection, or attention that the adolescent cannot find in family relationships. Conversely, a need to defy a parental figure, express anger about a chaotic home life, or act out sexual conflicts may lead an adolescent to become sexually exploitative.

A parent's difficulties with past personal issues of sexual abuse is also associated with teen incest perpetrators. For example, in a study conducted by Kaplan, Becker, and Martinez (1990), mothers of adolescent incest perpetrators were compared with mothers of nonincest perpetrators. Significantly more of the incest group mothers reported a history of physical and sexual abuse, sexual dysfunction, and prior psychotherapy.

Prentky and Cerce (1989) studied 81 adult sex offenders in an attempt to determine the severity of both sexual and nonsexual aggression. They examined four areas of developmental pathology during childhood and adolescence: caregiver instability, institutional history, sexual abuse, and physical abuse. They found that the severity of sexual aggression is predicted by caregiver instability and sexual abuse; however, the severity of nonsexual aggression is predicted by institutional history and physical abuse. People who experience frequent changes in caregivers and grow up in sexually deviant or abusive contexts are more likely to become sexually aggressive. Conversely, those who spend long periods of time in institutions, frequently change institutions, and experience physical abuse and neglect in childhood are likely to become nonsexually aggressive.

To summarize, experts on juvenile sex offenders state:

The family and environment are essential influences in the development of sexuality and, therefore, family trauma, physical and sexual abuse, neglect, scapegoating, undefined family relations, and exposure to sexually traumatic material in the environment may contribute to the development of sexually offending behavior. (National Task Force on Juvenile Sexual Offending, 1993, p. 31)

A MODEL OF THE ETIOLOGY AND MAINTENANCE OF ADOLESCENT SEX OFFENDERS

Becker and Kaplan (1988) note that, at the present time, there is no empirically validated model that explains the development of deviant adolescent sexual behavior.

This section presents a model of the etiology and maintenance of the adolescent sex offender (see Figure 5.1). This model, the etiology and maintenance of adolescent sex offenders (EMASO) model, shares elements of adolescent and adult sex offender models.

O'Brien (1986) develops the general schema for laying out social factors, individual factors, and the abuse cycle related to adolescent sex offenders that were adopted for the EMASO model. In his four factor model, Finkelhor (1986) suggests that the offender must overcome internal inhibitors and victim resistance for child abuse to occur. These notions are extended to victims of all ages. Ryan, Lane, Davis, and Isaac (1987) inspired the abuse cycle paradigm.

The EMASO model attempts to organize in a logical manner the many social, family, individual, and situational factors suggested in the literature. These factors contribute to adolescent sexual offender development and maintenance of the abuse behavior. As such, the EMASO model summarizes historical and current factors in abuse behavior.

The model is based on clinical and research data and designed to be a conceptual tool for organizing assessment and treatment issues. The clinical use of the EMASO model is presented in chapter 6. Caution is needed in applying the model because, like other models, it is not empirically validated.

The following sections define each element of the model.

Social Factors

Factors pertaining to society and its organization include gender stereotyping of male and female roles and relationships, values of

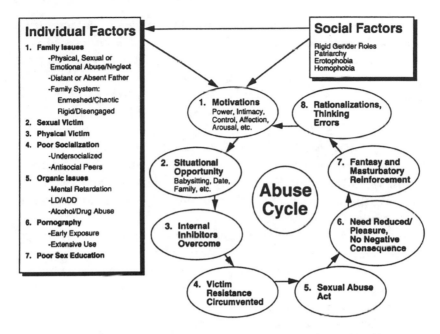

Figure 5.1. Etiology and Maintenance of Adolescent Sex Offenders
SOURCE: Adapted from O'Brien (1986).

patriarchy, homophobia, and erotophobia. Such social attitudes may set the social or cultural context in which sexual abuse behavior develops (Finkelhor, 1986). (See chapter 1 for discussion of these factors.)

These factors contribute to the development and maintenance of the individual factors and offender abuse cycle.

Individual Factors

Following is a list factors, some of which contribute to an individual's development of offender behavior and contribute to or help maintain the abuse cycle.

Family Issues

Family issues include physically, sexually, or emotionally abusive parenting, emotional abuse/neglect, and a distant or absent father (Steele, 1986). Smith (1984) reports that in his sample of juvenile sex offenders, 41% experienced intrafamilial violence or neglect during childhood, compared to only 15% of the non-sex-offender sample.

Family systems can appear as "enmeshed and chaotic" when poor emotional boundaries, chaotic role boundaries, or reversals exist among members. Such a family system tends to be in the backgrounds of people who commit incest and child molesters (Bera, 1985; Olson, Sprenkle, & Russell, 1979; Trepper & Sprenkle, 1988). Another pattern is the "rigidly disengaged" family system, where there are very rigid role boundaries between members and members are emotionally distant. This family system is more often associated with sexually aggressive, sexually compulsive, and disturbed impulsive behavior (Bera, 1985).

Other forms of family dysfunction seen with some adolescent sex offenders are homes where the adolescent has witnessed violence, such as husband/wife battery, or abuse among siblings of a physical or sexual nature (Longo, 1982). Such a history of witnessing violence is associated with violent behavior in the juvenile (Smith, 1988).

Lewis, Shankok, and Pincus (1979) studied extremely violent and less violent incarcerated boys. In addition to a higher reported history of physical abuse, 79% of the more violent children had witnessed extreme violence directed at others, usually in the home, compared with 20% of the less violent children.

Marshall, Hudson, and Hodkinson (1993) argue that such troubled familial history, particularly the failure of the parents to ensure secure attachment bonds between them and their children during infancy and childhood, creates developmental issues for those who will become sex offenders. Secure attachments provide children with an affectionate and empathic view of others that instills the skills, desire, and confidence to achieve intimacy with peers in adolescence. The failure to establish secure attachments results in problematic relationships that can lead to sexual misconduct.

Although further research is needed to confirm that aspects of the family environment differ for juvenile sex offenders as compared to other juvenile populations, the question remains how this contributes to a juvenile becoming sexually abusive. Davis and Leitenberg (1987) offer some possible explanations. For example, when a family tolerates physical abuse and neglect, the adolescent may learn this as acceptable behavior, may seek revenge on substitute targets, may offend to restore self-esteem, and may socialize with and then sexualize relationships with much younger children. Sex is then used as an expression of power, anger, and control.

Sexual Victim

Experiencing sexual victimization is reported in a significant percentage of adolescent sex offenders (Groth & Birnbaum, 1979; Ryan & Lane, 1991). As previously noted, it is not a complete explanation for perpetrator development.

Physical Victim

The experience of being physically abused may lead to physical aggression that, at times, is acted out in a sexual manner (Lane & Zamora, 1985).

Poor Socialization

Membership in a delinquent peer group may lead to becoming a sexually aggressive or a peer-group-influenced type sex offender. Fehrenbach et al. (1986) show that 65% of adolescent sex offenders evidence serious social isolation. Davis and Leitenberg (1987) reviewed the literature on juvenile sex offenders and found consistent reports that these perpetrators have little skills establishing and maintaining close friendships. Undersocialized adolescents may gravitate toward younger children, providing opportunities for child molestation or incest (Bera, 1985; Groth & Birnbaum, 1978).

Organic Issues

Attention deficit disorder, mental retardation, or alcohol/drug abuse contributes to sexual acting out when the individual overcomes the normal inhibitory mechanism or judgment for sexual impulses (Haaven, Little, & Petre-Miller, 1990; Lightfoot & Barbaree, 1993; Stermac & Sheridan, 1993). These issues have an organic or psychophysical impact on the adolescent.

Pornography

For a young adolescent who is sexually naive and lacks a clear and comprehensive knowledge of sexuality versus sexual abuse issues, exposure to pornography may lead to mimicking the behavior seen in the pictures. For others who have extensive exposure to pornography, it may act as a disinhibitor, rehearsal, or rationale to sexually aggress. (See Rosenberg, 1990, and Kutchinsky, 1991, for extensive inquiries on pornography and sexual aggression from varied perspectives.)

It has been clinically observed that when asked where he got the idea to commit the abusive act, a juvenile may mention having been exposed to explicit or pornographic material through magazines, cable TV, or videotapes. At other times he will say that peers had talked about sexual behaviors in very graphic and intriguing ways.

Poor Sex Education

Some adolescents may be vulnerable to abusive "experiments" with sexual behavior due to a combination of inadequate sex education, nonawareness of sexual abuse and its effects, cultural erotophobia, and the onset of hormonal changes in adolescence that increase normal sexual drives (Becker & Kaplan, 1988; Goldman & Goldman, 1982).

The Abuse Cycle

The social factors and individual factors reviewed above can begin a cycle of events that leads to the initiation and repetition of sexually abusive behavior (Lane, 1991). The cycle of behavior often occurs in the following stages.

Motivations

As a result of learned social attitudes and the predisposing factors in an individual's history, a number of motivations may develop such as the need for intimacy, affection, power, control, affiliation, or arousal. The adolescent may attempt to fill this void through victimizing sexual behavior (Lane & Zamora, 1985; O'Brien, 1983).

Situational Opportunity

An opportunity can arise where an adolescent has access to a vulnerable and available potential sexual victim. In these situations, the objectification of the victim is supported by the individual's social attitudes and individual history. A baby-sitting situation can be the site for the first incident of child molestation. A dating situation can be the site for acquaintance rape. After repeated success at perpetration, the offender may plan to put himself or herself in situations where abuse opportunities exist (Ryan et al., 1987).

Internal Inhibitors Overcome

The offender must overcome or rationalize internal deterrents to begin to offend sexually. Various "thinking errors," minimizations, or excuses can act as disinhibitors (Finkelhor, 1986; Yochelson & Samenow, 1977). Failure to predict or to hold oneself accountable for a negative impact on the victim results in a lack of empathy.

Victim Resistance Circumvented

The offender can "groom" the victim by winning a position of trust or authority in a child molestation or acquaintance rape (Finkelhor, 1986). In window peeping, the victim may not know the abuse is occurring. Shock, surprise, or threat overcome the victim in exhibitionism and stranger rape. Coercion may be covert to achieve compliance, or may be excessive and violent.

Sexual Abuse Act

A sexual perpetration occurs with a child, peer, or adult.

Need Reduction/Physiological Pleasure and No Negative Consequence

As a result of the sexual misconduct, the adolescent can experience a feeling of psychological need reduction and physiological pleasure. If there are no negative consequences such as an abuse report, arrest, or confrontation, the experience may become the basis for continued rehearsal and fantasy of abusive scenarios (Becker, Kaplan, & Temke, 1992).

Fantasy and Masturbatory Reinforcement

Aspects of the abuse can be replayed through fantasy and reinforced through masturbation (Abel, Barlow, Blanchard, & Guild, 1977; Becker et al., 1992).

Rationalizations/Thinking Errors

The offender will rationalize his behavior in a number of thinking errors: "it was no big deal," "he or she asked for it," "they didn't resist much and therefore must have liked it," "it won't happen again." Such rationales are needed to allow continued fantasizing or to overcome internal inhibitions for future abuse (Yochelson & Samenow, 1977).

Without intervention, the offender can return to the beginning of the cycle at "motivations"—motivations that could continue to be met in abusive ways. If this abuse cycle is repeated enough, the offender may develop a deviant arousal pattern that necessitates considerable intervention to modify (Becker & Kaplan, 1988; Groth, 1979).

Case Example

Bill was a 15-year-old with learning disabilities and general social immaturity. As a result, he often played at the park with younger children with whom he felt comfortable and authoritative. He developed a club for his 9- and 10-year-old friends. Membership soon required certain "secret rituals." One day Bill convinced a 10-year-old boy in the club to allow Bill to fondle him. Bill found this to be extremely arousing. He replayed the fondling scenario in his mind while masturbating that evening and again at subsequent times. He considered the touching "harmless." This increased the erotic power of the child abuse scenario and led to planning additional abuse on that child, as well as grooming future victims.

The adolescent can repeatedly replay the sexually abusive act and reenforce it through masturbation. This process of cognitive rehearsal paired with physiological arousal can strongly predispose the adolescent to seek another abuse opportunity. The sequence of motivations, situational opportunity, internal inhibitors overcome, victim resistance circumvented, sexual abuse act, need reduction/pleasure, no negative consequence experienced, pleasure experienced or need reduced, fantasy and masturbatory reinforcement, and misattributions/thinking errors becomes a repetitive cycle that can repeat many times until intervention occurs.

TYPOLOGIES OF ADOLESCENT SEX OFFENDERS

Various typologies of adolescent offenders have been used over the years to help organize clinical and research studies. These typologies have arisen because the heterogeneity of offenders is evident and combining the whole pool of offender data can readily undermine the usefulness of the results (Finkelhor, 1986). Such typologies can help in developing a meaningful explanation of a particular offender type's dynamics as compared with other types, and in suggesting more specific and appropriate intervention strategies (Knight & Prentky, 1993).

Most typologies of adolescent offenders are general classifications with two or three categories. Atcheson & Williams (1954) conducted a 10-year longitudinal study of 2,516 male and 596 female juvenile delinquents. One-hundred-sixteen boys were convicted of sexual misbehavior and classified in the following three categories:

1. Specific sexual offenses (includes exhibitionism, indecent assault, immorality, rape, and indecent acts)
2. Nonspecific charges (includes vagrancy, incorrigibility, and sexual promiscuity)
3. Unrelated charges

Groth and Loredo (1981) differentiated 26 older adolescent males into those who raped ($n = 14$) and those who molested children ($n = 12$). The rapist was slightly older and had a higher incidence of interracial assaults, and the victims were more likely to be strangers. A weapon was more likely to be used and sexual intercourse was more likely involved. The child molesters had the highest percentage of victims who were friends and relatives. Eighty-six percent of child molesters had prior peer-age sexual experience, which discredited the idea of child molestation as naive sexual exploration.

Lewis, Shankok, and Pincus (1979) studied 17 violent boys (with an average age of 15) who had been convicted of sexual assault. Eight were convicted of rape or attempted rape of females, and two were convicted of assaulting women and younger males. Seven were convicted of other forms of sexual assault on females such as grabbing breasts and/or buttocks or beating women. The comparison sample was 61 boys who had been convicted of committing other serious violent acts such as murder, assault, armed robbery, and arson.

Of the 17 sexual assaulters, 10 had committed two or more sexual offenses. Victims ranged in age from 4 to 60. The study attempted to determine whether this violent subgroup of juvenile sexual assaulters differed psychiatrically or psychoeducationally from other violent juveniles. The author found that the violent juvenile sexual assaulters suffer from significant psychological problems more often than other violent juveniles, usually commit other types of violent acts, and have had serious behavioral disorders since early childhood. Sexual assaulters are characterized by violent childhoods, and their behavior throughout childhood and adolescence resembles that of violent nonsexually assaultive boys. Both the violent and the sexually assaultive groups function far below their expected reading grade, had been abused physically and/or sexually by their parents, and are likely to have witnessed extreme violence.

Deisher, Robinson, and Boyer (1982) studied 83 male adolescent sex offenders 12 to 17 years of age (mean age = 15). They used a classification system of three distinct types.

The first group included adolescents who sexually victimized young children (n = 31). Male teenage child molesters typically have a long history of underdeveloped peer relationships and social isolation. They are often scapegoated in their own families. A combination of poor social skills, isolation from peers, and conflicting family relationships contributes to low self-esteem and attraction to younger, more submissive children with whom they are more comfortable. The offenses against children usually take the form of forced mutual fondling of genitals or other sexual contacts of penetration.

The second group committed violent assaultive sexual behavior against a peer or adult (*n* = 23). The teenager referred for rape or indecent liberties with a peer or adult is more likely to use physical force or a weapon. Superficially, such forceful offenders may be involved in peer group activities, yet unable to identify one or more friends. Despite appearances, these teenagers are usually disturbed, as shown by their severely limited ability to empathize with the victim and their unwillingness to see their behavior as problematic. To protect the community, residential treatment must be considered for this group of offenders because they generally do not engage in outpatient treatment.

These teenagers are usually manipulative and attempt to avoid incarceration or therapy. Court-ordered therapy is crucial for outpatient treatment of the assaultive sexual offender because of the otherwise high attrition. Professionals are often fooled and manipulated by the smooth and articulate interpersonal style of the adolescent rapist. It is precisely this smooth, personable style that allows the youth to negotiate the sexual situation that results in an assault. The behavior toward the victim apparently has little to do with sexual needs but rather with violent aggression and reflects serious conflicts about anger and personal power.

A third category of sexual offenders included adolescents whose crimes did not involve physical contact with their victims; their crimes included stealing women's underwear, exposing themselves, and compulsively peering in windows. Although physical harm is not a factor, this activity is not in accord with normal adolescent sexual development. It can cause significant psychological distress and trauma to the victim. Teenagers in this category report feelings of inadequacy, are often unable to develop dating relationships, and have significant difficulties managing feelings of anger and frustration. These behaviors may precede more serious, hands-on offenses.

There has been a notable recent effort toward developing a typography of the sexual offense behavior and the inferred motivation of the offense behavior of sex offenders. Knight and Prentky (1990) have devised two separate typologies: one for child molesters and another for rapists.

These classifications are complex multiple-factor arrays or decision trees of dichotomous variables that represent important features of the offender groups. This is a research-oriented typology based on an incarcerated adult population at the Massachusetts Treatment Center in Bridgewater, Massachusetts. This typology was recently used to classify juvenile onset sex offenders (Knight & Prentky, 1993).

Knight and Prentky (1990) classify child sexual molesters on two separate axes. Axis 1 uses two independent dichotomist decisions that result in four types. The first classifies the offenders as either high or low in fixation on children, with highly fixated subjects as those whose thoughts and social interactions focus primarily on children. Offenders low in fixation do not show the same focus on children. The second decision judges social competencies high or low, depending on the offender's success in employment, adult relationships, and social responsibilities.

Child molesters are classified on Axis 2 according to the nature of their contact with children using a series of decisions that result in six separate types. The first decision classifies the offender according to the amount of contact he or she has with children with those who have high contact, further divided into whether the meaning of the contact for the offender is "interpersonal" or "narcissistic." Interpersonal contact with children means contact over a broad range of activities (not simply sexual interactions), and sexual interactions are not primarily directed toward orgasm. Narcissistic contact is directed primarily toward achieving sexual orgasm. Offenders who do not have significant contact with children are further subdivided into four subtypes: high or low degree of physical injury to victims, and those who do or do not have sadistic fantasies or behaviors.

The Knight and Prentky (1990) rapist taxonomy classifies subjects according to four primary motivations for raping: opportunistic, pervasively angry, sexually motivated, or vindictive. These types are well described by their title. The authors further subdivide the opportunistic, sexual nonsadistic, and vindictive rapists into two subgroups according to levels of social competence, as defined for their child molester typology in terms of success in employment, adult relationships, and social responsibilities.

This typology was applied to 564 adult male sex offenders who had been committed as sexually dangerous to the Massachusetts Treatment Center, a locked treatment facility. This group was divided between those who had been abusive as juveniles and those whose onset of abuse behavior was in adulthood. This division resulted in 61 rapists with juvenile onset and 55 child molesters with juvenile onset.

The result of the taxonomic analysis of group differences between adult and juvenile onset perpetrators was that only a subset of the types found in the adult onset samples was appropriate to the juvenile onset samples. Specifically, for both the rapist and the child molester typologies, the low social competence, high antisocial types appear to be most prevalent among juvenile onset sex offenders. Interrater reliability was .80 to .98. Abstracts of the subjects' files were used for classification purposes.

The study further corroborated the hypothesis that juvenile sexual offenders are heterogeneous and that the development of cohesive subtypes is possible. Although not yet applied to juvenile sex offenders in a clinical setting or for treatment planning, important and sound methodological procedures in chart review for developing research and clinical typologies have been demonstrated by Knight and Prentky (1993).

The PHASE Typology

As of 1993, more than 1,000 teenagers and their families had been assessed and/or treated in the Minnesota-based Program for Healthy Adolescent Sexual Expression (PHASE), which began in 1981. (Also known as the O'Brien-Bera PHASE typology, it is usually cited as the PHASE typology.) As a result of the large number of clients and the pressing need to diagnose and develop disposition or treatment plans, a rudimentary clinical typology of adolescent sex offenders and their family systems was developed.

A typology was originally proposed by O'Brien in 1983 and presented as a paper in 1984 (O'Brien, 1984). In 1984 and 1985, Bera elaborated and refined the typology. In developing such a typology from clinical experience, it was hoped that the typology would be heuristic and parsimonious—that is, it would help in decision making with different clients, developing a clearer explanation of overall offender dynamics, and suggesting the appropriate treatment strategy.

Bera (1985) investigated the validity and reliability of this typology of adolescent sex offenders, and began analyzing their corresponding family systems. The present version of the PHASE typology (O'Brien & Bera, 1986) has become a widely used adolescent sex offender typology. This typology of offenders and their family systems can help organize clinical impressions and is a classification system that can guide practitioners through ethical and therapeutic decision making. The typology is clinically based, however, and future empirical research is needed.

Type 1: The Naive Experimenter/Abuser

Case Example

Johnny was a 13-year-old boy who had been asked to baby-sit a 5-year-old neighbor girl named Nicky. Johnny had been baby-sitting for only a short time and the situation was new to him. While there, he discovered a *Playboy* magazine hidden under the couch; Johnny found the explicit photographs arousing. While helping Nicky change into her pajamas, he wanted to see what it was like to kiss her and touch her in the way that had been depicted in the photographs. After a short time he felt guilty and stopped. Later that week, Nicky told her mother and Johnny was arrested for criminal sexual conduct.

Based on clinical experience, the naive experimenter/abuser is generally a younger male, age 11 to 14, who has little previous history of acting out. He usually has adequate social skills and peer relationships. He tends to be sexually naive and the abuse event appears to have been situationally determined (e.g., baby-sitting, family gathering, camping). Psychological testing and family history tend to be unremarkable. He typically engages in a single or a few isolated events of opportunistic sexual exploration with a victim who is usually a young child between the ages of 2 and 6. There is usually no recourse to any force or threats. His primary motivation for the abuse is to explore and experiment with his newly developing sexual feelings. The DSM-III-R psychological diagnosis is often an adjustment disorder.

Type 2: Undersocialized Child Molester

Case Example

Jerry, 15, had no close peer relationships and only a few school acquaintances. He could be considered a loner, and he spent a good portion of his time watching television or playing video games at home. He was well liked by his parents and was no trouble at home or at school. When playing outside he often was by himself or with considerably younger children. In the course of playing with the younger children, he became sexually involved with them and required fondling and oral-genital contact as a necessary part of being a member of a club he had formed. There were no threats or force used, but he did maintain secrecy with the children by telling them not to tell their parents. One of the children broke the secret to a teacher at school and Jerry was arrested for criminal sexual conduct.

The undersocialized child molester is clinically observed to suffer from chronic social isolation and has little peer acceptance. He gravitates toward younger children who admire or accept him, and is internally dominated by feelings of inadequacy and insecurity. Psychological testing often reflects social isolation, insecurity, and low self-esteem. He has little history of acting out socially and the family often has a distant or absent father figure. The sexual abuse behavior can reflect a chronic pattern of sexual behaviors with children that includes the use of manipulation, trickery, enticement, and rewards. The victim is usually a young and available child in either incest, baby-sitting, neighborhood play, or family situations. The molester's motivation for the abuse typically is an attempt to achieve intimacy or a sense of self-importance, self-esteem, self-identity, or autonomy. The DSM-III-R diagnosis of the offender is often conduct disorder-undersocialized aggressive, or paraphilia.

Type 3: Pseudosocialized Child Molester

Case Example

Norm was a 17-year-old boy, the youngest of six children. He was an exceptional achiever: an A student in school, a member of the theater department, and in the top bracket of students completing the SAT.

This religious and college-bound youth had engaged in kissing, oral-genital sex, and penis-vaginal rubbing with a niece 6 years younger. The abuse events occurred regularly over a 3-year period, and it appeared he had trained her into her victim role and coaxed her to remain silent. Vaginal redness led to questions by the girl's physician and the final disclosure. The entire family was shocked when Norm was arrested for criminal sexual conduct.

The clinical impression of the pseudosocialized child molester is of an older adolescent in the 16- to 18-year-old bracket. He has good social skills and is comfortable, but not intimate, in peer settings. There is little or no history of acting out socially, and he usually expresses confidence and security in most arenas. Psychologically he tests as "normal" on the Minnesota Multiphasic Personality Inventory (MMPI) and the Millon Adolescent Personality Inventory (MAPI). He is often a victim of some early childhood abuse such as physical, sexual, or emotional abuse or neglect. A "parentified child" family role is apparent. He is often intellectually gifted and a hard worker at home and in school.

The pseudosocialized child molester's abuse behavior reflects a more chronic pattern that can last years. The sexual abuse behavior is highly rationalized by the offender and little remorse or guilt is clearly demonstrated. The abuse events are characterized by the offender as mutual, intimate, and noncoercive. His motivation appears to be the narcissistic exploitation of a vulnerable child to meet his own sexual needs.

This type is often underdiagnosed during assessment because of his social skills and intellect. But this type has the greatest potential of achieving significant social status as a result of these intellectual gifts and coping mechanisms that can help place him in a position of trust and authority over children or adolescents: minister, school teacher, or youth leader. The DSM-III-R diagnosis can include pedophilia, conduct disorder, or personality disorder.

Type 4: Sexual Aggressive

Case Example

Troy, 15, was a victim of severe physical abuse at the hands of his stepfather, his mother's third husband. The mother often suffered from physical beatings from her husband as well. Troy had a history of fire-setting, theft, vandalism, and truancy. Very social and flamboyant, he took a 14-year-old girl out on a date and when she refused to "go all the way," Troy slapped her and forced her to perform oral sex on him, threatening to use a screwdriver if she didn't. Afterwards, she stumbled home and told her mother what happened, and Troy was arrested that evening by police for first-degree criminal sexual conduct.

Sexual aggressives are clinically observed as products of disorganized and abusive families. They have good peer-age social skills and are often charming and gregarious. Often having a long history of antisocial behaviors and poor impulse control problems, they typically fight with family members and friends and are likely to abuse chemicals. The sexual abuse usually involves the use of force, threats, or violence, and the victims can be peers, adults, or children.

Psychological testing often reveals an antisocial and character-disordered teenager. The offender's motivation for abuse is the use of sex to experience personal power or express anger when his desires have been frustrated. DSM-III-R diagnosis is often conduct disorder, socialized, aggressive.

Type 5: Sexual Compulsive

Case Example

David, 16, was an enthusiastic football player and good student at school. His mother was a traditional homemaker and his father was generally absent, working two shifts in a hospital. David committed a series of exposing incidents in front of high school girls near his school, and was identified and arrested by the police. In the course of therapy, it was discovered that he had exposed himself numerous times to his older sister, who kept it a secret and just yelled at him. The total abuse history spanned a 2-year period.

The family of the sexual compulsive is usually clinically observed as having rigid role boundaries and being emotionally disengaged. The parents are often emotionally repressed and have difficulty expressing intimacy. The offender has an inability to express negative emotions in a clear and straightforward manner. This type of offender typically engages in a repetitive, sexually arousing behavior of a compulsive nature. Such offenses often include nontouch behaviors like window peeping, obscene phone calls, exhibitionism, and fetish burglary (e.g., stealing women's underwear). A minority of this type are compulsive child molesters.

This behavior is generally seen as an autoerotic with no clearly apparent relationship to the victim. The offender is self-controlled, self-determined, and narcissistically absorbed. The offender appears to experience relief of anxiety or mood elevation by the behavior. DSM-III-R diagnosis can include one of the paraphilias, conduct disorder, or identity disorder.

Type 6: Disturbed Impulsive

Case Example

Bill, 15, was living with his father, who had been awarded custody of him and his sister following an acrimonious divorce. Bill had grown up in a house where tension and anxiety were present as a result of the marital discord, and he generally learned to keep to himself. One day while retrieving the vacuum cleaner from his sister's closet, he turned to his sister, who was sitting in her underwear, and grabbed her, tore off her underwear, and attempted to mount her while she yelled "Stop! Stop!" Finally she pushed him off and he seemed to "come to his senses," grabbed the vacuum cleaner, and left to complete his chores. Because of the family tension, the sister kept the event quiet. A second incident occurred with a girlfriend of his sister, whom Bill suddenly accosted while ice skating with her, grabbing her breast and buttocks. This incident was reported to the police and Bill was questioned and left in the custody of his father. He was finally arrested after accosting an adult female in the laundry room of his mother's apartment building. Again, the assault was sudden and unpredictable. Bill was subsequently placed in a psychiatric hospital.

Disturbed impulsives may have a history of psychological problems, severe family problems, substance abuse problems, or significant learning problems. Thorough history and psychological testing are imperative. The sexual abuse is characterized as impulsive or reflecting a disturbance of reality. It can be a single, unpredictable, uncharacteristic act, or may be one among a pattern of sexual abuse acts. The offense may reflect a malfunction of normal inhibitory mechanisms due to organicity or thought disorder, or as a result of chemical abuse. The motivation is complex and individually determined. DSM-III-R diagnoses are varied.

Type 7: Group Influenced

Case Example

Greg, 12, was a lonely boy whose only friend was Travis, 14. One evening they went to a neighbor's house after the parents had left. While there, Travis encouraged a group that included Greg and a 12-year-old boy and his 11-year-old sister to engage in a game of strip poker. During the game, when her brother went to the bathroom, the girl was accosted by Travis and Greg, who kissed and fondled her. The whole group told her not to tell, but the next morning she told her parents, and Travis and Greg were arrested for criminal sexual conduct.

The group-influenced offender is usually a younger teen who is not likely to have past contact with the juvenile justice system. The sexual abuse occurs within a peer group and the victim tends to be known by the offenders. The offender tends to defer responsibility for the sexual offense to the victim and/or other offenders in the group. The motivation for the sexual abuse can be the result of peer pressure or expectations—a "follower" dynamic; or an attempt to gain peer attention, approval, or leadership—a "leader" dynamic. DSM-III-R diagnosis is usually one of the conduct disorders.

Preliminary PHASE Typology
Research Support and Application

The PHASE typology is generally supported in preliminary research (Bera, 1985). The PHASE typology is clinically supported by a high interrater agreement of 81%. The typology is also supported by statistically significant findings on empirical variables, which provide an empirical base for the PHASE typology; significant differences exist among the seven types.

In the Bera (1985) study, the 51 adolescent subjects were placed into the following offender types:

- Type 1: Naive experimenter/abuser (n = 8)–15.7%
- Type 2: Undersocialized child molester (n = 6)–11.8%
- Type 3: Pseudosocialized child molester (n = 5)–9.8%
- Type 4: Sexual aggressive (n = 6)–11.8%
- Type 5: Sexual compulsive (n = 5)–9.8%
- Type 6: Disturbed impulsive (n = 7)–13.7%
- Type 7: Group influenced (n = 9)–17.6%
- Not sure (n = 5)–9.8%

The undersocialized child molesters and the pseudosocialized child molesters tend to view their family as "high cohesion/high adaptability types" on Olson's circumplex model as measured by the FACES-II test, a measure of family systems (Olson et al., 1983). They generally view their families as emotionally very close, loyal, dependent on each other, connected, spending time with each other, making decisions based on family needs, focused, and sharing interests. Members of this group also generally see their family roles as fluid, changing, unclear, lenient, flexible in decision making, and inconsistent.

The majority of sexual aggressive, sexual compulsive, and disturbed impulsive types see their families in the low cohesion/low adaptability quadrant of Olson's circumplex model. They see their families as emotionally separated, independent, open to outside people and ideas, having fluid generational boundaries, valuing time alone, preferring separate space, having few family friends, making most decisions individually, and supporting individual activities.

The PHASE typology has been applied usefully in the prevention, triage, and research of adolescent sex offenders. The SHARP program is the first video-based adolescent perpetrator prevention education curriculum available for middle school and high school students (Minnesota Department of Human Services, 1986). The PHASE typology is the basis of the offender types portrayed and interventions recommended. It is now used in hundreds of school violence prevention programs.

The Oregon Department of Family Services (1986) used the PHASE typology as the basis of its matrix of treatment interventions for juvenile offenders, and the typology continues to be used as a clinical and research tool in PHASE.

Rasmussen, Burton, and Christopherson (1990) modified the PHASE typology for sexually aggressive children into six types: sexually curious, reenacting trauma, socially motivated, egocentric, behaviorally disordered, and group influenced.

Some Reservations
About Offender Typologies

Offender typologies, like the PHASE typology, are an improvement over undifferentiated categorization of all sex offenders. Although the PHASE typology differentiates seven types, the differentiation should be understood as preliminary. Continued clinical experience, theory development, and research are needed to confirm the model, and more types and subtypes probably will develop. For example, Knight and Prentky (1990, 1993) suggest an adult offender typology of as many as 24 different types.

The PHASE typology was derived on a large outpatient population. It does not appropriately describe a residential population. For a residential population, the typology should be considered a starting point, in combination with Knight and Prentky's (1990, 1993) typology. Professionals should not be blinded from seeing offenders who do not fit the model or falsely label those who share a type's characteristics and are not offenders.

Meyers, Bays, Becker, Berliner, Corwin, and Saywitz (1989) caution about the dangerous temptation of having behavioral scientists appear as expert witnesses in child sexual abuse cases to testify that an individual fits a particular offender profile or type. No offender typology, including the PHASE typology, can be used to differentiate offenders from nonoffenders and should not be used to support guilt or innocence.

The PHASE typology is developmentally sensitive, recognizing age differences, motivations, contexts, and peer influences. Still, as with all typologies, it does not account well for individuals who may cross multiple categories.

SUMMARY

This chapter briefly reviews common clinical issues observed in adolescent sex offenders with a focus on the prevalence of family dysfunction reported in the literature. Family issues are demonstrated as significant factors in adolescent sex offender development and maintenance. A model of the adolescent sex offender, the EMASO model, is presented to organize the clinical literature logically, and the PHASE typology of adolescent offenders connects the individual and family factors reviewed. Chapter 6 builds on the EMASO model and PHASE typology as they apply in clinical intervention.

Research on models of etiology and maintenance of juvenile offenders and offender typologies with the inclusion of involved family members could provide relevant context and meaning to the numbers generated. The models presented here are an attempt to create such a context and to be useful tools for clinicians and researchers working within the sexual abuse domain. These models also attempt to overcome the limits of the models critiqued in chapter 2.

As sexual abuse research continues to broaden and deepen in scope, the EMASO model, the PHASE typology, and other models and typologies will change or be elaborated. Although such research on multiple, interacting individual, family, and social variables is complex, the task can be simplified by such theoretical models (Finkelhor, 1986; Gurman & Kniskern, 1981, 1992). The potential rewards of addressing the serious issues that juvenile sex offenders present is significant.

6

Treatment Approaches
for Adolescent Male Sex Offenders

CHAPTER 5 REVIEWS the behavioral and cognitive-behavioral treatment techniques that currently dominate the adolescent sex offender treatment field;this chapter focuses on the adolescent offender's family as a primary resource for assessment and therapy. The PHASE typology's treatment implications are explicated. A model outpatient adolescent offender program structure is summarized, and a seven-stage model for family-based adolescent offender therapy is provided. Levels of family-based involvement are presented to help guide clinicians wishing to augment their current family therapy approaches.

OVERVIEW OF TREATMENT METHODS
AND TECHNIQUES FOR JUVENILE SEX OFFENDERS

Knopp, Freeman-Longo, and Stevenson (1992) conducted a national survey of sex offender programs and received responses from 755 juvenile sex offender services. This section uses that survey as a base from which to structure a brief overview of the present major treatment methods and techniques used with adolescent sex offenders. Results of the survey are included for each method, and the percentages used in this chapter are from this survey.

Settings and Modalities

Juvenile sex offenders are treated primarily in community-based outpatient programs, which account for 75% of all services surveyed. Sixty percent of these outpatient services are private services and 40% are public services. Residential services account for 25% of all services, with 55% public and 45% private.

When asked "Do you use family treatment with offenders?" 92% of the community-based services and 86% of the residential-based services said "yes." No differences were found between low-level family information or education sessions rather than regularly scheduled family therapy.

Eighty-four percent of respondents identified peer group therapy as the preferred juvenile sex offender treatment method. This type of therapy utilizes the developmentally typical peer group social orientation of teenagers for therapeutic support and confrontation.

Cognitive-behavioral and behavioral methods were identified in some form in 65% of the services. The most important example of a cognitive-behavioral technique is a clear definition of the offender's "sexual abuse cycle" (Lane & Zamora, 1984). Elaborating on Lane and Zamora's original "rape cycle," Ryan et al. (1987) state:

> In order to prevent further sexual offending behaviors, the offender must understand the cognitive, behavioral, situational and psychological events which contributed to the offense. The cycle concept provides a framework in which the offenders can attach their individual feelings, thoughts, and behaviors, seeing themselves as unique individuals while identifying what they have in common with each other. After mastering their understanding of the cycle and seeing how it applies to them as individuals, the offenders then practice identifying the times in their past in which they responded similarly and situations in their present life which trigger the beginning of the cycle or signal that they are at the early stages of the cycle. They must identify the areas in their thinking which enabled them to progress through the cycle, and practice new ways to respond which will interrupt the cycle before the offending behaviors occur. (pp. 386-387)

Lane (1991), Lane and Zamora (1984), and Ryan et al. (1987) identify the following points from the beginning of the cycle to the sexual offense.

1. Negative self-image
2. Predicting rejection
3. Isolation
4. Fantasies
5. Planning the offense
6. The sexual offense
7. Return to negative self-image as a result

Various exercises are used to define the cycle in individual, group, and family therapy: paper-and-pencil exercises, use of a tape recorder, negative and positive consequences, and other cognitive behavioral techniques. Workbooks are available to help define these offense cycles and develop prevention strategies (Kahn, 1990).

Relapse Prevention

The offender can develop abuse prevention strategies by building a series of internal interventions or self-management skills to break this abuse cycle. A modified "relapse prevention" model, with an external supervisory component (Gray & Pithers, 1993; Pithers, Martin, & Cumming, 1989), is a systematic approach to teaching these strategies to the offender. Families, friends, probation officers, school officials, and employers are educated on how to assist the offender's process of avoiding relapse. Pithers, Martin, and Cumming (1989) explain:

The external, supervisory dimension serves three functions:

1. Enhancing efficacy of probation or parole supervision by the monitoring of specific offense precursors.
2. Increasing efficacy of supervision by creating an informed network of collateral contacts to assist the probation officer in monitoring the offender's behaviors.
3. Creating a collaborative relationship between the probation officer and mental health professionals conducting therapy with the offender. (p. 23)

The importance of aftercare issues, community safety, and community supervision is emphasized through the modified or expanded relapse prevention model (Freeman-Longo & Knopp, 1992). (For a detailed review of relapse prevention models, see Laws, 1989.)

Cognitive-Behavioral
and Behavioral Approaches

Yochelson and Samenow (1977) developed a cognitive-behavioral approach now used in some form in most programs. The original model suggests that sex offenses may be one outcome of irrational thinking patterns and an antisocial way of looking at life. The approach generally consists of helping the offender define and then confront the "thinking errors" that lead to criminal behavior. Examples of common thinking errors of sex offenders are "she/he asked for it"; "my life's so bad, I deserved a little fun"; and "it's not that big a deal."

Among the most widely used techniques is a combined cognitive-behavioral exercise called "covert sensitization" that pairs thoughts of negative consequences with thoughts of offending.

A controversial behavioral technique is masturbatory satiation, which "attempts to reduce (deviant) arousal by boring the patient with his own deviant sexual fantasies" (Barnard, Fuller, Robins, & Shaw, 1989, p. 819). The offender masturbates to a healthy sexual fantasy then switches to a part of his abuse fantasy for a long period without ejaculation. This is often done while talking into a tape recorder. The goal of this procedure is to have the offender associate abusive fantasy with boredom and frustration. An example of a protocol for masturbatory satiation tapes can be found in Steen and Monnette (1989).

In practice, this technique can be difficult to evaluate because it relies on the offender's self-report. If the offender lies about the nature of his fantasies, this technique can reinforce a sexual compulsive's victimizing arousal pattern. Some clinicians try to control this through use of plethysmography. Because of resistance to the use of directed masturbation in the course of treatment, the principles of this technique can be translated into a cognitive-behavior exercise called "verbal satiation," in which the "boring" process depends on repetition of fantasy material.

An even more controversial technique is aversive conditioning, which is used in 29% of the community-based services and 16% of the residential services. Aversive conditioning is the use of an aversive stimulus, such as a sharply snapped rubber band, noxious odors, or electrical shock, to stop sexually abusive thoughts. An example of one procedure is for the client to make an audiotape that describes the initial stages of approaching a potential victim. The client can then train himself in a behavioral lab by employing a noxious odor to stop the negative sexual thoughts.

Another method rarely used with juveniles is for the client to indicate to a behavioral trainer the arousal of the negative thought and then receive a semipainful electrical shock. This "thought stopping" can continue outside of the lab by using a rubber band on the wrist to be snapped with the arousal of negative sexual thoughts (Steen & Monnette, 1989). Typically, the procedure also employs complementary training for positive, nonabusive sexual thoughts during masturbation, often called "masturbatory reconditioning."

For motivated adolescents with compulsive or distressing sexually deviant thoughts, these procedures can be effective and offer a sense of control and rapid relief. For others, emotional distress has been observed. These forms of aversive conditioning are often used in conjunction with a penile transducer (Knopp, 1984).

Finally, an example of an extreme aversive technique is Smith and Wolf's (1988) report of an "aversive behavioral rehearsal" technique primarily developed by Wickramasekera (1980). No published reports of this technique as used with adolescents were found, although there are anecdotal reports of similar techniques being used in some adolescent programs.

This technique involves the use of male and female mannequins and other props with which the client rehearses the entire abuse scenario eventually in front of a video camera, therapist, treatment group, spouse, relatives, and friends. Out of 154 cases using the technique, only 5% of those completing the procedure are known to have reoffended over a mean 2-year follow-up period (Smith & Wolf, 1988). A small control group of 10 who refused the procedure or went through other components of the program are reported to have a 20% rate of known reoffense over a shorter period of time.

Exhibitionism encompasses the bulk of the reoffensive behaviors. The authors note that clients can experience this powerful technique as humiliating and state that careful preparation is important.

Psychophysical and Psychopharmacological Approaches

Penile Transducer

The penile transducer is used in 22% of juvenile sex offender programs. A sexual arousal assessment using the penile transducer is conducted in a private laboratory. A transducer is a small rubber gauge that the client is directed to place around his penis while he is alone in the lab. This transducer is connected to instruments that measure the degree of erection the adolescent gets while watching slides and videos or listening to audiotapes that depict various appropriate and inappropriate or abusive forms of sexual interactions. The procedure attempts to get direct measures of deviant arousal versus nondeviant arousal.

The penile transducer has been used in individual cases where there is the likelihood of recidivism based on a high degree of denial, minimization, or lack of awareness of arousal cues. This is a special concern for the adolescent who has a considerable history of sex abuse. This method can be useful in breaking through therapeutic impasses and measuring progress.

However, there is also evidence that oppositional, denying, or unmotivated offenders are able to suppress arousal and "fake" the exam. There are also concerns that behavioral arousal changes may not generalize outside of the lab. For example, Becker et al. (1992) found that 58% of the juveniles who denied their sex offense were "nonresponders," and concluded that plethysmography is of limited use with this subgroup of perpetrators because it does not differentiate between cues. They believe that the deniers have the ability to suppress arousal in the laboratory.

The early hope that penile transducers could be used to "prove someone is a sex offender" has been thoroughly discredited; today it is used primarily for research or therapy. (For a recent review of the major methodological issues concerning the validity of phal-lometric tests, see Schouten & Simon, 1992.)

The benefits of laboratory assessments include a measurement of arousal patterns that informs both the client and the therapist re-garding the role of arousal and/or preference in the offending behav-ior, a measurement of change over time, and the offender's conscious or unconscious ability to avoid deviant arousal. Posttreatment change is affected by the offender's application of cognitive change (i.e., motivation to avoid deviant thoughts and employ treatment tools).

Polygraph

The polygraph ("lie detector") is used in 25% of the community-based services and 19% of the residential services. It can be used to support more accurate self-report histories by the offender and as a progress check in therapy (Barbaree, Marshall, & Hudson, 1993; Steen & Monette, 1989).

The clinician should be aware that the polygraph has significant limitations and is prone to abuse, especially for assessment (Lykken, 1981). The polygraph is an instrument that shows general, nonspe-cific, somatic arousal responses. It is prone to having significant false positive errors that can lead to condemning an innocent party (Gale, 1988).

Depo-Provera

Depo-provera is used in 11% of the community-based programs and 8% of the residential services. Depo-provera is a form of me-droxyprogesterone that lowers the testosterone level in the blood stream. There is some evidence that a lower testosterone level de-creases the frequency and degree of sexual thoughts and behavior, as well as overall aggression (Barnard et al., 1989). However, such anti-testosterones are rarely used with adolescents except for those who are extremely aggressive or compulsive. Side effects can include interference with bone growth, a decrease in testicle size, weight gain, increased lethargy, and decreased sperm count. (For an excel-lent review of pharmacological treatments of the adolescent sex offender, see Bradford, 1993.)

CRITIQUE OF CURRENT METHODS AND RATIONALE
FOR A FAMILY-BASED ASSESSMENT AND TREATMENT APPROACH

The major treatment approaches currently in use are predominantly individual or group focused in therapy format and behavioral and cognitive-behavioral in technique. Family therapy is infrequently emphasized. This is probably the result of the application of adult sex offender methods to adolescents. Based on learning theory, adult methods treat sexually offending behavior as negative thinking or learning in the individual, the basic theory is that if you change a person's thoughts and behaviors in treatment, the person will change his thoughts and behaviors in the community (Greer & Stuart, 1983).

Unfortunately, individual-focused therapies and behavioral methods may suffer from generalization; that is, the behavioral changes displayed during the treatment process may not continue to be displayed over time in the family and community. Reliance on the client's self-report of change in the home and community is particularly problematic. Strategies currently used to minimize these problems have a strong emphasis on confrontational group therapy approaches, plethysmography and polygraph monitoring, and teaching relapse prevention strategies (Knopp, Freeman-Longo, & Stevenson, 1992).

Although there is much consensus in this field regarding intervention with the juvenile sex offender, not all experts in the field support the same techniques (National Adolescent Perpetrator Network, 1993). The use of intrusive behavioral methods such as olfactory aversion therapy, satiation, aversive behavioral rehearsal, or depo-provera for changing juvenile arousal patterns is still experimental. Many clinicians and experts, including this author, believe that teenagers, whether having been sexually abusive or not, should not be induced or "court ordered" into experimental therapies that include possibly dangerous or humiliating procedures until the long-term benefits and risks of these therapies are clearly known.

Although most clinicians acknowledge the benefits of family involvement, the field fails to employ family therapy to the extent possible with adolescents and often limits therapy to "fix the kid" strategies. To improve the effectiveness of adolescent sex offender treatment and to maximize generalization, further expansion of therapy utilizing a holistic, family systems approach and victim/family sensitivity throughout the process is important, along with expert application of the strategies already reviewed.

Chapter 5 describes family system issues that are significant to the etiology or maintenance of the abuse behavior. Given the importance of these family variables in the development or maintenance of an adolescent's sexually abusive behavior, the need for a family-based assessment for the juvenile sex offender is significant. Such an assessment can help develop abuse prevention strategies, diagnostic protocols in the assessment phase, family treatment goals, and strategies in the treatment of adolescent and family. With successful family therapy, the resources of the family members can be mobilized to maintain adolescent behavioral changes after termination of treatment (Gurman & Kniskern, 1981, 1991).

General Recidivism and Treatment Studies

Recidivism and treatment follow-up studies are noted for their methodological difficulties. Finkelhor (1986) notes that most studies use subsequent offenses that come to the attention of authorities or a follow-up sex crime as recidivism criteria only if a legal conviction occurred. Most studies only follow offenders over a short period of time (less than 5 years) and therefore probably underestimate true recidivism. Many early studies failed to distinguish between treated and untreated offenders, and others failed to distinguish between different types of offenders.

Of more value from the studies are results that distinguish offender variables most predictive of reoffense. Here there is general agreement. As summarized by Finkelhor (1986), adult child molesters of boys are about twice as likely to offend again as adult offenders of girls (27% to 40% versus 13% to 18%, depending on the study). Exhibitionists also have high reoffense rates (41% to 51%). Adult incest offenders appear to have lower recidivism rates (10% to 12% versus 18% to 24% for other sex offenders). These figures should be cautiously interpreted, given evidence that some also abuse outside the family or later in life with grandchildren.

Some preliminary adolescent recidivism studies are available. Smith and Monastersky (1986) found that a sample of 223 juvenile sex offenders (most of whom had been in some form of treatment) had a 7% reoffense rate over a 20-month follow-up. Bremmer (1992) found a similar low recidivism rate.

Lieker (1986) studied 154 adolescents in Utah convicted of a sex offense between 1974 and 1984. Records were searched for any sexual crimes committed after age 20. Of this sample population, almost 17% were known to have committed further sex-related crimes once they became adults. Fifty-six percent of these juveniles received no treatment. The recidivism rate of these adolescents is two to three times larger that the 5% to 7% rate mentioned in the previous studies. The lack of systematic sex abuse treatment can be speculated as the reason for the difference.

In a review of the recidivism literature, Davis and Leitenberg (1987) conclude that recidivism data provide "reason for some optimism about the long-term progress for most adolescent sex offenders" (p. 425). They also note that treated juveniles have lower recidivism rates than adults.

In summary, the evidence suggests that early intervention with a juvenile offender may reduce future victimization and lower the potential for continuing the deviant sexual abuse patterns into adulthood. Caution is still needed, because comprehensive recidivism studies find that the longer the follow-up the greater the recidivism, and the findings are dependent on how recidivism is measured. Well-designed, clearly controlled, empirical follow-up studies of treated and untreated adolescent offenders that span a number of years are needed to confirm these early impressions.

NEED FOR ASSESSMENT AND
CLINICAL PROGRAM STRATEGIES AND TOOLS

Criminal justice and mental health professionals face increased numbers of juvenile offenders to assess, process, and treat, and a growing literature on offender assessment and treatment. They are called on to diagnose offenders regarding degree of dangerousness and potential for reoffending, decide whether treatment should be residential or outpatient, and face other complex and ethically troublesome decisions that may affect all involved: Should such treatment be behavioral, family systems based, individual or group therapy based, residential or hospital based? Should it include psychiatric drugs, focus on sexuality or other personal issues, be of short or long duration, and include what kinds of aftercare plans?

The problems are similar to diagnosis problems in teenage chemical abuse. When a juvenile is found abusing alcohol or drugs in a school, community, or home or when driving, he or she is ideally referred for chemical dependency assessment. The assessment results in a label of experimenter, chemical abuser, or chemically dependent. If judged an experimenter, he or she is often referred to a drug education program. If judged a chemical abuser, he or she is likely to be referred to an outpatient treatment program that may include groups in school or at a local center. If judged chemically dependent, he or she is may be referred to an inpatient treatment program, often followed by an aftercare plan. (Note that in practice there is often over- or underdiagnosis of chemical dependency in adolescents.)

Similarly, criminal justice and sexual abuse professionals attempt to triage the sexually offending teenager toward receiving the appropriate degree of intervention. In practice, such an assessment is much more difficult than chemical health assessments because of the greater emotional reaction to the topic, the newness and lack of sophistication of the field, and the often more complex individual and family dynamics. Broader issues such as treatment options, competing theoretical orientations, costs, and insurance are significant as well.

While similar factors lead to over- and underdiagnosis of chemical dependency in adolescents, such diagnostic errors have a greater consequence in the sexual abuse field. Underdiagnoses could lead to the sexual victimization of additional people. Overdiagnoses label adolescents as dangerous "sex offenders," at times for life. As a result, juvenile sex offender treatment recommendations place greater demand on professionals in a much younger field of inquiry.

This chapter attempts to provide some direction to criminal justice and sexual abuse professionals by outlining the Program for Healthy Adolescent Sexual Expression (PHASE), the PHASE typology, and the benefits of maximizing family involvement. Chapter 7 addresses broader system issues and the coordination of treatment with the victim and victim's family.

PHASE: A FAMILY-BASED OUTPATIENT TREATMENT MODEL

The Program for Healthy Adolescent Sexual Expression (PHASE) was created in 1981. PHASE is an outpatient, family-centered program in the Minneapolis/St. Paul metropolitan area for the assessment and treatment of adolescent males and females who have behaved in sexually abusive or victimizing ways. PHASE provides a comprehensive program of clinical services involving psychological assessment, sexuality education, and individual, family, and group therapy.

PHASE has a significant emphasis on family involvement and therapy. Some of the primary aspects of PHASE are reviewed below, followed by an overview of the PHASE typology and its treatment implications.

Eligibility

Client eligibility requirements for entrance into PHASE are as follows:

1. Adolescent males, age 12 to 17, who have committed a sexual offense
2. No chronic history of physical violence
3. No active chemical dependency
4. Referral by juvenile courts, social worker, probation officer, or parents
5. Requirement of ongoing family participation and/or the participation of other involved persons such as foster parents, social workers, or probation officers

PHASE clients' sexual offense histories range from a fairly isolated experience to multiple offenses extending over a number of years. Offenses include obscene phone calls, exposure, sexual fondling, child molesting, incest, fetish-burglary, and rape.

Intake and the Assessment/Education Program

At first, the adolescent offender and his parents or concerned persons meet with staff for a 2-hour intake interview. Program philosophy and content are discussed, and background information on the juvenile's offenses as well as family dynamics is gathered. A psychological test battery can include the MMPI for age 16 and older, or the MAPI for age 15 and younger to assess symptom and personality issues; a sexual attitude questionnaire to assess general sexual opinions; and a sentence completion test that provides a qualitative, projective assessment. Other tests may be based on the concerns of the intake staff. The theme of the intake and testing is to assist in the assessment process and to determine the family's appropriateness for the monthlong assessment/education portion.

If appropriate, the adolescent and his family next enter into a 1-month, structured assessment/education program. Here they join six to eight other families who are working on similar sexual concerns. Each young person is assigned an individual therapist who works with him and his family throughout the program. Meetings include a weekly 2-hour adolescent group, two to three scheduled individual sessions, and two designated family sessions.

The adolescent groups explore the laws concerning sexuality, attitudes regarding sex roles and sexual expression, and the differences between consensual touch and exploitative touch. The various nontouch offenses are defined. Discussion includes a variety of safe, responsible ways to express one's sexuality.

Parents and/or concerned persons attend four support groups that meet while the adolescents are in group. In these meetings, the parents and concerned individuals are provided the same information given to the adolescents, as well as an opportunity to share concerns and progress with each other and provide support.

Upon conclusion of this component, each case is presented to the treatment team, decisions are made, and a diagnostic conference is held where decisions about the need for further treatment or referral are discussed. Adolescent offenders whose abuse behavior was nonviolent, with incidents few in number, and whose behavior could be best characterized as naive or experimental may be terminated at this time, with or without recommendation for continuing non-sex-offender-specific therapy. The offender must write a letter of apology to the victim as therapeutic restitution and reconciliation.

Adolescents with a more severe or chronic history and dynamic of sexual acting out are referred to PHASE outpatient treatment or other outpatient treatment programs. Sibling incest perpetrators often continue to live out of the home while in an outpatient program. If an adolescent also poses a significant risk to the community, an intensive residential treatment program is recommended.

Treatment Program

Juveniles entering the treatment part of PHASE continue in individual, group, and family therapy under the direction of their personal therapist or case manager. The treatment program typically runs for 7 to 8 additional months, but may continue for as long as 1 year. Each adolescent, working with his therapist, develops an individually tailored treatment plan.

Family participation and family therapy are considered crucial in the treatment program. Parents, siblings, and extended family members are affected by the consequences of the adolescent's behavior. The focus of family therapy is to improve family relationships in order to maximize the family's strengths, to support the adolescent as he proceeds through treatment, and to maintain his nonabusive behavior after graduation.

Weekly group therapy helps the teenager develop a better understanding of others' values and beliefs, in addition to improving self-awareness, social skills, and self-esteem. One-on-one therapy sessions provide a psychologically safe environment in which to address personal issues.

General treatment goals include recognizing and accepting responsibility for sexually abusive behavior; understanding the consequences of sexual abuse actions on themselves and on others; developing healthier ways to meet sexual, emotional, and interpersonal needs; and integrating these new skills and insights. Treatment dura- tion of PHASE ranges from approximately 6 months to more than 1 year.

Staff

The PHASE staff consists of a director and a program coordinator who supervise clinical staff, and an intake worker who coordinates incoming referrals, the assessment/education program, and testing. A number of treatment therapists have psychology, social work, or family therapy backgrounds and provide long-term psychotherapy in the treatment program. Supervision is provided by a doctoral-level clinical psychologist with expertise in child and adolescent development and a psychiatrist certified in child and adolescent psychiatry.

The PHASE Typology and Its Treatment Implications

Based on the PHASE typology, differential treatment issues and strategies are suggested according to the offender type and dynamics outlined in chapter 5. The treatment addresses offender and family issues and offers brief suggestions for how to address these issues in a structured, family-based program such as PHASE. Offenders who are likely to benefit from short-term therapy rather than a longer-term outpatient program or who may need to be referred to an out-of-home placement or residential setting are defined.

Type 1: The Naive Experimenter/Abuser

The naive experimenter/abuser commits one or a few acts of naive, opportunistic sexual exploration with no recourse to force or threats. A concrete education in adolescent sexuality versus sexual abuse is imperative for both the adolescent and his parents. This type appears to develop more open family communication on issues of sexuality in order to minimize future potential for problematic sexual behavior. The treatment of the naive experimenter/abuser typically ends at the conclusion of a short-term yet intensive assessment/education program of about 2 months.

Type 2: The Undersocialized Child Molester

The undersocialized child molester tends to be a younger teen with abuse that typically spans a number of months demonstrating a chronic sexual abuse pattern involving one or more child victims. Typical therapy issues include helping the family become a less enmeshed-chaotic system in which the offender is very family centered. Role reversals usually need to be addressed as well. The communication pattern of such families requires change, as do the peer communication and socialization skills of the offender.

Typical referrals are for outpatient adolescent sex offender treatment including individual, peer group, and family therapy.

Type 3: The Pseudosocialized Child Molester

Typically bright and social, the pseudosocialized child molester tends to be an older teen with a more chronic abuse history of a year or more. Therapy goals include breaking through the offender's denial and minimization, which are well defended because of his facile social skills. The offender often lacks genuine motivation for therapeutic change because his ability to compartmentalize his life is an effective defense.

This type of offender poses a significant danger of developing into a lifelong pedophile or personality disorder. This is the type that has the potential to evolve into the professionally successful minister, teacher, or youth leader who shocks the community by his unexpected arrest for years of child molestation.

These offenders are usually referred to an outpatient sex offender treatment program that includes individual, peer group, and family therapy. If a lack of compliance or heavy denial is demonstrated through the initial assessment/education program, an out-of-home placement or a residential program may be necessary.

Type 4: The Sexual Aggressive

Most rapists and violent sadistic child molesters are placed in this PHASE type. The offender is often antisocial and character-disordered with a significantly dysfunctional and abusive family system. Therapy includes effectively addressing the disorganized family system and abusive family members' tendency to undermine the adolescent's constructive therapy goals. The offender must develop more appropriate ways to express his anger and ways to satisfy his needs in a nonexploitative way. It is difficult to maintain the character-disordered offender's motivation in treatment.

The usual referral is to a residential adolescent sex offender treatment program or a trial attempt in an outpatient adolescent sex offender treatment program with a high level of supervision. All treatments should include intensive individual, peer group, and, where possible, family therapy.

Type 5: The Sexual Compulsive

The sexual compulsive engages in repetitive, sexually arousing acts such as window peeping, obscene phone calls, exhibitionism, and fetish burglary, or may also have a history of compulsive hands-on offenses. As a result, this type is considered a high recidivism risk.

Therapy typically focuses on the need to understand the behavioral sequence that led to the abusive events and to develop numerous interventions in that sequence that could be practiced in individual, group, and family therapy. Such therapy is done with the other PHASE types, but the sexual compulsive requires an intense focus on "relapse prevention" therapy.

The typical referral is to an outpatient adolescent sex offender treatment program with the option of out-of-home placement or residential treatment if the behavior is so compulsive that the offender cannot remain nonabusive in an outpatient setting.

Type 6: The Disturbed Impulsive

This is the most heterogeneous of the PHASE types in terms of abuse behaviors. The disturbed impulsive's offenses, whether a few or many in number, tend to reflect a malfunction of normal inhibitory mechanisms due to thought disorder, organic brain syndrome, intellectual or developmental disability, or chemical abuse. Therefore, the motivation is complex and individually determined, which makes effective assessment time consuming.

The therapist must complete in-depth psychological testing and a complete family and individual history in order to develop a concrete treatment plan. The families are often very dysfunctional and difficult to engage in therapy. Because of the complexity and impulsive nature of this type, it also has a high reoffense potential.

Depending on the results, referral could be to an inpatient psychiatric unit, a residential adolescent sex offender treatment unit, or a trial treatment in an outpatient adolescent sex offender program.

Type 7: The Group Influenced

The group influenced offender is typically a younger teen whose abuse occurs in concert with other peer offenders. Offenders should be split into separate therapy groups if referred at the same time, and the various offense stories should be compared and contrasted with the victim's testimony in order to develop a clear picture of what really happened. The offenders must be confronted about inconsistencies, rationalizations, projections, and blame. Each offender then must own his fair share of responsibility for the abuse and its effects on the victim. The usual referral is to an outpatient adolescent sex offender program unless the "leader" is actually a member of one of the more severe offender typologies.

The PHASE Typology:
Discussion

The PHASE typology is widely used in training and increasing awareness of those who must detect, assess, or treat juveniles with sexual misconduct behaviors: teachers, police investigators, juvenile probation officers, therapists, and social workers.

The PHASE typology is helpful in emphasizing that adolescent sex offenders are an aggregate of several distinct and discontinuous types. These types do not lie on a "continuum" and are not amenable to treatment by one particular therapy theory. For example, it may be inappropriate to use an "addiction" model on any type except perhaps the sexual compulsive. A "psychodynamic" approach may be inappropriate for the naive experimenter/abuser, who warrants a more direct and efficient psychoeducational approach.

Differentiating types helps "sort" those who are appropriate for a particular setting and model and address individual characteristics. The following factors determine the treatment a certain type will receive.

Setting. Is the adolescent a danger to himself or the community and therefore in need of inpatient treatment or residential treatment versus outpatient treatment? Are his victims or potential victims present in the home, requiring some period of separation?

Duration. What is the appropriate length of treatment? For example, it can be short for the naive experimenter/abuser and the followers in the group-influenced types, and medium or long for the more severe offender types such as the child molester, sexual compulsives, and sexual aggressives.

Therapeutic Strategies. What therapy and combinations of therapy are judged most appropriate? What therapists and therapeutic settings and orientations might be most appropriate for a particular client?

The PHASE typology can help guide individual/family assessment, suggest criminal justice restrictions, and differentiate therapeutic needs relevant to the issues of the particular client types.

A FAMILY SYSTEMS APPROACH: PERSPECTIVES AND EARLY STRUCTURING

Juveniles presenting to treatment nearly always have a parent or parent figure involved and present at intake. Bera (1985) found that out of 51 adolescent offenders studied in an outpatient program, all but one had a mother or stepmother and all but 12 had a father or stepfather involved in the current family constellation.

Early involvement of family members in therapy helps mobilize and maintain their commitment to the process, thereby maximizing the potential for comprehensive, effective assessment and treatment of the juvenile offender while in the program and after discharge. Significant family members provide important data in order to make a comprehensive assessment. An assessment is incomplete without the family to confirm and contextualize the adolescent's self-report and police, victim, or probation reports.

Early family involvement serves two key functions: it maintains the family members' awareness of and lowers the denial of the sexual abuse and it maintains the family's responsibility for abuse prevention and support of treatment strategies. The therapist frames his or her role as a "temporary consultant" to the caregivers, who bear the long-term responsibility. This critical early structuring enjoins the responsible caregivers as the "most important part of the treatment team" from the beginning of the assessment and therapy process. This encourages, maintains, and respects the family hierarchy (Minuchin & Fishman, 1981).

Such a therapeutic frame helps minimize the "abdication dynamic" by which temporarily overwhelmed caregivers attempt to give over responsibility for the care of the troubled adolescent to "professionals." The therapist hired to treat the adolescent can be triangulated to the point of suffering blame by parents, the adolescent, or both when inevitable difficulties occur.

A family-based intake assessment and therapy perspective also makes it possible to assess unrecognized victims and offenders in the family, extended family, and community. It allows these victims to get help early in the offender's therapy process.

Many practitioners agree that family involvement is potentially very useful. However, as many therapists are aware, a variety of roadblocks can appear when trying to recruit family members to take part in the treatment process. Many of these roadblocks are rooted in resistance on the part of the family. The following section offers strategies to deal with some of these potential roadblocks.

STRATEGIES TO INCREASE FAMILY INVOLVEMENT

Therapists can use a number of strategies to increase family involvement, especially before and during the intake session, when the critical early structuring of the therapy process occurs (Gelinas, 1988). The program should encourage parents, stepparents, and other family members to attend the intake assessment. This should include significant extended family members as well as the adolescent's siblings.

The intake assessment is an excellent opportunity to frame the sexual abuse in a nonshaming manner that emphasizes its effect on the whole family. For example, the therapist might state, "We're aware that Tony's behavior has affected everyone in the family, and it is important that they get some information and a chance to address their concerns as well." Such a statement helps the family feel their connection to the sexual misconduct without feeling blamed, thereby establishing a foundation for their participation in the treatment process.

Scheduling

Scheduling is one of the biggest headaches therapists encounter in their daily work. Most therapists are quite familiar with the emergence of resistance symptoms at this stage in the treatment process. Therefore, scheduling should be flexible in order to maximize the caregivers' involvement and to minimize potential schedule conflict excuses. A good way to respond to a parent's schedule conflict is simply by saying, "Well then we will schedule some other time" and offer alternative times and dates.

Missing Family Members

A strategy developed by Whitaker (1982) is to refuse to see any member of the family unless the whole family comes. The therapist can make himself or herself available by phone to answer resistant family members' concerns, which in turn help structure the first session.

Similarly, intake staff can make themselves available by phone to clarify and explain the intake and therapy process. This can be especially important to fathers who are often not "psychologically minded" or feel "dragged into therapy" or blamed. It is important to provide clear information and reassurances in a cordial and non-shaming manner. Some parents are concerned about what siblings, especially younger siblings, might hear. It can be clarified that the younger siblings will be in another room during the graphic descriptive portions of the intake.

Parents who are strongly resistant to involvement can be pressed to attend by the referring agency, usually the court system. This situation allows the intake therapist to avoid being the "bad guy," and frames the intake as an opportunity to address the entire family's concerns and develop support for an ongoing therapy process.

The Intake Session:
Structuring the Therapist/Family Relationship

In the intake session, it is useful for a therapist to maintain the role of "family consultant" or "advisor" to the parents, and to provide information that can help the family now, during the program, and after the program.

The therapist's personal limitations of time, knowledge, and power to change the presenting problem can be emphasized while the therapist provides general structure and leadership. Taking a personal "one-down approach" with such statements as "You know your child better than anyone could and you know clearly the problems he has" can help convey to the family a sense of safety, authority, and esteem. This frames the family as the crucial part of the treatment team. Treatment can be described as an opportunity to learn about how the sexual abuse began and develop ways to prevent it so that everyone can "pull together" to avoid being "dragged through this whole thing again."

The involvement of significant siblings and extended family members is especially important in minority and ethnic families. Martin and Martin (1978) state that the African American extended family provides a myriad of services such as informal adoption of children whose parents cannot care for them, financial support for unemployed members, childcare for working single parents, food, and shelter. The therapist's openness, respect and sensitivity to ethnic and minority differences can help increase significant family members' involvement and distinguish the program from past negative experiences with the majority "establishment."

A SYSTEMIC APPROACH
TO ADOLESCENT SEXUAL ABUSE

Treating the sexual abuse behavior is necessary but not sufficient in complete treatment of the conditions that allowed the development or maintenance of the problem. To reduce the risk of future sexual abuse, the systems to which the adolescent is connected in relationship to his sexual abuse must be dealt with. Relationship

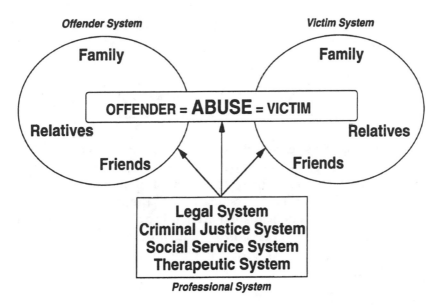

Figure 6.1. Systems and Perspectives Involved in a Sexual Abuse Case

dysfunctions often precede the sexual abuse behavior and are exacerbated by the abuse behavior. They can be dealt with most effectively in a family therapy context. The previous sections develop strategies to increase family involvement, "get them in the door." This section describes the development of a coherent systemic approach or "what to do once they're here."

In addition to family systems concerns, there are the "ecosystemic" issues of the social, racial, class, ethnic, and community contexts in which the abuse occurred (see Figure 6.1). As chapter 2 describes, these issues have a significant impact on how sexual abuse is defined and responded to. There are also the concerns of the other involved parties or stakeholders. The safety and needs of the victim and the victim's family are of first concern, whether the abuse occurred inside or outside of the family. In the initial stage of treatment of incest cases, the offending sibling is usually placed outside the home with a relative or in a foster home. Managing and coordinating the victim's issues are necessary aspects of a complete treatment plan. Criminal justice, social service, and therapeutic professionals are also involved, as may be extended family, community, school, and church figures.

STAGES OF FAMILY THERAPY
FOR ADOLESCENT SEX OFFENDERS

The therapy of adolescent sex offenders can be viewed in a series of stages. Each stage addresses particular goals that can be met using specific processes and techniques. Accomplishment of the goals at the preceding stage sets the foundation for the following stage. A stage approach helps demarcate therapeutic progress for the client, family, and involved professionals, and provides an orderly and structured plan to deal with the numerous issues present in adolescent offender treatment.

Therapeutic Context

The stages that occur in individual, group, and family therapy settings form the therapeutic focus for the treatment modalities of each stage. The therapeutic goal for a particular stage is introduced in individual therapy. Individual concerns and fears can be dealt with in this context of privacy, intimacy, and support.

An example is the abuse biography that is part of Stage 2; the individual writes the abuse biography detailing his history of sexual/physical/emotional abuse victimization and experience that led to and maintained the perpetration. He then shares the biography with his individual therapist, who provides feedback to help fill in gaps and clarify language in the biography. When an abuse biography is done, it can then be brought to group therapy.

In group therapy, the client can read his abuse biography and receive feedback and support from other group members. The sharing of this very personal history with others who have similar problems is an important part of developing group cohesion, overcoming shame, and giving up the secrecy associated with the sexual abuse.

Finally, the abuse biography is shared in family therapy. The family members ask questions concerning aspects of the abuse biography, because they often know the time frames and individuals involved, and therefore have a contextual grasp of the client's behavior. The therapist helps the family members ask questions that they previously may have been afraid to ask. This is an important stage in increasing family cohesion and breaking through denial, secrecy, and misattributions.

In this model, a therapeutic goal is first introduced and developed in individual therapy and then brought to group and finally to family therapy. Individual therapy is then used to help process the reactions of the group and family to the therapeutic task, setting the foundation for the next stage.

Structured family-based outpatient treatment programs such as PHASE coordinate individual, group, and family treatment modalities and can safely treat some fairly severe offender types by appropriately coordinating services. For example, a sibling incest offender can be placed in a relative's home, foster home, or group home setting where there are no vulnerable children present, thereby providing the victim safety and the offender therapeutic motivation. This allows the offender to be treated in or near his community, and it is easier to coordinate with the other therapists or caregivers involved, such as the victim's therapist or social worker. Many of the adolescent sex offenders and families served by PHASE receive primary treatment in a 6-month to more than a year time frame, with followup therapy as needed afterward. (Note that average length of treatment is longer nationally, reflecting possible differences in offender population served and program philosophy.)

Roles of the Therapist

In helping adolescent sex offenders and their families face juvenile sexual abuse, it is useful for the therapist to have a particular vision of his or her roles with the client, family, and other involved professionals through the stages of therapy. These roles change when the therapist is acting as an "individual therapist" versus a "family therapist" versus a "group therapist" versus an "organizational consultant." It is important for the therapist to clarify his or her role in each context.

Primarily, the therapist frames the problem; provides leadership, information, and support; and helps set direction for the troubled families and concerned persons who have enlisted this "expert's" help in dealing with the sexual abuse behavior.

It is useful to analyze the problem of sexual abuse therapy by levels of interaction. Individual therapy can deal with intrapsychic issues such as the individual's thoughts and feelings surrounding the abuse, the consequential misattribution or thinking errors, and the learning of the sexual abuse sequence. Another level of interaction is between family members and the family systems from which the offender came or in which the abuse occurred.

Another level involves the issues surrounding the victim/offender dyad explicated in chapter 7. Another level is peer interaction as demonstrated in group therapy and in reports from the school, community, or foster home. Finally, there is the professional level of involved social workers, therapists, attorneys, probation officers, and the like. Failure to look at the systemic and ecosystemic issues with which adolescent offenders present can lead to incomplete or abortive therapy results.

The therapist must consciously interrupt dysfunctional communication and interaction patterns demonstrated by the client and family and work toward changing the family structure. At each stage, the intervention is also diagnostic, as the therapist observes how the client and family respond. The response clarifies the issues to struggle with in the next stage. For example, as the parents read the teenager's abuse biography, it is not unusual that one or the other will recall personal abuse experiences. Such repressed experiences can explain a mother's protectiveness or a father's distance. With such issues uncovered, the family can more freely change in the desired direction.

The effective therapist working with adolescent offenders and their families plays a variety of roles and assumes leadership to provide complete treatment. The therapist, therefore, needs supervisory support to provide role clarity and share decision making. A sensitive and supportive team of treatment professionals and staff with good clinical direction can help therapists work with challenging families while minimizing professional "burn out."

Overview of Stages

The stages of therapy are as follows:

1. Assessment, education, and admission
2. Abuse biography: facts and behaviors
3. Abuse biography: thoughts and feelings
4. Abuse cycles defined
5. Relapse prevention training
6. Letters of apology and restitution/closure where possible
7. Graduation/aftercare

Each stage is defined and then illustrated by the case example of Peter and Jenny.

Case Example

Peter is a 14-year-old white male referred by the county probation service for a sexual health assessment. He had reluctantly admitted during a police investigation that he had sexually fondled a 4-year-old neighbor girl named Jenny while baby-sitting.

During the 2-hour intake interview with his family, Peter presented as a serious, responsible boy from an upper-class and very religious family. The youngest of four siblings, his brothers and sister were not involved because they lived out of the home. Peter and his parents were ashamed and did not know how to explain his sexual abuse. The family demonstrated strong discomfort and difficulty discussing any issues of sexuality.

Despite their reticence in informing the rest of the family of the abuse, Peter and his parents were open to signing a release-of-information form so the therapist could contact Jenny's parents. The two families had known each other for several years and attended the same church. Peter had baby-sat Jenny for 2 years, and all expressed concern about how Jenny and her family were doing. The two families had not talked to each other since the police investigation demanded that no contact occur between the two families. The victim and her family completed release-of-information forms, as did past and current therapists. Psychological and family tests were given to Peter and his family to complete.

As a result of Peter and his parents' motivation and Peter presenting as able to be nonabusive in an outpatient setting, they were accepted in the PHASE assessment/education program.

Stage 1: Assessment, Education, and Admission

Stage 1 frames and develops the treatment plan. The three initial
major goals—assessment, education, and admission—work together
synergistically.

Assessment involves interviewing and collecting data from the
individual, family, involved professionals, and the victim or victim's
family. Private sessions are held with the client, family, and siblings.
One goal is to obtain individual and family reports on sexuality and
sexual abuse history.

In the course of this assessment, individual and relationship dynamics are clarified. In addition, a review of chemical health, mental
health, and other issues is performed. Psychological testing is scored
and interpreted.

Ongoing education on the terminology, concepts, and differences
between healthy sexuality and sexual abuse are presented in group
sessions. This provides the words and concepts necessary to describe experiences the offender and family may have had but were
unable to articulate fully.

Because therapy is primarily a verbal activity, the provision of
concrete sexual information and terms is critical. This occurs in a
four session assessment/education group that includes peers who
are at the same stage as the offender. The parents benefit from a
parent education/support group because they are frequently unfamiliar with fundamental sexuality/sexual abuse knowledge. The combination of individual, group and family education with the ongoing
assessment provides the foundation for an initial or more complete
disclosure of sexual behaviors.

During these initial assessment/education sessions, the client and
family develop more comfort and ability to talk about sexuality and
sexual abuse. At the same time, the therapist is contacting other
involved professionals and the victim or victim's parents. The collateral information is used to confront the offender and family appropriately and tactfully regarding discrepancies, denial, minimiza-

tion, and projection, which are typically a part of the defensive mechanisms used. Without a clear admission of sexual abuse, it is inappropriate to refer the client to an ongoing sex offender treatment program because there is no clearly defined basis for a therapy contract.

The assessment, education, and admission stage provides data to share with other involved professionals. It is important for the therapist to share this information with the other involved professionals either over the phone or in a face-to-face "treatment planning session" in order to develop a unified treatment plan. This also creates a network to prevent relapse during outpatient treatment.

Dynamics common in sexual abuse can triangulate professionals against each other. These triangulations should be confronted early to develop a unified treatment plan to maximize the likelihood of complete success. Without a cohesive plan and early resolution of differences, therapy may be aborted when the issues between professionals reoccur. Without a unified plan and clear mandate from the "stakeholders" in the case, treatment should not proceed.

Case Example

For Peter and his parents, the assessment/education groups for Peter as well as the parents support groups proved important in their development of sexuality and sexual abuse information and appropriate language. Over the course of Stage 1, Peter's parents became noticeably more able to talk about sexuality, sexual abuse, and the abuse Peter had perpetrated on Jenny.

In the last group, Peter was able to state for the first time that he abused Jenny many times, not just the one time that he had previously admitted. He admitted the abuse continued over a 3-month period during his weekly Friday night baby-sitting. The abuse included fondling Jenny and encouraging her to fondle him. Peter made Jenny promise not to tell or he would not be her "friend."

Peter denied a history of physical or sexual abuse. He said the idea to touch Jenny came about because of his own curiosity with some peers' frequent discussion of sexuality and sexual exploits. Peter's initial experimentation became a patterned sexual abuse cycle that included masturbating after the sexual contact.

During Stage 1, Jenny's parents were contacted by phone. They were relieved to know what was going on with Peter and his family, since their information was at least 3 months old. They were also gratified to learn that Peter had made a full admission that concurred with what their daughter had told them. The victim-sensitive offender therapy process was outlined for them.

When asked what they would like at this time, Jenny's parents asked if Peter could attend Sunday church service at another time. Jenny and her parents often saw Peter there. She was also reminded of the incident by seeing him when he rode his bike past their house. Peter and his parents were happy to comply with these requests to attend another service and not to have Peter ride by the house.

Jenny's parents said that Jenny had been to therapy and that she was no longer having nightmares or other symptoms. As a result, Jenny was presently not seeing her therapist. Her parents agreed to sign a release-of-information form and have her therapist contact PHASE to share information and coordinate future therapy.

The PHASE number was provided to the parents for future reference if needed. The therapist promised to contact the family later in the course of therapy to provide other information, options, closure, and restitution. The probation officer was called and agreed with the treatment plan that Peter should begin the long-term outpatient adolescent sex offender treatment at PHASE. Jenny's therapist was also called and agreed to coordinate therapy as needed.

Stage 2: Abuse Biography: Facts and Behaviors

After there has been a clear admission of the sexual offense by the offender, he is ready to enter an ongoing adolescent sex offender treatment program. The focus of this stage is to develop a complete "abuse biography" that details in chronological order the adolescent's physical abuse, sexual abuse, and other abuse events he suffered or perpetrated.

In writing this abuse biography, the offender should segment the task in small steps; that is, write about the first five years of the client's life, followed by kindergarten, first, second, and third grade, and so on. Simultaneously, it is useful for the family to develop a family history that can parallel and place the adolescent's history in context. At this stage, the therapist generally "restrains" the client and his family from too great a focus on the emotional aspects of their histories. This helps protect the client and his family from being flooded with emotion, which increases resistance and slows this recollection and fact-gathering stage.

During this stage there is clarification of the exact details of the abuse and the language or meaning the client uses to understand these details. In this phase, the therapy is more supportive than confrontational. In individual, group, and family sessions, the therapist uses Rogerian-style active listening skills and positive reframing. These individually and family-generated abuse biographies are then shared by reading them aloud (if possible) in individual, group, and family therapy.

Case Example

After settling into the adolescent treatment group, Peter began working on his abuse biography. He was the youngest of four, with very active older siblings, and frequently felt powerless and left out of significant sibling and family events. The family's rigid religious beliefs and discomfort in discussing personal matters seemed to result in little discussion of sexuality, much less sexual abuse issues. The parents' own recalling of Peter's early development confirmed Peter's impressions. The parents had learned a lot that they "should have" known before about sexuality and sexual abuse.

As a result of his lack of information on sexuality, Peter had been extremely intrigued by his peers' graphic information about sexuality and sexual experience. Peter was jealous and again felt insignificant and powerless. He saw a ready opportunity while baby-sitting one Friday night.

Peter's writing of his abuse biography went very slowly. In a halting fashion, he tried to describe in detail each of the sexual abuse incidents that occurred over the 3-month abuse period. The therapist was very supportive and encouraging. At times, when Peter was barely able to get the words out, the therapist even helped write down Peter's words. If Peter became emotional and felt overwhelmed, the therapist would back off, acknowledging and appreciating Peter's guilt and remorse, at times saying, "It is a very good sign of health that you feel this bad for what you did." After a few minutes, Peter would feel settled and the therapist would return to the task of having Peter describe "just the facts" of what occurred, stating that "We will deal with these feelings and emotional pains in the next stage." It was in this way that the abuse biography was completed over a 2-month period.

Stage 3: Abuse Biography: Thoughts and Feelings

With the facts and memories clearer, the effect of writing and then reading the biography aloud in individual, group, and family settings can be very powerful. At this point, the therapist elicits the feelings and rationales the offender experienced in order to keep perpetrating. Emotional consequences of the abuse and the effects on involved parties are clarified, as are the defenses and misattributions utilized by the individual and family. This process of working through feelings and developing insights from the abuse history is critical in later defining the sexual abuse cycle that the offender has developed.

Case Example

Peter shared the biography in group and in family therapy. The therapist wrote on a copy of the abuse biography, making notes of feelings, misattributions, and insights developed during the readings in group and family therapy. Peter read slowly, sometimes in a shaking voice, and the remorse and tears came out.

Peter was especially anguished sharing the abuse biography with his parents, which resulted in tears for all involved. The seriousness of Peter's molestation of Jenny and the shame and guilt for his behavior was clear.

Stage 4: Abuse Cycles Defined

The sexual abuse cycle is defined in individual, group, and family therapy until what happens cognitively, emotionally, and situationally before, during, and after an abuse event is clear (see Figure 5.1). Developing a detailed understanding of the cycle enables well-founded and effective interventions.

With a clear abuse biography, the abuse cycle is easily defined. Now the misattributions of fault, blame, denial, and other thinking errors can be directly addressed. Heretofore, the therapist has maintained a generally "neutral," nonjudgmental stance in order to elicit the offender's history, thoughts, and feelings. The defenses are now laid bare in the individual, group, and family sessions.

If necessary, the therapist can use a powerful technique of highlighting the misattributions that involves the offender writing a therapeutic letter of apology to the victim. Offenders who have been merely complying with the treatment to this point often find this task onerous, because the therapist has had contact with the victim, the victim's family, and/or the victim's therapist and incorrect self-reports are easily countered. The offender knows that attempts to attribute blame or minimize abuse effects would be fruitless. Such a letter forces the offender to face his responsibility for the sexually abusive behavior and to increase his understanding of the consequences on himself, his family, and the victim. Letters of apology to the victim's parents (if a child victim) and to the offender's own parents can also be helpful.

An exercise for offenders who have been victims of physical or sexual abuse is to write a letter to their offender. This step can be done before or after the letter of apology to the victim. Another exercise involves writing the abuse history as seen from the victim's eyes. This is an excellent means of developing empathy for the victim; lack of victim empathy is key to misattribution to overcome internal inhibitors in the abuse cycle.

If the offender has been displaying appropriate victim empathy, the letter of apology writing can be delayed to Stage 6.

Case Example

Peter's abuse cycle became evident as a result of the facts and feelings developed in Stages 2 and 3. This included the minimization of the seriousness of what he was doing ("just touching each other") and Jenny's apparent lack of resistance. Peter now realized Jenny had been obedient and compliant only because Peter had baby-sat her for a long time—not because she "wanted to do it." Because of the therapist's contact with the victim's family, concrete information of the effects of the abuse (e.g., nightmares and hypervigilance) allowed no room for minimization.

The therapist now used a large piece of paper to outline Peter's abuse cycle as developed from Stages 2 and 3. The cycle was defined as follows.

Motivation: Power, intimacy needs, and sexual experimentation, and after a time, the baby-sitting situation were combined with sexual arousal.

Situational opportunity: Regular Friday night baby-sitting of Jenny provided a consistent opportunity.

Internal inhibitors overcome: Peter denied to himself that what he was doing was really abuse, so he was able to believe it was OK.

Victim resistance circumvented: The long-term baby-sitting relationship created a situation of authority and trust. Peter called it a secret and special game, threatening that if the secret was broken, he and Jenny would never be friends again.

Sexual abuse act: Fondling Jenny's vagina; having her touch his penis.

No negative consequences and pleasure/need is reduced: Abuse remained a secret for 3 months. Pleasure was experienced, and Peter's power, intimacy, and sexual needs were reduced.

Fantasy and masturbatory reinforcement: Abuse events were replayed through fantasy and reinforced with masturbation between baby-sitting times.

Rationalization and thinking errors: To Peter it was "only" fondling. He rationalized that because Jenny did not actively protest, maybe she "liked it." When he felt sorry for himself, he thought he "deserved" what he "got" from Jenny.

Peter's motivation for power, intimacy, and arousal appeared to be met through sexual abuse, and the abuse cycle was reinforced and repeated over Peter's 3-month abuse career.

Peter wrote his therapeutic letters of apology to Jenny, her parents, and his own family. Despite his increased insight and awareness, three drafts were necessary before a final draft was approved in group. Rationalizations and thinking errors continued to creep in. The letters were an important step toward taking full responsibility for his sexual molestation of Jenny.

Stage 5: Relapse Prevention Training

Stage 5 develops effective interventions in the abuse cycle. The context and history has become clear and insights are present. Family members are developing new roles and relationships. The offender and his family have an increased awareness of the emotional, psychological, and situational processes that led to the offense. They are now able to develop appropriate alternative behaviors and interventions.

By identifying the stressors, arousal patterns, fantasies, and reinforcers involved in the abuse pattern, the offender and his family can identify the stressful "high risk" situations and accompanying effect. The offender can identify underlying needs for affection, power, competence, and acceptance that were precursors for sexual acting out. The roles of the family, social, and peer system in allowing the sexual abuse (covertly or overtly) are clarified. Nonabusive ways to meet these underlying needs, as well as healthy, nonabusive interventions in the abuse cycle, are practiced in individual, group, and family therapy. The probation officer is informed of the relapse prevention plan for court support and supervision.

Case Example

A number of interventions were developed to minimize Peter's potential for future abuse. He and his family agreed that Peter should never baby-sit again or be in situations where he had power over or responsibility for children. He practiced stopping his abusive thoughts whenever they arose. Peter's masturbation fantasies were restructured using masturbatory reconditioning. While masturbating, Peter practiced stopping inappropriate/abusive fantasies (e.g., thoughts of Jenny) and reinforced positive, age-appropriate and nonaggressive sexual fantasies (e.g., thoughts of romantic, caring interactions with consenting peer-age mates).

Peter's need for empowerment and intimacy was addressed in family therapy with the entire family, including the siblings. In addition, Peter became active in appropriate peer-age groups at school and the community such as the choir, athletics, and the Boy Scout program. The probation officer was informed of the relapse prevention plan.

Stage 6: Letters of Apology and Restitution/Closure Where Possible

The letters of apology can now be refined for actual use. The therapist attempts to set up a closure session between the victim and victim's family and the offender and the offender's family. (Details and outcomes of these sessions are contained in chapter 7.) If the victim and victim's family prefer, the letter of apology can be sent through the mail in lieu of a face-to-face meeting, and/or the no contact contract can continue.

In a subsequent session, the offender can make amends and closure with his own family concerning the abuse events. For this closure ritual, the offender is also asked to write a letter.

Case Example

Peter completed the final versions of his apology letters to Jenny, Jenny's parents, and his own parents and family. These letters were therapeutically refined to the point where it became clear that there was no misattribution of fault or blame to others. Peter's full acceptance of responsibility for the sexual abuse was evident.

The therapist called Jenny's therapist, informing her that the letters of apology had been completed and were appropriate. She called Jenny's parents and asked if they would like to receive the letters through the mail or in a face-to-face session or to continue with no contact between the two families.

Jenny's family chose to receive the letters in a face-to-face session. The session was scheduled to be held at Jenny's therapist's office, where Jenny's parents had a sense of control and power. A remorseful Peter read the letters of apology to Jenny and her parents. This session was later said to be healing by both the victim's and offender's families.

A family session was then held for Peter's parents and siblings in which he read his letters of apology to them. These sessions were emotionally powerful and significant therapeutic closure was evident.

Stage 7: Graduation/Aftercare

In this final stage of primary sex offense therapy, the individual and family can review what was learned in therapy. This review of the therapy and the changes that the offender and his family has experienced can refine intervention strategies for future risk situations. Therapeutic closure in the individual, group, and family sessions occurs when issues that have not been addressed in the sex abuse program are identified and aftercare therapy is facilitated. For example, for those clients who continue to have social skills deficits, an ongoing social skills group or activities are recommended. Another common referral is ongoing marital therapy for parents whose marriages are troubled.

The last session ends with a series of "predictions" that sexuality and/or sexual abuse issues can emerge at different points in the future. Sometimes called "developmental prescriptions," these points often occur at developmental transitions that remind the offender of some aspect of the sexuality/sexual abuse issues for which he had been treated. Examples include when the offender starts dating, marries, has children, or when his children reach the same age as when he was abused or abusing. It is emphasized to the offender and his parents that this is normal, and that he will have to separate current situations from the past in a positive way. It is recommended to the recovering offender and his family that it is best to inform those he becomes intimate with about his past history and to see a competent therapist at these points.

Case Example

Peter and his family completed their sex offense specific therapy. Ongoing recommendations included Peter's continued commitment to no future baby-sitting or supervision of children, and continuation of his peer-age activities in school and the community. Relapse prevention strategies were reviewed and developmental prescriptions were discussed.

The therapist, Peter, and his family predicted some of the future developmental transition points that may give difficulty. When Peter begins peer-age, consensual sexual relationships, he may experience some inhibitions resulting from confusion between the present positive sexual intimacy and his past negative sexual abuse. Or when he has his own children, concern about his past sexual behavior may be activated. Such concerns were addressed, with possible interventions and resources defined.

The parents felt they had learned so much in this difficult experience that they instituted a sexual abuse prevention education program at their church for the families and children in the congregation.

Follow-up check-in sessions were scheduled at 3 months and 6 months after graduation to confirm Peter's ongoing positive behavior.

FUTURE DIRECTIONS

This chapter argues for the family systems perspective in understanding and treating the adolescent sex offender—a critical point of intervention in sexual abuse. It offers a critique of the current state of clinical knowledge from a theoretical and clinical perspective. The family is suggested as a usually available, important, but underused clinical resource. Practical strategies for increasing family involvement in therapy are offered.

No attempt is made to review the many schools of family therapy that contribute to this clinical issue. However, two schools are suggested as examples of the rich possibilities available to clinicians. Structural family therapy has much to offer, especially due to its success with low socioeconomic families, juvenile misconduct, and ethnically/racially diverse families. Minuchin and Fishman (1981) demonstrate how to turn an institution for boys into a treatment for families—a lesson that many juvenile offender institutions could learn.

Strategic family therapies offer creative ways to deal with the resistance and persistence in families. Other models to consider are contextual family therapy and behavioral family therapy. (For an excellent overview of family therapy, see Gurman & Kinskern, 1981, 1991.)

Levels in Family-Centered Treatment

In a nationwide survey of juvenile sex offender treatment programs, Knopp, Freeman-Longo, and Stevenson (1992) state that family therapy is used in the vast majority of juvenile sex offender programs. The survey did inquire about the degree of intensity of family therapy. The literature suggests that more intensive family-centered therapy is underutilized for two probable reasons: the current dominance of cognitive behavioral methods in sex offender treatment, and the individual and group therapy modalities that are the focus of most psychology and social work clinical programs. The following material will help the clinician understand how to build increased awareness and skills in family-based adolescent sex offender therapy logically.

Figure 6.2 is a prototypical developmental sequence for family-centered treatment as developed by Doherty and Baird (1986). Though first used in training family physicians and in research, this model has also been applied to the development of family-centered school psychologists (Doherty & Peskay, 1992).

This model can be used to assess adolescent sex offender therapists' current skills in family therapy and to encourage them to build on these skills. The model provides a series of levels based on the therapist's interest and competence in negotiating the therapist, client, and family therapeutic triangle. A knowledge base, personal development level, and course skills are delineated for each level. The model is adapted to the adolescent sex offender therapist with permission from the authors and the Society of Teachers of Family Medicine.

Each level of involvement can stand on its own as a valuable way for therapists to interact with families. Each level represents a knowledge base and set of skills to be mastered, which should not be discarded when a therapist becomes more sophisticated and moves to the next level.

A sense of competency and safety at one level sets the stage for the next, such as knowing how to talk about the facts of sexual abuse before talking about feelings that result from sexual abuse before moving into systemic family therapy. This developmental level paradigm helps avoid inappropriate attempts to use sophisticated family therapy "prescriptions" before having a solid base of family information and interaction patterns.

Family therapy is a promising area for future scholarly and clinical development in the field of juvenile sex offender treatment.

Level 1: Minimal Emphasis on Family

In this baseline level of involvement, the therapist deals with the family only as necessary for practical and legal reasons; communicating with the family is not integral to the therapist's role. The therapist who concentrates on the individual cognition and behavior of the adolescent offender is characterized as the sole conscious focus of change.

Level 2: Ongoing Therapeutic Information and Advice

Therapist's Knowledge Base: This stage is primarily information based, plus requires an awareness of the triangular dimension of the therapist, client, family relationship.

Therapist's Personal Development: Openness to engage clients and families in a collaborative way.

Therapist's Skills

1. Literally and clearly communicates therapy findings and treatment options to family members.
2. Asks family members questions that elicit relevant diagnostic and treatment information.
3. Attentively listens to family members' questions/concerns.
4. Advises families about how to handle the therapeutic needs of the client.
5. For large or demanding families, knows how to channel communication through one or two key members.
6. Identifies gross family dysfunction that interferes with treatment and refers the family to a family therapist.

Level 3: Feelings and Support

Therapist's Knowledge Base: Normal family development and reactions to stress.

Therapist's Personal Development: Awareness of one's own feelings in relationship to the patient and family.

Therapist's Skills

1. Asks questions that elicit family members' expressions of concerns and feelings related to the patient's condition and its effect on the family.
2. Empathetically listens to family members' concerns and feelings, and normalizes them when appropriate.
3. Forms a preliminary assessment of a family's level of functioning as it relates to the patient's problem.
4. Encourages family members in their efforts to cope as a family with their situation.
5. Tailors therapeutic advice to the unique needs, concerns, and feelings of the family.
6. Identifies family dysfunction and fits a referral recommendation to the unique situation of the family.

Figure 6.2. Levels of Therapist's Involvement With the Family in the Treatment of Adolescent Sex Offenders

SOURCE: Adapted from Doherty and Baird (1986) with permission from the authors and the Society of Teachers and Family Medicine.

Level 4: Systematic Assessment and Planned Intervention

Therapist's Knowledge Base: Family systems.

Therapist's Personal Development: Awareness of one's own participation in the systems, including the therapeutic triangle, the treatment system, one's own family system, and larger community systems.

Therapist's Skills

1. Engages family members, including reluctant ones, in a planned family conference or series of conferences.
2. Structures a conference even with a poorly communicating family in such a way that all members have a chance to express themselves.
3. Systematically assesses the family's level of functioning.
4. Supports individual members while avoiding coalitions.
5. Reframes the family's definitions of its problem in a way that makes problem solving more achievable.
6. Helps family members view their difficulty as requiring new forms of collaborative efforts.
7. Helps family members generate alternative, mutually acceptable ways to cope with their difficulty.
8. Helps the family balance its coping skills by calibrating the various roles in a way that allows support without sacrificing anyone's autonomy.
9. Identifies family dysfunction that lies beyond primary care treatment and orchestrates a referral by educating the family about what to expect from the therapist.

Level 5: Family Therapy

Therapist's Knowledge Base: Family systems and patterns whereby dysfunctional families interact with a therapist and other involved professionals.

Therapist's Personal Development: Ability to handle intense emotions in family and self to maintain neutrality in the face of strong pressure from family members or other professionals.

Therapist's Skills

Following is not an exhaustive list of family therapy skills but rather a list of key skills that distinguish level 5 involvement with families.

1. Interviews family members who are quite difficult to engage.
2. Generates a testing hypothesis about the family's difficulties and interaction patterns.
3. Escalates conflict in the family in order to break a family impasse.
4. Temporarily sides with one family member against another.
5. Constructively deals with a family's strong resistance to change.
6. Negotiates collaborative relationships with other professionals in other systems who are working with the family even when these groups are at odds with one another.

Figure 6.2. Continued

7

Victim-Sensitive Offender Therapy: A Systemic/Attributional Perspective

THIS CHAPTER PRESENTS a new paradigm for understanding interpersonal violence: the systemic and attributional model (Bera, 1990). A systemic and attributional critique of society's current response to sexual abuse is presented and a victim-sensitive offender therapy (VSOT) model is proposed as an essential part of comprehensive treatment for both victims and offenders.

A system perspective emphasizes the whole of a problem rather than its parts (Bateson, 1972; Whitchurch & Constantine, 1993). It emphasizes the contextual and interactional dynamics of abuse, the behaviors of the offender-victim dyad. This "system view" points out that, although the vast majority of sexual abuse occurs within intimate family and social systems (i.e., between family members, relatives, friends, or acquaintances), victims and offenders are generally treated in a fragmented, inadequate, and isolated manner, ignoring the context in which the abuse occurred. Furthermore, because both victims and offenders verbalize and act on misattributions of responsibility, they can be most completely treated by coordinated victim and offender communication and intervention in a carefully prepared, safe, and controlled manner.

The VSOT model is not the entirety of sex offender treatment but one part of the processes outlined in previous chapters. Offender-victim interactions potentially have the most positive impact on victims and offenders of any contact with the legal or social service systems. But if such interactions are not utilized or if they are done primarily for the offender's benefit, they can have a profoundly negative impact on victims.

A primary goal of victim-sensitive offender-victim interactions is to empower victims while protecting their safety. A second goal is to enhance the offender's sense of responsibility for his or her actions while increasing the offender's awareness of the true impact of his or her actions on victims and others. A final goal is to maximize the potential for therapeutic closure between the offender and victim.

In VSOT, the treatment provider can carve out a role of being sensitive to the victim within the offender's social service, legal, psychological, and family milieu. That role involves using offender-oriented systems to address the victim's concerns about the offender's past, present, and possible future abusive behavior. The sex offender therapy provider clarifies his or her role by stating, "I'm your therapist, but I will also be sensitive to the victim's concerns in the course of therapy." Being sensitive to the victim's issues enables the therapist to maximize the potential positive outcomes for both parties.

In general, offenders and victims may get similar three-stage treatment: their treatment needs are assessed; individual and/or group therapy works toward confronting and correcting the clients' mis-attributions of responsibility (victim's self blame or guilt, offender's victim or system blame); and clients write letters reflecting their new attributions and resulting feelings (confrontation letters by victims, apology letters by offenders).

The letters in many programs are not sent. The difference in this model is that the letters are sent. If the victim permits, the offender sends a letter of apology. If the victim and/or the parents choose to participate, meetings with the offender are held, enabling a real closure on the abuse experience rather than a symbolic one.

Further research is needed in the form of sensitively designed longitudinal studies on outcomes for both victims and offenders who participate in restorative offender-victim interactions. Early empirical studies on the positive impact of treatment strategies using victim-offender communication in the treatment of sexual abuse can be found in Yokley (1990). Outcome studies mediating other types of victim-offender conflict can be found in Umbreit and Coates (1992).

Although the model presented here is for juvenile sex offenders, it has also been used with adult sex offenders as well as juvenile and adult sexual abuse victims. The treatment stages are significantly longer for adult offenders than for juveniles. This three-stage model can be applied to the task of organizing the multiple issues in sexual abuse cases in general.

CONTEXT AND CRITIQUE OF CURRENT APPROACHES

Sexual Abuse Occurs Within the Victim's Family or Social System

The majority of victims of sexual abuse are assaulted by someone they know and should be able to trust: a family member, a relative, a neighbor, or an acquaintance. More than 80% of all child victims are sexually abused by people known to them. Parents, stepparents, or relatives are responsible for 30% to 50% of all cases, with neighbors, baby-sitters, or friends involved in most of the remainder (Finkelhor, 1986; Herman, 1992; Peters, 1976; Sgroi, 1975). In these studies, over one third of the assaults occurred in the child's home, whereas 20% occurred in the home of the offender. Adolescents and adult victims are more likely to encounter physical force or violence, usually in acquaintance or marital rape situations (Keller, 1980).

These studies demonstrate that incidents of forced, tricked, or manipulated sexual touch are usually committed by people who use their intimacy with the victim to perpetrate abusive behavior. Such incidents represent a fundamental breach of trust in society's most basic and precious relationships. These crimes of intimacy shake the victim's basic "faith in the world" and lead to the well-documented sequelae of abuse: victim guilt, shame, phobia, fear of risking intimacy, nightmares, and developmental disturbance (Briere, 1992a; Burgess & Holstrom, 1975; Finkelhor, 1986; Herman, 1992; Keller, 1980; Peters, 1976; Resick, 1993).

Treatment Is Often Fragmented, Inadequate, and Isolated

The treatment perspective traditionally adopted by professionals working with victims or offenders focuses on the individual's personality or family background, thereby ascribing etiology and treatment strategies to individual psychological dynamics. Classic criminology suggests that the offender's personality develops from his or her sociocultural conditions and, indeed, ascribes the offender's criminal behavior to those conditions (Sutherland & Cressey, 1978). The sexual abuse event is divided into at least two parts—victim and offender—and leads to the kind of fragmented responses critiqued here.

Social service and criminal justice systems can respond to sex crimes in an inadequate, fragmented, and piecemeal fashion (Wilson & Pence, 1993). Typically, reports of child abuse are investigated by county child protection workers with the help of the police. If the offender is a family member (e.g., father), the offender is often removed from the home to avoid a traumatic and revictimizing experience for the victim.

In cases where the victims are adults, the police investigate the abuse while support may be provided by victim assistance programs or rape crisis center workers, where such programs are available.

Both child and adult victim cases are usually referred to the courts, where restraining orders and confidentiality laws (intended to protect the victim) and attorneys' strategic advice (intended to protect the alleged offender's rights) may further alienate the participants and exacerbate their trauma (Briere, 1992a).

"No talk" rules embodied in these legal devices increase the misattribution of responsibility: the victim assumes blame for the abuse and its consequences (often based on direct or indirect messages from the offender and/or other family members) while the offender (often aided by his or her lawyer) projects all blame onto the victim and paints him- or herself as the innocent victim of circumstance, a misunderstanding, or the system. Thus the adversarial legal process tends to cement countertherapeutic mindsets in victims and offenders (and often their therapists).

Although offenders may be ordered into treatment by the courts and may receive coordinated state- or county-funded services, a significant portion of sexual abuse victims receive no treatment for their abuse-related trauma (Sgroi, 1991). Officials often pay inadequate attention to the concerns of these victims. In cases where children are victims of extended family members or neighbors, the only help offered may be a pamphlet handed out after the evidentiary interview.

Although psychotherapy might help, often it is unavailable or too expensive. Many parents do not pursue professional help because of embittering experiences with the system and conflicted loyalties to the offender. Child sexual abuse forms the largest category of all reported sex crimes, yet of the offenders with whom we have worked, only a minority of victims has any contact with a professional therapist.

Although adult victims may receive help from rape crisis centers (available primarily in urban settings), the victim must actively search out the services and maintain therapy for complete treatment. For a number of reasons, however, rape crisis centers often fail to provide adequate support. In most cases they define their mission in terms of crisis management and advocacy rather than treatment. Although this constitutes a necessary first step, it is incomplete as a therapeutic process (Briere, 1992a).

After the abuse report and if there is a confession or legally "sufficient" evidence, sex offenders may be placed in a criminal "correctional" facility or residential treatment facility, or court ordered into outpatient treatment as a condition of probation. Usually some combination of the above is recommended. Prison and residential treatment facilities usually treat the offender in isolation from the community, using an individual and group therapy format (Swartz, 1989).

Even in incest cases there is often no sensitive opportunity for the victim to express his or her issues vis-à-vis the offender—no forum is offered for the victim to develop a therapeutic sense of power. Often, the next time the victim hears about the offender after the initial investigation or trial is through an announcement of the offender's impending release. "Untreated" victims may contact rape crisis centers or mental health clinics for help at this time.

Generally, victims and offenders are treated together in outpatient programs only if both are members of an intact nuclear family (Gelinas, 1988). If there has been a divorce or the victims are outside the immediate family, attempts at achieving a therapeutic resolution of the abuse between the victim and offender are rarely made. In extra-familial pedophilia and rape, the victim is not considered a part of treatment and no attempts are made to confront the issues between the two people most involved.

In contrast to current fragmented isolated treatment modes, Gulotta and deCataldo-Neuberger (1983) argue for a very different, holistic perspective: a systemic and attributional approach to the whole field of criminology and victimology:

> It should be no longer concentrated only on the victim's [or offender's] personality and on his sociocultural condition, but should embrace the dyad, criminal-victim, a system which cannot be separated without inciting the same criticism aimed at all psychological currents of individualistic trend. (p. 5)

MISATTRIBUTION ISSUES FOR OFFENDERS AND VICTIMS

Offender Misattributions:
Blaming Victims, Excusing Themselves

Attribution theory was developed within the field of social psychology and offers a useful perspective on sexual abuse. As Kelley and Thibaut (1969) define it, "Attribution theory describes the process by which the individual seeks and attains conceptions of the stable dispositions or attributes" (p. 5).

An action such as sexual abuse can be attributed to causes in the environment or in the situation, or to the underlying dispositions of the persons involved. The mainstay of the attributional process is that "intent" is imputed rather than observed. Heider (1958) was the first to call the attention of psychologists to the fact that actions are controlled more by how an event is perceived than by what actually happens.

Offender misattributions are well documented in the literature. Scully and Marolla (1984) interviewed 114 convicted male rapists to examine the motivations and attributions they used to explain their behavior. They report that these convicted rapists' attributions of blame or minimization to the victim fall into five major categories: women are seductresses, women mean "yes" and say "no," most women eventually relax and enjoy it, nice girls do not get raped, and the sexual assault is only a minor wrongdoing.

Similar attributions of fault to the victim are also found in various analog studies using male and female college undergraduates (Shotland & Goodstein, 1983) and medical students (Gilmartin, 1983). A possible explanation for the similarity of attribution to the victim by diverse subject pools is posited by Lerner (1980). He theorizes that people are inclined to believe in a "just world," a place where individuals "get what they deserve and deserve what they get."

According to this belief, the quality of "goodness" or "evil" is attributed to the personality or the behavior that brings about the good or the evil result. In order to maintain their view of the world as "just," people need such attributions of fault—or a negative disposition—to victims. If bad things can happen to good people, the same could happen to them. The "just world" view thus becomes "defensive attribution."

Study subjects attribute fault to sexual abuse victims regardless of age. Using scenarios involving child and adolescent victims with an adult offender, Waterman and Foss-Goodman (1984) replicated many of the adult and peer assault victim-blaming results. Regardless of the victim's age (7, 11, or 15 years) and the offender's adult status, respondents placed some responsibility for the sexual abuse on the victim. The major reason respondents gave for blaming child victims was, "The victims should have resisted." Significantly, subjects also blamed the nonparticipating parents of the victims because they "should have protected the victim" or they in some way contributed to the victimizing event.

Both subject characteristics and victim characteristics relate to how much victims are blamed. Respondents whose answers exhibit sexual conservatism and acceptance of interpersonal violence are more likely to find fault with the victim's behavior. Subjects who report histories as victims of molestation blame victims less than subjects who do not report such past incidents. Waterman and Foss-Goodman further suggest that "blaming the victims may contribute to a climate conducive to child-molesting" (1984, p. 347). A better understanding of the determinants of victim blaming may lead to strategies for changing these attitudes.

Scully and Marolla's (1984) findings also include rapists who admit responsibility for their behavior. These men developed excuses permitting them to view their behavior as idiosyncratic rather than typical; therefore they believe that they are not really rapists.

The men's self-attributions sort into three main categories: they were under the influence of alcohol or drugs and thereby had diminished responsibility for the rape; their act was a result of emotional problems that diminished their responsibility; and they painted an image of themselves as "nice guys" in an attempt to minimize the crime and negotiate a nonrapist identity.

Admitters project the image of someone who has made a serious mistake, but who in every other respect is a decent person. Their severe minimization of the effects of the abuse and their responsibility for them is readily apparent. Scully and Marolla (1984) note that this lack of personal acceptance of responsibility is fertile ground for the development of future sexual misconduct.

In Waterman and Foss-Goodman (1984), respondents attribute blame to the adult offender in child sexual abuse scenes for the following reasons (in descending frequency of report): the offender abused power, the offender was "sick," the offender was morally wrong, adults should know better, and the offender must have ignored the victim's protests.

In the same study, respondents attribute fault to the nonparticipating mother and father of the victim because the parents should not have left the child alone, the parents should have taught the child how to prevent abuse, and the parents did not elicit the child's ability to confide in them.

Furthermore, when the offender is the spouse of the parent, the nonabusive parent (usually the mother) is faulted for not sexually satisfying the offending spouse, not teaching the child how to prevent abuse, and not being the kind of parent in whom the child could confide.

Work continues on offender misattribution. Pollock and Hashmall (1991) focused on the themes and structures of the excuses of 86 child molesters and found similar results as the studies described above.

Misattributions by Victims:
Guilt and Self-Blame

Numerous studies (Burgess & Holmstrom, 1975; Herman, 1992; Landis, 1956; Peters, 1976; Sgroi, 1991) have found that child victims of sexual abuse tend to keep the secret from their parents because they feel the abuse is in some way their own fault and they fear rejection, blame, punishment, or abandonment for this confusing and often terrifying event.

The personal and psychological effects on the victim and family can be multiple: fear of safety at home, eating and/or sleeping disturbances, nightmares, learning disorders, and numerous other symptoms that are now suggested as constituting "post-sexual abuse trauma syndrome" (Briere, 1984, 1992b).

Because of the many attributional dynamics and their serious consequences, therapists who work with sexual abuse victims emphasize that the sexual abuse is never the victim's fault, that it is serious, and that victims may experience it as life threatening. Becoming angry about the abuse and going through a grieving process are therapeutic for the victim in "letting go" of the abuse events (Herman, 1992). Developing a sense of self-control and mastery over their own life situations is enhanced by such techniques as assertiveness training and self-defense classes (Bera, 1980).

These misattribution-laden mindsets on the part of both victims and offenders warrant coordinated assessment and treatment planning that benefits the clients, families, and professionals involved. Unfortunately, few current treatment approaches provide such a holistic approach. Most fail to offer any therapeutic closure options for the individuals most involved and affected by the abuse events: the victim and offender.

Systemic Perspectives
for Victim-Offender Issues

A systemic and contextually based process involving controlled interaction between the victim and offender is a common therapeutic strategy in incest treatment (Goodwin, 1982; Trepper & Barrett, 1986). This process is coordinated by the family therapist and provides critical information and therapeutic experiences for completing treatment in a systematic way. This process empowers the victim with additional information, a sense of safety and respect, and choices that can lead to a more satisfying and complete resolution of the abuse.

Gelinas (1988) emphasizes that individual and group therapy for trauma "is necessary but not sufficient to resolve the negative effects of incest on the victim's life. It is also therapeutically essential to work with the particular relational issues surrounding incestuous child sexual abuse" (p. 5). These issues are worked through with face-to-face family therapy that includes both the offender and the victim.

Another example of a systemic approach aimed at increasing appropriate avenues for therapeutic closure is the victim-offender reconciliation programs (VORPs) that have existed for a number of years (Knopp et al., 1976; Umbreit, 1985; Wright & Galaway, 1989). These programs bring victims and offenders together in a controlled, safe, and supervised process, and have been used successfully in robbery, assault, vandalism, and other crimes (Green, 1984). A body of literature and a number of professional associations have been developed within the VORP movement.

Concerns regarding the VORP approach focus on the inappropriateness of using a reconciliation or mediation model in crimes of interpersonal violence because of the significant power disparity between offender and victim. "Mediation" and "reconciliation" imply that two sides compromise and agree on some middle ground. The movement recognizes that such language is clearly inappropriate in cases of sexual abuse or physical violence.

This process is more accurately portrayed in new language and conceptual frames (most clearly developed by Zehr, 1990) as seeking "restorative justice" when injustice has occurred. Sexual and physical abuse is an abuse of power and authority, most often from a position of trust, over a vulnerable and available victim. The aim of VSOT is to empower the victim and restore justice by having the offender take responsibility for the offense and offer appropriate contrition, restitution, and apologies in a personal and meaningful way. (For a detailed history and discussions of these issues with illustrative cases, see Wright & Galaway, 1989.)

Victim-sensitive offender therapy attempts to be victim sensitive in both conceptualization and language. Ethically, it values the safety, rights, and needs of the victim as a primary aspect of offender treatment.

In workshops on the VSOT model, the traditional training of therapists, psychologists, and social workers is challenged because the issues of sexual abuse are outside the boundaries of discrete "disciplines" and demand a holistic or systemic view. Such a view helps overcome the dilemmas forced by "normally defined" disciplines while safely attempting a more complete therapeutic resolution of interpersonal violence.

An overview of those involved in many sexual abuse cases is presented in Figure 6.1. Sexual abuse connects the offender and victim and, as a result, their respective families.

The professional system includes the legal, criminal justice, social service, and therapeutic professionals connected to the victim or the offender. Because of the recognition of the involvement of these professionals in child sexual abuse, many counties have multidisciplinary child abuse teams to develop effective coordinated responses (Wilson & Pence, 1993). The VSOT model recognizes the need for coordinated treatment beyond simple investigation of the abuse.

TREATMENT DESCRIPTION

Systemic or multisystemic approaches represent today's most promising direction for sex offender treatment and control strategies (Freeman-Longo & Knopp, 1992). For example, Pithers et al.'s (1989) modified relapse prevention model integrates the offender system and professional system depicted in Figure 6.1. The model and its advantages are reviewed in chapter 6.

Victim-sensitive offender therapy was designed to overcome the aforementioned systemic dilemmas while redefining the VORP or mediation model from a victim-sensitive, ethical, safety, and rights position more appropriate for sexual offense treatment. It adds the victim system to the modified relapse prevention model.

To use this model, therapists working with sex offenders need to view the rights, feelings, and safety of the victim(s) (or potential victims) of their client's behavior as a primary concern. At the same time, therapists must avoid jeopardizing the rights of the offender. This ethical posture should guide every view, insight, and decision the therapist makes regarding the offender.

STRENGTHS OF THE VSOT MODEL AND VICTIM-OFFENDER COMMUNICATION MODELS IN GENERAL

Although the VSOT model runs counter to traditional, individually focused treatments, it is a logical consequence of a systemic, ethical, and attributional analysis of sexual abuse and has the following strengths.

1. The model keeps the offender fully responsible for his abusive behavior.
2. The model minimizes misattribution of fault to the victim.
3. The therapist is prevented from inadvertently colluding with the offender against the victim because of limited data, coming primarily from the offender.
4. The model keeps the offender out of trouble by confronting early on any malicious gossip and indirect "get-backs" directed against the victim or family.
5. The therapist maintains a clear ethical perspective throughout treatment, minimizing confusion at decision points.
6. The model maintains a victim-offender system view throughout that can maximize the degree of therapeutic closure for both victim and offender.
7. The model helps ensure completeness of treatment for the offender and thereby minimizes the potential for victimizing behavior.
8. The model gives the therapist more complete information at each stage to make sound treatment plans by supplementing traditional reliance on the offender's self-report with ongoing victim input.
9. The therapist is able to maintain a high level of credibility with other involved professionals (e.g., judge, child protection worker, social worker, probation/parole supervisor) by keeping the victim's interest at heart and soliciting the input of all concerned.

Yokley (1990), writing on sexual abuse victim-offender communication intervention models, summarizes a number of potential benefits for the victim:

1. The victim receives assurance of the reality of the abuse.
2. The victim feels relief of guilt/self-blame.
3. The victim has the means for appropriate expression of anger.
4. The victim can reconsider (misattributed) responsibility and empowerment through confrontation.

The offender can potentially benefit in the following ways (Yokley, 1990):

1. The offender accepts responsibility.
2. The offender develops victim empathy and awareness.
3. The victim earns emotional restitution.

Cautions and Guidelines

Yokley (1990) offers a number of guidelines for victim-offender communication interventions:

1. Victim safety and benefit is primary.
2. Victim-offender communication interventions should always be voluntary, at the victim's discretion, and in the victim's best interest.
3. Victim-offender communication interventions should involve only treated offenders who accept full responsibility and are remorseful.
4. The offender and the victim should be carefully prepared.
5. The offender should use responsible, victim-sensitive language.
6. The victim can be empowered and supported through early provision of information about the offender. This improves the victim's understanding of the offender's behavior.
7. Apology sessions should be timed prior to the end of offender therapy. It should be clear to the offender that further rehabilitation and supervision is often warranted.
8. Only trained sexual abuse professionals should be used.

THE VSOT PROCESS

The three-stage VSOT process was originally developed in the Program for Healthy Adolescent Sexual Expression (PHASE) and continues to be refined. Chapter 6 provides a description of concurrent clinical treatment of offenders' sexually abusive behavioral patterns. A brief description of the VSOT process follows.

Ideally, the VSOT process should be undertaken only after the offender has pled guilty and no lawsuits are contemplated by the involved parties. If either the victim or the offender has unusual life events or stresses, VSOT should be delayed to a more appropriate time. Examples of such stresses include significant thought disorder, psychiatric mental illness such as active schizophrenia, manic-depression, major depression, or unremitting rage or anger at the offender that precludes any chance of nonabusive communication. Such anger is most likely if a parent of the victim has been a victim himself or herself and has significant unresolved abuse, shame, and rage. There is no way to predict or guarantee the participants' behavior and foster reasonable expectations. Both the victim and the offender have the right to stop at any point in the process. Clinical judgment and the circumstances of each case should guide the application of this or any resolution model.

A summary of the VSOT process appears in Figure 7.1.

Stage 1: Communication Switchboard

The first stage sets the context and expectations for the assessment and VSOT process. At intake or shortly after the juvenile sex offender begins the assessment process, the therapist assumes a central role as communication coordinator or "switchboard" among all concerned participants, including the probation officer, previous therapists, the offender, and the victim (or parents of victims who are underage). The therapist explains the VSOT model, its stages and goals, and why certain information must be shared with other treatment personnel, agencies, the victim, his or her family, and their therapist.

The offender (or parents/guardian) signs release forms allowing the therapist to get the offender's police statements and to contact the victim(s) (or parents/guardian). This is the point at which the therapist clarifies to the client, "I'm your therapist, but I am also sensitive to the victim's concerns." Just as the family therapist is challenged to maintain multiple roles that must be clarified in the course of therapy, the VSOT therapist must openly clarify his or her roles with the victim and the offender.

Stage 1: "Switchboard" (intake to 2 months)
A. Process for Offender
  1. Offender (or guardian) signs releases of information for:
    a. Victim and offender's police/child protection statements
    b. Permission to contact victim(s) (or parents/guardian)
B. Process for Victim
  1. Therapist initiates contact with victim (or parents/guardian). Therapist answers questions, provides support for reporting, lets victim know disposition of case and offender's current status (i.e., on probation and in treatment).
  2. Therapist discusses victim's need for treatment of abuse effects and provides current information and therapy referral.
  3. Therapist solicits reports of offender's ongoing intrusive behaviors and responds with appropriate measures to curb them.
  4. Therapist explains the purpose of release-of-information forms, requests cooperation, and sends release form to victim (or parents/guardian).
C. Goals
  1. To complete a contextually sensitive offender assessment.
  2. To ensure a complete and therapeutic exchange of all abuse-relevant information among involved systems and persons.
  3. To establish the identity of the VSOT therapist as the victim's advocate within the offender's milieu.
  4. To enlist victim's (et al.) involvement in the VSOT process.

Stage 2: Confront Misattributions and Check Progress (3-5 months)
A. Process for Offender
  1. Therapist checks offender's misattributions toward victim(s) or system.
    a. Offender fully accepts blame/responsibility for acting on his decision to abuse.
    b. Offender clearly knows effects of abuse on victim.
    c. Offender owns full responsibility for abuse consequences to himself.
  2. Offender completes a sexual abuse biography and writes a clear letter of apology to the victim(s) (and victim's parents) for his abusive behavior.
B. Process for Victim
  1. Therapist checks progress of victim therapy.
  2. Therapist provides needed information and a progress report of offender to victim and/or guardians.
C. Goals
  1. To confront any continued sexual abuse misattributions.
  2. To complete a progress assessment of the offender and victim.
  3. To revise the treatment plan and closure expectations in preparation for Stage 3.

Stage 3: Closure Choices (6-12+ months)
A. Process for Victim(s) (or Parents)
  1. Choose closure option.
    a. Offender continues a no contact contract with victim (and family).
    b. Offender mails a letter of apology to the victim.
    c. Offender attends a face-to-face closure meeting with the victim (and family), reads apology letter, answers questions.

Figure 7.1. Overview of the VSOT Process

2. Prepare for closure.
   a. Victim processes new questions and feelings.
   b. Victim clarifies expectations.
   c. Victim chooses ways to make the meeting room (if closure meeting is chosen)/home/neighborhood/school feel safe.
B. Process for Offender (and family)
   1. Offender understands and complies with the expressed choices of the victim(s) (or parents).
C. Goals
   1. Offender faces the personal effects of his abusive behavior and makes apology.
   2. Victim develops a sense of personal closure and control.

Figure 7.1. Continued

The communication switchboard stage allows the VSOT therapist to do a complete and contextually sensitive assessment of his or her client by getting all sides of the sexual abuse experience. Only a small minority of teenage sex offenders are completely honest about their sexual abuse or fully recognize the effects of the abuse on their victim(s), but they often are open to their therapist contacting the victim in hopes of making therapeutic progress and increasing the potential for achieving closure.

The VSOT therapist calls the victim(s) (or parents/guardian) to let them know the disposition of the case (e.g., "Frank pled guilty and is now on probation; he's in our outpatient treatment program."). It is not unusual for a long period of time to have passed since the abuse report, and victims may wonder about the results of the investigatory or legal process. This telephone call is often the first concrete information the victim has received about the offender since the investigation or trial.

In this phone call, the therapist supports the victim or parents for reporting the abuse, despite any frustrating or traumatizing interactions they may have had with the social service and/or legal systems. In our experience, only about 25% of the victims or their concerned persons who are contacted have been involved in any kind of therapy. Often they are embittered by the investigatory and legal process they have gone through, and do not trust asking for further "professional" help. During the time since the investigation, however, new thoughts or concerns may have come to mind that they may wish to share with a therapist.

The VSOT therapist educates parents about the need for victim treatment, where and from whom they can get it, and how it can be funded (victim-assistance programs, victim compensation, and/or restitution provisions in the offender's sentence). The VSOT therapist solicits any concerns the victim and/or parents have about the abuse, the victim's trauma-based behavior changes, or continued emotionally intrusive behavior by the offender. The therapist helps the parents sort out their primary concern (helping the victim heal) from their feelings of loss of relationship to the offender or the offender's family.

Because the offender is usually a neighbor or family member, some level of emotionally intrusive behavior may be continuing: The baby-sitter offender rides his bike past the victim's house every day; the two families encounter each other every Sunday at 9 o'clock Mass; gossip targeting the victim as "promiscuous" or "easy" haunts the victim at school. The VSOT therapist justifies the victim's trust and confidence in him or her by intervening whenever possible through alterations in the offender's behavior contract or amplified interpretations of existing court orders.

The VSOT therapist encourages the victim to ask any questions about the abuse he or she would like the offender to answer and to continue reporting any inappropriate offender behavior. By talking with the offender's therapist and seeing results, the victim may develop a sense of power and control of his or her situation. Ideally, the victim feels that what he or she went through then—and is currently experiencing—is important and is finally being heard.

The victim and/or parents have a direct impact on the offender's treat- ment by providing corroborating or contradictory evidence regarding the offender's disclosure of offense behaviors, and by exposing the offender's subsequent intimidation or power/control behaviors.

After explaining that the information will be used to confirm or confront information in the offender's disclosure, the VSOT therapist asks the victim or parents/guardian to sign releases of information for copies of the victim's police statement and interview with the child protection services worker. If the victim is in therapy, the family is asked to give permission for the victim's therapist to consult with the VSOT therapist.

In this initial stage, the VSOT therapist begins to enlist the victim(s) and his or her concerned persons in an ongoing information-sharing and therapy process. The victim learns that her or she will be provided with information, options, and choices as needed, and that the VSOT therapist is a significant supportive contact within the offender's milieu who will be at the victim's service in the months to come.

Stage 2: Confront Misattributions and Check Progress

Stage 2 occurs 3 to 4 months into the treatment program. The offender must complete a verbal or written abuse biography detailing his history of abusive sexual behavior. The VSOT therapist checks this document for misattributions the offender continues to hold against the victim and determines whether the offender fully accepts blame/responsibility for deciding to engage in his abusive behavior, whether the offender clearly knows the effects of the abuse on the victim, and whether the offender accepts full responsibility for the consequences of his behavior to himself (in other words, he does not blame the victim or "the system" for where he is now). All three conditions must be met before going on to Stage 3.

After the offender completes the abuse biography, he writes a letter of apology to the victim and victim's parents to begin making amends for his crime. The offender reads his biography and letter in individual, group, and family therapy sessions. The offender's therapist, family, and/or treatment group may reject the documents.

The offender rewrites and/or rereads these documents until they are accepted as both convincing and sincere. Sincerity is assessed by looking at omissions of fact or feeling, victim-blaming language, or incongruent affect while the offender is reading. Any inappropriate content or incongruent affect is confronted with feedback from the therapist, family, and group ("If the victim were here listening to this, I don't think she'd/he'd believe you").

Writing the letter (often only one or two paragraphs) is usually more stressful for adolescent offenders than writing several pages of abuse biography, perhaps because the letter is a more personal and direct admission of responsibility.

If the victim is in therapy and has given permission, the VSOT therapist consults with the victim's therapist to check on the progress the victim has made. The consultation provides two-way "reality checking." First, the VSOT therapist can compare the effects of the abuse and the victim's memory of events with the offender's self-reported abuse biography. Second, the victim's therapist (or parents/guardian) can gain access to the offender's abuse biography and police statements as a reality check for the victim (especially valuable when the victim has dissociated during the abuse). New information from the offender may help explain victim behaviors or phobias that were not thought to be abuse related.

The offender should not be allowed contact with the victim until his biography and letters are approved, he shows no tendency to blame the victim, and the victim does not blame himself or herself.

Finally, the VSOT therapist provides a progress report on the offender's readiness to continue the process, offers other information that may be useful, and again solicits any questions the victim may have regarding the abuse.

Stage 2 has three major goals: to confront any continued sexual abuse misattributions, to complete a progress assessment of the offender and the victim, and to revise the offender's treatment plan and expectations in preparation for Stage 3.

These goals are important in developing plans and expectations for the level of closure the victim chooses in Stage 3. Offenders and victims and their families may have high hopes that the closure session will "fix" everything so that their lives can go back to "normal." The therapist must clearly outline what can be accomplished at each level of closure to prevent the victim or the offender from being disappointed or having a sense of failure. The VSOT therapist helps the victim and his or her family plan what to expect so they do not feel "used" in the process and to save the offender from an inappropriate blast of rage that could be countertherapeutic.

Stage 3: Closure Choices

Stage 3 may occur when the adolescent sex offender has been in treatment for 5 to 12 or more months. Closure is the last major task in the VSOT process. The offender is nearing completion of his other treatment components: His abuse biography and letters of apology have been accepted by his therapist, family, and peer treatment group; he accepts full responsibility for all aspects of his abusive behavior; and he has some understanding of the effects of his behavior on his victim.

The VSOT therapist contacts the victim (or his or her therapist and parents) to discuss the closure process. The VSOT therapist outlines three levels of closure and gives the victim time to decide which one he or she will choose.

1. The offender will continue to comply with the no contact contract into the future. The VSOT therapist makes a commitment on behalf of the offender that the contract will be honored, backing up that commitment with a promise that the therapist will relay any breaches of the contract to the offender's probation officer.
2. The offender will mail a letter of apology to the victim. The VSOT therapist offers (with the offender's informed consent) whatever closing information about the offender's process that the victim asks for or that might be helpful to him or her.
3. The offender (and his family, if appropriate) attend a face-to-face meeting in a setting the victim chooses with any support people the victim chooses. At the meeting, the offender reads his apology letter(s) to the victim and his or her family and answers their questions.

After hearing these choices and processing the ramifications of each, the victim chooses a route. In the process of choosing, the victim may develop new questions he or she wants the offender to answer and may experience new feelings and emotions to work through with his or her therapist.

Among the victim's options is changing his or her mind about closure choices at any time, including at the face-to-face meeting. Victims are invited to contact the VSOT therapist any time they have questions or want to talk about the abuse and feel the VSOT therapist may be helpful—even years after the event. Referring a therapist for the victim may be necessary as well.

The victim's therapist prepares the victim (and parents/guardian) for the closure meeting by reviewing questions and clarifying the family's expectations for the meeting. The therapist reaffirms that the offender is at fault and helps the victim choose how to make the

Stage 1 Therapist Letter
Following is the initial letter sent by the VSOT therapist to Tammy's parents.

Dear Theresa and Tom:

Thank you again for spending so much time with me on the phone
this week telling me your side of what happened between Michael and
Tammy. I know that talking about the abuse again can be uncomfortable
and even painful. Yet it is just that detailed information of what
you know happened and the effects it had on Tammy and yourselves
that allows me to do a complete assessment and treatment plan. This
ensures that Michael is held fully accountable for his actions and
their consequences.

Enclosed is a copy of the release-of-information form signed by
Michael's parents. I am glad I could answer questions you had concerning Michael and his therapy. Please call if other questions or concerns come up.

Also enclosed is a release-of-information form for you. I would
like you to sign and return it in the stamped envelope. This will
confirm the verbal release you gave me this week so I can include
your information and concerns as part of the assessment and therapy
goals. A second release allows me to talk to Tammy's therapist.

Finally, you will find a brief description of the victim-sensitive
offender therapy stages of treatment [Figure 7.1] that summarizes
the process in which Michael and you can participate, if you so
desire.

Again, thank you. And do call if I can be of any help. I'll write
again as Michael approaches the last stage of his therapy.

Respectfully,
Walter Bera, LP

Stage 3 Therapist Letter
Note that many if not most cases in which the VSOT model is used are hindered by
the lack of an active victim therapist, and each case has unique features. Letters
need to be modified to reflect the actual circumstances of the case. Following is an
example of the letter from the VSOT therapist used in Stage 2.

Dear Theresa and Tom:

Michael has been making steady progress over the last several
months. He will be completing the primary phase of treatment in the
next few months. I promised to write you at this point to provide
you with some options that you and Tammy might find personally helpful
or therapeutic.

Part of Michael's tasks near the end of treatment is to write
letters of apology to you and Tammy—personal apologies he owes you

Figure 7.2. Therapist Letters in VSOT

for the sexual abuse he perpetrated. I would like to define some possible options for you that I reviewed with Tammy's therapist for your consideration.

1. You and Tammy can meet with Michael, his parents, and myself. You are in charge of who attends or does not attend. You can ask any questions you want and receive the letters personally. I suggest my own or Tammy's therapist's office as a neutral site, or you may choose any other site that you think might be appropriate.
2. You can receive the letters through the mail. Feel free to call me if you have any questions after receiving them.
3. You can continue the no contact contract.

Take some time to talk it over and call me if you have any questions or when you make your decision. When, where, and how you want to meet or receive the letters is completely your decision. My role is to attempt to provide options for healing or closure and convey or facilitate your wishes to Michael and his family.

I can be reached at 555-1212.

> Respectfully,
> Walter H. Bera

Figure 7.2. Continued

meeting room feel as safe as possible, including bringing favorite stuffed toys and providing seating arrangements.

The offender is also prepared for the closure choice the victim has made. The VSOT therapist asks the offender any questions raised by the victim and relays the answers. The no-contact contract is continued, the letters are sent, or the meeting is scheduled. The VSOT therapist prepares the offender emotionally for the meeting, if that is the victim's closure choice.

The goal of Stage 3 is to facilitate the most complete therapeutic closure possible, given the specific circumstances and personalities of all involved. The case example that follows is a simplified composite. Baby-sitter offenders may molest children in several families, but to focus on the process, this history concentrates on just one victim family.

Case Example

Michael was a 15-year-old boy living with his mother and 10-year-old brother in a college neighborhood. His parents had divorced 8 years before, and his father moved to another state soon after. The children continued to see their father for extended visits and on holidays. Michael's mother, Mindy, was an instructor in the college's English department and the custodial parent of Michael and his brother.

Michael had always been characterized as very family centered, shy, and sensitive. He also was considered a good baby-sitter and regularly cared for the neighbors' 5-year-old girl, Tammy.

Suspicions were aroused when Tammy told her mother that her "gina" hurt, and her mother observed some irritation around Tammy's vaginal area. In answering questions, Tammy made it clear that Michael had been sexually abusing her under the rules of a "special and secret game."

Shocked, Tammy's mother called Child Protection Services for advice. A social worker interviewed Tammy and there was a follow-up medical exam. The police interviewed Michael who, after considerable questioning, admitted a few instances of fondling. The police told Michael not to contact Tammy. The two families stopped communicating as well.

After Michael's limited offense disclosure, the courts sent Michael and his family to PHASE for assessment. He and his family were accepted for the initial PHASE assessment/education program. In Stage 1, during the first month of treatment, the therapist explained that releases of certain information were needed in order to do a complete assessment and to inform Tammy's parents that Michael and his family were involved in therapy. Michael and his mother signed releases of information for the therapist to receive copies of Michael's statements to the police. They also gave permission for the therapist to contact Tammy's parents to find out how Tammy and her parents were doing and to begin a potential process of healing.

After receiving the signed releases, the VSOT therapist called Tammy's parents, Tom and Theresa, the next day. Theresa answered and the VSOT therapist explained who he was and let her know that Michael was currently in the assessment/education phase of an adolescent sex offender treatment program. He also explained that Michael and his mother had signed releases of information so the therapist could talk to Theresa and Tom about Michael's case. The VSOT therapist followed up with a letter detailing the conversation (see Figure 7.2).

Theresa said she was thankful the therapist had called because there had been no communication between the two families since the investigation 3 months before. The family had been concerned about how Michael was doing and wondered if Mindy was mad at them for reporting the abuse and if there was any new information on what Michael had done to Tammy.

The therapist told Theresa that Michael was slowly opening up and that Mindy was not angry at them, but there was little new information on the abuse itself since Michael was just beginning the program. The therapist assured Theresa that she and Tom would receive new information as it came out in Michael's therapy.

Tom and Theresa shared information about Tammy's reactions to the abuse that had manifested since the initial investigation. Tammy had remembered more abuse incidents involving Michael. She had nightmares, enuresis, and phobias that appeared to be abuse related. Tammy's parents asked for a therapy referral, saying that they were beginning to realize that the abuse had more of an effect on her—and on them—than they first thought. Theresa disclosed that she had been a victim of sexual abuse herself as a child; she worried about whether that had "contributed" to her not seeing or realizing that Tammy was being sexually abused. Tom wanted to know whether the *Playboy* magazines he had in the bedroom might have been used in Michael's abuse of Tammy.

The VSOT therapist assured Tom and Theresa that this new information would be used in Michael's assessment and that their specific questions would be followed-up in the course of Michael's therapy. They were referred to a victim therapist who was comfortable working with an offender therapist. The VSOT therapist asked the family to sign release forms allowing him to get copies of Tammy's statements to the Child Protection Services worker. The victim therapist asked the family to sign releases of information so she could consult with the VSOT therapist. After hearing why it was necessary, Tom and Theresa agreed to sign.

During Stage 2 (Michael had been in treatment just over 3 months), Tammy disclosed more specific details of the abuse to her parents and therapist, who relayed the information to the VSOT therapist. The VSOT therapist confronted Michael with the new information, and he finally admitted a 2-year history of regular sexual contact with

Tammy, including fondling, oral sex, and "humping" Tammy until he ejaculated. Michael wrote an abuse biography detailing his new information on how he abused Tammy. He had, for example, abused Tammy in the bathroom, and this information helped explain Tammy's fear of the bathroom and her enuresis. After the VSOT therapist shared this information with Tammy's therapist and parents, who talked about it with Tammy, Tammy's bathroom phobia and enuresis stopped.

Michael expressed increased remorse as he realized that his abusive actions were having long-term effects on Tammy and her family, as well as on him and his family. In addition, he clarified that while he did use one of Tom's *Playboy* magazines in the course of abusing Tammy, he had discovered them after he had already started his abuse behavior.

Michael was now able to write sincere letters of apology to Tammy and to Tom and Theresa. In family therapy, Michael made a heartfelt apology to his mother for all he had put her through. Mindy said she forgave him and told him she was satisfied with his progress so far. She also said she was glad to know that Tammy, Tom, and Theresa's needs were taken into consideration in the therapy process.

The VSOT therapist contacted Tammy, Tom, and Theresa's therapist to give a progress report on Michael and to let the family know that they could receive his letters of apology at the end of Michael's therapy, if they wished. Tammy's therapist reported that Theresa was dealing with her own childhood sexual abuse in the course of Tammy's victim therapy, but that Theresa's childhood sexual abuse trauma did not add an additional emotional burden to Tammy's experience. In fact, processing Tammy's experience of abuse was helping Theresa work through something she had buried for years.

The VSOT therapist wrote Tom and Theresa, along with Tammy's therapist, to outline their closure options: continuing a no contact contract, receiving Michael's letters of apology through the mail, or having a face-to-face process session with Michael (see Figure 7.2). The VSOT therapist talked to Tammy's therapist before sending the letter and offered to answer any questions Tammy's parents might have about their closure options. Tom and Theresa, after talking with Tammy's therapist and Tammy, decided they wanted a face-to-face meeting in Tammy's therapist's office.

The goals of Stage 2 were completed with the progress assessment of Michael and Tammy. The treatment plan and expectations were revised accordingly.

Michael was assessed as being ready to prepare for closure. He was demonstrating remorse for his actions in the content of his abuse biography and letters, by complying with treatment plan and program contracts, and by expressing worry about Tammy's welfare. His language in therapy had shifted from blaming Tammy and Child Protection Services for his current problems to accepting responsibility for both his abusive actions and their consequences to himself. In fact, Michael went a little overboard, turning "accepting responsibility" into self-blame and self-hate. He became very depressed for a short time until he was reminded that, although he had done something very wrong, he was now in the process of making amends. At this time, he rewrote and reread his abuse biography and letters and they were accepted by his therapist, his mother, and his offender-treatment group (see Figure 7.3). Michael's treatment plan was revised to focus on encouraging him to provide honest, open answers to the questions Tammy and her parents had asked and on preparing for the in-person closure meeting.

Tammy's therapist used play therapy, among other techniques, to create an environment safe enough for Tammy to talk more freely about Michael's abuse. Including Tammy's mother in some sessions was an important step in showing Tammy that, despite what Michael had told her, she had not been "bad" and would not be punished or abandoned for breaking the secret-keeping rules of Michael's "game." It was explained to Tammy that Michael broke the rules in making her play such a mean game with him and making her keep a secret that hurt her. Tammy expressed appropriate anger at Michael (represented by a male doll) for tricking her and making her keep "bad" secrets.

The therapist prepared Tammy for not ever being alone with Michael because he had done a hurtful thing. When Tammy expressed sadness that she would not get to play the "good" games with Michael any more, the therapist explained that Tammy's friends and family could not be positive that Michael would never hurt her again, and they wanted to keep her safe. The therapist asked Tammy if she would like Michael to say he was sorry for tricking her and hurting her, and Tammy said yes. The therapist, Tammy, and her parents worked on some questions they wanted Michael to answer. The therapist re-layed their questions to Michael's therapist.

In Stage 3, after Michael had been in therapy for 8 months, a meet-ing was arranged at Tammy's therapist's office. The meeting format was agreed on in consultation between the parents, Tammy's therapist, and the VSOT therapist. Michael would take the initiative in review-ing his abuse biography and answering any questions asked by Tom, Theresa, or Tammy. Michael was prepared for the meeting with role plays in his offender-treatment group. Tammy's therapist prepared her clients at the same time, working on their questions and what they could reasonably expect from the closure session.

Tammy and her parents arrived at their therapist's office ½ hour before the scheduled meeting time so they could feel settled, comfort-able, and in control before Michael, Mindy, and the VSOT therapist arrived. Michael and his support people arrived and were seated fac-ing Tammy's family and therapist. After the VSOT therapist reviewed the structure of the meeting, Michael began.

With the help of his therapist, Michael summarized his abuse biog-raphy. Michael and his therapist answered Tammy's, Tom's, and Theresa's questions as they arose. As Michael read his letter of apol-ogy to Tammy, he started to cry, saying he felt really bad because he sin-cerely liked Tammy and realized how he had used her affection for him to hurt her, as well as abusing Tom and Theresa's trust. Tammy ap-peared unmoved—she could not seem to believe that Michael, who had been in such a position of power over her, was reduced to tears and guilt. The VSOT therapist offered Michael's letter of apology to Tammy, and she accepted it. After she looked at the letter, Tammy asked her mother to hold it for safekeeping.

Michael read his letter of apology to Tom and Theresa, who gra-ciously accepted it. Tammy said that the abuse was not her fault but Michael's, and her statement was confirmed first by Michael and then by all the participants. Tammy said she was glad he had gotten the help that he needed, especially because she had been worried he might do it to other little girls. Tom and Theresa were satisfied with the process and relieved to get information they needed. They also said that they forgave Michael. Mindy observed that she and Michael had grown closer as a result of facing Michael's abusive behavior.

Dear Tammy,

I don't know what words to use. I'm sorry for sexually abusing you. It wasn't your fault in any way, it was all mine. It will never ever happen again to you or any one else. I hope this letter will help in overcoming the bad experiences I put you through.

> Sincerely,
> Michael

Dear Mr. and Mrs. Smith,

I'm very sorry for sexually abusing your daughter. You don't have to believe me, and I will not go on and on and try to say I'm sorry the amount of times it would take to heal your wounds. I don't think there are any words that can describe the deep feeling of hate in my heart for the things I did. I really am very sorry, and I hope that in time you won't hate me. But if you do, I can't blame you. I did such a bad thing, I just can't express my feelings of how very sorry I really am.

> Sincerely,
> Michael

Figure 7.3. Michael's Letters of Apology

The families discussed what level of contact would be appropriate in the future. They clarified that it would take some time to trust Michael fully but that they wished to continue to communicate as neighbors, with the parents freely exchanging phone calls. Both families agreed that Michael could never again be placed in a position of trust with Tammy. This session ended with handshakes, and a few weeks later Michael graduated from PHASE.

TREATMENT RESULTS

The VSOT program was designed to be victim sensitive throughout the treatment process. At the time of the initial assessment, the safety of the victim is put foremost during offender placement recommendations. Throughout the program, language is encouraged that benefits the victim by confronting all offender misattributions and by teaching offenders to use self-responsible language. During the final closure choices, sensitivity to the victim involves restoring power and control by having the victim decide what type of closure will occur and where and with whom it will take place.

Following is a summary of closure choices made in the VSOT program over a 3-year period, categorized by offense type. The closure method chosen can usually be predicted by the frequency of contact and degree of intimacy between the offender/family and the victim/family prior to the abuse disclosure.

Sexual Abuse Within the Nuclear Family (Incest)

The vast majority of incest cases are resolved with a face-to-face closure meeting between the offender and his younger siblings. This is typical of the practice now used with family-based incest treatment programs. A handful end with a letter of apology (see Figure 7.4) when the family has other abusive or very disorganized features or the offender (or victim) has been rejected by the family and is in an out-of-home placement.

Sexual Abuse by an Extended Family Member (Incest)

This type of sexual abuse typically occurs in a baby-sitting situation or family gathering, where an uncle or cousin takes advantage of his niece/nephew or other related child. The majority of these cases end with a face-to-face reconciliation meeting. Some end with letters of apology (see Figure 7.4), usually because the victim's family lives some distance from the offender's family and they have only occasional contact.

Sexual Abuse by a Neighbor

A minority of cases in this category resolve in face-to-face meetings. Those that do commonly involve the next-door neighbor, a close family friend, or others who live very near to the family and where there are firm social ties with regular contact. Less intimate

The following letters were written by adolescent sex offenders who participated in PHASE. They are for illustrative purposes only. These letters should be written in language that is clear and sensitive to the age and needs of the recipients. The letters are not complete or exhaustive in themselves, but are a part of the overall VSOT model.

Brother-Sister Incest
These letters were written by a 15-year-old boy to his 5-year-old sister and his parents.

Dear Nancy,

    I am very sorry for sexually abusing you. I took advantage of a trust that should not have been broken. This isn't at all your fault; it's all mine. I will work to make sure it will never happen again, because I love you and am getting help from Walter and the guys in the group.

    Love,
    Your Brother,
    David

Dear Mom and Dad,

    I'm very sorry for sexually abusing Nancy. I know it was hard on you both and still is. I will work to ensure that it will never happen again through the help I am receiving from Walter and the group; but the main reason is because I love you both and I don't want to hurt you or Nancy again.

    Love,
    Your Son,
    David

Extended-Family Sexual Abuse
This letter was written by a 16-year-old uncle to his 6-year-old nephew, who had trusted and loved him and feared he was angry at him for breaking the abuse secret.

Dear Bill,

    I'm sorry. I'm sorry that I sexually abused you. There are a few things I want you to know. First of all, I'm not mad at you for telling others about what I did to you. What happened was not your fault, and in this way, I will be able to get some help straightening myself out. What I did to you was very wrong, and the counseling I'm receiving now is helping me to realize that.

    Sincerely,
    Matt

Figure 7.4. Sample Letters of Apology

Exposer
This letter was written by a 17-year-old male to a 34-year-old woman to whom he had
exposed himself from his car in a parking lot.

Dear Janet,

   I feel that you have the right to an apology from me. I honestly
don't know exactly how to begin apologizing for the terrible episode
I caused you. I have no explanation to offer you for what I did.
You mustn't take it personally, because you did nothing to cause my
actions. You were only an innocent victim. I know I've caused you a
great deal of pain. It must have been very shocking to you. I feel
that I have directly insulted you, and I know you were very offended.
I hope you can accept my apology, and even if you don't, I can understand that.
   It was my personal problem only. The legal system has helped me
very much. I have learned many things through being given information
and getting counseling. I've learned better morals and respect. Right
now I have a better understanding of myself and other things that
can help me control or even completely diminish my problem. I'm going
to try very hard to put this all behind me and get started on the
right track toward a better life.
   I'm very, very sorry.

      Brian

Fetish Burglar
This letter is from a 16-year-old fetish burglar who stole underwear from his mother.
She had been quite frightened by her son's behavior because she discovered her
cut-up underwear under her son's bed. In time he was able to explain that he cut
the underwear's leg holes so that he could get them over his large thighs in order
to cross-dress, not as an angry action against his mother.

Dear Mom,

   I am sorry for what I did, and I am sorry for all the pain and
fear that I caused you. As you know, I am getting help for my problem
of cross-dressing and stealing women's clothes. I feel I am making
progress with this problem as well as with our relationship. I promise
that it will never happen again but I also know that there is nothing
I can say to get rid of the grief. I hope to prove in time that you
can again love and trust me.

      Love,
      Ned

Figure 7.4. Continued

relationships typically end with a letter of apology (see Figure 7.4) because the victim's family wishes for a "less formal" resolution.

A few cases involving baby-sitting by a neighborhood acquaintance (e.g., where the offender was a baby-sitter known to the community or the son of a daycare provider) end in face-to-face meetings. Because the relationship was simply functional, the victim's family usually severs all ties. Most choose to learn the details of the abuse through the VSOT therapist and elect to receive a letter of apology through the mail. A significant minority of the families opt for a continued no contact contract monitored by the VSOT therapist and probation officer.

In a park or playground child-molestation, because there was no prior relationship with the offender, most victims choose to receive the letter of apology in the mail. When they are first contacted by the VSOT therapist, most express thanks for being able to learn the results of their reporting the abuse. Again, a significant number of these families choose a continued no contact contract and say they will keep the therapist's telephone number should any problems arise in the future.

The Nontouch Sex Offender

The category of nontouch offender includes those who steal underwear, expose their genitals, window peep, or make obscene phone calls. If the underwear stealing or exposing is directed toward close family members, the cases necessarily resolve with face-to-face closure meetings. The meetings help the victim understand a behavior that seems bizarre and inexplicable.

Nontouch cases involving neighbors and strangers to the offender usually end with letters of apology (see Figure 7.4) received through the mail. The VSOT therapist answers the victim's questions and offers explanations of the offender's behavior to help put some of the victim's concerns to rest.

The Group-Influenced Offender

The victims of this type of abuse are typically peers of the offenders. The abuse occurs in a group setting, such as a party, school bathroom, playground, or sporting event. Characteristically, the offenders blame the victim. The victim usually feels humiliated and confused. Peer gossip and rumor tend to isolate the victim further. As a result of the situational and attributional processes involved, all of these cases end with an emotionally distant letter of apology, supplemented by a detailed explanation from the VSOT therapist. Many victims in these situations move to new schools and neighborhoods in an attempt to sever all ties and escape the lingering social impact of the abuse.

The Acquaintance Rapist

The victims of date-rape are generally very angry and traumatized by the forced sexual abuse. They usually express relief that the offender is in treatment and anger about the assault, the legal process, and the emotional aftermath. Because the victim's experience is typically very different from the story the offender tells, the therapist can use that information to confront the offender. Some victims accept a letter of apology from the offender on the condition that it is sincere, and all request an assured no contact contract.

SUMMARY AND IMPLICATIONS

The systemic/attributional perspective and the VSOT model offer a fundamentally new approach to the treatment of sexual abuse. Increasing numbers of programs are implementing victim-offender communication components, and guiding protocols are being established (National Adolescent Perpetrator Network, 1993; Yokley, 1990). In a study of 323 juvenile offender treatment programs, 232 (or 72%) use victim apology as a treatment technique, ranking 10th in techniques of greatest use (Knopp, Freeman-Longo, & Stevenson, 1992). This chapter demonstrates that the VSOT process can occur in clear, safe, structured stages from the initial assessment to final closure. The treatment section demonstrates the broad range of offenses that can benefit from such an approach and provides an indication of the type of closure often selected. In fact, closure choice can often be predicted by the frequency of contact and degree of intimacy of the victim-offender dyad and their respective families prior to the abuse disclosure.

This chapter concludes with some examples of VSOT model implications for therapy and the organization of research and treatment of interpersonal violence in general.

It is possible to treat sexual abuse successfully despite an "untreatable" offender. As occurs in some incest cases, the offenders can be so sociopathic that they cannot be treated with conventional therapy. But the VSOT model can help the victim, spouse/parent, and other siblings in the family gain a rational view of the abuse and the offender; the hurt parties can heal by growing beyond the offender's limitations.

Such offenders usually agree to participating in marital and family clarification (not reconciliation) sessions in which their sociopathy quickly becomes obvious. This helps an enmeshed spouse and blaming siblings "let go" of their distorted view of the offender and become more sensitive to how the victim was isolated and used by the offender.

Victim/offender treatment coordination teams should become an integral part of offender therapy. Just as the field now sees the need for multidisciplinary teams for effective and efficient investigation and adjudication of child abuse, so too could the treatment of victims and offenders of sexual abuse and other interpersonal violence benefit from coordination teams. Setting up such teams would involve defining the team (the "professional system" in Figure 6.1), and its task around the victim-offender dyad and their respective needs. Coordination of information and efforts leads to treatment and management that is significantly more informed, safer, and complete, while being shorter in duration and less costly than traditional approaches.

The unit of research in interpersonal violence should be the victim-offender dyad. Sexual abuse studies and interpersonal studies in general focus on either victims or offenders and the data analyzed in their respective groups or subgroups. If the organizing unit of research becomes the victim-offender dyad, the contextual interactional dynamics of sexual abuse could be richly studied. Questions such as the voracity of abuse memories, descriptions, and attributions could be addressed by having members of the victim-offender dyad relate their version of the abuse events. Research on issues of prevention and treatment could also be enriched by analyzing the victim-offender dyad.

The VSOT model offers a structure for possible closure years after the sexual abuse has ended. One case example involves a 30-year-old incest victim. Her father abused her from age 6 through 12. She only revealed the abuse after she moved away and engaged in therapy. For a variety of reasons, she decided not to prosecute. The father, although not denying the abuse, only sought general psychoanalysis.

The victim came to therapy to complete her incest work. The father was contacted via phone, and after discussion about the VSOT model and process as well as reviewing potential legal concerns, he agreed to participate. After some months, correspondence, and phone calls, the daughter received the confirmation of the full truth of her experience and the apology she had always wanted. In addition, the father offered economic restitution, which further helped heal the relationship between these estranged family members.

It is possible for victims to receive information and an apology for abuse that occurred when they were too young or not ready to remember. A couple came to therapy to create closure in an unusual situation. The father had been a sexual compulsive whose behavior included penis-vaginal rubbing, a form of incest with his two daughters, 6 months and 2½ years at the time of discovery. The behavior had gone on for some months with the older girl and a shorter time with the infant. The father had been sentenced to out-of-home placement, workhouse time, and treatment, which he by all accounts successfully completed.

The victims were now entering their early teens and had no recollection of the incest. Therapists had previously recommended against bringing up the abuse, as the memories could be potentially traumatizing to the girls. The present dilemma revolved around the fact that the extended family and relatives were aware of this abuse history, but the victims were not. The parents feared that the victims would learn of their abuse through an awkwardly and potentially traumatic slip at a family gathering. They felt the girls were old enough now and deserved to learn their history in a complete, coherent, and responsible process.

After some preparation, the girls did hear their father's abuse history and later received a heartfelt apology. Rather than being made uncomfortable, they were relieved because both knew "something" had happened in their past but never knew what kind of questions to ask or of whom.

Many questions remain in the application of various victim-offender communication models. Legal, confidentiality, ethical, and therapeutic issues will become clearer and protocols will be established as more programs begin to use these emerging models. The successful negotiation of these details will determine the ultimate limits of this promising new direction.

PART III

A Model for Working With Adolescent Male Prostitutes

DON LeTOURNEAU

8

Adolescent Male Prostitution: A Social Work/Youth Work Perspective

CHAPTER 1 OFFERS a brief historical perspective of childhood and adolescence as well as a discussion of erotophobia, homophobia and sexual identity development as they relate to adolescence. An understanding of these issues is critical to understanding the foundation and context of the social institution of street youth, particularly adolescent male prostitutes. This chapter explores those themes in more specific ways and provides perspective to an area of adolescent male sexuality that has been tragically ignored.

As chapter 1 points out, few adult prerogatives are more firmly protected than sexual behavior. And few adolescent behaviors create the kind of adult discomfort that adolescent male prostitution manages to achieve. Such prostitution represents adolescents engaged in willful sexual behavior, adolescents involved in the illegal activity of prostitution, and most anxiety producing, adolescent males involved in significant amounts of homosexual behavior. It is hard to image any social phenomenon that combines such a powerful mix of social taboos and neuroses.

The available cultural paradigms for viewing and understanding adolescents have a clear gender differentiation. On the one hand, young women are increasingly viewed as the victims of a patriarchal male society that oppresses, sexually exploits, and sexually assaults them.

On the other hand, young men are increasingly viewed as threats to society and in need of control. The rising level of violence, characterized by sexual assaults, gang violence, juvenile crime (predominantly perpetrated by young men), and seemingly random attacks by young men, are seen as evidence to support these perceptions.

Lost in these gender-polarized dichotomies is a way to view adolescent males involved in prostitution. This view contradicts the popular theory that young males who are sexually abused grow up to become sex offenders. It contradicts the image of adolescent males as violent and perpetrators of crimes (many adolescent male prostitutes do engage in criminal behavior other than prostitution but in no greater proportion or level of violence than adolescent female prostitutes). And it contradicts the images of adolescent males as sexually aggressive and exploitative of their sexual partners.

The distorted cultural dichotomies have contributed to the lack of research, inquiry, and attention to adolescent male prostitution, despite the fact that its reported incidence has increased dramatically in recent decades (Boyer, 1989).

The author's efforts to research, serve, advocate, and educate about the issue of adolescent male prostitution have consistently been met with resistance from most areas of human services, research, and professional education. The resistance is seldom overt and hostile and is probably unconscious and not deliberate, but it is resistance nonetheless. It is as though information about male prostitution threatens passionately held "beliefs" about males or there is simply no theoretical framework within which the information can reside.

It is our hope that the information presented here will make its way into the repertoire of mainstream human service professionals and that a framework can begin to be constructed that allows for more diverse and authentic paradigms of adolescents. Current views are one-dimensional and limiting ways of understanding adolescent "victims/survivors" of both genders and obscures their potential for adaptation and survival.

This chapter begins with a review of the historical and recent research literature that is relevant to male prostitution. It then offers a critique of the research, its findings relative to the "causes" and "effects" of adolescent male (and female) prostitution, and the conventional view of adolescent prostitution. The variety of methods and types of intervention and prevention aimed at adolescent prostitution are discussed; chapter 9 presents a model of intervention called detached youth work.

THE HISTORICAL LITERATURE

Male prostitution is described in two bodies of literature. The historical literature includes both the history of prostitution (Amos, 1877; Bailey, 1956; Benjamin & Masters, 1964; James, 1951; Sanger, 1937; Scott, 1968) and the history of homosexuality (Bray, 1982; Burg, 1984; Foucault, 1980, 1986, 1988; Weeks, 1981). The second body of literature is research literature on adolescent male prostitution in the last 40 years (Allen, 1980; Boyer, 1989; Boyer & James, 1983; Butts, 1947; Caukins & Coombs, 1976; Coombs, 1974; Craft, 1966; Deisher, Eisner, & Sulzbacher, 1969; Fisher, Weisberg, & Marotta, 1982; Gandy & Deisher, 1970; Ginsburg, 1967; Hoffman, 1972; Jersild, 1956; MacNamara, 1965; Reiss, 1961; Weisberg, 1985).

The historical literature is only reviewed in the modern research by Boyer and James (1983). However, the historical literature provides a valuable perspective for understanding the present configuration of adolescent male prostitution. Much of the literature on the history of homosexuality has only recently been available, but it is critical in understanding homosexual prostitution. Adolescent male prostitution is certainly not older than homosexual behavior, but it is thousands of years older than homosexuals as an identifiable class of individuals.

Recent research literature tends to view adolescent male prostitution as a post-World War II phenomenon that emerged with the contemporary male homosexual subculture (Fisher et al., 1982) or as a logical construction in the social identity of young males who are homosexual in contemporary society (Boyer, 1989). Although there is little doubt that "hustling" has become an integral part of the modern gay male community and that cultural attitudes toward homosexuality predispose adolescents with this orientation to view themselves as "deviant," the historical literature indicates that the parameters of male prostitution are much broader. Pederasts and women have played major roles in the history of adolescent male prostitution, yet are virtually ignored by researchers. Few writers have attempted to integrate the history of male prostitution prior to the 18th century with current information.

From a historical perspective, three major assumptions can be made about adolescent male prostitution. First, male prostitution is as old as female prostitution. The earliest records of prostitution refer to "religious" or "temple" prostitution (James, 1951). Although the term *prostitution* is not particularly accurate to describe these temple ministrants, who were dedicated to a deity and performed ritual intercourse with supplicants as a part of worshiping their deity, there is evidence that some people offered their sexual services along with temple ministrants for less than ecclesiastical motives (Bailey, 1956).

Benjamin and Masters (1964) state: "Male homosexual prostitution is, so far as we know, about equally as ancient as the female hetero-sexual variety. Homosexual temple prostitutes existed among the Hebrews and in India. Boy harlots plied their trade in the antique civilizations of Egypt, Persia, Greece, Rome, China, and Japan, as else-where" (p. 284)

These male temple prostitutes were the source of the Biblical denouncements of sodomy, sodomites, and catamites and created the linking of homosexual behavior and idolatry in Western cultures (Scott, 1968). The Hebrews, like most other cultures at the time, employed female temple prostitutes under a variety of euphemistic titles, but male temple prostitutes were a part of rival religions, and therefore condemned (Scott, 1968).

This connotation of sodomy and idolatry is further evidenced in the translations of the Greek word *hierodoulos* (temple ministrants). Most Biblical translations render the word as "whore" or "harlot" for females and "sodomite" or "catamite" for males (Bailey, 1956). These translations display a limited understanding of the role and function of these early temple ministrants while obscuring the role of males.

The second major assumption that can be derived from the histori-cal perspective is that male prostitution has always been as prevalent and extensive as female prostitution, even more so at certain times in history. Most texts indicate that the earliest temple prostitution was as prevalent by males as by females. During the classical period of the Greeks and Romans, male prostitution probably exceeded female prostitution (Bailey, 1956; Benjamin & Masters, 1964; James, 1951; Scott, 1968).

Although there is little specific information about male prostitution from the Middle Ages, there is little reason to believe it was less prevalent. The Roman system of licensing and taxing brothels remained the practice in Europe throughout the Middle Ages and accounts survive that indicate that males were as much a part of the brothels as females and provided sexual services to both men and women (Bailey, 1956; Scott, 1968).

Throughout the Renaissance and Victorian period, there are well-documented accounts indicating the prevalence of male prostitution in European cities (Bray, 1982; Burg, 1984). Weeks (1981) notes that Havelock Ellis, Iwan Bloch, Magnus Hirschfeld, Sigmund Freud, and Alfred Kinsey all commented that male prostitution was little less evident than female prostitution.

The final assumption that can be derived from the historical literature is that children and adolescents have always been a significant portion of those involved in male prostitution. Boys as young as 4 years old were bought on the slave markets of Rome and taught passive pederasty for work in the brothels (Lloyd, 1976). Many young boys during the Middle Ages and the Renaissance who could not secure an apprenticeship were recruited or forced to work in brothels or as "kept" servants with overtones of prostitution (Bray, 1982; Burg, 1984). Many of the age-of-sexual-consent laws that were passed at the close of the 19th century were aimed at protecting children from recruitment to prostitution (James, 1951).

These assumptions raise more questions than they answer. If male prostitution is as old and as prevalent as female prostitution and has always involved young boys and adolescents, why does so little literature describe and analyze it? Foucault (1988) points out that what has changed is not the behavior but the way in which the questions are asked and the importance they are given in philosophical and moral debate:

> In the first centuries of our era, compared with the lofty formulations of the classical period, reflection on the love of boys lost some of its intensity, its seriousness, its vitality, if not its topicality,

This does not mean that the practice disappeared or that it became the object of a disqualification. All the texts plainly show it was still common and still regarded as a natural thing. What seems to have changed is not the taste for boys, or the value judgment that was brought to bear on those who had this partiality, but the way in which one questioned oneself about it. An obsolescence not of the thing itself, but of the problem; a decline in the interest one took in it; a fading of the importance it was granted in philosophical and moral debate. (p. 189)

Weeks (1981) observes that "writings on male prostitution began to emerge simultaneously with the notion of homosexuals being an identifiable breed of persons with special needs, passions, and lusts" (p. 113). Bloch suggests that the first use of the term *prostitute* to describe males appears in Duchesne's (1853/1909) *De la prostitution dans la ville d'Alger la conquete.* Yet historical accounts indicate that males have been involved in behavior that can be labeled prostitution (even if it was not called that at the time) since the earliest cultures.

The linking of male prostitution and homosexuality has more to do with cultural categories and perceptions of human sexual behavior than with natural categories of human sexual behavior. Is male prostitution viewed as homosexual prostitution because it involves exclusively homosexual behavior or because of the homosexual identities of the customers? In the historical accounts, the proportions of which customers were male, female, or pederast is debatable and virtually impossible to determine. But evidence suggests that homosexual men were not the only customers of male prostitutes and, as Weeks (1981) points out, "historians and social scientists alike have failed to fit everyone who behaves in a homosexual manner within a definition of 'the homosexual' as a unitary type" (p. 113). As is explored latter in this chapter, current research literature indicates that a significant number of customers are women.

The most recent research suggests that young male prostitutes are more likely to identify as homosexual than previous research indicated (Fisher et al., 1982), yet a common approach of most of the studies of male prostitution is to collapse the homosexual and bisexual categories together as homosexual. Even though this practice has been criticized for implying that homosexuality is a homogeneous category and that sexual orientation is a polarized and immutable state

(De Cecco, 1981), Boyer (1989) defends the practice on the grounds that her study is one of cultural categories rather than natural ones.

The biases of early researchers against homosexuality, the collapsing of bisexual and homosexual identity categories of the more recent research, the inability of historians and social scientists to fit everyone who practices homosexual behavior into a homosexual identity, and the lack of data concerning sexual orientation development in adolescence that is based on natural rather than cultural categories creates skepticism concerning the labeling of male prostitution as homosexual prostitution. This focus on the homosexuality of male prostitution is more the result of the cultural discomfort with the image of males as prostitutes than because of the truly homosexual nature of the phenomenon. The most bisexual period of the male life cycle is usually during adolescence, and attention should be focused on the adolescent aspect of male prostitution rather than its "homosexualness."

THE RESEARCH LITERATURE

There is little research on male prostitution, and much of what has been done is not particularly useful in understanding adolescent male prostitution. In many cases, the research tells us more about the researchers than the subjects being studied. Perhaps the biggest limitation of the literature is that it displays dated attitudes toward homosexuality in general and adolescent homosexuality in particular. Most researchers tend to accept obsolete pathological diefinitions of homosexuality (Butts, 1947; Caukins & Coombs, 1976; Craft, 1966; Coombs, 1974; Jersild, 1956; MacNamara, 1965; Reiss, 1961). Boyer (1989) suggests that "subject and researcher agreed on a mutual denial of homosexuality" leading to research that offers little insight into the phenomenon (p. 155). This illustrates a consistent problem in researching youth in prostitution. These youth become very adept at perceiving adult biases and tell adults what they want to hear (Baizerman, Thompson, & Stafford-White, 1979). To these youth, researchers may be just a different variety of customer.

Other limitations of the research include sampling biases that limit applicability to broader populations. Only two studies have been based exclusively on adolescent populations, and these were done with boys who were incarcerated or from a researcher's psychiatric practice, limiting their value (Craft, 1966; Hoffman, 1972; Reiss, 1961; Wienberg, 1972). Most research has studied only small samples in one or two locales (Caukins & Coombs, 1976; Coombs, 1974; Deisher et al., 1969; Deisher & Gandy, 1970; Ginsberg, 1967). Many studies look at only one type of prostitution and fail to reflect the diversity of male prostitution (Craft, 1966; Deisher et al., 1969; Ginsberg, 1967; Hoffman, 1972; Reiss, 1961; Wienberg, 1972). Finally, most of the research was done during the 1960s and early 1970s before an awareness of the social problems of runaway behavior and physical and sexual abuse of children, and therefore fails to look at the relationship these social problems have to adolescent prostitution.

The most ambitious recent research on adolescent male prostitution is that performed by Urban and Rural Systems Associates (URSA) between 1979 and 1981 as a result of federal hearings on juvenile prostitution and pornography in 1977 (Weisberg, 1985). These hearings resulted in funding for a number of research projects that examined the sexual exploitation of juveniles (males and females) and led to the work by Boyer and James (1983) on adolescent male and female prostitution. URSA (1982) looked at data from several cites around the United States and combined ethnography, service provider surveys, profile analysis (data supplied by service providers on clients involved in male prostitution), and a literature review to generate the first nationally based study on adolescent male prostitution. Seattle-based researchers played an especially important role in this research because of the work of Deisher, James, and Boyer at the University of Washington, and because two agencies in Seattle supplied nearly one-half of the profiles for URSA's profile analysis.

The Findings of the Research Literature

The "typical" adolescent male prostitute can be described as a white, 14- to 18-year-old boy from a broken/neglectful, low- to middle-income family. He has a history of physical and/or sexual abuse, is a high school dropout, and is unemployed, unskilled, and self-identified as gay or bisexual. He is a runaway or throwaway (often the result of his emerging sexual orientation) who regularly uses drugs and alcohol, has a juvenile justice record, and is increasingly reliant on social service systems for food, housing, medical, and employment assistance (Boyer & James, 1983; Deisher, Robinson, & Boyer 1982; Fisher et al., 1982).

With some subtle variations, the research and historical literature describes four basic types of adolescent male prostitution: street hustling, bar hustling, kept boys, and call service or "professional" hustling (Allen, 1980; Caukins & Coombs, 1976; Fisher et al., 1982). These types primarily reflect the locale of the hustling and are fluid when used to identify boys. A boy may engage in one or all of these types during his entrance into, participation in, and exit from prostitution. These four types also reflect the classes of hustling and are reasonably consistent with the historical literature (Bray, 1982; Burg, 1984).

Street Hustling

A 17-year-old hustler recently met a 15-year-old hustler:

> *"Girl, how long you been hustling the streets?"*
> *"About a year and a half."*
> *"You must not be any good then. If you been out here that long you shoulda done had yourself a book full of names and be sittin' by the phone instead of out here peddlin' your ass on the street corner."*

The street hustlers of the literature and experience are boys who are the relatively permanent inhabitants of the "streets," as opposed to those who visit or pass through the streets. The streets are where most boys are introduced to and begin their careers in prostitution, which means this locale is inhabited by boys of all types. Street hustlers are distinguished as the lower class hustlers by their inability to anticipate and conduct their lives with the future in mind (Banfield, 1973). Those who visit or pass through the streets may choose to be present oriented and live moment to moment, but are capable of moving on or out of this milieu.

Street hustling is the most wide open of all the types of hustling. One can encounter all types of people looking for all types of sexual encounters. This is the very reason many hustlers look for more predictable and reliable ways to hustle, yet it is also this adventure and risk that keeps (traps) some and draws others back. In the most general terms, street hustling means standing on a street or corner and establishing contact with a customer in a car through eye contact. Although virtually anything is negotiable, the most common sex sold on the streets is fellatio and it most often involves the customer preforming fellatio on the hustler.

Although seldom defined, the streets as described in the literature is really a metaphor for the meeting ground of a variety of *deviant* subcultures (drugs, prostitution, strip shows, bookstores, gangs, homeless, criminal) that exist in all cities. The term is often loosely used in an attempt to describe a milieu of these overlapping subcultures and the social space common to them. It may refer to a specific physical location (such as Polk Street and the Tenderloin in San Francisco, Times Square in New York, West Hollywood in Los Angeles, Hennepin Avenue in Minneapolis) but is better conceptualized as a metaphor for the confluence of these marginal subcultures. Gang members, prostitutes (male or female), delinquents, or homeless youth have their own as well as shared territory on the streets. Sometimes these territories are relatively stable over time (such as those mentioned above), but more often they are subject to migrations and changes. Police intervention/harassment, public awareness/attention, urban gentrification/development, and the interests of the youth themselves are but a few of the variables that influence the actual physical location of the streets.

Because of the illegal and/or marginal nature of these subcultures that inhabit the streets or public space, it is difficult to obtain "hard" or quantifiable data describing the individuals who live and/or work there. Ethnographies (Fisher et al., 1982) or other qualitative methods are more suited to studying these subcultures. There is an identifiable gay male subculture within which street hustling by boys takes place, but these boys may also participate in the activities of the other subcultures that are a part of the streets.

The boys who street hustle are often the most troubled and delinquent of the boys who engage in prostitution. They are survival oriented and live by hustling whatever they can (e.g., drugs, sex, larceny, panhandling) and are likely to identify as heterosexual or bisexual. They are also likely to have extensive histories of physical and sexual abuse and involvement with the juvenile justice system (Boyer, 1989; Deisher & Gandy, 1970; URSA, 1982).

A useful way to conceptualize these boys is to understand them as having traumatic histories before coming to the streets or early in their street careers, and becoming trapped by the cycle of exploitation they are exposed to on the streets. The resiliency and/or adaptive skills of these boys is minimal and they become the easiest targets for exploitation by street predators. That predation further damages the resiliency of these boys and perpetuates further exploitation.

At times, this group can appear to be either "victims" or "predators," depending on the behavioral sample observed. The high prevalence of sexual abuse histories and prostitution behavior combined with delinquent activities make these boys among the most difficult to work with.

Street hustlers are in the most need of basic social services. Their inability to anticipate the future means they live from crisis to crisis. Needs for food, housing, and medical care are the immediate priority, but street hustlers often need educational services, employment and training services, legal advocacy, mental health services, and case management services. They are often, however, unable or unwilling to maintain participation in these services, and so leave social service providers feeling like a revolving door when these boys drop out of programs only to present themselves again when they are in a crisis. This lack of continuity often leads to a permanent termination from services they have frustrated, leaving these boys to turn increasingly to the streets for their survival needs.

Case Example

Mark first "ran away" from home when he was 13. His mother was an alcoholic who divorced when he was 4. He had a sister who was in foster care because one of his mother's boyfriends had molested her, and Mark had been in foster homes and group homes for his delinquent behavior. He was molested when he was 10 by a friend of the family his mother had recruited to be a "positive male influence" on him, but he had never told anyone.

In school, Mark was in special education classes for his behavior. He got in fights often, was caught stealing in school, and was referred

to juvenile court for his truancy. This and shoplifting led to his placement in foster care. His "bad attitude" and "oppositional behavior"
landed him in a group home. He barely graduated from the group
home and was returned home at 12.

Mark would not listen to his mother and her rules, and one night
when he came home late and found his mother drunk, they got in a
huge fight and she kicked him out. By now Mark knew plenty of kids
on the streets; he started hanging out with them and sleeping where
he could. When he became desperate for money, a friend told him
about a guy who would pay him to give him a blow job and Mark decided to try it. The guy had lots of drugs and alcohol and offered
Mark a place to stay for a while.

Mark met other guys who would let him stay for a while and he
sold small amounts of drugs for some of them. He also got pretty good
at stealing cars and breaking into the houses of guys he used to stay
with. By the time Mark was 17, he had spent time in a couple of juvenile correctional facilities for his delinquent behavior, but none of
the counselors or therapists had ever suspected his prostitution behavior and he never told anyone. Everyone, including Mark, was
more comfortable talking about his delinquency.

On the streets, Mark would hustle and deal while staying with one
of his friends or until he got enough money for an apartment. He was always running out of money and getting evicted. He also got ripped
off and in fights a lot. Somebody he had crossed or the cops were
always looking for him. Mark always had grand plans for getting a
"straight" job and going to college after he got his GED, but not long
after he got a job he would lose it because he was up late partying
the night before and could not get up for work.

Bar Hustling

Bray (1992) describes the brothels of male prostitution in London
during the Renaissance as "likely to have been taverns where prostitutes could entertain their clients. Such taverns, together with young
male prostitutes walking the streets and alleys of Elizabethan London,
probably offer the principal way we should envisage homosexual
prostitution in the London of the time" (p. 89). Bray also describes
the "molly houses" (places where homosexual men would meet) of

the time as being taverns or private homes where drink was sold and one could have sexual encounters.

Weeks (1981) observes that "the most basic purpose of the homosexual subculture in the nineteenth and early twentieth centuries . . . was to provide ways to meet sexual partners," and "As early as the 1720s, these meeting places had been known as 'markets,' corresponding to the contemporaneous use of the term 'marriage market' " (p. 121).

Bar hustling differs from street hustling primarily in that it is more focused and more gay oriented. The distinctions can be fairly subtle and the overlap between the two is often considerable. Bar hustling occurs around the edges of the "markets" where gay men meet to find sexual partners. In many cities this is the gay bars, but it can also be gay neighborhoods, parks, bookstores, or, in the past, bath houses. The territory is more exclusively gay than where street hustling occurs, which can be territory shared with other subcultures.

The boys who hustle in these areas are more likely to be gay identified and to have run away or been kicked out because of their emerging homosexuality, are as likely as street hustlers to have been sexually abused, and are drawn to the gay markets as a part of making meaning out of their emerging sexuality (Boyer, 1989; Boyer & James, 1983; Fisher et al., 1982). URSA found that, in comparison to street hustlers, bar hustlers are from slightly less dysfunctional families, have completed slightly more school, were older when they ran away, and were older when they first had sex and when they first started hustling; neither type was likely to have been involved with social services and juvenile justice agencies (Fisher et al., 1982).

Bar hustlers are generally more competent and more able to anticipate the future in their lives than street hustlers. Bar hustlers often look for "sugar daddies" and can look like kept boys in this respect. They are very mobile and can act as travel companions for men who take them on trips or who are from out of town and offer them rides to new places, particularly in winter. This is especially true of the west coast between Seattle and Los Angeles and the east coast between Miami and Boston, where there are corridors of cities boys can move between with relative ease.

These boys enjoy the attention and power they derive from older gay men, but, as some researchers have noted, there can be a hostile dependency between these boys and their customers/sugar daddies (Allen, 1980; Boyer & James, 1983; Caulkins & Coombs, 1976). Some of these boys hustle to stabilize their lives and identities as gay men, whereas others become trapped by the cycle, resenting the exploitation by adult gay men while lacking the skills or abilities to escape it, in part because of how lucrative it can be.

Bar hustling also includes what URSA and other researchers have described as situational or part-time hustlers (Allen, 1980; Fisher et al., 1982). These are usually older adolescents and can include college students, who hustle in the bars when they need extra money or for the excitement. (URSA's typologies describe situational hustlers participating in street hustling as well as bar hustling.) There are stories of young men who have put themselves through college and graduate school this way (URSA, 1982).

Bar hustling is the area of male prostitution that has grown the most rapidly during the last two decades, and no doubt reflecting the growth and visibility of the gay male community in most larger cities (Boyer, 1989; Fisher et al., 1982). The boys who hustle in and around the gay bars are increasingly gay identified with a probable history of sexual abuse. Although somewhat less acute, their social service needs are similar to those of street hustlers, but bar hustlers are less likely to receive those services in an atmosphere that understands or accepts their homosexuality. The homophobia (or, at the very least, heterosexism) of most youth-serving agencies leads many of these boys to be wary of such programs. The most effective service provision is usually the result of programs by or in conjunction with local gay and lesbian social service organizations.

Case Example

Greg began running away from home when he was 14. He was well known to the juvenile police officer in his suburb for his habitual running. There was never any indication of delinquent behavior other than running. Greg lived with his older sister and mother, who had never married. His mother was eccentric and controlling, but there was no indication of abuse or serious problems at home.

Greg knew he was gay when he was 13; he began running to hang out downtown and at a local gay park. He soon met other gay-identified boys and plenty of gay men who let him stay with them. It did not take long for Greg to figure out how to make money, since most of the boys he knew hustled and most of the men he stayed with would spend money on him. Greg soon had a regular clientele and only spent time on the streets to party and hang out with the other boys.

In a somewhat neurotic way, Greg's mother would regularly call and harass the local juvenile officer and chastise him for not finding her son and getting him away from those "perverts" who were "poisoning" her son with ideas about homosexuality. A few times the officer was successful at tracking Greg down and bringing him home, but Greg never stayed for long due to his mother's incessant lectures about perverts and homosexuals. Eventually the officer was successful at having Greg arrested while he was turning a trick, and Greg was sent to a group home.

Greg continued to hustle occasionally while in the group home (without their knowledge) for extra spending money and clothes, but this behavior eventually dissipated. He would still hang out in the same places, but more for the peer relationships than for sex or money. While on the streets, Greg had stayed high most of the time, primarily on marijuana but frequently on cocaine. The group home tried to get him to go to outpatient treatment or at least AA groups, but Greg was not interested. He continued to smoke marijuana while in the group home (without their knowledge), but, like the hustling, this behavior dissipated over time and eventually Greg no longer got high.

Over his mother's vociferous objections, Greg was eventually placed in a gay foster home, graduated from high school, and went to college.

Call/Professional Hustling

Hetaera and male courtesans are at least as old as the Greeks; Bailey (1956) notes a revival of hetarism and courtesans in the 12th and 13th centuries. Today, call boys/men service upper-class men and women who require discretion and can at least imitate an acceptable level of social status.

As described in the literature, these boys usually work the upper-class bars and hotels and occasionally work for call services or upper-class houses of prostitution (Allen, 1980; Caukins & Coombs, 1976; Fisher et al., 1982). Those that provide their services to men are mostly gay identified and see themselves as professionals (Fisher et al., 1982). They may engage in prostitution on a part-time or full-time basis, or, as URSA describes it, on a vocational or avocational basis (Fisher et al., 1982). Those who provide their services to women most often identify as heterosexual and often work the strip shows for women and/or for private dance circuits.

In most of the research, professional hustlers are a small percentage of those studied, but it is not clear whether this is the result of this group making up a small portion of males involved in prostitution or the result of their skill at concealment. Whatever their numbers, they exist and are the most competent and least troubled of the young men who are involved in prostitution. They represent the "upper-class" of male prostitution in that they are able to anticipate a future in their lives and conduct their lives accordingly.

Call boys are the least likely of all types of male prostitutes to request services from social service agencies and are not likely to see themselves as needing such services. On occasion they may involve themselves in individual psychotherapy, but often this is not related to their involvement in prostitution, and they may not even reveal that information to their therapist.

Case Example

Tony was kicked out of the house when he was 16. He was a straight-A student from a middle-class family in the suburbs with three kids and mom and dad. Tony had never been in trouble, but, as the oldest child and male, his father had high expectations for him. However, Tony did not want to play sports, and it was getting harder and harder for him to hide his homosexuality from himself and his father. When Tony finally told his father, his dad kicked him out.

Tony quit school and stayed with a friend's family until he got a job and his own place. Free to pursue his sexuality, Tony managed to get into the gay bars and started experimenting with sex. One of the bars that had regular strip shows had an amateur night, and some of Tony's friends talked him in to trying out. He liked it, and was recruited to do it on a regular basis. The money was the most appealing part for Tony, since he made only a little above minimum wage at his job. Through the other guys that danced, Tony also learned how to make even more money with men who booked him for private parties and for sex. With his looks and intelligence, Tony soon had a regular clientele and quit dancing. He became so popular that he raised his prices and became more selective.

Tony finished his GED and financed his college education through hustling.

Case Example

Ed's mom divorced when he was 2 and never remarried. His mother had gone back to college and law school, and was a workaholic. Ed and his mother got along, but he always had the feeling that he reminded his mother of the mistake she made in marrying his father, whom he never knew. Ed's first sexual experience was with his best friend's mother when he was 13. She was wealthy and divorced and no one seemed to question that he spent a lot of time at his best friend's place, even if his friend was not there.

Ed had learned to be very charming with older women and began to notice how they looked at him and acted toward him when he was downtown or at the mall. When Ed was 16, a woman in her 30s picked him up at a shopping mall, and he wound up staying with her for several days. She took him to bars and out for dinner and told him that he acted older than his age that he seemed to know what a woman wanted. After this happened a few more times, and Ed was not coming home much or going to school, his mother and he began to fight; Ed finally quit coming home. One of the women he stayed with took him to a bar that did a male strip show for women, and talked him into trying out. He did and pretty soon he had enough money to get his own place. Through some of the guys he danced with Ed learned about a service that booked guys for private parties, and pretty soon he had developed a clientele that paid him to do more than dance.

This form of prostitution often presents the dilemma of whether prostitution can be a "healthy" career choice for an individual or whether it is inherently exploitative and/or abusive to the prostitute. Free from most of the debilitating effects of the streets and lower-class forms of prostitution, professional hustling's effects are more limited to the impact of fee-for-service sex. The arguments for and against these perceptions are most often constructed around passionately held beliefs about human sexuality and the theology of sex and seldom on the basis of research.

Kept Boys

Emperor Hadrian of Rome was so captivated by his "kept boy," Antinous, that statues of the boy were set up all over the Roman Empire (Lloyd, 1976). (Although earlier writers on this subject display fairly homophobic attitudes, more recent accounts suggest the relationship between a kept boy and his "master" to be quite complex; see Yourcenar, 1954.) Bray (1982) describes boys of Renaissance England who lived in households with the status of servants but whose relationship with the masters of the household had strong overtones of prostitution. Boys who were conscripted to the expanding navies of the 17th and 18th centuries often ended up being known as the "carpenters, cooks, or fiddler's boy" (Burg, 1984, p. 38). Today one can read the newspapers to find stories of local and national public figures who are embarrassed to be caught employing young men in dubious roles that have strong overtones of prostitution.

Kept boys are a type of male prostitution because of the obvious financial arrangements that are a part of a primarily sexual relationship. Other than acknowledging their existence, the research literature offers little insight into the lives of kept boys. The overlap between kept boys and bar hustlers in older adolescent boys even leads many to combine the types as one (Allen, 1980; URSA, 1982). However, there are actually two very distinct groups of boys who can be considered kept.

The first group is the kept boys of the literature, who are older adolescent boys and might hustle the bars or work the call services when they do not have a sugar daddy. The fluidity in the types of hustling they participate in indicates that they are a part of the upper class of hustling. Kept boys in this group are almost exclusively gay identified and often form complex relationships with the men who keep them. Their relationships can have a difficult mixture of "trick," lover, mentor, friend, and parent. There is a mutually manipulative quality to these relationships that can create hostile dependencies for both parties, adding to the complex nature of the relationship.

Although homophobic attitudes can lead some to oversimplify these relationships, there are obvious parallels to these relationships that are not interpreted so simplistically in the heterosexual world. The practice and tradition of kept girls and mistresses offer the most insight into the world of these kept boys.

Case Example

Damion grew up in a rural area as the son of a local sheriff's deputy. He had some minor troubles with the law (shoplifting and theft) and began drinking a lot when he was about 15. His father kicked him out of the house when Damion started identifying as gay at 15, and Damion made his way to the city in search of other "queers." He found the local "cruising" area and began hanging out and sleeping where he could. Soon he was hustling, and before long he "fell in love" with one of his tricks.

Damion moved in with his lover (he never called him a sugar daddy even though Damion was 17 and his lover was 43), but he still hustled on occasion. His lover would try to get him to get a job, quit hustling, and finish school, but Damion only wanted to get high, party, and shop. They would have fights and Damion would leave for a while until his lover would beg him to come back.

After that relationship ended, Damion found others, which would last several months until the hostile dependency of both parties would blow it up. Sometimes Damion's lovers would get violent and beat him up, but this would only give Damion more ammunition to make them feel guilty and a chance to extract a large favor (such as shopping) to make up.

Damion even learned to hook up with men who would take him to Los Angeles, Miami, or the Caribbean on trips. As he got older (20s) and his appeal diminished, Damion began staying with men longer and would even help some find younger boys on the streets.

The second group of boys who can be considered kept are those who are kept by pederasts. Pederasts, as the word is used here, represent a subculture of men whose primary sexual interest is pre- through postpubescent boys. Clinically, these men can be considered pedophiles and/or hebophiles, but these diagnostic categories,

although accurate, fail to capture the community these men participate in, the historical traditions they share, and the patterns they
develop. Although recent research illustrates that the data about
pedophiles has broadened considerably in recent years, little clinical
or research data are available about men who molest adolescents.

The pederasts referred to here are best typified by the membership
of the North American Man Boy Love Association and the types of
individuals involved in boy-sex rings that are reported by journalists
occasionally. One of the most infamous examples of such a report is
documented in *The Boys From Boise,* a ring that involved over 100
boys and numerous public officials (Gerassi, 1966). These pederasts
should not necessarily be considered gay men, though they can present themselves as such. Pederasts move through the gay male subculture and the streets and are alternately parasites and predators in
those worlds.

The boys who are kept by pederasts are much younger (8 to 15)
than other kept boys and are most often recruited to the relationship
while they are still living at home or early in their runaway/throw-
away career. They may be ambivalent or confused about their sexual
orientation and are likely to have been involved in pornography. This
pornography is seldom the commercial pornography that attracts
public attention but the private pornography that is more characteristic of the pederast community. Local and national networks of
pederasts facilitate the exchange of private pictures and home videos
with other interested pederasts.

These boys most often come from abusive, neglectful, or dysfunctional families and are initially the most isolated of the boys in prostitution. Gradually, these boys may be exposed to the world of the
streets and/or prostitution through their association with the pederast,
and eventually either the youth or the pederast severs the relationship and the boy moves on to street hustling as a means of survival.

Boys kept by pederasts are difficult to research because of their
inaccessibility, but there is some description of this phenomenon in
the literature on investigation of sexual abuse and missing children
by law enforcement agencies (Burgess, 1984). This literature is more
relevant to the prosecution of pedophiles than to the boys who are
kept by pederasts and seldom acknowledges the relationship of this
phenomenon to male prostitution.

Case Example

Joey was the middle of five children in a two-parent household in the suburbs. Both of his parents worked and Joey was on his own a lot by the time he was 10. Joey and some of his friends in the neighborhood would hang out at the home of a man named Dave. Dave worked nights and was around a lot during the day and let the neighborhood boys play his stereo, smoke, and even drink once in awhile. None of the boys told their parents about what went on at Dave's for fear of ruining a good thing, and, since Dave helped coach a little league team in the community, none of the parents worried too much.

After Joey got in some trouble in school and for shoplifting, Dave suggested to Joey's parents that Joey come along on a camping trip. Everyone thought it might be good for Joey. While on the trip, Dave molested Joey, and when they came back Joey's behavior continued to deteriorate. Even though Joey was uncomfortable with what was going on, Dave made it sound like it was a natural thing.

Joey was eventually placed in a group home because of the trouble he was getting into, but he ran away and went to Dave, who promised not to turn him in. Joey stayed with Dave for several months. Dave had lots of camera equipment and talked Joey into posing for him, saying he could be a model. He even got him to pose nude by showing him some art books on nudes.

Joey eventually got arrested while trying to shoplift and was sent to a residential treatment program, which he also ran from. He stayed with Dave a few days but started hanging out downtown and learned fairly quickly that there were other men like Dave who would let him stay with them. He also quickly learned about hustling.

This graduation of sorts is often the path to the more obvious forms of prostitution for many boys. Many researchers note the early sexual abuse histories of the boys who become involved in prostitution and theorize a correlation between these histories and the boys' subsequent involvement in prostitution (Boyer, 1989; Coombs, 1974; Deisher et al., 1969; Fisher et al., 1982; Jersild, 1956). A weakness of the literature is that little or no distinction is made regarding the types of abuse boys experience prior to their involvement in prostitution. There is no information about the duration, frequency, or specific sexual acts involved and often little or no data about the relationship between the abuser and the boy.

The author's experience suggests that a significant amount of the abuse documented by the research could be accounted for by the prolific careers of pederasts. There are many pathways into prostitution for boys; it is impossible, based on the literature, to determine how many find their way through pederasts, but the topic certainly deserves more attention than it has received.

There is a possible parallel between the young pimps who do the recruiting and early socialization of young women prostitutes and the similar role that pederasts play in recruiting and socializing young men. The parallels lie primarily in the skills that pimps and pederasts have at identifying youth who are most vulnerable and in the elaborate seductions they are able to employ. Pimps and pederasts are much more able than social service agencies to supply vulnerable youth with housing, food, clothing, and affection.

An important difference between pimps and pederasts, and possibly the reason for the lack of inquiry into pederasty, is the difference between what drives male and female prostitution. Female prostitution is more profit or economically driven, whereas male prostitution is more sexually driven. The subculture of female prostitution (pimps and prostitutes) is generally organized around business principles and what is profitable. The subculture of male prostitution and the role of the pederast are organized around sexual tastes and/or obsessions, and often subjugate profits to those interests. In this sense, adopting the mind of the pederast is not as easy as adopting the mind of the pimp. Most people understand the profit motive and capitalism, but few are comfortable with the world of the pederast. A more thorough understanding of how this pederast subculture operates would shed light on adolescent male prostitution.

WHAT IS MISSING FROM THE RESEARCH LITERATURE

Following are examples of areas the research has ignored or contributed little to but that offer much potential for increased knowledge and understanding of not only male prostitution but adolescent male sexuality.

Drag Queens

Roman boys who were castrated and dressed as girls were in great demand in the brothels of Rome. Benjamin and Masters (1964) report that in the 19th century Dr. Jacobus Sutor found boys of 11 and 12 in the brothels of Beijing who had been partially castrated and taught to cross dress and assume a feminine gender role when he visited China. Cross-dressing male prostitutes are a common and prominent feature of male prostitution in the Middle and Far East.

Drag queens or cross-dressers have been and are a common feature of male prostitution throughout the world, yet there is virtually no research on this unique aspect of prostitution. The adolescent boys who cross-dress and prostitute on the streets of American cities today raise important questions about ethnicity, homosexuality, and gender role expectations in our culture. They are disproportionately boys of color, primarily African American, Hispanic, and American Indian. This situation leads to pointed questions about gender role rigidity for males within different ethnic and cultural milieus.

Drag queens are not transvestites, as they are often called, because of the primarily public nature of their cross-dressing and because their cross-dressing is not primarily related to sexual arousal. Rather, it is primarily related to gender role presentation. They are also not transsexuals, as they sometimes are diagnosed, or at least few of them meet the criteria necessary for surgical consideration. Drag queens often talk of feeling more feminine than masculine, which can mislead clinicians into thinking they are transsexuals, but seldom do they actually want to be a woman. This is often a metaphorical way for them to talk about the qualities of being feminine. Most striking is that the same behavior in women is seldom, if ever, considered a sign of pathology or even deviant.

Case Example

Allen/Alexis was 16-year-old African American male who had been doing "drag" since he was 13. He said a customer had first gotten him to try it, and he felt safer dressing as a woman than as a man. In his predominantly African American community he reported less harassment for dressing as a woman than as a male who identified as gay. He and the group of "queens" he socialized with would confuse and confound uninitiated youth workers with their mixing of pronouns. A favorite phrase of Allen's/Alexis's was "I'm more woman than you could ever handle and more man than you could ever hope to be." He also once commented that a therapist was more "woman" than he was, which was interpreted as a reference to the therapist's nurturing qualities.

Allen/Alexis would prostitute with a variety of customers. Some were "closeted" gay men who wanted to pretend they were having sex with a woman but knew he was male. Some were openly gay men who were extremely "butch" and wanted a "feme" counterpart. Often he would prostitute in areas where he could pass as a woman with men who did not know he was male. On those occasions he would restrict the transaction to preforming fellatio on customers to prevent them discovering his genitals.

Allen/Alexis had briefly taken black market hormones to stimulate breast development but had no desire to have a sex change. He also had several different wardrobes corresponding to different styles such as "slut," "businesswoman," and "entertainer."

Heterosexual Male Prostitution

Badgley (1984) found that 50% of the 229 adolescents (145 females, 84 males) interviewed reported that they had been approached for sex by women. This is one of the few studies to ask the question, what would we learn if we asked more?

Informal interviews with clients and street outreach workers from around the country reveal that virtually all have anecdotal accounts of boys who trick occasionally to exclusively with women. The accounts vary greatly as to the type and style of prostitution with women, but the one consistent theme is that women seldom to never want brief and orgasm-focused sex from the boys. It is virtually always a kept-boy style of prostitution. The boys always spend at least the night and often days with the woman and the sex is qualitatively different than that which occurs with male customers.

There is little doubt that the phenomenon exists, likely in numbers that would surprise most practitioners, but there are virtually no data on which to speculate. Perhaps the more pertinent question is why have these questions not been asked more?

The Effects of Prostitution

Boyer (1986) is the only researcher who has conducted longitudinal studies to analyze the exit process from street life and the impact of social services directed at street youth. The bulk of the research on prostitution consists primarily of field interviews and case studies that describe the phenomenon, its causes and motivation, and the needs of the youth involved.

Because of the wide diversity of the types of prostitution boys may engage in and the similar diversity of the boys themselves, it is impossible to say much in a general way about the effects of prostitution on young men. It is important to distinguish the effects of the streets from the effects of prostitution. The lower-class forms of prostitution such as street hustling can have much more debilitating effects than the higher-class forms such as the call services, but this is more likely the result of the higher levels of predation and deprivation that are characteristic of lower-class prostitution as the result of actual fee-for-service sex. The violence, drugs, and frequent arrests that are more common in the lower classes of prostitution create effects that can be independent of the effects of sex for money.

There are at least three important variables to consider in assessing what impact prostitution may have on individuals who are involved. The first is the life experiences of the boy prior to his involvement in prostitution. This is important in evaluating the resiliency and/or adaptation skills the boy possesses. Boys who have extensive histories of deprivation, poverty, physical/sexual abuse, neglect, or institutionalization become much easier targets of predation by everyone from customers to the police. It is as though prostitution has an exponential effect on the history a boy brings to prostitution. The more troubled he is before he becomes involved in prostitution, the more troubled he will become by his involvement. This does not mean that those who manage prostitution with more competency have not experienced significant trauma. Resiliency in children allows some to adapt more effectively than others and to show less effect from trauma, but it is unlikely that those who are getting the most "beat up" by their involvement in prostitution were not the most "beat up" before they got involved in prostitution. As is explored later, however, one must not automatically assume that all boys in prostitution have significant histories of abuse and neglect.

The second variable in assessing the impact of prostitution is the extent and duration of the boy's involvement in prostitution. Boys who make brief forays into prostitution and move on suffer fewer effects than those who remain involved for a long time. Those who prostitute on a part-time basis with regular customers suffer fewer effects than those who prostitute many times a week with customers off the street. Those who begin their prostitution careers in early adolescence and are still involved in late adolescence, regardless of the class of prostitution, are likely to have lasting and significant effects. The most immediate and obvious of these effects is in the domain of living skills such as housing, education, employment, money management, and relationship skills, all of which may be minimal and crisis oriented. The less obvious effects are in the domain of mental health and self-esteem. Many boys are adept at masking the latter effects even if they are significant.

The third variable in assessing the impact of prostitution has to do with the sexual orientation of the boy. Weeks (1981) observes that "homosexual roles and identities are historically constructed" and that "the social definitions and subjective meaning given to the orientation can vary enormously. . . . If this is the case for the clients of male prostitutes, how much more true is it for the prostitute himself who must confront two stigmatized identities—that of the homosexual and that of the prostitute" (p. 115). The fact that homosexual behavior, especially in the context of child abuse or prostitution, does not necessarily give rise to a homosexual identity makes sorting out this issue extremely difficult. Hence the obsession of the research literature with "Are they gay or are they not?"

Although Boyer's (1989) research has contributed greatly to the understanding of homosexual identity formation in young male prostitutes, there is little or no corresponding research on young men who identify as heterosexual or bisexual. It is important to note that over one-third of the boys in Boyer's prostitute sample identified as bisexual or between a 2 (mainly heterosexual/substantial degree of homosexual) and a 4 (mainly homosexual/substantial degree of heterosexual) on Kinsey's 7-point scale.

If it is difficult for researchers and clinicians to make sense of the sexual orientation of young males in prostitution, it is even more difficult for the young men themselves. The only conclusive thing that can be said about the sexual orientation and identity development of young males in prostitution is that it is likely to be problematic and confusing for both the young man and those who work with him.

Case Example

By the time Johnny was 17, he had been arrested over a dozen times for offenses ranging from soliciting to shoplifting. He had been beaten up by cops, customers, and other street kids and was a permanent fixture of the "gay ghetto" street hustling scene. Johnny had been severely physically and sexually abused from 4 to 8 and had grown up in 12 foster homes, 3 residential treatment centers, and 1 correctional facility.

Case Example

Greg started running away when he was 13 to explore his emerging homosexuality. His suburban middle-class family was reasonably functional but homophobic. After hustling with regular customers for about a year, Greg was arrested and spent time in a group home and a gay foster home. Greg had more difficulty dealing with the homophobia of his mother and the juvenile justice system than with his prostitution experiences.

Case Example

Bob ran away from his foster home at 14 and learned to hustle after being approached many times in the bookstores he liked to hang out in. When he was 16, he identified as homosexual and moved in with an older lover who turned out to be abusive. After leaving that relationship, Bob started having sex with women and became confused about his sexuality. After identifying as bisexual for a period of time, Bob settled on a heterosexual identity.

Case Example

Jeff had been hustling since he was 13 but adamantly stated he was not homosexual. He was involved in a lot of delinquent behavior and spent some time in correctional facilities. Jeff had been violently sexually abused by a man when he was 10. Jeff finally realized he was in love with his best male friend when he was 16; after the realization, both quit hustling. They eventually both identified as homosexual but continued to have sex with women on occasion.

THE CONVENTIONAL VIEW

Much of the current research and literature concerning adolescent male prostitution focuses on how entrance into prostitution is a problem manifesting "deviance" and/or "pathology" that is caused or influenced by a number of possible variables such as early sexual experience, sexual abuse, homosexuality, dysfunctional families, low self-esteem, and drug/alcohol abuse (Mathews, 1989).

In the conventional view, the variables mentioned are thought to work singly or in combination to induce an adolescent to enter prostitution. There is an implicit assumption that the sexual activity of prostitution violates the norms of acceptable sexual behavior, and therefore involvement in it is considered "sick" and/or deviant. This is even more true of male than female prostitution because the sexual behavior often involves homosexuality. Although there is little doubt that these variables contribute to the vulnerability of some youth to become involved in prostitution, the generalizabilty to all youth in prostitution is suspect and these variables provide little insight into the more fundamental processes that place adolescents at risk of involvement, contribute to their continued involvement, and present barriers to exiting street life and prostitution.

Before reviewing the variables, it is important to note two methodological issues in the research on adolescent prostitution that affect the results. The first is the problem of sampling or who is studied; the second issue is how data are collected once the subjects are identified. The most accessible subjects for research are those who are arrested, incarcerated, in treatment, requesting help/services, or most visible on the streets. If one assumes that a significant proportion of young people involved in prostitution is not accessible through these means, then it is difficult to generalize the research findings to all youth who are involved in prostitution. These types of methodological problems have parallels in the research on homosexuality (Gonsiorek, 1982, 1991) and sexual abuse (Finkelhor & Browne, 1986) yet are seldom acknowledged in the literature on adolescent prostitution.

The reliance on primarily quantitative methods of data collection is inherently problematic in regard to adolescent prostitution. It usually means the young person must fit his or her reality into a predetermined set of questions and/or categories that convey to the youth a lot about what the researcher already thinks and wants to hear about, rather than what the youth sees as important and relevant. For example, a young hustler was having a conversation with a social worker. The young man began to relate his family history, and was asked why he was sharing that information, to which the response was, "Isn't that what social workers want to know?" At 16, this young man was already adept at perceiving the professional biases of social services professionals and responding to those biases in the manner the professional were most comfortable with.

These qualitative methods also rely on the relative honesty of the subjects and the interpretations of the interviewer. These are somewhat unreliable given the legal and moral judgments of the behavior being studied and the extremely short-term nature of the relationship between the youth and the researcher.

Finally, these methods assume that the answers that youth give do not change over time. In reality, the answers to such simple questions as who are you, where are you going, and where did you come from change significantly over time.

Early Sexual Experience/Sexual Abuse

The research literature clearly indicates that a significant number, if not the majority, of young males in prostitution were sexually or physically abused and/or psychologically maltreated while they were growing up (Boyer, 1989; Deisher et al., 1969; Fisher et al., 1982). Yet many young men are abused and maltreated and do not become involved in prostitution and many young people involved in prostitution were not abused. Clearly there is a need to consider other variables that, in combination with abuse, lead to a young person's involvement in prostitution. It is also misleading to overemphasize one variable to the exclusion of others, such as the disenfranchisement of youth, the mixed and double messages about sexuality that are targeted at youth, the inability of social services to provide assistance to street youth, the disintegration of families and communities, and the climates of futility that many young people grow up in.

Homosexuality

The percentage of young men involved in prostitution who identify as homosexual has increased significantly over the last 2 decades; prostitution can be understood as a logical construction in the social identity of young males who are homosexual (Boyer, 1989). However, many young men are involved in prostitution who do not identify as homosexual, some male prostitution does not involve homosexual behavior, and considerable prostitution is bisexual. Researchers commonly ignore the diversity in the sexuality of males in prostitution by dichotomizing the samples into groups of homosexual and heterosexuals and suggesting that bisexuality is the same as homosexuality. Boyer (1989) defends this practice by suggesting "that the study is not one of natural categories but of cultural ones" and arguing that "individuals draw upon the existing cultural categories in their attempts to gain self-understanding" (p. 179). This dichotomization has also been criticized because it implies that homosexuality is a homogeneous category and that sexual orientation is a polarized and immutable state (DeCecco, 1981). The relationship between homosexuality as a socially/culturally constructed identity and male prostitution is poorly understood. Because adolescence is perhaps the most bisexual period in the human development life cycle, more research is required to uncover the depth and meaning of sexual orientation as a variable influencing an adolescent's involvement in prostitution.

Dysfunctional Families

Every year over 1 million young people run away from their families to escape problems or seek adventure on the streets (Children's Defense Fund, 1990). If the young person is unable or unwilling to return home, survival becomes a serious issue. As needs for basic food and shelter become more acute, prostitution becomes a realistic and viable alternative to meet these needs. A difficult family or living situation may bring an adolescent to the streets, but the decision to engage in prostitution depends on other factors such as the length of time a person has been on the streets, the intensity of survival needs, and the influence of friends and street peers.

Low Self-Esteem

A common perception is that a poor self-image leads adolescents to become involved in prostitution. In a study of personality characteristics of 30 young women who had been involved in prostitution for over a year, Thompson (1988) found that most had a positive self-image, and the young women who had the worst self-images had all spent time in residential treatment programs because of their prostitution activity. When asked why they used some of the negative labels they employed for themselves, the women commonly responded, "that's what they told me in treatment." Mathews's (1989) study of adolescent prostitution in Toronto found that the low self-esteem reported by adolescents after they began their involvement in prostitution resulted not from the work itself but from the harassment, judgment, and persecution from police, social workers, and others.

Drug/Alcohol Abuse

The myth persists that drug or alcohol addiction drives some people to prostitution to support an ever-increasing habit and harder drugs. Although many young people involved in prostitution use drugs and alcohol, it is not known how this usage is in any way different from the drug- and alcohol-using population in general. The relatively recent development of crack addicts prostituting to get more crack is as yet poorly understood. The more common scenario is a development of or increase in drug or alcohol abuse as a means of coping with the loneliness and stress of street life.

The Problem With the Conventional View

The tendency of traditional social research and social work practice to view involvement in prostitution as a symptom of personal
pathology or as deviance implies a preunderstanding that is normative. A view that if a young person is a prostitute, it can be assumed
that certain things must be true about his or her background, personality, and motivation gives rise to uniform intervention approaches
and labeling that is one-dimensional. Personal pathology/deviance
explanations isolate the phenomenon of adolescent prostitution in
the individual. This view is limited in that it deflects awareness of
the broader social and economic forces that place many youth at
risk for involvement in prostitution (or gangs, homelessness, delinquency, or drug abuse) and it fails to illuminate the social interactions that affect a youth's life once he or she enters prostitution. Not
surprisingly, social policy and social service interventions based on
the conventional view have failed to reduce or contain the number
of adolescents involved in prostitution (or gangs, homelessness, delinquency, or drug abuse).

Viewing prostitution as the symptom of personal pathology/devi-
ance also fails to address the consumers of adolescent prostitution.
There are definite and identifiable markets for the sexual services of
adolescents. The question should not be what is wrong with adolescents that they prostitute, but why do so many adults want to have
sex with adolescents? If there are such clear markets for the sexual
services of adolescents, how come more young people do not become involved? The customers are usually adult males, but a study
in Toronto found that half of the adolescents interviewed had been
approached for sex by women (Badgley, 1984). The lack of research
and attention directed at the consumers of adolescent prostitution is
difficult to defend and raises questions about the focus on the adolescents involved.

The conventional view also minimizes or ignores the economics
of adolescent prostitution. For young people with acute survival
needs who posses few employment skills and have no permanent
address and possibly no identification, prostitution presents a viable
option for quick money. Working for minimum wage at a fast-food
restaurant can appear as exploitative to some adolescents as prosti-

tution. The economics of street survival has been expressed as, "Once I was on the streets, I knew I could steal, sell drugs, or sell sex. There was less chance of getting busted if I sold sex, and I figured I didn't hurt anybody else." For many young people on the streets, prostitution is not a moral or a mental health issue but one of economics. These young people decide that, at some level, prostitution is acceptable, though indeed this decision is made in desperation and with a very limited range of options.

Individual pathology/deviance explanations fail to recognize that prostitution is not a monolithic form of behavior. There are many different types of prostitution and many different types of prostitutes, each with his or her own reasons and explanations for why he or she got involved in prostitution and why he or she stays or leaves. If one listens long enough, those reasons and explanations are likely to change over time as the young person's awareness of himself or herself and the world he or she lives in changes. As Mathews (1989) states, "The conventional view fails to consider the lived, felt reality of adolescents on the street, and as a result social work programs based on this theoretical orientation are meaningless and irrelevant to these young people" (p. 8).

A CONTEXTUAL VIEW

Mathews (1989) is one of the few researchers to address the social context in which prostitution occurs. His social effects model "rejects the individual pathology concept and attempts to ground adolescent prostitution in a wider social context" and "views entrance into prostitution not as a problem for the adolescent but as a solution" (p. 8).

Mathews identifies two types of "social effects." The first are "factors which originate in society and social relationships and which inform and/or influence an adolescent's process of entrance into, and maintenance in, prostitution as an income producing activity" (p. 8). These factors include elements such as the convoluted media images about sexuality targeted at adolescents, tacit social acceptance of prostitution, and the "contradictory messages that come from a government that finances itself, in part, through drinking, smoking, and gambling (lotteries), yet advocates restraint and morality when it comes to sex" (p. 8).

The second factors "consist of more negative elements and are best understood as being consequences suffered by the adolescent prostitutes as a result of society's judgment against what they do" (p. 8). These include the loss of traditional support structures (family, friends, school, church), the narrowing of life choices available, the acquisition of a "criminal" role, and the entrenchment in street lifestyle and values that makes transition back to the straight world more difficult.

Mathews's model details how needs, skills, values, models, and subculture interact and lead to an adolescent's decision to enter prostitution, to become entrenched in prostitution, and to exit from prostitution. This model views prostitution as a satisfier of basic needs (work—for money to buy food and shelter) and as a consequential choice for young people with few resources (skills, contacts, and emotional support).

Mathews suggests that the most important factor in a young person's decision to exit prostitution is a highly supportive significant other or model (this could include youth workers, social workers, exprostitutes, family members, boyfriends, girlfriends, or street workers) outside of the prostitution community. As a young person leaves prostitution, he or she frequently loses income, status in the street community, and stability and control over his or her life. The establishment of a significant relationship provides more incentive for a young person to change than anything else.

Mathews's research falls within the tradition and is consistent with a re-emerging body of literature and new research that confirms the importance of significant adult relationships in fostering resilience, protective factors, and healthy development in adolescents, especially high-risk adolescents. This growing body of recent research and scholarship complements older literature on the role of youth workers and mentors as powerful agents in helping adolescents overcome significant obstacles to their development. (This research is discussed in more detail in chapter 9.)

Young people exiting prostitution also have a variety of street friends and other models exerting influence in the opposite direction, and can vacillate between the streets and the straight life for considerable periods of time. They experience great ambivalence as they contemplate choosing between competing cultural patterns of work, remuneration, and lifestyle that make the prospects frightening and imposing. This ambivalence leads many professionals to question the "true" motivation of the young person who vacillates between hanging out with old friends and trying to stay out of prostitution while developing the resources to maintain a nonstreet life.

This can be a particularly dangerous period of time for some young people both emotionally and physically. Emotionally because significant others outside of the subculture of the streets can question the motives and genuineness of the youth's desire to leave prostitution and withdraw their emotional support at a time when the youth needs it most. Physically because the cultural rules, values, and norms of behavior are different in the street subculture than in the straight world. In the straight world, police and social workers are the "good guys" and friends can be trusted not to hurt you if you disagree with them. On the streets, police and social workers are the "bad guys" and no one can be trusted not to use physical force or intimidation if they do not like what you are doing.

For example, frequently a youth leaving prostitution has considerable knowledge and information about a host of criminal activities (drug dealings, theft and burglary rings, sex rings, political corruption) that police and others are interested in to use to prosecute the "bad guys." The new values the young person is learning (trust the "good guys") often leads him or her to want to cooperate with the police in investigating and prosecuting the individuals the youth has knowledge about. This makes the young person a threat and a target for those same individuals. In the 15-year history of the Street Program at the Lutheran Social Services of Minnesota, eight young people were murdered and many others were harassed and intimidated during this stage of exiting prostitution. The irony is that many young people who cooperate with authorities in these types of investigations because they want to help and want to do the right thing end up feeling as betrayed by the "system" as they did by individuals on the street. In both situations they are used and manipulated for goals that have nothing to do with their own well-being.

This points to the young person's need for the emotional support of a significant other as he or she attempts to make the transition between cultures. The young person's ultimate decision to leave appears to be strongly affected by a need for genuine emotional relationships. Once a young person begins to experience the genuineness and stability of a relationship with a positive model, the young person can begin to sort out his or her other needs, values, and skills (resources) in order to establish priorities and determine a plan for leaving the streets.

Through a relationship with a significant other, a young person can find access to his or her needs for work, housing, support, and assistance. This greatly enhances the likelihood of leaving prostitution. This also opens up the possibility of getting the young person involved in specialized training programs to develop the skills that will enhance his or her prospects of maintaining traditional types of employment. Although the street values the young person acquired are likely never forgotten, the person can reevaluate them in light of new emotional relationships and the stability of a new living situation.

9

Prevention of and Intervention With Male Prostitution

THROUGHOUT HISTORY, "interventions" with prostitution have ranged from licensed regulation to suppression and control through law enforcement. Licensed regulation has most commonly been utilized. Suppression and control through law enforcement are primarily a development of the late 18th and 19th centuries.

Because the most visible adolescent prostitution is on the streets, and most adolescents are introduced to prostitution through the streets (even if they move on to higher-class forms of prostitution), interventions or attempts at prevention tend to focus on the social phenomenon of street youth. Although adolescent male and female prostitution have a range of similarities and differences, the approaches to working with male and female prostitutes have been relatively similar. This chapter discusses some of the approaches to interventions and presents a detached youth work model. Unless otherwise noted, the discussion and model apply equally to both males and females. A thorough knowledge of the uniqueness of each form of adolescent prostitution is necessary for effective service provision, but it would be a mistake to build separate programs or interventions for males and females.

Baizerman (1989) suggests a public health model and vocabulary to organize and analyze the discussion of intervention and prevention attempts. It is important to distinguish the different levels of prevention and, although all interventions may be preventive, it is possible and useful to specify precisely, if abstractly, what one hopes to prevent.

In public health, distinction is made between and among three levels of prevention: primary, secondary, and tertiary. Primary prevention means keeping a phenomenon from occurring, secondary prevention means keeping a phenomenon once present from occurring again and/or becoming debilitating, and tertiary prevention means rehabilitation.

Public health also distinguishes between a social group of actual people and a population/group as a logical or empirical category of people. There is also distinction among the levels of intervention called clinical (e.g., Joe), population/group (e.g., 14-year-olds; runaways; left-handed, blue-eyed boys) and social institutional (e.g., street youth).

Prevention of adolescent prostitution may mean controlling its magnitude and configuration by eliminating or preventing the recruitment of certain populations/groups (e.g., younger youth) and/or by changing how the street subculture is connected to a variety of other social institutions (e.g., police, child protection, youth-serving agencies), social structures (e.g., the job market), and social phenomena (e.g., exposure to HIV). This does not represent a moral acceptance of street youth or prostitution, rather an acceptance of the phenomenon as being real and beyond the current willingness and/or ability to make it go away. Adolescent prostitution is morally unacceptable, but it exists and persists. Its consequences can be diminished on youth who are on the streets for whatever reasons or causes.

This raises the question of whether the prevention of a phenomenon is possible without an understanding of what caused it. The short answer is yes; controlling a phenomenon also prevents it from becoming more serious, lasting longer, and entailing more debilitating consequences. Of more significance when thinking about cause is the distinctions among individuals, population/group, and social institutional. The causes for each are themselves different phenomena, with increasing complexity and abstractness as one moves from the specific, concrete individual to a theoretical entity such as the social institution of street youth.

Even more important may be the choice to pay more attention to continuance than to cause. The key analytical and action questions may be what and how adolescent male prostitution and street youth are sustained. Adolescent male prostitution as a part of the larger subculture of street youth (e.g., prostitutes, homeless, gangs, delinquents) is embedded in a reticulum of social structures and processes. Adolescent prostitution is sustained by its interconnections to functionally and geographically related social systems.

Table 9.1 organizes these concepts and grounds them to an understanding of services to youth involved in prostitution.

These levels of prevention (primary, secondary, and tertiary) and levels of intervention (clinical, population/group, and social institutional) are used to organize the following review of intervention models for youth in prostitution.

THE SOCIAL INSTITUTIONAL LEVEL

Prevention and intervention at the social institutional level are complex and difficult due to the multiple variables involved and the difficulty in mobilizing support in social, economic, and public policy within which the social institution of street youth is embedded. This section does not analyze in detail the social, political, economic, and religious contexts that contribute to the cause and continuance of street youth and prostitution, but provides a brief overview of some of the major trends and issues related to the social phenomenon of street youth. Having no more youth on the streets, making it poss- ible for all youth to get off the streets, making street life different (i.e., more bearable or less damaging), making it possible for youth to have a nonstreet life, and creating a healing environment (i.e., making services and opportunities for nonstreet life available) are indeed difficult if not impossible tasks to accomplish fully, but there is ample room for improvement.

At this time in American history it is not possible to escape the conclusion that we face an imminent crisis regarding our nation's children and youth. It is not necessary to recite the litany of reports and research that document the multitude of ways that youth are in crisis. One of the most recent documents reports that fully one half

TABLE 9.1 Public Health Prevention

	Clinical Level	*Population Group*	*Social Institutional*
Primary Prevention	Keeping Joe (a youth) off the streets	Keeping X type of youth off the streets	No more youth on the streets
Secondary Prevention	Helping Joe get off the streets	Helping X type of youth get off the streets	Making it possible for all youth to get off the streets
	Preventing Joe from being further damaged by his street life	Keeping street life from becoming more damaging to X type of youth	Making street life different (e.g., bearable or less damaging)
Tertiary Prevention	Helping Joe have a nonstreet life	Helping X type of youth have a nonstreet life	Making it possible for youth to have a nonstreet life
	Reversing the damages caused by Joe's street life	Reversing the damages caused by X type of youth's street life	Creating a healing environment (i.e., make available services and opportunities for nonstreet life)

of America's youth are at serious to moderate risk of not reaching productive adulthood (Carnegie Corporation, 1992).

There is growing consensus in the reports that chronicle the troubles of youth that the most important influences on young people today have arisen as a consequence of social and economic upheaval and injustice. This consensus argues that the various ways of getting into trouble—not just trouble with the law—can be seen as statistically probable reactions to these influences. In other words, troublesome adolescent behavior says more about the situation than about the young person. In the Carnegie Corporation (1992) report, James Comer, a cochair of the Carnegie Task Force, describes the changes that have influenced youth:

> Two massive sets of social and economic changes have occurred along parallel tracks, and they intersect most acutely at the point when young people attempt to make the transition from adolescence to adulthood, from dependence to independence—or, better yet, interdependence, for that is what productive adulthood in our country really means. I see these two tracks as the following: a significant increase in the number

of skills needed for successful adulthood and a significant decrease in the ongoing support and guidance offered to young people during their growing up years. These two trends have created a serious problem in our country—indeed, I believe, a crisis. (p. 18)

Comer describes the nation's postindustrial shift from a manufacturing and industrial base that was able to absorb almost all workers to an economy rooted in an information and service base. With this shift came new and greatly accelerated educational requirements that necessitated higher levels of individual development and adequate family and community functioning to promote that level of development.

What has actually occurred has been a decrease in the support young people feel from their families and communities as they struggle to move through their development and meet the more accelerated educational and skill requirements for successful transition to adulthood. Some of this decline in support is the result of poor or nonexistent public policy related to youth development, but the decline also reflects the greater demands for work placed on many parents and the disintegration of neighborhoods and communities as safe and nurturing environments for children and youth.

The results of this lack of support for children and youth can be seen in the rising levels of adolescent violence, delinquency, and self-destructive behavior. As young people grow up without the support and guidance they need, in conditions of great stress and adversity, such as poverty, neglect, abuse, parental inattention, depression, alcoholism, criminality and unsafe neighborhoods, the probability of engaging in high-risk behavior increases. A sad reality of American life is that when families, schools, and communities fail to provide for the needs of children and youth, some people attempt to exploit those unmet needs with little or no regard for the welfare of youth. The current rise in gang behavior among adolescents is perhaps the most striking example of this reality. Young people's needs for safety, protection, support, discipline, structure, and meaningful interaction with adults is exploited by organized adults who use the youth for their own political and financial gain. Pimps and pederasts have long used these same tactics with youth at risk.

As young people grow through adolescence without the support they need and with ever higher levels of development necessary for a successful transition to adulthood, many are left in a social and economic backwater. This enforced marginalization gives rise to feelings of anger, rage, alienation, and hopelessness, which can be seen in their behavior.

It is this aspect of risk that defines the popular term *high-risk youth.* More youth today are at risk not because they have some personal qualities or pathologies that identify them, but because the conflict between social and economic policy has affected greater numbers of youth, increasing the statistical chances that greater overall numbers of youth will "crack" under the strain. Some groups of youth are more at risk than others owing to factors such as class, ethnicity, gender, and locale, but a significant number remain marginal in every meaningful social and economic sense until they reach their mid-20s and possibly longer. It is no surprise that there is increased crime, mental illness, drug abuse, homelessness, and prostitution due to this enforced marginalization.

The trouble in which young people find themselves reveals far less about them than it does about the environment in which they grow up. The terms *at risk* and *in trouble,* common concepts in working with young people today, are often misunderstood. The implication is often that to describe a young person in either of these ways is to point to some enduring characteristics that can be attributed to the individual concerned. Developmental theory is often employed to describe how a young person is implicated in his or her own "trouble" or risk. We suggest that at risk and in trouble are not adjectives that describe individuals, but they are prepositional phrases that refer to the situations in which people find themselves. Risk and trouble, in other words, denote circumstances; they do not define people.

This position does not exclude the possibility that there are some young people for whom risk is in some sense a personal characteristic, or whose troubles are deep-seated. But it does imply that this situation is not easy to demonstrate, that it is unlikely to be true for more than a small minority, and that a "situational" perspective should always be the one to which first consideration is given.

Much attention has been paid in the last decade to the educational and family situations of young people, but the "third leg," so to speak, of the human development triangle has received far less attention. If family and school constitute two of the primary sources of development and support for young people, the third leg represents those experiences that young people have in their neighborhoods and the larger community. An ancient African proverb admonishes that "it takes an entire tribe to raise a child."

With the exception of infancy, no time of life compresses more physical, intellectual, social, emotional, and moral development into so brief a span as the period called adolescence. The importance of community environments and institutions in contributing to that development is well supported by both research and practice. The opportunity to make those contributions arises largely during non-school hours, yet few American communities work consciously to seize that opportunity.

The Carnegie (1992) report states:

> The passage through early adolescence—guided by family, encouraged by school, and supported by community—should result in healthy outcomes. That is the case for many American youth but not for many others. Instead of safety in their neighborhoods, they face physical danger; instead of economic security they face uncertainty; instead of intellectual stimulation they face boredom; in place of respect, they are neglected; lacking clear and consistent adult expectations for them, they feel alienated from mainstream American society. (p. 9)

Historically, the social and behavioral sciences have followed a problem-focused approach to studying human and social development. This "pathology" model of research traditionally examines problems, disease, illness, maladaptation, incompetence, and deviance. The emphasis is placed on identifying the risk factors of various disorders such as alcoholism, mental illness, criminality, and delinquency. The identification of risks does not necessarily provide a clear picture of what strategies are needed to reduce the risks.

More recently, there has been a growing amount of literature and research on "protective factors," "resiliency," and "youth development" (Benard, 1991; Garmezy, 1991; Gibbs & Bennett, 1990; Search Institute, 1993; Watt, 1984; Werner & Smith, 1982). This research, which is well reviewed by Benard (1991), examines the high-risk children who become healthy, competent young adults and have found "remarkable evidence of strength, courage, and health in the midst of disaster and adversity" (Watt, 1984, p. 22).

This research, along with the increasing theoretical acceptance in the child development field of the transactional-ecological model of human development, in which the human personality is viewed as a self-righting organism that is engaged in active, ongoing adaptation to its environment (see Bronfenbrenner, 1974), has resulted in a growing interest beyond the identification of risk factors for the development of a problem behavior to an examination of the protective factors: those "traits, conditions, situations, and episodes that appear to alter—or even reverse—predictions of [negative outcome] and enable individuals to circumvent life stressors" (Garmezy, 1991, p. 421).

The importance of this research to the prevention and intervention fields is obvious: If the personal and environmental sources of social competence and wellness can be determined, better preventive interventions can be planned and focused on enhancing the personal and environmental attributes that serve as the keys to healthy development. This is especially true for the social institution of street youth, who live, work, and play in among the most high-risk environments. Too often, prevention and intervention strategies with these youth underestimate their resiliency and overemphasize their risk for disorders such as alcoholism, mental illness, criminality, or delinquency. Such strategies also unduly individualize the problems of street youth and ignore the social and environmental factors that contribute to the phenomena of street youth and adolescent prostitution.

Although this discussion is general with regard to adolescents, young males have been particularly hard hit by the social, economic, and political changes of the last few decades and the extension and marginalization of adolescence. Unlike the biological rite of passage of menses for young women, the rites of passage for young men have always been culturally defined and determined. Modern societies have been unable to maintain coherent rituals for males to identify their passage out of childhood and into adulthood. Chronically high unemployment rates and a 25% drop in earning power over the last 2 decades for young males (a 60% drop for young African American males) have left these young men more dependent for longer periods of time and further undermines their transition to adulthood (The Forgotten Half, 1988). During this extended dependence and marginalization, young men are murdered, assaulted, incarcerated, and complete suicides more than any other age or gender group in America, and far more than in any other industrialized nation ("More Young Men Killed in U.S.," 1990; Search Institute, 1993). This book also suggests that young males are sexually abused in greater numbers than is reported or generally believed. Young men are not just the perpetrators of increased levels of interpersonal and sexual violence, they are also the victims of it.

A question that needs to be asked of current public policy is the extent to which it assumes (or does not) that individual problems have environmental roots. Policies and resource allocation seem to reflect the view that young people and their parents are largely responsible for their own problems. Unemployment, bad housing, run-down schools, racial and sexual violence, and questionable police behavior not only do not excuse individual or collective acts of rage or despair, but they often do not even explain them.

A particular gender differentiation in this last policy shift is disturbing. It is reflected in the fact that the majority of the adolescents in juvenile correctional programs are male, and the majority of the adolescents in community and institutional mental health programs are female. The common stereotypes are that young men are "delinquents" or "criminals" and that young women are "troubled" or "victims." Although both labels (delinquent/criminal and troubled/victim) create responses that young people do not necessarily want or need (i.e., control), the rationale for the one is to protect the com- munity and the rationale for the other is to protect the individual. The situation and/or environment are likely to be used to explain, even if they do not excuse, the behavior of young women.

The statistical categories or situations in which young people are at risk or disadvantaged (e.g., abused children, ethnic minorities, school dropouts, inner city youth, youth from broken homes) can be facilely described. Membership in any of these categories makes it much more likely, in a purely statistical sense, that trouble of some kind will occur. Young people in one or more of these categories are at risk because some feature of their social environment puts them at a disadvantage. It is worth noting that the term *disadvantaged,* a less fashionable term these days, implies a fundamental issue that *at risk* does not, namely social justice.

These trends and policies refute the popular notion that youth make up a privileged group, and suggest that today is an especially difficult time for the young, particularly if they are in any way disadvantaged. Young people are in the front lines of the economic and political battles that rage around them and in which they are not allowed to actively participate. They attract the stereotypes and images that portray themselves as the ultimate causes not only of their own troubles but of other people's problems as well. And youth are on the receiving end of regressive social policies that seem to overpower attempts to liberalize and enrich the experience of growing up.

THE POPULATION/GROUP LEVEL

Population/group interventions target logical or empirical categories of youth who are at risk or involved in prostitution for prevention efforts (primary, secondary, or tertiary). Examples of these kinds of interventions are shelter and services for runaway and homeless youth, HIV-risk reduction for youth in prostitution, drug abuse prevention for homeless pregnant girls, and employment and training services for homeless youth.

In the last 20 years, most models of intervention at this level have grown out of adolescent health programs and runaway shelters for youth. Adolescent health programs have their roots in adolescent medicine, which represents the collaboration of the schools of medicine, public health, and social work in universities during the 1960s. These programs were a response to the unique medical, developmental, psychosocial, and health-care needs of adolescents. Deisher, who conducted research on male prostitution in the 1960s and has been instrumental in developing programs for youth in prostitution in Seattle, was among the early pioneers of adolescent medicine. Los Angeles Children's Hospital, which has long been involved in providing health care and coordinating services to youth in prostitution, is an example of an adolescent health-care program that grew into a comprehensive service system for these youth.

Runaway shelters developed out of a response to the youth who dropped out in the 1960s; these shelters expanded greatly during the rise in runaways in the 1970s. The expansion of these programs was in part a result of the federal Runaway Youth Act of 1974 and the funding made available through the Youth Development Bureau of the Department of Health and Human Services. Some of these programs continue to evolve and now attempt to serve homeless youth through funding from the legislative renewal of the Runaway Youth Act and the National Network of Runaway and Youth Services. Like adolescent health programs, these shelters and programs have experienced the increasing population of runaway and throwaway children in the last 20 years and have attempted to adapt to the changing service needs of the population of youth most likely to become involved in prostitution.

With the emergence of homeless youth and the threat of HIV infection in the 1980s, adolescent health-care programs and runaway shelters joined forces in many locations and developed the concept of multiservice centers and service provider collaborations in an attempt to consolidate resources and provide a more comprehensive range of services for street youth. The alliance arose because the shelters had access to the youth, and adolescent health programs had expertise in health care issues. The services these collaborations provide include street outreach, drop-in centers, shelter, health care, employment and training services, educational programs, transitional living skills programs, advocacy, and case management services.

A key development in the inclusion of services in such programs of adolescent males involved in prostitution was the emergence and growth of lesbian and gay social service organizations in the 1970s. These organizations gave gay-identified boys a reason to trust that their sexual orientation would be respected and that gay-identified, gay-sensitive staff would be available to them. The emerging expertise of lesbian and gay social service organizations added new insights to the problems facing gay youth and contributed to the development of services specifically designed for these youth, including prevention efforts such as support and coming-out groups.

Unfortunately, these organizations, which were at their high point in the 1970s and early 1980s, are often consumed by the need for AIDS services or have not survived or retained their effectiveness in more politically and fiscally conservative times.

Each of the last 3 decades has seen dramatic increases in the growth of disenfranchised and alienated youth due to social trends and policy shifts and the corresponding socially constructed definitions of the problems they face (Weisberg, 1985). The "hippies" became the "runaways" who became the "prostitutes" who became the "homeless" who have now become the "gangs." As the social alienation of these youth has increased, they have become less willing to participate in programs designed to meet their ever-expanding needs, and service providers have become increasingly reliant on outreach as the most effective means of involving youth in program participation.

These alienated youth are the easiest, although not the only, pool on which predators, such as pimps and pederasts, look to recruit youth to prostitution. These youth do not all become involved in prostitution but a significant number do, and those that do not are likely to become involved in one of the many other deviant or criminal subcultures of the streets, such as drugs or theft, thus increasing their alienation.

The theory behind intervention programs that target this population is that youth have a basic right to services that will allow them to grow and develop, and, if given access to services that respect their right to choose, most youth will choose alternatives to street life and prostitution. It is the simple idea of offering a carrot instead of a stick; or, from a behavioral perspective, offering reinforcement instead of punishment-based alternatives. These interventions allow youth to build, in their own way, on their competencies and adaptive abilities rather than focusing on their disabilities. These interventions allow youth to choose the time and place in which they will face their victimization and make their own meaning of it. If all they want is to get a job and housing so they can go back to school, that is what they are offered. The boundaries about who is allowed to get close and how soon are left to the youth to control. Adults earn the right to restore the trust that was betrayed; they cannot assume that because they mean well, youth should trust them.

Access to services and the changing needs of youth present problems for service providers. These two issues of access and needs are the points around which many programs or collaborations of programs struggle and/or fail in their efforts to serve youth involved in prostitution and street youth in general. A more basic concern is the integrity of the model itself, which is alien and suspect to many law enforcement, mental health, social service, and public welfare agencies. Maintaining a noncoercive approach to the direct and indirect challenges of such systems is a continuous struggle.

Access can be thought of as the entry point back into the broader society for youth involved in prostitution or street life. That gateway for youth is embodied in the outreach worker. The relationships outreach workers are able to form with youth are the basis for the access the youth has to the possibilities the youth worker has to offer. The youth worker represents an agency or program to the youth on the street. The youth do not trust programs, for which they have little concept (e.g., program philosophies, protocols, service flow charts, and bureaucratic structures), but may trust an outreach worker who works for an agency to work with them toward other possibilities.

Outreach workers are also gateways for the programs that employ them. It is through these workers that agencies have access to the youth they intend to serve. Outreach workers must keep the agency responsive to the needs of youth and can be the source of information and experience on the changing needs of alienated youth. This is reflected in the evolution of the programs that developed out of serving runaway youth in the 1970s.

Despite the critical role the outreach worker plays in the success or failure of programs designed to serve disenfranchised youth, outreach work is often assigned to entry-level staff with little or no training or support. They are overworked, underpaid, and seldom taken seriously. They work to establish credibility with youth on the street and similarly have to work to establish credibility at their agency. The management of this tension by both the worker and the agency is the key to whether a program can provide the access and maintain the growth necessary to achieve its goals of helping the youth it intends to serve.

Case Example

Establishing rapport with street youth often requires that an outreach worker be accessible by spending long hours hanging out with and listening to youth. This work often occurs in the evening or late at night on street corners, in coffee shops, or at other street youth hangouts. These youth are often not willing to show up for appointments during the day at an agency office until they have established a trusting relationship with the worker, which could take weeks or months.

This willingness to cultivate relationships with youth on the street runs counter to the ethic in many youth work agencies of "if the kid doesn't show up for the appointment he or she must not want help very badly." Other youth workers may suspect outreach workers of being manipulated by youth because they are willing to go out and find kids rather than wait until the kids come to them. They are also often suspicious of anyone who is willing to work the unusual hours that outreach workers are and of people who are seldom around the office.

THE CLINICAL LEVEL

Clinical intervention models target individuals who are at risk or involved in prostitution for prevention efforts (primary, secondary, and tertiary). Clinical intervention models most often view prostitution as a symptom of pathology or deviance, and tend to isolate the problem in the individual while paying less attention to the environmental factors. These models profess a desire to help youth but can end up punishing the "victim" because they are willing to use coercion to provide interventions. There are primarily two types of clinical intervention models: the criminal/legal and the mental health.

Criminal/Legal Intervention Model

The assumption that adolescent prostitution is child abuse is a common feature of most juvenile justice systems. There is typically a belief that prostitution is harmful to an adolescent and that his or her continued involvement is likely to lead to other criminal acts. This belief suggests that it is in the child's "best interests" to prevent continued or further involvement in prostitution, even if incarceration is necessary. If a youth is unwilling to accept whatever assistance or programs are offered, police, probation, child welfare, and child protective agencies often use the extensive powers of the juvenile court to coerce the youth into accepting services.

These actions are usually initiated by the police, who are aware of youth on the streets involved in prostitution. Patrol or vice officers (seldom juvenile officers) will bring some charge against a youth to initiate a court action and allow for the detention of the youth to prevent running away from a shelter. This varies with each local jurisdiction and is usually a result of agreement among the police, juvenile justices, and city/county attorneys as to what charges the prosecuting attorneys will uphold and the justices will not throw out of court. Because legislation often changes and civil rights abuses are sometimes challenged, there is an evolving nature to these charges. Generally, they comprise whatever will accomplish the goal of obtaining legal leverage over the adolescent. Once in the juvenile justice system, the youth is either given such unattractive "options" that he or she is coerced into "choosing" what the court intends, or the youth is ordered into criminal justice programs that are designed for a variety of criminal offenses. With the increase in juvenile sex offender treatment programs, it is not uncommon for juvenile justices to order youth involved in prostitution (particularly males) into these programs. The rationales for this are specious at best, and are often the result of the system's exasperation over not knowing what else to do with youth who refuse to be "helped."

Numerous problems are inherent in these coercive approaches. Weisberg (1985) offers an analysis of the difficulties in using law enforcement and the juvenile justice system as an intervention approach to adolescent prostitution. Most of the problems stem from inadequate investigation and prosecution of the real offenders in adolescent prostitution—the customers. Law enforcement agencies lack the training, resources, or willingness to perform the investigations necessary to prosecute these cases adequately. They therefore prosecute the victims of prostitution in attempt to force help on those unwilling to accept it, further alienating youth who have often suffered much already.

However, if law enforcement agencies were willing, trained, and equipped to investigate adolescent prostitution and prosecute the customers who demand the services and youth were processed through child protective agencies as victims of sexual abuse, different outcomes might ensue and different questions might be raised. Law enforcement agencies do not typically coerce other child sexual abuse victims into treatment. Such behavior might appropriately be construed as further victimization. Yet this is precisely what happens in adolescent prostitution.

The system unfortunately often violates youth in a way not unlike that of the perpetrator. At its core, child sexual abuse is a gross violation of personal boundaries and choice. A child's right to say no and personal and physical boundaries are violated. Whether the violations are the result of seduction, tricks, manipulation, or physical force, the child on some level knows a violation even when unable to put words or meaning to the events. Child protective and law enforcement agencies often perpetuate similar violations on adolescents involved in prostitution.

Instead of identifying and building on the resiliency of the child, the system often saps the youth's strength. Youth involved in prostitution, and street youth in general, exemplify this issue most dramatically. These youth, who most often have extensive histories of abuse, develop adaptive coping strategies that often are functional in that environment, though often not desirable or adaptive outside of it. They run away from abusive homes or situations. They become suspicious and distrustful of adults. They fight to regain and maintain control over their lives, and develop elaborate survival strategies beyond the abilities of many adults to cope with situations.

Instead of building on their resiliency, protective factors and adaptive skills and seeing them as resourceful within a dangerous environment, these youth are often returned to the homes they find abusive, reinforcing that they have little or no control over their lives. Their judgment is impugned for not trusting service providers to have their best interest at heart, and the resources that would allow them to avoid resorting to prostitution or crime for survival are withheld. It is paradoxical that juvenile justices often order a youth to a treatment or correctional program for extended periods of time at exorbitant rates, whereas less expensive programs that provide outreach, shelter, and employment training for the same youth are barely able to secure minimal funding, if they are funded at all.

Case Example

In Minnesota, Juvenile Court Judges refer young people involved in prostitution to inpatient or residential treatment programs that range from exclusive treatment centers that charge up to $900.00 per diem to county correctional facilities that cost $250.00 per day. By comparison, two transitional housing programs in the Minneapolis/ St. Paul area that provide housing subsidies and case managed health care, counseling, independent living skills training, employment training, educational opportunities, and legal advocacy do so for well under $50.00 per youth per day.

Mental Health

Mental health approaches generally assume the conventional view of prostitution as a symptom of personal pathology resulting from such factors as prior sexual abuse, family dysfunction, and/or chemical abuse by the youth or youth's family (Mathews, 1989). Interventions by mental health approaches can be psychoanalytic, cognitive/ behavioral, or behavioral, and settings can include correctional, inpatient hospital, residential, group homes, and outpatient.

Utilizing individual, group, and family therapy, mental health approaches seek to address the individual pathology or disorder of the adolescent and/or his or her family as a means of intervening in the youth's prostitution behavior. These approaches often include social services such as education, employment training, and independent living skills as part of their treatment plans but as secondary rather than primary issues. Because they generally assume that prostitution is a manifestation of personal deviancy and/or pathology, mental health approaches seldom are exclusively designed to treat prostitution behavior, and are more often general mental health programs designed to treat disorders in adolescence. Mental health approaches have significantly different configurations depending on their source of referral and intake. Those whose primary source of referral (and payment) are public agencies, such as juvenile court, child protection, and child welfare, most often are part of models that rely on law enforcement and coercion for interventions. Those that rely on referrals from individuals and other private social service agencies are usually parts of models that rely on participation by the client for interventions.

Because adolescents have far fewer patient rights than and are often considered the property of parents, "commitment" or coercion into mental health programs and institutions is far easier to accomplish with adolescents. Depending on state laws, parents and public agencies (child welfare and protection) often have few clear standards for such commitments. Independent review or appeal processes for the adolescent are rare.

A unique problem institutional and residential mental health programs face in working with boys in prostitution is responding to gay-identified boys who are sexually active in a residential living setting. Homophobic staff and residents often harass these youth, who are offered little or no institutional protection. Most residential programs are unprepared for sexual activity among same-sex residents. This discomfort and inexperience in dealing with homosexual behavior in adolescence is a reason why many programs minimize or ignore a boy's involvement in prostitution and focus instead on antisocial or delinquent behavior. The prevalent attitudes in residential and institutional mental health care for adolescents regarding adolescent homosexuality are that the boys are too young to know, it is a phase they will grow out of, or the same-sex orientation is the result of individual pathology. Seldom are these institutions able to embrace and affirm an adolescent's homosexual identity. This failing seriously impairs whatever treatment these programs offer.

Mental heath rationales for coercion are based on the belief that an adolescent's prostitution behavior is a danger to himself or herself and possibly to others; as such, it must be controlled for the youth's own best interests. In the service of corrections, mental health is primarily concerned with protecting the community. In the service of child protection and child welfare, mental health is concerned primarily with protecting the adolescent from himself or herself and from further exploitation.

Correctional mental health programs are either general and designed to facilitate change in the delinquent behavior of adolescents, or they are sex offender programs that also address delinquent behavior, but in more specific ways and with a major emphasis on sexuality that the general approaches often lack. Another distinction between general corrections and sex offender programs is the more frequent use by the sex offender programs of a broader variety of treatment strategies and techniques, whereas the general corrections programs are primarily dependent on behavioral techniques and strategies.

Although it is not unusual for adolescents involved in prostitution to be court ordered into sex offender programs, this is inappropriate. The rationales that prostitution is technically a sex "crime" and/or that sex offender programs work on victimization issues (which youth in prostitution often have) are dubious, and any possible gains from these approaches are contradicted by the overwhelming messages of blaming the victim and holding children more accountable for sexual behavior than adults.

Inpatient hospital and residential programs (such as residential treatment and group homes) are often used by corrections to treat adolescents in prostitution but are primarily used by child protection and child welfare agencies (or by parents who employ these agencies or their insurance to pay for and place their children). The treatment philosophies can range from psychoanalytic to behavioral, and the way these programs address issues can be general (e.g., "ranches" or "homes" for boys) or quite specific (e.g., inpatient chemical dependency treatment programs). Inpatient hospital and residential programs incorporate the treatment of prostitution into their strategies of treatment for the disorders of adolescence or the specific problems they are set up to treat. If a youth is in a residential treat-ment program for adolescent boys, such as a boys' ranch, the treatment plan may include some special attention to the boy's prostitution involvement, but this attention usually will be in the context of a more general treatment plan that addresses perceived "core" issues, such as prior sexual abuse or family dysfunction. If a youth is in a more specific program, such as a chemical dependency treatment program, prostitution may be addressed, but again as a manifestation of a perceived central issue such as drug or alcohol addiction.

Case Example

John would run away for months at a time and then come home. He had done it so many times his parents had quit calling the police when he left. When he was 16 and came home from one of his "trips" his parents talked him into checking into a chemical dependency treatment program. They knew he used drugs and convinced him he had a drug problem.

During treatment, John talked about his prostitution behavior, but the focus was always on his chemical use and "what he would do to get high." During family counseling, they talked about how physically abusive his father had been and how his family had a hard time accepting his homosexuality.

When used as parts of noncoercive models, mental health programs are based on the belief that adolescent prostitution is child abuse and that, as victims/survivors, these youth need access to mental health services as part of their recovery from that exploitation and the likely sexual abuse they have experienced. These primarily outpatient programs are usually a part of the continuum of services that are accessible through the outreach programs described earlier, although therapists in private practice or community mental health clinics often see youth and young adults who are self-referred.

Outpatient mental health programs can utilize individual, group, and family therapy and employ a full range of treatment strategies and philosophies when treating adolescent prostitution, but often programs that are designed to treat prostitution specifically emphasize group work and occasionally individual and family work in conjunction with that. This therapy commonly uses cognitive/behavioral or self-help approaches and focuses on prostitution and "the life" or lifestyle issues of prostitution. When these programs are part of the service continuums of outreach programs, these mental health services are often case managed with other social services.

Family counseling is often difficult for youth who are referred to mental health services through street outreach programs. Some have no family. Others have family who refuse to participate due to rejection of the youth (e.g., because of the youth's homosexuality or conflict with a stepparent who forces a choice on the biological parent) or because they are exhausted/disillusioned from past attempts at family counseling (e.g., they had bad experiences or have seen little or no results from their efforts), or because of denial of the family's dysfunction (e.g., alcoholism, incest, physical abuse). The work in outpatient mental health programs around issues of family dysfunction and family therapy often would be helpful to the adolescent; however, unlike adolescents, families cannot be coerced into treatment.

Another difficulty of family therapy with adolescents who have been on the streets is the result of managing a normal developmental process gone awry. It is quite normal for older adolescents (15 to 17) to begin individuating from the family and asserting independence. Adolescents who have experienced the freedom and autonomy of the streets and attempt to move home or reestablish ties with their family often find it very difficult to tolerate the control or guidance that parents quite rightly exert. For youth who have managed the horrors of the streets, being a "normal" child again is difficult. It is as though they skipped a step and are expected to come back and do it over, which can be difficult—if not impossible—to do, even if they want to.

A critical aspect of the configuration of mental health services for youth in prostitution is the issue of funding or fees. There is clearly more money in providing services through coercive models and institutional programs. These programs charge fees to either the county who refers or places the youth or the insurance company of the parents who place the youth. Youth in prostitution have very little money to pay for mental health services themselves, and as a result, mental health providers who wish to serve them through noncoercive models must recruit funding through grants. When available, this type of funding is limited and results in minimal outpatient programs.

The newest models of service to homeless youth are decentralized residential treatment programs. They provide shelter, transitional housing, a range of social services, mental health services, and case management, all accessible to the youth through self-referral. The funding for such programs is, however, difficult to construct (usually from a variety of funders) and falls far short of the per diem per person fees that traditional institutional mental health programs receive from insurance or counties.

These new service models have received the support of the Adolescent Services Division of the National Institute of Mental Health, which sponsored a conference in 1991 that invited runaway and homeless youth service providers to become a more integral part of the mental health service systems for "seriously emotionally disturbed adolescents." These runaway and homeless youth programs have demonstrated effective models for working with children's mental health systems despite their chronic underfunding, particularly in comparison with traditional mental health services.

Case Example

Greg found out about the prostitution group at a mental health clinic through a flyer at the drop-in center for street youth. He liked the support and understanding he got from other guys in the group about how hard it was leaving street life and how tempted he was to go and party with his old friends at times. Those had been his only friends for a long time. After a few months, the group therapist talked to Greg about trying to get his family in for counseling, but only his mother would come. It helped though: Greg was starting to get along with his mother and she was talking about how she was finally getting comfortable with his lover.

DETACHED YOUTH WORK: A MODEL

For a complete review of the history and practice of detached youth work, the reader is directed to the research of Thompson (1990). Much of what follows borrows heavily from her work and from the author's long professional association with her.

To understand the type of youth work involved in working with street youth, youth in gangs, and youth involved in prostitution, it is helpful to look at the history of detached youth work in the United States. Literature dealing with detached youth work can be found in law, sociology, psychology, social work, and criminal justice disciplines and in the popular press. For the sake of brevity, only information from the United States is included here; considerable foreign and international literature on the subject lends credibility to it being a cross-cultural model.

The History of Detached Youth Work

From the mid-1960s until the present, virtually no literature has been published in the United States on detached youth workers or detached youth work programs. Possible explanations for this include the following. First, by the mid-1960s, detached youth work was no longer a new and exciting approach to working with gangs; it had been around for 20 years and it was effective, according to those in the field (New York City Youth Board, 1952). Yet no one had developed a solid theory of detached youth work. No established discipline claimed it as its own, and there was no consensus regarding the roles and functions of detached youth work.

Second, the nature of gang behavior shifted. What consisted mostly of public fighting and terrorizing neighbors in the 1960s began to evolve into a more private (even secretive) behavior that involved more drug and organized criminal activity. In 1965, the New York City Youth Board noted this shift as it was beginning: "New demands of narcotic addiction, school and employment are replacing fights as the focal point of the gang's concern" (p. 58). The public began to see gangs as less troublesome. This continued until recent years with the attention given to drive-by shootings and increased levels of public violence.

A third explanation arises from the preceding one. The behavior of adolescent gang members was seen by many until the late 1960s as within the range of "normal adolescent" behavior, and the problem was defined as a societal problem ("social issue") of finding more appropriate channels and activities for young people. This view gave way to a more "medical" view of gang behavior as resulting from "troubled" or psychologically "disturbed" young people ("personal problem"). During this same time, social concern was shifting from the lower-class adolescent to the middle-class adolescent (i.e., the rise in the public attention given to the Flower Child Movement, the protests of the Vietnam War, and the Civil Rights Movement were driven mostly by middle- and upper-class young people).

The fourth reason for the lack of literature on detached youth work has to do with the biases of youth workers toward scholarly work, including research about their own practice. Youth workers did not develop their own literature, almost as a reaction against the academic and scholarly disciplines that declined to claim detached youth work as part of their discipline. Konopka (1972) describes the reluctance of social workers to adopt the methods of social group work on which detached youth work is based. For Konopka, social group work (i.e., detached youth work) is distinguished by its emergence from self-help groups and movements of democratic group action such as youth services, recreation, the labor movement, settlement houses, and community centers, whereas casework, which is the oldest method of social work, has its origins in philanthropy movements, such as the Charity Organization Society, which distinguishes sharply between the giver and the receiver of social services.

The early programs of detached youth work are important because they set the tone for later programs. And the detached youth workers themselves are important because they represent the essence of youth work itself.

Theory and History of Juvenile Gangs and Delinquency

To understand the emergence of detached youth work, it is important to examine the context of juvenile gangs and juvenile delinquency from which detached youth work is developed.

The wealth of writing and scholarship about juvenile delinquency from the late 1950s to the mid-1960s is an indication that juvenile delinquency was a "growth industry" for academics at that time. Among the research, the work of Shaw and Jacobs (1940) and the "Chicago School" had a significant impact on detached youth work. Shaw found that delinquency and crime tends to be confined to delimited areas and that delinquent behavior persists despite demographic changes in these areas. He speaks of "criminal traditions" and the "cultural transmission" of criminal values. In this tradition, "delinquency, for the most part was seen as a result of a reversible accident of the person's social experience" (Kobrin, 1959, p. 22).

Cloward and Ohlin (1960) expand the notion of cultural transmission and argue that delinquency arises because opportunities are blocked to lower-class youth who want the same things as other youth but cannot find socially legitimate ways to achieve "success." Cloward and Ohlin suggest that these lower-class youth move into criminal activity, prove their manhood through fighting, or retreat into chemical use as ways of responding to their lack of opportunities.

A third theory, the cultural approach (Kvaraceus & Miller, 1959) looks at lower-class neighborhoods as having developed a relatively stable subculture in which forms of criminal and delinquent values and behavior are accepted and normative. Lerner (1957) proposes a fourth theory that views delinquency as a manifestation of the general breakdown in community standards (i.e., social disorganization). A fifth approach is psychogenic: An adolescent's family and early childhood experiences are seen as predictive of later troubles (Aichorn, 1935; Redl, 1945). Another perspective is that delinquent behavior is related to "rites of passage" (Bloch & Niederhoffer, 1958). In this view, delinquency is seen as a normal process that some adolescents pass through on their way to adulthood, but that they "age out" of eventually.

A seventh approach views delinquency from a situational perspective where a youth is seen as acting out as a way of reducing personal tensions. This approach shows an obvious psychological-psychiatric theory base.

Bernstein (1964) subscribes to a multiple causation model. He suggests that "delinquency is not a unitary diagnostic category. It is behavior which is in conflict with the law within a designated age range. Its origins are diverse not only from one youth to another, but also within any one youngster" (p. 25).

The early views of gangs implicitly, and often explicitly, saw them as normal manifestations of adolescent developmental tasks and needs. A basic tenet of these views was the conception of delinquency as within the normal range of adolescent behavior and not pathological. The behavior was certainly not "typical" and was socially "deviant," but not "crazy." For example, Thrasher (1927) says:

> Gangs represent the spontaneous effort of boys to create a society for themselves where none adequate to their needs exist . . . the failure of normally directing and controlling customs and institutions to function efficiently in the boy's experience is indicated by the disintegration of life, inefficiency of schools, formalism and externality of religion, corruption and indifference in local politics, low wages and the monotony of occupational activities, unemployment, and lack of opportunity for wholesome recreation. (p. 37)

Freeman (1956) states that the "phenomena of the corner crowd is a natural function of the situation" (p. 15) and Lerman (1958) asserts that to understand gang behavior, one must consider factors other than personality dynamics, for example:

> The internal relationships of the group and the evolved roles, status, structure, norms, and persistency of interaction of the individual's immediate peer group; the pressures toward conformity and the potentiating effects of group participation, predominant values of the significant people and institutions within the neighborhood life space affecting the individual and his primary reference group; the mode and style of personal controls of behavior prescribed, permitted, and proscribed by outside sources, and the reality aspects of the specific problem situation with which the individual is confronted. (pp. 71-72)

Gang Work

Campbell (1984) comments on the decline in the number of articles and literature on gangs and gang behavior in the mid-1960s in a book on girls and gangs:

> In the sixties, for example, it was widely believed that gangs had finally disappeared. Absorbed into youth politics, some argued. Fighting in Vietnam, said others, or turned into self-destructive junkies. It seems likely that their disappearance was a media slight of hand. New York stopped reporting gang stories and the rest of the country followed suit. Gangs die out and are reincarnated regularly by the media whenever news is slow. As a phenomenon, gangs have never been put to rest. Though they may be inactive for a few months or a few years, they are quietly living in the tradition and culture that has sustained them for over a hundred years in the United States. (pp. 5-6)

In the last few years, the popular press has again picked up on gangs, resulting in a proliferation of attention on gangs and gang behavior. Public concern about crime is fueled by stories in the popular press about primarily minority youth involvement in gangs and criminal or delinquent behavior. The public dialogue, heavily influenced by a law enforcement perspective (i.e., the "war" on drugs), seems to ignore the long history of gangs in America and the lessons learned in understanding gangs and delinquency.

Much like the conventional view of adolescent prostitution mentioned in chapter 8, the popular public opinion of gangs seems to unduly locate the problem as within an individual youth and/or his or her family. Despite decaying and increasingly violent neighborhoods, poor schools, and chronic poverty, young people are expected to "just say no" to drugs and gangs. Even more, they are often seen as morally weak or corrupt if they succumb to these powerful influences in their lives.

The predominant early view of juvenile delinquency held that such behavior arose out of societal conditions and that gangs were a natural consequence of such conditions. That view also assumed that, although troublesome to society, gang behavior displayed "normative" adolescent developmental responses to conditions. Thus early social service agencies, churches, and leisure time organizations attempted to involve gang members in their programs. Thrasher (1927) describes this early work:

> In the early 1920's businesses, the YMCA, the Boy Scouts, the settlements, the parks and the playgrounds, and the Boys Clubs attempted to take over the gangs and turn them into social or athletic clubs. The politicians and the saloon keepers have also learned the trick of taking over these gangs and making clubs out of them, but their motives have usually been rather more for their own aggrandizement than for the good of the boys. (pp. 509-510)

These early programs and attempts to co-opt gangs were not very successful. These programs were unable to draw boys, or when they did, the boys were disruptive and seen as a threat to others. The failure to incorporate the boys into ongoing programs probably prompted the settlement houses and early leisure-time agencies to send some workers into the community to work with these boys. This was not done systematically, however, and was not called detached youth work. It probably involved the use of indigenous young men and was focused on involving male adolescents in athletic activities (Thrasher, 1927). Some of the neighborhood associations affiliated with the Chicago Area Project in the early 1930s used detached youth workers, but again did not label them as such. In a 25-year assessment of the Chicago Area Project, Kobrin (1959) states, "In all probability, the Area Project was the first organized program in the

United States to use workers to establish direct and personal contact with the 'unreached' boys" (p. 27).

Explicit Detached Youth Work Programs

More attention was not given to gangs until World War II, when there was an increase in adolescent delinquent gangs. One response to the reemergence of gangs was to create detached worker programs. These appeared almost simultaneously in many large cities, as social service agencies and governmental units came to recognize that traditional building-centered programs were ineffective in controlling and preventing gang disruption (Kobrin, 1959; New York City Youth Board, 1965). One study in 1947 reported that fewer than 10% of problem youth were attending in-building programs (Dumpson, 1949).

The words "detached youth worker," "gang worker," "area worker," "social group worker," "streetworker," "corner worker," "corner group worker," "extension worker," and "street gang worker" are descriptions of where the worker does his or her work and with whom he or she works.

Lerman (1958) provides a definition that fits most detached youth work programs reviewed here: "A non-membership, community located professional service provided through a single worker who works in an environmental situation over which s/he has limited control and who extends service to a group without prior request from them for service" (p. 45). A more comprehensive definition comes from the Boston Special Youth Project.

> Detached work involves intensive contact with a corner-group where the worker meets the teen age group in their natural environment. By close association with them and getting to know their needs as a group and as individuals, the worker forms a positive relationship and helps them to engage in socially acceptable activities which they come to choose. The basic goal is helping them to change undesirable attitudes and patterns of behavior. (Freeman, 1956, p. 21)

The first explicit use of the phrase "detached youth worker" appears in 1947 in a New York City Youth Board plan for the Central Harlem Street Club Project (Thompson, 1990). This plan suggested that such workers were part of the Youth Street Club Program. The detached youth worker programs in New York City, Los Angeles, Boston, and Chicago have received the most attention in the literature, although there are references to programs in San Francisco (Bernstein, 1964), Philadelphia (Bernstein, 1964; Philadelphia Department of Welfare, 1964), Detroit (Bernstein, 1964), and Cleveland (Bernstein, 1964; Welfare Association of Cleveland, 1959).

The Efficacy of Detached Youth Work

Until the literature on detached youth work began to dissipate in the late 1960s, it was replete with testimonials and claims as to youth work's effectiveness (Ackely & Fliegel, 1960; Bernstein, 1964; Caplan, Deshaies, Suttles, & Mattick, 1964; Dumpson, 1949; Freeman, 1956; Kobrin, 1959; Juvenile Delinquency Evaluation Project, 1960; New York City Youth Board, 1952, 1962, 1965). These studies of detached youth work document the efficacy of the approach and identified some of the major themes related to the work.

In terms of outcomes, these studies indicate that the most dramatic changes that occur from detached youth work are in the arena of public group behavior. Public delinquency (e.g., theft, vandalism, and fighting) is reduced the most. The second most dramatic changes occur in the area of individual public behavior, and the least dramatic in individual private behavior (e.g., drinking, gambling, sex). Bernstein (1964) believes that changes in private behavior are almost always linked to other changes such as school, jobs, and relationships with youth workers and adults. Among the other desirable outcomes from detached youth work are:

- More youth staying in or returning to school
- More youth involvement in organized activities of other agencies
- More successful referrals to other professionals
- More youth obtaining and maintaining employment
- More youth taking individual responsibility for their own actions
- Improved relationships between the target youth and the community
- Improved health care of the youth involved
- Improved attitudes on the part of youth toward his or her future and his or her ability to affect it

More dramatic and personal examples of the effectiveness of detached youth work can be found in Bernstein's (1964) study. He discovered several situations where groups of youth who were not being served by detached youth workers acted out in dramatic ways in order to obtain the attention and services of a detached youth worker.

The Evolution of Detached Youth Work

Even though the literature and research about detached youth work faded and disappeared, the practice of it did not. Youth work's origin, evolution, and practice parallel the work for which it was designed. It shares much with gangs, which move in and out of the spotlight of public and academic attention but do not cease to exist in the absence of that attention. It is possible to trace the evolution of detached youth work through the moral panics and youth crises that have ebbed and flowed over the years. Adolescent prostitution emerged as a dominant issue of the mid-1970s with news stories, congressional hearings, and ensuing research. Homelessness became the issue of the 1980s, and the conceptualization of homeless youth emerged out of the runaway programs of the 1970s designed, in part, to address and prevent adolescent prostitution. In the 1990s, the crisis is again gangs. There are youth workers (not many) whose careers have spanned the last 2 or 3 decades who find amusement in the changing language, symbols, and "problems" while they continue to do essentially the same work with the same client groups (sometimes even with the children of former clients).

That amusement does not belittle the evolving complexity of the problems that youth face or the increasing danger or severity of those problems. But it does serve to illustrate part of the essence of detached youth work. Thompson (1990) describes that essence as:

> a stance which is actualized as a praxis depending upon the unique moment, the unique youth, in a unique context. Detached youthwork then is contingent: it depends. Hence there is no single method, skill or approach. . . . If what a detached youthworker does "depends," how can (s)he be expected to tell you what (s)he does. Each youth, each moment is unique. Yes, there are commonalities and patterns, but they are abstractions. The concrete, specific is what matters. Here too, and

unknowingly, the detached youthworker speaks like an Existentialist:
it depends on the meaning, the moment, the choice, and the action.
(pp. 86-95)

Detached youth work, which seems intrinsically tied to work with the most marginal and alienated of youth, is not related to the work through the problems these youth display (e.g., gangs, prostitution, homelessness), but through the ability to create authentic helping relationships with these marginal and alienated youth and to effect more positive outcomes than would likely occur. The knowledge base of detached youth workers has been expanded to include a more diverse population of youth, and the language systems used to describe and define those youth has changed and gotten more complex, but the art of creating, sustaining, and "manipulating" relationships has remained the essence. Relationships are the skill of detached youth work:

> Given who these workers choose as youth clients, i.e., "street kids," their willingness and ability to create "real relationships" is impressive. It is the major rationale for this kind of youth work, as well as being at times a challenge to other human service professionals. These workers "connect" with the unconnected and (thought to be) unconnectable. (Thompson, 1990, p. 97)

Thompson's research documents that current detached youth work is the same as that which has been practiced historically, with three major differences. The first is that current detached youth workers do not work exclusively with gangs of youth but with individual alienated youth on the streets or with logical empirical categories of youth (e.g., youth in prostitution, youth at risk for AIDS, homeless youth). As in the past, the longer a youth worker remains in the work, the more he or she becomes involved in a variety of problems both on the individual and community level.

Another difference is that agencies that employ detached youth workers today do not have an explicit belief in the intrinsic value of detached youth work but rather see it as a recruiting method for agency programs. These agencies often call their workers outreach workers and define the function of these workers as marketers and public relations workers between the population of youth identified for service and the building-centered employer. One of the most extreme examples of this is the federal funding made available in 1991 for teen health clinics to employ outreach workers to promote prenatal care and clinic use in homeless, drug abusing, pregnant, adolescent females.

The third difference is that women are now commonly found among detached youth workers, as well as among clients. Historically, work with gangs was done by men with adolescent males.

THE THEORY OF ADOLESCENCE UNDERLYING DETACHED YOUTH WORK

The detached youth workers of the 1950s often challenged the more dominant psychiatric perspective of young men involved in gangs as troubled individuals; social group workers (i.e., detached youth workers) often challenged the distinctions social work's case-work method made between the giver and the receiver of social services. Today's detached youth worker often challenges conceptualizations of adolescents and adolescence (i.e., youth the person versus youth the stage of human development).

Kurth-Schai (1988) describes a conceptual continuum for mapping contemporary thought concerning the nature of adolescence. On one end of the continuum, youth are seen as victims of adult society, with the assumption that youth are vulnerable and in need of adult protection. She traces this image from the early years of the industrial revolution to the current images of youth as victims of physical, sexual, and emotional abuse. In addition to this overt victimization, Kurth-Schai includes as victims objects of adult sentimentality characterized by the view that youth are "economically worthless but emotionally priceless."

On the other end of the Kurth-Schai continuum is the view that youth are threats to adult society, with the assumption that youth are dangerous and in need of adult control. She also traces this image from the early days of the industrial revolution to the current images of gangs and juvenile crime, and attributes the perpetuation of this view to lack of contact and caring for other people's children.

In the middle of the continuum is the view that youth are learners of adult society, with the assumption that youth are incomplete, incompetent, and in need of adult guidance. Kurth-Schai traces this image to 20th-century academic models of child and adolescent development represented by the socialization and enculturation theories of sociologists and anthropologists and the universal stage theories of developmental psychologists. She further notes that:

> As guidance may include elements of protection and control, assumptions derived on the basis of this conceptualization may be used in support of either of the first two images. . . . [Y]outh therefore are perceived in terms of their incapacities and inabilities, and it is assumed that adult intervention is essential for their proper development. (p. 115)

Lacking from these conceptualizations of adolescence is the potential of young people to contribute to the social order. Kurth-Shai summarizes:

> By conceptualizing children as objects of sentimentalization we trivialize their thoughts and actions. By seeing youth as objects of socialization we obscure their "social insight and environment-shaping competence." By regarding youth as victims we obscure their potential for adaptation and survival. By perceiving youth as threats to society we ignore their potential as catalysts for positive social change. (1988, p. 117)

The consequence of failing to acknowledge the social potential of youth is serious:

> The secret message communicated to most young people today by the society around them is that they are not needed, that society will run itself quite nicely until they—at some distant point in the future—will take over the reins. Yet the fact is that society is not running itself nicely . . . because the rest of us need all the energy, brains, imagination and talent that young people can bring to bear on our difficulties. For society to attempt to solve its desperate problems without the full participation of even very young people is imbecile. (Toffler, 1974, p. 15)

Detached youth work challenges the definitions of adolescence as simply the transition period from dependent childhood to self-sufficient adulthood or as a "marginal situation" in which new

adjustments must be made, namely those that distinguish child behavior from adult behavior in a given society (Muuss, 1962). These
definitions of adolescence are guilty of what Goodman (1970) refers
to as the "underestimation fallacy." Konopka and the Center for Youth
Development and Research of the University of Minnesota (1973)
offer a more comprehensive definition of adolescence:

> We do not see adolescence exclusively as a stage that human beings
> pass through, but rather as a segment of continuing human development.
> We reject the common conception that adolescence is solely prepara-
> tion for adulthood, except that everything in life can be considered to
> be preparation for what follows. We believe adolescents are persons
> with specific qualities and characteristics who have a participatory and
> responsible role to play, tasks to perform, skills to develop at that
> particular time of life. The degree or extent to which an adolescent
> experiences such responsible participation will determine and maxi-
> mize his/her development. (Konopka, 1973, p. 2)

The key for Konopka and much of the recent research and literature on resiliency and youth development is responsible participation. Benard's (1991) review of the resiliency and protective factors
research points out that high expectations from families, schools,
and communities and meaningful participation and involvement of
youth are key factors in fostering healthy development and resiliency
in adolescents. Detached youth work has and does share this conceptualization of adolescence.

Rather than viewing adolescence as inherently problematic, difficult, and full of risks for health-compromising or disordered behavior, detached youth work views adolescence as full of opportunities,
possibilities, and potential, even with "troubled" youth. This is another
way in which detached youth work challenges the views and conceptualizations of adolescents. The population that detached youth
work selects as clients is generally viewed as troubled and the agencies
employing youth workers most often apply a pathology or disease
approach to working with youth. Yet, detached youth work shares
more conceptually and philosophically with the youth development
field (e.g., 4-H Extension programs, YMCA/YWCA, Boy/Girl Scouts),
which fosters healthy development and provides youth with oppor-

tunities to master developmental tasks rather than focusing on the elimination of problem behaviors.

Because of this development approach, an essential component of the knowledge base of detached youth work is child and adolescent developmental theory; an essential component of the practice of detached youth work is the critical analysis and evaluation of the applicability of developmental theory to the everyday lives of youth.

The work of Gilligan and others in recent years challenges and expands traditional developmental theories of adolescence. Gilligan, Ward, and Taylor (1988) note that, because Piaget's view of knowing and thinking is based on mathematical and scientific knowing and thinking, the revival of Piaget's work in the 1960s signaled a move toward stronger math and science education and the decline of curriculum that teaches history, languages, writing, art, and music. Implicit in Piaget's theories of cognition is the belief that young people have little insight and "knowing" that is valuable to adults (Gilligan et al., 1988). Erikson (1963) gave us the concept of adolescence as seeking identity, and emphasized separation, individuation, and autonomy, which seems at odds with the human condition of interdependence and has likely contributed to the egocentric and narcissistic behavior that is so common to adolescence today (Gilligan et al., 1988; Konopka, 1973). Erikson's moratorium as a condition of adolescent development is an explicit denial of the adolescent's ability to participate, contribute, and experience accountability in society. Kohlberg's general inattention to the moral development of young women has been challenged by Gilligan et al., who have created a whole new set of questions to ask about the meaning of self, development, and relationships. The deep sense of outrage, despair, and disconnection that Gilligan et al., Konopka, and Miller have tapped in young women has contributed to theories of adolescent development of both boys and girls (Gilligan et al., 1988).

Konopka (1973) suggests the concept of adolescence as an "age of commitment" in which the youth struggles between dependency and independence as he or she moves into the true interdependence of humanity. Konopka describes this age of commitment as including the search for self, but also points toward the "emotional, intellectual and sometimes physical reach for other people, ideas, ideologies, causes and work choices" (p. 11).

The key concepts of adolescence for Konopka (1973) are:

1. The experience of physical and sexual maturity
2. The experience of withdrawal of and from adult benevolent protection
3. The consciousness of self in interaction
4. The re-evaluation of values
5. Experimentation

Woven into these concepts are the qualities or characteristics of adolescents. Experimentation is coupled with a mixture of "audacity" and "insecurity," reflecting adolescents' unique willingness to try out new ideas and relationships as well as the uncertainty that comes with the withdrawal of protection. "Loneliness" and "psychological vulnerability" are qualities of adolescents that reflect the lack of a bank of positive experiences to draw on when experimentation results in defeat or the outcome is negative. "Mood swings" are the result of a series of tensions created by the move from dependence to interdependence. Omnipotence tangos with feelings of helplessness and inadequacy, "it won't happen to me" plays hide and seek with the fear that it will, confusion results from being expected to act like an adult one minute and being treated like a child the next. A strong "peer group need" creates a willingness to subjugate personal needs to cooperation and group acceptance. Finally, adolescents need to be "argumentative" and "emotional" because they are in the process of trying out their own changing values and relationships with the outer world.

Based on this concept of adolescence, Konopka (1973) believes that programs and systems for serving youth should be judged by the opportunities they afford youth and the credibility they enjoy. They should provide the opportunity for youth to experience making choices and commitments while experimenting with a variety of roles to try out those choices and commitments. They should enjoy credibility from the validity of the program in the eyes of those served.

One is hard-pressed today to find programs serving youth that meet these criteria. Such programs exist but are more the exception than the rule. Unless real options are available, "making choices" becomes an empty phrase for young people. Pseudo decision making does not promote developing commitment. Therefore, intervention should be focused on the removal of limiting factors, and law and policy should be used to support healthy development rather than to control and contain socially disapproved behavior.

KEY ELEMENTS OF SUCCESSFUL DETACHED YOUTH WORK PROGRAMS

The discussion of detached youth work so far has been abstract and theoretical, more about a "stance" than about practice. To an extent this is part of the nature of the work, but some things can be said about the characteristics of successful detached youth workers.

In addition to Thompson's research (1990), two research projects have focused on what works with youth: a joint research project by Search Institute of Minneapolis and the Minnesota Extension Service, University of Minnesota (Search Institute, 1992, 1993) was designed to identify the keys to successful youth work; and an ongoing project of the Community Fellows Program at the Massachusetts Institute of Technology (Starr, 1993) is conducting research on what techniques are effective in working with youth.

Virtually all the research points to the chief skill of youth workers as their ability to create authentic relationships with youth that demonstrate their genuine caring (Search Institute, 1992; Starr, 1993; Thompson, 1990). The deeper question is how that caring is demonstrated and how those relationships are created. Following is a summary of some of the chief characteristics of successful youth work

Respect

An essential characteristic of successful youth workers and youth work programs is a deep value and respect for young people. Good youth workers respect and strive to understand young people and their families (including their values and traditions) and to accept, learn from, build on, and celebrate their clientele's strengths.

Commitment

A part of caring and respecting youth is having a commitment to them—being accessible and available to youth as well as being consistent over time. Relationships are not like "cases" that can be transferred, and alienated youth cannot be dealt with en masse. Alienated youth need to see that youth workers as individuals are willing to commit to long-term relationships and are willing to be available to the youth when they need them.

High Expectations

Youth workers who respect and care about youth see them as intelligent, capable, and deserving. They want and expect youth to succeed and work to give youth opportunities that enable that success. These high expectations do not mean discounting a youth's pain or difficulty; youth workers focus on empowering youth to overcome obstacles by believing in their ability to succeed. Youth workers do not patronize or "coddle" youth by seeing them as "damaged" or unable to achieve much because of the trauma and difficulty in their lives. This can be extremely difficult with youth who have suffered much, and becomes a delicate balancing act between affirming and nurturing while challenging and holding youth accountable. These high expectations are usually applied to youth programs as well, and can lead to youth workers being critical of services that do not provide the best for youth. Although expecting much from young people, youth workers are simultaneously working for structural change that removes barriers for youth to succeed.

Indigenous Workers

There is considerable debate in the field as to the need for youth workers to have the same background (e.g., same race, same economic condition, same personal struggles) as the youth they are attempting to serve. Historically, indigenous workers have been preferred for detached youth workers, and it is fair to say that if youth workers have not come from the same background as the youth they work with, they start at a disadvantage. One youth worker in the MIT study put it this way: "All the degrees don't mean nothing to me. If you are intelligent enough about the streets, to me that's better than any degree that you can ever get, cause you know what's happening. . . . You can better understand and deal with these people" (Starr, 1993, p. 7).

Caring is put forth by some as an alternative to this experiential knowledge. If someone is sincere in his or her caring, the argument goes, youth appreciate that, even if the person is not from the streets. This is an area that needs further study, but it is safe to say that a youth worker who does not share the same background as his or her clients will need to work much harder to demonstrate caring and willingness to learn and understand the background and environment that the clients experience.

Self-Knowledge

Youth workers, particularly those working with street youth, need to know and understand themselves prior to facilitating someone else's growth. This involves assessing one's personal biases and prejudices, understanding one's motives for helping others, having a good sense of personal worth so that unhealthy needs are not being met through one's work in unhealthy ways, and establishing boundaries and limits to prevent becoming enmeshed or overinvolved with clients.

Professionalization

There is a long-standing debate as to the professional status of youth work, especially detached youth work, that most likely has its origins in the early debates about social group work as a legitimate method of social work. Youth work and detached youth work, with roots in social group work, emerged from self-help movements, settlement houses, and community organizations, whereas clinical social work and family therapy, with roots in social casework, emerged from philanthropy movements that distinguished sharply between the giver and the receiver of social services.

This long-standing debate aside, it is worth noting four dimensions of professionalization that detached youth work often challenges and that contribute to the ambivalence of its professional status: the enclosure of professional space, the specialist division of labor, the cult of theoretical training, and the fetishism of technique.

Enclosure. Enclosed professional space—offices, desks, interview rooms—is at once a defense against the outside world and a structure of perception, the gestalt in terms of which a young person's life is viewed. The defense function is particularly illustrated for those working with street youth in the language that workers use, with its talk of the "front lines," working in the "trenches," and client "bombardment." With the images of a hostile environment this language evokes, it is hardly surprising that professionals attempt to create a territory within which they can more easily control the environment.

Yet the sterility that these professional spaces create sets limits on what can be known about a youth and renders this knowledge one-dimensional; how young people function in interviews, classrooms, examinations, and assessments is unlikely to be much of a guide to the rest of their lives. The less willing professionals are to experience young people in a range of settings and the less prepared they are to work with them in a space that is genuinely shared, the more partial and selective their knowledge of young people and the greater their failure to understand what is really important to them will be.

Specialists. The rise in specialties and the fragmenting of young people based on the symptoms they display contribute to the mutual suspicions and stereotypes that infect one separately trained profession's view of another. This is constantly confirmed by the surprise of youth workers, social workers, health-care providers, chemical dependency counselors, teachers, psychologists, and employment/training counselors on those few occasions when they work together long enough to appreciate one another's standpoint. The fact that shared experiences can have such a liberating effect should create caution about the attempts to guarantee interagency cooperation through procedures and "channels of communication." The error is a pervasive one, it being regularly assumed that if only the "machinery" is set up right, an improved service will follow. The whole person cannot be discovered in a filing cabinet of assessments based on behavior observed in unnatural and unfamiliar settings. Young people can only be discovered by those brave enough to venture out into the unprotected and exposed environments where they live.

Theoretical Training. Professional aspirations tend to encourage two parallel developments: an overvaluing of abstract learning, detached from its moorings in experience, and a belief in the effectiveness of short-term interventions at the expense of the more traditional commitment to long-term relationships. Drawing on a range of theoretical disciplines does not mean overriding concrete situations and empirical experiences with distant academic concerns. It does not mean squeezing young people and circumstances into ready-made categories, ignoring the obvious dissonance. And it does not mean prizing erudition above material skills and a basic rapport.

Technique. The fetish of technique is to the professional what the fetish of procedure is to the organization. It is sustained by the vision of an expert reaching deeply into a distressed young person, pulling a few crucial levers, and letting nature or society do the rest. Such an uncompromisingly instrumental perspective, apart from fostering a cynical understanding of what people mean to each other, takes no account of the long-term nature of human processes. Nor does it explain why persistent evidence suggests that the most substantial social work achievements are based on relationships in which a great deal of time, patience, and empathy have been invested.

For detached youth work then, the whole-person theme is crucial in an analysis of professionalization and the organizational structure of services for street youth. The four dimensions reflect various ways in which young people are fragmented and their integrity is translated into a series of incomplete and selective images, though it is imagined that unity can be restored by recombining them. The hierarchical nature of organizations and the ways in which they preclassify according to established systems and procedures makes them resistant to innovation and oblivious to subtle changes in the environment, whereas the one-dimensional nature of the professional gestalt converts risky social situations into clients and individual clients into clusters of separate needs.

THE WORK OF DETACHED YOUTH WORK

What follows is an attempt to ground detached youth work in the everyday activities of a detached youth worker. This list is not exclusive, and is particular to detached youth work with street youth. It is meant to give the reader a sample, a feel, a taste of what it means to "do" detached youth work.

Dealing With the Everyday Life of Street Youth

Hanging out on street corners, shopping malls or all night restaurants until 4 a.m. watching, talking, and listening to street youth. Getting paged at 2 a.m. to help a young person who has been raped, beaten up, or stranded by a "trick" and does not trust the police or the service system to help and has no one else to turn to. Giving young people rides to free dinners offered by churches, the grocery store, the doctor or health clinic appointments, job interviews, counseling appointments, school, their families, or work. Mediating disputes between street youth, between lovers, between prostitutes and pimps, between hustlers and sugar daddies, between youth and parents, and between street youth and police.

Helping Street Youth Deal With the System

Attending court appearances, institutional staffing, agency meetings, and even family counseling sessions with street youth in the role of advocate and encouraging rapprochement and conciliation. Visiting street youth in detention facilities, residential treatment programs, group homes, and hospitals. "Networking" and case managing individual youth and groups of youth with social workers, probation officers, therapists, counselors, and parents. Using personal and professional relationships to help street youth gain access to services (shelter, housing, health care, education, employment and training, counseling, legal, recreational, spiritual, and cultural) and working to keep those services accountable to the young people.

Collaborating and Community Organizing

Educating and collaborating with service providers (shelter, housing, health care, education, employment and training, counseling, legal, recreational, spiritual, and cultural) to make their services more accessible to street youth and to develop new or expanded programming. Organizing and participating in community groups and coalitions around such issues as runaway and homeless youth, prostitution, gay and lesbian youth, children's mental health, HIV/AIDS prevention, gangs, missing children, and child sexual abuse. Working with public officials, legislators, and policy makers to advocate, testify, educate, and develop new programming for service gaps. Working with researchers to document and identify street youth and their needs better. Attending and presenting at local, regional, and national conferences and think tanks on runaway and homeless youth, prostitution, gay and lesbian youth, children's mental health, HIV/AIDS prevention, gangs, missing children, and child sexual abuse.

Thompson (1990), in describing the major skill of detached youth workers at developing relationships, states:

> Yet, when talking about their work (themselves working; themselves at work), youthwork means skill. Relationship is something they do well, something they know how to do. In their metaphor, they "build" relationships. This is their skill and how, when, and with whom it is used show how, where, and with whom detached youthwork is practiced (i.e., actualized). Given who these workers choose as youth-clients, i.e., "street kids," their willingness and ability to create "real relationships" is impressive. (p. 96)

Detached Youth Work and Supervision

The supervision and employment of detached youth workers can best be understood as a series of tensions that are cultural, structural, and often personal. To borrow a concept from the psychoanalytic

Supervisor = parents,
school,
"the system,"
society

Worker = youth

Figure 9.1. Supervision

literature, there is a "parallel process" (Kahn, 1979; Sachs & Shapiro, 1976) on a systemic as well as a personal level in which the relationship between the detached youth worker and the supervisor closely resembles the relationship between the youth and his or her troubles with the adult world. This relationship is illustrated in Figure 9.1.

The tensions between detached youth workers and supervisors can be seen in a variety of arenas, but they most often are metaphors for the struggle between the youth and society. The detached youth worker defines the work in terms of the youth (i.e., youth teach the worker how to be helpful and the "program" emerges from those needs), and the agency/supervisor defines the work in terms of programmatic and funding goals (i.e., which funders will fund and/ or what hierarchies dictate which preclassified and established systems and procedures of "programs" that squeeze young people and circumstances into ready-made categories of "service delivery"). This tension or strain between the detached youth worker and supervisor is best managed when it is understood, in the psychoanalytic parallel process language, as transference and countertransference or as the unconscious acting out of emotions displaced from one relationship/situation to another relationship/situation.

Many detached youth workers perceive supervision as control, and many agency administrators perceive supervision of detached youth workers as difficult (e.g., they are hard to control, accountability is difficult). Thompson (1990) describes this tension:

"Out of sight out of mind," as the saying goes. This is true for the youthworker while the agency personnel expected to supervise the youthworkers act on the adage "visibility is accountability." The more time the youthworkers spend with youth and the less time with agency staff, the more likely they were "to identify" with the youth. The long hours of listening, observing, and being with youth create, in the youthworker, the belief that (s)he is one of the few adults who can "really" understand the youth. They begin to look at the agency as if they were an outsider, questioning policies, procedures, and even the beliefs of the other agency staff. While the supervisor worries, "frets" and imagines what is happening and why, the anger and the frustration of the worker only increases the concern of the supervisor and a vicious cycle is created. (p. 95)

Baizerman (1988) describes another type of tension between detached youth workers and their agencies:

The detached youthworker wants the authority to be an agent of the agency in the name of the youth. Herein lies another source of tension between worker and employer. Employing agencies tend to be ambivalent about detached youthwork because the gains in status and funds which accrue due to their presence is offset by the tensions and problems attendant to their being employed. Since detached youthworkers work with youth at relatively high-risk to complicated personal and familial troubles, detached youthwork seems to get entangled in a wide array of never ending legal, moral and psychological "problems," as seen by the agency. Nothing is ever simple, neat or "cut and dried," i.e., routine. (p. 3)

This is illustrated by the work with gay-identified adolescents involved in male prostitution. Agency executive directors and boards may feel ambivalent about a detached youth worker's advocation for these obviously underserved youth because such advocacy makes the agency vulnerable to attacks by right-wing Christian and profamily organizations that could jeopardize agency funding or credibility.

Another area of tension is what detached youth work often calls "ethics" and agencies often call "boundaries." Detached youth work is always extending the concept of boundaries by challenging the ethics of the helping professions. The work itself is seen by some as "codependent" or guilty of "overidentifying" with the client. In addition, by the very nature of the work (being out on the streets), detached youth workers are witness to much that is illegal, "immoral," violent, and unjust. Helping and forming relationships with youth in this context means that "doing the right thing" is never an easy judgment. Professional detachment collides with a deep sense of moral outrage. Because detached youth workers are not usually members of an established profession, they often do not have professional socialization into the codified ethical codes of such groups and they often challenge the standards of practice of those professional groups. These challenges are well taken but without a process for reflecting on and understanding them, the worker can become frustrated and lose effectiveness.

Commenting on this, Thompson (1990) observes:

> Detached youthworkers may have psychological insight about them-
> selves and/or their clients. If such insight is present, they still lack a
> theoretical base or language in which to talk about these insights. Hence,
> supervision, which is often about what in the worker may be influenc-
> ing what the worker is doing, can be threatening. The supervisor
> represents the employing agency, and the detached youthworker tends
> to be in tension with his/her employer. Thus it is seen how the very
> ethos of detached youthwork, the lack of formal preparation and personal
> limitations of the worker join in an anti-supervision dance. (p. 96)

Thompson (1990) summarizes the needs of supervision as:

> Youthworkers appear to be open and willing to supervision if it is
> reflective, supportive and provides a means to remove barriers and obsta-
> cles to services to client youth. Youthworkers want someone to talk to
> about what they are experiencing, someone who will listen, challenge,
> confront, and accept. They need, in my opinion, supervision which
> provides for practical mastery, supervision that helps them put their
> experiences into personal and work contexts and supervision that can
> move from the levels of "real and concrete" to the theoretical, and back
> again. . . . Agencies need to understand the detached youthwork stance.
> It is important that agency personnel recognize and acknowledge the
> value of detached youthwork as understood from the perspective of the
> worker. Administrators must come to understand the inherent struc-
> tural sources of job strain. The anti-technocratic ideology, the lack of
> an identified code of ethics, the lack of professional identification and
> status, the relative isolation, the long hours, and the constant struggle
> to do the right thing in the right way. With such understanding, adminis-
> trators would help to prevent "burn out," would help to define "role
> boundaries." They would provide outside consultants for detached
> youthworkers and strongly encourage ongoing meetings with youth-
> workers employed at other agencies. (pp. 106-107)

Synopsis of the
Detached Youth Work Model

The model of detached youth work is presented as a method of working with street youth and youth involved in prostitution. It is a method with a history in the social group work method of social work that has evolved and survived but is usually practiced without formal training and education. This lack of formality reflects the long-standing debate about the professional status of the social group work method and the ongoing challenges that detached youth work presents to the professionalization and bureaucratization of youth services.

Detached youth work embraces the youth development theories of adolescence such as those of Konopka (1972, 1973) and Gilligan et al. (1982), rejects the notion of adolescents as incomplete and incompetent, and explicitly rejects attempts to pathologize and medicalize the problems of street youth. The practice, skills, and objectives of detached youth work are the art of relationships and the displacement of technique by principle.

Finally, although supervision of detached youth workers may be difficult, it is not impossible and can be made much easier by agencies valuing and understanding detached youth work and addressing the sources of structural, cultural, and personal strains of detached youth work.

Summary

Science is said to proceed on two legs, one of theory (or, loosely, of deduction) and the other of observation and experiment (or induction). Its progress, however, is less often a commanding stride than a halting stagger—more like the path of a wandering minstrel than the straight ruled trajectory of a military marching band. The development of science is influenced by intellectual fashions, is frequently dependent on technology, and, in any case, seldom can be planned far in advance, since its destination is usually unknown. (Ferris, 1988, p. 144)

Observations always involve theory. (Hubble, 1985, p. 12)

Our hope is that the information presented in this section will make its way into the repertoire of mainstream human service professionals and that a framework can be constructed that allows for more authentic and diverse paradigms of adolescents, particularly males. For this to occur, the prevailing theories or paradigms of adolescent males must be broadened to include the observations that history and research present; these observations must be accountable for the theories that shape them.

The historical literature illustrates that young men and boys have been the sexual objects of pleasure for men, women, and individuals both eclectic in their desires and exclusively pederast throughout human history, and that prostitution has always involved young men and boys. As Foucault (1988) points out, what has changed is not the "taste for boys," but the way in which the questions are asked and a fading of the importance they are granted in philosophical and moral debate.

In modern times, questions about male prostitution have been largely confined to whether the young men involved are homosexual or heterosexual and how that sexual orientation affects or influences their involvement in prostitution. Although these are intriguing questions, they are difficult to understand or investigate without being grounded in the larger questions of the nature of the "taste for boys" and why it is not granted more importance in philosophical, scientific, and moral debates.

Male prostitution is, in a sense, the visible tip of an iceberg. Above the surface is the activity of prostitution; below the surface are the disquieting issues of young males as "victims" or the objects of sexual exploitation, a range of sexual behavior and motivation that does not conveniently fit the culturally defined categories of homosexual or heterosexual, and gender role behavior that challenges conventional notions of maleness.

Attempts to define male prostitution as homosexual prostitution are but one way to obfuscate and distort the unique maleness of prostitution to fit cultural categories and definitions rather than to describe the reality of those involved. This completely ignores the roles of women and exclusive pederasts as customers, as well as making the erroneous assumption that male customers and the prostitutes themselves fit within a definition of homosexual.

Male prostitution is the most visible form of the sexual abuse and exploitation of young males. Below the surface is the issue of the high prevalence of sexual abuse prior to prostitution in the young men involved. This is but one indication that the documentation of sexual abuse of boys is underreported, and speaks to why it is so hard for boys and young men to voice their experiences and for those experiences to be heard. In a culture where men are defined, by both men and women, as sexual predators, it is difficult for them to tell of their experiences as prey.

In terms of social sex roles, the term *male prostitute* is itself an oxymoron. The term *prostitute* carries a host of negative images more associated with the social role of women than men, making the term *male prostitute* difficult to assimilate into everyday conceptualizations of males.

The framework must be renovated if more authentic paradigms of males are to emerge. More research with better methodology that includes the areas of male prostitution that have been traditionally ignored (e.g,. drag queens, pederasts, women customers) is necessary to better understand these enigmatic phenomena, but the information that research supplies must have somewhere to reside. The available cultural paradigms for males, especially adolescent males, do not easily allow for the incorporation of that information.

The other operative word in adolescent male prostitution is "adolescent." The parameters around the discussion of adolescent involvement in prostitution need to be expanded, the phenomenon needs to be contextualized in a wider social setting, factors in society (values, beliefs, and attitudes) and social relations that have a bearing on the process of entrance into and maintenance in prostitution deserve attention, and the dimensions fundamental to a deeper understanding of the phenomenon need to be delineated.

It is not our intention to condemn as worthless conventional research views and perspectives or to present as entirely oppressive all social service practice. Clearly some young people benefit from the existence of these services. It is also not our intention to appear supportive of adolescent involvement in prostitution, for we believe it to be sexual abuse. But the current simplistic "victim/perpetrator" paradigm does not capture the full nature of the abuse: the economic, social, and political exploitation; the impoverishment of constricted sex roles; and the considerable limitations of current theory and institutions.

Because street prostitution is the most visible form of prostitution (and the most accessible to the young person starting out), it receives the most public attention and tends to become the stereotype of what the life is all about. The truth is, prostitution is a diverse enterprise conducted in private homes, in hotels and nightclubs, and through escort services and pagers, as well as on the streets.

Perhaps the most difficult aspect for people outside the life to understand about street life is the shift in thinking that occurs once a young person has been living "out there" for a while. This thinking can best be described as a "survival mentality" characterized by desperation, hypervigilance, and a need for instant gratification. Most of these youth live a moment-to-moment existence and capitalize on any opportunity, illegal or otherwise, to meet their urgent survival needs.

There is a general tendency on the part of the public and some professionals to want to reduce adolescent prostitution, a complex social phenomenon, to a simple "problem" requiring a simple solution. In essence, the problem is seen as in and with the adolescent. Adolescent prostitution is both a mirror and a microcosm of many of the prevailing values, attitudes, and beliefs of modern society.

Prostitution is not simply the activity of prostitutes but is a phenomenon inextricably interwoven with the social fabric of our society. Consideration must be given to the many components that often get overlooked. A major one is the "markets" that exist for the sexual services of adolescents and the adult male and female customers who use these services.

Adolescent prostitution as an income-producing activity appears to be, for the most part, a short-term career, even when it is pursued on a full-time basis (Mathews, 1989). For many adolescents, it is simply a bridge between impoverished states in a directionless career path; for others it is an acknowledged stopgap en route to other areas of work. In any event, most young people do not appear to remain in prostitution much beyond 3 years, and intrusive interventions can be a factor not only in their entrance into the life but also in their staying in it longer. Criminal records, labeling, forced and irrelevant social service programs, and esteem-lowering persecution and harassment are not only ineffective but encourage the behavior they are trying to stop.

The moral repugnance of adolescent prostitution is difficult to reconcile with the acceptance that it is beyond the current willingness and/or ability to eliminate. This difficulty often leads to simplistic and quick solutions to try and make adolescent prostitution go away or a fatalistic resignation that nothing can be done about it. The intermediary, and more difficult position, is that it is morally unacceptable, but it is here and unlikely to go away. However, its consequences on the youth on the streets can be diminished, and interventions can control its magnitude and configuration by eliminating or preventing the recruitment of certain population/groups (e.g., younger youth) and by changing how the street subculture is connected to a variety of other social institutions (e.g., police, child protection, youth-serving agencies), social structures (e.g., the job market), and other crucial phenomena (e.g., exposure to HIV).

The problem of adolescent prostitution can be addressed on many levels; the most effective approaches are those that are able to develop multilevel and multiservice strategies. Because the social institution of street youth is embedded in a reticulum of social structures and processes and is sustained by its interconnections to functionally and geographically related social systems, approaches that flourish in one location cannot necessarily be transplanted to another location and produce the same results. If models of intervention have value, it is not because they can be replicated, component by component, somewhere else. Indeed, a mechanical metaphor is not appropriate here—an organic one is far more useful. No doubt it is possible to "take new cuttings" and "breed new strains," but this is quite different from the idea that one can engineer identical structures indiscriminately. Rather it is the way of thinking about these phenomena and the underlying principles that can be replicated and transplanted to new environments.

Any model of intervention with street youth needs to be built on at least four principles. The first is to identify situations, not categories, of young people. This means, on the one hand, that efforts should be made to study the wider context in which street youth occur, and, on the other, that those who find themselves in that situation must not be overly pathologized and labeled.

The second principle is that street youth are not aliens. This is a truism but nonetheless a necessary reminder. Economic, institutional, and cultural wedges have been driven between the worlds of street youth and adult society. The distorted images of street youth as prostitutes, gang members, drug addicts, and delinquents call for adults to bear the responsibility for rapprochement between the generations and build long-term relationships and support. Implicit in this principle is the respect for young people as persons.

The third principle is to relate services to needs, not needs to services. Among the layers of organization and bureaucracy, it has become increasingly difficult to see that a "need" is independent of the vast and complicated machinery of youth services. Needs today are most often defined in terms of whatever services are deemed viable. This principle argues for a more empirical approach to identifying and understanding needs. This means professionals must be prepared to gather as much relevant data as possible (about individuals, groups, and communities), be ready to experiment with new ways of asking questions, and be willing to listen carefully to the answers. It means professionals must have the tenacity to sift for clues and search for patterns without assuming that either they or the street youth already know the ultimate outcome. It means professionals must consistently think of themselves as researchers, analyzing data, hoping to be surprised, and trying not to take anything for granted.

The fourth principle is that when organizations and agencies consider the concepts of evaluation and accountability, they should look outward to street youth and the community rather than upward toward managers and administrators. Accountability should ultimately be to the client, not the organization. Tests of an agency or professional's ability have become tied to such criteria as recorded change in client behavior and the capacity to describe one's activities in language so convoluted that anyone outside the profession (and many inside) have difficulty understanding it. Reversing this would mean that a worker's skills would be tested by the client, rather than protected by records and the ability to convert accounts of activities into theoretical codes and organizational ciphers. Implicit in this principle is the belief that joint accountability and mutual evaluation are desirable where workers and clients have developed a relationship of cooperation based on mutual respect and a balance of power.

The detached youth work model presented here is an organic model whose emphasis is on a set of principles rather than a set of techniques or structures. As Thompson (1990) suggests, detached youth work is "a stance which is actualized as a praxis depending on the unique moment, the unique youth, in a unique context" (p. 86). It starts with a problem (street youth), not a program, and its primary tool is the relationships the worker is able to form with youth. Strategies and services emerge from these relationships and the nature of the problems the worker encounters.

At its simplest and most sweeping, the message of detached youth work is this: Youth-service agencies tend not to be able to cope with fluidity, uncertainty, change, and continuity—any form of "becoming" that transcends boundaries in time, space, or role. For both organizational and professional reasons, these agencies are more comfortable with fragments and factors, components and compartments, timetables and targets and everything else that can be defined, discriminated, determined or differentiated. To the degree that this is true, these agencies also fall short of the principles espoused here, and fail in their mission to serve youth.

10

Epilogue

A young man who had a bitter disappointment in life went to a remote monastery and said to the abbot: "I am disillusioned with life and wish to attain enlightenment to be freed from these sufferings. But I have no capacity for sticking long at anything. I could never do long years of meditation and study and austerity; I should relapse and be drawn back to the world again, painful though I know it to be. Is there any short way for people like me?" "There is," said the abbot, "if you are really determined. Tell me, what have you studied, what have you concentrated on most in your life?" "Why, nothing really. We were rich, and I did not have to work. I suppose the thing I was really interested in was chess. I spent most of my time at that."

The abbot thought for a moment, and then said to his attendant: "Call such-and-such a monk, and tell him to bring a chessboard and men." The monk came with the board and the abbot set up the men. He sent for a sword and showed it to the men. "O monk," he said, "you have vowed obedience to me as your abbot, and now I require it of you. You will play a game of chess with this youth, and if you lose I shall cut off your head with this sword. But I promise that you will be reborn in paradise. If you win, I shall cut off the head of this man; chess is the only thing he has ever tried hard at, and if he loses he deserves to lose his head also." They looked at the abbot's face and saw that he meant it: he would cut off the head of the loser.

They began to play. With the opening moves the youth felt the sweat trickling down to his heels as he played for his life. The chessboard became the whole world; he was entirely concentrated on it. At first he had somewhat the worst of it, but then the other made an inferior move and he seized his chance to launch a strong attack. As his opponent's position crumbled, he looked covertly at him. He saw a face of intelligence and sincerity, worn with years of austerity and effort. He thought of his own worthless life, and a wave of compassion came over him. He deliberately made a blunder and then another blunder, ruining his position and leaving himself defenseless.

The abbot suddenly leaned forward and upset the board. The two contestants sat stupefied. "There is no winner and no loser," said the abbot slowly, "there is no head to fall here. Only two things are required," and he turned to the young man, "complete concentration, and compassion. You have today learned them both. You were completely concentrated on the game, but then in that concentration you could feel compassion and sacrifice your life for it. Now stay here a few months and pursue our training in this spirit and your enlightenment is sure." He did so and got it. (Sohl & Carr, pp. 43-44)

Our initial attempts to create a more "unified" volume on males as victims and perpetrators of sexual abuse seemed premature, at least for us and perhaps for the field. We found ourselves most comfortable with an increasingly diverging set of perspectives that reflected what each of us believed in, felt we were good at, and respected but did not necessarily share in terms of perspective or skills in the others.

Despite the variety of our perspectives, from individual therapy in which the effects and meaning of the abuse interacts with the development of the self, to family therapy in the context of large and complicated systems, to gritty on-the-streets social work, we share important commonalities.

The first is a deeply felt need to place understandings of sexual abuse in a larger and richer context. This context includes the social forces that disenfranchise youth and drive them into the streets; the complex and changing function that prostitution has played in our civilization; the family systems of both victim and offender as well as the larger "institutional family" (perhaps the most dysfunctional of all) of social service, mental health, criminal justice, and related systems; and the ways in which the experience of sexual abuse resonates throughout the individual psyche. The phenomena of sexual abuse cannot be understood in a fragmented or atomized way. There is no real "field" of sexual abuse, nor should there be.

Rather, there are different ways of understanding the complexity of sexual abuse through the simultaneously limiting and enriching perspectives of particular disciplines. Treating sexual abuse as a specialty area apart from the individual psyches carrying the experience; the families and other systems affected; and the larger culture that is simultaneously horrified, condoning, shaming, and denying regarding sexual abuse merely repeats the alienation, fragmentation, and disenfranchisement that are the hallmarks of the experience. We are integrationist about sexual abuse and promiscuous about the levels on which it needs integration.

There is another commonality in our perspectives: A belief that a helping or therapeutic intervention cannot occur unless there is a pervasive respect for the client. Whether that client is victim or perpetrator, adult or minor, psychologically minded or lacking in insight, well defended or emotionally integrated, cooperative or obstreperous, normatively middle class or living on the edge, the patient or client deserves the good will, complete skills, respect, and understanding of the therapist or helper—concentration and compassion.

This is a truism in any kind of clinical work. However, certain kinds of clinical work, like working with victims and perpetrators of sexual abuse, more readily elicit violations of these norms. The helper who cannot feel warmth or empathy toward a client or class of clients and who cannot simultaneously risk challenging that client or clients should not be working with such individuals. Neglecting this basic stance is the danger of any overly politicized perspective. We suggest that any goal that interferes with or diminishes the overriding principle of operating in the best interests of the individual client is inappropriate and runs the risk of shading into seriously unethical behavior.

That is not to say that such goals are unworthy but rather that their place is not in clinical work. Desires to seek justice for victims, to make the world a less oppressive place for any class of people, to prevent further abuse, and the like, are only reasonable in clinical work if they do not deflect from the individual client's best interests. Interventions rendered in the interest of victims in general, to make examples of certain people or situations, or to create social change, invariably shortchange some individual clients.

The core feature of abuse, sexual or otherwise, is that the rights and interests of an individual are ignored and/or violated to serve the purposes of another. Intervention efforts that zealously attempt to remedy other abuses by deflecting from the centrality of the best interests of the individual client can easily end up as a more exquisitely rationalized form of abuse.

We share an attitude of wringing every drop of utility out of a theoretical perspective or clinical technique. We believe that there is little sacred and a great deal foolish about the theory and practice of clinical work. Such endeavors are only as worthwhile as they are respectful and useful. Clinical theories and techniques are not understandings of human nature, philosophical systems, spirituality, or important in their own right. Rather, they are tools to be used in ways intended, and perhaps in ways not initially intended (but cautiously), to reduce suffering in a way that serves the client's best interests.

We suspect Kohut would not have been pleased to see his ideas about early childhood processes applied to later childhood and adolescent developmental events. Many family system theorists might find tight adherence to specific goals intermingled with potentially high risk interactions with multiple systems at once, in victim sensitive offender therapy, too untidy. Many social workers might perceive the central allegiance to the youth served in the detached youth work model as unnerving indeed.

Our common goal is to utilize clinical theory and technique to accomplish the task of respectful and effective reduction of suffering and to facilitate change in the best interests of the clients. Slavish adherence to theoretical niceties and oppositional delight in trouncing on such niceties ignore the centrality of the needs of the client.

Finally, we share a curiosity about the meaning of our work. Regularly questioning the nature of what one does may not reliably produce wisdom, but we are confident it helps contain clinical arrogance.

We are disquieted by the peculiar convergence of recent cultural trends in the United States regarding children. The 1980s, which witnessed recognition of and "concern" for sexual abuse of children, also saw a massive erosion of social supports, health care, and economic services for children to a level that has not been seen for the better part of a century. Are we as a society concerned about the welfare of children, or are we using children to indulge yet another round of our cultural love-hate obsession with sexuality, our see-saw between excess and repression? Do we focus concern predominantly on child-hood sexual abuse so we do not have to address unnerving questions about the failure of our familial, social, political, economic, and health-care institutions to address the needs of children?

To allow so many children to be without adequate prenatal care, early childhood nutrition, health care, and a viable education or job skills within a violent environment with little prospect of meaning-ful adult employment; and then to be concerned about these chil-dren's vulnerability to sexual abuse seems a sham. If our concern for children is true and deep, we as a society must find ways to address all the ways children are abused.

In this "field" of sexual abuse, where the needs and the demands of clients are high, the database is thin, dogmatism seems to run ram-pant, and the internal contradictions and avoidance of substantive issues on a societal level make the mind reel, we heartily recommend concentration and compassion.

John C. Gonsiorek

References

Abel, G., Barlow, D., Blanchard, E., & Guild, D. (1977). The components of rapists' sexual arousal. *Archives of General Psychiatry, 34*, 895-903.

Abel, G., Rouleau, J., & Cunningham-Rathner, J. (1986). Sexually aggressive behavior. In W. Curran, A. L. McGarry, & S. A. Shah (Eds.), *Modern legal psychiatry and psychology* (pp. 14-37). Philadelphia: F. A. Davis.

Ackely, E. G., & Fliegal, B. (1960). A social work approach to street-corner girls. *Social Work, 5*(4), 27-36.

Aichhorn, A. (1935). *Wayward youth.* New York: Viking.

Allen, C. M. (1990). Women as perpetrators of sexual abuse: Recognition barriers. In A. L. Horton, B. L. Johnson, L. M. Roundy, & D. Williams (Eds.), *The incest perpetrator* (pp. 108-125). Newbury Park, CA: Sage.

Allen, C. M. (1991). *Women and men who sexually abuse children: A comparative analysis.* Orwell, VT: Safer Society Press.

Allen, D. M. (1980). Young male prostitutes: A psychosocial study. *Archives of Sexual Behavior, 9*, 399-426.

Allport, G. W. (1954). *The nature of prejudice.* Reading, MA: Addison-Wesley.

American Humane Association. (1981). *National study on child neglect and abuse reporting.* Denver, CO: Author.

American Psychological Association. (1985). *Standards for educational and psychological testing.* Washington, DC: Author.

American Psychological Association. (1986). *Guidelines for computer-based tests and interpretations.* Washington, DC: Author.

American Psychiatric Association. (1994). *Diagnostic and statistical manual of mental disorders* (4th ed.). Washington, DC: American Psychiatric Association.

American Psychological Association. (1992). Ethical principles of psychologists and code of conduct. *American Psychologist, 42*, 1597-1611.

Amos, S. (1877). *Laws for the regulation of vice.* London: Stevens and Richardson.

Arendt, H. (1968). *Men in dark times.* Orlando, FL: Harcourt Brace and Company.

Aries, P. (1962). *Centuries of childhood: A social history of family life.* New York: Random House.

Atcheson, J. D., & Williams, D. C. (1954). A study of juvenile sex offenders. *American Journal of Psychiatry*, *111*, 366-370.

Awad, G. A., Saunders, E., & Levene, J. (1984). Sexual abuse: Current issues and strategies. *International Journal of Offender Therapy and Comparative Criminology*, *14*(1), 105-116.

Badgley, D. (1984). *The committee report on sexual offenses against children: Vols. 1 & 2*. Ottawa, Canada: Ministry of Supply and Services.

Baer, M. (1976). *Ode to Billy Joe* [Film]. Warner Bros.

Bailey, D. S. (Ed.). (1956). *Sexual offenders and social punishment*. London: Hazel Watson and Viney.

Baizerman, M. (1988, November). Do we need detached youthworkers to work with street kids? *Street Children Update: Briefing*.

Baizerman, M. (1989). *Street kids: Where should we focus*. Unpublished manuscript.

Baizerman, M., Thompson, J., & Stafford-White, K. (1979). Adolescent prostitution. *Children Today*, *2*(3), 20-24.

Baker, A. W., & Duncan, S. P. (1985). Child sexual abuse: A study of prevalence in Great Britain. *Child Abuse & Neglect*, *9*, 457-467.

Banfield, E. (1973). *The heavenly city revisited*. Boston: Little, Brown.

Barbaree, H. E., Marshall, W. L., & Hudson, S. M. (Eds.). (1993). *The juvenile sex offender*. New York: Guilford.

Barnard, G. W., Fuller, A. K., Robins, L., & Shaw, T. (1989). *The child molester: An integrated approach to evaluation and treatment*. New York: Brunner/Mazel.

Bateson, G. (1972). *Steps to an ecology of mind*. Toronto, Canada: Chandler Publishing Company.

Beck, A. T. (1976). *Cognitive therapy and the emotional disorders*. New York: Internation Universities Press.

Becker, J. V., & Kaplan, M. S. (1988). The assessment of adolescent sexual offenders. In R. J. Prinz (Ed.), *Advances in behavioral assessment of children and families: Vol. 4* (pp. 94-118). Newbury Park, CA: Sage.

Becker, J. V., Kaplan, M. S., Cunningham-Rathner, J., & Kavoussi, R. (1986). Characteristics of adolescent incest sexual perpetrators: Preliminary findings. *Journal of Family Violence*, *1*, 85-97.

Becker, J. V., Kaplan, M. S., & Temke, C. E. (1992). The relationship of abuse history, denial and erectile response of adolescent perpetrators. *Behavior Therapy*, *23*, 87-97.

Benard, B. (1991). *Fostering resiliency in kids: Protective factors in the family, school, and community*. Washington, DC: Northwest Regional Educational Laboratory and the U.S. Department of Education.

Bender, L., & Blau, A. (1937). The reaction of children to sexual relations with adults. *American Journal of Orthopsychiatry*, *7*, 500-518.

Benjamin, H., & Masters, R. E. L. (1964). *Prostitution and morality*. New York: Julian Press.

Bera, W. (1980). *Self-defense/assertiveness training in the treatment of sexual assault trauma*. Unpublished manuscript.

Bera, W. (1985). *A preliminary investigation of a typology of adolescent sex offenders and their family systems*. Unpublished master's thesis, University of Minnesota.

Bera, W. (1990). The systemic-attributional model: Victim-sensitive offender therapy. In J. M. Yokley (Ed.), *The use of victim-offender communication in the treatment of sexual abuse: Three intervention models* (pp. 45-76). Orwell, VT: Safer Society Press.

Berger, L. (1974). *From instinct to identity: The development of personality.* Englewood Cliffs: Prentice Hall.

Berman, M. (1982). *All that is solid melts into air: The experience of modernity.* New York: Simon & Schuster.

Bernstein, S. (1964). *Youth on the streets: Work with alienated youth groups.* New York: Association Press.

Bloch, H., & Niederhoffer, A. (1958). *The gang.* New York: Philosophical Library.

Block, J. H. (1983). Differential premises arising from differential socialization of the sexes: Some conjectures. *Child Development, 54,* 1335-1354.

Bolton, F. G., Jr., Morris, L. A., & MacEachron, A. E. (1989). *Males at risk: The other side of child sexual abuse.* Newbury Park, CA: Sage.

Boorman, J. (Director). (1972). *Deliverance* [Film]. Warner Bros.

Boyer, D. (1986). *Street exit project* (Final Report to U.S. Department of Health and Human Services, Grant No. 90-CY-0360). Washington, DC: Office of Human Development Services.

Boyer, D. (1989). Male prostitution and homosexual identity. *Journal of Homosexuality, 17,* 151-184.

Boyer, D., & James, J. (1983). Prostitutes as victims: Sex and the social order. In D. E. J. MacNamara & A. Karman (Eds.), *Deviants: Victims or victmizers* (pp. 109-146). Beverly Hills, CA: Sage.

Bradford, J. M. (1993). The pharmacological treatment of the adolescent sex offender. In H. E. Barbaree, V. L. Marshall, & S. M. Hudson (Eds.), *The juvenile sex offender* (pp. 278-288). New York: Guilford.

Brannon, R. A., Larson, A. W., & Doggett, K. V. (1989). Sexual victimization among juvenile sex offenders. *Violence and Victims, 5*(3), 213-224.

Bray, A. (1982). *Homosexuality in renaissance England.* London: Gay Mens Press.

Bremmer, J. F. (1992). Serious juvenile sex offenders: Treatment and long-term follow-up. *Psychiatric Annals, 22*(6), 113-130.

Briere, J. (1984, April). *The effects of childhood sexual abuse on later psychological functioning: Defining a post-sexual abuse syndrome.* Paper presented at the Third National Conference on Sexual Victimization of Children, Children's Hospital National Medical Center, Washington, DC.

Briere, J. (1990). Accuracy of adults' reports of abuse in childhood: Dr. Briere replies [invited letter]. *American Journal of Psychiatry, 147,* 1389-1390.

Briere, J. (1992a). *Child abuse trauma: Theory and treatment of the lasting effects.* Newbury Park, CA: Sage.

Briere, J. (1992b). Methodological issues in the study of sexual abuse effects. *Journal of Consulting & Clinical Psychology, 60,* 196-203.

Bronfenbrenner, U. (1974). *The ecology of human development.* Cambridge: Harvard University Press.

Brown, M. E., Hull, L. A., & Panesis, S. K. (1984). *Women who rape.* Boston: Massachusetts Trial Court.

Browne, A., & Finkelhor, D. (1986). The impact of child sexual abuse: Review of the research. *Psychological Bulletin, 99,* 66-77.

Burg, B. R. (1984). *Sodomy and the pirate tradition: English sea rovers in the seventeenth century Caribbean.* New York: New York University Press.

Burgess, A. W. (1984). *Child pornography and sex rings*. Lexington, MA: Lexington Books.

Burgess, A. W., & Holmstrom, L. L. (1975). Sexual trauma of children and adolescents: Sex, pressure and secrecy. *Nursing Clinics of North America, 10*, 551-563.

Butcher, J. N., Dahlstrom, W. G., Graham, J. R., Tellegen, A., & Kaemmer, B. (1989). *Minnesota Multiphasic Personality Inventory-2 (MMPI-2)*. Minneapolis: University of Minnesota Press.

Butcher, J. N., Williams, C. L., Graham, J. R., Archer, R. P., Tellegen, A., Ben-Porath, U. S., & Kaemmer, B. (1992). *Minnesota Multiphasic Personality Inventory-Adolescent (MMPI-A)*. Minneapolis: University of Minnesota Press.

Butts, W. M. (1947). Boy prostitutes of the metropolis. *Journal of Clinical Psychopathology, 8*, 673-681.

Calvert, K. (1991). *Children in the house*. Boston: Northeastern University Press.

Campbell, A. (1984). *The girls in the gang*. New York: Basil Blackwell.

Caplan, N. S., Deshaies, D. J., Suttles, G. D., & Mattick, H. W. (1964). Factors affecting the process and outcome of street club work. *Sociology and Social Research, 48*, 207-219.

Carnegie Corporation. (1992). *A matter of time: Risk and opportunity in the nonschool hours*. Woodlawn, MD: Author.

Caukins, S. E., & Coombs, N. R. (1976). The psychodynamics of male prostitution. *American Journal of Psychotherapy, 30*, 441-451.

Children's Defense Fund. (1990). *Children 1990: A report card, a briefing book, and action primer*. Washington, DC: Author.

Cloward, R. A., & Ohlin, L. E. (1960). *Delinquency and opportunity*. Glencoe, IL: The Free Press of Glencoe.

Conte, J., Berliner, L., & Schuerman, J. (1986). *The impact of sexual abuse on children* (Final Report No. MH37133). Rockville, MD: National Institute of Mental Health.

Conte, J., & Schuerman, J. (1987). The effects of sexual abuse of children: A multidimensional view. *Journal of Interpersonal Violence, 2*, 380-390.

Coombs, N. R. (1974). Male prostitution: A psychosocial view of behavior. *American Journal of Orthopsychiatry, 44*, 782-789.

Craft, M. (1966). Boy prostitutes and their fate. *British Journal of Psychiatry, 112*, 1111-1114.

Dahlstrom, W. G. (1993). Tests: Small samples, large consequences. *American Psychologist, 48*, 393-399.

D'Augelli, A. R., & Patterson, C. J. (Eds.). (1994). *Lesbian, gay and bisexual identities across the lifespan*. New York: Oxford University Press.

Davis, G. E., & Leitenberg, H. (1987). Adolescent sex offenders. *Psychological Bulletin, 101*(3), 417-427.

DeCecco, J. P. (1981). Definition and meaning of sexual orientation. *Journal of Homosexuality, 6*(4), 51-67.

DeFrances, V. (1969). *Protecting the child victim of sex crimes committed by adults*. Denver, CO: American Human Association, Children's Division.

Deisher, R. W., Eisner, V., & Sulzbacher, S. (1969). The young male prostitute. *Pediatrics, 43*(6), 936-941.

Deisher, R. W., & Gandy, P. (1970). Young male prostitutes: The physician's role in social rehabilitation. *Journal of the American Medical Association, 212*(10), 1661-1666.

Deisher, R. W., Robinson, G., & Boyer, D. (1982). The adolescent female and male prostitute. *Pediatric Annals, 11*(10), 819-825.

Deisher, R. W., Wenet, G. A., & Boyer, D. (1982). Adolescent sexual offense behavior: The role of the physician. *Journal of Adolescent Health Care, 2*(4), 279-286.

deMause, L. (1982). *Foundations of psychohistory*. New York: Creative Roots.

Dimmock, P. (1990, August). *Myths about male victims* [handout]. Minneapolis, MN: The Treatment of Male Sexual Abuse Victims Workshop.

Doherty, W. J., & Baird, M. A. (1986). Developmental levels in family-centered medical care. *Family Medicine, 18*(3), 153-156.

Doherty, W. J., & Peskay, V. E. (1992). Family systems in the school in home-school collaboration: Building a fundamental educational resource. In S. L. Christenson & J. Connolley (Eds.), *New approaches in home-school collaboration* (pp. 37-46). Washington, DC: National Association of Schools of Psychology.

Dominelli, L. (1986). Father-daughter incest: Patriarchy's shameful secret. *Critical Social Policy, 6*, 8-22.

Doris, J. (Ed.). (1991). *The suggestibility of children's recollections: Implications for eye witness testimony*. Washington, DC: American Psychological Association.

Doshay, L. J. (1943). *The boy sex offender and his later career*. New York: Grune & Stratton.

Dumpson, J. D. (1949). An approach to antisocial street gangs. *Federal Probation, 13*(7), 22-29.

Ellis, A. (1962). *Reason and emotion in psychotherapy*. New York: Stuart.

Ellis, A., & Greiger, R. (Eds.). (1977). *Handbook of rational-emotive therapy*. New York: Springer.

Erikson, E. H. (1963). *Childhood and society*. New York: Norton.

Exner, J. (1986). *The Rorschach: A comprehensive system: Vol. 1* (2nd ed.). New York: John Wilcy.

Faller, K. C. (1990). *Understanding child sexual maltreatment*. Newbury Park, CA: Sage.

False Memory Syndrome Foundation. (undated). *Mission and purpose*. Mimeograph.

Fehrenbach, P., & Monastersky, C. (1988). Characteristics of female adolescent sex offenders. *American Journal of Orthopsychiatry, 58*, 148-151.

Fehrenbach, P. A., Smith, W., Monastersky, C., & Deisher, R. W. (1986). Adolescent sexual offenders: Offender and offense characteristics. *American Journal of Orthopsychiatry, 56*, 225-233.

Ferris, T. (1988). *Coming of age in the milky way*. New York: William Morris.

Finkelhor, D. (1979). *Sexually victimized children*. New York: Free Press.

Finkelhor, D. (Ed.). (1984). *Child sexual abuse—New theory and research*. New York: Free Press.

Finkelhor, D., & Associates. (1986). *A sourcebook on child sexual abuse*. Newbury Park, CA: Sage.

Finkelhor, D. (1990a). Response to Bauserman. *Journal of Homosexuality, 20*, 313-315.

Finkelhor, D. (1990b). Early and long-term effects of child sexual abuse: An update. *Professional Psychology: Research and Practice, 21*, 325-330.

Finkelhor, D., & Browne, A. (1986). Initial and long-term effects: A conceptual framework. In D. Finkelhor & Associates (Eds.), *A sourcebook on child sexual abuse* (pp. 180-198). Newbury Park, CA: Sage.

Finkelhor, D., & Russell, D. (1984). Women as perpetrators: Review of the evidence. In D. Finkelhor (Ed.), *Child sexual abuse: New theory and research* (pp. 171-187). New York: Free Press.

Fisher, B., Weisberg, K., & Marotta, T. (1982). *Report on adolescent male prostitution*. San Francisco, CA: Urban and Rural Systems Associates.

Foucault, M. (1980). *The history of sexuality*. New York: Vintage.

Foucault, M. (1986). *The use of pleasure*. New York: Vintage.

Foucault, M. (1988). *The care of the self*. New York: Vintage.

Freeman, B. A. (1956). *Techniques of a worker with a corner group of boys*. Unpublished master's thesis, Boston University School of Social Work.

Freeman-Longo, R. E. (1986). The impact of sexual victimization on males. *Child Abuse & Neglect, 10*, 411-414.

Freeman-Longo, R., & Knopp, F. (1992). State of the art sex offender treatment: Outcomes and issues. In *Recidivism in sex offender treatment: A packet*. Orwell, VT: Safer Society Press.

Freud, S. (1896/1946). The etiology of hysteria. In E. Jones (Ed.) & J. Riviere (Trans.), *Collected papers: Vol. 1* (pp. 183-219). New York: The International Psychoanalytical Press.

Freyd, P. (1992, May 1). *FMS foundational newsletter*. Philadelphia: FMS Foundation.

Friedrich, W. N., Beilke, R. L., & Urquiza, A. J. (1988). Behavioral problems in young sexually abused boys. *Journal of Interpersonal Violence, 3*, 21-28.

- Fritz, G. S., Stoll, I. L., & Wagner, N. A. (1981). A comparison of males and females who were sexually molested as children. *Journal of Sex and Marital Therapy, 7*, 54-59.

Gale, A. (Ed.). (1988). *The polygraph test: Lies, truth and science*. London: Sage.

Gandy, P., & Deisher, R. (1970). Young male prostitutes: The physician's role in social rehabilitation. *Journal of the American Medical Association, 212*, 1661-1666.

Garmezy, N. (1991). Resiliency and vulnerability to adverse developmental outcomes associated with poverty. *American Behavioral Scientist, 34*(4), 416-430.

Gebhard, P. H., Gagnon, J. H., Pomeroy, W. B., & Christenson, C. V. (1965). *Sex offenders: An analysis of types*. New York: Harper & Row.

Gelinas, D. J. (1988). Family therapy: Characteristic family constellations and basic therapeutic stance. In S. M. Sgroi (Ed.), *Vulnerable populations: Evaluation and treatment of sexually abused children and adult survivors: Vol. 1* (pp. 25-50). Lexington, MA: Lexington Books.

Gerassi, J. (1966). *The boys from Boise*. New York: Macmillan.

Gibbs, J., & Bennett, S. (1990). *Together we can: A framework for community prevention planning*. Seattle, WA: Comprehensive Health Education Foundation.

Gilbert, C. M. (1989). Sibling incest. *Journal of Child Psychiatric Nursing, 2*(2), 70-73.

Gilligan, C., Ward, J. V., & Taylor, J. M. (Eds.). (1988). *Mapping the moral domain*. Cambridge: Harvard University Press.

Gilmartin, Z. P. (1983). Attribution theory and rape victim responsibility. *Deviant Behavior, 4*(3-4), 357-374.

Ginsburg, K. N. (1967). "The meat rack": A study of the male homosexual prostitute. *American Journal of Psychotherapy, 21*, 170-185.

Goldman, R., & Goldman, J. (1982). *Children's sexual thinking: A comparative study of children aged 5 to 15 years in Australia, North America, Britain and Sweden*. Boston: Routledge & Kegan Paul.

Gomes-Schwartz, B., Horowitz, J., & Carderelli, A. (1990). *Child sexual abuse: The initial effects*. Newbury Park, CA: Sage.

Gonsiorek, J. (1982). Results of psychological testing on homosexual populations. In W. Paul, J. Weinrich, & J. Gonsiorek (Eds.), *Homosexuality: Social, psychological and biological issues* (pp. 71-80). Beverly Hills, CA: Sage.

Gonsiorek, J. (1988). Mental health issues of gay and lesbian adolescents. *Journal of Adolescent Health Care, 9*, 114-122.

Gonsiorek, J. (1989). Sexual exploitation by psychotherapists: Some observations on male victims and sexual orientation issues. In G. Schoener, J. Milgram, J. Gonsiorek, E. Luepker, & R. Conroe (Eds.), *Psychotherapists' sexual involvement with clients: Intervention and prevention* (pp. 113-119). Minneapolis: Walk-In Counseling Center.

Gonsiorek, J. (1991). The empirical basis for the demise of the illness model of homosexuality. In J. Gonsiorek & J. Weinrich (Eds.), *Homosexuality: Research implications for public policy* (pp. 115-136). Newbury Park, CA: Sage.

Gonsiorek, J., & Rudolph, J. (1991). Homosexual identity: Coming out and other developmental events. In J. Gonsiorek & J. Weinrich (Eds.), *Homosexuality: Research implications for public policy* (pp. 161-176). Newbury Park, CA: Sage.

Gonsiorek, J., & Weinrich, J. (1991). The definition and scope of sexual orientation. In J. Gonsiorek & J. Weinrich (Eds.), *Homosexuality: Research implications for public policy* (pp. 1-12). Newbury Park, CA: Sage.

Goodman, G., & Bottoms, B. (1993). *Child victim, child witness: Understanding and improving testimony*. New York: Guilford.

Goodman, M. E. (1970). *The culture of childhood*. New York: Teachers College Press.

Goodwin, J. (1982). *Sexual abuse: Incest victims and their families*. Boston: John Wright.

Gough, H. G. (1987). *California Personality Inventory (CPI)*. Palo Alto, CA: Consulting Psychologists Press.

Green, S. (1984). Victim-offender reconciliation program: A review of the concept. *Social Action and the Law, 10*(2), 43-52.

Greene, B. F. (1981). A primer on testing. *American Psychologist, 36*, 1001-1011.

Greer, J., & Stuart, I. (1983). *The sexual agressor: Current perspectives on treatment*. New York: Van Nostrand Reinhold.

Groth, A. N. (1979). Sexual trauma in the life histories of rapists and child molesters. *Victimology: An International Journal, 4*, 10-16.

Groth, A. N., & Birnbaum, H. (1978). Adult sexual orientation and attraction to underage persons. *Archives of Sexual Behavior, 7*(3), 175-183.

Groth, A. N., & Birnbaum, H. (1979). *Men who rape: The psychology of the offender*. New York: Plenum.

Groth, A. N., & Burgess, A. W. (1979). Sexual trauma in the life histories of rapists and child molesters. *Victimology: An International Journal, 4*, 10-16.

Groth, A. N., & Loredo, C. M. (1981). Juvenile sex offenders: Guidelines for assessment. *International Journal of Offender Comparative Criminology, 25*(1), 13-18

Gulotta, G., & deCataldo-Neuberger, L. (1983). A systematic and attributional approach to victimology. *Victimology: An International Journal, 8*, 5-16.

Gurman, A. S., & Kniskern, D. P. (Eds.). (1981). *Handbook of family therapy: Vol. 1*. New York: Brunner/Mazel.

Gurman, A. S., & Kniskern, D. P. (Eds.). (1991). *Handbook of family therapy: Vol. 2*. New York: Brunner/Mazel.

Haaven, J., Little, R., & Petre-Miller, D. (1990). *Treating intellectually disabled sex offenders: A model residential program.* Orwell, VT: Safer Society Press.

Hamilton, G. V. (1929). *A research in marriage.* New York: Albert & Charles Boni.

Hart, S. N. (1991). From property to person status: Historical perspective on children's rights. *American Psychologist, 46,* 53-59.

Hechler, D. (1988). *The battle and the backlash: The child sexual abuse war.* Lexington, MA: D. C. Heath.

Heider, F. (1958). *The psychology of interpersonal relations.* New York: Wiley.

Henggler, S.W. (1989). Sexual offending and violent behaviors. In S. W. Henngler (Ed.), *Delinquency in adolescence* (Vol. 18, pp. 72-83). Newbury Park, CA: Sage.

Herek, G. (1991). Stigma, prejudice and violence against lesbians and gay men. In J. Gonsiorek & J. Weinrich (Eds.), *Homosexuality: Research implications for public policy* (pp. 60-80). Newbury Park, CA: Sage Publications.

Herman, J. (1992). *Trauma and recovery.* New York: Basic Books.

Hoffman, M. (1972). The male prostitute. *Sexual Behavior, 2,* 16-21.

Homma-True, R., Greene, B., Lopez, S. R., & Trimble, J. E. (1993). Ethnocultural diversity in clinical psychology. *The Clinical Psychologist, 46,* 50-63.

Hubble, E. (1985). *The realm of the nebulae.* New Haven, CT: Yale University Press.

Hunter, M. (1990). *Abused boys: The neglected victims of sexual abuse.* Lexington, MA: Lexington Books.

James, T. E. (1951). *Prostitution and the law.* London: William Heineman.

Jersild, J. (1956). *Boy prostitution.* Copenhagen: G. E. C. Gad.

Johnson, R. L., & Shrier, D. (1985). Sexual victimization of boys: Experience at an adolescent medicine clinic. *Journal of Adolescent Health Care, 6,* 372-376.

Justice, B., & Justice, R. (1979). *The broken taboo.* New York: Human Sciences Press.

Juvenile Delinquency Evaluation Project. (1960). *Dealing with the conflict gang in New York City: Interim report no. XIV.* New York: Juvenile Delinquency Evaluation Project of New York City.

Kahn, T. J. (1990). *Pathways: A guided workbook for youth beginning treatment.* Orwell, VT: Safer Society Press.

Kaplan, M. S., Becker, J. B., & Martinez, D. M. (1990). A comparison of mothers with adolescent incest versus non-incest perpetrators. *Journal of Family Violence, 5*(3), 209-215.

Keller, E. (1980). *Sexual assault: A statewide problem* (LEAA Grant No. 4317013675). St. Paul: Minnesota Department of Corrections.

Kelley, H., & Thibaut, J. (1969). Group problem solving. In G. Lindzey & E. Aronson (Eds.), *Handbook of social psychology: Vol. 4* (2nd ed., pp. 1-101). Reading, MA: Addison-Wesley.

Kelley, S. J. (1988, April). *Responses of children to sexual abuse and satanic ritualistic abuse in daycare centers.* Paper presented at the National Symposium on Child Victimization, Anaheim, CA.

Kempe, R., & Kempe, C. H. (1984). *The common secret: Sexual abuse of children and adolescents.* New York: Freeman.

Kinsey, A. C., Pomeroy, W. B., & Martin, C. E. (1948). *Sexual behavior in the human male.* Philadelphia: W. B. Saunders.

Knight, R. A., & Prentky, R. A. (1990). Classifying sexual offenders: The developing and corroboration of taxonomic models. In W. L. Marshall, D. R. Laws, & H. E. Barbaree (Eds.), *The handbook of sexual assault: Issues, theories and treatment of the offender* (pp. 27-52). New York: Plenum.

Knight, R. A., & Prentky, R. A. (1993). Exploring characteristics for classifying juvenile sex offenders. In H. E. Barbaree, W. L. Marshall, & S. M. Hudson (Eds.), *The juvenile sex offender* (pp. 289-320). New York: Guilford.

Knopp, F. H. (1982). *Remedial intervention in adolescent sex offenses: Nine program descriptions*. Orwell, VT: Safer Society Press.

Knopp, F. H. (1984). *Retraining adult sex offenders: Methods and models*. Orwell, VT: Safer Society Press.

Knopp, F. II. (1985). *The youthful sex offender: The rationales and goals of early intervention*. Orwell, VT: Safer Society Press.

Knopp, F. H., Boward, B., Brach, M. J., Christianson, S., Largen, M. A., Lewin, J., Lugo, J., Morris, M., & Newton, W. (1976). *Instead of prisons*. Orwell, VT: Safer Society Press.

Knopp, F. H., Freeman-Longo, R., & Stevenson, W. F. (1992). *Nationwide survey of juvenile and adult sex offender treatment programs: 1990*. Orwell, VT: Safer Society Press.

Knopp, F. H., & Lackey, L. B. (1987). *Female sex abusers: A summary of data from 44 treatment providers*. Orwell, VT: Safer Society Press.

Kobrin, S. (1959). The Chicago Area Project: A 25 year assessment. *Annals of American Academy of Political and Social Science, 322*, 19-29.

Kohut, H. (1971). *The analysis of the self*. New York: International Universities Press.

Kohut, H. (1977). *The restoration of the self*. New York: International Universities Press.

Kohut, H. (1984). *How does analysis cure?* Chicago: University of Chicago Press.

Konker, C. (1992). Rethinking child sexual abuse: An anthropological perspective. *American Journal of Orthopsychiatry, 62*, 147-153.

Konopka, G. (1972). *Social group work: A helping process*. Englewood Cliffs, NJ: Prentice Hall.

Konopka, G. (1973). Requirements for a healthy development of adolescent youth. *Adolescence, 8*, 1-26.

Kurosawa, A. (Director). (1951). *Rashomon* [Film]. RKO Pictures.

Kurth-Schai, R. (1988). The roles of youth in society: A reconceptualization. *The Educational Forum, 52*(2), 113-131.

Kutchinsky, B. (1991). Pornography and rape: Theory and practice? *International Journal of Law and Psychiatry, 14*, 47-64.

Kvaraceus, W. C., and Miller, W. B. (1959). *Delinquent behavior, culture and the individual*. Washington, DC: National Education Association.

Landis, J. T. (1956). Experiences of 500 children with adult sexual deviation. *Psychiatric Quarterly Supplement, 30*, 91-109.

Lane, S. (1991). The sexual abuse cycle. In G. D. Ryan & S. L. Lane (Eds.), *Juvenile sexual offending: Causes, consequences, and correction* (pp. 103-142). Lexington, MA: Lexington Books.

Lane, S., & Zamora, P. (1984). A method for treating the adolescent sex offender. In R. A. Mathias, P. Demuro, & R. Allinson (Eds.), *Sourcebook for treatment of the violent juvenile offender* (pp. 347-354). Washington, DC: National Council on Crime and Delinquency.

Laws, D. (1989). *Relapse prevention with sex offenders*. New York: Guilford.

Leaman, K. M. (1980). Sexual abuse: The reactions of child and family. In *Sexual abuse of children: Selected readings* (pp. 21-24). Washington, DC: U.S. Department of Health and Human Services.

Lerman, P. (1958). Group work with youth in conflict. *Social Work, 3*(4), 71-77.

Lerner, M. (1957). *America as a civilization*. New York: Simon & Schuster.

Lerner, M. (1980). *The belief in a just world: A fundamental delusion*. New York: Plenum.

Lew, M. (1988). *Victims no longer: Men recovering from incest and other childhood sexual abuse*. New York: Nevraumont.

Lewis, A. N., Shankok, S. S., & Pincus, J. H. (1979). Juvenile male sexual assaulters. *American Journal of Psychiatry, 136*, 1194-1196.

Leiker, J. H. (1986). *A follow-up study on convicted juvenile sex offenders as adults*. Unpublished master's thesis, Utah State University, Logan.

Lightfoot, L. O., & Barbaree, H. E. (1993). The relationship between substance use and abuse and sexual offending in adolescents. In H. E. Barbaree, W. L. Marshall, & S. M. Hudson (Eds.), *The juvenile sex offender* (pp. 203-224). New York: Guilford.

Lloyd, R. (1976). *For money or love: Boy prostitution in America*. New York: Vanguard Press.

Loftus, E. (1993). The reality of repressed memories. *American Psychologist, 48*, 518-537.

Loftus, E., & Foley, M. (1984). Differentiating fact from fantasy: The reliability of children's memory. *Journal of Social Issues, 40*, 33-50.

Longo, R. E. (1982). Sexual learning and experience among adolescent sex offenders. *International Journal of Offender Therapy and Comparative Criminology, 26*(3), 235-241.

Lykken, D. (1981). *A tremor in the blood: Uses and abuses of the lie detector*. New York: McGraw-Hill.

Mackinnon, K. (1987). A feminist/political approach: Pleasure under patriarchy. In J. H. Geer & W. O'Donohue (Eds.), *Theories of human sexuality* (pp. 65-90). New York: Plenum.

Maclay, D. T. (1960). Boys who commit sexual misdemeanors. *British Medical Journal, 5167*, 186-190.

MacNamara, D. E. J. (1965). Male prostitution in an American city: A pathological or socio-economic phenomenon? *American Journal of Orthopsychiatry, 35*, 204.

Malyon, A. K. (1981). The homosexual adolescent: Developmental issues and social bias. *Child Welfare, 60*, 321-330.

Markey, O. B. (1950). A study of aggressive sex misbehavior in adolescents brought to court. *American Journal of Orthopsychology, 20*, 719-731.

Marshall, W. L., Hudson, S. M., & Hodkinson, S. (1993). The importance of attachment bonds in the development of juvenile sex offending. In H. E. Barbaree, W. L. Marshall, & S. M. Hudson (Eds.), *The juvenile sex offender* (pp. 164-181). New York: Guilford.

Martin, A. D. (1982). Learning to hide: The socialization of the gay adolescent. *Adolescent Psychiatry, 10*, 52-65.

Martin, E. P., & Martin, M. M. (1978). *The black extended family*. Chicago: University of Chicago Press.

Marvasti, J. (1986). Incestuous mothers. *American Journal of Forensic Psychiatry, 7*(4), 63-69.

Masson, J. (1984). *The assault on truth: Freud's suppression of the seduction theory*. New York: Farrar, Strauss & Giroux.

Matarazzo, J. D. (1986). Computerized clinical psychological testing interpretations: Unvalidated plus all mean and no sigma. *American Psychologist, 41*, 14-24.

Mathews, F. (1989). *Familiar strangers: A study of adolescent prostitution*. Toronto, Canada: Central Toronto Youth Services.

Mathews, R. (1987). *Preliminary typology of female sexual offenders*. Unpublished manuscript.

Mathews, R., Matthews, J. K., & Speltz, K. (1989). *Female sex offenders: An exploratory study*. Orwell, VT: Safer Society Press.

McCarthy, D. (1981). *Women who rape*. Unpublished manuscript.

McCarty, L. (1986). Mother-child incest: Characteristics of the offender. *Child Welfare, 65*(5), 447-458.

Mendel, G. (1971). *Pour decoloniser l'enfant: Sociopsychanalyse de l'autorité*. Paris: Payot.

Meyers, J. E. B., Bays, J., Becker, J., Berliner, L., Corwin, D. L., & Saywitz, K. J. (1989). Expert testimony in child sexual abuse litigation. *Nebraska Law Review, 68*, 1-145.

Millon, T. (1987). *Millon Clinical Multiaxial Inventory-II (MCMI-II)* (2nd ed.). Minneapolis: National Computer Systems.

Minnesota Department of Corrections. (1993). *State prison profile*. St. Paul: State of Minnesota Publications.

Minnesota Department of Human Services. (1986). *SHARP (sexual health and responsibility program): An adolescent perpetrator prevention program*. St. Paul: Minnesota Department of Human Services Publications.

Minuchin, S., & Fishman, H. C. (1981). *Family therapy techniques*. Cambridge: Harvard University Press.

More young men killed in U.S. than in 21 other nations. (1990, June 27). *Minneapolis Star Tribune*, p. 7.

Muuss, R. (1962). *Theories of adolescence* (2nd ed.). New York: Random House.

Nasjleti, M. (1980). Suffering in silence: The male incest victim. *Child Welfare, 59*, 269-275.

National Adolescent Perpetrator Network. (1993). Revised report from the National Task Force on Juvenile Sexual Offending [Special issue]. *Juvenile and Family Court Journal, 44*(4).

Nestingen, S. L., & Lewis, L. R. (1990). *Growing beyond abuse: A workbook for survivors of sexual exploitation or childhood sexual abuse*. Minneapolis: Omni Recovery.

New York City Youth Board. (1952). *Reaching the unreached: Fundamental aspects of the program of the New York City Youth Board*. New York: Author.

New York City Youth Board. (1962). *The summer of 1962: A report on the New York City's program of vigilance and services to youth*. New York: Author.

New York City Youth Board. (1965). *The changing role of the street worker in the council of social work athletic clubs*. New York: Author.

O'Brien, M. (1984, May). *Adolescent sexual offenders: An outpatient program's perspective on research directions*. Paper presented at the 13th Annual Child Abuse and Neglect Symposium, Keystone, CO.

O'Brien, M. (1986). *Model of adolescent sex offenders*. Workshop handout. St. Paul: PHASE.

O'Brien, M. (1989). *Characteristics of adolescent male sibling incest offenders: Preliminary findings*. Orwell, VT: Safer Society Press.

O'Brien, M., & Bera, W. (1986, Fall). Adolescent sex offenders: A descriptive typology. *Preventing Sexual Abuse*, *1*(3), 1-4. (Available from ETR Publications, Santa Cruz, CA)

O'Carroll, T. (1982). *Paedophilia: The radical case*. Boston: Alyson.

O'Donohue, W., & Geer, J. H. (Eds.). (1992a). *The sexual abuse of children: Theory and research*. Hillsdale, NJ: Lawrence Erlbaum.

O'Donohue, W., & Geer, J. H. (Eds.). (1992b). *The sexual abuse of children: Clinical issues*. Hillsdale, NJ: Lawrence Erlbaum.

Olson, D. H., Sprenkle, D. H., & Russell, C. S. (1979). Circumplex model of marital and family systems I: Cohension and adaptability dimensions. *Family Process*, *18*, 3-28.

Oregon Department of Family Services. (1986). Guidelines for treatment of juvenile sex offenders (Oregon matrix). In *The Oregon report on juvenile sexual offenders*. Salem: Oregon Department of Family Services.

Perry, N., & Wrightsman, L. (1991). *The child witness*. Newbury Park, CA: Sage.

Peters, J. J. (1976). Children who are victims of sexual assault and the psychology of offenders. *American Journal of Psychotherapy*, *30*, 398-421.

Peters, S. D., Wyatt, G. E., & Finkelhor, D. (1986). Prevalence. In D. Finkelhor & Associates (Ed.), *A sourcebook on child sexual abuse* (pp. 15-59). Newbury Park, CA: Sage.

Petrovich, M., & Templer, D. L. (1984). Heterosexual molestation of children who later become rapists. *Psychological Reports*, *54*, 810.

Phillips, E. L., & Wiener, D. W. (1966). *Short-term psychotherapy and structured behavior change*. New York: McGraw-Hill.

Pierce, R., & Pierce, L. H. (1985). The sexually abused child: A comparison of male and female victims. *Child Abuse & Neglect*, *9*, 191-199.

Pithers, W., Martin, G., & Cumming, G. (1989). Vermont treatment program for sexual aggressors. In D. Laws (Ed.), *Relapse prevention with sex offenders* (pp. 292-310). New York: Guilford.

Plummer, K. (1981). Pedophilia: Constructing a psychological baseline. In M. Cook & K. Howells (Eds.), *Adult sexual interest in children* (pp. 67-79). New York: Academic Press.

Pollock, N. L., & Hashmall, J. M. (1991). The excuses of child molesters. *Behavioral Sciences and the Law*, *9*, 53-59.

Pope, K. S., Butcher, J. W., & Seelen, J. (1993). *The MMPI, MMPI-2, and MMPI-A in court*. Washington, DC: American Psychological Association.

Prentky, R. A., & Cerce, D. D. (1990). Thoughts on the developmental roots of sexual aggression. *The Adviser*, *3*(1), 4.

Radbill, S. X. (1974). A history of child abuse and infanticide. In S. K. Steinmetz & M. Straus (Eds.), *Violence in the family* (pp. 173-179). New York: Dodd, Mead.

Rasmussen, L. A., Burton, J. E., & Christopherson, B. (1990, October). *Interrupting precursors to perpetration in males ages four to twelve*. Paper presented at the annual conference of the National Adolescent Perpetrator Network, Albany, NY.

Redl, F. (1945). The psychology of gang formation and the treatment of delinquents. In *The psychoanalytic study of the child: Vol. I* (pp. 367-377). New York: Internation Universities Press.

Reiss, A. J. (1961). The social integration of queers and peers. *Social Problems*, *9*, 102-120.

Resick, P. A. (1993). The psychological impact of rape. *Journal of Interpersonal Violence, 8*(2), 223-255.

Rogers, C. M., & Terry, T. (1984). Clinical intervention with boy victims of sexual abuse. In I. R. Stuart & J. G. Greer (Eds.), *Victims of sexual aggression: Men, women and children* (pp. 91-103). New York: Van Nostrand Reinhold.

Rosenberg, J. (1990). *Fuel on the fire: An inquiry in "pornography" and sexual aggression in a free society.* Orwell, VT: Safer Society Press.

Rush, B. (1974). The sexual abuse of children: A feminist point of view. In N. Connell & C. Wilson (Eds.), *Rape: The first sourcebook for women* (pp. 64-75). New York: New American Library.

Rush, B. (1980). *The best-kept secret: The sexual victimization of children.* New York: McGraw-Hill.

Ryan, G. (1986). Annotated bibliography: Adolescent perpetrators of sexual molestation of children. *Child Abuse & Neglect, 10,* 125-131.

Ryan, G., & Lane, S. L. (1991). *Juvenile sexual offending: Causes, consequences, and correction.* Lexington, MA: Lexington Books.

Ryan, G., Lane, S., Davis, J., & Isaac, C. (1987). Juvenile sex offenders: Development and correction. *Child Abuse & Neglect, 11,* 385-395.

Sandfort, T. (1982). *The sexual aspect of pedophile relations.* Amsterdam: Pan/Spartacus.

Sandfort, T. (1983). Pedophile relationships in the Netherlands: Alternative lifestyles for children? *Alternative Lifestyles, 5,* 164-183.

Sandfort T. (1984). Sex in pedophiliac relationships: An empirical investigation among a non-representative group of boys. *Journal of Sex Research, 20,* 123-142.

Sandfort, T., Brongersma, E., & van Naerssen, A. (Eds.) (1990). *Male intergenerational intimacy: Historical, socio-psychological and legal perspectives.* New York: Haworth.

Sanger, W. W. (1937). *The history of prostitution.* London: Eugenics.

Schoener, G., & Milgrom, J. (1989). Processing sessions. In G. Schoener, J. Milgrom, J. Gonsiorek, E. Luepker, & R. Conroe (Eds.), *Psychotherapists' sexual involvement with clients: Intervention and prevention* (pp. 345-358). Minneapolis, MN: Walk-In Counseling Center.

Schoener, G., Milgrom, J., Gonsiorek, J., Luepker, E., & Conroe, R. (Eds.). (1989). *Psychotherapists' sexual involvement with clients: Intervention and prevention.* Minneapolis, MN: Walk-In Counseling Center.

Schouten, P., & Simon, W. (1992). Validity of phallometric measures with sex offenders: Comments on the Quinsey, Laws and Hall debate. *Journal of Consulting and Clinical Psychology, 60*(5), 812-814.

Scott, G. R. (1968). *Ladies of vice* (rev. ed.). London: Tallis Press.

Scully, D., & Marolla, J. (1984). Convicted rapists' vocabulary of motive: Excuses and justifications. *Social Problems, 31*(5), 530-544.

Search Institute. (1992). *Training needs assessment for the strengthening our capacity to care project: Final report.* Minneapolis, MN: Author.

Search Institute. (1993). *The troubled journey: A portrait of 6th-12th grade youth.* Minneapolis: Author.

Sgroi, S. M. (1991). *Handbook of clinical intervention in child abuse.* Lexington, MA: Lexington Books.

Sgroi, S. M. (1975). Sexual molestation of children: The last frontier in child abuse. *Children Today, 4*(3), 19-44.

Shively, M. G., & DeCecco, J. P. (1977). Components of sexual identity. *Journal of Homosexuality*, *3*, 41-48.

Shoor, M., Speed, M. H., Bartelt, C. (1966). Syndrome of the adolescent child molester. *American Journal of Psychiatry*, *122*, 783-789.

Shotland, R. L., & Goodstein, L. (1983). Just because she doesn't want to doesn't mean it's rape: An experimentally based causal model of the perception of rape in a dating situation. *Social Psychology Quarterly*, *45*(3), 220-232.

Showers, J., Farber, E. D., Joseph, J. A., Oshins, L., & Johnson, C. F. (1983). The sexual victimization of boys: A three year survey. *Health Values: Achieving High Level Wellness*, *7*, 15-18.

Smith, T. A., & Wolf, S. (1988). A treatment model for sexual aggression. *Journal of Social Work and Human Sexuality*, *7*(1), 149-164.

Smith, W. R. (1984). *Patterns of re-offending among juvenile sex offenders*. Unpublished manuscript.

Smith, W. R. (1988). Delinquency and abuse among juvenile sexual offenders. *Journal of Interpersonal Violence*, *3*(4), 400-413.

Smith, W. R., & Monastersky, C. (1986). Assessing juvenile sex offenders' risk for reoffending. *Criminal Justice and Behavior*, *13*(2), 115-140.

Sohl, R., & Carr, A. (Eds.). (1970). *The gospel according to Zen*. New York: New American Library.

Spiegel, D. (1989). Hypnosis in the treatment of victims of sexual abuse. *The Psychiatric Clinics of North America*, *12*(2), 295-305.

Staats, G. R. (1978). Stereotype content and social distance: Changing views of homosexuality. *Journal of Homosexuality*, *4*(1), 15-27.

Starr, A. (1993). *What works with youth? A working draft of the research of the Community Fellows Program at Massachusetts Institute of Technology*. Unpublished manuscript.

Steele, B. (1986). Notes on the lasting effects of early child abuse throughout the lifecycle. *Child Abuse & Neglect*, *10*, 283-291.

Steen, C., & Monnette, B. (1989). *Treating adolescent sex offenders in the community*. Springfield, IL: Charles C Thomas.

Stermac, L., & Sheridan, P. (1993). The developmentally disabled adolescent sex offender. In H. E. Barbaree, W. L. Marshall, & S. M. Hudson (Eds.), *The juvenile sex offender* (pp. 235-242). New York: Guilford.

Streisand, B. (Director). (1991). *The prince of tides* [Film]. Columbia Pictures.

Strong, B., & DeVault, C. (1992). *The marriage and family experience*. St. Paul, MN: West.

Sutherland, E. H., & Cressey, D. R. (1978). *Criminology*. New York: J. B. Lippincott.

Swartz, B. (1989). *A practitioner's guide to the treatment of the incarcerated male sex offender*. Washington, DC: National Institute of Corrections.

Tharinger, D. (1990). Impact of child sexual abuse on developing sexuality. *Professional Psychology: Research and Practice*, *21*, 331-337.

The Forgotten Half. (1988). *Pathways to success for America's youth and young families*. Washington, DC: The William T. Grant Commission on Work Family and Citizenship.

Thompson, J. (1990). *The price you pay to wear tennis shoes to work: A phemomenological study of detached youthwork*. Unpublished doctoral dissertation, Union Institute, Cincinnati.

Thrasher, F. M. (1927). *The gang: A study of 1,313 gangs in Chicago*. Chicago: The University of Chicago Press.

Timnick, L. (1985, August 25). 22% in survey were child abuse victims. *Los Angeles Times*, p. 1.

Tobias, J. L., & Gordon, R. (1977). *Operation lure*. Mimeograph.

Toffler, A. (Ed.). (1974). The psychology of the future. In A. Toffler (Ed.), *Learning for tomorrow* (p. 15). New York: Vintage.

Trepper, T. S., & Barrett, M. J. (1986). *Treating incest: A multimodal systems perspectives*. New York: Haworth.

Trepper, T. S., & Sprenkle, D. H. (1988). The clinical use of the circumplex model in the assessment and treatment of families. *Journal of Psychotherapy and the Family*, 4(1/2), 92-111.

Tsang, D. (Ed.). (1981). *The age taboo: Gay male sexuality, power and consent*. Boston: Alyson.

Tufts New England Medical Center, Division of Child Psychiatry. (1984). *Sexually exploited children: Service and research project* (Final report for the Office of Juvenile Justice and Delinquency Prevention). Washington, DC: U.S. Department of Justice.

Umbreit, M. (1985). *Crime and reconciliation: Creative options for victims and offenders*. Nashville, TN: Abington.

Umbreit, M., & Coates, T. (1992). The impact of mediating victim offender conflict: An analysis of programs in three states. *Juvenile & Family Court Journal*, 43, 1-8.

Urban and Rural Systems Associates. (1982). *Adolescent male prostitutes: A study of sexual exploitation, etiological factors, and runaway behavior* (Final report to the Administration for Children, Youth and Families, Grant No. HEW 105-79-120). Washington, DC: Department of Health and Human Services.

Urquiza, A. J., & Crowley, C. (1986, April). *Sex differences in the survivors of childhood sexual abuse*. Paper presented at the Fourth Conference on Sexual Victimization of Children, New Orleans, LA.

U.S. Department of Justice. (1993). *Crime in the United States, 1992*. Washington, DC: Author.

van der Kolk, B. A., & Kadish, W. (1987). Amnesia, dissociation and the return of the repressed. In B. A. van der Kolk (Ed.), *Psychological trauma*. Washington, DC: American Psychiatric Press.

Vander Mey, B. (1988). The sexual victimization of male children: A review of previous research. *Child Abuse & Neglect*, 12, 61-72.

Vander Mey, B. (1992a). Theories of incest. In W. O'Donohue & J. H. Geer (Eds.), *The sexual abuse of children: Theory and research*. Hillsdale, NJ: Lawrence Erlbaum.

Vander Mey, B. (1992b). Incest. In E. F. Borgatta & M. L. Borgatta (Eds.), *The encyclopedia of sexuality: Vol. 2*. New York: Macmillan.

Veyne, P. (Ed.). (1987). The Roman empire. In P. Veyne (Ed.), *A history of private life: From pagan Rome to Byzantium* (pp. 5-233). Cambridge: Harvard University Press.

Wakefield, H., & Underwager, R. (Undated). *Magic, mischief and memories: Remembering repressed abuse*. Northfield, MN: Institute for Psychological Therapies.

Walker, L. (1989). *Terrifying love: Why battered women kill and how society responds*. New York: HarperCollins.

Waterman, C. K., & Foss-Goodman, D. (1984). Child-molesting: Variables relating to attribution of fault to victims, offenders, and non-participating parents. *Journal of Sex Research, 20*(4), 329-349.

Weeks, J. (1981). Inverts, perverts, and mary-annes: Male prostitution and the regulation of homosexuality in England in the nineteenth and early twentieth century. *Journal of Homosexuality, 6*(1/2), 113-133.

Weisberg, D. E. (1985). *Children of the night: Adolescent prostitution in America.* Lexington, MA: Lexington Books.

Welfare Association of Cleveland. (1959). *A community-wide approach; The United Youth Program, 1954-59.* Cleveland: Cleveland Group Work Council.

Werner, E., & Smith, R. (1982). *Vulnerable but invincible: A longitudinal study of resilient children and youth.* New York: Adams, Bannister, and Cox.

Whitaker, C. A. (1982). My philosophy of psychotherapy. In J. R. Neill & D. P. Kniskern (Eds.), *From psyche to system: The evolving therapy of Carl Whitaker* (pp. 31-36). New York: Guilford.

Whitchurch, G. G., & Constantine, L. L. (1993). Systems theory. In P. G. Boss, W. J. Doherty, R. LaRossa, W. R. Schuman, & S. K. Steinmetz (Eds.), *Sourcebook of family theories and methods: A contextual approach* (pp. 325-355). New York: Plenum.

Wickramasekera, I. (1980). Aversive behavioral rehearsal: A cognitive behavioral procedure. In D. J. Cox & R. J. Daitzman (Eds.), *Exhibitionism: Description, assessment, and treatment* (pp. 39-50). New York: Appleton-Croft.

Wienberg, M. (1972). Labels don't apply. *Sexual Behavior, 3*(2), 18.

Wilson, C., & Pence, D. (1993, October). *Uneasy alliance.* Paper presented at the Annual Midwest Conference on Child Sexual Abuse and Incest, Madison, WI.

Wolfe, F. A. (1985, March). *Twelve female sexual offenders.* Presentation at "Next steps in research on the assessment and treatment of sexually aggressive persons (paraphiliacs)" conference, St. Louis, MO.

Woods, S. C., & Dean, K. S. (1984). *Financial report: Sexual abuse of males research project* (NCCAN Report No. 90-CA-812). Washington, DC: National Center on Child Abuse and Neglect.

Wright, M., & Galaway, B. (Eds.). (1989). *Mediation and criminal justice: Victims, offenders and community.* Newbury Park, CA: Sage.

Wyatt, G. E. (1990). Sexual abuse of ethnic minority children: Identifying dimensions of victimization. *Professional Psychology: Research and Practice, 21,* 338-343.

Yochelson, S., & Samenow, S. E. (1977). *The criminal personality* (Vols. I, II, and III). New York: Jason Aronson.

Yokley, J. (Ed.). (1990). *The use of victim-offender communication in the treatment of sexual abuse: Three intervention models.* Orwell, VT: Safer Society Press.

Young, J. E., & Beck, A. T. (1982). Cognitive therapy: Clinical applications. In A. J. Giles (Ed.), *Short-term therapies for depression* (pp. 182-214). New York: Guilford.

Yourcenar, M. (1954). *Memoirs of Hadrian.* New York: Farrar, Strauss & Giroux.

Zehr, H. (1990). *Changing lenses: A new focus for crime and justice.* Scottsdale, AZ: Herald Press.

Index

About the Authors

John C. Gonsiorek received a Ph.D. in clinical psychology from the University of Minnesota and holds a diplomate in clinical psychology from the American Board of Professional Psychology. He is a Clinical Assistant Professor in the Clinical Training Program, Department of Psychology, University of Minnesota. He is Past President of Division 44 (Society for the Psychological Study of Lesbian and Gay Issues) of the American Psychological Association and has published widely in the areas of sexual exploitation by health care professionals and clergy, sexual orientation and sexual identity, professional ethics, among others. He is in independent practice in Minneapolis, focusing on forensic evaluations, expert witness work, and individual psychotherapy.

Walter H. Bera received an M.A. in educational psychology from the University of Minnesota and has worked in the field of sexual abuse and harassment assessment, treatment, and prevention since 1978. He has worked in the Family Sexual Abuse Program of the Family Renewal Center, Illusion Theater's Sexual Abuse Prevention Education Program, and the Program for Healthy Adolescent Sexual Expression (PHASE) with adolescent sex offenders. He has produced original research, articles, plays, and videotapes, most recently coauthoring the video-based adolescent sexual harassment prevention curriculum *Crossing the Line*. He is a Licensed Psychologist and Marriage and Family Therapist in Minnesota and an Approved Supervisor in the American Association for Marriage and Family Therapy. He is completing his doctorate in family social science at the University of Minnesota; his dissertation focuses on male victims of clergy sexual abuse. He maintains a private practice in Minneapolis and provides training and consultation nationally.

Donald LeTourneau received a CSWE accredited social work degree from Bethel College in St. Paul and a master's of social work from the University of Minnesota Graduate School. He has taught youth studies courses at the University of Minnesota Center for Youth Development and Research and is past President and Board Member of the Minnesota Association of Child and Youth Care Workers. For more than 20 years he has helped develop community-based programming for a wide range of youth issues, including street outreach; shelter and transitional housing; employment and training; alternative education; outpatient mental health; health education and health care; gay, lesbian, bisexual, and transgender youth; adolescent prostitution; juvenile justice and delinquency; and youth development. With long-time colleague Jackie Thompson, he recently started the Institute for Youthwork, a private nonprofit organization that provides youth work consultation, program development, evaluation, education, training, and staff development.